Part 1: Contents

Foreword **6**

Foreword

I have tried to write a book not for setting-up home but for setting-up garden, though I think the two are inseparable. The process applies to both the owners of new, unmade gardens and those who have established gardens with which they are unhappy. In whichever of these positions you find yourself, I cannot overemphasize the necessity of immersing yourself in the theories of design and styling before setting forth to devise your own solution, to peruse the book logically from the beginning so that the basic philosophy of garden planning is not neglected in your understandable enthusiasm for the final horticultural result. Unfortunately, the horticultural industry encourages a disregard for a preconceived garden plan – witness the lip-service most garden publications pay to design. Even books supposedly written on the subject do not allow garden design to progress beyond the 1920s. In no other field of design are we of the modern world so blind. Arguably, the garden is one's private antidote to modernism and progress, the place where the individualist in us all makes his last stand, introducing all manner of emotional overtones and fulfilling totally impractical aspirations. And why not? But the modern world need not necessarily be banned from the garden. Economic factors that have put a high premium on any outside space, and new construction and surfacing materials, demand useful and attractive garden designs to suit.

I suppose the grass is always greener in your neighbor's garden and, by the same token, many Continental ones embody for me much from which we in the British Isles can learn. Conversely, Continentals love the large gracious gardens of the British Isles that are open to the public. In the United States and Canada, the quite different climatic zones have of necessity influenced garden design and plant selections. More recently, American landscape design is responding to the reality of smaller properties and a demand for low-maintenance plantings. Shouldn't we seek some essence from all these influences, but conditioned by the practicalities of location?

John Brookes

A view of herbaceous planting in the walled garden at Denmans, West Sussex

THE COMPLETE GARDENER

JOHN BROOKES

Part 1
The Outdoor Gardener

Part 2
The Indoor Gardener

CRESCENT BOOKS
New York • Avenel, New Jersey

THE
OUTDOOR
GARDENER

Part 1

1994 edition published by Crescent Books, distributed by Outlet
Book Company, Inc., a Random House Company,
40 Englehard Avenue, Avenel, New Jersey 07001

Random House
New York • Toronto • London • Sydney • Auckland

WHAT TYPE OF GARDEN?

Your outside space, its location, orientation, climate and soil

The modern garden in the light of gardens past

Introduction

While many of us might not conform to what convention would have us wear for a particular time of day, or for performing a particular function, we all appreciate that for a special evening out, jeans, for instance, would not be appropriate. You would not normally go fishing in a suit either, or garden in a dressing gown, although all these garments would cover us adequately. Choosing the correct garment allows us to perform most comfortably, whether it be dancing, fishing or digging. The cut and fit of the garment matters as well, for the best tailored clothes go on for ever, being made of good material and being designed to fit the wearer.

The way in which you clothe the area around the house is subject to the same discipline as choosing a garment to wear, according to what you want of it, how it will be used and how it will serve the house which sits in the middle of it. Gardens which are well made and individually styled will work best for the user.

The type of garden that you evolve for yourself should depend on the demands you make of it. Long before setting pencil to paper to produce a plan from which to work, let alone setting spade to earth, you must ask yourself what it is that you want your garden to do for you and your family.

As soon as the word "garden" is used, common sense is often ignored. Pictures of lawns and grottos and ponds start to cloud the issue and we are soon going to the supermarket in an evening dress or "mucking out" in a dinner jacket. Get back to reality, forget the stately layouts that you might have seen and think about the type of garden that you really need. Your type of garden must depend on you and your family's lifestyle. This will provide much food for thought, for the permutations of possible requirements among even a family of four, considering their diverse ages, and various likes and dislikes, are endless.

You might not be able to afford to pave terraces or build walls in order to fulfil your plan in one operation. This is unimportant as long as you get the plan of action correct and work slowly towards its completion as and

Creating style, *below left. Traditional English architecture with mellow stone walls and leaded windows is emphasized by a traditional garden. The same stone has been used for the steps, and plants allowed to smother and soften the whole. The gray foliage of Leucanthemum sp. blends with the stone while red climbing roses provide contrast. Below, in completely opposite style, a crisp, modern approach has been used to tie in the building and plants of this house. Japanese influence is strong, with sliding glass doors allowing the inside and outside to merge.*

when it is possible to do so. Whether you can afford to construct all the garden or not, it is essential to start to use the site according to your plan – storing wood, building the rubbish heap, walking a certain path or siting the dustbins, for instance.

The good garden plan will also provide a setting for your house. Many homes will have more than one garden, with an area in front and an area to the rear. These areas have totally different functions, as different as those of a kitchen and a sitting-room, and their characters should reflect this. The front garden is usually a place for display, whereas the rear garden is essentially an area to be used and viewed by you and your family throughout the year.

Your garden design will obviously depend on your individual taste, and how you have designed and decorated the inside of your house, for the garden will often become an immediate extension of it. Your taste may be traditional or it may be modern; you might like masses of plants or be very spartan in your choice. But the initial controlling influence on your plan is the location of your garden – town, country or the vast suburban areas in which most people live. It is the first factor to examine in detail.

The rear garden, *above. Unlike the public display of the front garden, the rear garden should be thought of as a private, outside room used as an extension of the home in summer. Consider the variety of uses to which you and your family will put the garden and try to include as many as possible in your rear garden plan.*

Where is your garden?

Gardens with a similar layout can feel completely different depending on their location. Enclosed town gardens will seem much smaller than the same size garden in a more rural, open setting. But it is the very fact that you have a private, outside space within a tight urban mass that makes the town garden so attractive to use in the summer, and to look at throughout the rest of the year. In the town garden, planning must be influenced by the proximity and feeling of the buildings which surround it and by whether the garden is overlooked.

The hazards of the walled town garden include a lack of light throughout the year, making plants reach upwards and inwards to gain the most from it. Shade might come from surrounding buildings or from an overhanging tree growing in a neighboring garden. Conversely, the walled garden might be a sun trap and become far too hot for limited periods.

Taking these factors into consideration, the design for an enclosed town garden should be very simple, with the object of making an outside room furnished with permanent sculptural groupings of plants. In front of these you can contrast bright masses of annual plants, grouped and arranged in pots. You might consider some form of overhead canopy too, for seclusion. The character of the town garden should be quite different from that of gardens in any other situation and should not be a reduced version of the country model.

Gardens of a larger size – and they usually are in suburban locations – have greater demands made of them. Couples tend to move outwards from city centers as their families grow, giving themselves more space.

Vegetables might be included in the garden plan to supplement the table, and any open space will eventually be used for children's play. Whereas the design of the town garden promotes passive enjoyment, the suburban family garden design should provide for more active enjoyment with enlarged terrace areas for play as well as entertainment. The planting of such a garden will at first be limited to the screens required to give privacy, and only as the children of the family grow up will it come to include more specialized decorative groups.

While country gardens may be large, there is now a general movement to make them more manageable. The increasingly wide spectrum of pursuits which a family can now undertake inhibits time spent working in the garden. Weekenders in the country often prefer to enjoy the countryside, rather than achieve an immaculate plot by Sunday evening with the prospect of starting again the following Saturday. The whole outlook on rural gardening is now far more relaxed. The area of the garden which requires moderate maintenance might be restricted to the house surround, with alternative and less demanding treatments used for the garden beyond the house or cottage.

Town, suburban and rural locations are often indivisible, one flowing into the other. My concern is for the smaller garden area within any of them. Often the only difference between the locations is climatic conditions, or the altitude at which they are located, for the standardization of modern building has meant that new houses and their plot size are often similar anywhere. It is easy to end up with a standardized garden to match if you are not conscious of its location.

Rural garden, *right.*
This Swedish cottage yard epitomizes relaxed country gardening. The seemingly casual arrangement of poppies and marguerites has been allowed to self-seeds among the small elements of random paving.

Urban gardens, *below. The tiniest gardens in town, even on roofs or balconies, can be magical. They provide an escape from bricks and mortar and a link with the natural world beyond the city.*

Suburban garden, *left.
Out of the city center,
more space means less
intensive gardening and
more space for garden
activity. The sunken
area in this suburban
garden allows for a
sheltered meal table,
usable for many months
of the year. Changes of
level provide casual
seating places for less
formal entertaining.*

11

Climate and weather

The climate and weather of a location will have a major influence on its character. They will have molded the vernacular style of building and where wood and stone are available locally they will have been used traditionally for constructing walls, paths and fences. Indigenous herbage will have been used for hedging and infills, giving gardens a particular local quality. It has only been the development of the modern garden center that has changed this by offering universally available modern materials. It is sad that gardens north and south are now paved in similar materials, and are stocked with a similar range of alien plant material. Only more extreme climatic conditions prevent this universal approach and encourage a garden molded by its environment.

When considering what any particular climate will support horticulturally you can do no better than to look and see what is supported naturally and in agriculture, in rural and suburban situations, and, of course, what is growing in other gardens. The main climatic factors which influence plant growth in an area are its altitude and the intensity and length of its winters. An area's horticultural possibilities can also be greatly affected by wind. Wind off the sea, for example, will be salt-laden in diminishing amounts up to five miles from the coast. The range of plants which can stand its full blast is quite small.

Climatic conditions can also vary enormously from garden to garden. The presence of surrounding buildings, or trees, or a combination of the two, might inhibit the number of sunlight hours that the garden receives. In summer, when the sun rides high over obstacles there will probably be more than enough light even if bright sunshine is limited to only part of the day. But in the winter,

when the sun is lower in the sky, direct sunlight might not reach the garden for months on end.

Trees and buildings can funnel prevailing winds and cause considerable damage, although open fences or hedges can be sited to counter the force of the wind by filtering away its strength. A solid barrier, like a wall (which in other circumstances can do so much to promote plant growth by retaining the sun's heat) simply increases wind turbulance and is inappropriate as a wind break.

Homes and gardens which are comparatively close to one another, but one on a hill top and one in a valley bottom, will experience considerable differences in temperature in both winter (due to frost) and summer (due to wind). Frost is an important factor to consider on a local basis. You must remember that cold air flows downhill like water. If your garden happens to be in the way, any solid barrier will trap the cold. It is possible to deflect the flow of cold air with well-thought planting, though. Gardens in valleys, or otherwise below hills, are likely to be in frost pockets, causing their micro-climates to be surprisingly cold. Frost will remain in a frost pocket until dispersed by wind or sun. Such a situation may be lethal to spring-flowering fruit trees.

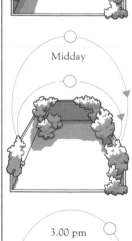

10.00 am

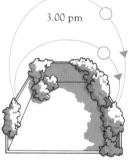

Midday

3.00 pm

■ Winter shade
■ Summer shade

Sun in walled gardens, *above. Only the central portion of an enclosed garden is guaranteed direct sunlight the year round. The low arc of the sun in winter dramatically increases the areas of shade through the day.*

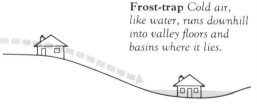

Frost-trap *Cold air, like water, runs downhill into valley floors and basins where it lies.*

Temperate climate garden *Adequate rainfall and mild winters allow for an amazing abundance of wide-ranging plant growth.*

Mild winter garden *Boxwood will not survive the coldest New England winters, but is used farther south and along the Coast.*

Hot climate garden, *left. Desert-type sun and lack of rain can produce striking examples of gardens molded by climate. Architecture, garden layout and choice of plants which can stand intense sunlight and possible drought, combine to reflect the spirit of place strongly.*

Cold climate garden, *below. This Continental woodland garden nestles beneath a plantation of poplars. The informal use of shade-loving plants merging with the established trees beyond, combines with the steeply-pitched roof line of the house to suggest a place of shelter against heavy winter snow.*

Aspect and site

The reasons which govern why we live where we do seldom include the suitability of a site for the creation of a garden. Access to place of work, proximity to relations, the suitability of the house and the potential of its internal space are the more usual concerns. When moving home, a pleasant view might be considered an advantage, or a property's closeness to the sea, but only the *size* of the garden is likely to be advertised as a feature of the space outside. Often you will have to adapt what you have bought from a previous owner, or, if you move into a newly built home, to start from scratch on a new site.

Even a brand new site can have encouraging features under the builders' rubble. Look for a change of level within the site, distant views, or even the shape of a neighboring tree in relation to your own plot. All can be used in your ultimate design. Older, established gardens will have existing vegetation with which to work. Small urban gardens, including basement areas, will have surrounding walls to establish the character of the garden, and with luck a little vegetation too.

The type of soil which you inherit – if there is any at all – will affect the character of the garden too (see p. 16) for certain plants prefer an acid soil, others a more chalky or alkaline one. The consistency of the soil will either allow it to warm quickly, encouraging early spring growth, or cause it to remain cold and sticky for longer and thereby slowing down plant activity. All too often a new

Dramatic aspect, *left. An Italian garden terrace in an established orchard setting exploits a magnificent view of the valley below. The simple line of an encircling granite block wall is all the garden design necessary in a site of such unusual aspect. In practical terms, the wall will shelter the seating from drafts blowing up from the valley floor far below.*

Considering aspect, *below. The dwellings illustrated have opposite aspects, the top with house front facing north, and the bottom with house front facing south. A rear seating area has been well-positioned in each garden to catch the sun.*

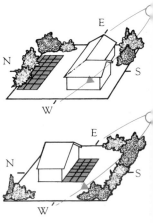

plot has a meagre layer of topsoil, perhaps only a dusting of it over clay compressed by building work. If you are moving to a new property, this problem is well worth checking since the removal of clay and its replacement with a more fertile topsoil can be an expensive operation and only possible if there is easy access.

The aspect of the house will rarely influence your choice of home but it will have a significant effect on the type of garden that you can make. The ideal aspect in much of the northern hemisphere is open to the south-west, gaining full benefit from long summer days. Remember that a sunny, south-facing frontage gives you a shady, north-facing rear garden, and while many plants will grow in the shade, your terrace will have to be a distance from the house if you want to sit in the sun. In hot climates, an area of reliable shade near to the house might be desirable.

There are very few aspects which present insuperable problems to garden planning, but frequently too little consideration leads to a plan which makes the garden difficult to live with. Tall planting or building in the line of the sun's regular path, for example, can cast shadows which restrict plant growth and give the garden a cold feel.

A garden on a slope often allows a good view, but if you are contemplating a new, steeply sloping site, and wish to work the garden, remember that retaining walls (see p. 120) may be necessary to create level areas in the garden. Such walls can be very expensive to construct well. Another problem to beware of, is that sites which fall towards the house may well produce drainage difficulties (see page 103), especially in winter.

Dramatic site, below. This terrace area blends into its woodland setting. Timber decking and random planting extend the rural mood right up to the house surround to the right of this photograph. The form and foliage of the many plants which will grow in light shade are often characteristic, with large leaves.

Analyzing your soil

The type of soil in your garden will be a guide to the type of plants that you can grow, provided that other variables, such as drainage, weather and the amount of sunlight that the garden receives also suit the plants you choose. Having said that, most soils which are in good condition, (in gardening terms, in "good tilth"), will grow most plants. Soil condition depends on its texture, and this can always be improved with the addition of organic matter. Only extreme soil types are particularly difficult.

The basic factor leading to regional differences in garden type is the soil. It has been formed over millions of years by the breaking up of the rocks of the earth's crust, so it is the nature of the underlying rock that influences the type of soil above it. For example, older, igneous rocks, like granite, and also sandstone, tend to form slightly acid soil, while limestone and chalk rocks will produce an alkaline soil (see below).

The texture of the topsoil – the bit we garden on – is determined by the size and consistency of the particles which make up that soil, and the presence or absence of organic matter in it. A clay soil is composed of very small particles packed so closely together that it retains moisture even in warm weather. It is often, therefore, a cold and sticky soil, but if it does finally dry out in hot weather it will crack. A sandy soil is composed of far larger particles than a clay one. It will drain well and warm up quickly in spring, and is therefore known as a warm soil. However, the line between draining well and draining too quickly is a thin one. A soil that drains too quickly will be a poor one as all the nutrients normally held in solution around each soil particle will leach away. The ideal soil, as far as texture is concerned, is a loam, consisting of a mixture of slightly more sand than clay particles, and with a high organic content.

The incorporation of organic manure in either a clay or a sandy soil will improve its condition enormously, not only by improving its texture but also by feeding the soil. The crumb-like consistency of well-rotted manure will bind together the particles of a loose, sandy soil, or divide up the fine grains of a sticky clay one, while the bacteria it contains will activate either soil type to promote plant growth. To test your soil for organic content, examine it closely and pick up a handful, running it through your fingers. Ideally, it should be of a crumbly consistency, neither too spongy and sticky nor too dusty. It should look dark in color and should also smell sweet.

As well as its sandy or clayey nature, a soil is judged by its relative alkalinity or acidity,

two opposing conditions. The relative alkalinity or acidity of a soil can be measured against a scale which has become accepted by gardeners and is known as the pH scale. This runs from pH0 to pH14 with pH7 as neutral. Plants grow in soils within the range of pH4.5 to pH7.5. A soil between pH5.7 and pH6.7 is ideal for the majority of plants. Above this reading the soil is too alkaline, and below it, too acid. A chalky soil has a high calcium (alkaline) content and will, therefore, have a high pH reading. It can be made more acid by adding heavy dressings of organic material, such as farmyard manure or compost. When adequately manured, a chalky soil will become quite fertile.

A peaty soil is at the other end of the pH scale, being acid. Unlike other soils, peat is derived from plants and is therefore organic itself. Occurring naturally, a peaty soil will often need to be drained. It can be made more alkaline ("sweetened") by adding lime in the form of ground limestone. A dose of 2.25 kg per 9 m² (5 lbs per 97 ft²) will raise the pH between 0.5 and 0.75 of a point. Bought peat has usually been sterilized and will therefore contain little or no food value, but it will still condition a soil by improving its texture.

To test your soil for alkalinity or acidity in America, a sample can be submitted to your county extension agents for analysis. Otherwise you can use a home testing kit, many types of which are readily available on the market.

Each soil type has a range of vegetation which will thrive upon it, from the smallest herb through, in many cases, to forest trees. The presence of any of this range on a virgin site will be a guide to the soil type. Neighboring gardens, too, will tell you what grows well there. For example, in many parts of Europe the rhododendron growing is a sure sign of an acid soil, and forms of viburnum usually indicate chalky (alkaline) ones. Birch, pine, gorse and broom usually indicate a light, sandy and often acid soil.

It is one thing to improve the texture and drainage characteristics of your soil and to make it suitable for healthy plant growth but it is a wasteful process to spend much time and effort trying to change the soil type of your garden completely in order to grow a particular range of plants that is alien to your locality. If necessary, you can use containers to hold a special soil type for plants that are not happy in your local soil.

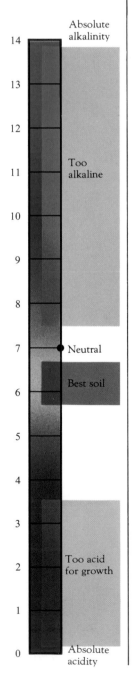

pH scale and values
The pH scale indicates alkalinity or acidity about the neutral value of pH7. Soil is usually acid or alkaline and has according characteristics. Soil testing kits are available which simply assess the pH value of your soil by measuring the hydrogen ion concentration in a suspension of soil in distilled water.

Absolute alkalinity

14

13

12

11 — Too alkaline

10

9

8

7 — Neutral

Best soil

6

5

4

3

2 — Too acid for growth

1

0 — Absolute acidity

Recognizing soil type from natural vegetation

Although soil type can be modified by the location of a site (sun or shade, and slopes, will alter the water content of soils), certain types of plant are attracted to and flourish in certain soil types. Plants which have seeded themselves in a garden plot, therefore, can be a good indicator of the soil type which you are to inherit with a plot.

Willow herb (*Epilobium* sp., fireweed in the United States), for instance, grows in a fertile, moist soil, as do nettles. Wild blueberries are standard vegetation on acid soils, which are usually sandy or peaty and poor. While ferns are adaptable plants and can be found growing on wet and dry soils, they mostly indicate a heavy, damp soil, suggesting clay. A sure incidator of a wet soil is the buttercup (*Ranunculus* sp.). It is often seen in low-lying garden corners and across poorly drained lawns. An alkaline, chalky soil is often the chosen home of saltbushes (*Atriplex* sp.) and yerba mansa (*Anemopsis californica*)

Willow herb – fertile soil

Heath and heather – poor, acid soil

Ferns – heavy soil

Buttercups – wet soil

Dog's Mercury – alkaline soil

A garden's uses

In the main, historic gardens that survive are those that have best met the requirements of the grand families for whom they were built, with their expansive life styles. That historic layouts have survived is a tribute to their architects, who not only fulfilled the requirements of their patrons but also created gardens of beauty that have proved worth preserving. The clue to their success is an understanding of the life and times of the families involved.

To tailor your own site to your requirements you too will need to analyze your family's needs and recognize that this is a continuing process. As the individual members of your family grow, so their interests and their resulting demands of the garden space change.

Before thinking about the trees and shrubs you would like to include in your garden, consider the practical aspects of your outside living space. These are usually centered on the service door from the house. Think of rubbish storage and access to it, of the compost heap, of gas storage if it is necessary, of a clothes drying area, and a place to store surplus household furniture, garden tools and machinery. All these areas will need to be serviced by hard, dry paving, preferably lit at night. This paving might link to a garage, or a workshop, or a glass-covered area perhaps, even a conservatory. Think about winter use as well as summer, and night as well as day. Some areas will need an electricity or water supply. A terrace for summer sunbathing, entertaining or for family meals outside should be an extension of these functional areas as well as the house.

Think where you might like a herb area (which ideally should be near to the kitchen entrance) and a vegetable plot. The size of a vegetable plot is an important consideration. Just how much time can you afford to devote to vegetable growing? Remember that vegetables will be cheap in the shops at the times of year when you will have to spend most time growing your own. Perhaps you only need to provide salad crops, or to grow soft fruit or even just a fruit tree. Whatever you decide, tough service paths to a vegetable and/or fruit growing area are vital.

The type of garden that you create within this framework will depend on the many possible demands that can be made of an outside space. Will children play in it, first perhaps in a sandpit but later football or tennis practiced against any available wall? These latter activities will mean that planting must be limited. A barbecue space will be useful to entertain the family throughout the summer and a further terrace which serves it might also be useful for table tennis in summer, and for more sunbathing and entertaining space. The growing, prosperous family might need a second garage space, or space to park a boat perhaps through winter or a camper.

As children leave home, parents often want to garden the area more, increasing its horticultural content. The addition of a greenhouse and a cold frame can be a means of extending this activity. Such detailed horticultural interest frequently lasts into retirement; then the maintenance of a detailed layout starts to take its toll, and areas of high cultivation can be reduced again.

Productive gardens
Vegetable gardens and herb gardens are demanding but very rewarding if your interest lies in using plants to produce food, spices, essences or medications. Well-planned sections of gardens, or indeed gardens devoted to vegetables or herbs, can be beautiful, as in the examples below.

Entertaining gardens, *above. Gardens made to serve their users must sometimes contain areas for active entertainment. For adults this often means an area for preparing and cooking outdoor meals and for children a sandpit can have endless attraction. There is no reason why such features should not be a bonus to the garden, as in this example.*

Relaxing gardens *If what you want from your garden is a place for relaxation that requires the minimum of upkeep, then this, too, is within your reach if you take the trouble to plan and build the garden well in the first place.*

How gardens have changed

The modern garden is very much a product of mundane practical considerations for, in the main, the space available is small and the design tempered by the time and money which is necessary to realize it. Gardens in the past were fewer, more spacious, and generally used for more gracious living. Moreover, such gardens were worked by staff. Those gardens which remain and which we visit, once served prosperous families, but running concurrently with them, and now lost to us, was always the laborer's cottage garden. Until the nineteenth century there was little connection between the two social extremes. Only after the Industrial Revolution in England did a middle class emerge which sought to copy grander gardens, albeit on a much reduced scale. The laboring cottager became urbanized, and he too gardened though with produce more in mind than decoration. These two developments converged to produce the garden which typifies suburbia.

A parallel horticultural development, starting in the eighteenth century, had provided an ever increasing choice of plant material, first collected from all corners of the world and then worked upon and hybridized by plantsmen to supply the clamoring horticultural market. Publishers provided volumes (and still do) of weekly and monthly journals to foster this market, and gardening societies were formed to exchange plants and information on their culture. This need for horticultural fact gathered real momentum with the formation of the Royal Horticultural Society in the mid-nineteenth century.

A lack of available labor to maintain the detailed garden altered the course of its development throughout the early twentieth century. However, it was not until the 1950s that any inspired new thinking changed the form of garden layouts in England. The spark which ignited new thought on garden planning originated in the sunny, open-air climate of California, where various streams of thought and circumstances converged to make this change.

The early Californian garden was of Spanish origin, arriving by way of Mexico. This was a garden of shaded patios and cooling sprayed water epitomized in the famed Moorish gardens of the Alhambra in Granada, Spain. A new ingredient was added to meet the twentieth-century requirement of living outside, centered on the swimming pool the fashionable venue of outside life in that climate. The horticultural content of the new garden was low, since the climate limited it. However, when planting was attempted it was often maintained by the Japanese labor which was so abundant and cheap in the 1920s and 1930s on the west coast of the United States. Some essence of the Japanese artistic tradition was inevitably added.

Tradition dies hard, *below. A 16th-century Flemish garden, portrayed in idealized form by Abel Grimmer. The design is attractive and crops abundant but a large work-force is needed.
Right, view of part of the garden at Sissinghurst Castle, Kent. Though a 20th-century construction, it is traditional in design and requires as much detailed husbandry as its 16th-century precursor.*

Japanese traditions had previously influenced the Modernist schools of architecture, painting and sculpture in central Europe. These had migrated to America in the face of Nazi antipathy and came to affect the design of gardens both in the pattern and use of new materials, paralleling the influence of new house designs as well. The best of the gardens which resulted are those of Thomas Church which he completed in the 1940s.

After the dull days of the Second World War, this sparkling emergent·style strongly influenced European landscape designers who were employed to enhance new building. The new style, however, had to take on a form more suited to the climates to which it was transferred. In Germany and Scandinavia, for example, the limitations of the winter climate restricted the range of usable plants, and a concern for shape and form outweighed the original demands for color.

In the United Kingdom, where the climate favors a far wider range of plants and the horticultural tradition is strong, the consideration of garden structure beneath the plants was much more discreet. Far more of a stimulus to considering design of the garden was the need to provide small, serviceable gardens for young, growing families on the new housing developments of the 1960s and 1970s. That the realization of even sensitive plans often produced mundane results is a criticism of the emergent garden center which has encouraged standardized materials for universal usage, and brought about the demise of the specialist grower and his discerning range of plant material. The suburban plot has been reduced to a depressing sameness wherever its location.

A marked concern for conservation and building in the vernacular style now spearheads a new approach to the garden, followed by the decreasing time available for garden maintenance because of the ever increasing spectrum of alternative interests. For those who are horticulturally concerned, and there are many millions, the garden will always be a place for growing plant collections, but for the millions more who are not it must become a usable home extension, but outside – a place designed to fulfil a cycle of family requirements furnished with plants. It is plants that will contain and articulate this outside room, giving it style and character. The hard materials for walling and paving must, of course, suit the style and location of the house that the garden serves.

The object of looking at gardens in history is to see how each evolved at a certain time, in a certain place, for the particular use of the family which owned it. That they survived at all is a tribute to their conception, and most of all to their maintenance through the years. A garden is a moving, growing entity and to maintain it in a particular style is an ever growing discipline.

It is at this point that there is an increasing realization that much of our current garden thinking is styled to an outmoded tradition. Does the owner of a small garden want to have to cut a lawn twice a week? And for the small family, with a supermarket nearby, are not bought lettuces, clean and packed, to be preferred to those grown by themselves? Then again, what of holidays and weekends – who maintains and waters the produce?

The undoubted charm of the eighteenth-century garden, which has been aped for so long in garden design, in town as well as country, is being superseded by a new approach, based on usage and available time. However, the modification of planting techniques, such as the mixed border or ground cover planting, is not enough if the underlying design concept is wrong.

And are we right to perpetuate the horticultural approach as a suburban ideal? What is wrong with longer, rougher grass, with plantings of subjects more naturally suited to their surroundings? We have been conditioned to the merits of perfected artificiality and seek horticultural excellence as the only yardstick of a garden's being, when the aspiration of an average gardener's personal paradise is far less discerning and, on a realistic level, a much more relaxed place.

Japanese style, *right. A garden at Okayama, Japan, in which plant forms and colors are sensitively combined with abstract shapes, creating a satisfyingly timeless composition.*

New styles demand new gardens, *below. A 20th-century garden designed by Christopher Tunnard within an earlier garden design. The lines and materials of a new house necessitate designing a new garden appropriate to the changed conditions. Bottom, the Dewey Donnell garden at Sonoma, California, designed by Thomas Church in 1948. The swimming-pool has been brilliantly interpreted in abstract form and works well with the landscape seen beyond.*

Inside-outside living

At first signs of sure sun in spring we (in northern latitudes at least) throw open windows and swing doors wide. Animals and children move naturally from indoors to out and the garden comes into its own as a usable space, realizing a potential which has been lying dormant all winter.

My own basement flat in London had a simple sliding glass door and through most of the summer, from early morning until evening, it was open, linking the small garden with my studio, and making urban life considerably more bearable. When the door was closed, the garden still gave enormous pleasure, even through the winter, when a solitary brave little winter-flowering cherry (*Prunus subhirtella autumnalis*) performed for months on end.

An inside-outside design is one where there is visual interaction of the inside of the house with the garden throughout the year. The link is effective from the depths of winter, when floodlit snow, for example, can look spectacular from the comfort of a warm sitting-room, to mid-summer, when easy coming and going can make the garden an extension to the home, for eating, for play and for entertaining.

The tradition of providing for outside living within a home originated in climates where sunshine is predictable. It started with the tight, enclosed courtyards of the Islamic world in a style which overlayed a previous tradition of the ancient Roman courtyard, or *atrium*. These two sources fused in the Moorish patio of southern Spain, which is a central well of light, enclosed by the stories of a dwelling – an arrangement not dissimilar to the medieval English courtyard. During the summer, much outside living takes place in such patio gardens. They are surrounded at ground level by open colonnades and furnished as a living-room might be, for daily usage. But rather than catching the sun, these outdoor rooms remain cool, being shaded from the sun by the surrounding high walls of the house. A simple central fountain cools the air and the noise of the trickle permeates the building.

This inside-outside Moorish way of life moved with the Spaniards to South America, to Mexico and latterly to southern California, where an enlarged version of the Moorish garden style provided a secluded surround to the fashionable swimming-pool-orientated life of the 1920s. New forms and constructional methods of Modern architecture emphasized light inside the house and allowed for easy movement in and out.

These are the roots and influences of a new interpretation of the garden as an area which extends the inside of a home outside. In summer, such a garden has a physical and visual link between inside and outside space – a link which is enforced by a use of similar flooring materials for both in and out, the use of indoor plants where possible, and furnished external terraces. If you can match colors too, inside and out, the bond is strengthened to give a feeling of increased size.

On the following pages you will find examples of successful designs which link inside with outside and so effectively increase the living area of homes. Some tend to take the feeling of internal decoration outside to balconies or patios, while others bring the style of the garden indoors. Your success in making the link between inside and outside in your own home depends on your willingness to use materials of both indoor and outdoor decoration inventively. And while an opening door allows the easiest movement between inside and outside, views in and out through windows provide similar opportunities for linking inside with outside increasing your use of the garden.

Conservatory feel, *right. Elegant though casual outside living is the theme for this conservatory-type grouping. Foliage complements upholstery, while hard flooring allows for watering through summer.*
Mediterranean terrace, *left. In hot, sunny climates, simple solutions for outdoor seating areas are often successful. The shade provided by a pergola engenders the feeling of total relaxation in summer months.*

Linking inside with outside

When there is nothing but glazing separating room and garden, you have a special opportunity to use the space of the adjoining garden fully. In summer the two are physically linked when you open garden doors. The sense of space remains through winter if the garden is well co-ordinated with the room and itself presents strong visual interest. Garden lighting will continue the effect after dark. An example of converging inside and outside spaces is shown in the photograph, below, where one end of a living room has glazed access to a paved terrace used for casual meals outside in summer. Alternative approaches are shown in stylized diagrams below.

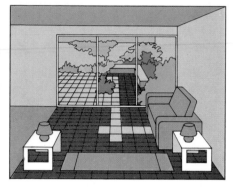

Alternative A, *left. A fully paved garden ideal for entertaining. The concrete slab ground patterning runs from outside, across the threshold, and into the room, linking inside and outside seating areas. Brick paving and matching colored walls emphasize the link.*

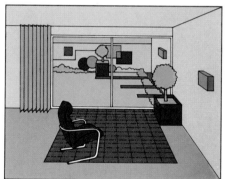

Alternative B, *left. Here, the space outside is designed for visual effect rather than use. The composition is abstract, using broad masses of a single plant, contrasted with clipped trees in square tubs. A mural draws the eye to the far wall beyond a ground design of lawn and paving brick.*

Existing living/garden room *This relaxing room has a large expanse of glass which opens on to a terrace used for dining.*

Terrace room, *left. The architect of this town house has used every available inch of space for an occupant who enjoys airiness and plants. Above, outside, is the roof terrace; below, inside, a music room. Both areas are equally full of plants.*

Relaxed outside dining, *right. The proportions of my own dining-room have been extended outside by the use of overhead beams stained to match the woodwork of the folding doors. The same styling is present in the garden furniture.*

Enclosed urban privacy, *right. A jungle of foliage outside your garden door, as in this example, has the effect of obliterating the rest of the world. Such an approach creates an outside living space of mood, atmosphere and fine detail.*

Rural space and light, *below. In complete contrast to the urban inside-outside plan, right, the space of a rural garden, below, allows a crisp, almost spartan approach. The uninterrupted garden view and large area of glass allow enough sunlight to illuminate the design inside perfectly.*

PLANNING YOUR GARDEN

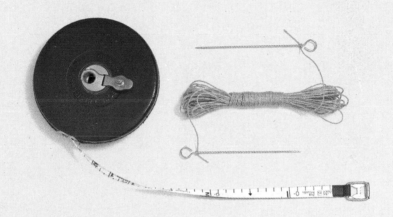

Measuring up

The principles of designing a garden

Making your plan

Looking at well-designed gardens

Assessing size and shape

Having estimated a site's potential and decided what you, the user, actually want from it, it is time to put some hard facts about the area on to paper so that you can start to produce a design to work to when constructing and then planting the garden. The first step is to take a blank sheet of paper, or graph paper if you prefer, and start to measure up, or outline survey, your site.

Start at the house. Most houses are built to a regular plan with angles at 90 degrees, so measure up the dimensions of your house working around it from face to face, taking running measurements to the windows and doors as you go, as shown opposite. In this way you will produce an accurate outline of the dwelling.

If you live in an older house which has many odd corners, or ancillary outbuildings, you might find it easier to seek out the deeds of your house. These will include a fairly detailed outline drawing of your property and you can use this as the basis for your measurements. If you have had any architectural work completed you might have a copy of the house plans ready drawn.

Once you have measured up your home, carefully draw up its measurements to a working scale. The scale should be at least 1/100, but preferably 1/50 for the smaller garden. Allow enough space to add the garden boundary around your house outline. The next procedure is to measure the garden. Go outside again and measure lines, or offsets, at 90 degrees to the house to the boundaries of your outside space. If necessary, mark these offsets on the site with string so that you can move down them and take further offsets, again at 90 degrees, to any existing features which are within striking distance. Then work around the lengths of the perimeter of the site, noting the measurements as you go.

If any elements within your garden are left "floating" on your layout and cannot be located by taking 90-degree offsets, take measurements to them from any two points already located. When you draw up your survey you will be able to use a pair of compasses set in turn to each of the pairs of measurements to establish the exact position of such features. This process is known as triangulation (see opposite).

Having established the positions and dimensions of the boundaries and major features of the site, work down in scale measuring the size and relative positions of smaller features including details such as the girth of a tree trunk and the span of overhanging foliage. Note also any internal walls or fences, any steps and manhole covers. Be as accurate as possible to make your survey worthwhile.

You will need to measure and plot any changes of level which may exist within your plot so that you can plan steps or retaining walls (see p. 119). Mark the positions of the top and the bottom of the level change to start with. If the change of level is great, you might need the help of a surveyor, who will quickly give you some spot levels to key points in the garden relating back to a datum or zeropoint, usually coinciding with a threshold into the house. For smaller changes of level, it is possible to take your own measurements by the system known as boning (see opposite). To do this, use a builder's plank, or a light aluminium ladder. The idea is that you measure the vertical descent of the slope against the plank or ladder which is held out absolutely horizontal from the top of the slope. If you cannot reach the bottom of the slope in one go, you can work your way down quite lengthy gradients plank- or ladder-length at a time, adding fall to fall to find the overall drop.

Mark clearly on your survey the direction of north as this will determine the ultimate pattern of the garden. Mark too the scale of your survey since it is all too easy to forget it.

Equipment for surveying and drawing your plan
The simple measuring and drawing equipment shown here is necessary for drawing up an accurate outline survey and then going on to make your garden plan.

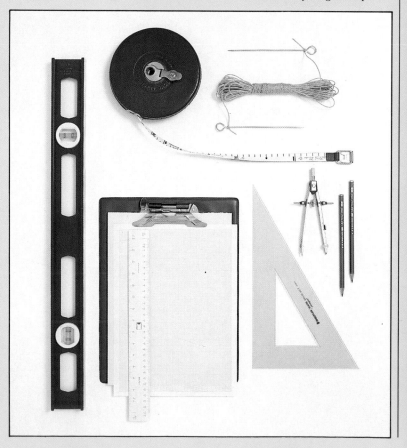

Making an outline survey

A simple survey, like the one shown right, shows all the relevant details of an existing plot, providing the owner with a basis for a new design. It has been drawn up to a scale where one unit of measurement represents a hundred units in the garden. If you can draw your complete garden on to your paper to a scale where one unit represents a smaller number of units in the garden, then do so.

First make a rough sketch of the area on which you can record measurements out in the garden. Ask someone to hold the end of the tape for you, or secure it to the ground with a skewer each time. As you measure offsets from your house to the boundary, make a note of any useful measurement along each one (running measurements).

Having filled in as many measurements as you can, you are ready to draw up the survey, turning your rough sketch into an accurate plan with ruler, set square and compasses.

Triangulation

Measure from any two points which you have already fixed (such as house corners) to any feature which is not within easy reach of a 90° offset. Set your compasses to the measurements required in scale, and make two intersecting arcs to locate the position.

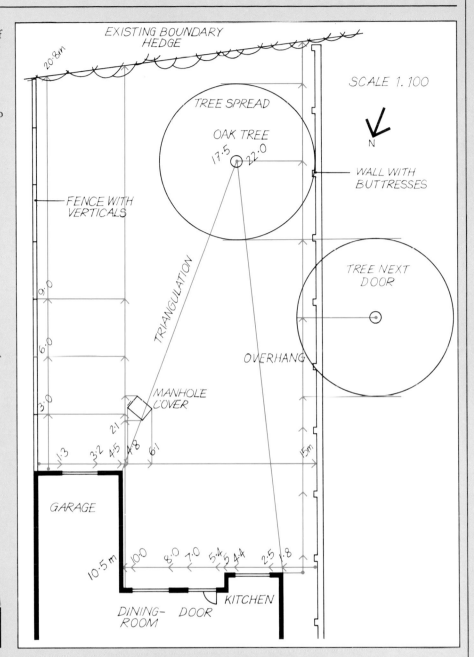

Measuring gradients

To survey a simple slope, a good practical way of boning, or judging the gradient by eye, and so measuring it, is to use a pole exactly one meter long, a plank and a spirit level. Nestle one end of the plank into the ground at the top of the slope and prop it horizontal using the meter pole, sliding it along under the plank as necessary and using the level. The slope falls a meter over the distance from the anchored end of the plank to where it meets the meter stick. Measure this distance. If necessary, repeat the process, moving the end of the plank down to the mark of the first meter stick. Add the vertical measurements and then the horizontal ones to find the overall gradient.

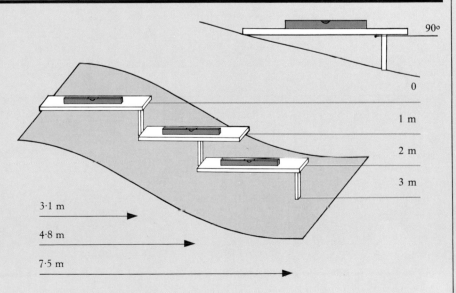

Line and pattern

Most people will recognize and relate to a garden which has been laid out formally, others will appreciate a freer-shaped, "natural" layout. In both cases the style of the garden is enforced by the way in which the plants have either been clipped to conform, or allowed to ramble, but the essential character of the design depends on its underlying pattern.

The lines which you use to produce the pattern of your garden plan will eventually mark the edges of the contrasting areas of the layout, whether these are for use as paths and service areas or for ornamental use as lawns and planting areas. Lines which run away from the viewer will make a site appear longer, and if you deliberately converge these (making a path get narrower for example) you will make the garden appear even longer. Conversely, lines which run horizontally across the view will give a site breadth.

Some patterns are static in feeling, others will appear to have movement in them, as can be seen in the examples of pattern below. We should be able to produce the right pattern for the right job. A garden with room for a focal point within its boundaries, or which has a view, will accept a pattern with movement in it. Lines in the pattern should lead the viewer to the view or the object. It is wrong to impose a pattern with movement on a garden if there is no goal for the viewer. Without some focal point his eye will wander aimlessly. On the other hand, a small walled garden area which has no outside interest, needs a patterned layout which will hold the eye within the site, so its design should be static.

There are permutations within these basic rules of course, the same effect being possible using curving lines as well as straight ones. The type of pattern which you use as the

Choosing a pattern

There are endless permutations of pattern, most of which can be adapted for garden planning. Those suggested here are drawn on a square grid so that they are all bound by the same scale. (You will eventually make such a guiding grid for your own garden, as on page 38.) Some of the patterns are in pairs showing positive and negative versions.

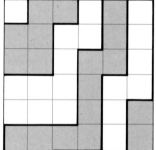

Static checkered

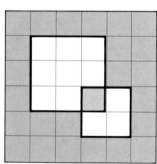

Static formal

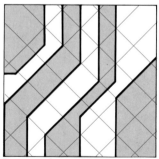

Abstract

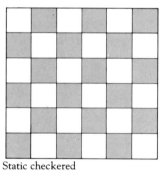

Dynamic

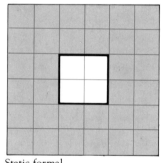

Static abstract

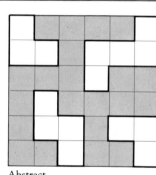

Dynamic diagonals

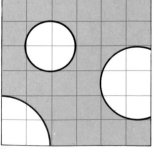

Positive abstract

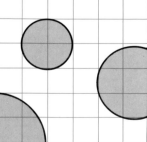

Negative abstract

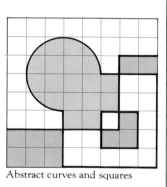

Dynamic curves

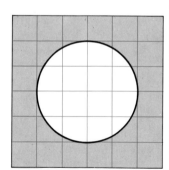

Abstract curves and squares

basis of your garden plan will depend on its suitability to the site, considering levels and views, and the period of the building it adjoins. A modern abstracted design, for example, would probably be unsuitable for an eighteenth-century house, while a modern, semi-detached house seldom requires a symmetrical, formal plan.

Remember that small elements, like bricks or granite blocks, can be used for quite intricate patterns, while larger elements of stone or concrete block, are mostly suitable for larger, or simple layouts, if they are not to need expensive cutting. Simpler shapes, too, are easier to fill with plants. Odd corners are seldom easy to fill with any garden medium – hard or soft. But having said that, it is better to think of a pattern first, and then decide how to describe its lines and fill it in. It is too easy to become bogged down at the start in plants and materials and how to use them. The patterns shown opposite illustrate a few possible choices on an idealized square plot. As yet, no decision has been made as to what the lines enclose (paths, planting, lawns or terraces), but each pattern creates a different feel and so will make a different garden. Your garden will have its individual shape and it will have its own character established by many variables, particularly your dwelling. You must try to emphasize this character through the lines you use to make the underlying pattern of your garden.

Dynamic pattern,
The bold lines which formed a simple pattern of interlocking circles, drawn boldly as the basis for a design, are very evident in this impressive garden. They now mark the boundaries of lawn, paths, steps, a plunge pool and planting.

Shape and texture

The lines which you have chosen to create your garden pattern will perhaps produce a satisfactory drawing in plan form. But the ultimate shape of that plan will only emerge as you take it into the third dimension, by planning the heights of different elements, be they walls or changes of level, or soft plantings of trees or shrubs. With these you build up the real shape of your garden so that it becomes a pleasant place to be in.

But what makes one plot a pleasant place to be, and another not, are the shapes and proportions of the grown masses of planted greenery that hold and surround those areas which we use to walk on or lounge in. Further, the shapes and proportions of these planted and non-planted areas can either complement or vie with the other three-dimensional shape on the site – your home.

These proportions, and whether they balance or not, are obvious in older, more mature gardens, where the planted masses – the trees and shrubs – are established and in front of you. What makes garden planning such a difficult art is that you must try to imagine the planted areas as they will appear in years to come while planting twigs now. It is difficult to grasp that even planners of the great English landscape parks of the eighteenth century had the same problem. They could reshape the landscape in the manner of "Capability" Brown, making lakes and shifting vast areas of earth, but they had to plant out their rolling parks with tiny trees which we see in their maturity more than two hundred years later.

Planted masses, of course, are not the only means of giving a garden shape. Walls, fences, raised beds, even built-in barbecues, mold the proportions of the smaller garden. The materials which you use will affect the feel of the garden considerably, reflecting or absorbing the light, or giving either a hard or a soft finish. However, within each planting

Composing on a small scale

Every grouping of elements in your garden should receive the same attention, however small the scale. Points of interest can be created with simple compositions that contrast shape and texture, like the one shown below. Plants of various shapes and textures are contrasted with a smooth stone or concrete ball.

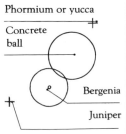

Phormium or yucca

Concrete ball

Bergenia

Juniper

Balancing shape and texture *The plan of this urban garden is bold and simple, holding the eye. The garden presents a green picture from the various levels of the house that it serves. While the firm shape of the design is softened by foliage forms, it is still strongly evident. A weaker layout would have become merely a collection of plants.*

Molding space, *right. In this layout, plants have moulded the space that we peer into through the shadow of foreground planting. The feeling of three-dimensional containment in a garden is important, and it is this aspect which makes a garden an effective retreat.*

area, you must eventually compose groupings, as you will see in the chapter on planting
design (see p. 167). The shape of each mature
plant and its components (leaves and stems)
is not the only consideration; its texture and
the quality of light which it reflects or dif-
fuses are also very significant. Consider and
compare a rhododendron leaf with that of a
camellia, for instance. The rhododendron
leaf is flat and dull while that of the camellia
is bright and shiny. Multiply this difference
by the number of leaves on an average bush
and the total adds up to a considerable
contrast. Deciduous species (those that drop
their leaves in winter) will obviously have
less all-year impact, but the appreciation of
the tracery shapes and the texture of their
bare branches and shoots is an acquired
pleasure in winter.

The garden in three dimensions

The shape of your garden is largely
created by three-dimensional effects.
Space can be molded by the siting
and subsequent growth of trees,
shrubs and smaller plants. The two
examples, below, show how the
same site can be manipulated to
create totally different effects.
That on the left, termed formal, has

a grouping of foliage that holds the
eye, the masses of trees and shrubs
balancing each other.
That on the right, termed informal,
has a grouping of foliage that leads
the eye around a central mass and
suggests hidden extensions to the
garden. In both gardens, foliage
(mass) balances the open area (void).

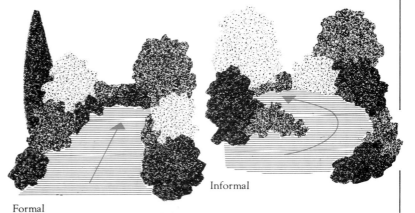

Formal

Informal

Color

Bright splashes of color, which every seedsman's catalogue would have you use, will only last for a limited period, for most plants actually flower for no more than one month in the year. Primarily, you should be concerned with more subtle color – the hues and tones of permanent foliage which last the whole year through. The foliage colors of both deciduous and evergreen shrubs and trees are remarkably varied, and, when well selected, will provide interest and cutting material throughout the year.

The "walls" of your outside room should be a background mass of subtle color. Seen in these terms, you will see that if this color is too strong it can become a disruption to the herbaceous or annual color that you might want to place against the background.

The colors of indigenous flowers are fairly low key in Northern Europe, with soft spring colors giving way to pale early summer ones which intensify through the months until the mellow tones of autumn appear. Harder, hotter flower colors originate in sunny climates, where their intensity is enhanced by the strength of the sun's rays. Be guided by nature and beware of man's interference. Plant breeders and hybridizers now strive to produce the most bizarre-colored varieties from even the simplest subjects. If

Subdued tones, *below. Compare the soft tones and beautifully blended foliage forms of this planting, with the striking blue border opposite. While the initial impact of the soft planting is not so dramatic, the subtle tonal range of this grouping creates a longlasting attraction.*

Theory of color
You should plan colors in the garden with the same care you give to decorating your home. To understand color, it helps to differentiate between hue (a pure color) and tone (a shade of a hue). The relationship of hues can be shown simply on the color wheel, below. The wheel has a warm half (magenta, red and yellow) and a cool half (green, cyan and blue). Hues next to each other on the wheel generally harmonize, while those opposite each other contrast.

Color wheel

Color harmony

Color contrast

Powerful warm colors, *right. The effect of this strong grouping of* Achillea, Helenium *and* Hemerocallis *is restful, despite the power of its warm colours. The secret lies in restricting the choice of colours to hues from a narrow sector of the colour wheel.*

there is a market for black roses, for example, then cultivators will produce them. Such plants are particularly difficult to use in juxtaposition with others, if they are not to dominate the scene.

Color outside should be used and controlled to back up the function and feeling of the garden, with herbaceous and annual color continuing the effect of your chosen foliage shrubs. Bright yellows and oranges, for example, are stimulating and are ideal in conjunction with a lively activity area. Softer colors, blues and pinks for instance, with a touch of purple or white, will produce a tranquil, calming effect. Both bright, stimulating colors and softer, recessive ones can be used in an area, but the effect should not be a pepper-and-salt one with both types mixed indiscriminately. Locate the strongest

colors within the foreground, and allow the colors to become paler with distance. A brilliant patch of color in the middle of a distant view is bound to be a visual disruption, as well as having a foreshortening effect.

So think carefully of the mood which you intend to underline with color, and when a selection of plants is to be seen against a backdrop of existing vegetation, grade the colors to compose the arrangement. The metallic blues and dark greens, contrasted with silver and gold in an average conifer selection, only produce tasteless discord.

Striking contrasts
The color impact of this border is breathtaking. Pinks and blues predominate, with gray in the selection of herbaceous plants and touches of lemon and white to enliven the whole. The border relies totally on color for its success but it has little form, with no bold foliage to subdue the color contrasts.

Evolving a framework

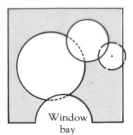

Furnished with your original survey (see pp. 28–29) and some basic ideas about designing a garden (see pp. 30–35), it is time to produce your own garden pattern, but to do this you need a framework to guide your design. No design, from that of Concorde down to that of the smallest piece of jewelry, is a random shape plucked from the air.

The most useful framework to use is a grid of intersecting equally-spaced lines. The spacing of the lines of this grid (its "modulation" in design terms) must usually depend on either the structure of your house, or on the boundaries which surround your plot. Study these structures closely, for your purpose must be to relate the scale of your grid to the scale of one or the other, or perhaps both, of these influences.

You might find that the external structure of your house suggests a strong, regular division of space. Look at the house wall facing on to the garden. If it has a formal design, for example, there will be a recognizable rhythm of the measurement which divides its doors and windows. These intervals might suggest the spacing of your grid. Modern houses are often built of pre-fabricated units which will similarly suggest the spacing. Many houses, however, have weaker, asymmetrical designs. If this is the case, it is better to look elsewhere for the scale of your grid.

Walls and fences are usually constructed in a regular pattern with vertical supports at regular intervals, in concrete, wood or brick, infilled with wood or brick. Such a boundary can provide an ideal starting point as you can use the post or pier interval as the spacing for your grid. Many sites will have little else to indicate a framework for the final plan.

To draw your grid, lay a separate piece of tracing paper over your original survey and, ensuring that you are working to the same scale, extend lines across the site starting from your reference points, either at 90 degrees to the house, or to the boundary, whichever you have chosen. Using the same interval which separates each of these lines, overlay another set at 90 degrees to the first set, covering the site with squares.

This square piece of tracing paper should now be used as a guide for positioning elements and creating patterns in your garden. Any pattern which you evolve within these guidelines will have a scale relationship either to the building which it surrounds and serves, or to the fences or walls which bound it. If you later reinforce this relationship by constructing your garden in materials which match those of the house or boundary, house and garden will inevitably link strongly and your design will support a variety of treatments when it comes to infilling the pattern.

When you come to draw the pattern that will be the basis for your garden plan, use the grid as a guide wherever possible, coinciding right-angles with the intersections of the grid lines and using the spacing of the grid as radii for any circles necessary. Although it is best to follow a grid where possible, to achieve a positive and bold plan, you can use your guiding grid in a flexible way. You can divide the squares of the grid in equal proportions, or even turn it through 45 degrees, to accommodate specific features.

Interlocking circles, *right. The pattern of this walled garden is a series of interlocking circles, inspired by the projecting bay window of the adjacent house, as can be seen in the diagram, above. The raised circle is edged in brick and surfaced in gravel with random planting and rock grouping.*

The grid as ground pattern, *below right. Although a grid should be used as a temporary overlay to guide your pattern, here it has been used as the finished pattern of a garden plan. A small area of the garden has been divided into three boxes of contrasting paving and uniform ground cover planting.*

Making and using a grid

The garden frontage of the house, shown right, has some interest, particularly in the projecting wing. However, more dominant is a boundary wall with piers spaced at 1.8-m (6-ft) intervals and these have provided the spacing for the guiding grid of a garden plan. The grid lines do, however, coincide with the important features of the garden elevation of the house as well, making this grid particularly successful. The beginnings of a pattern have been drawn on to the grid, circles and squares being included with equal confidence. It is unlikely that all the existing features of your garden will fit a grid exactly but it is important to establish a discipline for your plan that will encompass most elements of the layout.

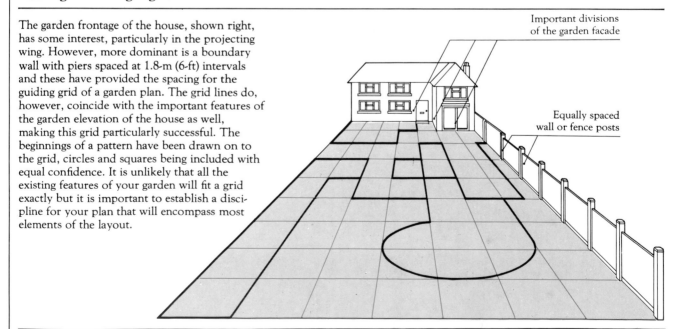

Important divisions of the garden facade

Equally spaced wall or fence posts

Linking house and garden, *above. In this urban garden the guiding grid has emerged strongly, linking the garden to the house façade rather than the public garden beyond the balustrade.*

The plan

On to your grid, which now overlays your basic site survey, you can next prepare to mark the areas that you have allocated for particular functions: the terrace to catch the sun, the vegetable area conveniently near to the house, an accessible area for rubbish bins, a greenhouse, an area of water, the soft fruit area and so on. Their positions will be influenced by convenience, the necessary positions of service paths and any safety precautions necessary for children. However, first you must consider the position of the sun in summer and winter, and prevailing winds, and make sure that you are neither blocking a particularly good view beyond the site, nor conversely, allowing too little room to plant a screen to hide a nasty one.

The positioning of these areas will sometimes suggest an overall pattern for the garden, or at least the run of the designated hard-surfacing. If no shape is forthcoming, evolve a pattern along the lines shown on pages 32 and 33, considering your preferences for regular or curved shapes. Always bear in mind, however, the contrasted effects which differing patterns create and their suitability to your site.

Often the area in which you are working will indicate the sort of pattern needed. A box-like garden, for example, surrounded by walls, will probably need a hard, straight-edged pattern which reflects the character of the site. You can later soften the whole with bold planting to achieve a balanced overall design. Curves generally need more space. Too large a circle within a square, for example, leaves corners which, in garden terms, are both hard to build and later to infill. Certain areas will of course require certain shapes. Although it is possible to cultivate vegetables in a circle, for example, straight rows are much easier to tend.

It is important to realize that all the parts of a garden design must work as a balanced whole, with no left-over corners and with positive balancing negative. The finished design should be clean and open, buildable, and ultimately workable. To achieve this clean, open plan, you must work within the discipline of your grid. Stick to its squares, fitting in angles at 90 degrees. Fit circles into the grid so that they run cleanly into each other and connect with the line of the house or a boundary. You might decide to turn the grid through 45 degrees and plan on the slant from your house and boundaries, or you might decide to divide the squares of your grid in half, thirds or quarters to facilitate a particular shape. But however you manipulate it, your guiding grid will provide an underlying strength to your plan. Your pattern will be positive, with bold sweeps to

Stages of the plan

The finished plan of your garden, shown as stage 4, below right, is achieved after completing stages 1 to 3 as carefully as possible, following the advice on pages 30–31 and 38–39. With this enclosed court-yard garden, stage 1 shows how a guiding grid can be evolved from the position and size of the garage, and the front and kitchen door-ways. Stage 2 shows the grid extended to cover the whole area and notes added on site conditions and potential features. Lines coinciding

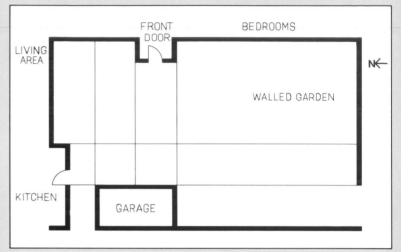

Stage 1

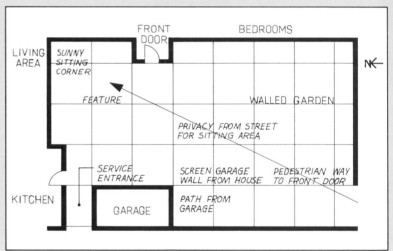

Stage 2

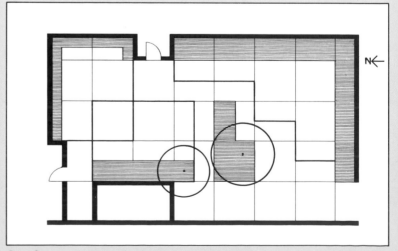

Stage 3

with, or bearing a relationship to this grid will ensure that the features of the garden will eventually bear a strong relationship to the house and garage.

Stage 3 involves the choice of pattern and areas to be planted, surfaced or otherwise given some sort of feature. As the finished plan emerges, decisions such as what type of paving and whether there should be changes of level have to be made. Planting will need further planning (see p. 168).

curves. There will be no weak, wiggling lines in the pattern and when the grid is removed and you draw up your final plan, the pattern will stand on its own as a meaningful shape, broadly encompassing differing functions and areas of activity.

Using a grid to help your design will work for any size of garden and for any style, whether you prefer straightforward traditional patterns, or those which are abstracted or flowing. Try to visualize the garden in a sort of patchwork pattern, with areas of cultivation, of lawn and of paving, rather than inhibiting yourself by too rigid a layout of paths which leave awkward, left-over plots. Your garden should be dominated by areas of attraction which are served by hard surfacing.

Your final working plan will be a two-dimensional guide. Its success will depend on how you have been able to imagine the three-dimensional results of your plan – a procedure that becomes easier as your experience of plants and garden materials grows. The sketched projection, below left, is a representation of my mind's-eye-view of the shape of this garden.

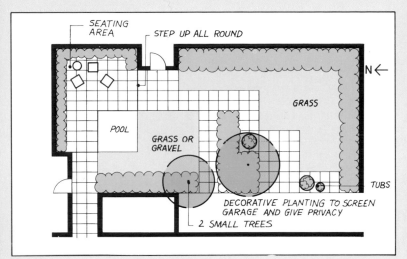

SEATING AREA
STEP UP ALL ROUND
N ←
GRASS
POOL
GRASS OR GRAVEL
DECORATIVE PLANTING TO SCREEN GARAGE AND GIVE PRIVACY
2 SMALL TREES
TUBS

Stage 4

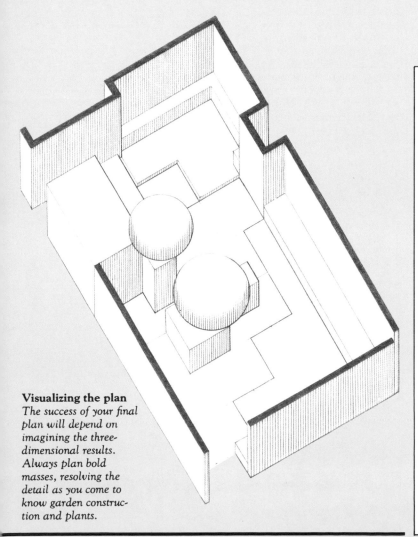

Visualizing the plan
The success of your final plan will depend on imagining the three-dimensional results. Always plan bold masses, resolving the detail as you come to know garden construction and plants.

How the garden might look
The impression, below, gives some idea of how this garden might come together when every detail of color and texture has been resolved. This is a stage you will see develop only after much preliminary work has been completed.

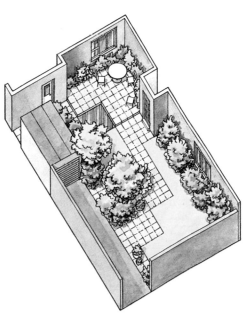

Well-designed gardens

Each garden illustrated in the following pages has been chosen as an example of successful garden planning. They show how the "rules" of good garden design have been used to produce gardens of individuality and character. Each garden is a composition in itself. What makes the compositions satisfying in each case is the effect of hard materials offset by softening planting and the enlivening influence of some sculptural element, often a simple pot or a group of boulders. Each, too, has a theme or a focal point, whether it be water, an outstanding tree or some other eye-catching feature.

The balance between structure and plants in a garden is difficult to achieve, for the horticultural content of a garden constantly changes with growth. Even when established, the balance has still to be maintained by pruning and thinning plants. In the following gardens, the balance is achieved, and its maintenance helped, by a simple garden plan – a crucial factor common to most well-designed gardens. Their outlines, in whatever material they are realized, can be appreciated even if the plan is thickly planted.

Gardens can be appreciated on a number of levels: from a design standpoint, from a horticultural standpoint and from an entirely emotional one. Emotional reaction to gardens is personal, while horticultural appreciation depends on knowledge and an interest in gardening. The appreciation of design, however, is an expression of personal likes and dislikes of a particular composition, for we all react differently to colors, patterns, shapes and textures. Once in a garden the senses of smell and hearing also play a part – the scent of a particular flower, the rustle of bamboo leaves, the singing of birds and the movement and fall of water affects all of us differently. The garden is one of the few art forms that can stimulate all our senses.

Unhappily, we cannot speak with the owners of these gardens, so the nuances of the compositions might elude us. We can only study them, seeking to understand how the elements and their arrangement are successful. But in seeing the use of line, pattern, shape, form and color in the following gardens, remember that your own garden must be planned to satisfy you and your family, and not necessarily others, so aping effective layouts will not be successful. It is up to the gardener to be his own designer, but looking closely at pictures of other people's designs can be an inspiration.

Water garden

This pool, the bridge and all the other, smaller components of the group work together as one sculptural unit and must give enormous pleasure to its owner throughout the year.

The pool is a rectangle, crossed by a timber bridge at right angles to it. The bridge structure is of softwood horizontals laid across metal braces. It is important that such a bridge, with no handrails, is wide enough for the pedestrian to feel safe. One edge of the pool is let into a bricked terrace, laid in a basket-weave pattern with a brick-on-edge surround. The treatment of the concrete pool at this end is informal, with rocks and boulders descending into the water.

The key plants are foreground fescue grass (*Festuca ovina glauca*) with the sword-like leaves of *Phormium tenax* beyond. In the foreground there is *Bergenia beesiana*, with its big, evergreen leaves. The far side of the pond is decorated with a sumach tree (*Rhus typhina*), while to the left of it the distant jar is highlighted against a bamboo (*Arundinaria* sp.).

In design terms the plan is quite formal, but subtle touches such as the counterpoise of the urns and the well-considered plant groupings make the arrangement appear pleasantly informal.

Key
1 *Miscanthus sinensis*
2 *Typha maxima* in pool
3 *Arundinaria* sp.
4 *Rhus typhina*
5 *Festuca ovina glauca*
6 *Phormium tenax*
7 Annual nasturtiums
8 *Bergenia beesiana*

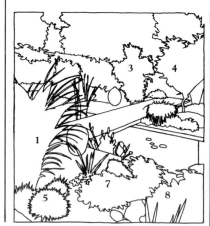

Deck garden

We tend to think of gardens as always being seen from ground level, but many gardens, especially in towns, are seen from above and need both a strong ground plan and plants with large leaves so that one can be appreciated through the other, as in the example above.

The garden, or outside room, illustrated here is constructed in timber and furnished with plants. The sunny part of the garden, against the house, is decked to form both a terrace and a surround to a small pond. The terrace provides a junction between house and garden. Built on to the deck is a low bench seat, which is backed by a herb bed. From this decking, one steps down into a private, outside dining-room, screened from neighbors, with planting areas contained by stained wood retaining walls, which match those of the decking.

The foliage that shades the garden is *Aralia elata* on the left, with *Rhus typhina* on the right. In the right foreground are the gray-green leaves of the perennial *Macleaya cordata*. Water lily pads are contrasted with rushes and water iris in the pond.

This is a designer's garden, for few others would be so restrained in their selection of forms and leaf shapes. A detail of interest is the concealment of the pool edge by the decked terrace. The pool container itself could simply be of fiberglass. Notice also the pleasant small-scale ribbed effect of the stable tile surface to the lower garden. The lesson to learn from this garden is the quiet calm that such a disciplined layout can produce.

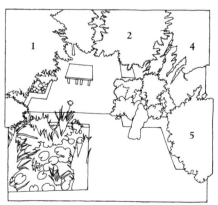

Key
1 *Aralia elata*
2 *Rhus typhina*
3 Small bed of mixed herbs
4 *Polygonum baldschuanicum*
5 *Macleaya cordata*

Suburban garden

This small garden is one in a row adjoining terraced, single story houses, built so that the wall of one house becomes the garden wall of another. Against this wall, a planting area has been retained with U-shaped pre-cast concrete blocks, and another adjoining row used to form a permanent garden bench, which can be provided with cushions in summer. This area looks into a small, private, paved space, bursting with plants and culminating in a single millstone fountain feature, set among boulders. The boulders are laid in a concrete saucer so that the overflowing water is retained and pumped back up through the center of the millstone. Pergola beams successfully divide the garden and frame a view to the small area beyond. A subtle detail that deceives the eye as to the size of the area is a mixing of paving materials. A coarse aggregate concrete block has been used and a pattern of granite works its way through them.

The planting is full and areas of planting interlocking with paving give movement to the garden, and this again makes it appear larger.

Key (plan joins split image)
1 *Miscanthus sinensis*
2 *Picea abies*
3 *Ligularia stenocephala*
4 *Kniphofia* sp.
5 *Arundinaria nitida*
6 Mixed planting including *Pinus mugo*
7 *Koelreuteria paniculata*
8 *Lavandula augustifolia*

Sunken garden

This small, sunken garden makes a handsome and secluded sunbathing area and can also be used for entertaining. It could work in either town or country, at ground level or on a roof. The designer has created a world on its own and, although the central space is open, the area is full of detail. The sympathetic use of hard materials, contrasted with softening plants, has created a visually satisfying balance.

The beds surrounding the central brick area are bounded by pre-cast U-shaped blocks used on their sides. They are wide enough to serve as bench seats. The stained timber detailing of the pergola, fencing and decking path hold the design together, while the subtly placed stones and an old millstone provide low key sculptural features. Such a garden layout would be hard and unsympathetic without a generous planting. The selection of plants is mainly evergreen for year round interest, though the deciduous weeping silver birch (*Betula pendula* cv.) makes an attractive feature even without its leaves.

Key
1 *Pinus sylvestris*
2 Mixed shrubs including azaleas
3 *Berberis* sp. with *Sambucus* sp behind
4 *Betula pendula* cv.
5 *Armeria maritima*
6 *Lavandula augustifolia*
7 Brick paving in basket-weave pattern
8 Old millstone
9 Stained softwood timber decking

Long, thin garden

The long, thin terrace site is a difficult shape to design satisfactorily. Some gardeners mistakenly try to resolve the problem by reducing a larger garden layout in scale to fit the site. This, however, creates small, unrelated patches of interest within too confined an area, whereas on a larger scale areas of grass or other surfacing would have held the concept together.

The designer of this 18 × 6 m/59 × 19 ft garden has taken the site as a whole and created a serpentine meander through it, providing an outside "room" for family use and another for play at the far end. The two are linked by strong architectural planting, which contrasts well with the hard paving materials and camouflages neighboring houses, to provide a real extension to the house.

A low seating wall of U-shaped concrete units also divides the two areas. The foreground space is paved with pre-cast concrete blocks, which run to the sanded play area. The latter is retained by timber sections, set in concrete.

The plant selection will look well throughout the year. Clumps of bamboo, sustained by, and combined with, tall summer grasses, are used to provide evergreen screening to the fence. The small tree with a sculptural quality on the left of the concrete seat is a cut-leaf sumach, *Rhus typhina laciniata*. In the middle distance is a shade-loving, large-leaved *Hosta glauca*.

The success of this small garden design stems from the balanced but generous arrangement of hard textures with soft planting infill, and a simple, yet positive, working layout.

Key
1 Sandpit
2 Herbaceous plants with roses
3 *Rhus typhina laciniata*
4 *Cotoneaster simonsii*
5 Paving interspersed with brick
6 Azaleas, *Arundinaria* sp. and trailing plants

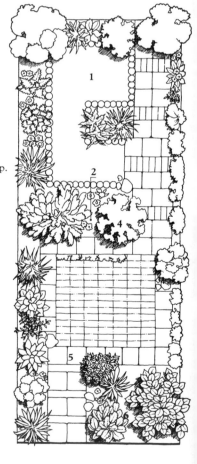

Shaded water-garden

Two raised areas of water make a visual center for the small, shaded town garden, shown above, that backs on to the rear wall of a neighboring dwelling. The design perfectly illustrates how to make a virtue out of necessity.

The layout is an abstract pattern of interlocking rectangular shapes in brick, though with the addition of a change in level. The plan culminates in a terracotta bust, offset by the painted, neighboring wall.

This simple subtlety in design works so well because it combines a carefully conceived modern plan with traditional materials that provide an attractive feature – the raised pools. The edges of the pools also provide casual seating. Planting in such a location is difficult because of shade and dripping rainwater from the overhanging trees, but ferns and mosses (growing on the left) do well in these conditions, as does bamboo. The positioning and form of the foreground shrub, a cotoneaster, offsets the shape of the pools. The only hard material used is brick.

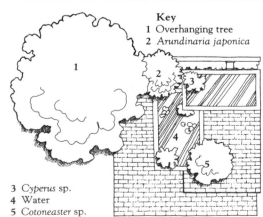

Key
1 Overhanging tree
2 *Arundinaria japonica*
3 *Cyperus* sp.
4 Water
5 *Cotoneaster* sp.

Front and rear town garden

The pattern of the small rear garden in this Milanese example has been turned at an angle of 45 degrees to the house; to work round a pear tree and thereby make what would have been a dull little garden into something quite unusual. There are many interesting corners which are not only servicable but make stimulating, abstract patterns of wood and water, centered on pieces of metal sculpture. The whole is designed to be appreciated not only from within the garden space but from the house.

The designer has used only two materials in its construction, giving the layout added strength: wooden block paviers and disused railway line ties and large, rounded cobbles. The cobbles have been used in such a way as to deter small children.

The railway ties have been used to form retaining walls, a bridge and a bench seat, and to provide an attractive end "wall" which also serves to screen a rubbish area by the far boundary. Unplanted, such a hard treatment might be thought overscaled, but when fully planted the relationship between hard and soft materials is fully balanced. Much of the planting is evergreen for year round interest, with bold clumps of foliage working with the ground pattern – fatsias, camellias, bergenias, rhododendrons and variegated *Hedera colchica* have all been incorporated with ferns (which are not evergreen) in the shaded corners. The rampant climber, *Parthenocissus tricuspidata veitchii* grows through the far boundary fence and provides brilliant color in autumn.

The frontage to this house is narrow but it is full of interest. The color is warm and welcoming and the garden plan is essentially a path straight to the door, but circulating round a large piece of sculpture. The same sort of wood blocks have been incorporated as in the rear garden, but they have also been used with granite blocks.

Above and top, rear garden
Right, front garden

Key

1 *Parthenocissus tricuspidata veitchii* on fence
2 *Iris pseudacorus*
3 *Ilex* sp., rhododendron and variegated *Hedera colchica*
4 Large pear tree
5 *Fatsia japonica*
6 *Yucca* sp., *Chamaerops humilis*
7 Camellias, *Hydrangea macrophylla*
8 Pots of bulbs and summer bedding

Rear garden

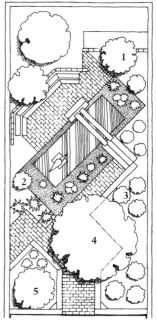

Front garden

Park-side garden

Most of the gardens illustrated in this section are of European origin. Their designs are impeccable – designs that work in a constructional sense and in the use of plant material in conjunction with the layout. There is, however, a lack of variety in their planting since cold continental winters inhibit many plants that can be grown in the British Isles and regions of similarly mild winters.

It is the abundance of plant material in English gardens that cold climate visitors find so attractive. Then, too, there is a more relaxed approach to garden design in the British Isles. This comparatively new garden in central London illustrates both points.

The setting is grand and monumental, for the crescent of houses, of which this is one, are of early 19th-century origin though with obvious 18th-century influence. Any gardening in the shadow of this type of structure calls for a strong layout if it is not to appear insignificant. The plan is therefore a simple checkerboard of brickwork, on the scale of the house, infilled with stone paving or grass. It was originally intended that the grass area should be of consolidated gravel, but the designer's client thought that grass, a continuation of the ground medium of the communal garden beyond, was more appropriate. To strengthen the bond with the communal garden, balustrading crosses the garden so that the two appear to be joined. The planting, though heavily shaded by trees, is full and, in the traditional English manner, is a bold mixture of masses, seemingly bursting from their confining beds.

Key
1 *Laurus nobilis*
2 *Cordyline australis* in pots
3 Old pear
4 Mixed planting in light shade

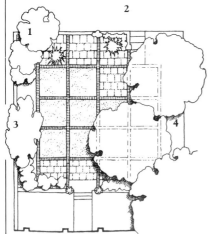

GARDEN-BY-GARDEN GUIDE

Gardens of different shapes, sizes and styles with
alternative possibilities for their design

*Alternative suggestions for plants in cold climate
gardens are included*

Small walled garden

You can grow an extensive range of plants in a small, walled garden, particularly if it catches the sun. The garden illustrated below is a good example of what can be achieved within a limited space. The view is from the upper story of the house, showing the garden's profusion of flower color. The high view-point also shows how the terrace is divided from the rest of the garden.

Both treatments opposite show the space opened up to provide a broader view of the planting when the owner is sitting on the terrace or within the house at ground-floor level. In the top suggestion the pattern is turned at 45 degrees to the house, so that a meander is created in the design; the end of the garden is lost but the eye is led to a piece of sculpture.

The lower suggestion is a more formal design but the view is again stopped, this time by a pergola running across the area. An arresting feature is provided by a timber bench surrounding the tree sited half-way down the lawn. Both designs provide a paved edging so that foreground herbaceous material can overflow.

Enclosure and abundant planting *This garden has old-world charm with its mass of flower color and its feeling of seclusion. The terrace is enclosed and has a relaxed feel with plants allowed to spread into the jointing of the random stone.*

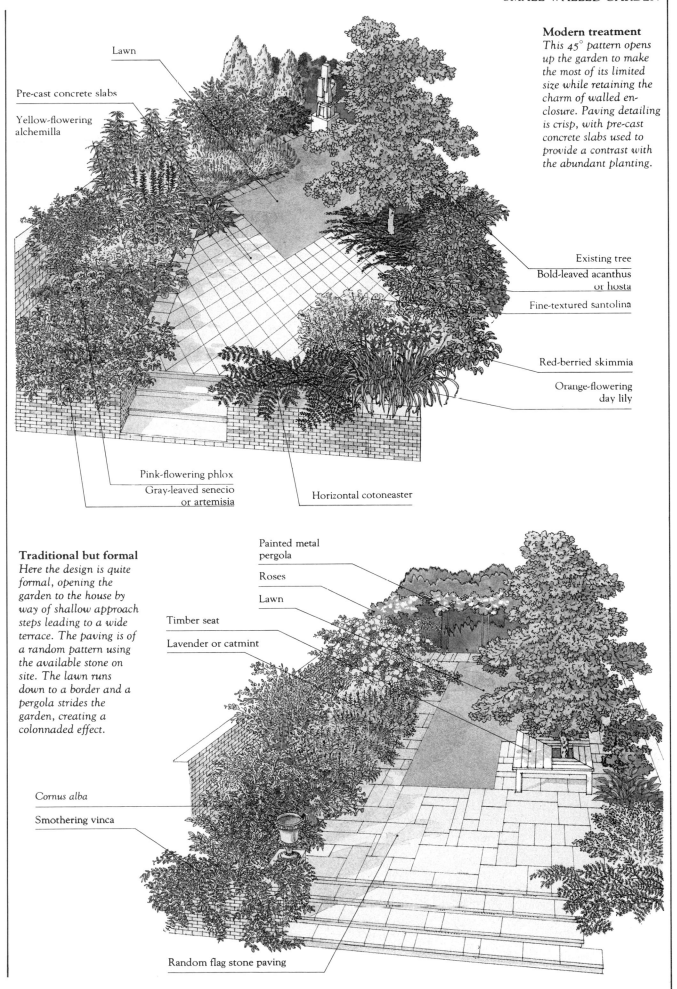

Lawn

Pre-cast concrete slabs

Yellow-flowering
alchemilla

Modern treatment
*This 45° pattern opens
up the garden to make
the most of its limited
size while retaining the
charm of walled en-
closure. Paving detailing
is crisp, with pre-cast
concrete slabs used to
provide a contrast with
the abundant planting.*

Existing tree

Bold-leaved acanthus
or hosta

Fine-textured santolina

Red-berried skimmia

Orange-flowering
day lily

Pink-flowering phlox
Gray-leaved senecio
or artemisia

Horizontal cotoneaster

Traditional but formal
*Here the design is quite
formal, opening the
garden to the house by
way of shallow approach
steps leading to a wide
terrace. The paving is of
a random pattern using
the available stone on
site. The lawn runs
down to a border and a
pergola strides the
garden, creating a
colonnaded effect.*

Painted metal
pergola

Roses

Lawn

Timber seat

Lavender or catmint

Cornus alba

Smothering vinca

Random flag stone paving

53

Spacious room outside

The garden to this house is a true outside room, for it connects directly to the building and is the only outlook from the windows. Vegetation provides shelter and privacy, so that the space is conducive to outside use.

The garden is slightly sunken, so that there is a step down to it from the boarded decking that adjoins the house. Beds, surrounded by brick paving, have been arranged to provide a small flower garden. Such a layout might with equal effect have been employed as a herb garden or, if the gardener were interested, a model vegetable garden.

The treatment in the top example, opposite, enlarges the decking area, which now projects into an area of water. Stepping stones cross the pool to a sitting bay, which is covered with a timber pergola over which a Russian vine grows. Planting includes a proportion of evergreen, with yellow spring-flowering *Cytisus* sp. and *Genista* sp.

The proposal below comprises a progression of brickwork bands, with tightly-packed granite paving between. Planting, which includes gray-leaved *Santolina* sp. and *Senecio* sp. with purple-leaved *Berberis* sp., runs through the pattern bands to give a staggered effect. The garden culminates in an L-shaped bench, facing towards the house. Tubs of blue-flowering *Agapanthus* sp. punctuate the design.

"Window" planting areas *The shape of the garden beds and the brickwork employed in this design resemble the wall and windows of a Romanesque church when seen from the house.*

Including water and a pergola, *right. In this proposal, the decked terrace has been extended to project into a pool. The pergola encloses an intimate space for summer use.*

Plan

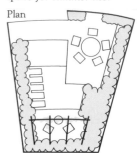

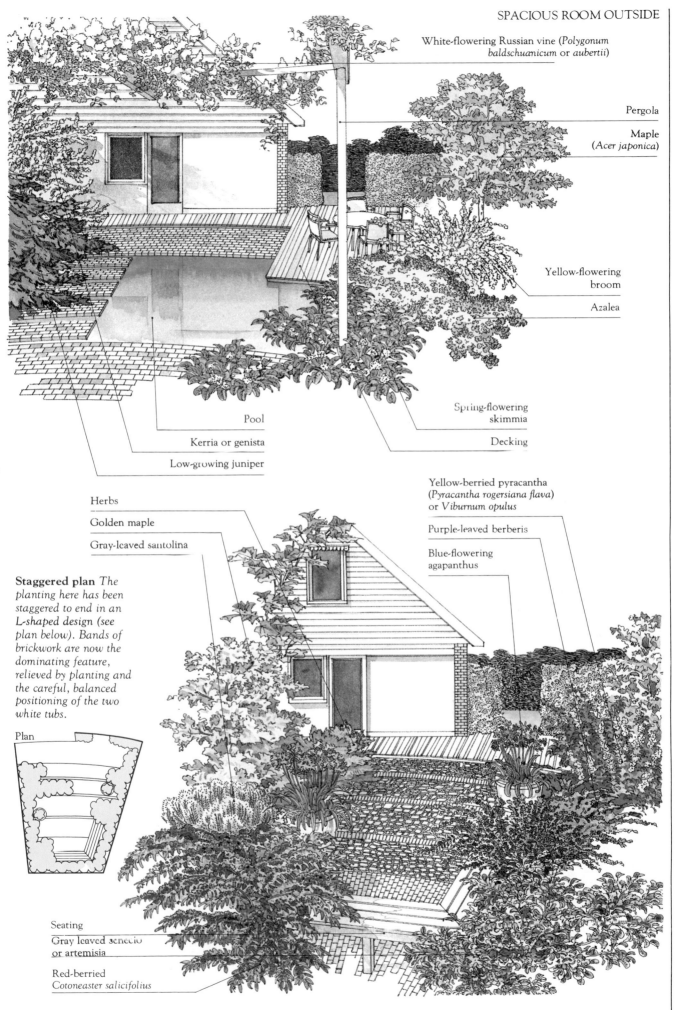

White-flowering Russian vine (*Polygonum baldschuanicum* or *aubertii*)

Pergola

Maple (*Acer japonica*)

Yellow-flowering broom

Azalea

Spring-flowering skimmia

Decking

Pool

Kerria or genista

Low-growing juniper

Herbs

Golden maple

Gray-leaved santolina

Yellow-berried pyracantha (*Pyracantha rogersiana flava*) or *Viburnum opulus*

Purple-leaved berberis

Blue-flowering agapanthus

Staggered plan *The planting here has been staggered to end in an L-shaped design (see plan below). Bands of brickwork are now the dominating feature, relieved by planting and the careful, balanced positioning of the two white tubs.*

Plan

Seating

Gray-leaved senecio or artemisia

Red-berried *Cotoneaster salicifolius*

55

Town garden with a backdrop

This town garden ends by the rear wall of a garage, which has been made the backdrop and focal point of the layout by extending a pergola from it to cover a decked terrace. The pool on the left has a raised stone surround; general surfacing is of granite blocks. Plants include foreground *Ilex* on the right, which face the large leaves of *Vitis coignetiae*. Bamboo (*Arundinaria* sp.) and Portuguese laurel make up much of the remainder of the planting.

The top layout opposite has a strong gridded pattern, which harmonizes with the proportions of the pool and garden. The ground pattern is composed of precast concrete slabs (the color of the stone pond surround), with an infill of brick to match the garage construction. Most of the existing evergreen planting remains, but a low species of *Cytisus* is included at the end of the pond. The Russian vine that masks an ugly height transition with neighboring buildings at the end of the garden in the existing design is replaced with a contorted hazel (*Corylus avellana* 'Contorta'), backed with pyracantha.

The garage in the lower proposal remains the focal point in the design but it has been further incorporated into the layout. Planting to screen the garage includes *Malus floribunda* on the right hand side, with evergreens in front; on the other side of the garden, behind the pond, are grouped *Rhus typhina*, with *Viburnum plicatum* in front. Perennial planting before them includes iris, and aster for autumn interest. At the rear of the garden, hellebores are planted in the shade, with small-leaved golden ivy that will grow up to cover the garage. The garden is then furnished with tubs of bright annuals and bulbs for early spring effect.

Backdrop as a feature
This garden terminates at the rear of a garage and in the existing design the roof of the garage has been extended to become a pergola over a decked terrace. The idea is a good one and works well to provide a private seating area within a small garden.

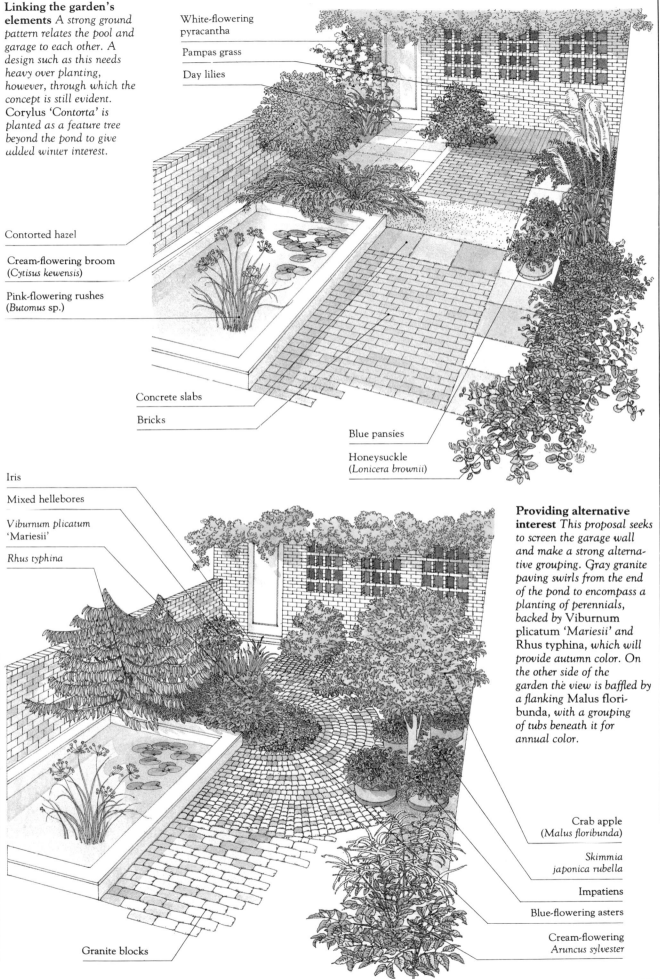

Linking the garden's elements *A strong ground pattern relates the pool and garage to each other. A design such as this needs heavy over planting, however, through which the concept is still evident. Corylus 'Contorta' is planted as a feature tree beyond the pond to give added winter interest.*

White-flowering pyracantha

Pampas grass

Day lilies

Contorted hazel

Cream-flowering broom
(*Cytisus kewensis*)

Pink-flowering rushes
(*Butomus* sp.)

Concrete slabs

Bricks

Blue pansies

Honeysuckle
(*Lonicera brownii*)

Iris

Mixed hellebores

Viburnum plicatum 'Mariesii'

Rhus typhina

Providing alternative interest *This proposal seeks to screen the garage wall and make a strong alternative grouping. Gray granite paving swirls from the end of the pond to encompass a planting of perennials, backed by* Viburnum plicatum 'Mariesii' *and* Rhus typhina, *which will provide autumn color. On the other side of the garden the view is baffled by a flanking* Malus floribunda, *with a grouping of tubs beneath it for annual color.*

Crab apple
(*Malus floribunda*)

Skimmia japonica rubella

Impatiens

Blue-flowering asters

Cream-flowering
Aruncus sylvester

Granite blocks

Woodland garden

The cultivated section and wild areas seen from this garden are clearly defined by the strong line of the hedge that divides the two. Natural woodland acts as a backcloth for the plant forms within the man-made garden and so creates a sense of seclusion and contrast.

In the proposal opposite below, the garden is made completely open to the woodland beyond with the removal of the distant garden planting, so that features are made of the silver birches (*Betula* sp.) and the trunks of the oak trees (*Quercus* sp.). The shape of the lawn is softened so that the cultivated grass disappears into the shadow of the woodland, with an outpost of "wild" garden planting (foxgloves) on the right. In spring, bulbs and later bluebells will grow in the areas of rough grass. With careful lighting, this garden could look magical at night.

When a boundary line must be defined, such an open solution is not feasible. In the proposal opposite above, silver birches have been established nearer the garden to link the natural woodland and the cultivated area even though the boundary hedge remains. Additional planting of wild grasses to the right repeats the original foreground planting but otherwise the distant garden planting has been removed to allow woodland and garden to blend. The far boundary is a single wire that allows a view through to the woodland.

Even though the woodland may not be part of the property, it is the "borrowed landscape" (features beyond the confines of the garden that provide visible background) of the garden. Few town gardens have so spectacular a backdrop as this but you can often reveal a view of a church tower or a neighbor's tree, simply by clearing the foreground. In attempting to create a view, however, be careful to maintain the privacy of your garden.

Contrasting garden and backdrop *The small, raised bed, the rectangular shape of the lawn and the shapes, forms and flower colors of the plants chosen, deliberately separate the existing garden from its woodland setting. The cultivated garden appears to be a protected, exotic area.*

Disguising the boundary *When a boundary line is absolutely necessary in such a setting, woodland planting can be introduced into the garden to soften the division between garden and surrounding woodland. Here the dwarf, fastigiate conifer has been removed from the foreground raised bed to allow a clear view of the nearest silver birches.*

Wire boundary line

Wild grasses

Repeated grass

Wooden container

Assorted alpines

Removing the garden boundary *Here the boundary hedge has been removed to open the view to the woodland and to allow the garden to flow naturally into tree shadow. The foreground grasses and the raised bed – a feature of the "cultivated" garden – have been removed to make way for plant forms that extend the woodland feel right up to the house.*

Foxgloves

Silver birches

Sedums

Areas of rough grass

Alchemilla mollis

Pinks

Mimulus or Veronica sp

Entrance garden

The entrance to a house can give clues about its occupants. Two factors influence this. As a general rule, the bigger the garden the less welcoming it appears, much as a large office with a single occupant seems intimidating. The second and most crucial factor, however, is the peripheral planting. If it is low and well-spaced, allowing an uninterrupted view to the house, the effect is welcoming. Conversely, tall, bunched planting that encloses the house gives the impression that the owner is unsocial. However, privacy may well be what you seek and this has been achieved in the garden below. The composition of structures and planting works throughout the year, with a mass of foliage established to hide the greater part of the house. An urn on a plinth makes a feature that points out an entrance way and marks the way to the narrow, but perfectly adequate, entrance path.

An isolated characteristic that will give a welcoming feel to your home is a wide access path, such as that shown in the top proposal opposite. The wide path has been enhanced by the use of alternate paving textures while the vertical line provided by conifer planting helps integrate the house with the garden. Other planting in this proposal is a mixture of the existing scheme with some new plants. The low-clipped hedging and ground cover masses to the left of the path have been retained, for example, while horizontal-growing junipers now edge the path on the right to emphasize the new width.

In the lower proposal, the entrance path has been opened out completely. Steps have become platforms, the shapes of which are repeated in ascending masses of clipped boxwood (*Buxus* sp.). To counteract the strong structure of the approach, multi-stemmed birches have been incorporated to soften the planting and to increase the scale of the design.

Private entrance, *below. If you seek privacy, this massed planting is effective and gives year-round cover and interest. Planting roughly balances the area of forecourt and the well-detailed path. Since the house is purposely masked and the entrance path is not deliberately linked with the front door, the effect suggests seclusion.*

Widening the approach, *right. The feeling of hospitality is strengthened by wide steps that give the pathway more importance in comparison with the low hedging on both sides of it. The fastigiate conifers that replace part of the original massed planting have the visual effect of joining the house to the garden.*

Reddish-purple maple

Low-clipped barberry

Fastigiate junipers

Horizontal-growing juniper

Low, shrubby pine

Small-leaved ivy

Spiky yucca

Random paving

Horizontal-growing juniper

Welcoming effect, *below. The effect here is very welcoming, for now the entrance path has been opened out completely and consists of platforms rather than steps. Both the use of a single paving material, brick, and the raised bed of scarlet impatiens, take the eye straight to the entrance way.*

Multi-stemmed birch

Raised bed with scarlet impatiens

Clipped box

Cobbles

Basket-weave brick paving

61

An enclosed corner

There is usually one favored corner in a garden, however small, that catches the sun the whole year round. You are lucky if your house is sited at such an angle that this corner is adjacent to it. Many have to make a sitting place to catch the warmth at a distance from the house and such an example – an enclosed corner – is shown below.

The ground rises 450 mm (18 in) into a corner formed by brick wall. In the existing design shown in the photograph, railway ties have been used to make the stepped levels into the corner. Stone slabs cross the levels and also provide a base for the timber seat. The warm tones of the brickwork are repeated in the mass of low shrub and perennial species. These mingle on the different levels to produce a patchwork of color. Such a country-garden-style mass can soon get out of hand, however, if the ground-covering species are not rigorously thinned each autumn.

The two alternative treatments for such a corner, illustrated opposite, show how sharply contrasted moods can be created by the selection and the location of plants to complement new structural elements. Any alternative treatment must be tempered by the existing conditions of the corner. You must choose plant species that like both warmth and a dry aspect because the foundations of the wall will soak up moisture. Bear in mind also that the strong root runs of certain species make them inappropriate for planting too close to walls.

The treatment you choose depends very much on the location of your garden. The summerhouse corner might best suit a town garden for it is crisp in its detailing, while the Japanese-style garden would be suitable anywhere if the style harmonizes with the rest of the garden.

While the existing country-garden selection of plants is of low, circular, colored forms, the summerhouse planting has a combination of larger circular forms contrasted with the stronger forms of evergreens and the summerhouse itself. The Japanese composition is altogether linear and, though low key in color content, has great visual interest throughout the year because of the strong forms of the plants used.

Country-garden corner *The existing country-garden corner is more random than the alternatives suggested opposite. Its effect depends on a massed carpet of aromatic prostrate perennials and shrubby herbs. The shrubby material includes thymes of various colors, low white lavender and fastigiate rosemary. Perennial gold creeping veronica forms a base for the tiers of wallflowers. Purple and silver variegated ajuga feature strongly. Much of the planting is evergreen, giving continued interest through the seasons.*

Summerhouse corner *The stepped levels to the summerhouse are in brick to match that of the walls. The canopy itself is tiled and the timber structure painted white. The lower level of loose gravel is planted with self-sowing perennial alyssum, while the shrubs and climbers are full and rounded to soften the hard lines of the walls, paving and building. The colors are soft; white, gray and a touch of blue.*

Fastigiate conifer

Ceanothus or dwarf Korean Lilac

White rambler rose

Large-leaved climbing ivy or clematis

Warty barberry or cistus

Low-trailing *Vinca minor*

Engineering brick

Spiky white-flowering libertia or day-lilies

Gravel

Spiky phormium or yucca

Japanese effect *The Japanese layout depends on the contrast between structural lines and the shape and form of plant material. Planting includes a craggy sumach, fronded bamboos and the drop of the branches of a small weeping willow which are repeated by wisteria flowers in season. The stepped levels and the seating platform are made up with railway sleepers but the infill is of cobbles. These elements combine with a water container to make a zig-zag of incidental interest.*

Blue-flowering tree wisteria

Weeping willow or 'Red Jade' crabapple

Craggy sumach (*Rhus typhina*)

Large-leaved bamboo

Railway tie

Loose cobbles

Low bamboo (*Arundinaria* sp.)

Large-leaved hosta

Luxuriant rural garden

This old garden runs parallel with the house and slightly above its base level. Instant character is provided by the dominant old apple tree at one end, which plays host to a profuse rambler rose. Shrubs on the right, facing the house, have become large and include a good proportion of evergreens.

In this situation, the gardener who wants to redesign his garden should accept the surrounding planting but rethink that at ground level. A modern layout would be discordant; far better to extend the old feel of the garden by turning it into an ecological area in which insects and birds are encouraged to find a home, and this is the purpose of the proposal, opposite top. For the young family especially, there is much to be said for a garden in which berries attract birds and various planting provides a sanctuary for small creatures. In my ecological garden a saucer-shaped pool has a stony

beach running down to the centre of it, giving access to the water; a grass path surrounds the pool and beyond, under the apple tree, a grouping of grasses provides good, natural protection for small creatures.

Alternatively, this garden could be revitalized to enhance its old world feel. More of a feature is made of the apple tree in the lower design by surrounding its base with a bench seat painted white. The right-hand side planting has been thinned and then extended. Perennials include traditional plants of phlox, aster, lupines and delphiniums together with low-growing herbs such as sage, chives and rue.

Traditional feel *The charming existing garden has reached a full-blown maturity with all of its plants grown to large proportions. There is a fine line between a mature garden and an overgrown one and any revitalization should be carefully considered if the original has charm.*

Ecological garden, *right. This version of the garden is planned to be attractive to wild life. The surrounding planting of grasses and berrying shrubs, such as Cotoneaster sp., is to attract birds, while flowering perennials will encourage butterflies and other insects. Foreground planting includes bold masses of Sedum sp., Helleborus sp. and Iris foetidissima for winter interest and to provide animal food.*

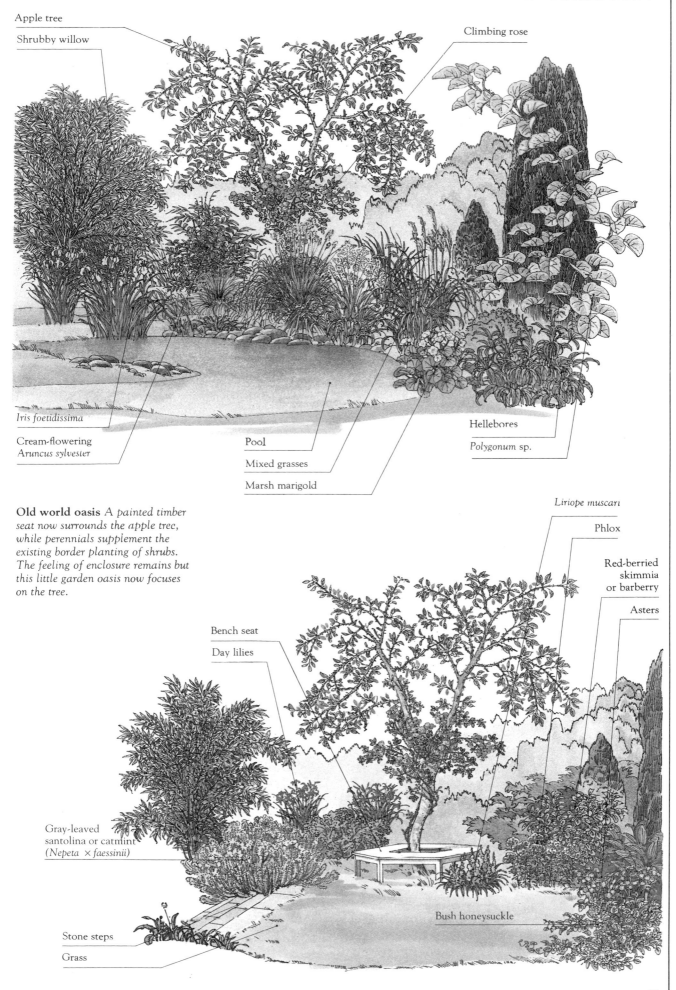

Apple tree

Shrubby willow

Climbing rose

Iris foetidissima

Cream-flowering
Aruncus sylvester

Pool

Mixed grasses

Marsh marigold

Hellebores

Polygonum sp.

Old world oasis *A painted timber
seat now surrounds the apple tree,
while perennials supplement the
existing border planting of shrubs.
The feeling of enclosure remains but
this little garden oasis now focuses
on the tree.*

Liriope muscari

Phlox

Red-berried
skimmia
or barberry

Asters

Bench seat

Day lilies

Gray-leaved
santolina or catmint
(Nepeta × faessinii)

Stone steps

Grass

Bush honeysuckle

Small courtyard garden

This modern atrium-type house has a central courtyard overlooked by all its rooms. From the existing planting of ferns and Japanese anemones (*Anemone japonica*), one would assume that it receives little light. The central shrub is a *Forsythia* sp. and all the plants are growing in gravel.

The existing garden area has been treated to provide an all-year visual feast. Such an enclosure, if it is to be treated as a garden, can be very exciting, for the conditions here are quite different from a normal exposed site. The courtyard has a micro-climate with still air warmed by heat from the house in colder weather. If it also receives sun, the vegetation in this environment can be exotic. A temporary roof in the winter would give extra protection.

The alternatives, opposite, treat the enclosure as an outside room for children's play or a water fantasy. The plan for a play area makes supervision from the adjoining kitchen easy and I have extended the tiled kitchen unit on the garden side of the window as a standing for plants and provided a small table at which children could sit. A sandpit could eventually be turned into a small pond. The rest of the area is paved, but slightly sunken so that the surrounding step becomes a seat, protecting the glazing from wheeled toys.

An entirely different feel has been achieved in the second possibility by making the whole enclosure a mirror of water, reflecting light into the house. The pool is lined with the same tiles as the kitchen and the water flows through individual tiles raised up on integral pillars.

A central feature is a bed of white *Iris laevigata*, with an underplanting of weed to keep the water clear. A few brightly colored koi carp, a mass of simple fountain jets or underwater lights for night-time will all help to bring the area to life.

A courtyard garden *In a courtyard garden such as this where plants are so minutely observed from all angles, it is asking a lot of them to provide continual pleasure and interest throughout the year. Strong and exotic plant forms pull this off though. Here ferns provide strong leaf shape against grasses and cobbles on a shingle bed.*

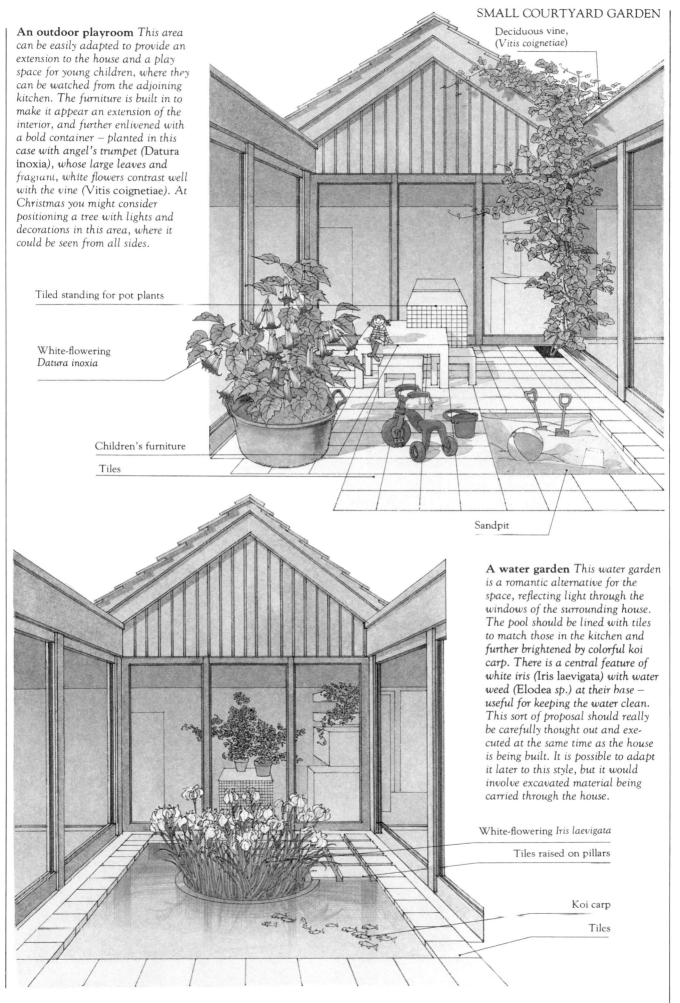

An outdoor playroom *This area can be easily adapted to provide an extension to the house and a play space for young children, where they can be watched from the adjoining kitchen. The furniture is built in to make it appear an extension of the interior, and further enlivened with a bold container – planted in this case with angel's trumpet (Datura inoxia), whose large leaves and fragrant, white flowers contrast well with the vine (Vitis coignetiae). At Christmas you might consider positioning a tree with lights and decorations in this area, where it could be seen from all sides.*

Deciduous vine, (*Vitis coignetiae*)

Tiled standing for pot plants

White-flowering *Datura inoxia*

Children's furniture

Tiles

Sandpit

A water garden *This water garden is a romantic alternative for the space, reflecting light through the windows of the surrounding house. The pool should be lined with tiles to match those in the kitchen and further brightened by colorful koi carp. There is a central feature of white iris (Iris laevigata) with water weed (Elodea sp.) at their base – useful for keeping the water clean. This sort of proposal should really be carefully thought out and executed at the same time as the house is being built. It is possible to adapt it later to this style, but it would involve excavated material being carried through the house.*

White-flowering *Iris laevigata*

Tiles raised on pillars

Koi carp

Tiles

Divided rural garden

This typical English garden was probably made 40 or more years ago, for the surrounding trees are mature. Gardens at that time were usually divided, with lawns and flowers near the house and a greenhouse and possibly a small vegetable garden beyond. Such an arrangement can produce extremely attactive results when the elements of the garden are linked by luxuriant foliage and when there is adequate dry paving connecting the various sections of the "working" garden – the vegetable and herb area beyond the greenhouse – to the house.

The two accompanying views, opposite, show how such a garden could be altered, though still within the original context. The top proposal is for a paved herb garden, working well with the greenhouse. A lattice plan of brickwork is infilled with further brick panels, alternating with brushed concrete. A raised brick pond is a focal point in the concept. The beds are filled with herbs, while the foreground barrel contains chives for a variation in plant forms. This layout makes the garden a lovely, scented place in summer, busy with bees, and will also provide an attractive, enclosed area in winter.

The lower design is a layout suitable for a modern cottage garden. The angles of the greenhouse roof have been repeated in the foreground metal arch and then again in the staggered pond and the path leading through the garden. This angularity is contrasted with soft, flopping herbaceous plants.

Separate lawn and greenhouse areas
View of a traditional English garden of the inter-war period, with grass at the rear of the house leading to a transitional greenhouse area with a vegetable patch beyond.

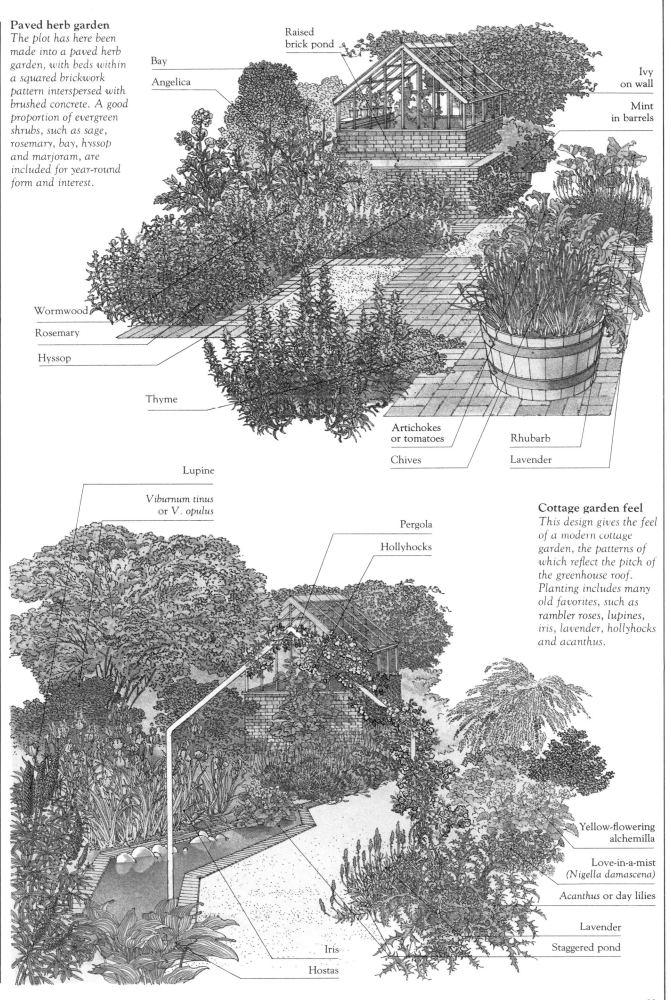

Paved herb garden
The plot has here been made into a paved herb garden, with beds within a squared brickwork pattern interspersed with brushed concrete. A good proportion of evergreen shrubs, such as sage, rosemary, bay, hyssop and marjoram, are included for year-round form and interest.

Bay

Angelica

Raised brick pond

Ivy on wall

Mint in barrels

Wormwood

Rosemary

Hyssop

Thyme

Artichokes or tomatoes

Chives

Rhubarb

Lavender

Lupine

Viburnum tinus or *V. opulus*

Pergola

Hollyhocks

Cottage garden feel
This design gives the feel of a modern cottage garden, the patterns of which reflect the pitch of the greenhouse roof. Planting includes many old favorites, such as rambler roses, lupines, iris, lavender, hollyhocks and acanthus.

Yellow-flowering alchemilla

Love-in-a-mist *(Nigella damascena)*

Acanthus or day lilies

Lavender

Staggered pond

Iris

Hostas

Sheltered corner

This small segment of a garden adjoining a house is enclosed and south facing, forming an attractive, sheltered corner. The area appears sunken as there is a surrounding retaining wall that creates an L-shaped raised bed to enclose the pool and waterfall. The scheme works well by combining a private section of garden with an area that also gives views to the garden and countryside beyond.

The proposals opposite completely separate the corner from its surroundings, to create an outside room screened for shelter and privacy. Both proposals retain the raised bed of the original to preserve the feeling of enclosure. The retaining wall is built of abutting U-shaped pre-cast concrete units, laid on their sides so that a shelf is provided for casual seating. In the example, top, similar concrete units have been used to provide an occasional table, and wooden screening in the mood of the existing structure baffles the view to provide extra seclusion.

The lower design makes more of the seating area with the addition of a wooden pergola, cantilevered from the existing timber surround to provide a canopy that hosts climbing plants

Major elements of the existing planting have been retained, but the top design has a simpler overall plan while in the lower suggestion the area is enclosed with dense evergreen planting to give additional shelter and a greater feeling of privacy.

Strong three-dimensional shape, *below. This sunken, sheltered corner adjoining a house is largely taken up with a pool and its waterfall inlet. An intermediate level has been created as a seating area. Structural elements and planting combine to provide a wealth of visual interest.*

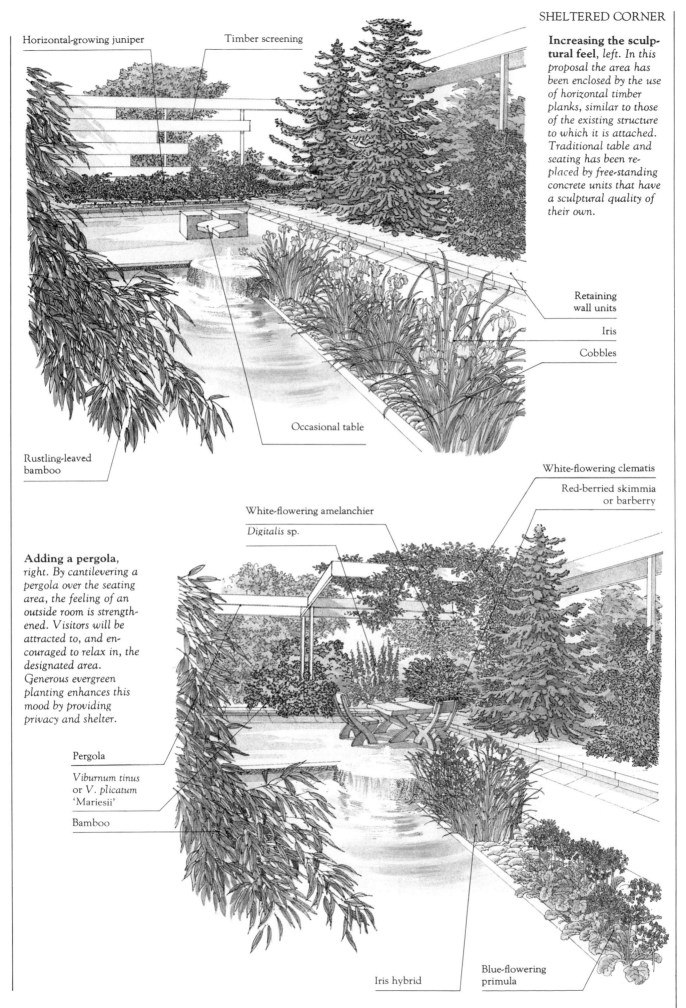

Horizontal-growing juniper

Timber screening

Increasing the sculptural feel, *left. In this proposal the area has been enclosed by the use of horizontal timber planks, similar to those of the existing structure to which it is attached. Traditional table and seating has been replaced by free-standing concrete units that have a sculptural quality of their own.*

Retaining wall units

Iris

Cobbles

Occasional table

Rustling-leaved bamboo

White-flowering clematis

Red-berried skimmia or barberry

White-flowering amelanchier

Digitalis sp.

Adding a pergola, *right. By cantilevering a pergola over the seating area, the feeling of an outside room is strengthened. Visitors will be attracted to, and encouraged to relax in, the designated area. Generous evergreen planting enhances this mood by providing privacy and shelter.*

Pergola

Viburnum tinus or *V. plicatum* 'Mariesii'

Bamboo

Iris hybrid

Blue-flowering primula

71

An unusual frontage

A small area of planting to offset the public façade of your house, and to lead to an entrance, is often a tricky one to design and plant, for the result must be satisfying the whole year round. If there is a gateway its appearance introduces another problem.

The existing frontage, below, has a garden area a little more than a meter wide. The gateway and fencing which back it are both as simple as possible in stained timber – a treatment in total sympathy with the uncompromising house façade. Planting is subordinate to the strength of the structures although the plant forms are helped by a "mulch" of large cobbles and pebbles. Name plate and latch are admirably clear and are illuminated at night by the well-positioned lighting pillar.

Any alternative treatments for this situation must also work in sympathy with the house frontage, perhaps softening it, but certainly not starkly contrasting with it. They should be eye-catching and strong in form,

utilizing plants that will stand the wear-and-tear of a situation alongside a busy path.

The two alternatives shown opposite both have strong visual elements close to the gate. The top version incorporates a small area of water, while below, the attraction is a sculptural grouping in timber, including a squared lighting pillar. In both examples, planting has been kept largely maintenance-free. The rising line of the planting towards the façade is also a constant factor. In this way the strong horizontal line of the house balcony is broken, when viewed at eye level, by the taller planting.

A modern front approach, *below. This front garden has simple fencing and paving to match the strong lines and tones of the house façade. The planting is lightweight by comparison.*

Introducing water, *right. Here the fencing is retained but the timber extended in simple trip rails to prevent people from walking into the small formal pool. The linear paving is also retained with the inclusion of a strip of cobbles which further protects the water. Planting between the water and the house has strong form and color, the leaves of stag's horn sumach (Rhus typhina) contrasting with a horizontal juniper (Juniperus sabina tamarscifolia) and the shrubby willow.*

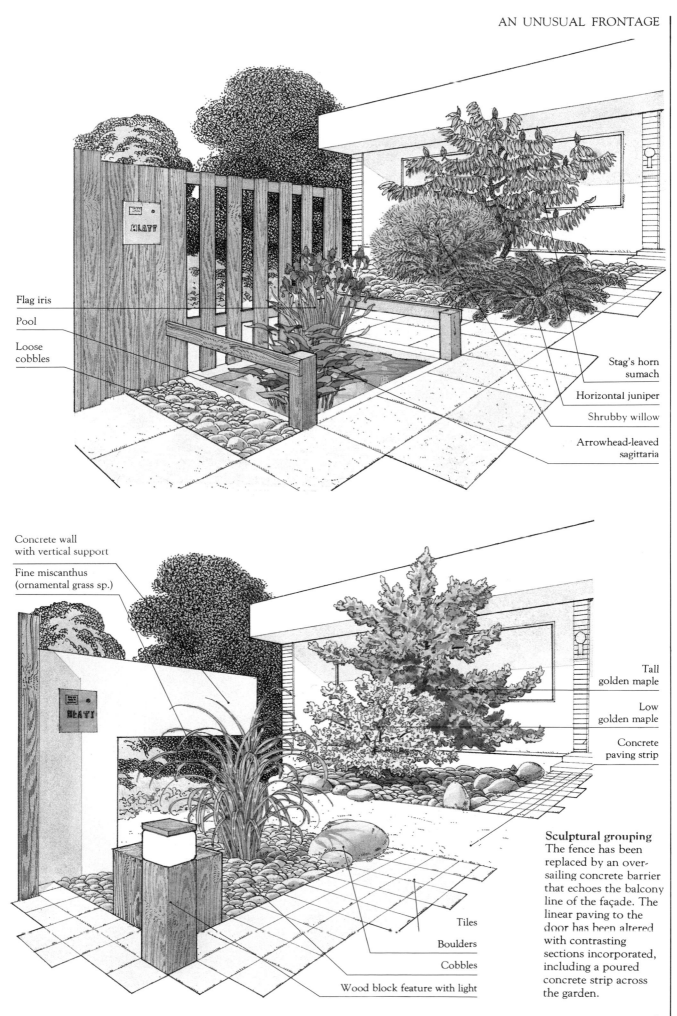

Flag iris

Pool

Loose cobbles

Stag's horn sumach

Horizontal juniper

Shrubby willow

Arrowhead-leaved sagittaria

Concrete wall with vertical support

Fine miscanthus (ornamental grass sp.)

Tall golden maple

Low golden maple

Concrete paving strip

Tiles

Boulders

Cobbles

Wood block feature with light

Sculptural grouping
The fence has been replaced by an over-sailing concrete barrier that echoes the balcony line of the façade. The linear paving to the door has been altered with contrasting sections incorporated, including a poured concrete strip across the garden.

73

Garden with a view

The garden with an imposing view has its own set of design problems. The example below highlights some of them. A pool has been chosen as the link between the garden and the country beyond and the result is dramatic. The far banking of the pool forms an invisible boundary. A small sculpture of a hawk, a bird of the countryside beyond, placed centrally on the far edge of the pool, further links garden and countryside. In such a situation the gardener has to decide on the balance between the attraction of the foreground garden planting and the attraction of the view beyond. This balance is altered by revealing more or less of the view and by altering the strength of the pool composition in relation to the whole.

The two proposals opposite show alternative arrangements. In the top example, the foreground detail has been cleared so that the far bank line has much of the feel of the hills beyond. The sculpture is now set higher and to one side so that it counterpoises the prospect against planting that complements the view without detracting from it.

The lower proposal reduces the width of the view. Larger planting on the left has been designed to create a feeling of the country encroaching into the garden. This planting is of garden forms of indigenous genera, such as shrub roses. In the left foreground, the stag's horn sumach (*Rhus typhina*) is a good compromise between rural and "domestic" plants and acts as a foil to a simple fountain.

The existing pool
Water can make an attractive transition between garden and countryside. Here the detailing of the pond is natural, with boulders used to make an informal surround.

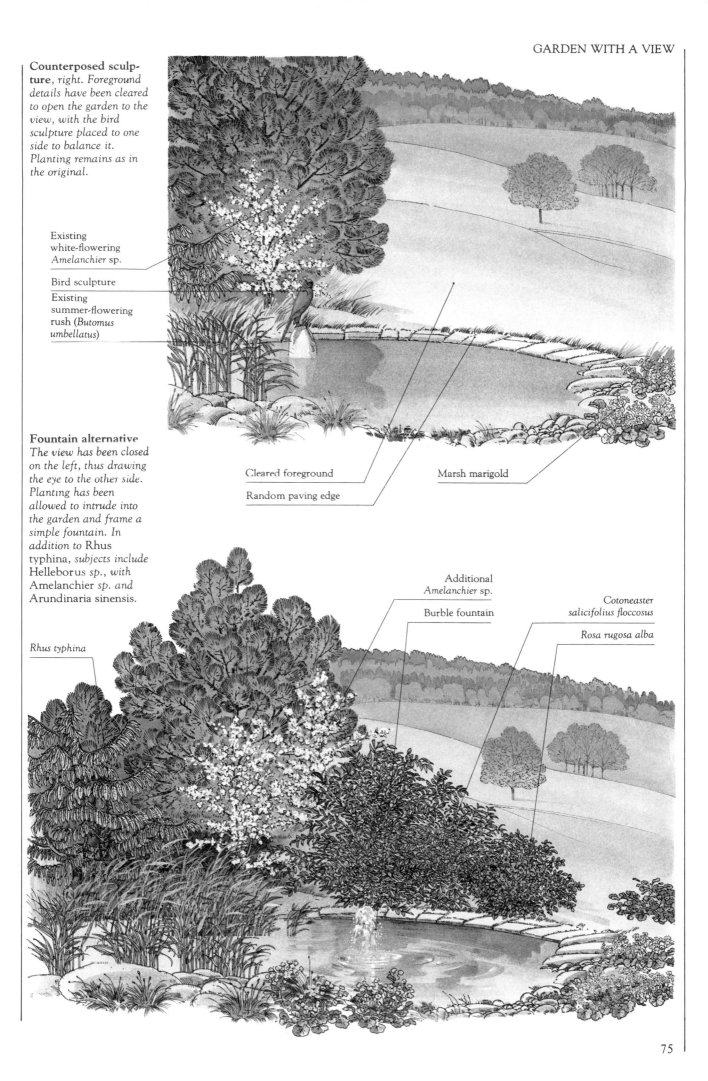

Counterposed sculpture, *right. Foreground details have been cleared to open the garden to the view, with the bird sculpture placed to one side to balance it. Planting remains as in the original.*

Existing white-flowering *Amelanchier* sp.

Bird sculpture

Existing summer-flowering rush (*Butomus umbellatus*)

Fountain alternative
The view has been closed on the left, thus drawing the eye to the other side. Planting has been allowed to intrude into the garden and frame a simple fountain. In addition to Rhus typhina, *subjects include* Helleborus *sp., with* Amelanchier *sp. and* Arundinaria sinensis.

Rhus typhina

Cleared foreground

Random paving edge

Marsh marigold

Additional *Amelanchier* sp.

Burble fountain

Cotoneaster salicifolius floccosus

Rosa rugosa alba

75

Flight of steps

Steps are expensive to build but, when well sited and well finished, give a garden added interest. All too often, however, gardeners economize, making steps too narrow and too steep. A flight should be a sculptural feature, leading you from one area to another or welcoming you and your guests when used as a house access.

The view below is of a meandering flight of steps, surfaced with cut granite and with a wood retainer forming the riser. The strong horizontal line of the steps contrasts well with the vertical shapes of the grasses and plants on either side. A light fitting has been added as an incidental feature that leads you on while providing nightime illumination.

An alternative treatment, top right, has gravel on the step treads and allows planting to flow into the landings, with boulder groups making the finished result more sculptural. The design center right is suitable for the entrance to a house, incorporating name plate and lighting. By turning some of the steps, added interest is given to the arrangement. The shallow retaining wall provides a casual seat and offers a measure of privacy to the garden beyond.

The steps in the example bottom right are more ornamental and incorporate a waterfall feature, which can be easily worked from a small, submersible pump located in a reservoir at the foot of the flight.

Random steps *These steps are well proportioned, being neither too long nor too steep. The textured surface, retained by timber verticals, makes them safe in all weathers and additionally the flight is lit for night use. Vertical plant forms have been chosen to complement the horizontal lines of the steps.*

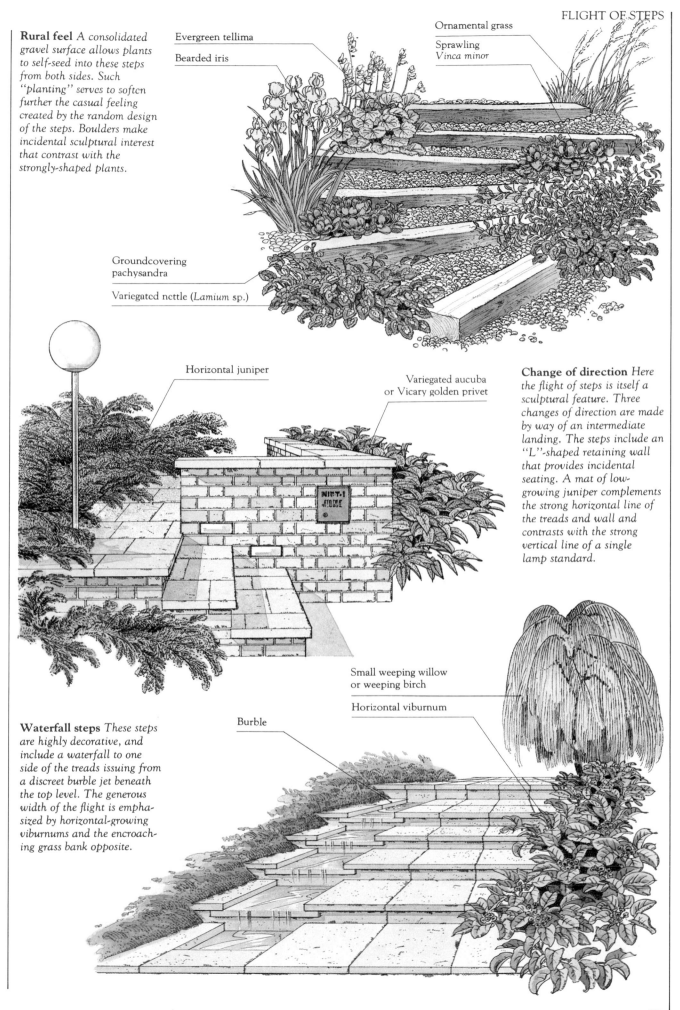

Rural feel *A consolidated gravel surface allows plants to self-seed into these steps from both sides. Such "planting" serves to soften further the casual feeling created by the random design of the steps. Boulders make incidental sculptural interest that contrast with the strongly-shaped plants.*

Evergreen tellima

Bearded iris

Ornamental grass

Sprawling *Vinca minor*

Groundcovering pachysandra

Variegated nettle (*Lamium* sp.)

Horizontal juniper

Variegated aucuba or Vicary golden privet

Change of direction *Here the flight of steps is itself a sculptural feature. Three changes of direction are made by way of an intermediate landing. The steps include an "L"-shaped retaining wall that provides incidental seating. A mat of low-growing juniper complements the strong horizontal line of the treads and wall and contrasts with the strong vertical line of a single lamp standard.*

Small weeping willow or weeping birch

Horizontal viburnum

Burble

Waterfall steps *These steps are highly decorative, and include a waterfall to one side of the treads issuing from a discreet burble jet beneath the top level. The generous width of the flight is emphasized by horizontal-growing viburnums and the encroaching grass bank opposite.*

77

Garden with a barn

An old barn is a great asset in a garden, not only for storage but to provide a feature in its own right. Too often a barn's potential is not fully realized, however, for some garden plans underplay this useful, and often attractive, addition. The solution is to fashion the surrounding garden to suit whatever function you want the barn to perform. In the photograph below, the garden's main feature is a barn with a corrugated iron roof. The barn is used as a retreat and as a place for storage. Whatever the original function of the barn, it is now very much part of the garden plan.

My two alternative designs, opposite, are aimed at strengthening the link between the barn and the rest of the garden. The top design uses the barn as a shelter and background to a swimming-pool. Barns and swimming-pools belong to different eras and careful planning is necessary if they are to tie together satisfactorily. The barn structure has been given greater emphasis by adding an ornamental turret. The roof has been tiled and the walls are now in brick. This material is used again in the square patterning of the terrace which surrounds the swimming-pool and which is then infilled with concrete poured *in situ* and finally given a brushed surface finish.

The lower proposal retains a rural feel and the planting is larger to create a sheltered corner in which to sit or sunbathe. Older-style plants with gentle forms and shapes enhance this mood. Both proposed designs have strong ground patterns that are evident through the plantings and features. These patterns emanate from a regular grid based on the spacing of the piers or walls of the barn so both layouts are bound to link garden and barn strongly. In the pool-house variations I have gone so far as to leave the grid complete as a ground pattern in paving brick.

An integrated rural feature *An old barn, such as this with a corrugated iron roof painted black, can either be a handsome addition or an eyesore in a garden. To combine the two successfully, ensure that your planting harmonizes with the structure.*

Pool-house variation, *right. In this rather extravagant proposal, the barn has become a pool-house. This new function is at odds with the character of the building but some restyling makes it work in harmony with the swimming-pool. Planting, which includes cypresses, phormiums and pelargoniums, strengthens the link.*

Cypress or juniper 'Skyrocket'

White-flowering rambler rose

Spiky phormium or yucca

White-flowering buddleia

Plumbago capensis or Jackman clematis

Red-hot pokers

Yellow-flowering koelreuteria

In situ concrete

Paving brick

Swimming-pool

Scarlet-flowering pelargoniums

Enhancing the rural mood, *below.*
Planting in this example, which in-
cludes pyracanthas, lilacs and irises,
dominates the structure to enhance the
rural mood and provide a sheltered area
for sitting or sunbathing.

Red-berried pyracantha

Verbascum olympicum or day-lilies

Mulberry

Blue-flowering wisteria

Brick edge

Iris

White-flowering lilac

Euphorbia wulfenii or *E. epithymoides*

Yellow-flowering alchemilla

White-flowering shrub rose

Lemon-flowering potentilla

Walled side-garden

One of the less pleasant aspects of many town gardens is the narrow section of ground at the side of the house which provides a link between front and rear. It is invariably a wind tunnel and mostly in the shade. Often the area is used to store rubbish and sometimes fuel, such as logs. Whether to incorporate the area decoratively into the rest of the garden is a difficult decision depending on the width of the passage way and the sort of view into the rear garden that is possible. If the passage is narrow, you might block direct access with a gate to give security to the rear of the house and to conceal household storage. If, as below, the side area is wider

there is an opportunity to create an enclosed area with its own character, or to incorporate the area into the rear garden.

The existing side-garden has been roofed over with a pergola in stained softwood. The paving is of granite blocks laid in a brick pattern. The house wall, to the left, projects to a timber extension about which the rear garden space turns to the left out of view. The side garden we see is passage-like since it is not specifically tied to the rear garden. In both the alternative treatments for the space, illustrated opposite, the side-garden has been considered as part of the rear garden, so apparently opening out the space available.

Enclosed walkway
Closely-spaced pergola beams and plant-supporting wall battens, stained to match, increase the feeling of enclosure in the existing side-garden. Yellow rudbeckia and incidental color in containers combines with sprawling planting to block the view to the rear wall of the garden.

Radiating pattern *A small planting area at the base of the vertical support for the rear roof canopy has been used as the center of a radiating pattern which extends into the side-garden. Spiky phormiums punctuate the center of the pattern and, from this, brick paviers have been laid in straight courses that diverge with distance. The resulting gaps have been infilled with random-size cobbles to match the cobble infill adjacent to the house wall. The angles of the pergola horizontals above echo the radiating pattern below. A paved space has been allowed for dustbins. Planting augments the strong ground patterning with a pampas grass (Cortaderia selloana) featured among the cobbles.*

Plan

Large-leaved ivy

Feathery pampas or fountain grass

White-flowering clematis

Spiky phormium or yucca

Winter-flowering cherry (*Prunus sibhirtella autumnalis*)

Cobbles

Brick pavier

Opening the view *In this version of the side-garden, an open view through to a piece of sculpture has been achieved by the removal of the pergola and careful planting in the foreground of this view. Low-growing junipers skirt the bottom of the buttress on the right-hand wall and do not block the view to the rear garden. This version is less linear and more relaxed than the one above, with paving of stone slabs set randomly in brick softened by planting of euphorbias and pyracanthas in bold groupings.*

Narrow-leaved pyracantha

Horizontal juniper

Brick

Euphorbia robbiae or *E. epithymoides*

Sawn stone slab

Plan

81

Square garden

A square garden, such as the one shown below, presents itself to the viewer in one go and so a bold and simple design is particularly important. The existing garden is well-used with features made of the terrace and a small raised pond. The terrace commands a view of the pretty, old-fashioned planting that surrounds areas of lawn.

I have tried to draw the layout together in the two proposals opposite. The top design is dominated by curves. A radiating brick pattern in front of the raised pool and a curved sweep of lawn tie the new terrace to the existing one, where brick is now used to form a step. Strong, curving shapes need equally bold clumps of planting.

If you do not like curves or if you want a more architectural shape to your garden, the second idea may provide the solution. This comprises a series of interlocking squares, culminating at the raised pool. Use a gravelled surface instead of grass if you are anxious to avoid heavy gardening, and then allow certain plants, such as hosta, day-lily, bergenia and ornamental grasses, to soften the effect by growing through it to make generous clumps.

Piecemeal charm, *left. This is a garden that has developed over a long time. Its original planting is now a foil to new features, such as the foreground terrace and a pond that is similarly raised, but within a brick surround.*

Interlocking squares, *right. Here, an overall effect is achieved by using brick squares. Gravel rather than grass forms the surface, in which plants can be allowed to seed themselves. Planting is full, with this mid-summer view showing the successful use of bulbs and annuals within a framework of perennials. Interest and form throughout the year are provided by the two Prunus subhirtella autumnalis, Viburnum plicatum, and the evergreen planting.*

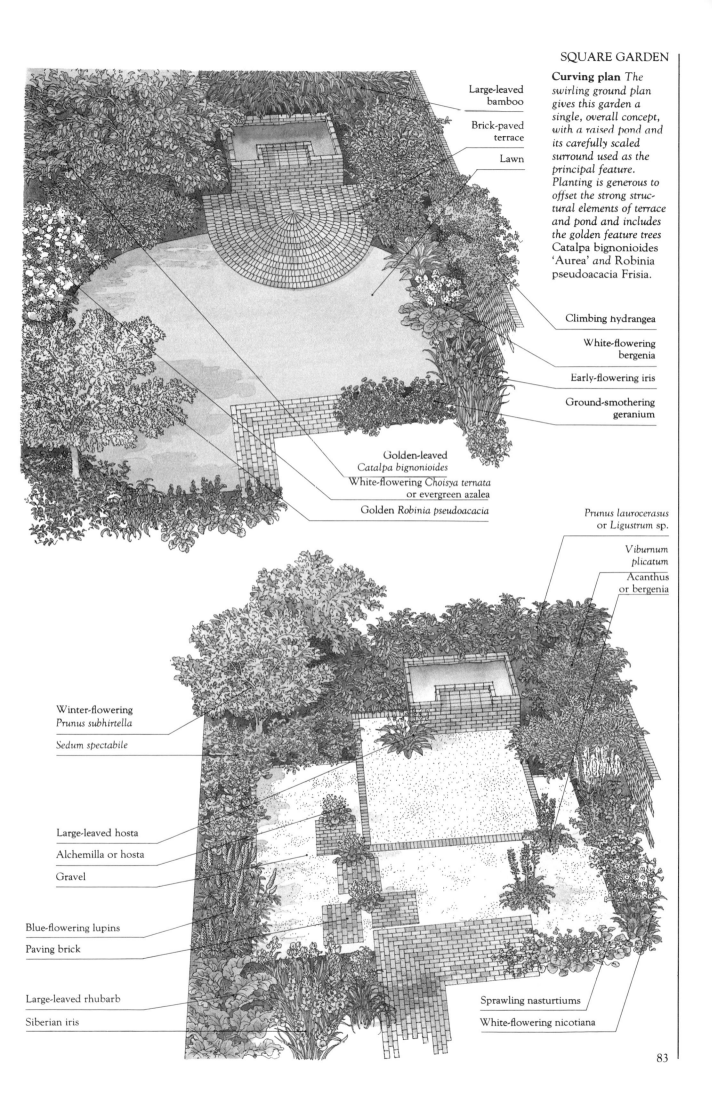

Large-leaved bamboo

Brick-paved terrace

Lawn

Curving plan *The swirling ground plan gives this garden a single, overall concept, with a raised pond and its carefully scaled surround used as the principal feature. Planting is generous to offset the strong structural elements of terrace and pond and includes the golden feature trees Catalpa bignonioides 'Aurea' and Robinia pseudoacacia Frisia.*

Climbing hydrangea

White-flowering bergenia

Early-flowering iris

Ground-smothering geranium

Golden-leaved
Catalpa bignonioides

White-flowering *Choisya ternata*
or evergreen azalea

Golden *Robinia pseudoacacia*

Prunus laurocerasus
or *Ligustrum* sp.

Viburnum plicatum

Acanthus
or bergenia

Winter-flowering
Prunus subhirtella

Sedum spectabile

Large-leaved hosta

Alchemilla or hosta

Gravel

Blue-flowering lupins

Paving brick

Large-leaved rhubarb

Siberian iris

Sprawling nasturtiums

White-flowering nicotiana

Terraced garden

The architect of this modern house excavated an area outside, both to form a garden and to provide light for the lower rooms. Surrounding the chief dug-out area, terraced steps have been constructed and retained by vertical timber posts sunk into the ground. The planting is of ericaceous species that have their own charm, with various conifers that punctuate different levels of the garden.

The garden design at the top of the opposite page tries to bridge the visual gap and provide a plant scheme matching the excitement of the house. For example, Italian cypresses (*Cupressus sempervirens*) have been used to give height to the planting. Bolder areas of growth, with open areas of gravel, are in harmony with the modern style of the angular concrete and glass building.

The lower proposal is simpler. The individual plants chosen are small but the areas of planting are generous, alternating with open spaces. This design includes patches of annual color as well as roses.

An alternative means of changing the garden completely would be to re-shape the terracing. My suggestions for the steeply rising site are shown below right.

Existing amphitheatre *The unusual terracing of the site links the striking building with its garden strongly and provides rank upon rank of interesting planting areas.*

Alternative terracing schemes, *below. This series of diagrams shows the existing terracing scheme and two proposals that would alter the feel of this rather unusual garden.*

1 Existing terracing
2 Abstracted pattern
3 Graded top level with a sunbathing "room".

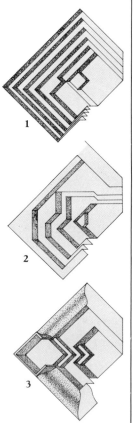

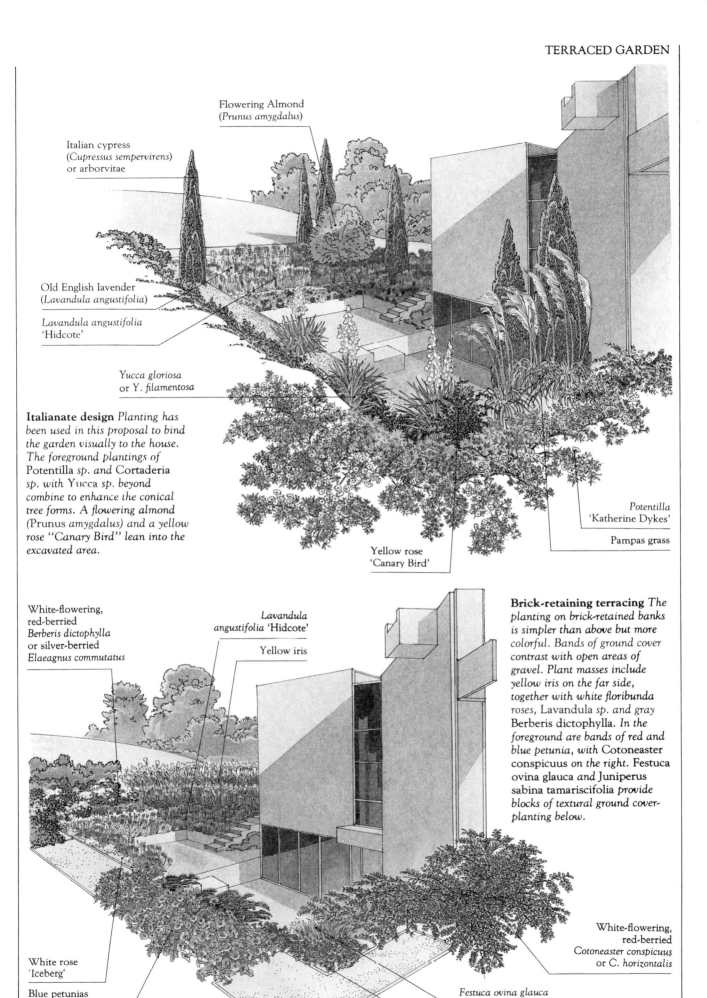

Italian cypress
(*Cupressus sempervirens*)
or arborvitae

Flowering Almond
(*Prunus amygdalus*)

Old English lavender
(*Lavandula angustifolia*)

Lavandula angustifolia
'Hidcote'

Yucca gloriosa
or Y. filamentosa

Italianate design *Planting has
been used in this proposal to bind
the garden visually to the house.
The foreground plantings of
Potentilla* sp. *and Cortaderia*
sp. *with Yucca* sp. *beyond
combine to enhance the conical
tree forms. A flowering almond
(Prunus amygdalus) and a yellow
rose "Canary Bird" lean into the
excavated area.*

Potentilla
'Katherine Dykes'

Pampas grass

Yellow rose
'Canary Bird'

White-flowering,
red-berried
Berberis dictophylla
or silver-berried
Elaeagnus commutatus

*Lavandula
angustifolia* 'Hidcote'

Yellow iris

Brick-retaining terracing *The
planting on brick-retained banks
is simpler than above but more
colorful. Bands of ground cover
contrast with open areas of
gravel. Plant masses include
yellow iris on the far side,
together with white floribunda
roses, Lavandula* sp. *and gray
Berberis dictophylla. In the
foreground are bands of red and
blue petunia, with Cotoneaster
conspicuus on the right. Festuca
ovina glauca and Juniperus
sabina tamariscifolia provide
blocks of textural ground cover-
planting below.*

White-flowering,
red-berried
Cotoneaster conspicuus
or *C. horizontalis*

White rose
'Iceberg'

Blue petunias

Gravel

Festuca ovina glauca

Red petunias

Suburban garden

The design below is an effective treatment for the side of a garden and, when seen from ground level and from the house, works as a visual progression down the length of the site. Interesting and detailed paving makes the junction between the lawn and the detail on the right. Some good planting in the foreground screens an informal pool in the Japanese manner.

The top example, opposite, provides more interest at the terrace end of the garden by means of a piece of sculpture, with descending areas of water beneath it. The concept is crisper than the original, with the strong form of both the pools and the sculpture softened by bold planting. The bamboo clump remains but it is now backed by a mass of yellow-flowering *Ligularia* sp., beyond which is a group of the horizontally layered foliage of *Viburnum plicatum* 'Mariesii'. Low junipers reach down to the water beneath the sculpture and these are backed by autumn flowering *Anemone japonica alba*. A formal, clipped hedge completes

the progression, from behind which the paving emerges to provide a balance to the sculpture.

The bottom idea makes more of a feature of the terrace that ends the garden, extending it back towards the house in an abstract concept of interlocking squares at different levels. These are tied together by a small, circular pool with *Sagittaria* sp. making strong foliage planting within it. Planting in this design is subordinate to the structural concept, with bamboo retained to sit among a low planting of *Hypericum calycinum*.

Formal approach, *right. This is a more formal approach to the use of water, with the flow allowed to descend at intervals and provide foreground interest to the concrete sculpture. The top, paved terrace now acts as a counter-balance to this feature. Planting complements the sculpture and bamboo is included for its bold leaf shapes, mixed with flower color.*

Finely-detailed flank *Attractive paving leads the eye down this half of a garden. Half-way is an informal Japanese pool, screened by a large bamboo. Seen straight on, this feature is well organized and handsomely displayed against a bold lattice fence with* Clematis montana *growing through it.*

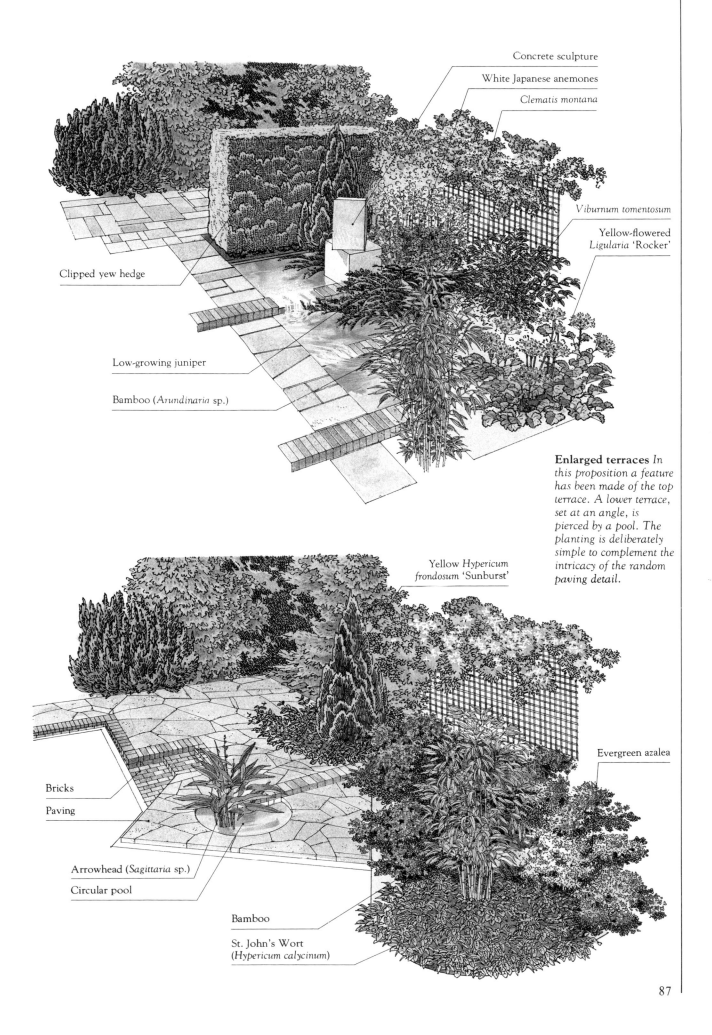

Concrete sculpture

White Japanese anemones

Clematis montana

Viburnum tomentosum

Yellow-flowered
Ligularia 'Rocker'

Clipped yew hedge

Low-growing juniper

Bamboo (*Arundinaria* sp.)

Enlarged terraces *In
this proposition a feature
has been made of the top
terrace. A lower terrace,
set at an angle, is
pierced by a pool. The
planting is deliberately
simple to complement the
intricacy of the random
paving detail.*

Yellow *Hypericum
frondosum* 'Sunburst'

Evergreen azalea

Bricks

Paving

Arrowhead (*Sagittaria* sp.)

Circular pool

Bamboo

St. John's Wort
(*Hypericum calycinum*)

87

Ground pattern garden

The layout of this garden makes a strong ground pattern to be looked down upon from the terrace that surrounds the house. The pattern is picked out in granite setts, mostly across lawn, and consists of pathways connecting circular islands. Granite blocks are laid below the level of the grass so that mowing is not impeded and so care of the complex lawn shapes is easy.

The treatment in the top example, opposite, is dramatic, for the centers of the setted circles have become simple pools of water, each with a small fountain jet. Surrounding these are swirling masses of ground cover planting of *Juniperus sabina tamariscifolia* and *Stachys lanata*, interspersed with yellow or white floribunda roses, colors that should not be mixed. The taller planting on the left is of *Cotoneaster salicifolius floccosus*, with evergreen or deciduous viburnums on the right.

Another way of changing the three-dimensional shape of the garden would be to use the existing ground pattern as the basis for a rose garden, an example of which is shown in the diagram right.

The lower treatment opposite overlays these existing features with an even stronger ground pattern, some of which remains grass while the rest is planted. This gives the garden more of a traditional feeling. Sculptural features have been made of the circles, which now include topiary plants from the range hornbeam (*Carpinus* sp.), privet (*Ligustrum* sp.) or bay (*Laurus nobilis*). In place of bay, which is not winter-hardy in cold regions, use yew (*Taxus* sp.).

Paving pattern, *below. The existing garden, with its pattern of interconnecting decorative paths linking all corners of the area, has been designed to be effective when viewed from the terrace.*

Rose garden alternative *In the plan below, I have superimposed a curving pattern over the design. The central swathe is of grass and the surrounding areas planted with floribunda roses. Grade the rose colors gently.*

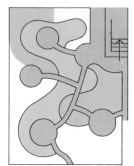

Including pools *In this alternative, beds of roses and ground cover plants weave between granite block circles, the centers of which now have simple pools and fountain jets. In addition to presenting a more interesting prospect from the terrace, this arrangement would also be pleasant to walk in.*

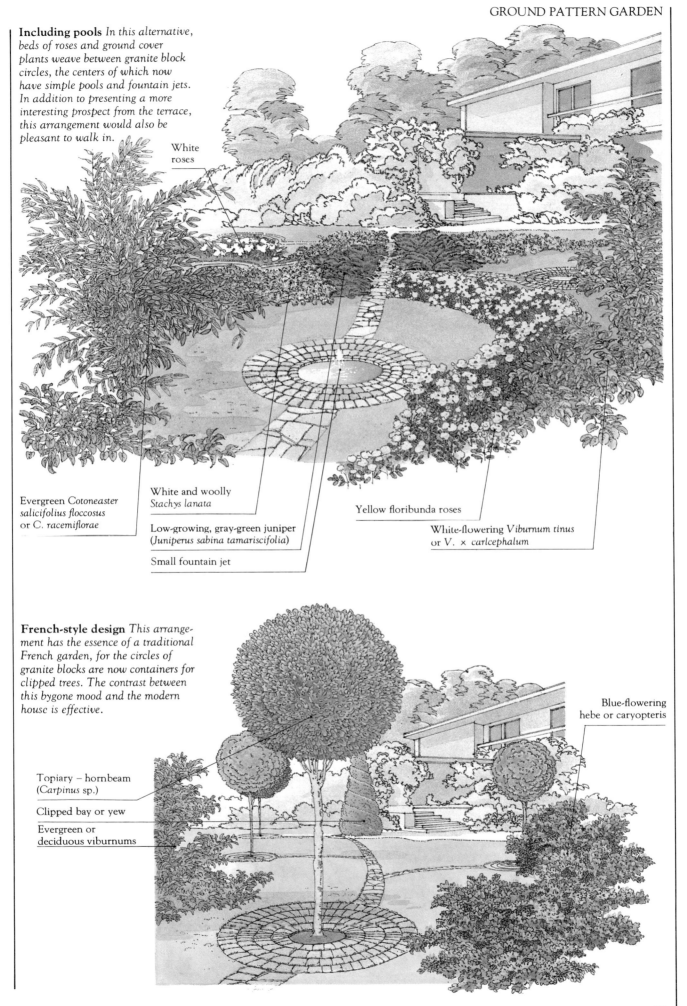

White roses

Evergreen *Cotoneaster salicifolius floccosus* or *C. racemiflorae*

White and woolly *Stachys lanata*

Low-growing, gray-green juniper (*Juniperus sabina tamariscifolia*)

Small fountain jet

Yellow floribunda roses

White-flowering *Viburnum tinus* or *V. × carlcephalum*

French-style design *This arrangement has the essence of a traditional French garden, for the circles of granite blocks are now containers for clipped trees. The contrast between this bygone mood and the modern house is effective.*

Blue-flowering hebe or caryopteris

Topiary – hornbeam (*Carpinus* sp.)

Clipped bay or yew

Evergreen or deciduous viburnums

89

Rural entrance

The stepped entrance to this house was designed at the same time as the building (or at the same time as extensive re-building) for the proportions and detailing are harmonious with the house. The combined structure of house and garden is successful as it seems to blend into the surround of natural woodland. An assortment of pots and planting on the stepped levels is centered on the stump of an old pine tree that must have once been a prime feature of the site. The steps themselves are set at wide intervals to create a relaxed approach to the house entrance.

In the first proposal opposite I have suggested clearing the levels of decoration completely and replacing the dead trunk with a young pine, similar to those behind the house. In the second proposal, I have chosen

to strengthen the strong natural character of the environment by using groups of boulders on the stepped levels.

In both alternatives I have suggested planting low masses of the shrubby *Pinus mugo* to link the garden with the natural woodland beyond. To add color, one might include "wild" plant forms such as the foxglove (*Digitalis* sp.) and spectacular giant cow-parsley (*Heracleum mantegazzianum*) with its large, handsome divided leaves and white flower heads up to three metre (9 ft) high.

Combining good looks with utility *This is a well-designed entrance that looks attractive while providing such useful features as a log store. The steps leading to the building are broad for a relaxed effect, with brick-on-edge risers and pre-cast paving stone treads.*

Strengthening the rural feel, *right. The design is made simpler and more sympathetic with the surrounding woodland by clearing the levels. The central, dead pine trunk, around which the existing scheme was designed, has been replaced by a young pine that becomes a prime feature. The scale of all new planting complements the long horizontal lines of the stepped levels.*

Existing
Rhododendron sp.

Existing
Cotoneaster sp.

Young Scots pine
(*Pinus sylvestris*)

Shrubby *Pinus mugo*

Dramatic boulder groupings, *below. A more
individual effect has been achieved here with
massive rock groupings and giant cow-parsley. The
strength of this design results from the contrast
between the rounded forms of the boulders and the
horizontal lines of the step treads.*

Giant cow-parsley

Boulder grouping

Pinus mugo

Cobble bed

A rock garden

The rock garden below is a successful feature. The "outcrops" of rock of which it is made look natural, resembling strata exposed by the elements. Much of the planting appears to be shaped by its site so that rocks and plants complement one another.

In each of the two alternative designs, opposite, a specific weathering process has been simulated. In the top example, the rocks are part of a composition that includes water—the "worn" rock faces looking in towards the water. A still sheet of water will reflect a rocky landscape and provide an area of calm that will balance the drama of rock and plants.

In the lower design, rock faces have been supposedly exposed by weathering from the right of the illustration. The rock group is split by a gravel path. In both alternative designs the plants used are mostly ground-hugging, with *Saxifraga* sp. and *Sempervivum* sp. used to simulate the hardy primary growth of exposed sites.

When planting a rock garden, think carefully about the natural form you are copying. An alpine bluff has characteristics that the gardener should note. An exposed rock face will produce a crumble of rock particles, or scree, at its base in which only hardy, tufted plants could find a home. Larger, less hardy plants only survive in the areas sheltered by the rock formation away from the exposed face. It is in such areas that any fastigiate plant must be sited. A well-sited vertically growing plant will relieve the otherwise horizontal forms that go to make a rock garden.

Rockery feature *In this garden, the rockery is a separate feature divided by paths from the rest of the garden. Lines of rock strata are discernible, giving the rockery island a feel of authenticity. Planting includes attractive, low-growing species in the foreground and shrubby masses behind the main rock grouping.*

Introducing water, *right. This alternative combines water with rocks, including a modest waterfall with its resulting pool. The fastigiate conifer, placed centrally, echoes the vertical line of the waterfall. The pool is made to look completely natural with no visible surround. Planting follows the plan for the original rockery except for a horizontal-growing juniper and low, poolside planting of sedums and primulas.*

Spiky yucca

Small, dense hebe
or candytuft

Fastigiate juniper

Water source

Spreading
hypericum

Pool

Low-growing
juniper

Lemon-flowering
day lily

Waterfall

Primula

Green-flowering sedum

Sloped site *Here the rockery feature has been re-shaped so that the rocks are revealed down the length of a slope. The vertical line of a fastigiate juniper to one side of the group balances the visual weight of the rocks below it. Low-growing plants, including delicate alpines, clad the planting areas.*

Evergreen
azalea

Ground-covering
cotoneaster

**Fastigiate
juniper**

*Cryptomeria
japonica* 'Spiralis'

Campanula carpatica

Yellow-flowering
alyssum

*Juniperus sabina
tamariscifolia*

Picea punges 'globosa'

Juniperus × media "Old gold"

Golden saxifrage

Pink-flowering sempervivum

93

Small urban garden

This small, colorful area is typical of many urban gardens, both in size and content.It is well designed and executed, with paving and raised borders in the same brick. The pattern is staggered to allow a screen for rear access to the parking space beyond but the chief concern has been to provide a pleasant space for family use.

The proposals suggested opposite are for an identical space, but that above is sheltered by a neighboring tree. A shaded garden is never as colorful as one in sun, but its mass of greenery can be cool and inviting in the summer. Winter interest is provided by broad-leaved evergreens such as rhododendrons and azaleas, leucothoe, pieris and hollies. One of the hardier hollies, inkberry (*Ilex glabra*), survives well in an urban environment. In those regions where winters are too harsh for broad-leaved evergreens, rely on tall-growing yews (*Taxus*) and hemlock (*Tsuga canadensis*) for background and screening. Fill in with small deciduous trees and shrubs such as amelanchier, redbud and winged euonymus for all-year, texture effects.

Grasses, as in the proposal, opposite, below, grow best in light, open gardens and will survive in dry ground. The diversity of leaf forms and height is considerable. Foliage color is also wide ranging and includes green, gold, blue, grey and purple and many of these colors are spotted and striped.

Bright enclosed space *This well-designed, small European garden is seen here at its most colorful in early summer. Planting includes roses, yellow Achillea sp. and, in the foreground, delphiniums and a small maple.*

Dry soil alternative, *right. In this alternative design I have imagined the garden to be overshadowed by a neighboring tree, which will make the soil dry. The plants used are less colorful than in the existing garden but greener and fuller. Emphasis is now on shape and much of the planting is evergreen to last the year through. Bulbs, hosta and foxgloves provide spring and summer interest.*

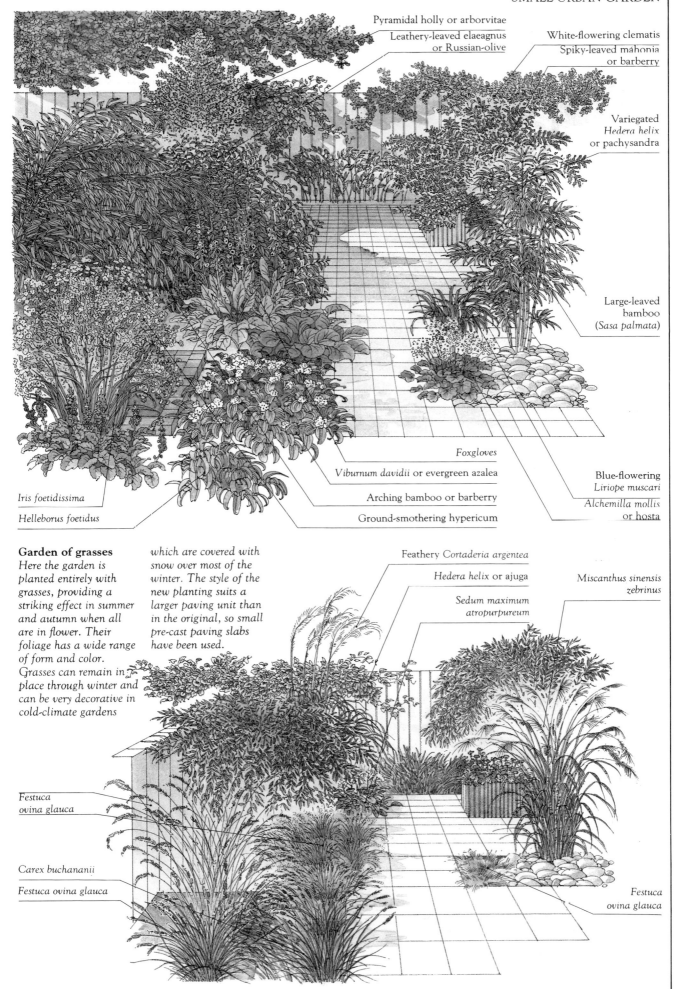

Pyramidal holly or arborvitae

Leathery-leaved elaeagnus or Russian-olive

White-flowering clematis

Spiky-leaved mahonia or barberry

Variegated *Hedera helix* or pachysandra

Large-leaved bamboo (*Sasa palmata*)

Iris foetidissima

Helleborus foetidus

Foxgloves

Viburnum davidii or evergreen azalea

Arching bamboo or barberry

Ground-smothering hypericum

Blue-flowering *Liriope muscari*

Alchemilla mollis or hosta

Garden of grasses
Here the garden is planted entirely with grasses, providing a striking effect in summer and autumn when all are in flower. Their foliage has a wide range of form and color. Grasses can remain in place through winter and can be very decorative in cold-climate gardens

which are covered with snow over most of the winter. The style of the new planting suits a larger paving unit than in the original, so small pre-cast paving slabs have been used.

Feathery *Cortaderia argentea*

Hedera helix or ajuga

Sedum maximum atropurpureum

Miscanthus sinensis zebrinus

Festuca ovina glauca

Carex buchananii

Festuca ovina glauca

Festuca ovina glauca

95

Southern frontage

The front of this handsome Southern house has an "L"-shaped covered way which provides shade from the sun as well as shelter from the rain. Beyond the covered way is a large cedar while, within the square formed by the path, there is a beautiful, established golden maple (*Acer japonica* 'Aureum').

A front garden is the setting for a house and, as the scene for coming and going, it should provide a balancing, tranquil and static appearance. The existing design of this garden consists of a long curving border surrounding a simple circular pond. The border divides the house from the garden and, having separated the two, the eye is then held by the fountain.

The first proposed design, opposite above, uses a simple gravel surfacing to bind together the disparate elements of the garden. Since the attraction of the existing house and trees is essentially one of form, the theme is continued with clumps of bamboo and masses of low-growing *Juniperus sabina tamariscifolia* complementing the pool,

which now has a small vertical fountain splash. A low azalea mound beneath the existing maple brings the eye down to ground level again. Gravel used in this way should be laid in quite a thin layer, rolled and consolidated into another layer of binding gravel (see p. 131).

Gravel is used again in the checkered pattern of the second layout, opposite below. Squares of gravel alternate with masses of boxwood in a more formal and architectural garden. Each square is edged in brick to match the surfacing of the entrance path. Other plants could be used instead, depending on soil, climate and the desired effect. Lavender, for instance, would provide a woolier look, though it should be clipped after flowering. Planting must be evergreen, however, in order to maintain the pattern throughout the seasons. It would be possible, though, by raising each planting area by even only a brick's height, to use either roses or a single color of annual bedding plants and still hold the pattern through the year.

Curved front garden
A front garden design, bordered by covered walks and dominated by fine trees, should essentially be a simple pattern offsetting the house beyond. A strong serpentine line divides lawn from planting and outlines the static shape of the well-proportioned circular pool.

Gravelled landscape *The anchor of this proposal is the use of one ground medium – gravel – in which new plants are set to complement those already present. They include bamboo (Arundinaria sp.), masses of low Juniperus sp., and a mound of azalea beneath the existing Acer japonica 'Aureum'. The fountain jet has become a single vertical, giving a restful effect.*

Cedar (*Cedrus atlantica*)

Covered way

Golden maple (*Acer japonica 'Aureum'*)

Covered way

Bamboo

Gravel

Low-growing juniper

Fountain

Slab edging

Azalea

Cedar

Golden maple

Checkerboard effect *This design is architectural and works by focusing attention on the covered ways. The pattern is created in brickwork. Squares filled with gravel alternate with masses of low, clipped boxwood (Buxus sp.). Such a solution makes features of the two fine existing trees, a golden maple and a cedar, complementing the simple formality of the house as well.*

Covered way

Gravelled squares

Low-clipped box

97

Narrow walled garden

It is in the walled urban garden that one can most safely be bold in design, for what is within the walls need relate to little else. Any garden pattern within the uncompromising lines of surrounding brick walls has to be strong and heavily planted to create a balance between greenery and the structure of the garden. The narrow, walled garden below is dominated by a large tree, so small-scale planting would anyway be inappropriate.

The present design is one of contrast. The crisp, hard lines of the brick-paved terrace are divided by a pool, which runs the width of the garden beyond. Beyond the pool a sense of mystery prevails, with a woodland-style path and fuzzy planting to soften the effects of the surrounding walls while underlining the seclusion the boundary offers.

I have suggested two abstract designs, both of which have strong patterns when seen from the house. The first proposal, opposite above, comprises a series of interlocking planting and gravel areas, separated by brick-on-edge. The simple planting scheme consists only of ferns, for these are ideal for a shaded, town situation.

The lower proposal is more formal and emphasizes the existing pond. Large masses of planting contrast with areas of brick paving, the whole culminating in a simple structure of a tiled roof on four verticals over the rear entrance.

Mixing two styles *It is difficult to combine two styles in a small garden but here it is achieved in dramatic style in a very narrow garden. Being totally enclosed, the garden's surroundings have been ignored and a place of mystery created inside. Brick has been chosen to match the walls for the terrace and pool details.*

Curved abstract design, *right.*
Here the garden has an overall
concept of interlocking planting and
stepped gravel areas. If such a
garden is in shade, as has been
assumed here, it can be planted
solely with ferns, which thrive in
these conditions. Spring bulbs and
lilies are added for early season
interest and color.

Plan

Athyrium filix-femina

Brick-on-edge

Osmunda regalis

Trachelospermum
asiaticum or
Akebia quinata

Gravel

Pool

Catalpa bignonioides

Polystichum achrostichoides

Viburnum tinus
or V. × carlcephalum

Tiled roof

Large-leaved bergenia

Arundinaria viridistriata
or Molina 'Variegata'

Ground-covering
hypericum

Paving brick

Large-leaved rhubarb

Large-leaved ivy

Arundinaria
murielia or
Glyceria 'Variegata

Shrubby
potentilla

Small typha
(cattail)

Pool

Paving brick patterns *This garden*
pattern is abstract, based on asym-
metrically-placed squares of paving
brick that culminate in a simple
structure over the rear entrance in
the far boundary wall. Various
grasses or bamboos dominate the
planting but it also includes large-
leaved genera such as rhubarb
and Bergenia sp. The pool has been
retained but altered in shape.

Plan

99

Balcony garden

This attractive balcony is obviously a source of great pleasure. The large opening doorway gives easy access to the outside space, extending the room in summer months and allowing an unrestricted view to greenery in winter.

The chief feature of my alternative suggestion is a metal or wooden box (which could be watered automatically), planted with box wood (*Buxus* sp.) and trimmed to the same shape as the valance. Annuals planted in spherical containers reflect the bobble edging of the valance. These planting spheres are constructed in metal mesh on the principle of the hanging basket, welded to a metal vertical set into the planting box below. They are lined with moss and filled with compost. Annuals such as lobelia and impatiens are planted through the moss. They will need daily watering from above.

The existing flooring of the balcony is of lightweight tiles with asbestos content. Red or brown quarry tiles are an alternative or, where there is no hazard of frost, colored ceramic tiles.

Summertime balcony, *right. The collection of potted plants helps this balcony to become an interesting and colorful extension of the room it adjoins. The floor covering and plant containers are plain to offset strongly-colored blooms.*

All year alternative *In this substitute treatment, the balcony becomes a place with strong form that continues to give pleasure and protection through the winter months. The evergreen box hedge provides much of this form. In summer, the balcony is enlivened with spheres of color provided by annual planting in containers, such as that far right.*

Blue-flowering lobelia mixed with pink impatiens or petunias

Box hedging clipped to echo the pelmet frill shape

White-painted wooden planting boxes

Lightweight colored tiles

Planting sphere, *below. A spherical mesh container, such as that shown here, is easy to construct with wire netting, or even by connecting two hemispherical hanging baskets. In my alternative design, such spheres are welded to verticals.*

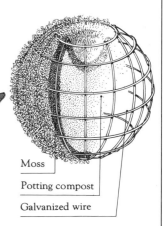

Moss

Potting compost

Galvanized wire

CONSTRUCTING YOUR GARDEN

Drainage, irrigation and electricity

Selecting and making boundaries, screens, levels and surfaces

Introducing features and structures

Preliminaries

By now you should have a clear idea of the pattern and form you are planning for your future garden. The time has come to create it in hard materials, such as walls and paving, which you will later infill with shrubs, mixed planting, and grass or other ground cover. Built features, such as garden sheds, must also be considered so that they can be integrated into the plan rather than merely added later.

It is at this stage that you decide on the materials that you will use: consider what is available locally, what would look appropriate for your area and what the cost of different materials is. In a traditional setting, stone looks well either for walls or paving. The smaller elements of brick or granite blocks are also suitable and, being crisp in outline, are equally suitable in a modern setting. Much depends on the way you use the materials to infill your pattern. Broadly, the smaller the element the more the details will be noticed. For this reason, brick paths are less dynamic than those made of concrete slabs that merge and lead the eye to the path's termination. Pre-cast concrete slabs tend to be modern in feeling and, although many are modified with rusticated finishes, this will not deceive anyone into thinking they are real stone. Concrete in its many forms is a universal material and, laid *in situ* for paving, one not to be despised. Combinations of materials can be used to break up a large hard area, though the detailing should never become fussy.

The suitability of wood for garden use also depends on your location and what is available at a reasonable price. Cedarwood, for instance, is found throughout the United States, though it is no longer cheap. Other softwood can also be used and it is available in most areas of Europe. In the United Kingdom, softwood is widely available but unfortunately the climate does not lend itself to its use for outside flooring or decking since the long, damp winters make it wet and slippery no matter how well treated. Railway and the smaller landscape ties are excellent for garden use and are heavily impregnated with preservative. Their proportions are generous and they therefore take many years to decompose.

The pattern you have on paper, albeit a working drawing, is still only two-dimensional. By incorporating wall and step heights, depths of ponds and so on, you make the plan three-dimensional. Remember that it is the different levels, the feeling of enclosure given by planting, and also the areas of void contrasted with the mass and height of solids, that makes a garden such a pleasant place in which to be. It is a fallacy to suppose that the abundance and brilliance of flower color in a garden affects this basic feeling in any way at all.

Before pegging out the design which you have evolved on paper to see whether it will be satisfactory, you will probably have to clear the site. If you are starting from scratch in a new garden, it may be builders' rubble that will have to go. Older gardens may need someone else's unsuitable planting removed. Nevertheless, think hard before removing any major item, such as a tree, an area of paving or a line of hedge, for it might be possible for you to incorporate them into your new plan. Trees can be thinned and branches removed or braced to make a new shape, although this is work best done by a qualified tree surgeon. Hedges, if overgrown, can also be cut back.

Clear all weeds from the site, either by using a herbicide (being sure to keep pets and children away when newly applied) or renting a sickle bar mower or even resorting to bulldozing.

The plan so far *If you have worked your way through the section on planning your garden and have perhaps been inspired by the gardens illustrated in the Garden-by-garden guide, your own garden plan should look something like this. You should have resolved the positions of surfaces, boundaries, features and the areas for planting, although as yet there will be no detail about the materials to be used.*

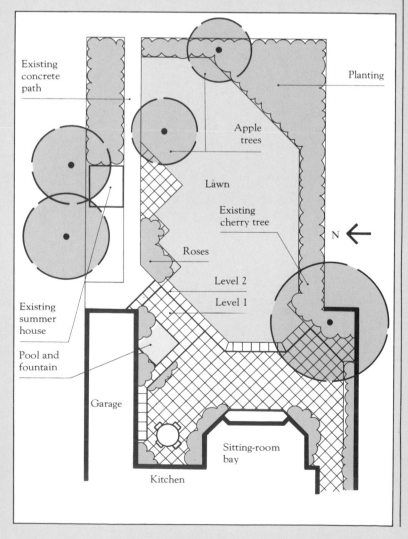

Marking out the design on the site

You can now translate your plan into reality outside, using white string and pegs, to see if your ideas really work. At this stage you will be rewarded for keeping to a grid system in your design for it will be easy to line up your shapes with the buildings which you used to evolve it, and any unpleasant little corners will now become apparent.

Having pegged out the straight runs, tackle the circles (easy to deduce if you have worked to a scale plan) by using a central peg and string attached to it. Scrape out the necessary arcs in the earth with a nail or stick and peg these lines out too.

Once you have described all your patterns with pegs, join them with string. This will enable you to read the overall layout when you stand back from the garden. Look at the pattern from several vantage points – from an upstairs window, from ground level and from outside the site. Then walk on the pathways you have outlined, ensuring that there is room for a wheelbarrow or a mower and that you can easily get round corners. If there is an access path to the front door, make sure that there is a comparatively straight way down the middle, even if the outline twists, for otherwise visitors will cut unnecessary corners. If you have marked out a terraced area that is supposed to be in sunshine, estimate the course of the sun in summer and ensure that there is no unexpected area of cast shadow.

If you are planning a drive, ensure that it is wide enough for you to get out of a car on either side and that there is room to turn it, if needs be. In short, check that your planning ideas are practical as well as visually satisfying from all angles.

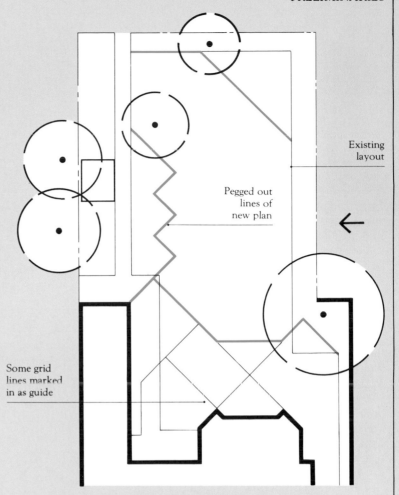

Existing layout

Pegged out lines of new plan

Some grid lines marked in as guide

Pegging out, *above. Having evolved your plan on paper, peg out the outlines on the ground using stakes and string. If you have worked to the correct scale, from an accurate outline survey, your measurements will translate to the real garden. Adjust your outlines to delete any awkward corners and angles that you notice.*

Assessing the layout, *right. Before you start digging or building, go indoors and study the pegged out pattern from all the windows that look on to the garden, imagining steps and changes of level where necessary. You might see aspects of the plan that require slight modification to make all views from the house satisfying. The view from upstairs windows is particularly useful and can provide the mind's eye with a clear impression of the future garden.*

Drainage

Few small gardens need a full drainage system but where drainage is necessary it will be obvious, for the garden, or parts of it, will be wet underfoot for long periods. It is possible, however, that your site is on low-lying ground and, while dry in summer, the water-table will rise in winter to make the area wet again. The natural vegetation will indicate this – rushy grasses and little else.

By far the most likely cause of dampness, especially in a new garden, is a layer of clay from excavations that has been dumped and spread on site by the house builder. Often he disguises this with a thin layer of topsoil but the clay soon becomes an impervious layer that prevents drainage. Break this layer and the water will disperse.

Dig an inspection hole, a meter square and a meter deep, if you are in any doubt about the need to drain a particular area. In this way you will be able to see the soil profile and know how much topsoil and subsoil there is. After rain, you will also see how quickly water drains away. It is possible that your hole will fill with water when it is not raining, indicating that you have reached the water table. However, if you do at so shallow a depth your house will have needed special foundations and you are probably aware of this from a surveyor's report.

If the site is on natural clay, you have no alternative but to replace it with fertile topsoil. However, a soil with a proportion of clay may have become consolidated by heavy machinery working on it. Often this can be greatly improved by cultivating the surface to break-up the clay deposits that have been consolidated.

If your site really does need draining, you will have to install an underground system with pipes of either clay or flexible plastic. These are laid to a pattern according to the site, with feeder runs to the main outlet pipe running to a neighboring ditch or to the surface water drainage system of the house. Never connect a garden drainage system to the mains drainage system. In the United Kingdom this, in fact, is illegal.

The depth of the drainage runs, and their proximity to each other, will depend on the consistency and composition of the soil. It is important to realize that to overdrain a site is as pointless as trying to garden on one that is wet, for you are facilitating the rapid escape of all the essential minerals which are held in soluble form and feed the plants' roots.

The kind of drainage that a garden is much more likely to need deals with only a small area, which, for a number of reasons, may have standing water on it after rain. To drain this may only need a simple pipe run to a soakaway or dry well. It is a hole, a meter square ($3 ft^3$) and at least a meter (3 ft) deep, which is filled with rubble. It will act as a reservoir to hold drainage water, allowing it to disperse gradually. Such a soakaway should be sited under areas that will later be planted and at a distance from the house. The lifespan of a soakaway may only be five years or so, but this again will depend on the soil.

Soakaways can also drain areas at the base of contoured mounds or be sited along the edge of an area of paving, which has been laid to fall to it.

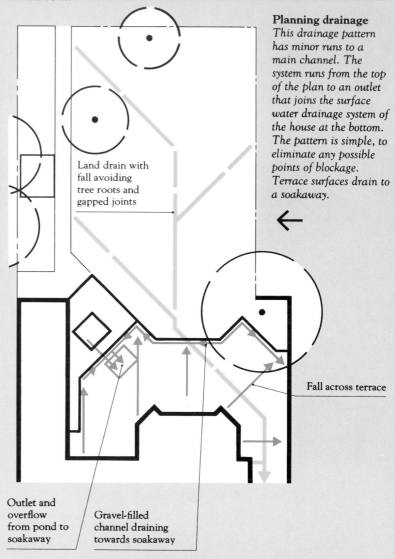

Land drain with fall avoiding tree roots and gapped joints

Fall across terrace

Outlet and overflow from pond to soakaway

Gravel-filled channel draining towards soakaway

Planning drainage
This drainage pattern has minor runs to a main channel. The system runs from the top of the plan to an outlet that joins the surface water drainage system of the house at the bottom. The pattern is simple, to eliminate any possible points of blockage. Terrace surfaces drain to a soakaway.

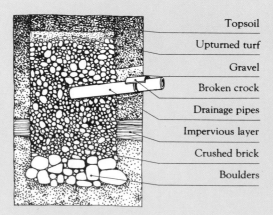

Topsoil

Upturned turf

Gravel

Broken crock

Drainage pipes

Impervious layer

Crushed brick

Boulders

Soakaway or dry well
A soakaway might well be all the extra drainage you require. An ideal example penetrates any impervious layers in the soil and so allows any water draining in to pass down quickly through the layers of gravel and crushed brick to soil that is less likely to become saturated.

Irrigation

Watering a garden, no matter what its size, is traditionally done by a hand-held can or hose. This is time-consuming and laborious, however, and other methods are readily available today.

The simplest, non-manual irrigation system is a perforated hose, passing across a planted area or over pots on a roof, which when turned on produces a gentle trickle of water. A hose can, of course, be laid when a garden has been fully constructed.

At the other end of the scale, there is a sophisticated grid system of pipes that can be sunk just below ground surface at an early stage of garden planning. This has countersunk nozzles, with a metal recess above each at ground level. When the system is switched on, the pressure of water pushes the nozzles just above ground level to release a spray, the coverage from one nozzle reaching that of the next to soak the whole area equally. On switching off, the nozzles sink down – a facility that is particularly useful on a lawn since it allows even mowing of the area. These systems can be timed to switch on and off automatically, much as a central heating system does.

Between these two extremes of irrigation system are oscillators which sweep water to-and-fro across an area to a distance determined by the pressure which drives them.

Electricity

It is usually necessary to bury cables for outside lighting under, or possibly around, structural elements before the garden plan is completed to avoid subsequent disruption.

Gardens need electricity for lighting, and to power equipment such as a fountain or a swimming-pool filtration plant. Power is also needed in the greenhouse, for an electric saw in the workshop and, if you have an electric mower, an outside socket is useful at a distance from the house to avoid an inconvenient length of cable.

All cables should be located along the bottom of a wall, or be contained within protective piping and buried at a level below that likely to be pierced by cultivation tools. Cables need full external-type insulation, with outlet sockets having screw caps and sited above the height at which a small child could reach them, as shown right.

When planning cables and lighting points to entrance paths, ensure that you have places for low lights at any changes of level you are likely to use at night.

It is worth investing some time and money to achieve really effective lighting, for not only does it allow you to enjoy a view of your garden from inside during winter evenings but it is also a worthwhile burglar deterrent. See an electrician for intricate systems.

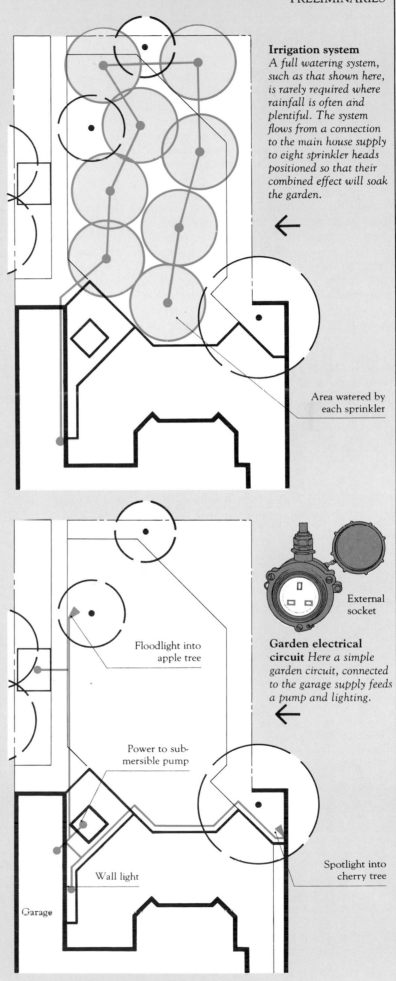

Irrigation system
A full watering system, such as that shown here, is rarely required where rainfall is often and plentiful. The system flows from a connection to the main house supply to eight sprinkler heads positioned so that their combined effect will soak the garden.

Area watered by each sprinkler

External socket

Garden electrical circuit *Here a simple garden circuit, connected to the garage supply feeds a pump and lighting.*

Floodlight into apple tree

Power to submersible pump

Wall light

Garage

Spotlight into cherry tree

Boundaries and enclosures

While boundaries delineate the perimeter of a site, a garden might be divided up internally with more decorative screens. Many people inherit a boundary fence or wall with their property, but as with every other feature in the garden the particular type of boundary and the degree of enclosure which it offers must depend on location.

The shapes of gardens tend to be regular, especially with newer properties, and the mistake is often made of surrounding the site with some standard form of structure that only emphasizes the regularity. The simplest way to relieve this monotony and to break the confines of a boundary visually is to vary the material of which it is made. Use brick or stone adjacent to the house or terrace, and perhaps timber for the rest, or build a boundary of the same material throughout, but vary the height to work with your overall pattern. More interesting still is to allow the line of the boundary to break into the site itself as part of your design so that the layout appears to flow round corners, making your garden appear larger.

Your choice of boundary construction should not ignore security or the need for privacy, a necessity to keep your children or dog in, or other people's out. But these considerations should not inhibit your attempts to mold a more interesting space.

Walls

Walls can be built of brick, stone, of concrete blocks, or of concrete poured *in situ*, though this latter method is usually reserved for retaining walls within the garden as it is stronger. Different wall materials (see p. 109) are used in different ways, the thickness of the structure depending on its height. Thickness will also influence the frequency with which piers or buttresses are used to support the wall. You can get away without these supports by staggering the wall in zig-zag fashion, or by simply stepping the line of the wall forwards and backwards by the thickness of a brick. Curving or serpentine walls will also support themselves, although they require much more space.

The elements of a stone wall are usually thick enough to support themselves without buttressing. Concrete blocks are now available in a variety of acceptable and attractive finishes and sizes and the larger ones do not require buttressing.

The way in which you finish, or cap, your wall can make an enormous difference to its final appearance. Stone walls have traditional cappings in various areas, such as a course of slate. The capping of a brick wall will depend on its thickness, but a course of bricks on edge is the usual finish. Concrete block walls can be finished with concrete slabs (to match a neighboring terrace perhaps), or brick can be used. Tile, slate or metal cappings might also be considered for a crisp, architectural appearance to the retaining wall.

Before embarking on a major fence or wall project along a boundary, check with your building inspector to be sure you are not violating any local ordinances.

Wall strength

Below are some of the ways of building a strong and stable wall without the need for piers. The one-brick-thick wall takes its strength from overlapping at intervals of not more than 2.5 m (8 ft) no more than 1.75 m (5½ ft) high. The zig-zag and crinkle-crankle walls take strength from their deviations.

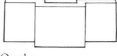

Overlap

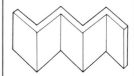

Zig-zag

Crinkle-crankle

Stone

Almost any kind of stone can be used for wall construction – granite, limestone, slate or sandstone. The two main types of wall stones are known as ashlar and rubble stones, of which the latter comprises three groups. Random rubble, which is of uncut stone, is laid coursed or uncoursed. Squared rubble, which is of roughly dressed stone, is laid regularly coursed, irregularly coursed, or uncoursed. Miscellaneous rubble walls use traditional materials and construction methods.

Most stone walls are built in random rubble. No cutting is done to fit the stone together and they are so placed within the wall that there is an adequate distribution of pressure over a maximum area, with no continuous vertical joints. To stabilize the wall, header stones are used every square metre (1.19 yd²) and should ideally run right through the wall. Whether this type of wall is coursed or uncoursed, all joints should be well-filled and flushed with mortar. A decorative variation can be achieved by filling some of the joints with soil and growing alpines in them. To construct a wall in stone of which one side only is to be seen, you can erect a concrete block wall first and face this with stone, tying the two with galvanized cleats.

Traditional stone wall *No mortar has been used to joint the miscellaneous rubble of this wall, just patience to ensure vertical joints do not coincide.*

Brick

Brick is the most commonly used material for building walls. There are three types that are suitable for external use. Commons, which are made for general purpose building, are the cheapest. They have no finish and are particularly subject to weathering. Facings, used where appearance is of prime importance, have either a hand finish or a wire-cut weather resistant finish on the side facings only. And lastly, engineering bricks, which are the hardest and most impervious bricks.

Bricks which are laid horizontally in the direction of the wall are known as stretchers, while those laid end-on, across the direction of the wall, are known as headers. The arrangement of bricks within a wall is known as the bond. The virtues of different bonds are mainly aesthetic. Bonds do have marginally differing strengths, so the bond will, to some extent, depend on the thickness of the wall.

For a wall one brick thick, the bond is usually of stretchers alone. Such a wall should not be much higher than one meter (3 ft). In construction of higher walls, use a Flemish or English bond, both of which have headers periodically binding the double thickness of brick. A more decorative bonding can be used on the facing side of a 300-mm (1 ft) wall. A suitable mortar mix for most exterior walls, subject to normal exposure, is of cement:lime:sand, in the proportions 1:1:8–9. Brickwork which is liable to water saturation, or which is subject to severe exposure and freezing temperatures, might have a mix of 1:1:5–6.

Mellowed brickwork, *right. Walls mellow with age and will become the home of ivy and lichens. However, ivy will eventually damage brick walls.*

Building with used bricks, *below. Different types of old brick have been used here for a multi-colored effect. Now clean of old mortar, they make an open-work wall.*

Brick wall construction

A wall must be built on stable and adequate foundations to eliminate any risk of subsequent movement. It is not possible to make exact rules as to the dimensions of foundations for various types of walls, since the bearing capacity of soils vary, particularly those with a high moisture content, such as many of the clays.

The depth of foundations depends on the level at which frost or the movement of ground moisture occurs. In most cases, a depth of 450 to 600 mm (1½–2 ft) is sufficient. Unless there are difficult site conditions, such as poor drainage (when you will need to take expert advice), a concrete mix of 1:2:4–6, cement:sharp sand:aggregate, is correct for normal wall foundation work.

The brick courses are built up from the foundation with great care taken to keep the wall square, both horizontally and vertically, and the amount of mortar used consistent.

English bond brick wall *This brick wall is the usual two-brick thickness (300 mm) (1 ft) and is being laid in English bond, with one course of headers and the next of stretchers.*

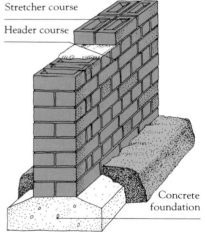

Stretcher course
Header course
Concrete foundation

Brick bonding

The four standard types of brickwork bonding, shown right, are generally used in wall construction, although they might equally be used as a paving pattern (see p. 129). The crispness of the bond is either emphasized or subdued by the style of pointing (the method of trowelling the joints) and the color of the mortar you use.

Running bond

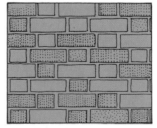
Flemish bond

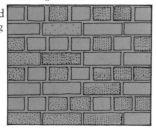
English bond

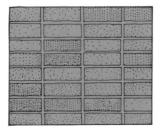
Stack bond

Cappings

It is usually necessary to put a protective capping, or coping, along the top of a wall since most bricks are only weatherproof on the finished face. Below are two standard cappings. On the left is the traditional method known as brick-on-edge. On the right, paving slabs have been used with an overhang proportionate to their thickness.

Brick-on-edge

Concrete slab

107

Concrete block

Standard concrete or reconstituted stone blocks are available, which have been molded to look like worked stone. These are perfectly sound for wall construction, but personally I do not like one material made to look like another. Most materials are quite valid in their own right and concrete is no exception. Plain concrete blocks are hard to beat for their strength, economy and speed of construction and they are now available in a variety of colors and finishes. There is a far wider range of finishes available than the crude, gray aggregate finish of the early material. Colors vary to match local brick or stone, these materials sometimes being crushed and used as a part of the aggregate of the block. The blocks may be utilized in a variety of ways to produce either a decorative finish or a perfectly simple one. Concrete blocks can be colored after construction. Concrete blocks are available in a standard exterior heavyweight grade, or as lightweights which are composed of lightweight aggregate in a more porous texture. The latter may have to be rendered for outside use but are ideal for roof garden construction where weight is a problem (see p. 160).

see p. 160

Wall designs

Some ideas for using solid boundaries to break up your site are shown below. Using your own invention for the boundary of a site is an important step towards creating interesting shapes within it. Plan the boundary in conjunction with your two-dimensional plan, and relate it, as far as possible, to the scale of your house and the scale of your garden.

Enlivening concrete with colour *This concrete block wall is of the course aggregate type and is used as a retaining wall with a paving slab finish. The wall is coloured to brighten a dull section of rear garden.*

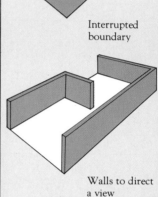

Interrupted boundary

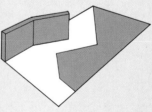

Walls to direct a view

Wall at an angle

Walls to create interest

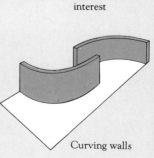

Curving walls

Concrete block wall-construction

Concrete blocks are considerably larger than bricks, so building a wall in this material is much faster and, therefore, far cheaper. The large size of cavity wall blocks makes piers unnecessary for a standard wall, although such blocks are usually reserved for retaining walls (see p. 120). Solid concrete wall blocks are half the thickness and will require the support of piers used with the same frequency as for brick walls (see p. 107). A similar concrete foundation is also required.

see p. 120
see p. 107

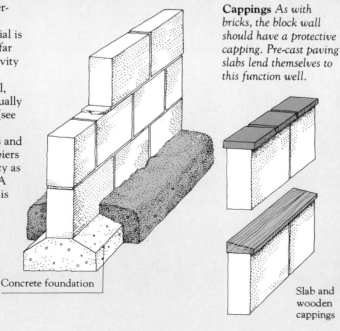

Concrete foundation

Cappings *As with bricks, the block wall should have a protective capping. Pre-cast paving slabs lend themselves to this function well.*

Slab and wooden cappings

Wall materials

There is a vast range of wall materials in brick, stone and concrete but their suitability will depend on your location. Using local materials is often the right decision and it also makes sense economically to use what is to hand. The scale of each component you use is important and must be sympathetic to the scale of other materials already present. You might consciously contrast the scale, using smooth runs of concrete with random stone, large concrete blocks with small bricks, or just different sizes and types of brick. With this last method you will also need to consider differences of texture.

Brick
The textural and color differences of the brick samples below are obvious. The engineering brick, top, is hardest. It is therefore the most resistant to damp. Below this are three types of "infill brick", which are the cheapest, and facing bricks.

Reconstituted stone
Different areas produce different rock, which can be crushed and used as the aggregate in the composition of reconstituted stone blocks. Reconstituted stone block is easier to transport and lay than natural stone.

Pre-cast concrete units

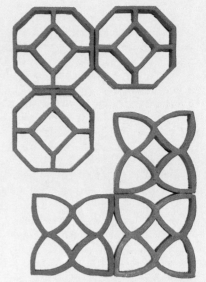

Terracotta units

Open screen wall units
Scale, texture and pattern will help you decide the type of open screen unit you need. An open screen is generally more successful when used sparingly, only piercing a solid wall, for example, as a decorative element, since any great area becomes boring. The finer elements in terracotta, being lighter, may be used on roof terraces as wind baffles, rather than barriers that cause turbulence.

Concrete block
The concrete block is a much maligned element for garden construction work. It is comparatively cheap, easy to erect and is an honest contemporary material. Hollow blocks or cavity blocks are approximately 300 mm (1 ft) deep, while solid blocks are about half that. Finishes vary from coarse to smooth and glazed.

17 Cavity block
18 Smooth solid
19 Rock-faced solid

1 Engineering brick
2–4 Flettons
5–10 Facing bricks

11–14 Split aggregate blocks
15–16 Pre-cast blocks

Stone
Where suitable, the scale and texture of various stones cannot be bettered and will usually mix well with other hard materials. However, the cost of labor, cartage, and handling difficulties often make its use prohibitive.

20 Sandstone
21 Granite
22–23 Limestones

Fencing

A fence serves the same function as a wall, although its construction need not be so massive or its form solid. Like a wall, its type and height should be dictated by situation and location – urban or rural. Strict attention should be paid to the siting of a fence which is set up along the line of demarcation between two properties to ensure that no encroachment is made on either side. It is usual practice to face the best side of the fence outwards from your site with the supports on the inside.

The materials most used for constructing fences are wood, metal and concrete. Concrete is usually reserved as a supporting material while there is an infinite variety of combinations of materials for possible infills, see-through or solid, which you can either design yourself or buy ready-made. Some types of prefabricated, fixed length panel are widely available. Local types of panel are made on the spot and are easily adapted to non-standard intervals.

A fence is no stronger than its weakest part, so the detailing of a fence to make sure that it has no weaknesses is important. A well-detailed fence will not only be more resilient but it will also last longer. Consider both the types of infill and support, the way in which you intend to fix the supports in the ground and, with wooden fences, the way in which you can further protect against rot with cappings and gravel boards.

The type of wood used in fence construction will considerably alter its lifespan. The principal European woods used for fencing are oak (English and European), larch, western red cedar and sweet chestnut, although other woods may be used when suitable, such as Douglas fir, Scots pine, ash, elm or beech. Redwood or cedar are used in the United States, split redwood being referred to as grapestalk since it is used traditionally to support grapevines.

Bark must be stripped from wood to prevent premature decaying of the wood, and the exposed grain must be treated with a preservative or sealed and painted. After using a creosote preservative on wood it cannot then be painted. Plants will not grow against it for a season, as newly applied, creosote gives off fumes which burn vegetation. Exposed metal components liable to rust, should be galvanized, zinc-coated or painted. Use screws rather than nails for fixings for a longer lasting finish.

When using poured concrete as a supporting material to fix fence posts, there are two alternative methods. The posts can be positioned independently, with careful measurement, and left standing until the concrete sets before the infills are attached. If there is a necessity for a completed boundary in one step, the posts and infills can be constructed at the same time if you make sure to support the posts with temporary wooden stays until the post foundations have set. The fence will need supporting for at least two days.

Novel urban fencing
Espalier fruit trees have been trained against latticework attached to the front boundary wall of this residence. The effect is crisp and urban.

Picket or palisade

Picket fencing is a see-through, decorative version of close board fencing which can have either a cottage or urban feel. It has a similar construction with post and arris rails, but its height is considerably less and the verticals, or pales, are spaced battens with rounded or pointed tops. To achieve a crisp, New England look, this type of fence should be painted white.

For an individual finish you can design your own end decoration for the palings of a picket fence. Six ideas for decorative palings are shown below, from a simple curve to complicated sawn shapes.

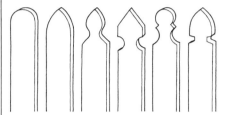

Traditional rural fencing, *right. White-painted picket, or palisade, fencing continues the cottage garden feel of the planting beyond in this garden. Such a fence needs annual maintenance if it is not to look shabby.*

Post and rail

Post and rail describes the simplest way of fencing with wood, or wood and metal, with one, two or three horizontal rails, between regularly spaced posts. There are a number of different construction methods with the rails either nailed to the posts or mortised into them. In the former, the verticals should be 1.8 m (6 ft) apart, while the latter method allows a greater spacing of 2.8 m (9 ft). The horizontal rails can be infilled decoratively as below.

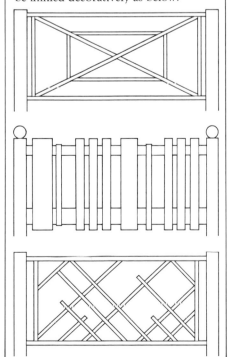

Ranch style

Known as baffle fencing in the United States, ranch fencing is made up of horizontal boards, spaced at regular intervals and secured to posts set not more than 2.75 m (9 ft) apart. Height of the fence should be between 1.35 and 1.85 m (4½–6 ft) high.

Board on board fencing is a variation of the ranch style fence, where the horizontals are secured alternately to each side of the verticals, providing a fence which looks equally good on both sides. Ranch style boarding can also be attached vertically to arris rails (the horizontal rails which are usually associated with close board fencing, as described on p. 112) to produce a totally different effect. Ranch fencing is either painted or treated with a wood preservative.

Shared boundary fencing *Open ranch-style fencing, which looks equally good from either side, is ideal as a boundary demarcation between properties. Whether open or close board (as in the diagram below), this fencing is an ideal plant support.*

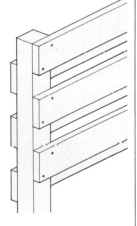

Close board

This type of fence will give privacy and shelter, and is available in pre-fabricated panels but is usually built on site. It is built of overlapping, feather-edged boards, between stout timber or concrete posts about 2.75 m (9 ft) apart, nailed to two or three horizontal arris rails which slot into mortises cut into the posts. Fitting a gravel board between the posts and just clear of the ground will protect the light feather-edged timber from wet rot. A capping strip along the top of the fence will prevent weathering of the end grain from above. This type of fence is suitable for most locations, rural or urban.

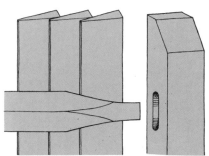

Close board construction *Arris rails slot into mortises cut into the posts to form the support for the overlapping verticals.*

Woven panel

Various weaves and sizes of pre-fabricated wooden slat fence panel are available. The life span of this type of fencing depends on the quality of the wood used for making the slats. Oak and cedar need little maintenance and are best, while soft-woods require regular treatment with a preservative. Use stout concrete or wood posts to support the fence panels and wood string cappings and gravel board to counter rot.

Fence and wall combination *Tough woven panels of cedar make up this fence which sits on a low brick wall.*

Bamboo

Bamboo makes an ideal screening panel which can be used on a boundary, particularly as a backing for growing bamboo or any plant of strong "architectural" shape. Make up panels of bamboo, lashing the stems, or culms, to cross members of a heavier wood with wire or heavy cord. Bamboo should not be nailed as it will split. When trimming the culms, they should be cut just above a joint to prevent moisture collecting in the hollow stems. Ensure too that the bases of the culms do not come in

Wooden trellis

In Europe, trellis work is relatively simple, being of diamond or square patterns in light softwood and made into panels about 1.8 m (2 yd) square. Folding trellis should be set within a rigid frame to give it stability. Much of this prefabricated material is lightweight and rots quickly, if the plants which it supports do not break it first.

The American market offers a far larger range of trellis work much of which is suitable for overhead shading as well as see-through fencing. French provincial, Spanish and Chinese-style patterns are available. The more ornate the infill to your framework, the more important the siting of it. If a particular pattern works with your house frontage, trellis work can provide a handsome boundary, but if isolated from the house, trellis is probably best used as a screening material (see p. 118).

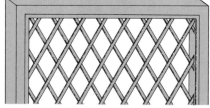

Framing trellis *To extend the life of trellis it should be fitted into a timber surround, and held by a timber fillet.*

contact with the ground, as they will rot. It is also possible to buy rolls of split bamboo (the type used for shading) which can be attached with wire to any openwork fencing, like chain link, in order to provide instant privacy or shelter. The lifespan of such temporary fencing, however, is limited.

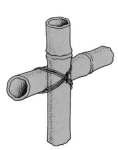

Traditional use of bamboo *A section of the bamboo fencing used in the gardens of the Katsura Palace, Kyoto. The vertical stems, or culms, are lashed to a horizontal, as below.*

Hurdling and snow fencing

In England, you can buy 1.8 m (6 ft) panels of hurdling in either willow or hazel. These vary in height up to 1.8 m. The traditional use of hurdling is to provide a temporary shelter for sheep during lambing, but it also makes excellent garden screening. In California an unusual low rustic fence can be made from grape stakes. Snow fencing – wire-bound pickets in redwood stain or white – is widely available and sturdy and attractive if properly installed.

Plastic

There are various types of plastic fencing system available which imitate painted post and rail, post and chain or palisade-style fencing. These can be used to mark boundaries and need little maintenance but they are lightweight in structure and are not tough enough for general garden use. Plastic posts are usually hollow and should be filled with aggregate for better anchorage. Plastic is better considered as a material to be used in conjunction with others, such as wood or metal. Various types of rigid plastic sheeting infill might be used in the same way as the corrugated fiberglass sheet is used opposite.

Metal

There are two common groups of metal fencing. One, for urban use, is the painted iron railing which is made up of vertical bars and often finished with a spike or dart to provide a substantial see-through barrier. This is the type of fence that fronts many late eighteenth- and early nineteenth-century town houses throughout Europe. The other group comprises line wire, wire mesh and chain link (sometimes plastic coated), all of which are strained between concrete, metal or timber verticals, the end posts taking most of the strain. Such fencing is manufactured by the roll so the distance which you set the posts apart is a matter of choice. It provides the minimum in privacy when used as a boundary, but can provide a worthwhile measure of security if well constructed. Wire mesh is a good support for light climbing plants.

Less common fencing materials

Panels of sheet fiberglass can be used to make light and decorative fencing panels if incorporated within a wooden frame, as below, within the fence verticals. Varying degrees of opacity and a variety of colored finishes are available. Corrugated panels are also available. Exterior plywood can also be used as a fencing element.

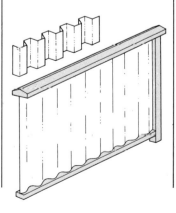

Fence post construction

It is essential to have sound verticals to hold your fence.

Timber posts should always be treated with preservative. But no matter how well protected, wooden posts set directly into earth will rot relatively quickly, and wooden posts set directly into concrete will also rot, if after a longer period. Where you can, fix the post at ground level to a metal plate or proprietary metal fixing, and then set that into concrete. Alternatively, you can use a concrete spur set in concrete to bolt the post to.

If you must set wood directly into earth or concrete prevent the wood from decaying for as long as possible. Where the soil is stable, place a large stone at the bottom of each post hole, to preserve the wood end grain, and backfill a little at a time with earth keeping the post absolutely vertical and tamping the earth in around the post. The odd piece of stone wedged hard against the post will help to keep the post firm. When locating posts in lighter, sandy soil, where less stability is possible, you must backfill with wet concrete. Do not set the end of the post directly into concrete, which might hold water, but again set the post on a large stone. Backfill for 100 mm

or so with gravelly soil before pouring concrete mix around the post. A standard mix for concrete used for post fixing is 1:3:5, cement:sand:aggregate. To cut down on the amount of concrete needed, bed the odd stone around the post as well.

Where heavy frost is likely it might bring with it the problems of cracking concrete and heaving of the earth. To minimize the damage caused by heaving, dig the post holes 300 mm (1 ft) below depth that frost can penetrate in your area, and shovel in a little gravel for drainage. Drive galvanized nails part way into the sides at the foot of each post, then position each post into the gravel before pouring the concrete around the nailed sections. Complete the backfill using gravel or gravelly soil.

To prevent the concrete collars around posts from cracking when wet posts freeze and expand, cut wooden wedges to the width of the posts, oil them, and place them alongside each post before you pour in the concrete. When the concrete has set, remove the wedges and fill the cavities with tar or sand.

If you are using concrete or metal fence posts, these are best set directly in concrete.

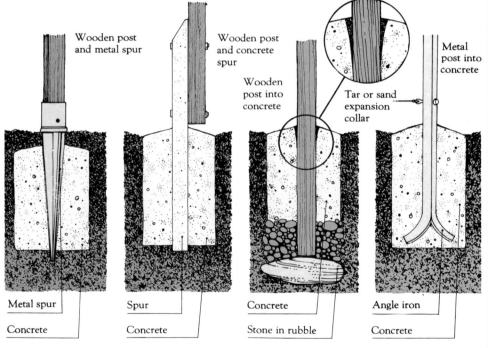

Wooden post and metal spur

Wooden post and concrete spur

Wooden post into concrete

Tar or sand expansion collar

Metal post into concrete

| Metal spur | Spur | Concrete | Angle iron |
| Concrete | Concrete | Stone in rubble | Concrete |

Post cappings

Hardwood fence post tops can be simply shaped to repel rain water. The life of soft-wood posts is considerably lengthened by fitting caps to prevent water from permeating the exposed end grain. These can be made of wood or non-corrosive metal sheet.

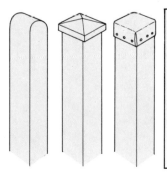

Post hole borer
A very useful tool to buy or borrow when constructing a fence, is a post hole borer. It allows you to remove the minimum of earth when digging post holes.

Fencing materials

Ready-made fencing panels available on the market are fairly standard; the major types are illustrated here. The purpose of the fence and its location will help you decide on the type you need. Plastic is obviously slick and urban, wattle fencing rural in feel, and the range available between these extremes is large. It is generally a false economy to invest in too cheap a fence, made of inferior material that will deteriorate quickly.

If you choose wooden fencing, ensure that it is well impregnated with preservative, either dipped in it or treated under pressure. Fit it with a protective capping and a gravel board beneath the lowest panel which can be renewed on its own, for the lowest area of the panel will always rot first. None of these maintenance points will be of any use, however, if the verticals which hold the fence are not of the soundest material and well pinioned into the ground.

Panel fencing

Illustrated below are three standard types of wooden fence, of which there are many permutations according to the size and weave of the wood used in their construction. Most are made of soft wood. Larchlap fencing cannot be seen through, while inter-woven panels may be. Trellis fencing is ideal for plant support, the combination of wood and greenery providing a pleasant see-through background. This can be enhanced by an evergreen planting of shrubs in front.

Larchlap

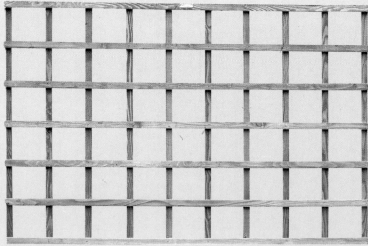

Inter-woven

Plastic fences

Maintenance will be reduced to a minimum if you select a plastic fence, and it will not rot either. Visually, such a crisp fence is attractive but physically it can be weak and unable, for example, to support the weight of children playing on it. Plastic fence is useful to define boundary divisions in an urban situation rather than to give privacy.

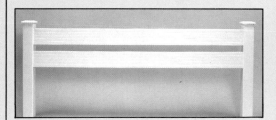

Ranch

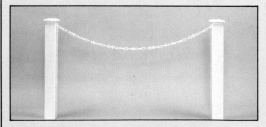

Post and chain

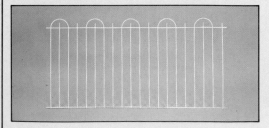

Picket

Trellis

Picket and hurdle

Picket fencing, when painted, has an urban feel about it, and when stained makes an admirable boundary and looks well in most other situations too. Its height can vary according to its function. Such a fence should be set at least 75 mm (3 in) above ground, if the base of the verticals are not to rot.

Wattle fencing is not built to last; traditionally it provides seasonal shelter during lambing. Its lifespan can be up to five years, however, and as a temporary measure, until planting has grown, or as a wind shelter to protect young or tender planting, it cannot be beaten.

Netting

Use netting fencing over large boundary runs where wood is too expensive, or where you want to define your site but retain any view from within it. Verticals can be wood but concrete is better, since they must support stressing wires along the top and bottom of the mesh. Chain link fencing, which is wire, or wire covered with colored plastic is the strongest mesh. Plastic chicken wire is less tensile than chain link but is ideal for more general garden use, for infilling decorative panels and to support rampant climbers such as pole beans and sweetpeas. Plastic-coated wire picket is usually used as a temporary measure and needs strong support at close intervals.

Picket

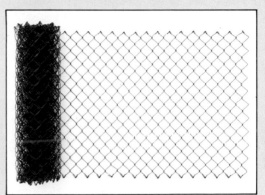

Plastic-coated chain link

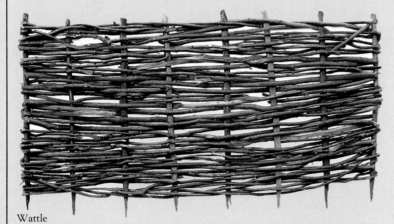

Wattle

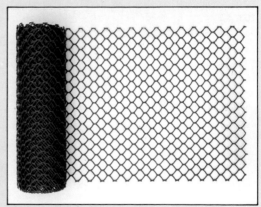

Plastic-coated chicken wire

Posts

Whatever your particular fencing infill, it is the strength of its supports that will make the structure work. Concrete posts set into concrete below ground undoubtedly provide the most solid support, and when well matched with the infill look perfectly acceptable. In wet ground, or when stock might rub or brush the fence, concrete is wise.
For a more sympathetic feeling, wood to match the infill panel is often necessary. The verticals may be sawn or left natural. All bark, however, must be removed, since it harbors pests and encourages rot.

1 Concrete spur
2 Metal foot
3 Concrete post
4 Softwood post
5 Larch post

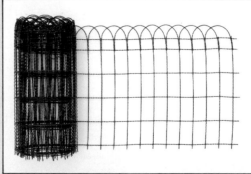

Plastic-coated wire picket

Gates

Why have the same front gate as your neighbor? Try to design your own gate so that the entrance to your garden is special and avoid the standard catalogue approach of cheap, overdecorative ironwork.

First decide exactly what you want of your gate. If it is a gate on to a public thoroughfare, should it stop people from looking in, or give them a glimpse of your garden? Is it just to keep children or pets in, or should it be a security gate? Is the gate to be decorative, or a utilitarian entrance and exit for pedestrians and/or cars? Answer these questions and you should be able to decide on dimensions and whether the gate should be a solid one, or openwork. Then decide on style, considering the style of your house (against which the gate is often seen) and the type of boundary it will pierce. If a wooden gate is to pierce an existing wooden fence, vary its construction or the gate will be lost when closed.

Consider the mechanics of your gate well – there is nothing more irritating if it fails. The piers on either side must be sturdy enough to support the gate and the hinges should be strong enough to prevent it from sagging. Always use three hinges in preference to two, and ensure that the lock or latch is durable and childproof as well as easy to see. If your gate carries your name or the house number, fit a spring to close the gate so the information can be seen at all times.

An entrance of character *A beautifully detailed, white-painted wooden gate, which is wholly in character with the house to which it leads as well as being decorative in its own right.*

Construction

Build your gate to last, for it will take heavy wear from undiscerning visitors. The construction details, right, are for a wooden picket gate which has both horizontal and cross braces to support the verticals. The horizontals are mortised into the hanging and closing stiles, and these are glued and secured with wooden dowels so that any rusting of screws is avoided.

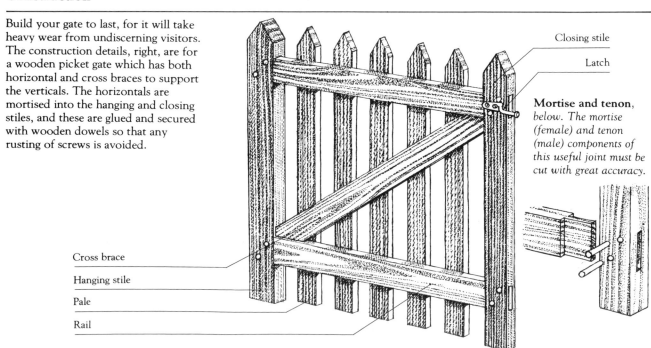

Closing stile

Latch

Mortise and tenon, *below. The mortise (female) and tenon (male) components of this useful joint must be cut with great accuracy.*

Cross brace

Hanging stile

Pale

Rail

Traditional oak gate
*left. The stout supports,
which balance the heavy
detail of this gate, are in
dressed stone. Also note
the tough-looking latch
which has been chosen to
match the style.*

Gates with style *below.
This beautiful white-
painted wooden gate
with a lattice top, pierces
an old stone wall.
Bottom, one half of a
pair of sunray entrance
gates in white-painted
wood. The supporting
wood pier is massive,
but in scale.*

Matching gate to boundary

Below are four examples of
gates set into a variety of
boundary types. The secret of
their success lies in the
relationship between the
proportions of fence or wall
to gate. The character of the
gates also reflects or offsets
the character of the boundary
they pierce.

Wooden gate in brick wall

Iron gate in brick wall

Ranch fencing and
gate

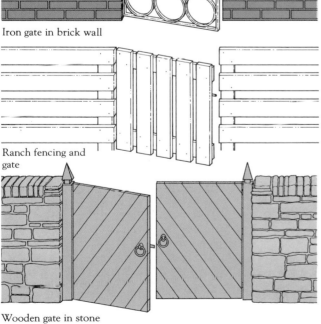

Wooden gate in stone

Internal walls and screens

You saw on page 106 how a boundary can be used to break up a site without necessarily dividing it up completely, like commas in a sentence. The use of screens within the garden, whether walls, fencing or hedges (see p. 196), goes one step further in the molding of space. As with boundaries, any internal screen should work within the original framework and pattern of your plan as described in Planning Your Garden.

A screen might be used to shelter a sitting area, or to partially hide a gas tank, the area for hanging washing, the rubbish dump, or even the vegetable patch if it cannot be well integrated. The density of such a screen can be less than for a boundary as no security measure is necessary, but to be effective it should provide screening throughout the year. A framework which supports a deciduous climbing plant will not be an efficient screen in the winter.

Various openwork concrete or terracotta building units are available which can provide an admirable screen. The simpler their pattern the more effective they are as a backdrop to any plants grown in conjunction with them. An openwork brick wall will perform a similar function.

Many forms of wooden fencing can be adapted to accept patterned infills within a simple surrounding frame, as shown right. Screens for special purposes, such as to shelter a swimming pool, may be see-through and constructed of more unusual screening materials. Heavy, expensive sheet material, however, such as glass, requires professional advice and specialist construction.

Open block screens

Screen blocks are of Middle Eastern origin, and intended to baffle a view while allowing a cooling breeze. Used incorrectly, they have the reverse effect of drawing the eye and, in northern climates, allowing a draft! Use the screening block sparingly therefore, and contrast its bold shape with large-leafed evergreen plants, as in the photograph, right.

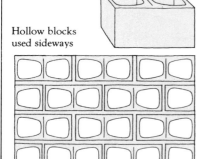

Hollow blocks used sideways

Making your own screens

On the right are some ideas for screens to be used within the garden in conjunction with planting.

1 *This idea uses driftwood within a framework, although any bough might be incorporated, provided that you remove its bark and treat it with preservative.*

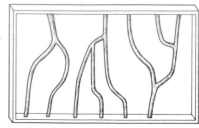

1

2 *Here the frame has a simple infill of bamboo verticals which would look particularly well if bamboo were planted on either side.*

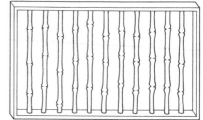

2

3 *Chain link fencing, or plastic-coated netting, can also be used as an infill material. Grow large-leafed vines, climbing beans or ivy through the link to thicken the screen through the year.*

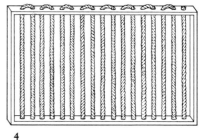

3

4 *Rope, threaded through a surrounding frame, and finally knotted, will give a nautical flavor to a swimming-pool surround screen. The rope can be natural hemp, or a colored man-made type.*

5 *The louvred screen is a good way to direct a view, while blocking it from straight on.*

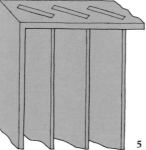

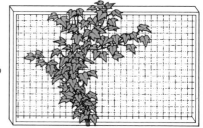

5   4

Changing levels

It is easy to end up with an ideal residence set in a garden of totally unmanageable levels. A solution to the difficulties of a sloping site where space is limited, is to build retaining walls to hold the earth back. A retaining wall will provide a strong, structural change of level and is the most suitable method of changing levels in a built-up area. However, a more economic solution is to grade out the site in banks or contoured mounds. This requires more space but can result in a pleasant rolling effect, perhaps backing up rocky outcrops, or a more carved and chiselled effect.

However you decide to change levels, the major practical consideration is the stabilizing of soil on your banks to stop loose soil from washing downhill in heavy rain. Pegged turf will stabilize a bank immediately (see p. 198), but the gradient which you grass should be gentle in section so that your mowing machine, of whatever type, can operate. Planting of a decorative ground cover (see p. 200) will also stabilize a bank, but make sure to use bold masses of individual types so as not to disrupt the flow of your ground shaping.

A gradient of 30 degrees to the horizontal is considered a reasonable gradient for a cylinder mowing machine. A gradient of 45 degrees can be managed by a rotary type of mower and is just practicable as a planted bank once the subjects are established. When planting a bank like this, it is advisable to plant through a coarse netting which is pegged into the earth and will retain it until roots establish themselves.

Importing earth to create garden banks can be an expensive business when you consider that shrubs require a minimum depth of 450 mm (18 in) of topsoil (grass can do with as little as 75 mm (3 in) however). But an advantage of molded banks is that you can hide any unwanted rubble or surplus spoil from building operations, or the excavations from a pool, beneath them.

Any ground shaping which you intend to appear natural should not look like a man-made dump on the top of natural earth. Always remember to clear topsoil to one side before building the bank or mound, then rake the topsoil back over it. If the spoil which you want to hide is not consolidated enough it will be liable to sinkage. Another pitfall to beware is that consolidated builders' rubble will provide such an excellent drainage system that topsoil over a mound will drain and become impoverished more quickly than other areas of the garden. In addition, surplus rainwater will tend to collect in puddles at the bottom of your banks, unless you provide for this with a drain run or soak away (see p. 103).

Gentle ground shaping *Gentle ground shaping has been used in this garden to encompass a swimming pool and to give it shelter. The material used to make the mounds was probably the excavation from the pool.*

Banks and steps

Various ways of creating banks, and so shaping your site, are shown in the series of sketches, right. The effect might be chiselled (1), or rolling (2). To achieve a complete undulating landscape, however small, requires space (4) unless you fake half of the roll with a retaining wall (3). To create ground interest with a slight change of level in a site, excavate a shallow step on the cut-and-fill principle (5). Always remember to remove topsoil before starting land shaping so that it can be replaced to form the new surface for planting.

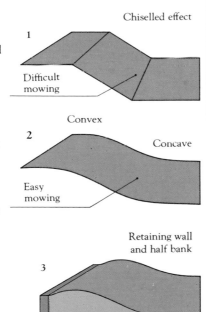

Chiselled effect

1

Difficult mowing

Convex

2

Concave

Easy mowing

Retaining wall and half bank

3

Spacious landscaping

4

Creating a change in level, cut equaling fill

5

Retaining walls

The construction of a retaining wall more than 750 mm (30 in) high is a project that should not be undertaken lightly, particularly if the soil which you are to retain, and into which you must dig, is heavy and needs draining. Any retaining structure will have to fight against the full, wet weight of earth behind it since you are creating a barrier to the natural drainage flow downhill. Provision for drainage is essential if your structure is to be sound and lasting. Do not take any chances where the proposed retaining wall is near a building. Seek expert advice, epecially where the slope to be altered is steep.

It is often not necessary to build a retaining wall at all if you grade out the bank in a series of "cut and fill" exercises, that you then turf or plant to retain. If you do decide to use retaining structures to support a particularly steep bank, you can use a similarly piecemeal approach, choosing a series of small walls.

The strongest type of retaining wall is one of concrete poured *in situ*, reinforced with metal rods or welded wire mesh – a specialist engineering job. Hollow concrete blocks, which have been reinforced with metal rods and then filled with poured concrete (see Appendix for the mix to use) will also make a solid retaining wall. Brick has less strength, being a smaller element, and when used for retaining walls should not be built more than a meter (3 ft) high unless as a fascia for reinforced concrete backing. Natural stone which has been cut on one side, or roughly dressed, makes a good solid retaining wall, particularly if it is built on the batter (sloped into the earth which it is to retain). A dry-stone wall with provision for planting within its structure, gives a charming rustic effect where it is desirable. However, stone is neither available, nor suitable, everywhere.

Wood may be used as a retaining material either in the form of railway line ties, or of logs, set into the ground vertically. Planks can be used horizontally, but with this method the vertical supports for the planks must be tied back into the bank with, for example, metal rods set into buried concrete and bolted to the supports. Depending on its imperviousness, wood will rot comparatively quickly, however.

To eliminate the build up of water behind your retaining wall, it is essential that it is pierced regularly by weep holes. These can either take the form of a gap in the jointing, or preferably a drain pipe set through the wall, angled downwards to a flush finish on the wall's face 150 mm (6 in) above ground level. Direct the water behind the wall to the weep hole by backfilling against it with a thickness of ash or rubble. A land drain at the base of the retaining wall may be required to take surplus drain-off. You will extend the life of a retaining wall by incorporating a damp-proof course and backing the wall with a waterproofing agent as well.

Retained banks *Massive lumps of stone have been beautifully ground to form this random retainer to a garden bank. Steps traverse the gradient, with a sculptural stone grouping beyond.*

Retaining-wall designs
Four designs for retaining walls are shown below. The top example uses concrete building blocks stepped back into the bank, and the one below it is constructed with pre-shaped concrete units. The poured concrete retainer has an angled shape for added strength. Such a wall should not normally be built higher than one metre. For higher construction you should seek specialist building advice.

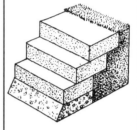

Building blocks

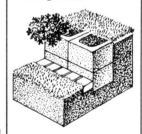

Pre-cast units

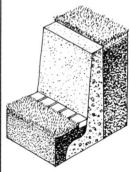

Poured concrete

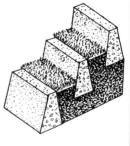

Poured concrete units

Retained lawn *Stepped retaining walls in stone, with planting between each, retain this lawn area. Across the wall is a random run of steps.*

Construction

It is essential that a retaining wall is strong, as the weight of wet earth it holds is very heavy. The higher the wall, the stronger it has to be. In general, the larger the individual elements of the construction, the stronger the retaining wall will be.

Water build up behind the wall must be allowed to escape through weep holes at the base. An infill of ash or clinker behind the wall will direct water to the drainage area and the weep holes. Whether the wall is damp-proofed or not will depend on its location and the type of wall, and whether you want plants in it, or only over it. It is not possible to damp-proof a wall partially filled with earth and plants.

A brick or concrete retaining wall will obviously last longer if it does not absorb water from the earth which it retains. To achieve this you must put a waterproof layer (of which there are many proprietary varieties available) behind the wall and the earth behind.

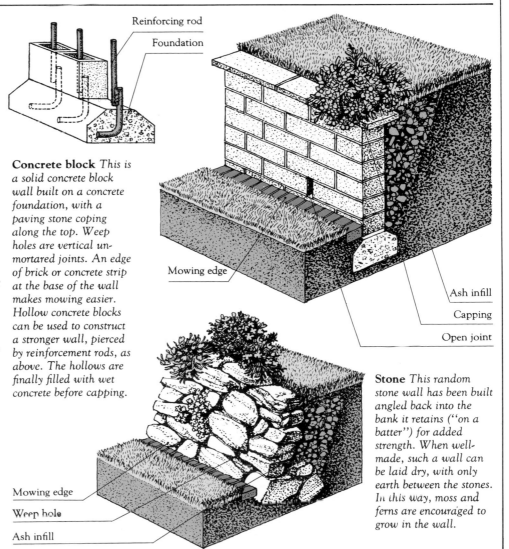

Reinforcing rod

Foundation

Concrete block *This is a solid concrete block wall built on a concrete foundation, with a paving stone coping along the top. Weep holes are vertical un-mortared joints. An edge of brick or concrete strip at the base of the wall makes mowing easier. Hollow concrete blocks can be used to construct a stronger wall, pierced by reinforcement rods, as above. The hollows are finally filled with wet concrete before capping.*

Mowing edge

Ash infill

Capping

Open joint

Mowing edge

Weep hole

Ash infill

Stone *This random stone wall has been built angled back into the bank it retains ("on a batter") for added strength. When well-made, such a wall can be laid dry, with only earth between the stones. In this way, moss and ferns are encouraged to grow in the wall.*

121

Steps and ramps

Few people can afford sculpture for their garden, but a good run of steps – not necessarily a huge flight – well-sited and interestingly composed, can more than compensate for its lack. Steps used in the rhythm of the garden can become not only a focal point, but an interesting and useful feature. They can provide a feature, a vantage point and a temporary perch.

Steps must be gentle, low and wide. Too steep a flight will quicken the pace unnecessarily. Making the steps as wide as you can will have the effect of making them look as gracious and inviting as possible. Plan your steps as a means of getting from level A to level B, but not necessarily in the shortest time. Consider them as part of the patchwork of materials which make up your garden pattern.

The materials you use for constructing the steps will dictate their form to a certain extent. In addition, the paving materials you intend to use at the top and bottom of the steps, or for any retaining walls nearby will also affect your choice.

After making a flight of equally-spaced steps fit into a bank, you will often be left with an awkward cut or fill area on each side of the flight. The treatment of this area can be a problem. If it is grassed, it can be difficult to mow. Sometimes a retaining wall holding the steps on either side is the neatest solution.

There is often no necessity to run your steps straight up and down the slope. If space allows, the run might go left or right for a period, with a landing on the turn. In this way, flights of steps can become more sculptural. For a similarly dramatic effect, you might decide on a more unusual construction still, such as steps cantilevered from a solid retaining wall.

There are flat gardens that can be considerably improved by simply constructing the occasional step right across the site. Such steps should articulate the garden plan, providing ground interest and encouraging the eye to remain within the site.

Gardens constructed on different levels with steps between them, will present a problem when it comes to using wheelbarrows or lawn mowers. These tools can be given a ramped route of their own if the area is large enough, or failing this, you might run a ramp at the side of any steps. If the ascent is gentle enough, it is possible to have ramped sections between two or three steps. Whatever the solution, such a garden will not be an easy one to work.

The consideration of safety must be a priority when building steps. Treads which are too smooth, or will wear quickly to an unstable surface, are equally dangerous. Treads set absolutely level will not shed rainwater quickly so presenting a hazard which is increased in icy weather when any standing water will freeze.

Shallow steps *This romantic flight of steps sweeps up a gentle incline under an overhanging wisteria. The retaining wall which edges the flight, would be more successful if it encouraged the eye to move with the curve of the steps, but the overall effect is inviting and altogether grand.*

Turfed steps *In this example, bricks have been used on end to form the risers to a turfed flight of steps. While appearing pleasantly rural, this method of construction will be difficult to maintain, since mowing will be difficult and edging of the grass necessary against the riser. The coping to the retaining wall which edges the flight has been specially shaped to match.*

Construction

Step construction is similar to paving (see p. 126), and building retaining walls (see p. 121), for each step riser (the vertical component) is a miniature retaining wall. You must pay particular attention, however, to the treads (the horizontal components). Each must be well set in concrete, with allowance for water runoff to left and right. Whether the edges of the treads meet with the edges of the risers to make right angles, or whether you make the treads overhang the risers, depends on the effect you want. The former is crisp and architectural, while the latter method creates a shadow line along each riser which makes each tread appear to float. The height of each riser should be approximately 150 mm (6 in), with the treads about 380 mm (15 in) wide. To decide on the number of steps that you require, first measure the change of level across the slope (see p. 31) and then divide it by the riser height. It is often necessary either to cut into the bank, or to build it up, at top or bottom, to make the slope fit the steps.

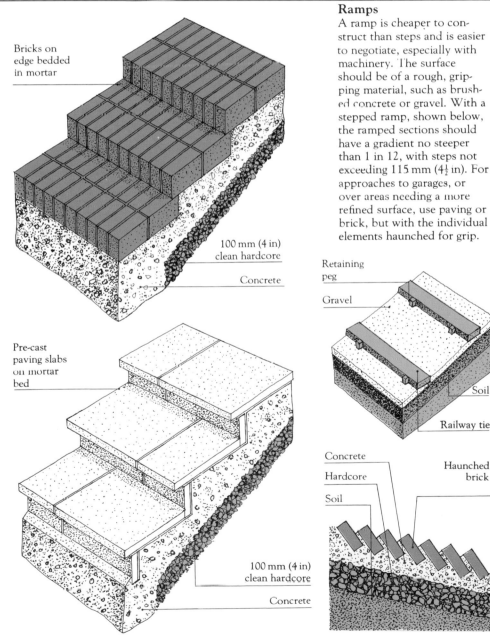

Bricks on edge bedded in mortar

100 mm (4 in) clean hardcore

Concrete

Pre-cast paving slabs on mortar bed

100 mm (4 in) clean hardcore

Concrete

Ramps

A ramp is cheaper to construct than steps and is easier to negotiate, especially with machinery. The surface should be of a rough, gripping material, such as brushed concrete or gravel. With a stepped ramp, shown below, the ramped sections should have a gradient no steeper than 1 in 12, with steps not exceeding 115 mm (4½ in). For approaches to garages, or over areas needing a more refined surface, use paving or brick, but with the individual elements haunched for grip.

Retaining peg

Gravel

Soil

Railway tie

Concrete

Hardcore

Soil

Haunched brick

123

Using different materials

Most types of paving material may also be used for steps, and it makes sense to connect paths at the top and bottom of steps by using the same material between. Architects have particular rules for step heights and tread widths which conform to various building regulations. But in the garden, the general rule is the gentler the flight of good wide treads, the more pleasant the steps. However, be ruled by the appearance of the materials you use. The tree trunk slices, bottom, for example, make attractive "stepping-stone" treads.

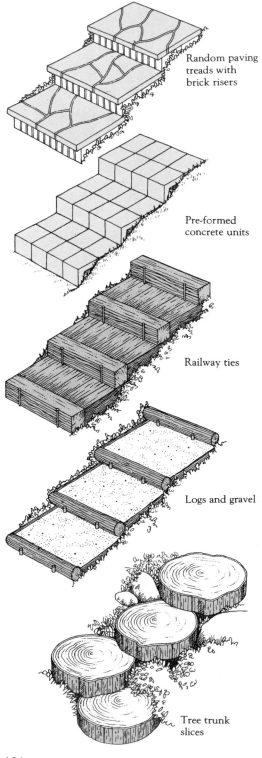

Random paving treads with brick risers

Pre-formed concrete units

Railway ties

Logs and gravel

Tree trunk slices

Random steps *A flight of stone steps, such as that above, is suitable for crossing a rockery or rough bank where it will complement a rural feel.* *It would be totally unsuitable, however, in a more formal setting, such as the approach to a house.*

Cantilevered treads

When space is limited, steps should be tucked into a corner, as in the photograph right. The structure is of stained softwood, supported on a central wooden rib which is let into the wall beneath a landing. Alternatively, treads may be cantilevered from a wall as in the diagram, below.

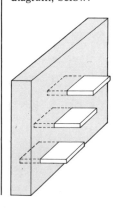

Step designs

We tend to be too rigid in our ideas for steps, making simple flights that run straight up and down. With a little ingenuity, the direction of the flight may be altered so that the finished effect is more casual and more of a sculptured feature in the garden. If your garden plan lends itself to it, you can incorporate a landing in the flight of steps, changing the course through 90 degrees, or even 180 degrees if there is room for two landings.

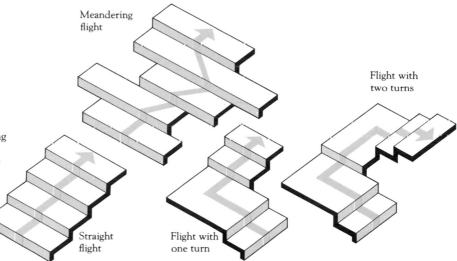

Meandering flight

Flight with two turns

Straight flight

Flight with one turn

Sympathetic planting for steps

The plants that you choose to flank or cover steps are important if the flight is to be properly integrated into the garden. A "weedy" look can create a magical effect. To achieve the feeling of longstanding random growth, leave planting pockets at the sides of the flight, or leave jointing open for planting. Select species that will not become too rampant, and that can take a certain amount of wear. Herbs are ideal as they will smell when brushed. Try chamomile (*Chamaemelum nobile*), catmint (*Nepeta* × *faassenii*), or mixed-colored, low-growing thymes (*Thymus* sp.).

The way in which you plant the areas bordering a flight of steps can change the character of the steps completely. A straight flight can be made to appear curved or staggered from side to side, by letting plants encroach on to the sides of the flight in a planned fashion. Starkness can be softened, or purely functional steps given a lift with strong "architectural" planting.

Soft planting, *above. Woodland strawberry* (Fragaria vesca) *covers the risers of these stone steps and gives a pretty, edible result. The flight has been further softened with planting at the sides of the steps.*

Abundant planting, *left. The effect of the herbaceous planting on either side of this straight flight of steps is to give it a meandering line. This is an example of excellent grouping of plants to complement a structural feature.*

125

Surfaces

Now that you have shaped up the garden, with all its walls, changes of level and steps positioned and built, you are ready to get down to filling the areas of ground pattern with planting, lawn, water or a hard surfacing medium of some kind. Whatever medium you choose from those shown on the next pages, hard surfacing should provide the stepping off point to enjoy the garden as well as providing a link between buildings and the soft, planted areas of the garden.

Paving

In the gardens of northern Europe and much of the United States, paving is the principal surfacing medium. The choice of paving you make will depend on the character of your site and the materials you have chosen to use so far, but more significantly on the price of different pavings. With a limited budget the choice must be between having a larger paved area in a cheaper medium, or a smaller area in a more expensive one.

Decide on the feeling of the paving you need. If it is to be the base of an outside room, that is a terrace next to the house, or in a sunny location elsewhere in the garden, it will provide a full stop in the garden plan and must therefore be strongly detailed. If it is simply to be a hard surface connecting point A with point B, it need not be decorative. I prefer simple paving patterns that provide a background to any elements placed on, or planted around, the surface. Remember that paving near the house has the additional purpose of setting off the building.

When paving is being laid adjoining a building, it should only butt the wall if 150 mm (6 in) below the damp proof course. Where this is impossible, allow for a gap of about 75 mm (3 in) between the edge of the paving and the wall of the building, and fill it with clean pea gravel.

All paving should be laid with a slight fall across its surface (away from the house in adjacent paving) of about 50 mm (2 in) in two metres (6½ ft). Over a small area, drain off into neighboring planting or to a lawn if your soil drains well. For larger areas, lay a drain run at the edge of the paved area, linked to a soakaway (see p. 103). Where this is not possible, as in an enclosed yard, lay the paving to fall to·a central gully, which might link to a soakaway, or to surface water drainage from the house.

Whatever paving you choose, try to avoid having to cut too many elements. Keep the outlines of paved areas simple and consider the possibility of working out the framework grid for your garden design (see p. 38) to fit multiples of the paving unit dimensions.

Pre-cast paving slabs

Most pavings for family pedestrian use will need to have a hard-core base of 100 mm (4 in), according to the soil conditions (on clay you might manage with a little less). Over this, the slabs should be laid in 50 mm (2 in) of builder's sand, if each slab is heavy, or sand and cement if the slabs are smaller and require firmer support. Considering the thickness of the slabs them- selves, say another 50 mm (2 in), it will be necessary to dig to a depth of at least 200 mm (8 in) if the finished paving surface is to be flush with surrounding levels. Brush sand or sand and cement (depending on your chosen bedding materials) dry into joints.

Slab path, *above. Pre-cast paving slabs in a simple walling bond pattern.*

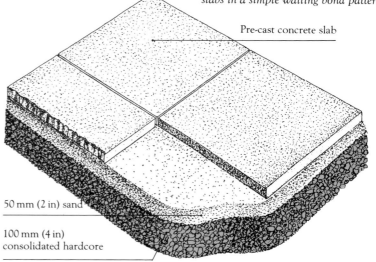

Pre-cast concrete slab

50 mm (2 in) sand

100 mm (4 in) consolidated hardcore

Poured concrete

Concrete laid *in situ* should only be used on perfectly stable soils which are not liable to frost upheaval, or where the water table is high. It is one of the cheapest methods of laying a large area of hard surfacing. You pour newly mixed concrete, on the spot, into a frame of your own construction. The frame need only be temporary, but might be formed by other surfacing, such as brick or paving stone. Make a temporary frame from 25 mm by 75 mm (1 × 3 in) planks held rigid and level allowing for the necessary fall) by stout pegs, over a well-consoli- dated 75-mm (3-in) base of either fine hardcore or binding gravel. Temperature changes will make a poured concrete surface crack if you make its area too large for its thickness. A good thickness in the

garden is 100 mm (4 in) and you should keep sections of *in situ* concrete to 4 m by 4 m (13 × 13 ft). Divide larger areas with wooden expansion joints. Lay concrete paths in 4-m (13-ft) sections.

100 mm (4 in) concrete (see Appendix for mix)

Temporary wooden shuttering

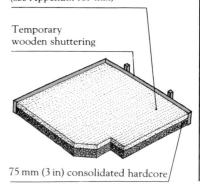

75 mm (3 in) consolidated hardcore

Stone

Quarried stone may be split and given a sawn or rubbed face for use as paving. The choice of a particular stone will depend on several factors. These include its durability and whether its surface will become smooth and slippery, particularly when wet, or fracture in the frost. The stone thickness will vary from 50 to 75 mm (2 to 3 in) depending on the size of the flags.

On normal soils (light or sandy clays, fine sands, sand and gravel, or gravel), lay the stone flags on a 75-mm (3-in) layer of clean hardcore, or similar granular base material, blinded over with sand. If large and heavy enough, the flags may be laid directly on to the sand. Spot bedding, where a dot of mortar is put at each corner and in the center of the underside of each flag, will assist the levelling process. Allow for a cross fall of 1:32 across the paved area. Brush in a dry 1:1 sand and cement mix to seal the joints.

Random paving

Random paving (where each unit is of nondescript shape) should be laid on exactly the same foundation as pre-cast paving slabs. When laid badly, this type of paving is known as "crazy", which rather speaks for itself. It soon becomes weed infested and uneven. Laid well, the sizeable individual elements should be tailored to fit each other so that the joints are no wider than those of regular forms of paving, and the overall area is level. The jointing should be as for pre-cast slabs.

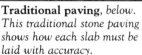

Bold use of stone, *above.* *Stone paving should be laid in simple, bold areas, as in this stepped terrace.*

Traditional paving, *below.* *This traditional stone paving shows how each slab must be laid with accuracy.*

Paving patterns

A heavy paving pattern is only attractive when it is used to fulfil a particular function, such as to draw attention to a particular area. It is preferable not to mix colored slabs in your pattern but simply to use designs as below.

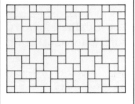
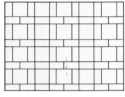
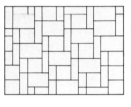
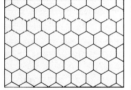

Paving and plants

The inclusion of plants amongst paving can create a very pretty effect as in these two photographs. The effect is strongest if only one type of plant is used but it is only possible with large, stable paving elements.

Combining paving and plants, however, will restrict the usage of the paved area. Plan open joints for planting carefully so that the character of the paving is enhanced rather than obliterated.

Small unit paving

Paving with small units, such as those shown on the next pages, and including brick and granite blocks, gives easier paving of awkward shapes in the garden and provides a richer surface texture. However, small-unit paving is usually more expensive than putting down larger units, such as pre-cast concrete slabs. It is not always the material itself which is more expensive, but the cost of having a mass of small elements, such as bricks, laid. And to try to save on laying small-unit paving well by cutting cost on the base materials, or how the jointing is finished, is a false economy. You will only end up with a weed-infested, uneven and probably dangerous, surface. Well-laid and finished, small-unit paving can be very impressive over relatively small areas. It will attract the eye and will be a feature in its own right.

Plain coursing In this European garden, bricks have been laid in straight courses to give an architectural feel to the path. The walls and steps are built of a standard concrete unit, with large cobbles laid loose to fill the beds at the base of the walls.

Construction

Any small paving unit (whether it be brick, patio blocks, or any of the proprietary paviers now available) is prone to shift after laying because of its relative light weight and small surface area. To prevent this, and for normal wear, each element needs to be buried in a 25-mm (1-in) mortar base, over a 75-mm (3-in) solid hardcore base. When the area is complete, simply brush a dry mix of sand and cement (4:1) between the joints. This mixture will gradually take up moisture from the ground and slowly set. In places where small unit paving is to take heavy wear, it should be laid on a concrete base over a con-solidated sub-base as explained for *in situ* concrete on page 126.

However, you can use a less durable concrete mix of 1:1:6, cement, sand and aggregate for this purpose, making the base about 100 mm (4 in) thick. When the concrete has set, the paving units can be laid on top, pointing them with mortar as if you were building a horizontal wall. When nearly dry, the mortar should be rubbed back.
Before fixing a single element, make sure that your pattern will work by laying out the paving loose. Some intricately shaped paviers are now available which interlock to form a predetermined pattern. You will find that there are alternative ways of interlocking the elements, however, to alter slightly the overall effect of the paving.

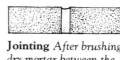

Jointing After brushing dry mortar between the joints of small-unit paving, wait for it to absorb some moisture and start to dry. Before it dries completely, run the rounded end of a stick along the joints to produce a neat concave finish between each unit.

Small-unit edging
The usual method of supporting edges is an outside row of bricks edge-on. The edging row can be laid to give a zig-zag effect or, to give a raised edge. Alternatively, you can use a reinforced concrete edging strip.

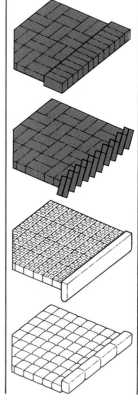

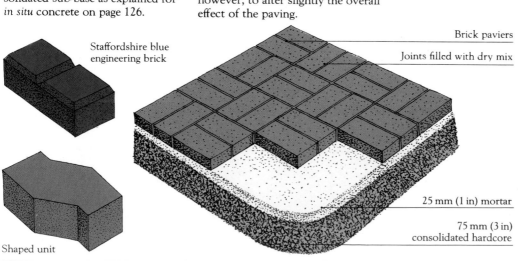

Staffordshire blue engineering brick

Shaped unit

Brick paviers

Joints filled with dry mix

25 mm (1 in) mortar

75 mm (3 in) consolidated hardcore

Brick paving

More houses are constructed of brick than of any other material, and a similar brick used to pave garden areas adjoining the house is a sure way of achieving integration of building and site. This will create a pleasant wrap-around feel.

When considering walls in the section on boundaries and enclosures (see p. 106), you will have seen the variety of facing bricks which are available for building and you might be able to match the brick of the facing walls of your house. But although facing bricks are made for exterior walls, they are not specifically recommended for exterior paving. Used for paving they will sooner or later flake and become uneven through the action of frost. This effect can be desirable, particularly in a period setting. For a crisper, longer lasting brick surface, use brick paviers. These have been fired to become harder than wall bricks, and although they are more expensive they are easier to lay because they are thinner, slightly wider and longer. Another alternative is to use engineering bricks which, although the same size as facing bricks, are, like brick paviers, much more durable. Take care not to lay too large an area of brick paving in too fancy a pattern, for the mix soon becomes too rich. There is something special about good brick paving, but too much of it becomes indigestible.

Patterns in brick

Brick (or brick pavier) is an adaptable paving medium. It can be laid face down to present the bottom, or bedding face of the brick, or laid on edge to present a side, or stretcher face. You can interlock bricks in a variety of ways and bricks can be cut. These variables give you a great variety of possible paving patterns, five of which are shown below. Over larger areas, the richness of color and the quantity of elements required should encourage you to choose a simple ground pattern. Such patterns include all-aligning coursing and simple wall bonding patterns.

Bedding faces

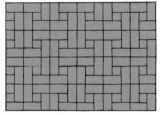

Bedding faces using halves

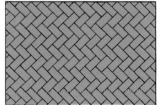

Bedding faces

Stretcher faces

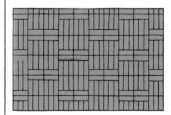

Stretcher faces

Recessed pointing, *above. This terrace has a surface of broken courses of brickwork. The pointing of the bricks has been recessed so that each element is clearly defined.*

Stepped terrace, *left. External building bricks have been used to create a crisp step in a terrace which is surfaced in alternating courses of paving bricks, and paving bricks on edge.*

Granite or Belgian blocks

Blocks are a hard, quarried stone surfacing material. They are gray and either roughly brick shaped, or half this size and roughly cubic. They were used originally as an extremely durable road surfacing material, close-packed in sand. Where old road surfaces are being removed it is sometimes possible to obtain used blocks from your local supply outlet. New blocks are mostly imported and are therefore an expensive medium to use. However, granite is a material which is alien to many situations so consider its use carefully. Granite blocks are laid in a 50-mm (2-in) bed of sand and cement (3:1), close-packed, over a 100-mm (4-in) solid hardcore base. More of the sand and cement mix should be brushed between the blocks where possible before lightly watering the surface and allowing the mortar to harden.

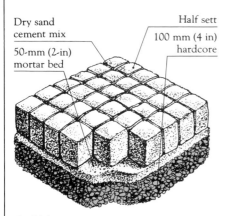

Dry sand cement mix

Half sett

50-mm (2-in) mortar bed

100 mm (4 in) hardcore

Squared granite blocks, *above. The feeling of granite blocks is hard and urban. Here they have been used as both a retaining curb to a planted area and as a surfacing material.*

Concrete paving blocks, *right. These are blocks made of concrete, giving a more refined finish than granite.*

Cobbles-on-end

Engineering brick

35 mm dry sand cement mix

75 mm hardcore

Concrete

Cobbles

Cobbles are rounded stones which have been formed by glacial action or by the action of the sea. They are graded and sold in various sizes for use in the garden. Laid loose and in contrast with bold foliage plants, they create a Japanese effect. Cobbles are difficult to walk on and they may be used as a deterrent, infilling corners which would otherwise be trodden on.

For an altogether crisper effect, cobbles may be laid on end, tight-packed together like eggs in a carton. Such paving makes an admirable infilling when creating a paving pattern. When using cobbles in this way they will need to be retained by a curb of some type, such as brick-on-edge, granite blocks or concrete. The cobbles are laid in 35 mm (1½ in) of dry sand and cement (3:1) over a 75-mm (3-in) layer of consolidated hardcore or hoggin. Brush a little of the dry mix through the cobbles when the laying is complete and then water them. The finished result should show little mortar.

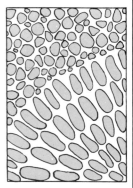

Cobbles for paving *These cobbles, laid in a random pattern on their sides, with a flattish side uppermost, are obviously for walking on. Usually cobbles are laid end on to discourage pedestrians.*

Inventive use of cobbles, *above. Different patterns are possible using cobbles of varying sizes and thicknesses.*

Soft surfacing

Between the extremes of hard paved surfacing and soft ground cover planting or lawn, there is the technique of "soft" surfacing. It is more relaxed in feel than the former and needs less maintenance than the latter, and being cheap has great potential for the small garden. The usual soft surfacing media are various sizes of gravel and stone. Also used are wood and bark chips, materials which are often used as a mulch spread over planted areas to reduce evaporation. Used as a soft surfacing material, bark looks best in a woodland setting.

Soft surfacings are an ideal alternative for small areas or for people who want a restricted amount of planting that will always look crisp and clean in its surround. They are equally usable in country courtyards, suburban front areas or tight urban gardens.

A retaining edge is important for all soft surfacing materials as without one they tend to spread. Within this retaining edge soft surfacings only require periodic maintenance as described in the chapter on care and maintenance. Weeds in gravel or crushed stone can be hoed or hand pulled after rain with ease. But the finished effect should be random and casual, with plants allowed to self-seed, so a weed-free approach is not always essential.

Pea gravel and gravel

Pea shingle is small chippings of stone which have been smoothed by the action of water. It is dredged from low-lying, inland pits or taken from the beach. It is the smallest sized gravel and requires raking periodically to maintain a neat appearance. Other gravel grades consist of the sharp chippings of natural rock obtained from a quarry. Both gravel and crushed rock have marked regional differences depending on the type of rock from which they originated. The traditional use of rock or gravel is for surfacing drives or roadways, where it is rolled into a bituminous preparation. It can also be laid loose, but consolidated, as a cheap garden surfacing. The material should be retained by a curb and 20 mm ($\frac{3}{4}$ in) should be rolled into a 75-mm ($\frac{3}{4}$-in) hard, gravelly base, otherwise it becomes difficult to walk through. The surfacing layer needs replenishing each summer to retain its crisp effect. Increasingly, stone and gravel are being used as media in which to plant. The preparation of the ground beneath depends on soil type. If limestone or gravelly roll the 20-mm ($\frac{3}{4}$-in) surfacing layer on to the soil and plant through it. Where the soil is sandy or clayey, you need to hold the gravel by spreading it over a 75-mm (3-in) base. Pockets will have to be made through both layers for the roots of plants to penetrate to the soil below. After some time, however, there is a build up of soil within the layers and you will be able to plant directly into the gravel.

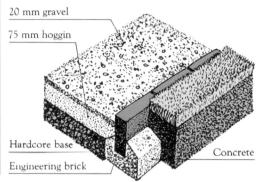

20 mm gravel

75 mm hoggin

Hardcore base

Engineering brick

Concrete

Planting in gravel, *below. Random planting in consolidated gravel is possible, as shown here in my own garden. Bold clumps of* Verbascum bombyciferum *feature in the foreground with masses of* Alchemilla mollis *and* Limnanthes *sp. beyond.*

Paving materials

There is a bewildering selection of types of paving though most people settle for concrete in one form or another since it is the cheapest and most universally available material. But it is all too easy to be conditioned by what your local supplier holds. So remember that the range is varied and shop around. Do not be afraid of mixing materials, though be sure in your mind of the finished result you seek.

Textured paving

In selecting your paving, first choose a color to blend with your house. Wet an area of the slab to see what it looks like. Then determine the size of each slab, to fit with your ground pattern or grid and to avoid too much cutting. Where you need to cut and tailor the slabs (usually a sign of your ground pattern not working) use a good quality slab since cheaper ones tend to crumble. Lastly, select for texture, bearing in mind the function of the paved area.

Shaped slabs

Smooth paving

If you want to stand chairs and a table on your paving, choose a smooth finish. When introducing a pattern into a large area of smooth paving, make sure that the outline of the overall plan and the pattern of the infill do not fight each other. As for textured paving, choose the color of smooth paving to match your house and wet the slabs before making your final choice to test change in color and slip-resistance.

Riven and "pointed" slabs

Regular slabs

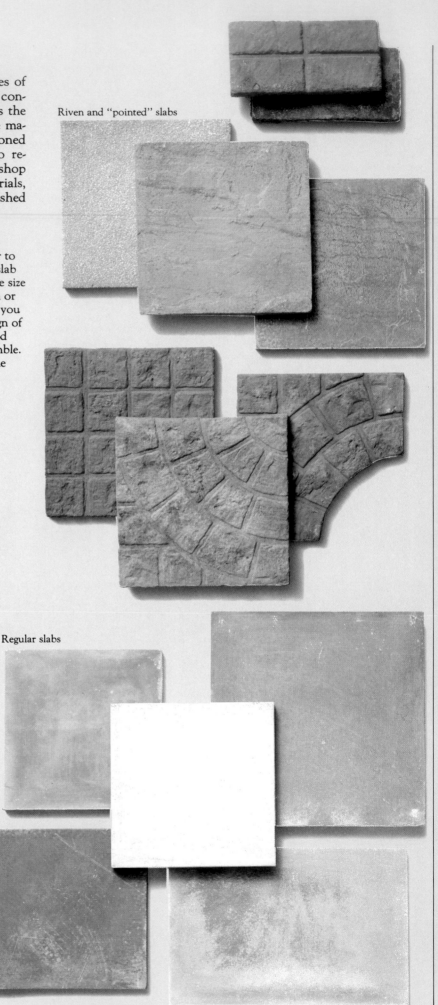

Gravels

There are as many gravel types as there are stone types, for one is a chip off the other. The chipping sizes vary as well, so there is considerable variety in color and texture, as shown below.

Small unit paving

It is the correct use of the smaller units of paving that often sets the style of your garden, roof terrace or conservatory. Broadly, the more sophisticated the mood you seek the finer the finish should be. Granite blocks and paviers are for heavy wear, but are unsurpassed when well finished. Finer brick and tile finishes are excellent for interconnecting use, joining indoors and outside. The new concrete interlocking pavier supports vehicles yet is refined enough for domestic use. Too large a laid area of the more refined small units can create a back-yard feeling.

1 Granite blocks
2 Granite paviers
3 Brick pavier
4 Stable tile
5 Brick paviers
6 Interlocking paviers
7 Quarry tiles

Cobbles

When a sea-washed pebble is large enough to make a usable element on its own, it is known as a cobble. Laid close together, they make a simple but positive finish.

Pea gravel

This is excavated from saline or fresh-water pits and does not have any sharp edges.

Stone paving

There is a timeless, massive quality about stone paving that seems correct in almost any situation. However, its variable thickness makes it difficult to lay. Old York stone, used for English interior flooring and for street pavements, is very handsome although its availability is decreasing.

8–9 Sawn sandstone
10–11 Dressed sandstone
12 Random sandstone
13–14 Random limestone
15 Random ironstone
16 Random slate

Mixing materials

The dividing line between a successful mix of paving materials and an unrestful muddle of them, is very thin. So when you find yourself with a few slabs or bricks left over from this or that job and want to combine them in a random way, the rules for success are to keep the areas of each material as large as possible and to interlock the materials so that the transition from one to another is smooth.

Various types of paving can be mixed to produce a more calculated pattern. The stronger the pattern, the larger the area should be. The decision to lay a particular combination of paving materials is generally dictated by economics. A large area of brick might be too expensive, for example, but a brick pattern infilled with concrete or gravel, will make the project considerably cheaper.

Be very careful about introducing a mix of colors into your paving design. Remember that too rich a mix is likely to produce paving that vies with any planting or other feature that abuts it. Some of the paving colors manufactured clash violently with foliage.

Stone mix *The transition in surfacing from granite blocks, through cobbles, to random stone and then back to blocks, has been handled with sensitivity. The stone trough is related in size and texture to the stone slabs of the paving.*

Wood in gravel, *left. These slices of tree trunk have been used as stepping "stones" through coarse gravel. During the winter, the wooden areas can become slippery unless wire-brushed.*

Slabs in cobbles, *right. Here, hexagonal pre-cast concrete slabs are laid in pebbles. The bevelled edge of the slabs will prevent them breaking.*

Ties and cobbles
Old railway ties are here set to radiate round a gentle curve. Loose cobbles are used to infill the joints and will provide a better grip in winter. The scale of the cobbles offsets that of the ties well.

A complete mix, *right.*
This consciously designed mix of paving materials dominates the flower beds piercing it and the furniture set upon it. Pre-cast concrete slabs form a grid that has a wooden infill. In the foreground, coloured bricks have been used.

Mixing brick and slabs
When mixing materials, be positive about your plan. On the right are three ways of paving a small terrace. Assume that it adjoins the house on one side, so that brick is a linking material between house and garden. The top terrace is entirely in brick with an area left open for random planting. It is important to leave enough uninterrupted space for table and chairs if they are required. The middle terrace has an equal amount of brick and slab that has been laid in a conscious pattern. The last version uses the slabs predominantly, with a random infill of brick, to give what is perhaps the most satisfying effect.

The inclusion of larger paving units, such as pre-cast concrete slabs, will cost less than paving entirely with small units. Be careful, however, to compare the dimensions of the larger and smaller units so that your pattern allows for the least possible amount of cutting.

Cesspool covers
Irritatingly, a cesspool cover is often sited in the area that you have designated for a terrace, and at the wrong angle compared with the planned direction of your paving units. You can deal with this problem in a number of different ways. Whichever you choose you must be positive about the solution or you will end up making a feature of the cover rather than hiding it. You can buy replacement covers which have an inverted metal tray into which you cut and fit a section of the surrounding surfacing material. However, these lids are too shallow to take earth for plants or lawn. Or you can plan for the inspection cover to sit within a cobbled or gravelled area that is strong enough to dominate. An adjacent shrubby crawler, such as a cotoneaster, will screen the cover. Failing all else, pave or grass the surrounding area and paint the cover black. You will soon forget the cover if you do not draw the eye to it by doing anything such as placing a planted tub on top.

Decking

Decking (areas of wooden planking) is not an English form of surfacing but it is often used on the Continent and in the United States. Climatic factors are the prime reason. Long, moist winters in the British Isles make wood slippery and unattractive while more extreme climates with longer, hotter and drier summers are appropriate for decking even though decks may be snow-covered in winter. Such a climate makes for extended periods of outside summer living when the wooden deck can be put to many uses.

Cost is another factor which controls the use of decking in the garden. In areas where wood is relatively cheap, decking becomes an attractive method of surfacing. Where wood is plentiful decking will provide a sympathetic link between garden and surrounding countryside.

There are three types of decking. The simplest type is low level and provides an alternative to terracing. It is usually supported by concrete piers or short timber or metal posts. In towns, such decks are often useful as a transition between a turn-of-the-century house and its garden. These often have basements and a well-sited deck can be a useful bridge between the garden level and the ground floor.

Hillside decks provide a method of creating level space where none exists. Correctly sited, they can provide a platform for spectacular views. This type of deck is costly to construct and might require the expertise of an architect, especially if the deck adjoins the house. An architect will also be aware of any local building regulations with which you must comply.

The third type of wood decking is used to provide a surface for a roof garden where the original roofing material was unsuitable for pedestrians and garden elements. Where any major construction is envisaged to convert a roof space for use as a garden, you should take the advice of an architect or a structural engineer so that the load the roof can bear is established. Plant containers alone can be extremely heavy.

A successful deck depends on the quality of the wood you use and its maintenance. It is obviously necessary to choose a wood with high resistance to decay, splintering and warping. Redwood is the ideal decking wood, and is only available in the United States. It does not require treatment with preservative. Red cedar is similarly durable and available on a wider scale. Pines, larches and spruces also provide wood that is usable for decking but all require preservative treatment. It is important that the wood you use can be sawn without splintering and will accept nails readily. The number of fixings required in deck construction necessitates the use of galvanized nails rather than screws.

Construction

Low level decking is relatively easy to construct once you have made your choice of wood. The deck depends on firm, poured concrete footings (foundations) below ground level. Dig out holes for these beneath the final positions of the piers of the proposed deck, and use temporary wooden formers to establish a substantial slab of concrete. You can buy proprietary pre-cast concrete piers which sit on the footings and provide the bases for the wooden posts which will take the wooden frame of the deck. The wooden posts must be cut to allow for any changes in ground level so the 100 × 100 mm (4 in) beams that form the basis of the deck structure are indeed level. These beams support 100 × 50 mm 4 × 2 in) joists which support the decking planks. The structure is nailed together, the wooden posts being nailed to nailing blocks let into the wet concrete of the footings. Where decking is used at low level, make sure that weed growth is suppressed beneath the deck. One method is to spread black plastic sheeting between the deck supporting posts. The visible sections of sheeting can then be covered with pebbles or gravel.

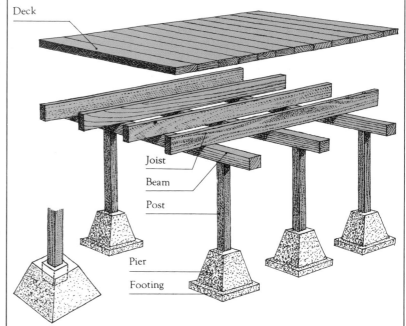

Deck

Joist

Beam

Post

Pier

Footing

Stepped terrace *This timber deck is well-detailed and extensive, with full-width steps between two levels. The timber used for the decking matches that of the house façade and is simply laid.*

Decking patterns

The simpler the pattern of wood you devise for your deck, the simpler the supporting structure need be. Less wood and construction time are other advantages. If you want a fancy pattern, however, relate it to the patterns of neighboring wooden structures, such as fencing.

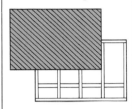

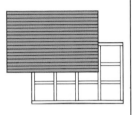

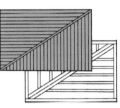

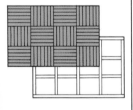

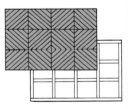

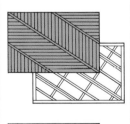

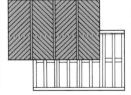

Linked decking, *above. In this example, bold decking steps have been used in conjunction with retaining walls constructed of railway ties. These elements have a solid feel and* *this characteristic is emphasized by intermediate concrete block steps. The staining of the wood used in the construction, and its proportion, marry with the wooden house fascia.*

Deck design

The design for a wooden deck, shown in the diagram, right, provides useful terrace space which might adjoin any house. In place of a handrail or balustrading, the edges of the deck have been built up to surround the area and to provide casual bench seating. A further raised section, doubling as a table, lifts to provide useful storage space, possibly for cushions or garden equipment.

Seating

Facing boards

Storage space

Deck level

Step

Foundation and supports

Features

Having established the basic layout and working areas of your garden, you can now start indulging in flights of fancy and think about realizing any eye-catching features that you want to incorporate, such as raised beds, rockeries or water areas in their various forms, including streams and channels.

Nowadays, few gardens are large enough to include many features and, in a small area, you should make your special interest set the character for the whole garden. Avoid at all costs a series of unrelated eye-catchers, divided by grass or planting, making the garden a collection of oddments. The most common cause of such a state is misjudgment of scale. The rockery, for instance (that peculiarly English garden feature), can all too easily become a pimple in your layout. To have any measure of success, a rockery must look natural, as though it were an escarpment of natural rock exposed through the action of wind and rain. It is this outcrop which is planted about with alpine plants. Water is often incorporated with rock outcrops in the garden, either as a pool or as a stream. Both can look charming but can also easily become pretentious unless you keep the concept bold and simple.

Rockeries and raised beds

Making a rock grouping look natural is not only the result of placing the rock in strata but also in the selection of a rock indigenous to your area, if indeed there is one. You must also make sure that the build-up of land to the outcrop looks natural. On flat land the build-up should be gradual and so considerable space is required, as shown in the diagram opposite.

If you do not have room for natural groupings of rock, there is no reason why you should not grow alpines in contrived changes of level which create various raised beds. Such beds are effective and far more at home than a rockery in an urban setting. Given that many alpines are small plants, it makes sense to grow them in raised beds where their often exquisite forms can be better appreciated. The raised bed can also provide the well-drained, open situation that alpines thrive in. In the wild, many alpines root in scree or shale, which can be substituted by gravel or pebbles in the garden. You might consider incorporating raised beds in a terrace to provide shelter from drafts and screening.

Natural rock groupings *In these two groupings, stone is well-integrated into the garden surround. Notice how, in both cases, the stone sits in a bank, looking as though weather has exposed it. The stratification, or graining, of the rock runs in the same direction as it would if occurring naturally. The rocks used do not look like currants stuck in a cake.*

Rockery construction

You do not need a mountain of earth to make a realistic rock outcrop. You can utilize any gentle gradient in the garden; otherwise you will have to change levels (see p. 119), either creating a simple mound or by constructing a retaining wall. You will see from the diagram below, however, that the mound should not be too high, nor too cramped. Try to use slabs of rock to let into the bank so that you can create the impression of naturally occurring strata. Much of the rock will be covered by backfilling with earth and a substitute for scree, such as gravel (see the scree bed, below). The backfill should be

well-drained – a prerequisite for all alpine plants – but it does not need to be rich. Soil accompanying granite or ironstone tends to be acid, while soil accompanying limestone is alkaline so you should recreate this and choose your plants accordingly (see pp. 16–17).

If you do not have enough room for both sides of the mound, the lower diagram shows how you might fake the mounded effect with a low retaining wall. This construction is particularly useful for siting a rockery at the edge of your site. In this case, however, do not allow the retaining wall to be seen or you will spoil the effect.

Rockery set into a mound

Rockery set into a bank held by a retaining wall

The realistic rock garden *This example shows how much space can be required to harmonize the scale of outcrops with the environment.*

Scree bed construction

In a natural situation, a bed of scree is composed of chippings of the parent rock. It is not only uncomfortable to walk on, but also dangerous, since it is liable to slip. It is naturally well-drained and so dries out quickly. Plants growing in scree tend to be in semi-shade in the lee of larger rocks and this is a situation which you might seek to recreate in your garden, building up the bed as shown right.

You can site a scree bed in a similar position to a rockery, you can

combine the two or you can raise the scree bed within retaining walls of brick (as below), stone or railway ties to show off small alpine plants to best effect. Below is a series of brick retaining walls which might be backfilled with scree beds to support a selection of alpine plants which will crawl through the gravel finish and cascade over the low walls. Brick steps have been incorporated to negotiate the bank which sweeps into the structure on the right.

Section through a scree bed in the garden

Rock bedded in gravel

Ground level

Gravel

Rough peat

Hardcore

Scree beds in retaining walls *This corner idea combines steps and retaining walls to provide raised beds for alpines. Anyone using the stepped route across the beds will be encouraged to stop and study the plant groups.*

Water

Water has an attraction which will draw the eye more than any other feature in the garden. It has almost the strength of a building in a garden layout, while having the unique attribute of reflecting light. It is a feature which, if well-integrated into a garden, can be an enormous addition, but if used badly, will spoil any progress you have made, becoming an irritation and rivalling other features of far gentler attraction. To avoid such problems, water should be used with discretion and as part of the structure of your garden design. In small gardens, it is probably best to use water in a formal way, in conjunction with the building or as a sculptural feature, such as a water container of some sort, or a fountain. The informal use of water (that is water in free-form shapes that imitate naturally occurring ponds) calls for greater space than the small garden allows, unless the whole garden is given over to congruous informal styling.

It is necessary to be absolutely clear about which category of water you want to include in your garden, then to decide whether it is to be flowing or still, and lastly, to ensure that it will be safe for children using the garden. There is little sense in planning a magnificent decorative pool, only to have to cage it for safety. Many suburban gardeners have to wire over their pools to prevent birds from stealing their fish and to prevent falling leaves from contaminating the water.

Decide on the depth of the pool according to its purpose. Shallow pools of about 300 mm (1 ft) depth appear deeper if sides are painted black, using a waterproof paint. A greater depth is necessary if you want pond life. Fish must be able to get under ice if the pond freezes in winter.

Whatever the type of water you want to include in your layout, whether formal or informal, it must always be clear and sparkling. To achieve this, water must either be running, using a pumped recycling system, or you need to establish a balance of pond life which includes oxygenating plants (at least ten per square metre (10.76 ft²) of water surface), snails and fish. A balance creates a food chain which excludes the green algae that stain surfaces and cloud water. Small water containers should be drained and refilled regularly.

Finely-detailed pool *Sympathetic planting and detailing masks the rigid outline of this beautiful pool. There is a fine balance between water, planting and hard surfacing.*

Types of pool

First consider the shape of pool you want, for this will determine how well-integrated it will look in your garden. Below are designs based on circles. While a plain circle is formal, pool shapes devised from interconnecting circles (as in the bottom two examples) can be treated formally or informally.

Formal circle

Interconnecting circles

Shape devised from intersecting circles with graded beaches

Formal use of water

"Formal" use of water in the garden refers to strictly geometric-shaped containers, pools or channels. Crisp detailing of edging and of any steps which might run through such elements is vital. Edgings should usually overhang the water by at least 50 mm (2 in) so any variance in the height of the water due to evaporation is hidden in the shadow of the overhang. Without the overhang you will also see the green line which stains the rim of any pool. Stepping stones through the water should be detailed in the same way so that they appear to float on the surface.

Formal pools are often constructed in waterproofed and reinforced concrete or are of concrete block or brick, rendered with a waterproof facing. The former method is stronger. Fiberglass pre-molded pools are also available up to a considerable size in formal shapes but they do not have outlet or overflow facilities. A formal pool can be still and reflective, its surface broken only by the occasional iris or rush clump or it may be agitated by a fountain. Avoid too great a fountain display for the area of water. The height of a fountain jet should not be more than the distance from the source of the jet to the edge of the pool.

Formally contained water can be most attractive when it is raised rather than sunken. There is a great charm associated with sitting on the edge of a raised pool and it is safer if children use the garden regularly.

Formal pool, informal planting, *above. The outline of this pool is "L"-shaped, although the wooden tie surround has been extended laterally to form an adjacent step. Informal planting softens the rigid shapes.*

Hexagonal raised pool *The strictly formal lines of this hexagonal pool in brickwork are broken by a solitary clump of irises.*

Construction

Small pools should be constructed in waterproof concrete (see Appendix for a suitable mix), allowing you to incorporate in the construction both an outlet to a dry well, for occasional cleaning, and, more important, an overflow to prevent flooding in heavy rain. Where frost is likely, the concrete should be reinforced and the pool made with

sloping sides to allow the ice to expand upwards as it freezes. Failing this precaution, a softwood plank can be floated in the pool, which will allow the ice to expand into it.

You may also build into the pool a shelf recess for marsh-type plants. Allow all edgings to overhang vertical faces by 50 mm (2 in) to conceal any variance in

water height due to evaporation. This will also hide the inevitable green scum line of algae at the edge of the surface of the water.

To plant in the water you will need special containers which are designed to hold a rooting medium and the root systems of water plants (see p. 214).

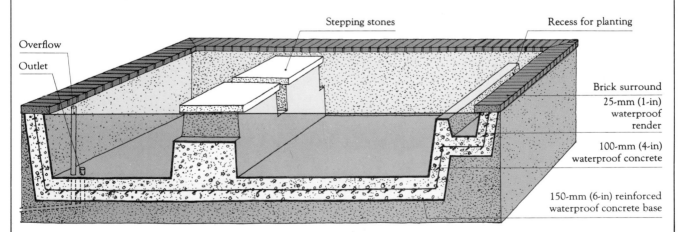

Overflow

Outlet

Stepping stones

Recess for planting

Brick surround

25-mm (1-in) waterproof render

100-mm (4-in) waterproof concrete

150-mm (6-in) reinforced waterproof concrete base

Informal use of water

Water used informally needs space to be successful, for you are trying to simulate a natural pool with eddies and bays of planting running into the water and contrasting with beaches of pebbles. To sustain this effect convincingly, the whole of a small garden needs to be planted and designed informally. Alternatively, a more contrived, Japanese, informal boulder pool is possible, backed with bamboos. Anything between these extremes is too demanding of a pool in a small area.

A plain, planted circle of water in an informal setting can be attractive, where you are creating a contrast of form. On a small scale, however, the dribbling stream and informal pool emanating from a rockery always looks contrived. Informal pools can be constructed in concrete, though the edging seldom looks convincing, and small, concrete-lined streams tend to crack.

The most successful pools today are constructed by excavating a hole, adding a layer of sand, and then lining it with a strong gauge plastic or butyl rubber sheet, preferably black. The edges should be held down and screened with a cobble or gravel beach. Planting, however, is difficult if it is to be convincing and hide the very edge of the sheet. The bottom of the pool can be lined with rounded pebbles and planted, the plants being held in purpose-made underwater containers. Care must be taken not to perforate the sheet lining since a small leak is practically impossible to locate.

Japanese effect *The boundaries of this informal pool, in the Japanese manner, are carefully screened by boulders and planting. The effect is enhanced by the sharp contrast of the simple wooden bridges that cross it.*

Construction

The area of an informal pool must be larger than that of a formal one if the effect is not to be pretentious. Plastic or butyl rubber sheeting makes an ideal lining for these larger amorphous shapes. The drawback to such a lining, however, is the need to hide the edge of the plastic carefully, together with any folds. Two ways of edging such a pool, when the sheeting has been laid on a 75-mm (3-in) sand layer, are illustrated

On the left is the informal beach effect, in which the gradient is shallow enough to hold the boulders laid over the sheet, and to prevent them from slipping to the bottom of the pool. An alternative is to lay the sheet over pre-formed steps, cut into the earth, to hold the beach. On the right, a straight edging is achieved by wrapping the sheet over a block retaining wall and laying a brick or stone coping over it.

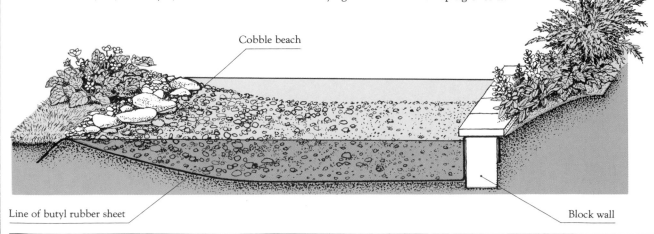

Cobble beach

Line of butyl rubber sheet

Block wall

Waterfalls

The gentle ripple of falling water has a more subtle attraction than the play of a fountain, but falling water needs bright sunlight to enliven it. Some of the most successful small waterfalls are those between level changes of small, formal pools, for as a design element they provide a strong vertical connection between sheets of water. Technically, one should not seek too large an over-flow or the amount of water to be pumped back will demand a huge pump. The amount of water that a gentle overflow uses can easily be returned by a submersible pump. When constructing an overflow, the design of the lip over which the water passes is crucial if the water is not to cling to it and then dribble down the face beneath. A flat stone that projects 50 mm (2 in) at the overflow might reject the flow of water; failing this, use a tile or piece of slate with a groove cut near its edge, along the underside to break the water flow.

For pumping larger heads of water, the pump should be located "onshore" just outside the pool area, at the lowest level and be placed in a waterproof brick box with a slab over it. Whether you require a submersible pump or an onshore version, pumps require an electrical supply (see p. 105).

A waterfall effect, *right. Each of the lipped saucers in this arrangement over-flows into the saucer below and finally into a simple, concrete, circular pool.*

Stepside waterfall, *above. The idea of water running at the side of steps or a path originates in the Middle East, where running water is used to cool the air. Here it is used as a decorative device.*

Simulated mountain stream *Rocks and water are used here to simulate a mountain stream. The water needs only to trickle gently to create the desired effect. A simple submersible pump maintains the supply.*

Fountains

Wind can play havoc with fountains, quickly emptying the pool if the jet of water is too high. The height of the fountain should therefore be no more than that of the distance from its source to the pool surround. In a domestic setting, keep the jet simple. It should either be placed centrally or allowed to play diagonally.

Vertical

Diagonal

Swimming-pools

Nothing is so demanding in a garden as a swimming-pool. Size can be played down by reducing the intensity of color of its lining and by altering the edging to it, but such an area of water will always dominate its surroundings. For this reason, its shape should fit carefully into the overall garden plan to minimize its bulk. It is a fallacy to suppose that the more bizarre the swimming-pool's shape, the more it integrates itself into a site. In fact, the simpler the pool's shape and that of the terrace which surrounds it (for pool and surround should be considered as one), the easier it is to fit a garden plan. Remember that you can use the shape of the swimming-pool terrace to adjust the shape of the pool slightly, so that the combination of pool and terrace better fits the site. However, it is best to tailor the shape of your pool to your garden plan from the outset, keeping it as simple as possible. Simple shapes are also more practical, since they are easier to heat, cover and swim in. Remember that, unlike a hotel swimming pool, the pool at home in a small garden has to be lived with throughout the year. Nothing is more depressing than a summer blue pool under leaden winter skies and to cover it with stretched canvas is unsightly, so consider a darker color.

The site for a swimming-pool must be open, sunny and away from deciduous trees to prevent fallen leaves from littering the water and poolside. It should not be constructed where the water table is too near the surface, or the whole structure will be subject to movement. There should be easy access to the site for digging machinery and a use to which the excavated soil can be put (see p. 119) as cartage is expensive. With the completed pool you will need storage space for maintenance gear, a site for the filtration plant and ideally a place for changing.

The actual structural work of building a pool should be undertaken by specialists who will advise you, but it is as well to know the questions to ask.

Pool types vary. When constructed of concrete they are either built and reinforced *in situ* or wet concrete is sprayed on to concrete block walls. Alternatively, they may be of cast fiberglass, or polythene or butyl rubber sheet within a metal casing or frame. The framed varieties are usually not built into the ground and, though cheaper, are not particularly attractive. However, with a decking surround, they can be successfully integrated into their site. They have some advantages. They can be moved at the end of the season and, being shallow and above ground, warm up quickly. Those contemplating a heated pool might consider using solar energy, but the panels have to be correctly sited to catch the sun.

The epitome of summer *A well-sited pool in the garden epitomizes the essence of summer – hot days and lazy lounging. The fixtures at this pool side (see p. 233), as well as the pool itself, combine to make the ideal setting.*

Pool shapes

The shape of a swimming-pool should be dictated by site, use (for play or for serious swimming too) and, of course, cost. A one-off shape will be more expensive than a standard-shaped model and may well need more heating, for warm, underwater convection currents tend not to permeate tight angles. Below are some simple pool shapes.

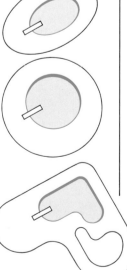

Pool edging

A swimming-pool's edging provides the trim to the pool as braiding completes a cushion. Above all it should not be slippery. Lighting and a scum trap can be well-integrated into proprietary moldings, which are pre-formed. Example (1) has a recessed scum trap below the level of the edging. Example (2) allows the raised pool surface to overflow into a surrounding scum trap. The two lower examples, (3) and (4), play down the fact that the pool is for swimming because they could surround an ornamental pool being in concrete slab, quarry tile or brick. Such edgings do not complement bright blue pool linings, but rather gray or black linings.

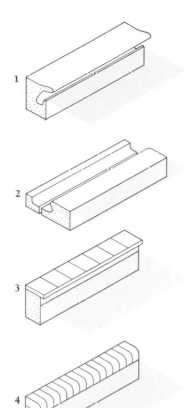

Successful integration *The decking for sunbathing and the tailoring of this poolside to a garden setting, make this example so attractive. Simple planting provides a useful partial screen between terrace and pool.*

Successful pools

The successful swimming-pool fits the garden design rather than dominating it. It should be a useful feature that serves its purpose – both for swimming and poolside relaxation. Ideally, it should also be a feature of beauty which has some of the attributes of a formal ornamental pool.

A feature of beauty, *below. Few have such a dramatic location for their swimming-pool. But this free-shaped pool above an Italian lake exemplifies how successful the swimming pool can be as a water feature.*

Divided functions, *above. This pool has been wisely divided to provide a shallow pool area for young children's play away from the deeper swimming area. Children are at constant risk by a swimming-pool and, unless they can swim well, should always wear a life jacket for safety.*

Plants near a pool

The obvious hazard when planting too near a pool is that leaves from deciduous species will drop into it; evergreens, too, will shed some leaves. Plants that are spiky or poisonous should also be avoided, especially if children use the swimming-pool.

Plants too close to a pool can suffer from the effects of chlorine, though this depends on how the chlorine is administered. Seek the advice of a pool purification expert as to the suitability of the system that is installed.

Despite the problems, planting is often necessary to shelter a pool from drafts and to relieve and soften large areas of paving with which pools are usually surrounded. Where grass is used as an alternative surface, care must of course be taken to ensure that cuttings do not get into the pool. You might consider using plants in portable containers as temporary decoration when the pool is not in use.

Recreational areas

The term "recreational area" is here used to mean those parts of a garden that are reserved for special activities – play areas, for example, or the barbecue corner.

Children can be very destructive within a garden if it is not designed to accommodate their play. Since the garden is often the only safe area for their games, it is sensible to orientate it to them, for balls and bicycles will otherwise inevitably end up among growing things. However, a child's play facilities will have to be changed as it grows older. Toddlers need a small grassed area, within sight of the house but well away from water or steps, and they appreciate bold splashes of color at this stage. When they are a few years older, they enjoy simple changes of level, for example grass steps or a gentle bank to roll down.

A sandpit is always popular. Where possible, make it large enough for the children to get in it, so that it can become a house or a desert island for them – fantasy is a major part of their play. Allow for a flat space within the sandpit on which they can make sand pies or castles, for otherwise this will be done on the surround of the sandpit, with an unsightly result.

Very shallow water for splashing in is usually greatly enjoyed, but keep it well away from the sand or the result will be mud everywhere. Shallow water raised to a toddler's eye height is safer and can be used for sailing boats. Both sandpit and pool can ultimately be adapted to become decorative garden pools.

As children get older, they will want more space for their activities – a route for bicycles, somewhere to kick a ball, to play with a tennis racquet and so on. Some hard surfacing will allow for table tennis outside. Often, space is needed for tinkering with machines and a corner for pets. Most of these areas will, however, inevitably be at the expense of more pleasant landscape amenities.

The major purpose of the recreational area of a garden, as far as children are concerned, is to have fun. Children must be allowed to run about, kick a ball, cycle and climb without being inhibited. If you incorporate a climbing toy, site it on grass or within an area surfaced in a soft medium, such as pulverized bark. This will make falls a little less dangerous for children.

Fun in the garden *If the garden is a place to be used for recreation, especially by children, careful planning will make playtime more enjoyable, safer and less of a strain on the fabric of the garden. Use durable materials and planting where they are necessary.*

Sandpits

It is essential that a sandpit is large enough to play in, is well-drained and is filled with the correct sand. A depth of roughly 300 mm (1 ft) of sand (not builders') is needed. The sand should be contained within a concrete, brick or wooden structure and be laid on paving slabs, which are themselves laid over a layer of fine hardcore or ash. To allow for drainage, the slabs should not be jointed.

In towns, the perennial hazard of a sandpit is of cats using them. Construct a simple lid, with a wooden surround and infilled with netting of some sort. This can be put on when the sandpit is not being used.

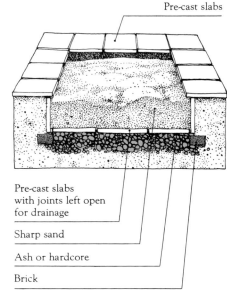

Pre-cast slabs

Pre-cast slabs with joints left open for drainage

Sharp sand

Ash or hardcore

Brick

Climbing frames

Most proprietary climbing frames quickly become defunct as children develop. Try to build your own adaptable climbing frame from an old tree trunk that will provide a point of minor sculptural interest, and can eventually be sawn for logs. remove rough bark and splinters by wirebrushing.

Barbecues

An adults' recreation area needs as much careful consideration as children's play elements in the garden. The barbecue area can become the centerpiece of a terrace garden in summer, but to be really useful it has to be designed and built to work as smoothly as the stove in your kitchen. There must also be adequate and convenient storage space for cooking implements and charcoal. Various forms of mobile barbecue are on the market but it is fairly easy to construct your own in brick. You can also build-in lighting and a worktop, which the movable barbecue always lacks.

Such a structure can be designed into a terrace layout and will still be attractive when not being used. Care must be taken, however, to ensure that prevailing winds will not blow smoke from the barbecue towards the house, your neighbors, or where people are likely to sit. When the barbecue is not sited directly within a line of vision, it may be used as a place for burning garden waste in winter, if locally allowed. Allow for plenty of space surrounding the structure, both for the cook and for guests. On a chilly summer evening, hot charcoal is compelling and will attract a crowd when the barbecue is over. Flat raised surfaces to the sides of the barbecue structure are necessary for serving, depositing plates, for relishes, glasses and bottles. After a summer party, it is very annoying to have to retrieve empty glasses and cups from planted areas.

Construction

If you are likely to have a number of people to serve from the barbecue, the cooking grill should be about 1 m by 500 mm (3 ft × 2 ft) in size. A smaller size will guarantee that some of your guests will have to sit waiting for their food while others eat. The cooking grill can be held neatly in the coursing of a well-built brick structure, such as that shown below. The charcoal tray slots below the grill and is similarly removable. Allow at least a square meter (10 ft²) to the right and left of the cooking area for preparation and serving food.

Make sure that the overall height of the barbecue unit is convenient for your height, comparing it with the height of your kitchen worktops. You can build in cupboards, as shown, beneath the worktops, ensuring that the doors are waterproof.

Electricity supply from the house to a sealable socket will allow you to install a portable spotlight or standard lamp (see p. 105).

The barbecue structure will sit directly on a well-constructed terrace or on its own concrete foundation (see p. 126). A poured concrete infill beneath the grill is a useful protection.

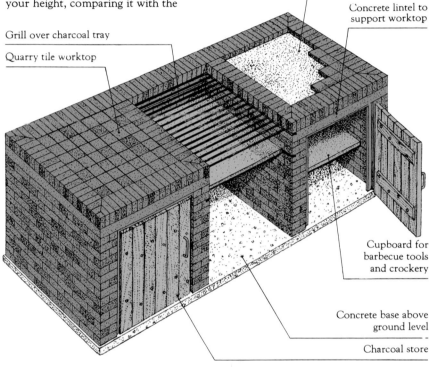

Sand and cement screed over concrete lintel

Concrete lintel to support worktop

Grill over charcoal tray

Quarry tile worktop

Cupboard for barbecue tools and crockery

Concrete base above ground level

Charcoal store

An outdoor kitchen
A well-designed area for preparing and serving food can be the perfect complement to an area for outdoor entertaining. This integrated food preparation area, with its wealth of storage space and worktops, is possible in a hot, dry, predictable climate.

Structures

No matter how well you planned your garden, it is often necessary, after a number of years, to add structures within it, as a new hobby is taken up, you buy an additional car and garden tools proliferate. The available range of pre-constructed buildings is considerable, as is the selection of materials of which they are made. You must make a firm policy, however, to choose the same materials or from one manufacturer's range, to prevent the new buildings appearing haphazard. Manufactured structures are usually modern and crisp in line, so if your house is of another period you will have to screen your new buildings from view.

Price will affect the buildings you buy but, as a general rule, the larger the building the easier it is to integrate into a garden, for it is the difference in scale between house and new structure that is difficult to reconcile. With the smaller pre-constructed buildings there is also the problem that their height is often out of scale to their ground plan.

Unity can be achieved by grouping your structures – a shed, a greenhouse, frame, compost area and possibly gas tank – so they can be served by one path. Another method is to employ a windowless wall to support lean-to structures. The rule is to build-in your new structures rather than merely add them.

Conservatories and garden rooms

Conservatories and garden rooms are often listed together but their function is quite different. A garden room is an extension to a house, while a conservatory, although attached to a house, is part of the garden. The emphasis in a conservatory is on growing decorative plants under glass. Its furnishing and flooring will therefore have to sustain frequent watering and general plant husbandry. The garden room, on the other hand, is furnished as part of the house and is merely decorated with plants.

A garden room can be used as a summer sitting-room, but since large areas of glass are essential it will become too cold in winter and too hot in summer without double glazing. Windows can be opened, of course, but drafts become a problem. Unless well controlled, therefore, the uses to which a garden room can be put are limited by temperature. Nevertheless, it makes an excellent work space or a games room for children.

There is an increasing range of conservatories on the market, from traditional Gothic to modern styles. Most conservatories are constructed of softwood and then painted white, but this treatment demands regular maintenance and re-painting. Plants may be sited in beds or in pots on the ground or raised on shelving. Considerable care and maintenance of plants is required, however, unless you invest in an automatic watering device, since in warm weather plants may need watering twice a day.

But a conservatory amply repays all the work entailed, for it will provide you with a growing garden through the long dark days of winter, with hyacinths and narcissus, cascading mimosa or a Banksian rose, as early as January. In summer, a conservatory makes an ideal area for evening entertaining.

For the best effect, keep your planting and furnishing to a particular style and on no account let your conservatory degenerate into a collection of potted oddments. Make it tropical with large-leaved plants, or light and pretty within a particular color range, but at all costs be positive in your approach.

Purpose-built unit A *loggia-type conservatory, this was purpose made to connect two buildings, to accommodate a limited number of plants and provide an entrance to the garden. The construction is made into an attractive feature in a garden area that would otherwise be both drafty and perhaps uninteresting.*

The plantsman's conservatory *This conservatory has been designed more for growing plants than for family use, but space has been found for some incidental seating within a bower of planting in the 19th-century manner.*

Occasional dining-room, *below. In this example, the conservatory has been made into a handsome dining-room for summer use. The floor is tiled, both to facilitate maintenance of the plants and to provide a practical medium on which to stand furniture. The blinds, which are adjustable, keep the conservatory cool throughout the summer.*

Making use of the conservatory

A corner of your conservatory can be used as a small greenhouse, but you must first build staging at a convenient height (see p. 151). On this you can divide, pot up and pot on your plants, along with propagating from your existing stock or striking cuttings collected along the way. Propagating the sort of exotic plant that makes a conservatory particularly special can become a passion. Illustrated below are two types of propagator for the enthusiast. Both have electrically heated wires running through gravel. The top unit is enclosed for greater humidity.

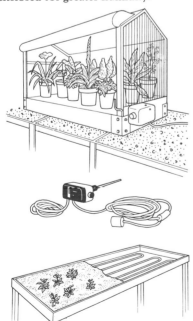

149

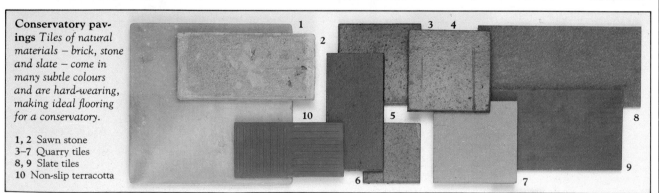

Conservatory pavings *Tiles of natural materials – brick, stone and slate – come in many subtle colours and are hard-wearing, making ideal flooring for a conservatory.*

1, 2 Sawn stone
3–7 Quarry tiles
8, 9 Slate tiles
10 Non-slip terracotta

Period home extension, *left. This conservatory, a home extension for year-round use, provides ample space for both plants and a dining area. The mood is predominantly of the Edwardian period, characterized by the tiled flooring and the basket-work seating.*

Modern garden room, *right. The feeling of this glazed extension, which forms a garden room, is modern. There is plenty of space for family use, punctuated by bold masses of foliage and color. Potted plants can be moved about to adjust the room for different numbers and uses.*

Alternative types of staging

Standard, commercially-produced staging systems are often more decorative than purpose-built structures but will not necessarily fit into awkward spaces. Moreover, some types of bought staging are little more than shelves, which soon become dirty from drainage. The top example illustrated below is of simple metal shelving. Below this is a metal framework containing deep trays for gravel, a useful way of keeping pots moist during absences from home. The third system is another example of stepped metal shelving. The two bottom systems have a metal frame with a wooden duck-board infill. However, these horizontals are subject to rotting.

Staging construction

Your staging must be of stout construction to support the considerable weight of gravel and of pots when filled and watered. Use 50 mm (2 in) angle-iron for legs, which should be set in concrete, and the tray, which must be welded to the legs and hold corrugated asbestos sheeting. Braces are needed under the sheeting and at the angle between the legs and the horizontal tray. At this point, paint the iron to prevent rust. Then cover the corrugated sheet with a layer of fine, washed gravel into which pots can be set. The gravel will both soak up surplus drainage moisture and at the same time help maintain moisture in the pots, which will soak up water by capillary action.

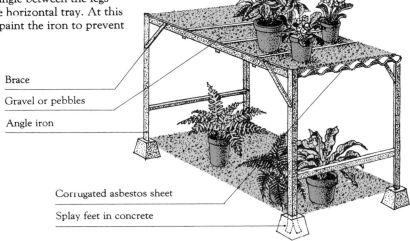

Brace
Gravel or pebbles
Angle iron
Corrugated asbestos sheet
Splay feet in concrete

151

Storage structures

Where to put garden tools, outdoor furniture in winter, bicycles, toys and the many other items that are used periodically in the garden is a common problem. Storage for these items seems to be totally overlooked by modern architects. As a family grows older the problem increases with discarded toys and leisure equipment accumulating. Apart from the obvious bulky items, such as a lawn mower, gardeners often collect a wealth of fertilizers and pesticides. Many of these are highly poisonous and should be kept in a waterproof place at a height beyond the reach of children. Then there are growing media: for seeds, mixes for cuttings and perhaps mixes for house plants. Add your gardening boots to the list and you end up with quite a storage problem.

Where possible, make a virtue out of necessity and use an out-building, where available, or consider building a new one that fits your garden plan, perhaps adjacent to an existing wall or fence. Failing this, you might consider a storage shed, but before constructing one it is advisable to consult your local bye-laws as some are quite strict about where you can build and to what dimensions. Choose a simple structure that fits your plan and you will be surprised how inconspicuous a utilitarian building can be. If you do want advice on screening, however, see page 118.

On the public side of the house there is often a need to place dustbins or to enclose gas or electricity meters. Simple units that conceal these items are played down when they, too, support your overall garden plan.

Traditional garden potting-shed *The diversity of well-used tools in this storage area and potting-shed indicates the sort of storage problem a keen gardener can have. Most people are unlikely to need such a large storage space but a smaller potting-shed can have similar character.*

Purpose-built storage structures
Specific storage problems can sometimes be solved with a purpose-built structure to suit the dimensions of the items that need storage. Such units are successful if they harmonize with the construction of your garden. Wooden structures, for example, might match the style of fencing.

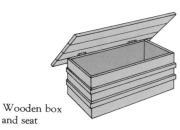

Wooden box
and seat

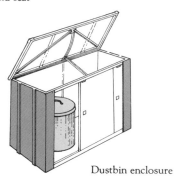

Dustbin enclosure

Corner shed

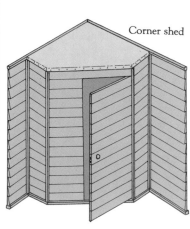

Garden sheds

The structures illustrated below give an impression of the range available. The size of unit you choose must be influenced by the size of your garden, but it is often easier to integrate a larger unit into your layout than a smaller one. If you already have another free-standing structure sited in the garden, such as a garage or a greenhouse, consider siting your shed next to it to avoid too many service paths and too much hard surfacing.

Wide-doored shed in metal and plastic

Simple wooden shed

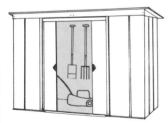

Metal section shed with sliding doors

Half-sized shed in metal

Shade house, *above. A shade house, such as this lattice-framed example, is used for storing house plants that like cool conditions and some shade.*

Simple storage structure, *below. This structure is built of concrete block. The roof is of hardboard with a felt covering, and the doors are wooden.*

Foundations

Solid foundations are essential for any structure. The recommended foundation for a substantial garden storage structure is a poured concrete float at least 150 mm (6 in) thick (see Appendix for a suitable mix), over a consolidated hardcore base. Alternatively, you can use any well-laid hard surfacing which matches other areas in your garden layout. Wooden sheds are usually bought with a wooden floor which sits on joists to allow ventilation under the structure.

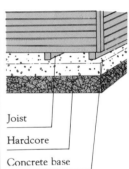

Joist

Hardcore

Concrete base

Storing tools

Garden tools should always be put away clean. Oil the tines and blades of steel tools and periodically oil any untreated wooden handles. It is very disheartening to work with ill-kept, rusty equipment. Many of the new garden tool "systems" have plastic-coated handles that accept a range of attachments. These might save space. Whether you have new-design or traditional tools, it is a good idea to hang as many of them on the walls of your storage area as you can. This will keep the tools in good condition and leave vital floor space free for bulky equipment. A racking system, such as that shown right, grips handles neatly and provides hooks, all on an adjustable base.

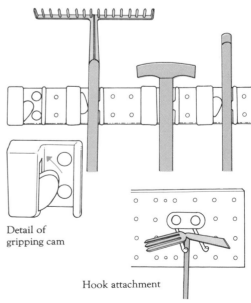

Detail of gripping cam

Hook attachment

Greenhouses and frames

Many specialist books have been written on the siting and structure of these useful additions to the garden but our primary concern here is with their appearance. Appearance, however, has to be tempered with practicality, for some of the greenhouse models on the market are too small and contrived in shape to be of much use. The "plantsman" will first decide on the greenhouse that is suitable for his growing needs, considering its appearance second. The determining factors will be the type of crop he wishes to grow and how much time he can spare on the maintenance of the greenhouse.

The siting, as well as the function of the greenhouse, will to an extent determine the type you need. The materials of which it is constructed can be painted or stained softwood, cedar or metal. The shape may be of the ridge type, the lean-to, the hexagonal or many sided, which themselves might be ridged, or it can be dome-shaped.

Greenhouses can now be fully automatic, in watering, ventilation and shading, but such sophistication becomes practicable only when there is a reasonably large area of glass. Most people settle for a greenhouse which they use for over-wintering, and then for seed sowing in spring and the propagation of cuttings for later summer use. Tomatoes and peppers can be grown throughout the summer, but without automatic equipment their watering can become a chore. The smaller the greenhouse the more difficult it is to control the temperature, and therefore the watering. A frame with underground heating would provide most people with all the glass they really need. The range of frame types is limited. It is reasonably easy to build your own of brick or, less permanently, of wood, with a simple lift-up framed glass top. If frames are not heated with underground wires, they can still be used to harden plants which have been raised from seed.

Both frames and greenhouses will need to be sited where sunshine is plentiful and therefore free from the overhang of trees. You must remember that in winter, snow is liable to build up on a greenhouse roof and must be cleared regularly. Overhanging trees will deposit collected snow with what might be disastrous results.

Frames and greenhouses should be serviced by hard, dry paths, wide enough for a wheelbarrow. Allow plenty of space around them for standing pots and boxes. Treated as small, efficient working units, frames and greenhouses can make handsome features on their own and need little screening.

Greenhouse as a feature *In this Dutch garden, the greenhouse has been treated as a prime feature of the layout and partially screened by decorative planting. The surround to the wooden-framed house has been hard-surfaced.*

Greenhouse types

The basic types of greenhouse for small gardens are shown below. They are constructed in metal or cedar (both needing little protection) or in softwood (requiring regular painting). Whether you choose free-standing or lean-to, glass-to-the-ground or half-bricked, is a matter of personal taste.

Wooden-walled

Wooden-walled span roof

Metal frame, glass-to-floor

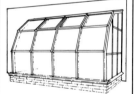

Lean-to on brick base

Metal-framed dome

Siting the greenhouse

Make sure that your greenhouse gets adequate sunlight away from the shade of trees and buildings. Ideally, the longest axis of a free-standing greenhouse should be positioned north/south, so that the sun crosses it during the course of the day, giving equal shares of direct sunlight to both sides. However, the final siting of your greenhouse must be dictated by your overall garden plan which should provide water and electricity (see pp. 104–105).

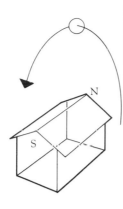

Colorful lean-to, *left. A lean-to timber greenhouse is often easier to site in a small garden than a free-standing model, as you can utilize any sunny wall. Here, use of colour increases the feel of summer.*

Window-sill greenhouse, *above. A south-facing, window-sill greenhouse is a neat solution to the problem of siting a full-size greenhouse in a small garden or where there is none at all.*

Cold frame construction

A simple cold frame, used to harden off plants in transition from a greenhouse to open ground or to germinate annual or vegetable seeds, can be easily constructed. A wooden, sloping-sided box should be made (about 1.2 m square/1.4 yd²) to fit the size of glazed panel available for the lid of the frame. This panel can either be purpose built, or you might use an old window frame. The lid to the frame illustrated simply rests against the low side of the construction. It can be lifted, slid and propped at the back of the frame. If your frame is to last you will need to treat the unprotected wood with preservative. Creosote fumes will kill seedlings so make sure that you use one of the "safe" wood preservatives on the market and give the frame plenty of time to dry. Alternatively, paint the frame, perhaps to match the white of a painted greenhouse. If the frame is used for growing plants in containers it can be positioned on hard surfacing where rot is less of a problem than if the frame stands on soil.

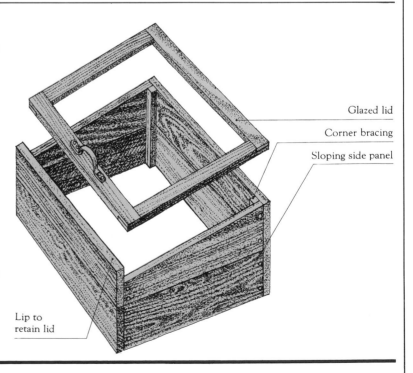

Glazed lid

Corner bracing

Sloping side panel

Lip to retain lid

Pergolas

In climates sunnier than that of northern Europe, the pergola is traditionally used to shade a path. In the British Isles it is more usefully employed as a roof transition from inside the house to the garden; alternatively, it can act solely as a support for ramblers or climbing plants. In urban areas, where gardens are overlooked, the pergola gives some measure of privacy to anyone sitting beneath it and, provided that you consider which way to run the horizontals of your structure, it need not inhibit sunlight. The pergola structure over a terrace area is one of the ways of creating an outside room, a place in which, rather than on which, to be. When a pergola abuts the house, it controls the view from inside, framing a portion of the garden while at the same time extending the proportion of the room from inside.

The detailing of the pergola must match the period of your home, for it will be seen both against your house and from within it. The proportions of the various parts of a pergola must balance. All too often the verticals that hold the pergola's horizontals are disproportionately large. The scale of the wooden horizontals (and wood is the material most suitable for this bridge on a domestic scale) must depend on the length it has to span between supports, and this too will depend on the sort of wood, hard- or softwood, that you propose using. The scale suitable for most terraces ought not to require a span of much more than 3–3.5 m ($11\frac{1}{2}$ ft), for if the wood is too large it is oppressive and if too narrow it warps. Traditional wooden horizontals in the British Isles are of massive oak spars, though in Mediterranean areas unsawn softwood was, and is, used. In the United States, red-wood is the first choice. Cypress and cedar are also durable but any good wood can be used if treated with a preservative, being kept stained or painted as necessary.

The verticals for a pergola of appropriate period might be columns of stone or of a reconstituted substitute. Alternatively, they can be of timber or metal. Unless the situation demands something different, the detailing of the material should be as simple as possible. The structure has a function to perform, that of supporting plants, so let them be the featured item rather than the clever detail of your structure. When a pergola adjoins masonry, it can either be let into the structure or, more easily, it can sit into an L-shaped metal shoe plugged to the wall.

If wood is too heavy a material for the horizontals of your particular situation, you might consider using strained wire, either over a roof garden or from wall to wall in a town garden. Trained vines or hops along these wires give shade in summer and let light through in winter.

Although the pergola is a simple and very effective way of linking inside and outside when constructed as an extension to a house wall, it can also be used to establish an enclosed space away from the house. Where two walls meet at right angles in the far corner of a larger garden, for example, a pergola can create a secluded seating area of great charm. In this case the style of the pergola is not so dependent on the style of the house, allowing you more freedom in the choice of materials.

Pergola for strong sunlight *This beautifully detailed pergola makes the area it encloses an extension of the house from which it leads. Such clean lines complement bright sunshine as the shadows from the pergola create linear patterns on walls and floor. The steps leading to the terrace area are of concrete poured in situ. The paving also has a consistent linear pattern.*

Traditional pergola
This covered walkway designed by the British architect, Lutyens, is built in traditional materials – oak and stone. Gertrude Jekyll, the English horticulturist, planted the "room" through which the path leads.

Sheltered rural corner, *right. Lightweight softwood has been used to give a rustic, restful feel to a cottage terrace pergola.*

Pergola construction

Stained softwood beams and scaffolding poles can be used to make a simple pergola, as shown right. The beams sit in proprietary metal joist shoes where they meet the supporting wall. At the opposite end of each beam, scaffolding poles have been let into the wood for half the thickness of the beam. These poles must be firmly bedded in concrete foundations beneath the surface they pierce. The run of beams is braced laterally with a metal tie. Plant support wires should be fixed along the underside of the beams and climbing plants (see p. 212) trained along them. Terrace paving units should be spaced so that pergola verticals coincide with a joint if possible.

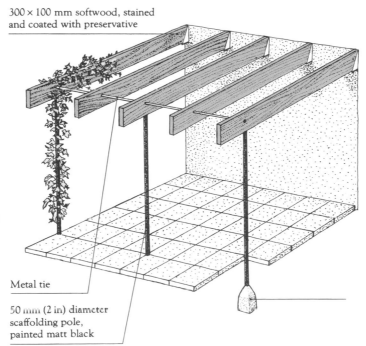

300 × 100 mm softwood, stained and coated with preservative

Metal tie

50 mm (2 in) diameter scaffolding pole, painted matt black

Metal shoe fixing *This metal joist shoe is let into the wall and fixed to the mortar.*

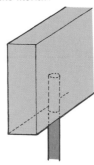

Vertical housing *Drill the horizontal to accept the upright.*

Structures for shade and decoration

The garden structures in this category include shelters, sunrooms, gazeboes and arbor supports. Such structures should provide shade from the sun and shelter from the wind while also giving a feeling of protection, for it is easier to relax comfortably outside with your chair or lounger against or near a structure than in an open position.

There are many different sizes and styles of prefabricated structures available. They are mostly of wood, either painted or treated with a preservative. If the shelter is close to your house or other structures, it should match or complement them. However, the charm of such structures is that they are usually secluded in larger gardens and can therefore create their own style.

I think it is important, when constructing a sunroom, that there is adequate ventilation to prevent overheating.

A simple, roofed shelter providing shade is a structure which lends itself to your own design. It does not need to have a waterproof roof but one that merely shades the sun's rays. Where there are existing walls or fences you might be able to use them partially to support a canopy. Corners formed by walls are particularly useful in this respect as very simple techniques can be employed to join wood or a metal frame to fill the corner.

Simple frameworks make ideal supports for climbing plants that will help to provide shade. Purpose-built plant supports in painted iron are a traditional feature that could suit the style of your garden, providing a crisp outline to an arbor. They can be combined with climbing plants or pleached trees to form an enclosed space.

Ideas for summerhouses
All the structures illustrated below could be sited as garden features to punctuate the rhythm of your plan. They can also be used for numerous practical purposes, such as providing a shaded seating area, a space for children to play or for storage of garden seating and equipment.

Brick-built sunroom, *right. This purpose-built garden structure has a sliding glass door, making it ideal for outside entertaining in summer. With the doors closed, the room is still useful in cool weather.*

Arbor support, *below. An open metal structure such as this can be used either unadorned as a decorative focal point or as a support for climbing plants, making a shaded garden room.*

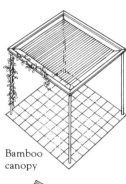

Bamboo canopy

Slat-roofed "A" frame

Tiled canopy

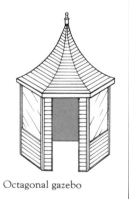

Octagonal gazebo

Carports and garages

As with all ancillary structures, try to incorporate a carport or garage within the overall design of your house, but if the building must be separate, the use of similar materials to those of the house will provide a visual link, as will repeating the roof pitch of the house. If you are constructing a flat roof make the line of the fascia of the garage extend some building line of the house. When there is a path between the house and the new structure, design gates or fencing to unite the buildings across the gap.

Here and in England, the garage is often the first thing you see as you turn into the drive. The detailing of a garage frontage, including the doors, is therefore important, as is the hard-surfaced area leading to it. The approach should be wide enough for easy access and egress from the car on both sides; it should also be provided with suitable drainage so that it can be used as a car washing area. Remember that driveways and the bases for carports and garages have to be specially constructed to take the weight of vehicular traffic. This involves thicker-than-normal layers of consolidated hardcore and surfacing. Take professional advice about the exact dimensions, depending on the surface material you choose and your soil type.

When constructing a new carport or a second garage adjacent to an existing one, consider turning it at 90 degrees to the other, to produce a courtyard feel, but ensure that you provide adequate turning space for cars.

Incorporating a garage

When building a garage try to incorporate it into the overall house design. Here this has been achieved by fitting it into a corner and using the same materials, roof angles and window and door sizes as those of the house.

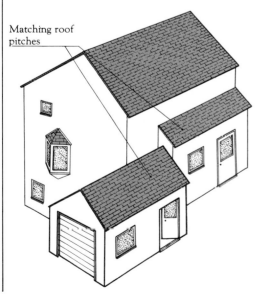

Matching roof pitches

Carport designs

A carport is a significantly large structure in the garden and deserves thoughtful planning. Consider the range of materials available to you and use the open-sided nature of the structure as an advantage to allow easy access to and from your car. The two examples, right, include space for useful storage at one end. One example is constructed in wood, the other in exterior grade concrete building block.

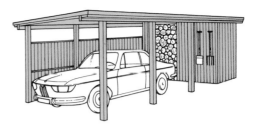

All-wood construction

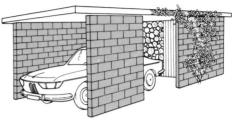

Concrete block construction

Successful carport, *above. A wood carport extended to provide a covered way to the house entrance, tying the two structures together.*

Hiding a garage, *below. If you have an unattractive garage, disguise it with planting. Here pyracantha has been clipped to garage shape.*

159

Roof gardens

To turn part of a domestic roof area into a garden is only possible if the roof was specifically designed to be load bearing. The overall weight of wet earth is enormous and considerable depth of earth is needed to grow anything other than shallow-rooted plants.

When starting a roof garden, it is essential that you determine what weight your roof will bear and to do this accurately you will need the advice of an architect or structural engineer. You may also need the permission of your ground landlord and, should you propose any structural alterations, planning permission too. Some authorities will not even permit any screening structure round the roof which is visible from the street below. Remember that structural additions must be tough to withstand winter buffeting by wind and rain. The combination of wind and intense sun makes watering a major undertaking through the year. Moreover, we tend to think of a roof garden only in summer, but the pots, plants and structures need tending the whole time.

Having done your preliminary homework, draw up the dimensions of your roof area and proceed to plan the space as if it were a living-room, orientating your seating to the sun and attractive views, much as you would to the fire or television set inside. When you have estimated the working areas, consider screening from neighbors as well as wind. In such cases you may need top screening in addition to that at the sides. When planning allows, an overhead pergola, from which panels can be hung, gives this facility.

Decide whether any planting you contemplate is to be contained within permanent structures or within movable pots. If the former, and the roof structure allows, build up your containers in as light a material as possible, allowing for drainage and adequate root space for the mature plants of your choice. 500 mm (20 in) depth of soil on drainage, is the minimum quantity for most planting. Trees need almost double this amount of earth.

After the planting positions, the next point to consider is surfacing. Weight again is important: thin tiles are ideal, in terracotta or even glazed flooring tiles; paving brick is good and slate should be considered. Marble, too, might be used, for it remains cool underfoot in summer. Wooden decking is the ideal flooring over an existing bitumen roof surface.

As with every garden setting, style your arrangement to produce a dramatic effect. Your plants will then become features within the outside room. Ensure that any pots are deep enough and constructed in fiberglass or plastic for lightness. All containers should be filled with a specially prepared lightweight mixture, over adequate drainage material. These lightweight soilless mixes contain little, if any, fertilizer, which must be compensated for by regular feedings.

Watering will be much easier if you install an irrigation system by threading a hose through your planting, regularly punctured with holes and fed from a gently trickling tap.

The plants which you select for your roof should be tough and able to withstand wind. For this reason, keep the planting low. Go for quantity which will screen and couch you in greenery, rather than delicate quality.

A garden on a roof is an expensive indulgence in materials, plants and their maintenance, but most of all in its installation for, unless the materials can be manhandled through your house, they must be winched or otherwise lifted up the outside of the house. Despite this, a private roof garden in town is a marvellous addition to any home.

Roof terrace planting containers
Architects designing roof terraces often build-in large planting containers, such as that below.

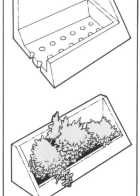

Screening

One of the hazards of roof gardening is the wind, which can whip the area throughout most of the year. Wind not only flattens plants but dries them out, particularly when combined with strong sun. A high, solid barrier protects only those plants directly in its lee, causing turbulence elsewhere. Better is a slatted wooden boundary, or even a mesh of some sort, to filter the full force of the wind.

The other reason for a screen boundary, of course, is to achieve privacy. If tall boundary screens are not possible, try to establish inner partitions of planting, and possibly a light pergola structure to provide screening.

Wooden screen, *left. This cedarwood screen not only looks decorative but would be an extremely effective wind filter on a roof.*

Vine support, *above. Light metal supports are here threaded with wires to support vines. When mature, vines provide an ideal protection from sun.*

Construction idea

When weight allows, build areas for planting using hollowed bricks, and try to establish a lush growth. In this way, you shelter the roof space and provide yourself with corners around which chairs can be moved as the prevailing wind or draft dictates. Allow for adequate drainage and use a growing mix with a high proportion of lightweight fill. Plants will root into this but will need plenty of feeding, preferably with liquid fertilizer. It is worth considering some form of automatic watering to save labor. In order to provide storage space for tools, pots and feeds, consider using built-in seats, as illustrated, with lift-up lids. They may not be the most comfortable of seats but they are ideal for parties.

Large scale roof garden *A roof garden can serve the rooms which surround it. This example has permanent, built-in seating and broad islands of quarry tiling. Bold masses of evergreen planting divide the view when seen from the different overlooking rooms.*

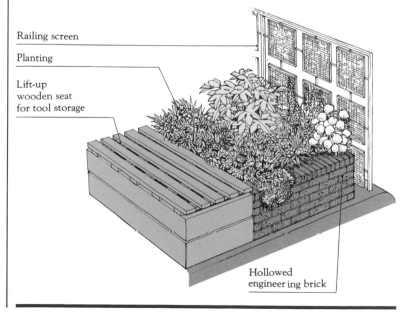

Railing screen

Planting

Lift-up wooden seat for tool storage

Hollowed engineering brick

Balconies

Many of the rules for roof gardening are applicable to the balcony, although the styling of the finish should be in character with the room it adjoins as opposed to the fantasy world one can create on a roof. The balcony, however, is usually more sheltered than the roof, often being covered by another balcony above, which will not allow rain water to reach your plants.

Decide exactly what it is you want from your balcony. There is inevitably a feeling of vulnerability when standing on it and this has to be overcome by screening if it is to become a place on which to sit and take the sun. Glass panels, if not structurally part of the building, can be fitted within an existing metal railing to provide this, without detracting from the building's façade. Few planning authorities will allow anything more. Screening, of course, should not impede the view; neither should planting, particularly when seen from inside the house.

Weight will always be a problem on balconies and before making any radical changes, or even introducing a single tub, check whether it will be safe. Where applicable, you should also check the strength of any structure above your balcony, since hanging containers can make a pleasant alternative treatment, as can a light, removable screen of zig-zag yachting rope.

One of the hazards of many balcony gardens, unless designed with containers built-in, is that water can drip on your neighbors beneath when pots are watered. If you are not using self-watering containers, therefore,

ensure that you have trays under pots to take surplus moisture once it has passed through the compost and drainage materials.

The type of plants you select should be tough, like those for a roof garden, but make sure they are in accord with the building. You might also consider using herbs in containers, for they will grow well in these situations and are, of course, useful too.

Many balconies are not suitable for greenery or, receiving no sun, are rarely used as a seating area. In such cases you might consider siting a piece of statuary or sculpture on the balcony (in fiberglass for lightness), set in an area of cobbles for textural variation if the structure will tolerate the additional weight.

It is important to think about what your terrace or balcony will look like from within the house, for it is from there that it will most often be seen. Consider lighting it to make a feature of the space and station plants within it accordingly. Then try to connect the two areas, inside and outside, with fabrics, such as awnings and internal curtains. You can further enhance this interconnecting feel by using the same flooring, since quarry tiles, slate and brick are all suitable for both inside and outside use.

Tented enclosure *An awning covers this balcony, turning it into an attractive tented enclosure for outside summer living. Surrounding greenery increases the privacy.*

Balcony ideas

Below are some different possibilities where space is at a premium and the balcony is overshadowed from above. Any fixtures are best built-in to save space.

For wind shelter or privacy, fix a stout wooden roller blind to the balcony above.

Build a small bench seat with a lifting lid for storage of cushions in summer months.

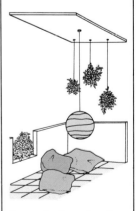

Leave the floor clear by hanging baskets for annuals from above, with a light fixture.

Outward-looking arrangement *A magnificent view dictates an outward-looking style for this balcony, as opposed to the inward-looking balcony on the opposite page. The boldly-shaped furniture and railing surround suggest the scale of a ground level garden.*

View from above, *below. The appearance of a balcony as seen from above is often important in towns. In this case a balcony has been entirely furnished with plants in containers to a design best seen from above. There is a glass infill to the metal balcony surround for draft protection.*

Self-watering pots

Self-watering pots have a reservoir of water which is drawn into the growing medium by a wick. They overcome the daily chore of watering required on windy and sunny roofs and balconies.

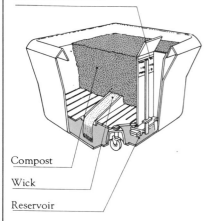

Water-level indicator

Compost

Wick

Reservoir

The balcony from inside

A balcony is more often looked at through windows and doors than walked on. Some balconies are not for walking on at all, being too noisy or shaded. If this is the case, plant the balcony or use it in a way which benefits the room which looks on to it. Make a composition of the balcony wall, the access and the balcony beyond.

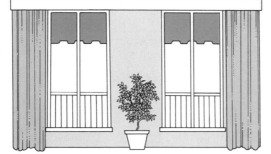

Crisp styling *The windows are connected internally by the curtain track and pelmet. The curtain material blends with the canopy over the balcony.*

Oriental feel *Here windows are connected visually by bamboo roller blinds. More bamboo is planted in pots on the terrace and a large jar placed inside.*

Using plants on balconies

The key to the selection of plants for the balcony container must be to select those species that can withstand a certain amount of draught and wind. There must, of course, be easy access to the plants for watering and dead heading. Remember that the arrangement that you establish in the first flush of enthusiasm in early summer has to be maintained throughout the season, including any holiday period, so do not overreach yourself. It is far better to have a fine display of something quite simple than an unsatisfactory showing of rare or bizarre plants. Conversely, you might consider a permanent planting of perennials and small shrubs, in which case you will need only incidental spots of colourful annual plants on the balcony.

Spectacular display, *above. This planting style is for the balcony enthusiast, providing total summer privacy. The selection is mainly of geraniums in differing tones of pink, but with some petunia and convolvulus distributed throughout. Plants are hung individually in pots on a wooden frame.*

Color and form, *left. A small Italian roof terrace is bright with yellow daisies and the bold form of agave. Color planting gives instant impact and character. The display is enhanced even by the inclusion of a caged canary, a feature which is hardly to be recommended, however.*

Stackable pots

Various units and containers are on the market that can be stacked against a support to produce an interesting textured surface in themselves and which, when planted, can create a waterfall of colour.

Each terracotta unit, right, needs only one retaining fixer to hold it, for the weight of the earth stabilizes individual units. On the far right are concrete units that can be used for planting against a wall, although some form of waterproofing is necessary if damp is not to penetrate the wall. Plants in units such as these require regular watering in the growing season.

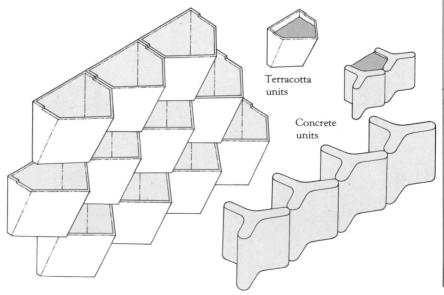

Terracotta units

Concrete units

Window-boxes

For many an urban dweller the window-box is his only contribution to landscape, but a row of houses ablaze with window-box color is an enormous pleasure in a town. Plants most often grown are geraniums and begonias, but you may wish for a greater variety of plant material in your box. Before considering what it might contain, however, you must select the container itself.

The type of window-box you need will depend very much on your window and how it opens, and whether, indeed, you will site your box outside. It is possible to have one for herbs, for instance, along the inside of the kitchen window. If your windows open outwards, your window-boxes will need to be suspended on strong metal brackets below the window so that any growth within them does not impede the opening. European windows tend to open inwards and old houses have sash windows that make the fixing, planting and subsequent attention of your box a far easier task. Sometimes "window"-boxes are sited around a low retaining wall, on a roof or balcony. Wherever the box and whatever its material, it must be securely fixed.

Window-boxes at one time were always constructed of wood; later they were of metal and today the most favored material is plastic. Many are often too shallow for a plant to be healthy throughout the whole season. The best boxes are still made of wood, but with a lift-out metal lining for easier planting. This gives the plants' roots insulation from what can be the lethal intensity of sunshine. A thin layer of lining plastic is not sufficient to protect them.

The compost for a window-box should be rich in organic material or peat to retain moisture, but plants will still need regular feeding with a proprietary liquid fertilizer since frequent watering will leach out minerals fairly quickly. Drainage should obviously be good. A reasonable drainage layer – say 50 mm (2 in) of broken terracotta pot – should line the base of the window-box, which must have drainage holes through the base to allow for the escape of surplus water. Standing water in an undrained container will cause roots to rot, which will ultimately kill the plant. Over the broken crock, put coarse organic matter to stop the soil from percolating into the drainage. Allow a 50-mm (2-in) space to the rim of the box when you have consolidated the soil for watering. The choice of plants for the window-box has traditionally been among bulbs for springs, then impatiens, geraniums, begonias, ageratum and petunias. All these provide spring to summer color in sunny situations.

Conventional display *This is a conventional, but nonetheless attractive, window-box planting of evergreens and conifers, together with begonias.*

Attaching boxes
It is essential that your window-box is securely fixed, especially when it overhangs a public way. Boxes on ledges with inward opening European or sash-windows may have a brace on either side, attached to the window surround. Boxes beneath an outward opening window should be held within an angled bracket, securely fixed to the wall or window.

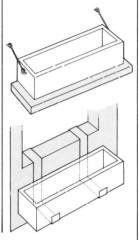

Window-box construction

There are many types of planting box on the market, and in a wide range of materials, but it is still sometimes necessary to construct your own to a particular size. Where possible use hardwood, for it will last much longer. Failing this, a serviceable container can be made using wood that has been seasoned and treated with preservative under pressure, then allowed to stand for several weeks. Use zinc-coated screws, counter sunk in the construction. Ensure that there is adequate drainage, using plastic inserts through the drainage holes so that the damp does not seep into the end grain of the wood. Make the structure stout for, when filled with wet earth, there is considerable outward pressure. Ideally, you should line the container with a metal tray, which can be easily removed for replanting.

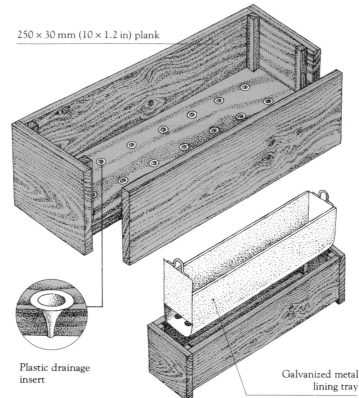

250 × 30 mm (10 × 1.2 in) plank

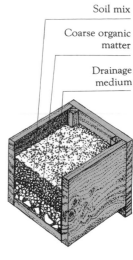

Soil mix

Coarse organic matter

Drainage medium

Filling the box *Line the bottom of the box with 50 mm (2 in) of broken pot, ensuring that large pieces cover the drainage holes. Then add coarse organic materials before filling with growing medium.*

Plastic drainage insert

Galvanized metal lining tray

City window-box, *above. The simplicity of this window and windox-box is an entirely satisfactory treatment in town – red geraniums in an asbestos box. The wooden wedges level the box and facilitate drainage, but when watering care must be taken to prevent the excess falling onto balconies beneath.*

Blending window boxes and façade
Use your plants dramatically to work with your house. Here geraniums and petunias suit the wall color. The shrubs on either side of the darker coloured doors are evergreen Choisya ternata.

CHOOSING AND USING PLANTS

Scale, form, shape and color

Selecting, positioning and combining plants, from
trees to ground cover

Planting the garden

Having completed most of the aspects of a garden's plan, plants, the life-giving element in any garden, can finally be considered.

Older, larger gardens were cut out of existing woodland or enclosed from surrounding countryside by clipped hedges. The modern, invariably smaller garden is now more likely to be formed by the surrounding walls of neighboring houses, fences and garage walls. The problem is no longer that of creating a growing frame of trees and hedges and using plants to decorate it inside, but rather that of using plants to soften and punctuate the space defined around your house following a consciously designed plan.

It is probable that you will be working with a relatively small area so the range of plants that you can use will be limited by their ultimate size. Your choice must support the scale of your garden space. You will have scaled your garden plan to the house (see page 38) and now the planting must be scaled to match the plan.

The range of plants from which to choose is further limited to those with strong shape, form, texture or smell, if you want to create or support a sense of character in the garden, all the year round. How they are grouped and in what numbers is also vital. A strong garden plan will always be weakened by the liquorice-allsorts effect caused by the one-of-this-and-one-of-that type of planting.

In choosing plants it helps to be aware of the period in which plants were introduced to particular locations. By choosing plants that are suitable for a specific situation according to their origin and to the period of their introduction a planting plan is strengthened. Cedar of Lebanon (*Cedrus libani*), for example, epitomizes 18th-century style, while the monkey puzzle tree (*Araucaria auracana*) is redolent of Victorian villa gardens. Both would seem incorrect – though they might well grow (where winter hardy) – in each other's location.

Some plants look well in a rural setting but are not usually acceptable in towns. The birch (*Betula* sp.) is an example of this, as is alder (*Alnus* sp.). Conversely, decoratively hybridized trees look out of scale and out of tune with indigenous rural planting. Japanese cherries (*Prunus* sp.), eucalyptus and the increasingly ubiquitous golden *Cupressocyparis leylandii* are amongst them.

Groups of plants have a particular character, according to their native location. And the cultivated forms of a native range of plants can usually make the bones of your garden selection. Some groups are modified by soil type. Rhododendrons and azaleas, for

Cottage garden-style planting *The selection of shrubs and herbaceous plants shown here is full and flowing, complying with the cottage garden tradition of relaxed planting.*

Structured planting, *right. Compared with the loose planting style above, here planting is tightly structured. Clipped masses contrast with freer plant shapes to make sculptural plant groups.*

example, like acid soil, while delphinium and lilacs respond to limestone. Then there are the ranges of plants growing naturally that are characteristic of certain climates, as for example the herbs and shrubs with resinous stems from hot Mediterranean regions. Rosemary, cistus, lavender, sage and the semi-desert types of plant, such as yucca, are other examples. Some plants prefer light, cool woodland shade, while the vast range of annuals and biennials are happier in open meadowland. Anyone who has climbed a mountain above its lower reaches will know that as the climate becomes colder the range of plants, and indeed their size, is rapidly reduced, until only tiny alpenrose or eidelweiss cling in the lee of rocks at the tops of mountains. Another obvious range of plant material, having its own peculiar style, is that suitable for moist locations, though within this there are sub-divisions of plants which need just damp soil, through moist to wet.

I emphasize the natural locations of plants because though the cultivated forms of wild plants will grow in alien sites and conditions, they must be mixed within the garden carefully. A yucca will probably grow quite well next to a fern, but you should not site them in that way for their original locations were totally different and they will not look "natural" together. However, this is a difficult area in which to be specific, for it concerns the individual's personal response to plants in the light of his own experience.

All of the plants we have discussed have their own particular shape, leaf characteristics and flower color because they have adapted themselves to their location. Plants with large leaves, for example, tend to originate in shady areas, for the size of the leaves is designed to catch the maximum amount of light. Plants from desert areas often have fleshy, sword-shaped leaves, adapted to conserve moisture and deflect sunlight. When

European style, *left.*
The planting here relies
on form and shape
rather than colour.
Plants combine with rock
groupings and the water
feature to present a
complete composition.
The plants used are
hardy enough to with-
stand cold winter
temperatures.

English style, *right.*
This full English
planting places great
emphasis on flower
colour and diverse
foliage forms. There is
little conscious structure
in the arrangement of
plant groupings but their
effect is romantic and
grand. A classical
pedestal and planted
bowl provides a focal
point. In winter the
impact of the planting
will be much reduced.

mixing garden plants, it is these characteristics of shape with which you should juggle for they remain constant throughout the year whereas flower color is transitory. Only when you have built up the outline character of the planting of your site, and styled it according to its location, should you consider plant color.

Planting is fraught with hazards but these can be identified and, once a plant's suitability to a particular situation is established, you can begin to think of the plant's uses in building up your composition. There is a definite order in which this should be done.

You should seek to develop an ever-changing plant arrangement to make up your garden mass, remembering that ultimately you will see little earth. This is a basic theory of planting design. Your aim in choosing and using plants is to achieve a recognizable overall form and to fulfill your garden plan.

Plant classification

Whereas common names of plants vary widely from area to area, use of the scientific name allows you to be certain of a specific plant.

The first word in a plant's classification is the genus name, for example *Acer*, *Berberis* or *Cotoneaster*. There are, however, approximately seventy sorts of cotoneaster, of which half are generally available. Some are 30 mm (1.2 in) high while others become trees. The second name identifies the species of a genus (for example, *Cotoneaster horizontalis*) and it often describes the character of the plant in question. You might see *Cotoneaster* sp. written. This is the accepted abbreviation of

Cotoneaster species and refers to all the species of the genus *Cotoneaster* or, alternatively, one of the species of the genus *Cotoneaster* without specifying which. If there is more than one natural variety of the same species there will be a third Latin name to identify each. If a variety has been produced by human intervention it is known as a cultivated variety or cultivar (usually abbreviated to cv.). In this case the third name will be in a modern language, and may be something like 'Crimson Rose'. Sometimes two genera or two species are crossed (hybridized). A hybrid is usually denoted by a × (multiplication) sign before the species name.

Principles of planting

When a garden has been built it remains incomplete until it is planted. How many and which plants you choose and how you group them depends on many factors. Planting can simply answer a specific requirement, such as to disguise an unsightly view, to give shade, to provide food, to appeal to the sense of smell or to fill a damp and shady corner. But more often, plants make the green bulky infill of the framework to extend the design while giving pleasure throughout the year with seasonal changes of color and texture in foliage, stems, berries, fruits and flowers.

You should also remember that the garden, if not a conscious duplication of natural vegetation, as in the ecologist's wild garden, often contains features that imitate nature. Pools, rockeries and stream beds depend on plants and groupings that interpret the sort of planting that occurs naturally, no matter how stylized to suit your garden. There are, of course, other lessons to learn from nature's distribution. An area of natural vegetation is often dominated by one or two species with only the occasional intrusion of others. This fact gives an area its feel, whether it be pine woodland or heather moor. It is to the landscape of such areas that we retreat to relax on holiday, and it is a similarly simple and discreet planting scheme that will provide a place of enjoyment in the garden. It is not necessary to fill every corner with a different species of plant. True, a garden is a contrived place and many (including the horticulturist) see merit in the range of plants that it is possible to include, but my interest lies between the contrived flower borders in many gardens and the gentle spontaneity of natural plant grouping.

These days many people have neither the time nor the inclination to garden intensively, so the obvious answer is to settle for relaxed planting that allows nature to influence the result, perhaps letting wild plants remain alongside their hybridized relatives.

Contiguous to these reasons for choosing plants is the desire to make plant groupings that satisfy personal taste in form, shape and color. Successful groupings will strengthen a ground pattern, contrast with background planting or support a certain color scheme. Your increasing knowledge of plants, experience in the garden and, I hope, the examples in this book, will help you to make successful groups of plants that work on all scales from trees down to the smallest ground cover subjects.

Planting for year-round interest

The series of three pictures, below, show the same garden in (from top to bottom) spring, mid and late summer. All three examples show how plants have been grouped to provide handsome ground cover throughout the year. In spring, narcissus, planted between emergent perennials, are in flower as the young needles begin to sprout on the foreground larch (*Larix* sp.).

Then, in summer, bold masses of *Sedum spectabile* with *Gypsophylla* sp. provide ground interest for the two bold clumps of *Lasiagrostis* sp. There is yellow *Sedum spathulifolium* in the foreground, with invasive *Polygonum* sp. on the right. By the end of summer the grasses have died down but the massed sedums look spectacular.

Imitating nature

Nature's vegetation has always been an inspiration for garden planting where the gardener seeks to create his own section of the countryside. Natural features have their own characteristic vegetation and can only be successfully included in the garden if you first analyze the natural form carefully, as I have done with a stream bed, below. You will then be able to establish planting areas in the correct positions and choose plants of a scale and form that suit.

Garden as an extension of the countryside, *above. The foreground planting in this damp location is domestic, but it reflects its location for over the mown path wild planting folds naturally into the background of trees, with incidental sculptural elements on the left, such as the fern.*

Natural forms translated for the garden, *below. A stream bed has been recreated here through a dry swath of boulders that make a shoreline effect formed by a larger river. Such a treatment demands riverbank planting like the willows in this example.*

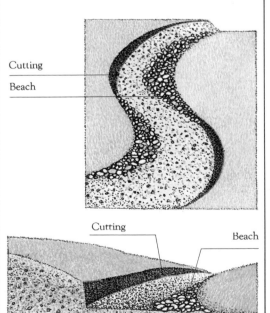

Cutting

Beach

Cutting

Beach

Considering shape, form and color

Once you have decided on the sort of planting you want, and the scale of plants needed to achieve it, you can consider other plant characteristics. For example, is a suitable plant deciduous, evergreen or even semi-evergreen; what is its flower color and the duration of its flowering period in relation to that of other plants in the grouping? Then consider leaf color, being sure to consider the entire year since some plants begin with pale green or gold leaves which become green by summer, while others are first green and then take on glowing autumn colors.

Stem color can also be extremely exciting in winter, when, for example, thickets of pollarded *Cornus* and *Salix* sp. may range in color from chrome yellow, through orange and red to dull burgundy.

After the color of flowers, you should consider fruit and berry color for autumn and early winter interest. Lastly, think about texture, both of leaf and stem. The textural differences of one leaf from another are the result of their adaptation to their original habitats. Many of the hairy gray leaves, which are invaluable for mixed borders, are from the southern hemisphere and have strong visual and tactile qualities. One of the most appealing is the silky gray leaf of *Convolvulus cneorum*. Other textures, like that of the holly (*Ilex* sp.) leaf, are smooth and glossy, while many of the Mediterranean herb plants have crisp leaves of culinary value. Do not overlook the texture of stems, for they may be smooth and glossy or soft and scaled, like some conifers.

These are the qualities with which you compose your plant groupings. The more diverse the shapes, colors and textures, the stronger the grouping will be.

Planting for foliage, left. All these leaves are small and create a light, feathery feeling of gray foliage. The groupings include *Anaphalis*, *Artemisia*, *Stachys* and *Rosmarinus* sp.

Planting for color, right. These strong colors suit bright sunshine. Pelargoniums and darker sweet peas (*Lathyrus odoratus*) are mixed beneath a fig and a vine.

Planting for form, below. Here the dominating feature is form. The leaves of *Hosta sieboldiana* and *Crocosmia* sp. are enclosed by yellow *Lysimachia thyrsiflora*.

Planning and planting a bed

You can compose your plants on site for small areas but you will find it is impossible to visualize a whole border, juggling with all the plant characteristics you want. It is far better to get an outline down on paper first.

Using your final garden layout as an underlay, trace off the areas to be planted and start working to scale on them. First list your priorities, starting with special feature trees or shrubs, which should emphasize or balance a design feature; then background skeleton or screening trees and shrubs.

According to the scale of your site, use a number of particular plants together, perhaps three of some and five of another. Plant through these if you like with a standard tree

or two for increased height and density, though you must remember that ultimately the shrubs beneath them will be in shade. Use plenty of evergreen so that the plan will work throughout winter.

Your catalogue will provide you with ultimate heights and spreads, which in turn will give you a clue to planting distances. Tall shrubs can be two meters ($6\frac{1}{2}$ ft) apart, medium shrubs 1.5 metres (5 ft) and so on (see p. 187). The earth between the plants will soon be covered over as the plants grow, but if you wish you can temporarily brighten gaps with sunflowers or nicotiana.

After your screen shrubs, start composing decorative species in front of them. Think

Putting your planting plan on paper

The garden plan that you decided on by the end of the chapter on Planning your garden left blank spaces for planting areas. When visualizing the plan you will have imagined the planting areas in three dimensions but the details of which plants you locate where can only be settled when you have some knowledge and experience of plants. Look at the examples of planting shown in this chapter for inspiration.

You will, by now, be used to drawing to scale. Taking dimensions from your plan, draw each planting area to a size that is useful, considering the detail that you need to include. Although you will be separating each bed from the overall plan, you must keep its location in the garden in mind. Decide on a system of symbols to denote the types of plants on your plan, remembering that every plant must have its exact planting position marked clearly. It is also important to show the amount of space you are leaving for the spread of plants. The best method of doing this is to draw center circles to represent the spread of each plant, again using scale measurements. Then use dots and crosses for smaller plants. A climbing plant can be indicated by a triangular symbol drawn with its flat side against the proposed support for the plant.

Stage 1 Select a feature tree that will either become the focal point of the planting area, or at least counteract another strong feature, such as the house itself or a view. In this example, two *Phormium tenax* have been chosen as a balancing feature within the same bed for the feature tree, *Acer negundo* 'Variegatum'.

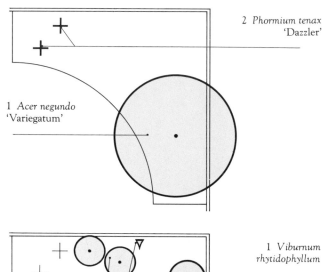

2 *Phormium tenax* 'Dazzler'

1 *Acer negundo* 'Variegatum'

Stage 2 Add evergreen peripheral planting of shrubs and climbers that will contain the site, giving privacy and shelter and making the green walls against which decorative planting is seen. This "skeleton" principle should also apply to smaller plants, including ground cover material. Here, hellebores, bergenia and an iris have been included as a framework.

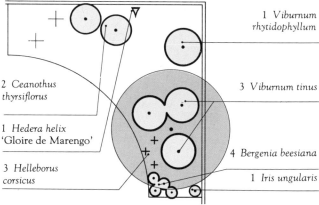

1 *Viburnum rhytidophyllum*

2 *Ceanothus thyrsiflorus*

3 *Viburnum tinus*

1 *Hedera helix* 'Gloire de Marengo'

4 *Bergenia beesiana*

3 *Helleborus corsicus*

1 *Iris ungularis*

Stage 3 Fill in with decorative shrubs of a smaller scale, considering color harmony and contrast, height, shape contrasts (winter and summer), leaf shapes, textures and stem qualities. Work down in scale, adding decorative herbaceous material (not included in this scheme) and finally ground cover.

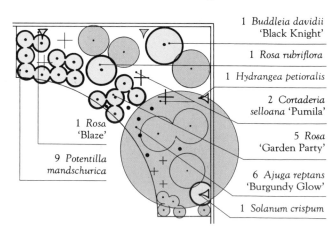

1 *Buddleia davidii* 'Black Knight'

1 *Rosa rubriflora*

1 *Hydrangea petioralis*

2 *Cortaderia selloana* 'Pumila'

1 *Rosa* 'Blaze'

5 *Rosa* 'Garden Party'

9 *Potentilla mandschurica*

6 *Ajuga reptans* 'Burgundy Glow'

1 *Solanum crispum*

first about strong architectural forms (*Phormium* and *Yucca* sp., for example) for the sunny parts, and the bold-leaved hostas and bergenias for the shadier areas. Contrast these strong shapes with softer, fluffier plants flowing around them. At this stage color as well as form must come into your thinking. Try to compose in ranges of color, a method which will also make your selecting process easier. Match the color of a wall, for example, or perhaps the color of your carpet in the room overlooking the planting. You might combine soft pinks and grays with a touch of purple and some white, for instance; or bright orange, yellow and red, lightened by gray and so on. Your colors help to set the mood of your garden, and this in turn should be suggested by your house and its location. Consider the same principles of form and color when deciding on

herbaceous planting, not necessarily using it in specific borders but perhaps mixing tall delphiniums with later-flowering summer shrubs, which will prop up the delphiniums and screen their dying tops. Then consider bulbs, not simply those for spring but lilies for summer, autumn crocus and so on. Site a rose or two against an old tree or some other suitable vertical support.

Put all this down on paper, ensuring that you have included all your favorite species. You must now be ruthless and eliminate about half the number you have selected. The most common mistake of the inexperienced is to plant too much.

If you have clearly defined each plant you want to include in your plan and indicated where each is to be sited, you can use this as a reference sheet and begin your planting in the garden with confidence.

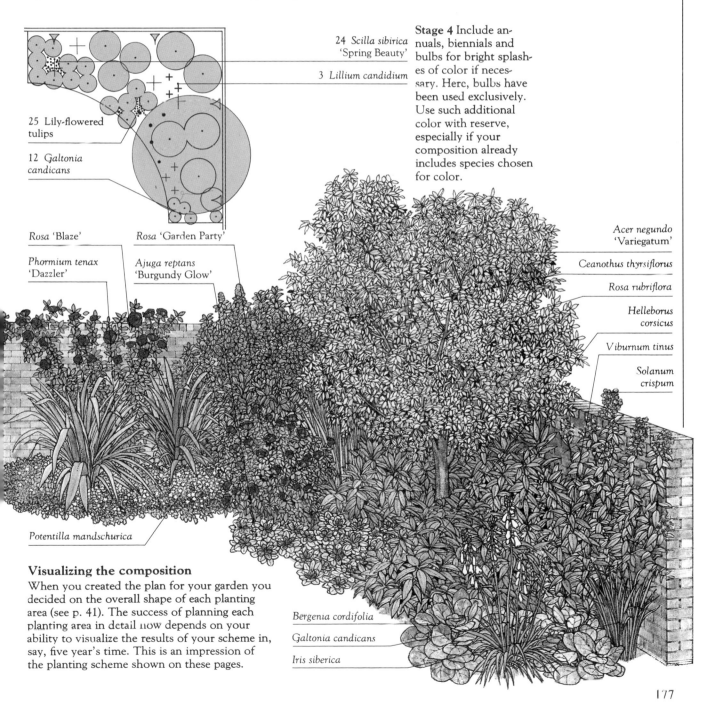

24 *Scilla sibirica* 'Spring Beauty'

3 *Lillium candidium*

25 Lily-flowered tulips

12 *Galtonia candicans*

Stage 4 Include annuals, biennials and bulbs for bright splashes of color if necessary. Here, bulbs have been used exclusively. Use such additional color with reserve, especially if your composition already includes species chosen for color.

Rosa 'Blaze'

Rosa 'Garden Party'

Phormium tenax 'Dazzler'

Ajuga reptans 'Burgundy Glow'

Acer negundo 'Variegatum'

Ceanothus thyrsiflorus

Rosa rubriflora

Helleborus corsicus

Viburnum tinus

Solanum crispum

Potentilla mandschurica

Visualizing the composition

When you created the plan for your garden you decided on the overall shape of each planting area (see p. 41). The success of planning each planting area in detail now depends on your ability to visualize the results of your scheme in, say, five year's time. This is an impression of the planting scheme shown on these pages.

Bergenia cordifolia

Galtonia candicans

Iris siberica

Trees

Whatever a tree's attributes, it will be the shape, both in summer and winter, that will be its abiding characteristic and the one that will influence the selection of other plants nearby. Trees will ultimately be the largest element in a garden and, when planting, one needs to think ahead since they grow quite quickly, not only upwards but outwards, when well maintained. So when making your selection be clear about the tree's eventual shape, size and color.

Broadly, tree shapes can be categorized as follows: fastigiate or columnar; pyramidal or conical; broadly columnar; broad-headed or round-topped, and pendulous or weeping. Within that grouping, the head of the tree may be thick, allowing little light through its foliage to plants beneath, sometimes inhibiting growth altogether, or light and fluffy, giving a dappled shade to growth below.

Although we see only the part of a tree that is above ground, the section below ground must not be forgotten. This is the feeding and anchorage system, not quite as large as the visible part but not far short of it in certain cases and in certain soils. As a general rule, the thinner the foliage the lighter the root run, since a heavy anchorage is not then necessary. Remember, therefore, that when planting in the region of existing trees, or adding new ones to an area of established planting, any nutrient held in solution in the ground will be absorbed by their rooting systems, to the deprivation of all else.

Contrasting foliage
Here the gray foliage of a mature eucalyptus and shrubby Atriplex halimus *is contrasted against the dark mass of a large clipped yew hedge (*Taxus sp.*). A willow-leaved pear (*Pyrus salicifolia*) backs the eucalyptus.*

Foliage backdrop, *above. The light foliage of an* Acer negundo *shades a seating area in this garden. To the right of the lawn is a whitebeam* (Sorbus aria 'Lutetiana') *grouped with the handsome red boughs of the evergreen* Arbutus unedo.

Root systems

It is as well to realize that some species of tree and shrub have almost as much root below ground level as they have branches above, especially when they are growing in good loamy soil. Much of such a root system consists of minute feeder roots that penetrate the film of water that surrounds each individual granule of soil. Wherever there is a water source, roots will grow towards it so large trees should not be planted too close to any drainage runs.

You must remember the extent of roots when you are caring for established plants and introducing new ones. Consider the vast network of roots beneath a mature tree, a clipped hedge or a number of pruned shrubs. Not only will these roots require such a vast amount of feeding that they will impoverish soil in their locality but they also present a barrier for new planting.

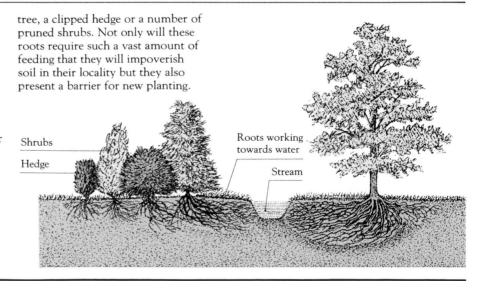

Shrubs

Hedge

Roots working towards water

Stream

The scale of the background trees that you propose planting should be carefully considered before you decide on their siting within the overall layout. Few small gardens can accommodate a forest tree – a beech (*Fagus* sp.), for instance, or an ash (*Fraxinus* sp.) or indeed any of the large conifers. Poplars (*Populus* sp.), which are often planted as screen trees, may be categorised as medium-sized trees, although they can grow to great heights. Even the notorious *Cupressocyparis leylandii* reaches 10–15 meters (33–50 ft) in height – and quickly. So have a care before planting and consult your catalogue to be sure of a tree's potential; then think carefully where to site it so that it will not block out the sun, infringe on a neighbor's garden or undermine your house with its invasive root run. Tree roots can be particularly damaging in areas with wet clay soils where coarse feeders will take up the

available moisture through a dry period, and so cause cracking of the medium surrounding their roots – including the foundations of your house, if they are anywhere nearby.

Hotter climates call for the use of taller trees near the house to shade it. Select trees with less dense foliage, to allow some light through. Such types invariably have shallow roots – as, for example, the false acacia (*Robinia pseudoacacia*).

Trees that are selected to provide a screen to a bad view may be more profitably sited closer to the house rather than at the garden's perimeter. Not only are more trees needed when planted along the edge, but they can all too easily draw the eyes to the precise point that you are trying to disguise.

Tree shapes
The basic characteristic tree shapes are shown below. These shapes relate to any size of tree, from forest species to small decorative hybrids. Some shapes, such as horizontal, suggest movement, while others, such as fastigiate, create static points in the garden that arrest the eye.

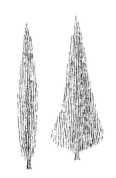

Fastigiate   Conical

Weeping

Round

Flat-topped

Horizontal

Woodland grouping *This grouping of trees resembles light woodland in a naturally occurring situation. Good groupings of trees always look attractive but especially so when bathed in autumn sunlight as here. In the foreground are species of white-barked birch.*

Small trees

The range of trees most suited to the smaller garden is extensive. While suitable when placed against existing, larger trees, they can equally well be grouped to provide either a screen within your garden or to become a decorative element in themselves. The life span of the smaller tree tends to be shorter than that of the forest tree, but maturity is reached more quickly. Smaller trees grow naturally on higher ground, where wind and cold inhibits taller growth, and this is worth remembering when selecting species for roof garden planting.

The type of small tree you might use can be divided into two categories: those that are decorative and those that may be used to infill and build up your screen planting. But here personal taste is involved, for what I consider decorative you may not.

It is generally agreed that the genera *Prunus* (cherry and plum), *Malus* (crab apple) and *Crataegus* (thorn), will fit into the decorative list, since they all flower, fruit and have a degree of autumn color. None, however, has any sculptural quality and you will look at a bare tree for half the year. Conifers, on the other hand, have their full shape the whole year round, but when used *en masse* provide a shape which is too demanding to fit most planting plans and too boring to view.

For me, the smaller variety of silver birch or the thin weeping head of the willow-leaved pear (*Pyrus salicifolia*) are preferable substitutes to conifers. I also admire gnarled old apple trees, dead or alive. More exotic, good value small trees are many of the maples (*Acer* sp.), admired not only for their leaves but for their branches and autumn color. They are not grown for flower, but magnolias are and the adult tree has a good shape. The golden catalpa (*Catalpa bignonioides*), growing 5 m (16 ft) in height, is spectacular when in flower, but it is most memorable for its huge heart-shaped leaves. The showering sprays of golden *Genista aethnensis*, and the midsummer gold of *Koelreuteria paniculata* followed by bronze bladder fruits, are also attractive. Golden robinia (R. pseudoacacia 'Frisia') develops into a pretty tree too. *Amelanchier canadensis*, the shadblow, is a charming white-blossomed spring alternative to the cherry that has distinctive sculptural qualities.

For autumn color you might consider *Cercidiphyllum japonicum*, the Katsura tree, for a lime-free soil. The leaves turn smokey pink, red or gold, and foliage is similar to the eastern redbud (*Cercis canadensis*) with its purple, rose-type flowers in early May forming on its bare branches.

In the wild garden, I enjoy the spring leaves of whitebeam (*Sorbus aria* 'Lutescens') and the autumn fruits of rowan (*Sorbus aucuparia*), but these are probably better used as infill between "feature" trees. This category also includes alders (*Alnus* sp.), hornbeam (*Carpinus* sp.) and hazels (*Corylus* sp.). A small tree for "feature" and "infill" is *Oxydendrum arboreum* with drooping flowers in summer and red foliage in autumn.

All these personal preferences have to be tempered with sound reason, however. Different locations at the same latitude might not support the same tree because of contrasted altitudes, for example. Climatic variations will also affect your choice of tree. The long cold winters and hot summers that occur in much of North America do not support the same trees as the less extreme conditions of the British Isles.

My personal dislikes within this category include trees with purple foliage, which I find too eye-catching and generally heavy and leaden within a composition. I hate deep pink-blossomed cherries, whose flowers

Dominating maple
The golden foliage of a Japanese maple (Acer japonicum 'Aureum') dominates this garden. Both this maple and the Acer palmatum dissectum 'Atropurpureum' in the left foreground, are often listed as shrubs but will become small, eye-catching trees.

Distinctive tree shapes *These four examples show the variety of tree shapes available. Right is a young Cornus florida with its layered branches Far right is a round-headed Japanese cherry. Below is the characteristic leaning form of an old apple tree, while below right is the drooping form of an aged pine.*

clash horribly with bright spring grass and deep yellow daffodils. I also shun laburnums, for while being spectacular when well-placed, finding the right place is very difficult.

My personal antipathy towards conifers stems from an upbringing in northern England where acre upon acre of once-open moorland has been struck ecologically dead by too rigid and too similar conifer afforestation patterns. This state of affairs is now tempered by contour planting and some inclusion of hardwoods, but my prejudice remains and it is not removed by the rows of bizarre coniferous subjects on display in any garden center. They epitomize the lengths to which our horticultural industry will go to achieve another sale at the expense of more natural plants and planting. However, certain conifers have a place within the garden's layout when carefully used, for their strong forms – whether prostrate, conical or horizontal – can be an asset to emphasize a point. Their strong coloring must be considered carefully though, for one glaucous blue spruce (*Picea pungens* 'Glauca'), for example, will, in maturity, dominate all around it.

Many of the dark, matt green conifers make admirable background and shelter.

Using trees within a garden presents a problem of scale unless you have acres of space. It is better to choose bold groupings if you can and to plant three or more of your chosen trees together. Parallel flowering can often be a problem, for in spring there is a flush of color, then a gap, then early summer color, and then another gap before the autumn crescendo. So try to choose your trees and plant them to provide a continuity of visual interest throughout the year.

Buying small trees *Small trees available commercially are categorized according to size and form (below). You should be very careful to establish the adult form of the tree you are buying, choosing specimens with healthy stems and shoots.*

Standard $(5\frac{1}{2}-6\,\text{ft})$

Weeping standard $(5\frac{1}{2}\,\text{ft})$

Half standard $(3\frac{1}{2}-5\,\text{ft})$

Quarter standard $(1-1\frac{1}{2}\,\text{ft})$

Bush

Planting a tree

For generations it was normal practice to plant most saplings in autumn, when trees are dormant, because all stock was sold bare-rooted. Today, however, it is possible to buy container-grown trees and shrubs so that they can be planted without disturbing roots more or less throughout the year, always provided there is not frost in the ground.

The hole in which the tree is to be planted should be excavated to about 1 m (3 ft) square. Fork over the ground at the base of the hole before putting in well-rotted compost, leafmold, peat moss and farmyard manure or the like to a depth of 200 mm (8 in). Then fork this in to the bottom layer of earth. Next, put the tree, which should have been well-watered, in the base of the hole, slit down the side of the container and gently remove it so as not to disturb the roots. You must clear the underside of the root ball, however, if the tree was potted in the traditional way with

a drainage medium in the base of the container. Ensure that the finished earth line will not be above that of the tree in its pot when you have planted it in your garden. If it is, lift the tree and add more earth and manure to the bottom of the hole. Before backfilling the hole, knock in a sound stake at the side of the root ball. In this way you will avoid driving the stake through the tree's young roots. Backfill the hole with as organic a topsoil as you can, gently shaking the stem up and down to ensure that soil settles between the roots, and firming the soil round the root ball as you go with your heel. You must be certain to examine the tree frequently as it will need regular, sometimes daily, watering during dry spells. This is especially important if the tree was planted out of its dormant period.

Staking and tying

Tie a newly planted tree to a stake with plastic cord. It is important, if you are planting a tree during the growing season, to keep it adequately watered, almost daily in most cases. This will encourage the roots to grow out of the tight ball that results from containerized growth into your prepared earth, quickly allowing them both to feed and support the tree. Trees planted in an exposed position must be provided with a stake set at an angle to the wind while those with particularly heavy heads may need additional staking and ties.

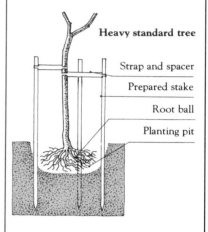

Heavy standard tree

Strap and spacer

Prepared stake

Root ball

Planting pit

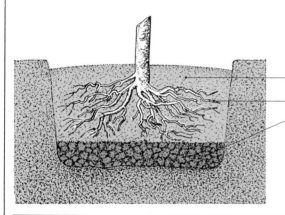

Topsoil with organic materials incorporated

Damaged roots pruned

Forked soil

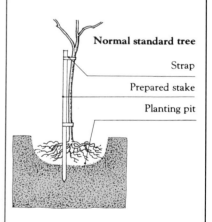

Normal standard tree

Strap

Prepared stake

Planting pit

Planting for contrast, *above. The handsome light gold foliage of* Robinia pseudoacacia 'Frisia' *stands out against a matt-green hedge.*
Highlit apple tree, *left. Many trees can be enhanced with lighting, but the source must be low for complete cover.*

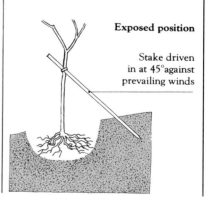

Exposed position

Stake driven in at 45°against prevailing winds

Training trees

Early medieval gardeners were enthusiastic shapers of plants for they needed to restrain and control their plants to achieve the formal symmetry of the patterned *parterres* so popular at the time. Successive moods of Romanticism encouraged a greater freedom and looseness in planting, even the copying of natural planting patterns, but today a greater awareness of form in the garden has renewed interest in tree shaping and encouraged the contrast of loose, natural plant shapes with trained plant forms. And together with topiary (the art of clipping) the training of trees is popular as a cheap alternative to sculpture in the garden.

Pleaching is the training of deciduous (sometimes flowering) trees upon a frame so that their branches entwine to form a green wall or canopy. An extension of this type of training is the topworking of fruit trees in the 17th-century French tradition. The shapes across the middle of this page show some examples of espalier and cordon forms trained against wires. The maintenance of shaped trees is outlined on page 251.

Pleaching laburnum and wisteria, *right.*
Laburnum trained over a metal frame gives the effect of a golden tunnel. Wisteria is interspersed to create a similar, purplish effect a little later.

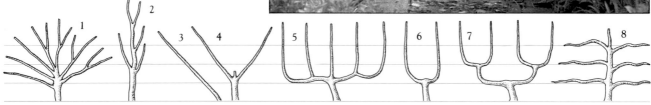

1 Fan
2 Feather
3 Single oblique cordon
4 Double cordon
5 Five grid
6 Single "U"
7 Double "U"
8 Espalier

Pleached Hornbeam
Carpinus betulus *has been pleached to give a tunnel effect, leading the eye to a white bench seat. Clumps of blue-gray rue* (Ruta graveolens) *are planted at the base of each tree to increase the feeling of enclosure at ground level.*

Hedges

The plants most commonly clipped are those that make garden hedges. These are of three types: the loose form, which needs little restraining and includes genera such as *Berberis, Escallonia* and *Pyracantha*; species that need pruning rather than clipping, such as laurel (*Prunus laurocerasus*), and, finally, hedges that should be kept tight and compact by clipping, including *Buxus* sp., *Carpinus* sp., *Cupressocyparis leylandii, Fagus* sp., *Ilex* sp., *Ligustrum* sp., *Lonicera nitida* and *Taxus* sp..

The type of hedge that you select will depend on its location, the character of the site and what you want the hedge to do. Location will dictate species to some extent, particularly with regard to the amount of snow that falls, for in areas of heavy snowfall the clipped hedge can be crushed unless snow is shaken off regularly. Shaping the hedge to a point can help but that may not be the shape you require.

A common mistake is to plant the components of a hedge far too close together in order to achieve a thick screen quickly. Few people then either water or feed the hedge, with the result that on reaching maturity individual plants within the hedge die down. So be sure to plant at recommended distances – and be patient. Remember, too, when selecting your species, that the quick growers do not miraculously stop their rapid growth when they have reached the height you want.

Clipped peacocks, *right. Topiary is part of the cottage garden tradition but its origins stem from the formal 17th-century garden.*

Traditional archway, *above. Yew (Taxus baccata) is here clipped to form an archway, with other clipped pyramidal forms of yew beyond. The architectural potential of this form of plant training is enormous, for it can be traditional, as here, or modern.*

Hedge designs

If you have the time, hedge plants give you great scope for designing in three-dimensions. This terrace is planted with hedge subjects, in a design containing contrasts of form, color and texture. The planting formation for a boundary hedge, below, should be combined with the planting distances shown right.

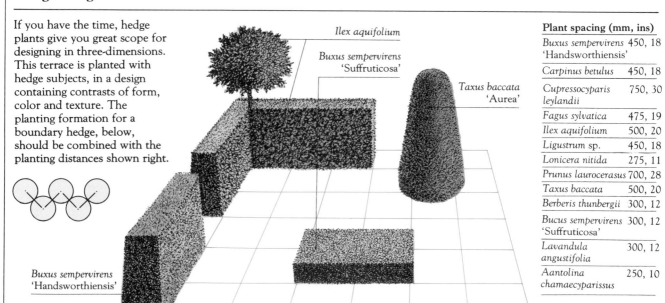

Buxus sempervirens 'Handsworthiensis'

Ilex aquifolium

Buxus sempervirens 'Suffruticosa'

Taxus baccata 'Aurea'

Plant spacing (mm, ins)

Buxus sempervirens 'Handsworthiensis'	450, 18
Carpinus betulus	450, 18
Cupressocyparis leylandii	750, 30
Fagus sylvatica	475, 19
Ilex aquifolium	500, 20
Ligustrum sp.	450, 18
Lonicera nitida	275, 11
Prunus laurocerasus	700, 28
Taxus baccata	500, 20
Berberis thunbergii	300, 12
Bucus sempervirens 'Suffruticosa'	300, 12
Lavandula angustifolia	300, 12
Aantolina chamaecyparissus	250, 10

Shrubs

When first looking at a garden it is often the brightest color or the most curiously shaped plant that catches the eye. However, the impact of these plants depends on their setting – the setting largely created by background planting. It is the background shrubs that do all the hard work, for it is against them that everything else is seen. They will also give the garden winter form, foliage for cutting and provide food and shelter for wild life if you are concerned about conservation.

The scale of this sort of planting will depend on the size of your garden, but as a general rule groupings of shrubs should be bold and simple.

Evergreens come into their own here, for they do the job the year round. Unfortunately the majority of broad-leaved evergreens lack winter hardiness and are limited to the South and West Coast. If you live here, consider evergreen forms of such genera as *Cotoneaster*, *Viburnum* and *Pyracantha*. You will see the diversity of sizes, forms and colors available. Next look at bamboos (*Arundinaria* sp.), the privets (*Ligustrum* sp., not to be despised), the laurels (especially *Prunus laurocerasus* and *Prunus lusitanica*), *Berberis*, *Mahonia*, *Elaeagnus*, *Escallonia* and *Enonymus* sp., yew (*Taxus* sp.), box (*Buxus* sp.) and bay (*Laurus nobilis*), ascertaining which are suitable for your soil, location and climate. Camellias are hardy to Washington, D.C. and grow in like climates. Where the planting is to be exposed to wind or sea spray, select hardy shrubs for they must provide a good line of resistance.

Rhododendrons are a special case since they will only thrive on an acid soil. Although

Shrubs for foliage color, *below. This mixed grouping of deciduous and evergreen shrubs, with small trees and some perennials, has foliage that is mostly gold in color. Compositions are often strengthened by selecting a single color range.*

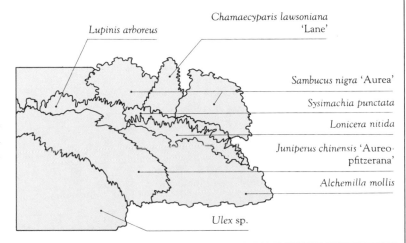

Lupinis arboreus

Chamaecyparis lawsoniana 'Lane'

Sambucus nigra 'Aurea'

Sysimachia punctata

Lonicera nitida

Juniperus chinensis 'Aureo-pfitzerana'

Alchemilla mollis

Ulex sp.

they (along with their near relatives *Pieris* sp., *Kalmia* sp., *Leucothoe* sp.) are more winter hardy than the previous evergreens, their culture is still restricted to the Pacific Northwest, Upper South and Northeast.

Amongst and in front of this evergreen background you can now start to choose and place your larger deciduous shrubs.

Azaleas must be first choice for late spring scent and flower. Others, just as useful, are winter-hazel (*Corylopsis*) for a wild effect, or gray-foliage sea buckthorn (*Hippophae rhamnoides*); buddleia and the spring-flowering spireas are quick growing, good flowering but short-lived shrubs, ideal for interplanting with slower evergreens and which can then be cut out in about five years' time. *Chaenomeles* sp. might be included in the list for both early season and autumnal interest, with species of the genus *Cornus* for their foliage, stem color or flowers. The flowering currants (*Ribes* sp.) also make useful infill, if you can stand their smell. Korean abelialeaf (*Abeliophyllum distichum*) has pretty white flowers that resemble those of forsythia but appear earlier. Late freezes can kill the emerging buds.

Some forms of forsythia have a strong yellow flower and an ugly upright stance. Much more attractive is the lemon, flaccid-growing *Forsythia suspensa* 'Atrocarpa' which flower arrangers love. For later flowering

Hydrangea combination, *above. A beautiful late-summer flowering grouping of* Hydrangea involucrata, *with its purplish flowers and large, sterile white ray florets, contrasted with the more usual mophead* Hydrangea macrophylla *'Ami Pasquier'. A proprietary hydrangea colorant is necessary in alkaline soils to retain blue flower shades, if this is wanted.*

Acid soil shrubs, *left. Heaths (*Erica *sp.) thrive in an acid soil. In the foreground of this view of a large garden, they are grown with low-growing, partially evergreen hybrid azaleas. The background is made up of species of deciduous Japanese maple.*

grow philadelphus for its delicious, evocative scent, the cream forms of which are particularly beautiful. The larger and more rampant forms of shrub rose make excellent background material where space is ample. The Japanese snowball (*Viburnum plicatum* 'Mariesii') is ideal for mid-to-late spring blooms, but none of the deciduous viburnums nor lilac (*Syringa* sp.) in its various forms should be overlooked.

Most of the shrubs mentioned so far are spring flowering. The later, summer-flowering shrubs – such as *Clethra alnifolia*, *Abelia grandiflora*, rose-of-Sharon, hydrangeas, vitex may need a more prominent siting. Where summer-flowering shrubs are to be spot planted (that is individually, perhaps in grass), the technique is the same as for container grown trees (see p. 182). Usually, however, shrubs will be planted in a prepared bed as part of your ground pattern.

Ideally, such an area should be hand dug. In the past, planting areas and vegetable gardens were "double dug", that is the earth was turned over, with organic manure incorporated and weeds removed, to two spits (spade depths) deep, provided that the depth of topsoil allowed for this treatment. Working in this way with earth, you increase topsoil fertility quite quickly. Nowadays gardens tend, if hand dug at all, to be turned to one spit deep only, with the incorporation of organic matter, but even this process can be expensive. But as you may get only one chance of cultivating a bed before planting a new garden, it is money well spent for it will create a good foundation for later growth. Machine cultivation of the earth, even with organic matter added, tends to be an altogether shallower process but can be satisfactory if done slowly.

A more up-to-date method of creating a bed is to "weed kill" a grass area to your bed's pattern. After a month or so, plant your shrubs directly into the brown mass of dead grass, then mulch over the surface with rotted manure or compost. This, however, should be done in autumn so that the organic material will be taken down by worms through winter and spring. A summer mulch of rotted manure tends to dry out and form hard little clumps, which are difficult to disperse and which will be constantly raked over by birds.

As with trees, if you are planting stock that is not bare rooted (that is, pre-grown in a container), you may plant throughout the season, although you must water well. Autumn, or spring for less hardy subjects (the time to plant bare-rooted stock), is still the best time for planting when the work is on a considerable scale.

Planting distances for shrubs

It is difficult to be specific about the spacing between shrubs for it depends on how quickly you want to achieve an interlocking mass of plants. You must also consider the rates of growth of different plants. Some rhododendrons grow to 5 m across, but slowly, so I would plant them 2 m apart. Five years is the maximum time you should have to wait for the desired result, given that in this time some shrubs will need to be cut right back or thinned drastically.

At the foot of this page there is a simple guide to the ultimate sizes of some commonly-used shrubs. Of these, I recommend that the large,

tall shrubs should be planted 2 m apart, medium-sized ones 1.5 m apart and small shrubs only 1 m. For other species, check ultimate sizes and then place them in one of the size categories for yourself. Generally, the beginner plants his material too close together, worrying that his newly-bought bundles of winter twigs will never burgeon out in spring. Until they knit together, you might want to cultivate the ground between shrubs. Cover it with a mulch or plant perennial bulbs or annuals. Try sunflowers (*Helianthus* sp. or *Nicotania* sp.) in tall shrub areas for bulk during the first few years.

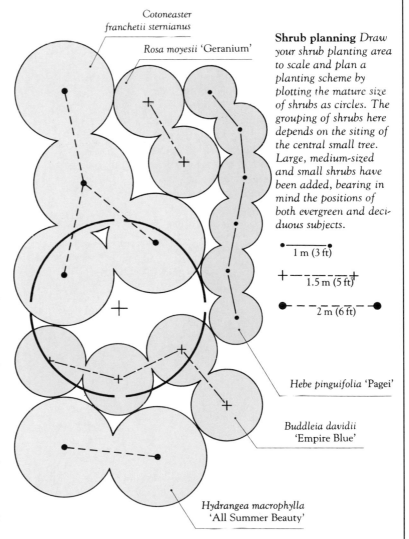

Cotoneaster franchetii sternianus

Rosa moyesii 'Geranium'

Shrub planning *Draw your shrub planting area to scale and plan a planting scheme by plotting the mature size of shrubs as circles. The grouping of shrubs here depends on the siting of the central small tree. Large, medium-sized and small shrubs have been added, bearing in mind the positions of both evergreen and deciduous subjects.*

1 m (3 ft)

1.5 m (5 ft)

2 m (6 ft)

Hebe pinguifolia 'Pagei'

Buddleia davidii 'Empire Blue'

Hydrangea macrophylla 'All Summer Beauty'

Tall shrubs	Medium-sized shrubs	Small shrubs
Buddleia sp.	*Berberis* sp.	*Deutzia gracilis*
Cotoneaster sp.	*Cytisus* sp.	*Skimmia japonica*
Philadelphus sp.	*Hydrangea macrophylla*	*Hypericum patuluma*
Pyracantha sp.	*Viburnum davidii*	'Sungold'
Viburnum sp.		*Iberis sempervirens*

Feature shrubs

Plant selection has so far been for its service-ability and its bulk. It is against this mass that you should now start to arrange your decorative plants, your star items, to maintain sculptural and color interest throughout the year. Much of your selection will, of course, depend on your location (whether hot or cold), on your garden's position (whether sunny or in shade), and on your soil (whether dry or damp). But there is a range of quite tough plants that seems to survive fairly well in most conditions, and which can provide the structural element of your decorative shrubs. For want of a better term, this range may be called one of "architectural" interest. In the same way as we placed "special" trees before considering infill between them, so one might work with architectural shrubs. No matter how brilliant your colour selection (if that is your aim), some element of form within the concept will help shape its appearance throughout the year.

Start with those plants that, if left unchecked, would become trees. Examples include *Aralia elata*, which if pruned back each autumn develop huge pinnate leaves a meter in length, and *Eucalyptus gunnii* which, if kept cut down, has beautiful, fine gray leaves that make a good foil to many colors. Spikey cordylines will also articulate your border, though they should have their heads tied up through cold winters. The suckering sumach (*Rhus typhina*, or its cut-leaved

form), makes a beautiful architectural addition to your garden, with brilliant autumn colours and a lovely skeletal shape in winter. Californians will know *Fatsia japonica* for its handsome, evergreen, fig-like leaves, and *Fatshedera lizei*, a more sprawling relative, crossed with ivy, that grows well in shade. Then consider *Magnolia grandiflora*, a magnificent free-standing tree in sheltered areas but a background wall shrub in more exposed ones, and the fig (*Ficus carica*), although it is not evergreen.

Tree peonies (*Paeonia delavayi*) have a statuesque quality, with ravishing flowers in spring, as has *Viburnum rhytidophyllum*, with lax ribbed leaves 75 mm (3 in) long. *Arundinaria palmata*, a bamboo, is not for mixing with smaller species since it is too rampant, but it also has vivid ribbed leaves.

Shrubs to establish character *Below, the grasses and bamboos of this garden are largely responsible for its character. All are evergreen and hardy. Bottom, in this mixed border the backing shrub rose is* Rosa moyesii, *with the strong horizontal form of* Juniperus chinensis *in front of it. These shrubs provide a foil to the vertical spires of foxglove (*Digitalis sp.*) and the spikes of perennial* Salvia superba.

Curving border

This example of planting relies heavily on feature shrubs and is shown above in the spring and in plan, right. The border combines shape, texture and leaf form and deciduous and evergreen species are well-balanced. While the color combinations are particularly attractive in spring, summer interest will be provided by white floribunda roses, by the magenta flowers of *Stachys lanata* and the cream flowering spikes of *Yucca filamentosa*.

Clematis montana 'Alba'

Cortaderia selloana

Taxus baccata 'Fastigiata'

Rosmarinus officinalis 'Miss Jessup's upright'

Stachys lanata

Yucca filamentosa

Iris × gernabuca 'Jane Philips'

Ceanothus thyrsiflorus

Potentilla fruticosa 'Katherine Dykes'

Rosa floribunda 'Iceberg'

Choisya ternata

→ N

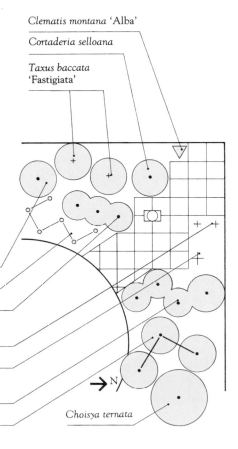

Bold grouping *Although the foreground hosta (Hosta plantaginea 'Royal Standard') is a plant of distinctive form it is made more dramatic by the background of* Phormium tenax *and* Lonicera nitida *'Baggesen's Gold'.*

It will always provide an instant Japanese effect. Coming down in size, use handsome yuccas grouped together in your composition, and New Zealand flax (*Phormium* sp.) if you garden in Florida or California. Consider the small *Viburnum davidii* (though it becomes 2 m (6 ft) tall), *Skimmia* sp., and *Choisya ternata*, the Mexican orange blossom, an evergreen with fleshy, pinnate leaves, for mild winter climates only.

Between these judiciously placed architectural species, start to blend and contrast in simple groupings the other decorative shrubs of your choice, keeping the interest dispersed throughout the season. Try to achieve a positive arrangement rather than a jumble of

plants, using two, three or four individual plants from the larger scale species and eight or nine from the smaller.

My particular favorites include many of the genus *Berberis*, for smaller subjects mix well with them; broom (*Cytisus* sp.) and *Ceratostigma* sp. for late-season blue, all the sweet-smelling species of *Cistus* for hot, dry places, and *Cotinus* sp. for purple foliage.

Herbs have summer flowering value and some, like the little herb *Ruta* sp., have the added attraction of being evergreen (gray). Hydrangeas, too, make summer color. I prefer the lacecaps to the more blatant blue or pink mop-headed *Hydrangea macrophylla* Much neglected are tree lupins (*Lupinus*

Shrub planting for scent
Although many scented shrubs bloom early in the year, their flowers are not spectacular and the plants seldom possess architectural form. Some of them, such as *Sarcococca* sp., *Mahonia japonica* (one of the few with a shape of character), *Choisya ternata* and forms of daphne, are not particular about their site so they can be put in a corner near a door or a window so that their perfume will waft indoors in the summer. But to make a visually satisfying border with shrubs of strong scent, you need to include plants with stronger shapes, forms or colors.

In this example, a corner bed is "pinioned" by two clipped, pyramidal *Carpinus betulus*. Around this point of emphasis are grouped shrubs that combine in form and color as well as providing a variety of scents throughout the season.

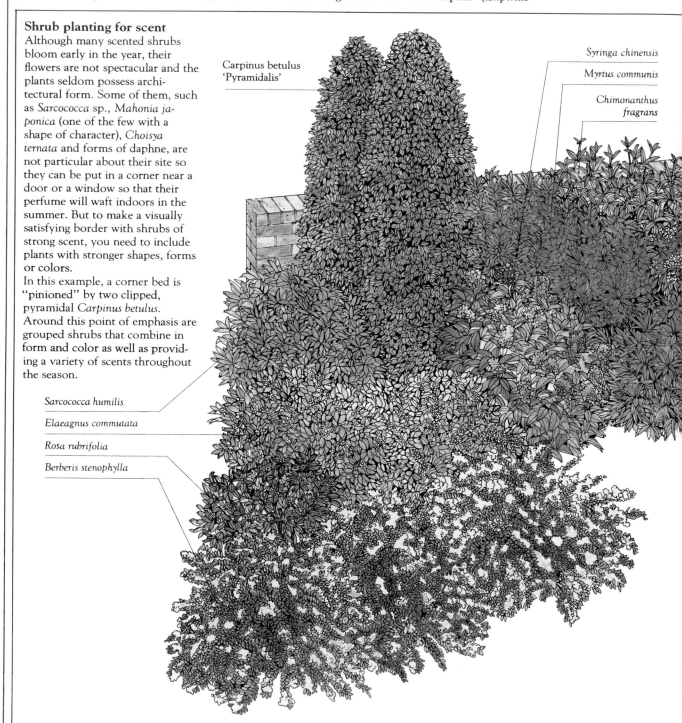

Carpinus betulus 'Pyramidalis'

Syringa chinensis

Myrtus communis

Chimonanthus fragrans

Sarcococca humilis

Elaeagnus commutata

Rosa rubrifolia

Berberis stenophylla

arboreus), which are easy to grow but are limited to their native California. Having more or less the same range of brightness, but being smaller in scale, is the ever increasing range of potentilla cultivars, which flower throughout the season until the frost. *Romneya coulteri*, the white Californian tree poppy, is exquisite but difficult to establish.

Many of the smaller, old fashioned roses are good all-rounders. For its foliage and hips, *Rosa rubrifolia* is splendid – indeed, all the *Rosa rugosa* cultivars, together with *Rosa moyesii*, have good autumn hips. I love the tight cabbage flowers of the Bourbon roses (*Rosa borboniana*), 'Madame Isaac Pereire' and 'Madame Pierre Oger'.

Certain floribunda roses will mix well with decorative shrubs, too; try mixing them with lavender and sage for a charming effect. Indeed, many of the shrubby herbs can be used decoratively in a border, but they are discussed separately (see p.217).

There is a wide range of shrubs which I have not included: those with gray foliage, *Artemisia arborescens* for example, will lighten the tone of any border. Although quite hardy in the British Isles, I have found many gray foliage shrubs almost impossible to obtain as little as 20 miles across the Channel, where they will not stand the winter's increased severity. Most need a good, open, warm and sheltered site.

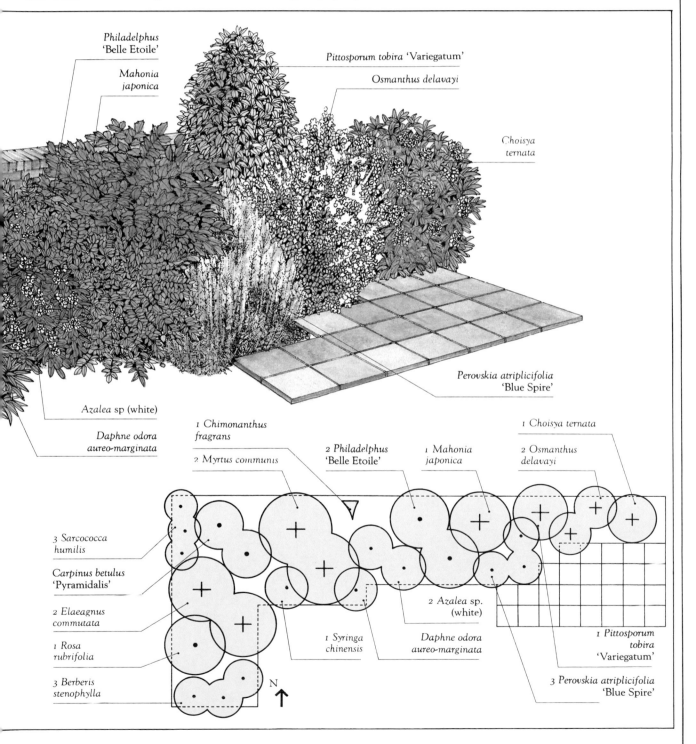

Philadelphus 'Belle Etoile'

Mahonia japonica

Pittosporum tobira 'Variegatum'

Osmanthus delavayi

Choisya ternata

Azalea sp (white)

Daphne odora aureo-marginata

Perovskia atriplicifolia 'Blue Spire'

1 Chimonanthus fragrans

2 Myrtus communis

2 Philadelphus 'Belle Etoile'

1 Mahonia japonica

1 Choisya ternata

2 Osmanthus delavayi

3 Sarcococca humilis

Carpinus betulus 'Pyramidalis'

2 Elaeagnus commutata

1 Rosa rubrifolia

3 Berberis stenophylla

N

1 Syringa chinensis

2 Azalea sp. (white)

Daphne odora aureo-marginata

1 Pittosporum tobira 'Variegatum'

3 Perovskia atriplicifolia 'Blue Spire'

Perennials

Perennials are the group of plants whose flowers give permanent summer color. Few are evergreen but most are fairly easy to grow. There are types of perennials suitable for every location and condition. The clue to their needs is often found in the soil types and climate of the country from which they first came. Many of the gray-foliaged perennials, for instance, originated in New Zealand, while many of the plants with brilliantly colored daisy-type flowers came from South Africa. Perennial plants that are indigenous to northern Europe tend to be those with flowers of softer hue, even though *en masse* they will provide a vivid spectacle, as is proven by successful "herbaceous" and "mixed" borders.

The difference between a pure herbaceous border and a mixed one is that the mixed border includes shrubs as well as perennials, which not only lengthen the period of attraction but physically support the arrangement. A mixed border is easier to maintain, for much free-standing, perennial material needs staking to support it throughout summer. This, I suspect, is because the earth we provide for them is over-rich. In the high desert areas of Iran many of the parents of our hybrid garden subjects survive in the most arid conditions, though perennials in the main prefer a moist, slightly acid soil.

When making your selection choose a suitable shape and size of plant before considering color, for these characteristics will last at least all summer while the flower may be present for as little as a week. Peonies, for instance, are in perfect bloom for only a few days, since it is usually too hot or too wet for their delicate flowers to survive. In a capricious way, however, it is precisely this fleeting quality we seek to capture. So it is vital that your peonies are sited in front of a bold and later flowering plant to make a virtue of their persistent foliage.

Within the range of plants I call architectural, high on my list of favourites are euphorbias for their year-round interest. They are closely followed by different species of hellebore. Grey verbascum, with its towering lemon spikes, improves any border, as do the huge leaves of the globe artichoke (*Cynara scolymus*). *Macleaya cordata* is equally handsome but needs space, as it spreads rapidly. The useful day lilies (*Hemerocallis*) sp. have an exceptional colour range and are extremely adaptable. Sedums are useful, too, for their late summer interest; the purple forms are particularly handsome, especially

Summer-flowering perennial planting
This is a fine selection of early summer-flowering perennials, including bulbous plants, with delphiniums dominating the scene, tall Eremurus sp. and then foxgloves behind. In the foreground are iris and large, leathery bergenia leaves, with the blue globe thistle heads of Echinops ritro.

when mixed with Japanese anemone (*Anemone × hybrida* 'Alba'). The humble bergenia is ideal for front row, evergreen interest, as is the high summer sprawl of *Alchemilla mollis*. Some of the cranesbills (*Geranium* sp.) are easy to grow and have dense foliage of character. They are also useful as ground-cover plants (see p. 201). Grasses are often worth including among these striking perennials that will form the skeleton of a planting area. They form a plant group in their own right from 2 m-high (6 ft) beauties, which rustle in the breeze, to minute, soft cushions of bright blue, gray or green foliage. Most grasses are hardy but can become invasive and need frequent dividing.

Incorporate into this framework your other perennial favorites of less imposing form, using their color to compose your picture. A genus that flowers very early each spring is *Doronicum*, soon followed by the myriad colors of iris. Behind their stands of sword-like leaves, the cool spires of delphinium soon rise and, later, campanulas of similar shades. As summer progresses, the colors of flowering perennials are warmer. Sun roses (*Helianthemum* sp.) range from pink to orange and yellow. *Helenium* and *Helianthus* sp. provide the hot colors, oranges and browns. Phlox can be used to follow these plants (use plenty of white forms to cool your planting) and then, for

Planting distances for perennials

It is impossible to be precise about planting distances for perennials, for some, such as globe artichokes (*Cynara scolymus*), grow to about a meter (3 ft) across while others are a few centimeters (3–7 in). As a general guideline to the number you need in a border, however, allow five to every square meter (10 ft²) (see diagram). Make your selection by shape as well as color. Here are tall blue lupines grouped with the blue heads of *Erigeron* sp. in front.

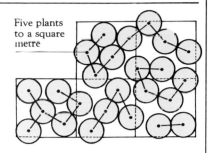

Five plants to a square metre

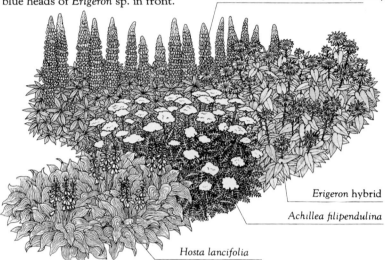

Lupinus (Russel)

Erigeron hybrid

Achillea filipendulina

Hosta lancifolia

Orange border *The perennials in this yellow and orange border include* Campanula *sp., with half-hardy* Gazania *sp., lemon* Antirrhinum *and gray foliaged* Helichrysum *sp. In the foreground are annual pot marigolds (*Calendula officinalis*).*

flowering into autumn, there are chrysan-themums and asters.

The colors of these summer flowers are bewildering in their variety, but one way to master this abundance is to plan your border and make your selection in a particular color range. Alternatively, stick to grasses in one area and plants with daisy flowers in another. Try to eliminate too many varieties and do not accept from friends snippets of those plants that you do not really want.

When you have made your selection, plant in bold clumps and drift one mass into another. If you are buying from a garden center, you will often find that one good young plant can be separated into two or three and, while the group will be thin in its first year, perennials grow rapidly.

Once established, some will need to be divided nearly every year. This is especially so of grasses. Perennials grow out from the center and eventually leave a hole in the middle of the plant. This dividing of plants is usually spring work (as described in Care and maintenance, see p. 255), so you must re-member which plant is which for in early spring you may not recognize them. Label each carefully in autumn so that you will know what is where when you come to deal with them in the new year.

Random spring planting, *left. A mixed and random spring planting in an English garden of foreground* Alchemilla mollis *backed by* Euphorbia wulfunii. *Over to the right are Spanish iris and* Primula sp., *with angelica (*Angelica archangelica*) behind.*

Mixed grasses, *right. The grass species in this example of perennial planting are clustered beneath an ailanthus tree at the front of an American house. Attractive, feathery seed heads indicate* Lasio-grostis splendens *and* Pennisetum orientale.

An evergreen perennial planting design

The range of perennial plants that will grow in light shade is more extensive than is usually supposed and it is this tolerance that is the common factor between the plants chosen for this scheme. The species included have adapted to their situation by modifying their leaf forms, making them particu-larly attractive. This, however, has been at the expense of bright flower color, for plants in shade usually have flowers of muted white, pink or blue.

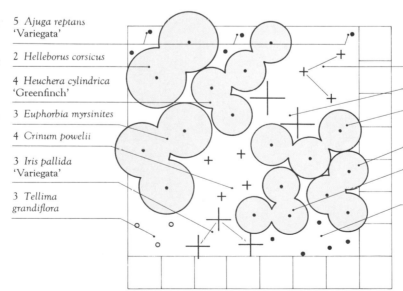

5 *Ajuga reptans* 'Variegata'

2 *Helleborus corsicus*

4 *Heuchera cylindrica* 'Greenfinch'

3 *Euphorbia myrsinites*

4 *Crinum powelii*

3 *Iris pallida* 'Variegata'

3 *Tellima grandiflora*

3 *Sedum* 'Coral carpet'

2 *Iris foetidissima*

3 *Bergenia beesiana*

3 *Geranium endressii* 'Wargrave Pink'

3 *Tiarella cordifolia*

5 *Stachys lanata* 'Silver carpet'

195

A mixed border planting design
This mixed border, shown as it would appear in mid summer, largely comprises evergreen subjects for year-round interest. At the back are the dense foliage shapes of *Cotoneaster wardii*, *Lonicera nitida* and *Stephanandra tanakae*. These not only form a screen against which smaller plants can be placed but provide a support for them, obviating the need to stake and tie. Plants in the middle distance include *Mentha rotundifolia variegata*, a spreading, decorative mint with attractive green and white leaves, *Anthemis*

tinctoria, which produces bright yellow, daisy-like flowers in mid summer, and *Allium flavum*, an ornamental onion with bright yellow flowers. Foreground material is mostly ground cover and includes *Salvia officinalis* 'Purpurea', a spreading purple sage with attractive foliage color, and *Limnanthes douglasii*, a California native which has profuse white flowers. The plants were chosen not only for their size and shape, but for colors – principally yellows, blues and white – that work harmoniously together.

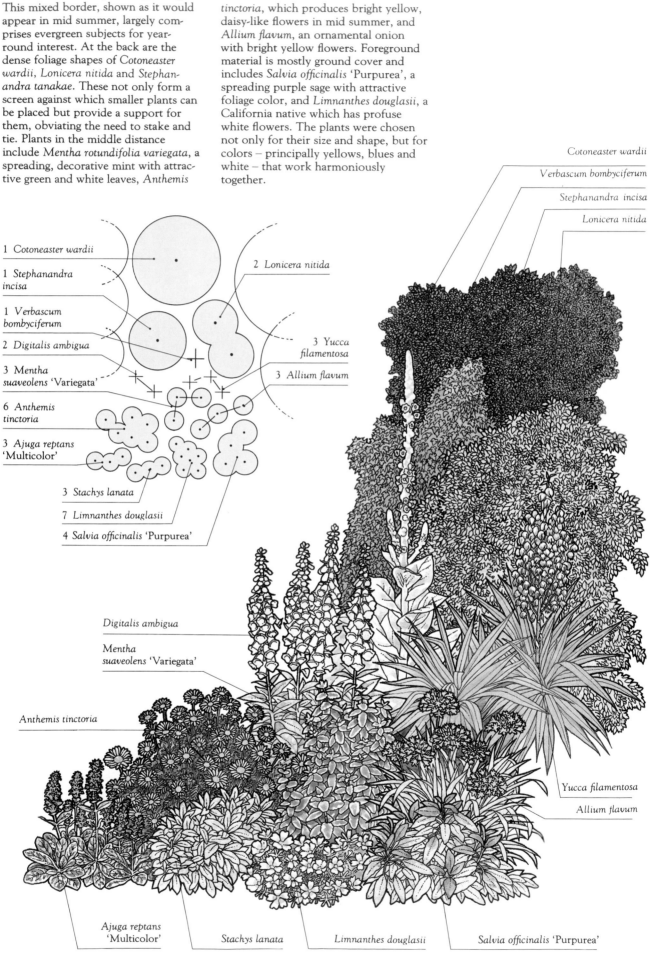

1 *Cotoneaster wardii*

1 *Stephanandra incisa*

1 *Verbascum bombyciferum*

2 *Digitalis ambigua*

3 *Mentha suaveolens* 'Variegata'

6 *Anthemis tinctoria*

3 *Ajuga reptans* 'Multicolor'

3 *Stachys lanata*

7 *Limnanthes douglasii*

4 *Salvia officinalis* 'Purpurea'

2 *Lonicera nitida*

3 *Yucca filamentosa*

3 *Allium flavum*

Cotoneaster wardii

Verbascum bombyciferum

Stephanandra incisa

Lonicera nitida

Digitalis ambigua

Mentha suaveolens 'Variegata'

Anthemis tinctoria

Yucca filamentosa

Allium flavum

Ajuga reptans 'Multicolor'

Stachys lanata

Limnanthes douglasii

Salvia officinalis 'Purpurea'

Annuals

Annual plants that develop from seed, flower, produce seeds and then die in one year. Many of their flowers are extremely bright and, in the main, they provide the colorful splashes in the garden, on the roof garden or in the window-box. With few exceptions, the flowering period of annuals is extremely short, so successive sowing of seeds or planting of seedlings is often necessary to maintain the display. There are some annuals, however, that self-seed and will continue to come up year after year in a random way, appearing in the most unexpected places. Among these are marigolds (*Tagetes*), the tobacco plant (*Nicotiana*), nasturtiums (*Tropaeolum*) and sweet-alyssum (*Lobularia maritima*).

Until a few years ago, gardeners prepared bedding schemes for annuals as the main feature of their gardens. Island beds would be prepared and filled with maturing plants that would be replaced *en masse* with later-flowering kinds at the first signs of fading. This sort of annual extravaganza is now restricted to public spaces since the labour costs and price of oil for heating greenhouses in which annual seedlings are nurtured has become extremely expensive.

Annuals differ somewhat in their hardiness and this can affect their propagation. The directions on most seed packets can aid you in determining when and how to sow. In general, the hardiest annuals can be sown in the open ground in early spring, even before the soil seems workable and before frosts have stopped.

Among my favorites in this category are sweet-alyssum (*Lobularia maritima*), pot-marigold (*Calendula officinalis*), larkspur (*Consolida ambigua*) and California-poppy (*Eschscholtzia californica*) and true annual poppies.

Less hardy and requiring a longer growing period before flowering size is reached are ageratum, the invaluable many varieties of *Impatiens*, *Lobelia erinus* and marigolds (*Tagetes*). Start their seeds indoors, either in a sunny window or under flourescent lights.

Annuals are today used to thicken out young shrub planting schemes and give quick height (cleome is ideal for this) or to enliven the front of a mixed planting scheme.

Use annual color in big bold splashes or intermingle colors to give the alpine meadow, cottage garden feel, depending on the effect you seek. Remember that taller species may need staking.

As soon as your annuals have died down, be decisive and either cut them back, when you will get another flowering if the season is young, or take them out and seed a quickly maturing alternative.

Informal annual color *This example shows zinnias and bedding dahlias growing beneath fruit trees. Dahlias can be grown from seed but it is customary to propagate by splitting tubers. Zinnia seed can be sown directly in the open ground after the soil warms. Or seeds can be started indoors.*

Using yellow, orange and red
Annual flower color in summer is predominantly yellow, orange and red in the northern hemisphere. These colors can be harsh and strident and must therefore be carefully sited, for they will inevitably dominate the surroundings, particularly in a natural, rural garden. To accommodate them best, plant these brightly-colored annuals either in the foreground or to one side of a main view. Avoid siting them at the far end of your garden, for this will have the effect of making the intervening space seem less, foreshortening the prospect. Used sensitively, however, yellows, oranges and reds can be extremely effective, particularly when muted by lighter flower color among them. Lemon and strong pink, for example, will dilute brighter colors when mixed with them; white, too, has the same effect and its addition brings instant sharpness to any color combination. Purple is another useful color when seeking to tone down these bright colors.

Warm color mix with white, *left.*
Nemesia strumosa is a plant whose mixed colors embody the essence of summer. Here, paler shades offset the hot colors.

Undiluted yellow,
below. Antirrhinums can be mixed with perennials or sited in front of shrubs but are most effective when planted in drifts.

1 *Thunbergia alata*

2 *Zinnia* 'Old Mexico'

3 *Antirrhinum* 'Topper'

4 *Gazania* 'Sunshine'

5 *Tagetes* sp.

6 *Helianthus* sp.

7 *Calendula* 'Pacific Beauty'

8 *Gaillardia* 'Gaity'

9 *Nemesia strumosa*

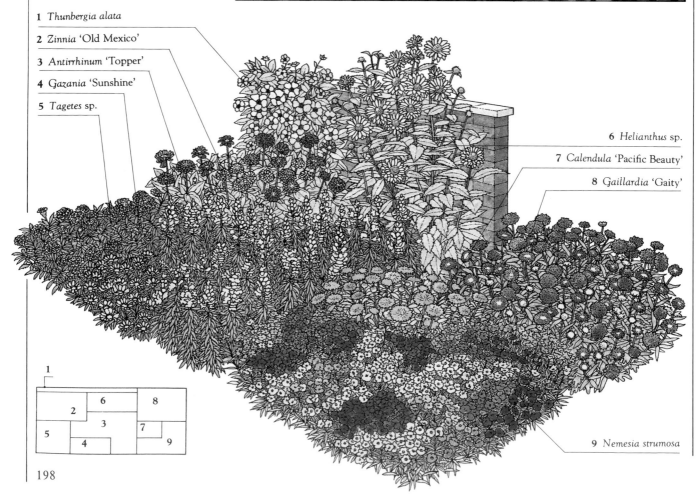

Using white and cream

White flowers mixed with other flower colors will always lighten the effect; when used entirely on their own, however, they will probably look cold, for white needs plenty of green to enrich it. Selectors and hybridizers of annuals have produced white plants that are so covered in flowers that their vital green foliage is masked.

White annuals look superb, however, when mixed with herbaceous plant material and while the justly-famed white gardens of England rely on perennials to create this effect, they are always supported by annual planting. Solid white planting in window-boxes over a whole façade also looks crisp, sharp and sometimes spectacular.

Cream should never be used as a substitute for white, for it has a warmth and quality of its own. As with lemon, use cream to soften strong, hot colors, or with green or gold flowers or foliage. Cream also looks well in conjunction with the vivid green of a well-kept lawn.

Cream contrast, *above. Soft and cream-colored* Mesembryanthemum criniflorum *flowers are especially effective when mixed with deep pink. The white* Arabis albida *strikes a harsh note, however, in the composition.*

Pure white, *left. White petunias have a striking purity about them and make some of the finest annual bedding material. They will only thrive, however, if they receive plenty of sun.*

1 *Ipomea* sp.

2 *Nicotiana alata*

3 *Dimorphotheca sinuata*

4 *Eschscholzia californica*

5 *Impatiens wallerana*

6 *Gypsophilia elegans*

7 *Cleome* 'Pink Queen'

8 *Phlox drummondii*

9 *Iberis* sp.

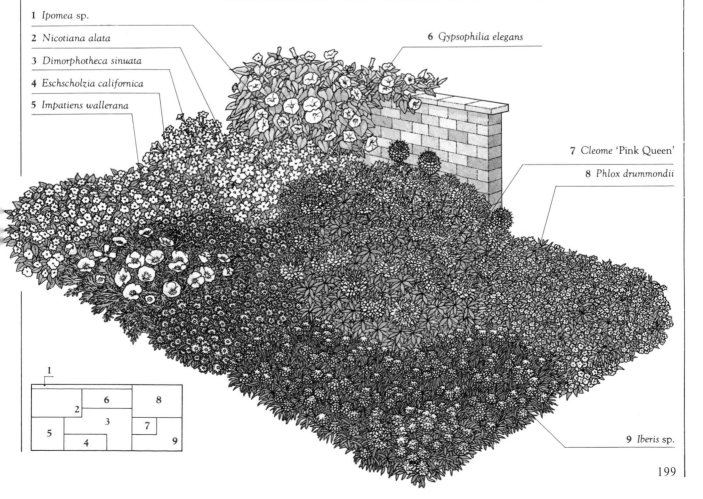

Using blue

Blue is a very strong color and should therefore be used with care in a garden. Too much will look brash, too little merely irritates. Siting is all important. Be guided by nature, for it is a color that occurs naturally in light shade or diffused through meadow grass.

Rich blue coloring is at its best when there is a cloudless sky and bright sun, for then it reflects the canopy. These conditions seldom obtain in the British Isles, for instance, and without them I personally find blue too demanding a color, unless carefully softened with pinks, grays and perhaps a touch of purple.

Blue is naturally a spring and early summer flower color, but I find blue crocus difficult to fit into a plan in spring and blue asters depressing later in the year. The rule is to be careful where you site blue annuals if you are seeking a natural effect. If, however, you want a grand, dominating sweep of color in your garden, this color cannot be bettered.

True blue clusters, *above. The Californian* bluebell, Phacelia campanularia, *produces the purest blue, bee-attracting flowers amongst a carpet of bushy, soft leaves.*

Evocative morning glory, *left. Nothing is as evocative of hot summer mornings as the purple-blue of morning glory* (Ipomoea tricolor). *This is an annual climber that will reach 6–7 m (19–22 ft) in height in full sunlight.*

1 *Ipomoea tricolor*

2 *Salpiglossis sinuata*

3 *Heliotropium arborescens*

4 *Callistephus chinensis*

5 *Ageratum houstonianum*

6 *Consolida ambigua*

7 *Nigella damascena*

8 *Campanula medium*

9 *Petunia* hybrid

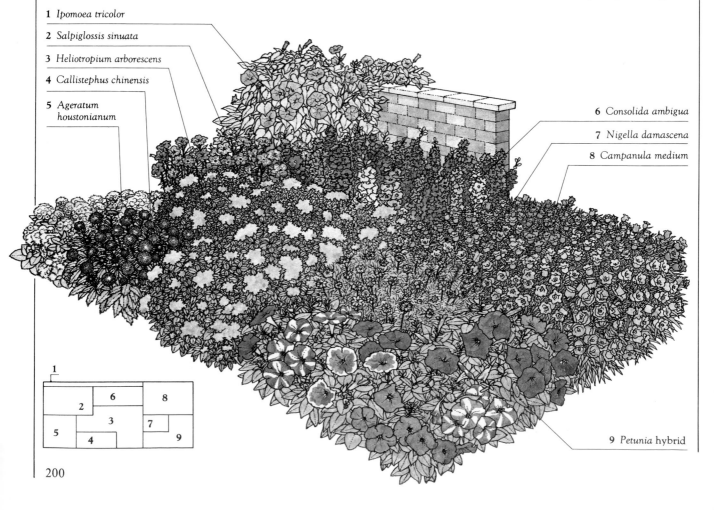

Lawns and ground cover

We are fortunate in northern Europe that grass, the primary natural ground covering mixed with herbs, grows so easily. Indeed, in the British Isles we carve out many of our gardens from this greensward, but there are few other parts of the world where grass will grow with ease.

Lawns take many forms. Real lawn enthusiasts treat their grass as though it were a bowling green, maintaining a weed-free, lurid emerald carpet of fine grass throughout the year, even during a drought, by mowing twice a week. This is both costly in time and finance, for this type of lawn must be fed and dressed regularly. And it will certainly not be the sort of place where children and pets can play. For normal family use, a coarse grade lawn is quite adequate and I do not mind seeing the odd weed within it.

The alternative to a closely mown lawn is one that is rough cut. By allowing the grass to grow longer, and mowing only a path or paths through it, you will cut down on the area which needs weekly care and you will also encourage flowers to grow within the rough area. Such treatment suggests a rural feel and can look charming with fruit trees grown in the longer grass. By leaving grass uncut for periods, you can successfully hide the inevitable raggy look of bulbs dying down after spring flowering in a mown lawn.

The establishment of wild flowers in a lawn is not as easy as one might suppose for, if you sow seeds, grass will inevitably swamp the tiny seedlings. So plant young plants by hand through the grass in drifts to establish a good coverage of wild flowers. The timing of your mowing will, of course, be dependent on the wild flowers that you establish and the length to which you allow the grass to grow.

To create a real flowery mead or alpine meadow, you should cultivate your ground freshly and sow a flower seed/grass mix suitable for your area. The grass seed must include a slow-growing type, with whose competition the emergent flower seedlings can cope. Coarse grasses will quickly swamp flowering plants and ruin the effect.

Large scale ground cover Epimedium *sp.* *has been used in this Dutch garden as ground cover between bold, brick stepping stones beside an attractive pool. The stone circles have been repeated in shape but on a larger scale in the paved area beyond to extend the overall garden design.*

Lawn variations

Lawn types vary enormously, from the emerald, weed-free suburban plot to the wild flower meadow. The type you make will depend on your taste, the lawn's function and the character of the garden of which it is part. It is therefore necessary to be clear about what you want the lawn for.

Is it simply to be looked at, or will your lawn be a place for playing and lounging upon?

Once your decision is made, you can buy the appropriate seed, for today there is a great variety. There are fine grass seed mixes available that will produce a lawn beautiful to look at but difficult to maintain and easily damaged. Or there are coarse grass seed mixes that will develop into a hard-wearing lawn. (See p. 280.)

Wild garden meadow, *right. A handsome example of dog- or ox-eye daisy* (Chrysanthemum leucanthemum), *growing in rough grass. This grass is roughly mown, as if mowing hay, after the daisies have flowered in July.*

Grass of different lengths, *below. This garden has a mixture of mown and rough grass, with some color provided by clover* (Trifolium *sp.*). *While a fine, mown lawn suffers from drought in high summer, longer grass, and particularly clover, remains green.*

Mowing edges *When you are laying grass, either turf or seed, against a wall or at the bottom of steps, make a mowing edge along the base of the structure, just below grass level, so that you can cut over the edge and reach all the grass. Without this, you will either have to hand cut the grass at the edges or leave a permanent tuft.*

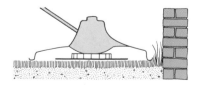

A useful lawn, *above. This "family" lawn is finely mown and carefully tended but composed of coarse grass to withstand hard wear.*

Plan for a mowing pattern, *right. You can mow patterns within a rough grass area, in this case between fruit and flowering trees. Within the rough grass plant a variety of bulbs.*

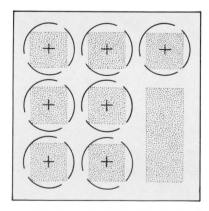

The establishment and proper maintenance of an all-grass lawn is a discipline of its own (see p. 256). You have the choice of using seed (see p. 280), which is relatively cheap to buy but costly in time while the seed is first growing, or turf, which is relatively expensive but fast to turn into a lawn.

Those with a small area to be covered, who do not want the chore of regular maintenance, the elderly or handicapped for example, and those without children, should consider other forms of ground cover planting. You will have seen in the section on establishing soft surfacing (see p. 131) how successful random planting in gravel can be. You can use the same technique of random planting within a growing framework. A beautiful clump of grass within a surround of low *Cotoneaster dammeri*, through which spring and autumn bulbs emerge, flower and then die down, can be very attractive. The natural form of this type of planting is the ivy (*Hedera* sp.) covering of a woodland floor, or the heath (*Erica* sp.) covering of heaths and moorlands. The technique can be used to plant decorative borders as well. The virtue of using either taller shrubs that sweep to the ground, like *Viburnum tinus* or *Hydrangea*

sp., or specific ground cover plants, is that they eliminate weeds, provided that you have first established the ground cover in clean ground. Weeds growing through ground cover are very difficult to remove.

Between the extremes of the lawn and informal ground cover planting, there are intermediate types of ground cover that can be walked upon occasionally. These include aromatic herbs that will release characteristic perfumes. Where climate permits, chamomile (*Anthemis* sp.) has been used as a ground cover planting since the Middle Ages. It was often employed to cover raised seating areas in traditional herb gardens and still can be in a full sun position. But chamomile tends to look bedraggled in winter and, while it can stand some frost, does not like being covered in snow for any length of time.

Mixed low-growing thymes are hardier and can create a rugged, aromatic ground cover, having waves of flower through it according to the species used. Both these ground coverings, however, need an open sunny position.

The various forms of *Ajuga* sp., though not traffic-proof, will grow easily anywhere and make excellent low ground cover. All

Roof garden treatment *Ground cover planting needs little thickness of soil, since sustenance usually comes to the plant through the multiple rootings of its runners. This makes them ideal for roof gardens, where weight is a critical factor. In this pattern English ivy* (Hedera helix) *is kept clipped to retain the plan's outline.* Rhododendron *sp. are planted through the ivy to provide color.* Pleached Platanus orientalis *surround two sides of the area.*

their leaves are purple or purple streaked. *Alchemilla mollis* becomes a wonderful summer carpet of green flowers with umbrella-shaped leaves that hold every drop of moisture. *Armeria maritima*, or thrift, is an alpine but makes dense evergreen cushions of foliage with rosy pink flowers in May and June. Various species of the genus *Berberis* have attractive flowers, foliage and berries, a good example being *Berberis thumbergii* 'Atropurpurea'. Within the wide range of cotoneasters, many are rampant and therefore useful as ground cover. Many will hang over a wall in a picturesque way. One of my favorite species is *Cotoneaster dammeri*, more particularly the cultivar 'Skogholm'. Cotoneasters will all grow under trees or shrubs or in the open.

Use *Dianthus* sp. to underplant roses, but remember that they prefer a sunny position in a well-drained soil. The prettily leaved genus *Epimedium* will grow in most situations and has divided, evergreen glossy leaves. Heaths (*Erica* sp.) can be grown on their own in a special area of the garden; they are better shown with other heaths than grouped with ground cover plants. They prefer full sun and nearly all hate lime, so are characteristic of a particular soil.

For a sunny bank, try the low-growing forms of the genus *Genista*, most of which are covered in bright broom-like yellow flowers in early summer. While usually used in the front line of the mixed border, cranesbill (*Geranium* sp.) makes an excellent and colorful ground cover, with pretty leaves in sun or light shade.

All the ivies are excellent ground cover plants in any situation. Once established, however, they can swamp everything else. The same can be said of the ground covering species of *Hypericum*, but both are useful for that corner in which nothing else will grow.

Horizontal-growing coniferous juniper makes good ground cover and grows remarkably fast. So does *Lamium maculatum*, a nettle, which not only romps sideways but will also work its way into shrubs. In hot places such as the southern States of the USA, *Liriope muscari*, with foliage like a rush and grape hyacinth-type flowers, can be used to cover large flat areas to make striking, but not walkable, lawns.

Lonicera pileata is a favorite evergreen plant of mine, having a pleasant spraying shape though no flowers that you would recognize as being from the genus. *Pachysandra terminalis* (Japanese spurge) is an almost prostrate evergreen carpeter and is a classic ground cover plant. For the wild area of your garden, the golden star (*Chrysoganum virginianum*) covers the ground, its bright green leaves dotted with yellow daisies from spring to late summer. It does well in any ordinary soil, including wet land. For a very shady situation, consider *Sarcococca humilis*, which is dull, shrubby and evergreen but has the most delightfully scented white flowers in spring. Sweet woodruff (*Galium odoratum*) forms low clumps of greenery with distinctive whorled leaves.

I personally find the much favoured *Vinca* genus invasive and ugly as ground cover, though there is no denying the beauty of its blue periwinkle flowers. Avoid *Vinca major* at all costs as it is just too smothering; *Vinca minor* is tolerable if you cut it back in spring after flowering to encourage bushiness.

Useful ground cover, *right. This ground cover planting within a scree or alpine garden has Erica sp. in the left foreground and a low Euonymus fortunei beyond. The central gold mass is of creeping Jenny (Lysimachia sp.), beyond which are marjoram and a low juniper. Low blue gentians appear at random.*
Far right, Hypericum calycinum makes striking ground cover on a bank retaining a flight of stone steps.

A ground cover planting design
This plan and projection is for a south facing courtyard, enclosed within three walls. "Spot planting" of feature shrubs punctuate the garden but most of the planting is ground cover. This provides year round interest with flower colour but more especially with texture and leaf shape. A design such as this needs careful maintenance to ensure that the plant masses remain separated and in the forms that the designer intended. A pattern of stepping stones helps to divide up the planted areas.

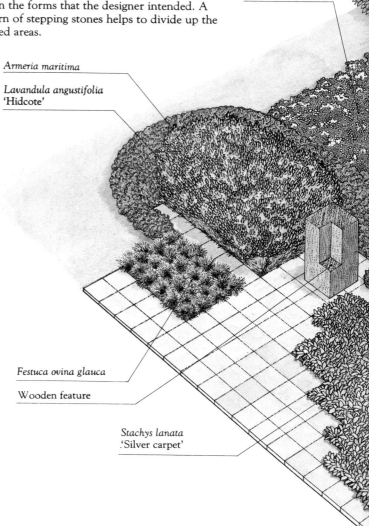

Prunus laurocerasus 'Zabeliana'

Rosa 'Sea Foam'

Armeria maritima

Lavandula angustifolia 'Hidcote'

Festuca ovina glauca

Wooden feature

Stachys lanata 'Silver carpet'

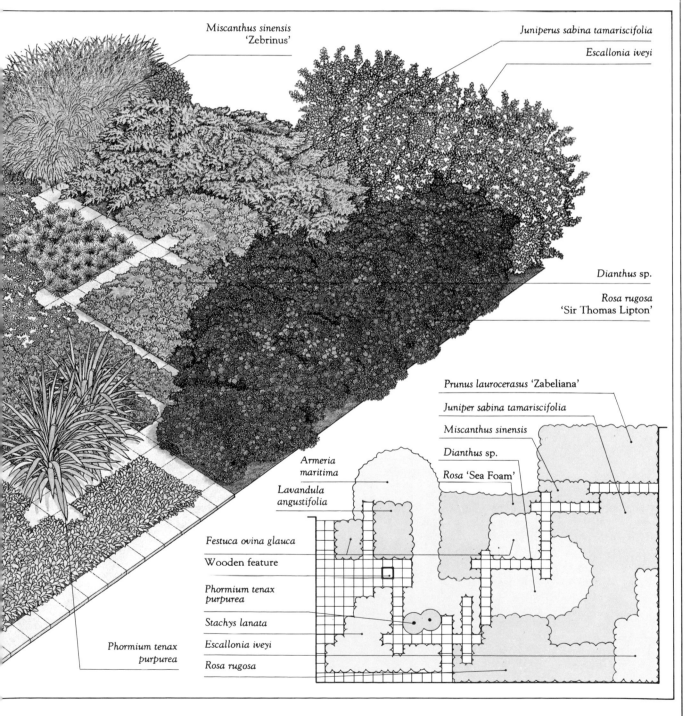

Miscanthus sinensis 'Zebrinus'

Juniperus sabina tamariscifolia

Escallonia iveyi

Dianthus sp.

Rosa rugosa 'Sir Thomas Lipton'

Prunus laurocerasus 'Zabeliana'

Juniper sabina tamariscifolia

Miscanthus sinensis

Dianthus sp.

Rosa 'Sea Foam'

Armeria maritima

Lavandula angustifolia

Festuca ovina glauca

Wooden feature

Phormium tenax purpurea

Stachys lanata

Escallonia iveyi

Rosa rugosa

Phormium tenax purpurea

Plants for shade

It is often thought that shade is one of the greatest problems of urban gardening for in cities and towns plants must often grow under overhanging trees or within the shadow of buildings and walls. In fact, there is quite a range of plants that have adapted to shade by developing larger leaves (often at the expense of brilliant flower color) and it is this characteristic that can be used to make strong planting designs.

There are two sorts of shady garden area, determined by location: those that are damp, perhaps getting no sun at all and subject to drip from overhead trees; and dry areas, which, due to dense overhanging plants that do not allow drips through, are sheltered from rain.

Most of the maples (*Acer* sp.) do exceptionally well in moist, shady conditions; use the snake bark forms for winter interest in addition to the usual Japanese type. Alder (*Alnus* sp.) does well, as do all forms of thorn (*Crataegus* sp.), poplars (*Populus* sp.) and willows (*Salix* sp.). The bird cherry (*Prunus*

Shaded urban garden, *left. An overhanging laurel (*Prunus laurocerasus*) shades this urban garden so a bold-leaved Fatsia japonica has been grouped with ferns against a small-leaved bamboo. The ferns are Athyrium filix-femina with the far smaller-leaved Polystichum setiferum 'Divisilobum'.*

Damp shade *Far left, Anemone japonica and the tender Aspidistra elatior make up a summer grouping with a stone birdbath against a background of Hedera sp. The green ground cover plant is Helxine sp., which not only tolerates but requires dampness.*
Left, massed Hosta undulata 'Variegata' make a striking composition with osmunda fern beneath Fatsia japonica. The plant to the left, at the base of the archway, is Helleborus corsicus.

Shade planting with a Japanese flavor *The
planting plan of this small rear garden reflects the
shaded conditions and makes a virtue of them.
Bamboo, Japanese maple and ferns create a leafy
scene beyond the simple sliding glass doors with a
distinct Japanese flavor. The simple wooden
decking and the sand bed add to the effect. The
encroaching bamboo is desirable but it will have to
be restrained to prevent it overwhelming everything
else, which it will do quickly.*

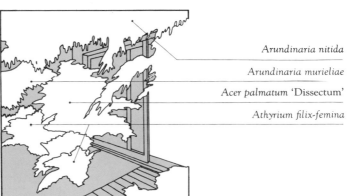

Arundinaria nitida

Arundinaria murieliae

Acer palmatum 'Dissectum'

Athyrium filix-femina

padus) flourishes, and so does *Cercidyphyllum japonicum*, a beautiful spring and autumn foliage tree.

On a smaller scale, from among shrubby subjects, goat's beard (*Aruncus sylvester*) will thrive and put on a huge show of creamy yellow flowers each summer. In a sheltered location, camellias thrive in moist shade and in mild winter climates are rewarding in both leaf and flower. They prefer neutral through to acid soils. Try *Clethra* sp. for white flowers with a seductive scent.

A hardy stand-by for damp shade conditions is the whole range of *Cornus* sp., which are good in leaf and retain attractive colored stems throughout winter. The large-leaved *Fatsia japonica*, for mild winter regions only, thrives in moist shade, putting on a mass of green flowers in late summer. For late winter flowers that stud their bare stems, consider witch-hazel (*Hamamelis* sp.), whose scented, twisted flower heads are long-lasting and immune to frost. Hydrangeas are essential for late summer interest in shade. Plant the gentle flowered lacecap varieties rather than the more common full-headed types.

Privet (*Ligustrum* sp.) should not be overlooked. There are many attractive large-leaved forms, and even the golden form of the common *Ligustrum ovalifolium*, when left untrimmed, is spectacularly bright throughout winter. Another often-despised plant, but which comes into its own in shade, is cherry laurel (*Prunus laurocerasus*).

Among the perennials, my favorites for shade include *Helleborus* sp. for early spring flowering, *Hosta* sp. and the dramatic leaves of *Rheum palmatum* 'Rubrum', a sort of decorative rhubarb.

Commonly-used ground cover plants for damp shade include *Hedera hibernica*, *Pachysandra* and *Vinca* sp. Many of the bamboos, being hardy and lovers of moisture, are excellent for this type of shade and will even succeed in very chalky soils. While one of the joys of bamboo is the sound of wind rustling through its fronds, it does not, in fact, like an open, windy situation. Once established, however, bamboos are some of the most beautiful and elegant of all evergreens and their height and forms vary considerably. Make your selection from the large genera of *Arundinaria* or *Phyllostachys*.

There is increasing interest in the hardy ferns – and with good reason, for most are easy to grow, are not fussy about soil, and prefer the cool, light-shaded, moist conditions on the north side of many gardens.

The range of plants suitable for a dry, shady location is smaller but, among trees, you can choose from the genera *Caragana*, *Gleditsia* and *Robinia* if you avoid the golden forms. Among shrubs are *Amelanchia laevis* for spring and summer interest and

many forms of *Berberis*. Sea buckthorn (*Hippophae rhamnoides*) grows fast and has striking gray foliage. Flowering currants (*Ribes* sp.) flourish in light, dry shade, as do elders (*Sambucus* sp.).

Ground cover plants for dry shade include many of the large-leaved *Bergenia* sp. and perennial blue *Brunnera macrophylla* that flower at about the same time. *Lamium* sp., though rampant, make excellent cover, as does *Lonicera pileata*, which is shrubby.

Many grasses grow well in dry shade. Most are easy to cultivate and many are evergreen. Pampas grass (*Cortaderia selloana*) is a standard favorite and thrives in dry shade, as do forms of *Festuca* and *Luzula* sp.

Grass and bamboos
Top, Cortaderia solloana, *a popular pampas grass. A much more compact form,* Cortaderia pumila, *is ideal for the smaller gardens.*
Above, Arundinaria viridistriata, *an unusual bamboo with rich yellow and green variegated leaves borne on erect, purplish canes. This plant can reach 2 m but shade stunts its growth.*

A planting design for dry shade

Plants suitable for dry shade are less numerous than those which prefer moisture; selecting species is therefore more a question of finding what will tolerate the conditions rather than what will flourish in it. The scheme planned on the right is for a corner of a house beneath an old pear or apple tree. To enliven what might be a dull area, plants have been selected for their gold leaves or flowers, with other foliage to complement them. A dark corner such as this will benefit from regular applications of organic compost, which will help to hold moisture in the dry soil. Otherwise, the pear tree will tend to extract much of the moisture and nutrients from the soil, leaving it impoverished.

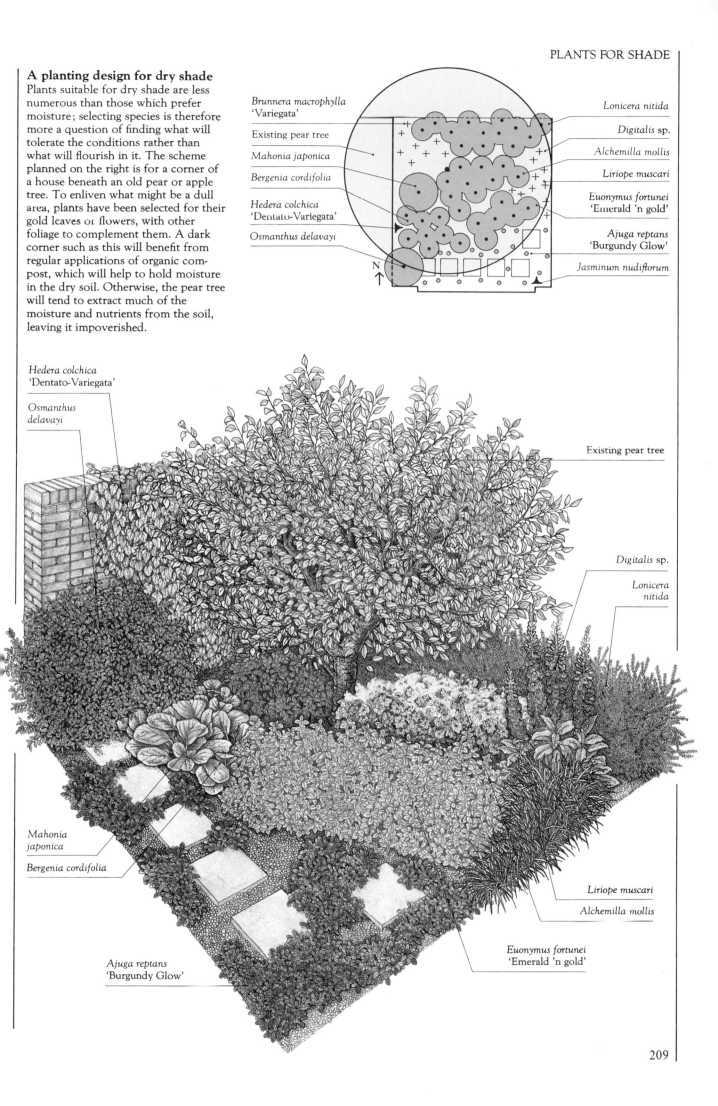

Brunnera macrophylla 'Variegata'

Existing pear tree

Mahonia japonica

Bergenia cordifolia

Hedera colchica 'Dentato-Variegata'

Osmanthus delavayi

N

Lonicera nitida

Digitalis sp.

Alchemilla mollis

Liriope muscari

Euonymus fortunei 'Emerald 'n gold'

Ajuga reptans 'Burgundy Glow'

Jasminum nudiflorum

Hedera colchica 'Dentato-Variegata'

Osmanthus delavayi

Existing pear tree

Digitalis sp.

Lonicera nitida

Mahonia japonica

Bergenia cordifolia

Liriope muscari

Alchemilla mollis

Euonymus fortunei 'Emerald 'n gold'

Ajuga reptans 'Burgundy Glow'

Bulbs

All too often we think of bulbs (a term I use to include corms, tubers and rhizomes) as spring features only, but in fact it is possible to have them in bloom throughout the year.

Plant bulbs either "naturally", that is as if scattered in drifts in grass, or incorporate them with mixed planting, where their dying leaves will not be so obvious. The secret to their correct use depends on their natural habitat, how they grow there and on their shape. Some, such as hyacinths and *Galtonia* sp., have a formality that needs to be offset by other plants, while others, such as *Narcissus* sp. and snowdrop (*Galanthus* sp.), are never successful within a border and need to be planted in a more natural way.

Winter and spring-flowing bulbs dominate planting areas during their flowering season, when they announce the demise of winter. In the British Isles, for example, the winter aconite (*Eranthis hyemalis*) and snowdrop appear as early as December. These are followed by crocus, then early narcissus such as the cultivar 'February Gold'. Anemones begin to show soon afterwards and are followed by other daffodils, *Chionodoxa luciliae* and grape hyacinths (*Muscari* sp.). Hyacinths are well-suited to tubs and formal beds, as are tulips. I love the lily-flowered types of tulip for their flopping informality and some of the parrot tulips for their bizarre colors. In early summer come the bright-colored forms of Dutch iris, followed by the architectural forms of *Allium* sp. and *Ixia* sp. from South Africa. Majestic crown imperials (*Fritillaria imperialis*) are also magnificent.

In high summer there are the white hyacinths (*Galtonia candicans*), all the lilies and the simple butterfly gladioli. Forms of autumn crocus then brighten the dying garden.

If you want bulbs to emerge through low shrubs in planted areas, place them in casual groups rather than regular, circular patches; they look more natural this way.

To plant bulbs in natural-looking drifts in lawn, scatter them casually across the growing area, as shown opposite, and then plant them where they land. Plant to the correct depth, of course, but do not space the bulbs out or you will lose the random effect. The late daffodils will not have finished flowering when you start to mow your lawn and will need a further six weeks after flowering to allow their foliage to die down before you cut the grass over them, for until their leaves have dried out bulbs are making their growth for the next year. You will therefore have an area of longer, rougher grass containing dying leaves within your lawn. It is important that the outline of this longer grass is part of the overall pattern of your garden.

Bulbs in containers, *above. Bulbous plants grouped in pots can make a bright splash of spring colour. This grouping includes narcissus and iris.*

Massed bulbs, *below. Mixed daffodils have been "naturalized" in grass in this English garden. Such profusion takes a number of years.*

Scatter planting
Within a prescribed outline, distribute your bulbs casually and then plant them where they have fallen. In this way you will achieve a pleasantly natural effect when they appear and later flower. Plant bulbs to the correct depth either with a special bulb planter or with a spade. Dig the spade in, lever up a section of turf while you put in the bulb and then firm down the earth.

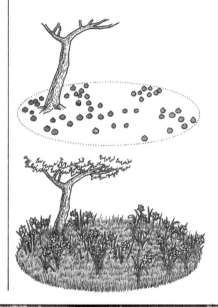

Unusual bulbs *All too often gardeners regard bulbs solely as spring plants, overlooking the contribution they can make to a garden through the year. Non-spring flowering examples include Allium sp., right, and Lilium odysseum, below. Some lilies require special treatment but others are easy to grow and will make an attractive, scented addition to your garden.*

Patterns with bulbs
To alleviate the untidy tufted appearance of dying bulbous-plant leaves on a lawn, plant your bulbs within carefully planned areas that can be left as long grass. About six weeks after the flowers have withered, the leaves will die down. You will then be able to mow that part of your lawn as well as the unplanted areas if desired, or maintain different grass lengths. After grass has been allowed to grow and seed, do not try to cut it close in one operation. Gradually reduce the height of cut.

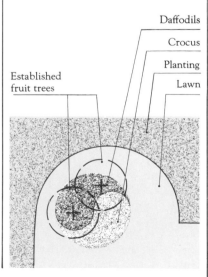

Daffodils
Crocus
Planting
Lawn
Established
fruit trees

211

Climbing plants

Plants "climb" in one of several ways. Some have aerial roots which adhere to a structure, like ivies (*Hedera*) and the climbing hydrangea (*Hydrangea anomala petiolaris*). Others cling by tendrils, a well-known example being the grape (*Vitis*). Other vines that climb by tendrils are Virginia creeper (*Parthenocissus quinquefolia*), clematis (leaf stalks become tendrils) and passion-flower (*Passiflora caerulea*). Boston-ivy (*Parthenocissus tricuspidata*) clings by means of rootlets attached to tendrils. Many vines, like the honeysuckles (*Lonicera*), wisteria, silver lace vine (*Polygonum aubertii*), fiveleaf akebia (*A. quinata*) and the rampant kudzu vine (*Pueraria lobata*), are twiners. Climbing and rambler roses can only support themselves by pushing their long branches in among a host plant or through a trellis.

Another category of "climbers" includes pyracantha and California-lilac (*Ceanothus* sp.) that like the shelter of a wall or fence and can be trained to grow against either support and become sturdy.

A few climbers are evergreen and these are ideal where screening is needed. For the South and other mild climate regions, there is trumpet vine (*Bignonia capreolata*), madeira vine (*Boussingaultia baselloides*) and Armand clematis (*Clematis armandii*). In the north there are varieties of winter-creeper (*Euonymus fortunei*) and ivy (*Hedera helix*). Hall's honeysuckle (*Lonicera japonica* 'Halliana') has evergreen or semi-evergreen foliage and *L. japonica* 'Aureo-reticulata' has yellow-veined leaves.

Remember that once vines have covered your fence, they will not necessarily stop growing. One of the fastest growing is silver lace vine which grows as much as 6–9 m (20–30 ft) in a season, quickly smothering its support with a froth of green-white flowers. A personal favorite is the non-fruiting *Vitis coignetiae*, another fast grower with huge leaves that change color in autumn to brilliant orange and crimson shades.

Discreet support, *below. The profusion of planting in this small town garden is dominated by a climbing rose. Climbing roses must be supported, although supports can be easily camouflaged. In this example, the support is detachable so that the wall behind can be painted easily.*

Versatile ivies, *above. This photograph shows the adaptability of ivy. In one case it has been allowed to ramble through a juniper tree, while in another it can be seen clinging to a wall. The varieties are* Hedera helix *'Buttercup' and 'Caenwoodiana'.*

Climbers on frontages

The supports that you choose for climbers on a house front should not dominate or be at odds with the symmetry of your frontage. Also match the scale of the support to the scale of the climber – a bold support needs bold foliage, while a fine tracery of leaves needs a fine support. Against masonry walls, consider running wires, supported on "vine eyes", parallel with the mortar courses. A wooden lattice should coincide with the proportions of windows and door-frames.

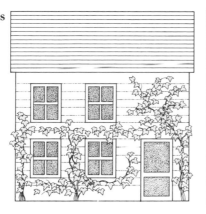

Above right, horizontal wires on "vine eyes". Below right, squared trellis is spaced to match windows and door.

Wall adornment, *above. Much of the charm of the old brick walls, above, is created by their climbing plants – in the top example, a climbing rose and a honeysuckle (Lonicera sp.) on the wall above. Both are attached to imperceptible wires that run parallel with the courses of the wall. The climbing rose will be detached from its support for reshaping (see p. 258) while the new shoots of honey-suckle are tucked under the wires as they grow.*

Climbers at night *The three-dimensional shapes of established climbing plants make them particularly good subjects for artificial lighting. Here, a variety of climbers combine with a house and make the floral walls of an enchanting seating area.*

Water plants

Water plants, like plants growing in normal ground, have characteristics that reflect their location and specific needs. The amount of moisture they require, for example, will vary, some liking only damp roots, others, such as certain reeds and rushes, grow in 500 mm (20 in) of water. There are also aquatic plants that are mostly submerged, allowing only their leaves to float on the surface of the water. Water lilies are typical of this group. Still others are fully submerged and act as oxygenators in water.

The condition that most affects aquatic plants is whether the water is running or still. Soil content is not of such vital importance as the depth at which the rooting medium is set to hold the plant roots. These two categories – nature of water and depth of planting – divide the range of water plants into two groups.

Because aquatics are not subject to the same needs as plants on dry land, many feeding from the water itself, they have adapted their form of growth; thus, they often have large leaves (as do those of plants living in shade) and it is this characteristic that makes them so attractive in planting compositions. There are many that grow horizontally, like water lilies; others have huge rhubarb-type leaves, such as *Rheum* sp., the decorative form of rhubarb, and the larger *Gunnera* sp. (suitable for mild areas). In contrast, some aquatics have leaves that are vertical and spiky. It is the contrast of vertical with horizontal that can make water planting so dramatic – consider, for example, the simple arrangement of a weeping willow over a sheet of still water.

The most effective groupings in water tend to be sparse and composed of two or three types of plant only. Look at natural water planting, and this point will become immediately obvious. Bold drifts of one subject against a mass of another, with areas of clear water between, offset each other. This is normal planting design procedure, but gardeners are often disconcerted by the presence of water.

Before choosing your plant material for use with water, decide where the plant is to grow and the depth of soil and water you are allowing it. You may have to build a ledge of

Complementing a basin feature *Water is recycled by a submerged pump into the stone basin and then the pond. Plants include arrowhead* Sagittaria lancifolia, *water lilies* (Nymphaea *sp.) and* Potamogeton densus, *notable for its elongated and close-packed leaves.*

specific height to suit some marginal plants. You can, of course, alter the height of plants in water when they have been planted in plastic containers by raising or lowering the container on bricks. These containers are specially made, with open lattice sides, and dark-colored so that they will not be seen when submerged. Larger, boggy areas should be planted to look natural, but remember to stick to simple groupings.

You must decide whether you want a truly natural look for your water planting or not, for decorative plants and ducks do not go together. Remember, too, that some weeds and floating plants become invasive in certain areas, so study local conditions when making planting decisions. The correct time of year for planting most aquatic plants is in April, May or June, as plant life is just starting to grow vigorously. By the following winter your water plants will have established good enough root anchorage to survive cold weather except for tropical water lilies.

Water lilies will make a great deal of growth in the course of one season if planted in good garden soil. Without this, the leaves will be stunted and plants will not flower. Ideally, the mix should be made up of six parts of good loam well mixed with one part of cow manure or coarse bonemeal. When the roots have been planted in loam and manure within containers, spread a layer of pure loam over it, then a layer of gravel to anchor the fine content when it is sunk into water. This ensures that the cow manure will not rise to the surface to decompose, foul the water and poison the fish.

Submerged oxygenators can be planted in pure loam, free of manure. Do not use dredgings from the pool, for this has little

Mature planting, *above. The planting in this attractive pond includes water lilies and reed mace (Typha latifolia), with Iris × germanica, which flowers in June, in the foreground.*

Early bloom, *left. These yellow-flowering marsh marigolds (Caltha palustris) brighten the side of the pond early in the year and often blossom again in the autumn. The variegated leaves are those of Iris sibirica 'Variegata.'*

Water planting methods

Different types of water plant (see p. 278) require different planting techniques so that they are set at the right depth. A built-in shelf at the side of a pool is an ideal site for marginal plants. In a pool with a well-balanced habitat for pond life, you can plant in soil established beneath sand and cobbles on the pool floor. Planting in a proprietary basket (as shown on p. 216) is more convenient. You can use blocks to adjust the height of the planting baskets.

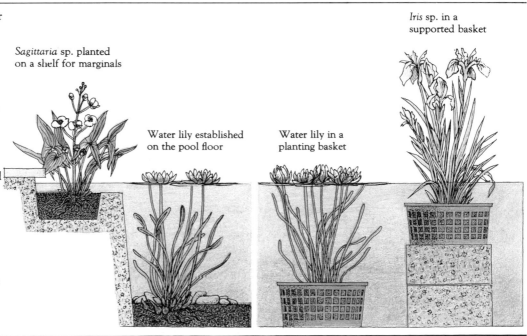

Sagittaria sp. planted on a shelf for marginals

Water lily established on the pool floor

Water lily in a planting basket

Iris sp. in a supported basket

food value and not even a weed will grow on it, as witness the heaps of uncultivated mud often seen by the banks of ditches and canals.

On receiving a new consignment of plants, remove any dead or broken foliage and lightly trim the roots. Often the remaining leaves will die off but new ones will appear in a few days.

When planting is completed, patience is needed filling the pool; it must be done gradually. The shock of cold water to plants that have already suffered from being moved during their growing period can prove fatal. To minimize the risk, fill the pool slowly and at first leave the water level only deep enough to cover the plant crowns. Then leave the pool for a few days before adding more water. To avoid disturbing dirt or mud, fill the pool by directing the flow from a hose into a plant pot set on the bottom. Do not run the water too quickly. When you are introducing plants into a full pool, lower them to their final position, if it is to be deep, over a period of days by altering brick heights standing beneath their containers.

New ponds and pools inevitably take time to clear, for you have to wait until the correct balance of plant life to fish, snails and the volume of water is achieved. This may take as long as a full season. Do not keep emptying your pool to clean it, since on refilling the whole cycle has to start again.

Water planter *Water lily ready to be introduced into the pond.*

Gravel

Rich compost

Hessian lining

Marginal planting *The bold leaves of Rodgersia sp. make a background to this boggy planting that includes* Primula japonica *in the foreground,* Astilbe sp. *on the left, and a form of* Polygonum.

Pondside grouping *Bamboos and grasses are not dependent on a boggy site but their vertical shapes can be very effective when planted in association with water, as in this example. Rushes (*Butomus sp.*) and* Scirpus sp. *– true water plants – complete the pondside grouping.*

216

Herbs

Herbs, whether shrubby or perennial, are useful decorative additions to a mixed planting in a garden. Certain herbs may also be included in your list of decorative trees, for bay (*Laurus nobilis*), myrtle (*Myrtus communis*) and witch-hazel (*Hamamelis* sp.) will reach such proportions. There are also good arguments for having a herb garden on its own. For anyone with a small area in an open and sunny position, herbs are ideal: they are not over fussy as to soil quality, they have decorative foliage and are more or less fragrant. Those that are not hardy can be grown as summer additions, if planted annually in the spring.

Perhaps more important than their decorative value are the culinary properties of herbs. Their value as an additive is being increasingly appreciated in times of tasteless packaged food. Certain herbs, of course, are classic additions to certain foods in different parts of the world: rosemary in Provence, sweet basil in Italy, marjoram in Greece and cumin in Persia.

In the East, spices are widely used for their medicinal properties. Even in the West, the use of herbs as medicine is becoming more widespread with the renewed interest in homeopathy as an alternative to the use of synthetic drugs and surgery. Herbs may be used in tissanes which can be sleep-inducive, tranquilizing, painkilling or purgative.

Herbs may also be used dried in *pot pourri* to scent your house in a natural way. The essential oils of many herbs can be extracted and compounded to produce scents and body oils, using the crushed root of orris (*Iris × germanica florentina*) as a stabilizing agent.

Herbs are a vital component in the increasingly popular treatment known as aromatherapy.

With all these healing and restorative properties, it is not surprising that over the centuries herbs have gathered a certain amount of myth, with extravagant claims made on their behalf. However, modern scientific methods of analysis are indicating that these claims are not entirely groundless and they are being newly quantified.

Many of the plants we commonly include in mixed planting are, in fact, herbs, including specimens for most types of location, such as *Gaultheria procumbens*, St John's wort (*Hypericum perforatum*), *Rosa damascena*, *Rosa gallica*, hollyhock (*Alcea rosea*), sunflower (*Helianthus annuus*), juniper (*Juniperus communis*) and one of the brooms (*Cytisus scoparius*).

Most herbs prefer an open, sunny position in which to grow, with moderately good, neutral soil. Mint, chives and parsley, however, will grow perfectly well in part shade.

In lighter, dappled shade you can grow angelica, celery (*Apium graveolens dulce*) and chervil (*Anthriscus cerefolium*). All these herbs are for use in the kitchen.

Many herbal books suggest that you grow your herbs within strict, formalized patterns edged with box, as was the practice in medieval times. Anyone who has grown herbs, however, will realize how invasive they can be, and it seems a waste of effort to be constantly restraining them to conform to a rigid design. The glory of a herb garden is its profusion, alive with the hum of bees on a hot summer day. Therefore build up your herb garden planting plan much along the lines of your general garden planting. Firstly, consider which herbs are deciduous and which evergreen; then ascertain their ultimate heights, color of foliage and form of

Herb border *A large box (*Buxus* sp.) backs this arrangement of herbs, which includes the gray-leaved curry plant (*Helichrysum angustifolium*), sage (*Salvia officinalis*), thyme (*Thymus* sp.), winter savory (*Satureia montana*) and a large purple plantain (*Plantago* sp.). Herbs will provide neat clumps of plant material, as in this example, provided that you have managed their autumnal trim and thin.*

growth. Consider their flowers but remember that while many herbs become laden with flowers, these are transitory and their other attributes will be dominant.

Eye-catching features can be useful foils in a herb garden. In the design below, changes of level are used, comprising a raised bed and a step. Another focal point is a simple pot feature. This might as easily be a piece of sculpture, or even an attractive bee-hive in which you could in fact keep bees.

You will need hard-surfaced access to your herbs as they need clipping, dividing and picking regularly. This surfacing can, however, be interspersed or bordered with low-growing thymes or chamomile to scent your way. An alternative is to devote a narrow border to herbs so that you have access along its length.

I do not include mints (*Mentha* sp.), horse radish (*Armoracia rusticana*) and comfrey (*Symphytum officinale*) among general herb

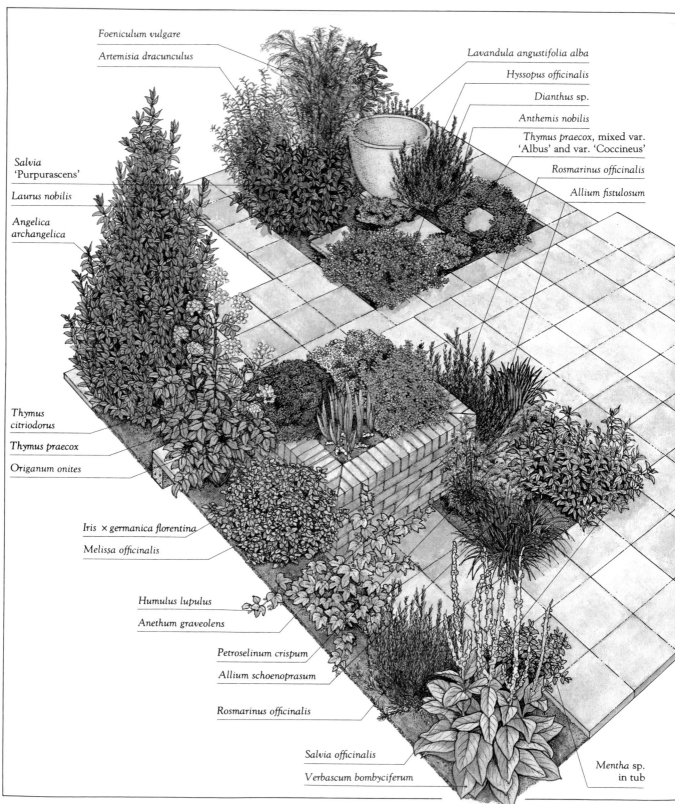

Foeniculum vulgare

Artemisia dracunculus

Lavandula angustifolia alba

Hyssopus officinalis

Dianthus sp.

Anthemis nobilis

Thymus praecox, mixed var.
'Albus' and var. 'Coccineus'

Rosmarinus officinalis

Allium fistulosum

Salvia 'Purpurascens'

Laurus nobilis

Angelica archangelica

Thymus citriodorus

Thymus praecox

Origanum onites

Iris × germanica florentina

Melissa officinalis

Humulus lupulus

Anethum graveolens

Petroselinum crispum

Allium schoenoprasum

Rosmarinus officinalis

Salvia officinalis

Verbascum bombyciferum

Mentha sp.
in tub

planting because they are so invasive. For these herbs, make a separate collection in individual tubs. Their foliage and flower colors are well worthwhile. Apple and Egyptian mint (*Mentha suaveolens*) are particularly handsome. I also keep the 'Dark Opal' form of sweet basil (*Ocimum basilicum*) in a separate pot as it likes a very hot position, is annual and can be kept quite dry.

Your herb garden will need regular attention, particularly the cutting back of dead flowers. Plants such as chives need to be divided and replanted on a regular basis (see p. 259) to retain shape and vigor.

Garden designs are often successful because they have a single underlying theme. Herbs can provide such a theme while offering a range of plant material that is interesting and useful.

A herb garden design

The herbal planting illustrated here would fit into any open garden, either as an item on its own or merging into the general garden planting around it. Alternatively, it might form a terrace, facing south if possible so as to be in full sun. The pattern is made up of three small beds, each between 2 and 3 m (6–10 ft) square. One bed is raised 450 mm (18 in) within a brick wall. Overall pattern is dominated by eight woody herbs: two *Rosmarinus officinalis* and a bay tree (*Laurus nobilis*, not hardy in cold climates) and sages (*Salvia* sp.), for all these are evergreen. In the growing season the planting is backed by the tall spikes of, first, the stately, yellow-green-flowering Angelica (*Angelica archangelica*) and, later, by lemon-flowering gray mullein (*Verbascum bombiciferum*).

An eye-catching herb is the Welsh onion (*Allium fistulosum*), whose spikey shape is repeated at a lower level by chives (*Allium schoenoprasum*). These are contrasted with clumps of parsley (*Petroselinum crispum*) and annual dill (*Anethum graveolens*). In the raised bed, the composition is of shrubby thyme species with orris (*Iris × germanica florentina*), bushy pot marjoram (*Origanum onites*) and low, golden forms of thyme.

The largest bed, on the lower level of the garden, has stepping stones within it to match the main paving. These support an attractive pot with a bold, simple form that contrasts with the tall lovage (*Levisticum officinale*) behind, the adjacent feathery leaves of fennel (*Foeniculum vulgare*) and intense blue flowers of hyssop (*Hyssopus officinalis*).

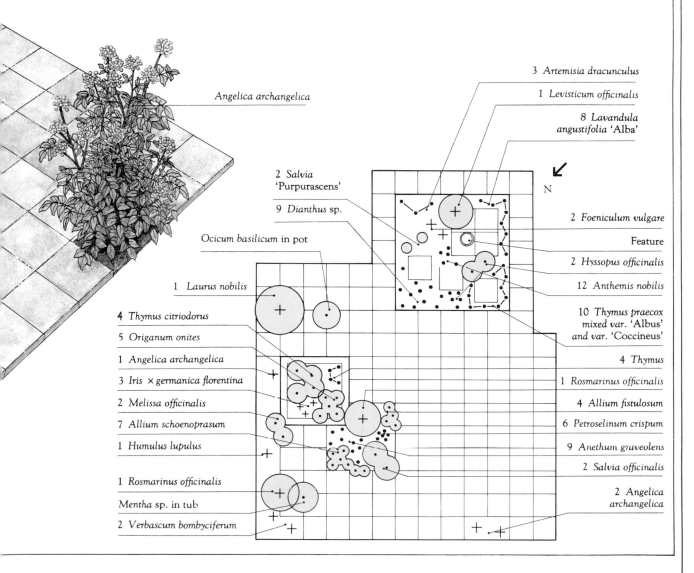

Angelica archangelica

3 *Artemisia dracunculus*

1 *Levisticum officinalis*

8 *Lavandula angustifolia* 'Alba'

2 *Salvia* 'Purpurascens'

9 *Dianthus* sp.

Ocium basilicum in pot

N

2 *Foeniculum vulgare*

Feature

2 *Hyssopus officinalis*

12 *Anthemis nobilis*

1 *Laurus nobilis*

10 *Thymus praecox* mixed var. 'Albus' and var. 'Coccineus'

4 *Thymus citriodorus*

5 *Origanum onites*

1 *Angelica archangelica*

3 *Iris × germanica florentina*

2 *Melissa officinalis*

7 *Allium schoenoprasum*

1 *Humulus lupulus*

1 *Rosmarinus officinalis*

Mentha sp. in tub

2 *Verbascum bombyciferum*

4 *Thymus*

1 *Rosmarinus officinalis*

4 *Allium fistulosum*

6 *Petroselinum crispum*

9 *Anethum graveolens*

2 *Salvia officinalis*

2 *Angelica archangelica*

Vegetables

Most people hide the vegetable garden as far from the house as possible because they do not think it decorative. I disagree. Vegetables may not be flowery but well-organized rows looking healthy and green can make a fine display. To have the vegetable patch adjacent to the kitchen door is also extremely convenient, provided there is an open, sunny space for it.

However, urban dwellers, if they have gardens at all, have little space for vegetables, so a rented allotment at the edge of the town may be the next best thing. In the British Isles there is a movement towards self-sufficiency and to have an allotment now is not solely associated with saving money but also with growing pure food. An allotment on the European continent has never been a place just to produce foodcrops. Individual plots usually have a small, carefully designed building incorporated within them, the style and scale of the structure varying from country to country. In parts of Germany, for example, the allotment is a private garden and the tool shed also acts as a weekend retreat in summer. Restrictions are placed, however, on electricity and other services to ensure that the structure is not used as a second home. The areas surrounding these "chalets" are usually given over to a combination of vegetables, flowers for cutting and herbs for culinary use. Unfortunately, the USA has always lagged behind other countries in community garden projects.

Even a small garden can make a productive vegetable and fruit area, for most families need only what may be called "convenience" vegetables – that is, summer salad material, snap beans, some tomato plants and herbs. If you have the space, larger crops, such as squash, broccoli, cucumbers and corn,

Fruits of the earth *The object of vegetable gardening, which is often arduous, is to provide fresh home produce, preferably grown in soil enriched only with organic materials.*

A vegetable garden
This garden plot is approximately 10 m square (107 ft²) and contains not only vegetables but a herb bed (raised for easy cutting), a compost area, a work bench and potting shed, all arranged to be both practical and attractive. Given the space, two more vegetable areas of similar size would allow greater flexibility of cultivation and a wider range of vegetables but you can manage perfectly well in such a limited space with careful planning. The cultivation area in the foreground is surrounded by a low, clipped hedge of santolina, rosemary and box, an arrangement that would look appropriate even in a small town garden. Paths, edging and raised beds are all constructed in the same brick. Softwood fencing has been used to support a corrugated, clear vinyl roof, supported additionally by pointed metal verticals.

Summer crop bed
This area includes climbing beans and salad vegetables, such as lettuce, radish, miniature tomatoes and cucumbers.

Covered potting area and store
A roofed area can be used very successfully as a place for sowing into seed trays and potting. If you are careful to clean and oil your tools after use (see p. 248) so that they are protected against damp, you can also use this area for their storage. The corner structure also gives the vegetable area a permanent shape independent of the growing crops.

can be sited elsewhere, together with a soft fruit area perhaps, if desired.

But be warned before you embark on making a vegetable garden. However enthusiastic you are there are practicalities to face. If you wish to be self-sufficient through the cultivation of your garden, the planting, care and harvesting of food crops must dominate the time you spend outside. To provide sufficient vegetables for an entire family throughout the year requires an area larger than most gardeners possess. Furthermore, the labor is heavy, the time needed considerable if the vegetable garden is to be kept fully productive and in good order, and to be truly organic you will need space and time to maintain a compost cycle. The resulting vegetables are therefore not cheap. Most people,

of course, do not price their own time and it is certainly true that home-grown vegetables are more wholesome and fresher than those bought from a shop. A deep-freeze is a valuable piece of equipment for anyone growing more than the minimum, since whole crops invariably come to fruition at the same time and you can end up giving away the majority of your produce.

It is impossible to estimate the ideal size for a vegetable area, for it will depend on the size of your family, what you want to grow and how much time you have to tend it. However, a vegetable garden measuring 335 sq m (3600 ft²) should meet requirements of a family of four. The location of the garden will determine the plants that will grow best; the balmier the climate, the

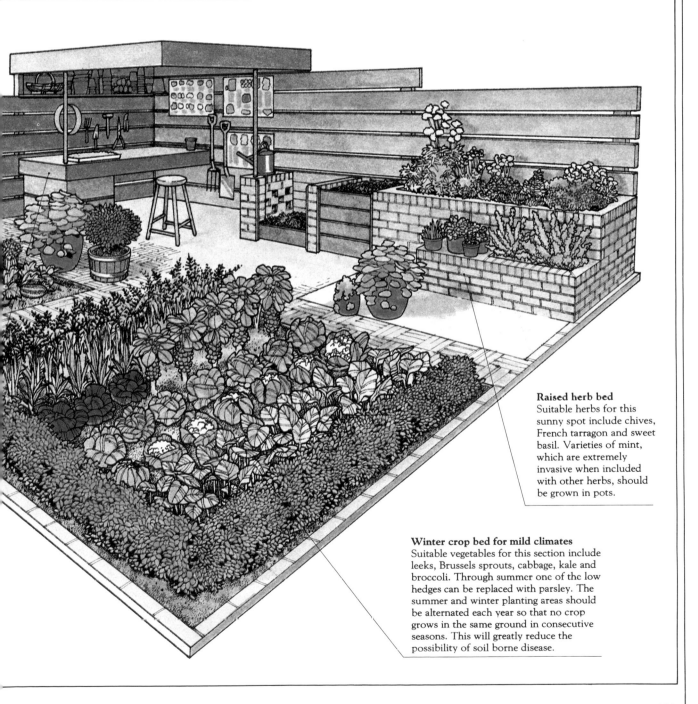

Raised herb bed
Suitable herbs for this sunny spot include chives, French tarragon and sweet basil. Varieties of mint, which are extremely invasive when included with other herbs, should be grown in pots.

Winter crop bed for mild climates
Suitable vegetables for this section include leeks, Brussels sprouts, cabbage, kale and broccoli. Through summer one of the low hedges can be replaced with parsley. The summer and winter planting areas should be alternated each year so that no crop grows in the same ground in consecutive seasons. This will greatly reduce the possibility of soil borne disease.

221

greater the yield. Production should increase over the years as you gain expertise and enrich the ground. It is always wise to look around at what other gardeners in your area are achieving and learn from their experience of various crops.

If, after considering all the factors, you decide to make a vegetable garden, ensure that its shape is strong and simple for it must be able to retain its character despite the constant change from bare soil to mature crop that occurs as you prepare the soil, grow the crop and harvest it. A bold, simple design is almost inevitable, since crops are traditionally grown in rows and should be served by hard paths for use throughout the year. The garden should also be divided into portions, so that different types of vegetables can be grown in different areas each year in rotation. In this way the soil will not become exhausted of any particular nutrient, nor will you encourage disease or pests to remain in the soil to feed a second year on a favored host plant. The vegetable area may be encompassed, and perhaps sub-divided, by some form of low surround. Edging box, a traditional garden surround, will har-

bor slugs which will feed on *Brassica* (the cabbage family) leaves, so it is better to use sage and rosemary for hedging, where hardy.

Traditionally, the vegetable garden was walled to keep out pests, and divided internally into four sections by wide paths, bordered with flowers for cutting, or with herbs or trained fruit trees, while other trained fruit trees lined the walls. There would be an adjacent potting-shed, a greenhouse, some frames and a place for storing sand and another for mixed soil, both for propagation and for making compost. One of the four working sections contained soft fruit or an asparagus bed or clumps of rhubarb, and possibly herbs, for its contents were semi-permanent. The other three cultivated areas housed crops which were rotated annually, both to deter soil-borne pests and to maintain a balance of nutrients in different parts of the garden.

The way such a traditional rotation works today is normally in the following manner. Planted in the first bed are leguminous crops (peas and beans), with onions, shallots, leeks, lettuce, celery and radish since they all need well-dug soil with plenty of manure or

Crop rotation

The object of rotating your vegetables is both to deter soil borne pests and to maintain a balance of nutrients in the soil. The two main enemies are clubroot disease in the cabbage family and nematode in potatoes, for these will rapidly infest the soil if cabbage family plants – the *Brassica* crops – and potatoes are planted in the same position in consecutive years. You must always ensure that when a crop is lifted the soil is suitable for the next growth you plant. Dividing your garden into four sections is ideal but fewer will suffice,

depending on what you want to grow. Here one section is planted with semi-permanent asparagus and seakale, a European favorite that has never caught on in the USA. Rhubarb can be substituted. Plot B contains leguminous vegetables and salad crops; *Brassica* crops occupy Plot C, while in the last quarter are found root crops. This is the ideal arrangement, but if you do not wish to grow so wide a range you can still do very well provided that you keep vegetables in the groups defined here and plant them in a different location each year.

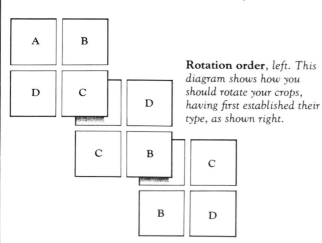

Rotation order, *left. This diagram shows how you should rotate your crops, having first established their type, as shown right.*

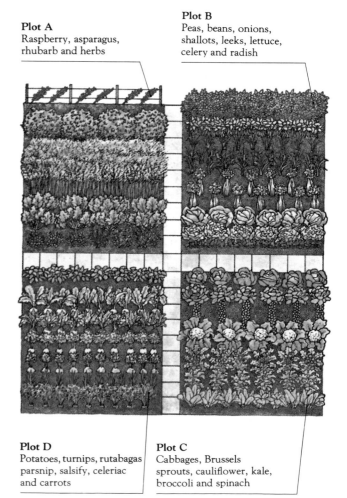

Plot A
Raspberry, asparagus, rhubarb and herbs

Plot B
Peas, beans, onions, shallots, leeks, lettuce, celery and radish

Plot D
Potatoes, turnips, rutabagas parsnip, salsify, celeriac and carrots

Plot C
Cabbages, Brussels sprouts, cauliflower, kale, broccoli and spinach

An established vegetable garden *The vegetable sequence in this garden has cabbages in the front, behind which are ripening peppers, strawed to protect them from damp. Farther back are French or snap beans, then Brussels sprouts and finally sweet corn. To the left of the growing area is a conveniently placed cold frame and a greenhouse at the rear.*

Vegetables with strong form and color *Useful vegetables can make very attractive planting. Below, green curly kale, left, and the dramatic ruby chard, center, and some ornamental cabbage, right, show the variety of stem and leaf textures and colors at your disposal. Such examples can be used in mixed planting throughout the garden and need not be restricted to the vegetable garden area.*

223

organic compost incorporated. The next quarter of the area contains mainly *Brassica* plants (cabbage, Brussels sprouts, cauliflower, kale, spinach and broccoli), and might need an inorganic feed to replace used minerals and possibly an application of lime if the ground is too acid. The third working quarter, where root crops are grown (potatoes, turnips, rutabagas, parsnips, salsify, celeriac and carrots) might need an initial application of inorganic fertilizer. Once the rotation is established, however, inorganic feed will not be necessary as the plots will remain in good health from the manure or

organic compost they receive every third year. This traditional system of rotating the crops of the kitchen garden is as applicable now as it was in the old walled vegetable gardens that existed until 50 years ago, though few of us can practice the system on the large scale of a traditional fruit and vegetable garden. If a newcomer to vegetable gardening, you need to scale the system down and to adapt it, especially when space is limited, to more intensive ways of inter-cropping vegetables.

Start by selecting varieties of vegetables that are of small growth (though not necessarily small cropping), which can be planted

Decorative vegetable and herb garden design

These two decorative borders are shown in their early autumn prime. The areas will certainly look bleak in spring but no amount of planning and selection can make a vegetable arrangement look well throughout the whole year. Some thought, however, will reduce dull periods to a minimum except in very cold climates. An arrangement such as this would be quite possible in a small garden, provided it were open and sunny in aspect and the gardener did not require too many vegetables. A tomato plant could be substituted for globe artichoke, a perennial that rarely survives northern winters. Bay (*Laurus nobilis*), also not hardy, can be grown in a tub and wintered indoors in a cool room.

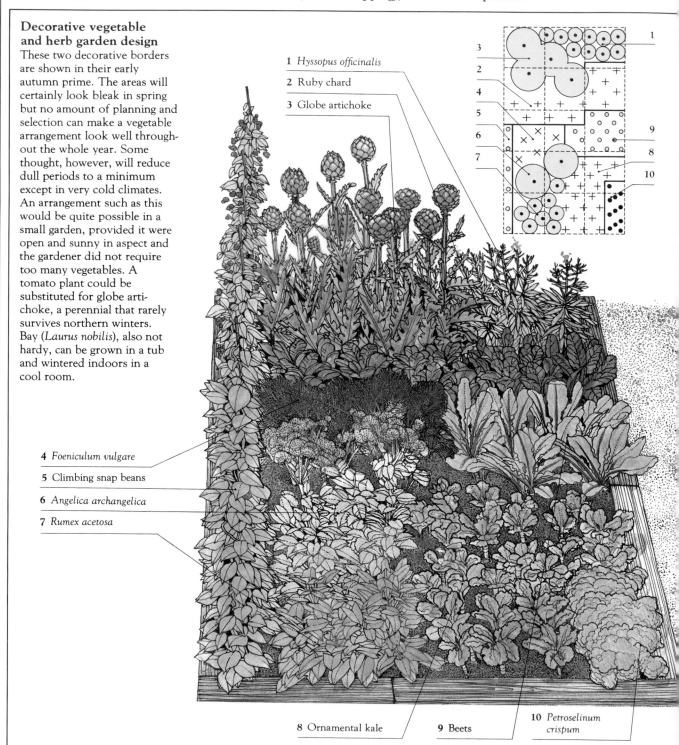

1 *Hyssopus officinalis*

2 Ruby chard

3 Globe artichoke

4 *Foeniculum vulgare*

5 Climbing snap beans

6 *Angelica archangelica*

7 *Rumex acetosa*

8 Ornamental kale

9 Beets

10 *Petroselinum crispum*

closer within the individual row. Then, between rows of slower, taller growing vegetables, plant quick-growing "catch" crops.

You will need to judge the different times of planting, rates of growth and size at maturity of your main crop vegetables, and then put in a quick-maturing crop before all the ground and light is used up. Quick-growing vegetables include radish, which reaches maturity within six weeks; kohlrabi and turnips, which grow in eight weeks, and Chinese cabbage and carrots, which take nine or ten weeks. Quick-maturing vegetables are also useful as "succession" crops to make use of

well-prepared ground once the main crop for the year has been harvested. Succession crops should not be confused with "successional sowings", which are sowings of the same vegetable at intervals to avoid a glut at harvest.

During the growing season be ready to fill any ground vacated by a previous crop, for if you do not nature will. It is usually wise to abandon a row of seedlings where germination has been poor in a small area and start again with another freshly-planted crop.

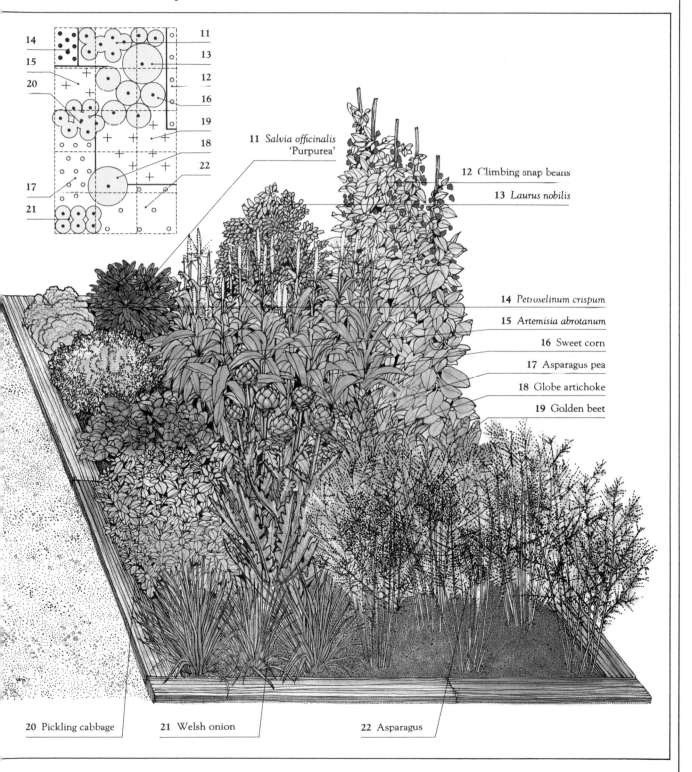

11 *Salvia officinalis* 'Purpurea'
12 Climbing snap beans
13 *Laurus nobilis*
14 *Petroselinum crispum*
15 *Artemisia abrotanum*
16 Sweet corn
17 Asparagus pea
18 Globe artichoke
19 Golden beet
20 Pickling cabbage
21 Welsh onion
22 Asparagus

Choosing vegetables

If you have space for a vegetable garden, and the time and enthusiasm to cultivate it, give careful thought to the choice of crops you grow and the growing area each will need. Details of 26 versatile vegetables are shown here. Sowing times given apply to most northern regions. Consult your county extension specialists for local recommendations. Yields in pounds are approximate as soil, climate and variety all affect results.

	Sowing time	Yield per 3 m row (10 ft)	Time to harvest (in months)
CHENOPODIACEAE			
Beets 	March–June	6.8 kg 15 lb	2
Spinach 	March, August	3.6–4.5 kg (8–10 lb)	From 2½
COMPOSITAE			
Lettuce 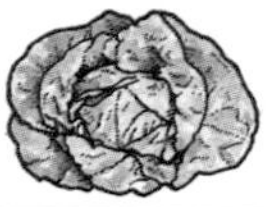	March–May, August	15 lettuces	2
CRUCIFERAE			
Cabbages 	March, July	5–8 heads	4½
Cabbage (Savoy) 	April, May (plant June)	5–8 heads	From 6
Brussels sprouts 	March, July	5 kg (11 lb)	6
Kale 	March, August	5.4 kg (11.8 lb)	8
Broccoli 	March, July	5.4 kg (11.8 lb)	4
Cauliflower 	March, July	5–8 heads	From 11
Rutabaga 	June–August	3.6–6.4 kg (8–14 lb)	From 7½
Turnips 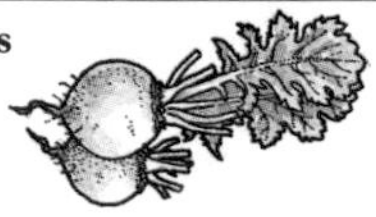	March–August	3.6–6.4 kg (8–14 lb)	5
Radish 	March, August	Plentiful	1½

	Sowing time	Yield per 3 m row (10 ft)	Time to harvest (in months)
GRAMINEAE			
Sweet corn 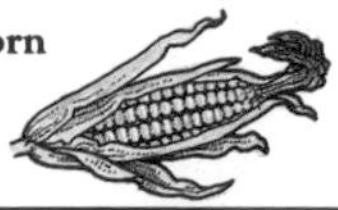	May	30–50 cobs	3
LEGUMINOSAE			
Beans (Broad) 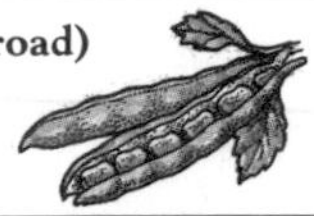	March	3.6 kg (8 lb)	3½
Beans (Snap) 	May–June	3.6 kg (8 lb)	From 3
Beans (Runner) 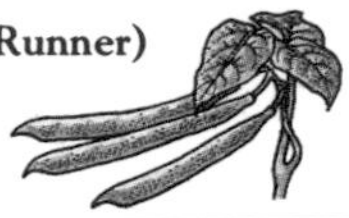	May–June	8–14 kg (17–30 lb)	From 4
Peas 	March, July	9 kg (19 lb)	From 3½
LILIACEAE			
Onions (from seed) 	March, April	3.6–4.5 kg (8–9 lb)	6½
Onions (from sets) 	Plant March, April	3.6–4.5 kg (8–9 lb)	5½
Shallots 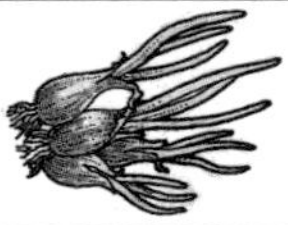	Plant March	3.6–4.5 kg (8–9 lb)	6
Leeks 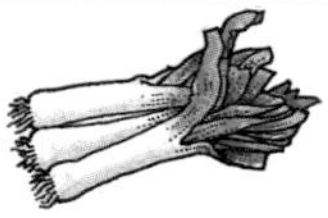	January indoors (plant March, April)	20 leeks	10
SOLANACEAE			
Potatoes 	Plant late February to May	11.3 kg (24 lb)	From 3½
Tomatoes 	February, March indoors (plant May, June)	9 kg (19 lb)	5
UMBELLIFERAE			
Carrots 	March–July	3.6 kg (8 lb)	From 5½
Parsnips 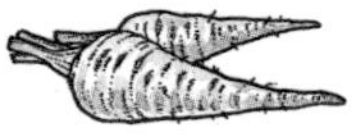	March–April	6.8-9 kg (15-19 lb)	From 7½
Celery 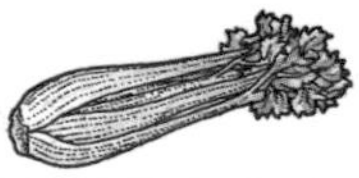	February–April indoors (plant June)	5.4–6.4 kg (11-14 lb)	From 7

FINISHING TOUCHES

Furniture, pots and containers, artificial lighting
and sculpture

Garden furniture

A garden seat is often the last thing that you add to a garden but it is often the first thing that catches the eye and provides the key to mood and style. A badly planned garden will seldom be rescued by adding attractive details but if a garden has been well-conceived and executed, the right finishing touches can make it special.

Choose your garden furniture much as you do that for your house, selecting pieces for specific purposes. Whatever you choose, however, should be relaxed in feel; few gardens are improved by overwrought little metal chairs. Another point to be remembered is that garden furniture should look decorative but be tough enough to stand outside throughout the year. The alternative is to buy furniture that can be stored.

Garden furniture is essentially of three types: tables and chairs for outside meals; chairs for relaxing and conversation, and, lastly, furniture for sunbathing, possibly beside a swimming-pool. There is a wide range of furniture on the market for each of these situations. Items may be of wood, which is attractive but heavy; of cane or bamboo; of metal, either painted or plastic-coated, or of molded fiberglass.

Purpose-built arrangement *A relaxed feel outside often stems from the compatability of seating areas with other areas for specific purposes. This happy arrangement consists of built-in seating adjacent to a barbecue.*

Metal

Metal furniture might look uncomfortable but, if well-designed, it can be quite the reverse, especially when combined with suitable removable upholstery. The lines of metal furniture should be crisp and its appearance lightweight, as opposed to the fussy, molded iron chairs and tables that are commonly sold.
The advantages of metal are its durability, which allows it to be left standing outside all year round, and its strength, which allows finely-detailed designs. Much metal furniture is plastic-coated to reduce the chore of re-painting that is otherwise required to maintain a crisp appearance. Indeed, the metal and plastic mix of materials is a useful combination for garden furniture, especially in urban and suburban locations where it is often in style.

Metal furniture as a year-round feature *This range of furniture is not only remarkably comfortable and practical when used outdoors, but it is also a decorative feature.*

Poolside furniture

Poolside furniture usually comprises tables and chairs for taking refreshment, and loungers for sunbathing. Poolside loungers must be able to withstand moisture and hot bodies covered in suntan oil and the frame must be tough enough to take children throwing themselves "aboard".

The plain-colored upholstery that you might choose for furniture positioned on a terrace would soon become soiled and probably rot if used at a poolside so many loungers are made with a covering of simple, fine-gauge nylon, or even woven plastic. These coverings have the advantage of allowing water to drain through while air circulates freely. If a lounger is upholstered in a textile, the design should be bold to disguise the inevitable stains.

Loungers range from simple canvas stretched over a metal frame, to more ornate metal or plastic-framed versions with backrests that adjust on the deck-chair principle. Most fold or dismantle for winter storage while the heavier types often have a pair of wheels for ease of movement.

Furniture for sunbathing is expensive and takes up a great deal of space. It demands a large terrace and this will look bare once the furniture is stored away for winter. In colder climates such furniture is best used on a large, sheltered balcony or in a sunny garden room where it can remain as a feature.

Plastic

Reinforced plastic furniture is light and weather resistant and, since plastic can be molded into an infinite variety of shapes, is available in a wide range of styles. Some molded plastic furniture is perfectly comfortable without upholstery, while some (the chair shown below is an example) is designed to accept detachable cushions. Bold, plain colors are often ideal for sunny terraces in summer.

Wheeled poolside lounger *This sprung, metal-framed lounger has a removable floral-patterned mattress.*

A pleasant place to pause *This bench is a successful sculptural addition to the garden. It is sited in front of an ingenious plant association of* Vitis coignetiae *and* Euonymus sp.

Stone and reconstituted stone

The function of stone and reconstituted stone furniture is quite different to that of the furniture discussed so far. It is certainly not for lounging on and it will be a permanent fixture. To be successful, stone furniture should be positioned to reveal any sculptural quality it might have. Well-sited, a piece of stone furniture can suggest a place to pause in a walk through the garden, or it might even be used as a focal point that is the culmination of your garden plan (see p 239).

Use of stone, because of its massive character, needs careful planning. Strong background planting is usually essential, so that plant detail will soften the stone in front of it.

It is possible to buy or construct simple stone slab benches that have attractive qualities. Much reconstituted stone furniture apes Renaissance styles. It is mostly too crude in its attempt to evoke "olde worlde" charm. Such furniture is part of the misconception that gardens should aspire to the uncomfortable grandeur of another age, although most people would think it strange to use anything but a 20th-century range in the kitchen and want a reasonably up-to-date car in the garage.

Wooden furniture

Wood, like stone and brick, is a material with natural attributes, such as bulk and grain, that are particularly suited to the garden. The detailing of unpainted wooden furniture should reveal these characteristics and, when sited, it should become a harmonious part of the whole garden scheme. When painted, however, wooden furniture has a completely different character. It instantly becomes part of the house rather than of the garden. It is also much more urban in feel. Softwood tables and chairs that were once used inside can often be bought cheaply in salerooms and at auctions. These can be stripped and then painted or stained to provide a far more attractive and cheaper seating arrangement for the garden than can be found on sale in garden centers and shops.

Wood is a very adaptable and readily available material so making your own furniture is another feasible economy if you are a reasonably competent carpenter. There are many existing designs for strong wooden furniture that you might choose to make. Simple designs are certain to be more successful than complicated ones. Alternatively, you might decide to design your own tables and chairs to complement your outside "room" perfectly. It is best to choose furniture that folds or dismantles for easy winter storage. Some such types are shown below. Choose a good quality wood such as redwood that has some natural weather resistance. Remember that hot sunshine can be as damaging to wood as damp and frost. Cedar, pine, spruce or similar softwoods are all adequate if seasoned and regularly painted or treated with preservative. A more resilient wood, such as oak, is ideal, if available, as it can be left untreated for longer periods and will weather to an attractive mellow tone.

A sturdy garden table, sited close to the house, is useful for much more than eating at. It is an ideal platform for potting house plants, flower arranging and so on. It is also useful for such incidental chores as cleaning shoes or grooming pets, if you cover it first.

Stowable wooden furniture *This style of furniture is designed for easy storage. The table folds flat and the chair pulls into two sections that interlock in a flat configuration for storing. Such furniture can be treated with a clear preservative, or one that stains the wood.*

Inventive wooden bench, *left. This substantial wooden bench is constructed from old railway ties. It is massive in scale but is in complete harmony with the planting and stone wall behind it. Bold planting of species with strong form and shape work with the bench to give a low-key sculptural arrangement.*

Oak and brick combination
Oak seating around an oak table is wholly in accord with the brick wall and paving on this terrace. Mature oak and mellow brick almost always work well together. The chairs are built to fit neatly up to the table top when not in use to keep the terrace tidy.

Stained softwood picnic table, *below. A well-designed, sturdy table of this sort can be invaluable with its built-in seating. You must be careful when buying or building furniture in this style, however, to choose a design that is substantial. Some examples are too lightweight and will not stand regular use for long before becoming unstable.*

Classic bench seat *If well-made and treated regularly with preservative, a bench seat should last almost indefinitely.*

Integrated furniture

Although most garden furniture should be considered a finishing touch and something that will attract the eye in its own right as well as providing a useful amenity, some very successful seating is built into the fabric of the garden as a permanent feature. Some of the gardens illustrated in this book make use of pre-cast concrete units that can be stacked or placed in a row to provide a bench. They might form steps or a retaining wall at the same time. In other gardens, wooden decking is built to include a bench section; alternatively a raised pool edge provides an inviting place to sit. Such "furniture" is part of the three-dimensional shape of many gardens. It is always low-key and harmonious compared with the eye-catching quality of some movable tables and chairs.

Built-in concrete seating corner *If the location is dramatic, even uncompromising reinforced concrete can provide a successful seating arrangement.*

Pots and containers

One of the ways of punctuating your garden layout is by grouping pots, tubs and other containers, either with or without plants, as incidental points of interest. You can also use color in containers to stabilize the mood of an area; pots around a terrace or pool can have this effect. Few groupings of this sort are large or important enough to become the focal point in a sizeable garden, but they can work well in a smaller area.

Having studied the various functions that a pot or collection of pots can perform, it is essential to choose a style that works for the particular spot on which you are to use them. The style of containers depends on the material of which they are made and also, of course, their shape.

Containers to enhance a terrace, *right. This splendid group contains daturas and lilies.*

1 Concrete dish
2, 4 Stoneware urns
3 Shaped concrete pot

Reconstituted stone, stoneware and china

Stoneware, including discarded sinks coated with a mix of mortar and moss or peat, are heavy and therefore difficult to move once filled with earth and planted. But they can look well in a traditional rural setting. Concrete or reconstituted stone can be as heavy as stone itself but containers exist which include lightweight materials. China pots for summer are often painted for a more refined effect.

Simple stoneware pot
The bold shape of this pot contrasts well with the agave backed by Coronilla **valentina glauca.** *Simple modern pots need a bold planting style to match.*

Gothic vase *The delicate tracery of this traditional container is complemented by the planting of a lacy species of pelargonium. Decorated pots need light planting styles.*

5 Stoneware "basket"
6–7 Lightweight containers
8 Glazed decorated vase

Terracotta

There is a vogue for using hand-made terracotta pots imported from Italy. They are often attractive, with patterns of swags and scrolls, but once on the ground, and especially if planted, it is difficult to see much of them. Moreover, the Renaissance form they ape is out of keeping in the average domestic garden. Far better to buy half a dozen cheaper containers, which will cost no more and can create a better effect.

Simplicity for success, *above and left. Simple containers are often the most successful. Here wood and terracotta containers are planted with pelargoniums and helichrysum.*

Wood

For a truly rural feel, you should use simple shapes in natural materials, such as wood. If you re-use wooden containers, such as old barrels, you must ensure that they have never contained poison and, if they were wine or beer barrels, treat the wood with paint or preservative, not omitting the hoops which will otherwise rust. Never let a barrel dry out, or the metal hoops that hold the planks together will become loose and ultimately drop off.

1 Half barrel
2 Versailles tub
3 Earthenware jar
4–5 Terracotta pots
6 Lugged terracotta pot

233

Hanging baskets

For the city gardener with little space, perhaps only a balcony, a hanging basket is an ideal way of containing summer color. Once established, however, a hanging basket is often difficult to water since it will be higher than eye level. Furthermore, being directly exposed to sun and wind it will dry out quickly. Plant hanging baskets with subjects that enjoy heat and exposure – pelargoniums, petunias, begonias and impatiens. In winter, you can fill the basket with ivies or in cold regions with cut evergreens.

It is essential to prepare your hanging basket properly, with a good mixture containing plenty of peat that will retain moisture.

Petunias and geraniums
This is how hanging baskets should look – full, colorful and overflowing.

Hanging baskets *The basket frame is traditionally lined with moss before being filled with soil. Today, however, it is possible to buy a porous composition pad, through which bedding plants may be grown.*

Moss lining

Composition lining

Plastic
The lightest materials for a container are plastic and fibreglass. The more simple shapes are attractive, but many are finished in unnecessarily bright colours which detract from anything planted in, or near, them. Plastic is well worth considering if you plan to move your containers during the growing season.

1, 4, 8–10 Tub containers
2, 5, 7 Pots and drainage dishes
3 Slatted container
6 Quadrant container
11 Split sphere container

Other materials

The variety of pots and containers on the market is considerable. It is possible to buy metal urns (right) which are specially made for plants and will last a lifetime, but you do not have to restrict yourself to these. Discarded objects of unusual shape, such as chimney pots (far right), can be extremely effective. Today there is also a wide range of man-made substitute substances (such as plastic and fiberglass) that are light, imitate many different styles of container and are almost indistinguishable from natural materials, such as china, clay and wood. When you require several containers it is best to have them all in the same material.

Containers of note, *left and above. This 19th-century metal urn (left) is wholly in character with the building behind. Old chimney pots make interesting containers if boldly planted.*

1 Plastic strawberry pot
2 Fiberglass panelled container
3 Plastic "wooden" container
4 Self-watering container
5 Plastic "pebble-dash" tub

Window boxes

The range of window boxes is enormous but the tougher and thicker their material the better. Boxes are often subjected to intense heat and wind, both of which dry out soil quickly, so the deeper and bigger they are the more the plants in them will thrive. Whatever their structure and material, boxes must have plenty of drainage holes to prevent waterlogging.

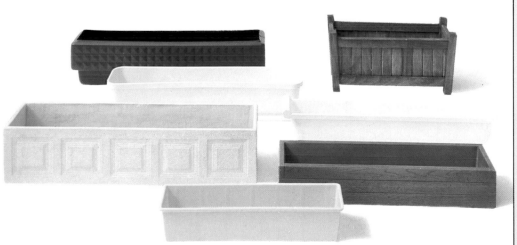

Artificial lighting

Garden lighting falls into two categories: useful illumination and decorative lighting. Necessary illumination includes the lighting necessary for seating and entertainment areas. It also covers the lighting that shows the way along a path to a log pile or illuminates your house number or name for the convenience of visitors. Such lighting should be subtle but strong enough to fulfil its function. It is especially important to illuminate steps used after dark.

Subtle decorative lighting can create a magical effect in the garden even when there is little growth to illuminate. The bare winter stems of a large tree, glistening with frost or decked with snow, can look even more spectacular than summer foliage. Successful decorative lighting must be low-key, directed away from the viewing point and usually from a low-level light source. You might choose to illuminate a scene – for example, a pond and its surround – or create a nighttime feature by illuminating a single subject such as a flowering tree, the arch of a gateway or a piece of sculpture, remembering that less attractive elements can be left in darkness.

Lighting fixtures are available in many shapes and sizes. It is imperative that all fittings are purpose-made for outside use. The design of a fixture provides either a spotlight effect or a more general floodlight effect. Generally, the simpler and more robust the design the better. Fixtures either screw to a wall, have a bracket that clamps to a convenient branch, have a bolt-down stand or a spike to hold the lamp in earth or gravel. Light fixtures on the external walls of a house can be connected to the internal main circuit; otherwise the fixture should be connected to the garden circuit (see p. 105) if you have one.

There are a number of illuminated decorative fixtures for the garden available where the light source itself provides the interest. These include Chinese lanterns and other low-wattage decorative lights for temporary decoration such as the very effective glowing spheres, or even imitation rocks, made in fiberglass and used to make sculptural groupings.

Decorative bollard, *above. This column provides illumination and is a feature itself.*

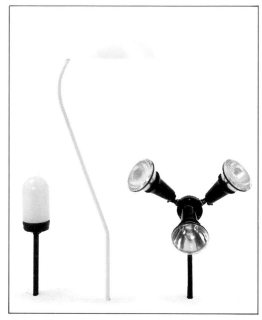

Spiked fixtures The three types of spiked lighting fixture shown below include, from left to right: a low bollard, suitable for use by a path or drive; a shaded floodlight for siting among bushes or flowers, and a three-way spotlight for featuring shrubs and trees.

Floodlit scene, *left. This magical scene represents the effect many seek to achieve when lighting trees and shrubs beyond water. Direct light on white blossom looks attractive, while deeper colors really glow. Note that the source of light is invisible, which should always be your aim. Visible light sources will detract from the lit area considerably.*

Attractive balcony,
*right. On warm summer
evenings, such a glowing
table setting on a
balcony is extremely
inviting. The trees and
shrubs beyond are
illuminated from below
the railings. Once
established, such lighting
greatly increases the
usefulness of an outside
entertaining area.*

**Lighting a garden
adjacent to buildings,**
*below. Here different
points of light pick out
elements of a building
and terrace groupings.
To achieve a balance
between inside and
outside lights you will
need to experiment with
the position and strength
of your light sources.*

Flares

Night lighting attracts bugs, moths and mosquitoes in summer. One way to combat this is to use candles that are impregnated with insect repellent. This type of temporary lighting is useful for a summer party and has the advantage of not being dependent on an electricity supply. The lights illustrated below are large and fairly expensive but smaller versions are available. The pointed frames can be hung from trees or stuck into the earth; they are of bamboo and enclose a candle. The bucket type can be used again and again throughout summer.

Care must always be taken with any naked flame, for in summer dry wood, bamboo clumps and thatch will catch fire instantly. It is advisable always to have water to hand for emergencies.

Sculpture

Sculpture may be the centerpoint of a garden or merely a side attraction, incidental to the whole. It may be overscaled for a dramatic effect or unobtrusive and in total harmony with the surroundings; it may be striking or incongruous, traditional in style or abstract. Groupings of pots or urns, boulders or stones, can all create a pleasing sculptural feature. Each location calls for a different style and treatment, although the dominating influence will be your personal preference.

As with all else in the garden, the selection of sculptural elements will depend on the style of your house, its setting and age, and of course on the style of your garden. Size is also important, for a large piece will always look pretentious in a small area.

The first question to answer, therefore, is whether you are designing a garden to show off a piece of sculpture or siting a sculptural object to enhance a portion of the garden.

For most people, sculpture is the last consideration in a garden, for usually an original piece is extremely expensive. Cast concrete sculpture, advertised in catalogues, is cheaper and you can always make your own arrangement in natural forms of wood and boulders. In any event, avoid mawkish sculpture, which is unsuitable for almost every kind of garden.

The ideal is a solid object, either representational or abstract, of simple shape, made in a durable material. This then needs sympathetic siting, either on a hard surround or contrasted by architectural plant forms. The final arrangement should be attractive at all times of the year and from all the angles from which it can be seen.

None of the sculptural groupings illustrated here could be described as extreme; you may like them or not but all demonstrate the importance of the correct siting of a piece. Sculpture must never be seen in isolation and it has to work visually within its paved or planted setting.

You can use a sculptural feature as a balance within your layout – to counteract a large tree, for instance, or on a roof terrace to detract attention from a neighboring eyesore. Not all sculpture has to sit in the middle of your site; move it around until you find it helps to create a satisfying and balanced composition.

It would be foolish to claim that much of the sculpture we incorporate in our gardens can be called great art, but there is no reason why it should not be attractive and fun.

Successful settings
Sculpture should give pleasure not only in itself but also in its setting. This Italian figure, of fiberglass impregnated with lead, would look well in either a modern or traditional garden. Here it sits on well-detailed brick paving, backed by a strongly architectural plant grouping.

Sphere in a courtyard, *above. This shining metal sphere is kept moist by a gentle central fountain. Water smothers the sphere, and then disappears into a reservoir below to be recycled by a pump. The arrangement is sited in a paved courtyard.*

Siting sculpture

The series of diagrams below shows how different styles of sculpture suit different locations and how the location changes a garden considerably. If the piece is located centrally and to the rear of an oblong plot it will demand instant attention and become the focal point of the whole garden. Placed to one side as a counterbalance to strong planting on the opposite side, a piece will become part of the incidental interest of the garden and encourage the eye to progrss from side to side. If you create a group, to which sculpture lends weight, to one side in the foreground, the garden space will seem to flow around the group.

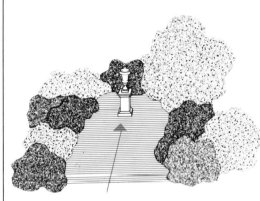

Sculpture as the focal point *A classical urn and plinth placed centrally dominate the garden and immediately draw the attention.*

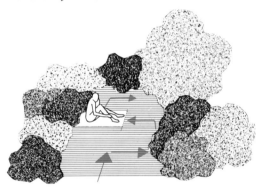

Sculpture to create a balancing feature *A modern seated figure strengthens one side of the garden to give it equal importance to planted masses on the other side.*

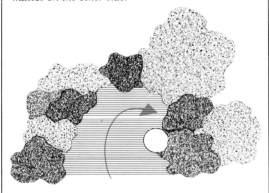

Sculpture to provide strong foreground interest *A sphere strengthens the foreground grouping considerably and encourages a feeling of movement around the group.*

Eye-catching arrangement, *above. A clever and humorous use of a number of sculptural pieces. The arrangement is on a roof terrace and disguises surrounding urban ugliness.*

Sculpture and water, *below. Water makes an ideal medium to offset sculpture. This landing swan has an ingenious fountain effect at its feet. Hosta leaves enhance the whole.*

Lion in a jungle
A terracotta lion placed within an arrangement of lush, tropical planting imitates the animal in its natural habitat. The grouping is intended to amuse and, in conjunction with the terrace, is highly effective and visually harmonious.

Importance of setting, *below. The setting for modern abstract sculpture has to be correct. This piece has a strength that blends with organic shapes. If the piece is minimal, however, it should be seen against the sky as strong plant forms will detract from a slight structure.*

Classic sculpture in a modern setting, *right. The main piece in this group sits well on a concrete plinth and the jar at the base of the plinth complements it. The bold foliage of Hedera colchica 'Dentata Aurea' forms a year-round backdrop.*

CARE AND MAINTENANCE

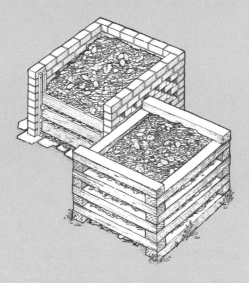

Looking after the structure of the garden and the
plants that fill it

Maintaining your new garden

Experienced gardeners know that there is no such thing as a completely maintenance-free garden, for even the simplest, those with large expanses of hard-surfacing, need periodic attention. The more subtle your garden plan, the more maintenance it will need. However, a good basic layout, well-designed and then well-constructed and planted, can greatly reduce subsequent maintenance throughout the year. For example, well-routed paths, laid to discourage weeds between the joints, save a great deal of seasonal upkeep.

We tend to think of garden maintenance solely as plant husbandry. This is far from so, for all structures will need attention. There are, in addition, certain seasonal tasks to be undertaken, such as maintaining soil fertility and cleaning garden pools.

I am not here seeking to describe essential day-to-day routines in the garden but rather to draw attention to the major seasonal duties which are necessary to maintain the initial standard of your garden throughout the years. Unlike most forms of design, gardening involves a constant modification of all the components of a garden.

Because of this, it is important that middle-aged people should realize that what they are capable of doing at present may be too much for them in 10 or 20 years time. For this reason, any alterations or improvements in the garden's layout should be directed towards ultimately reducing maintenance work. This is the last stage in a natural progression, for in the early years your garden can be more demanding when it serves the needs of a growing family.

For the reader's convenience, I shall discuss the maintenance of the elements that make up a garden in the order they were considered in the chapters on constructing and planting the garden. Reading through the maintenance necessary for the various elements of a garden before deciding on the sort of garden you want is a sensible step. This is especially so concerning your choice of plants.

Boundaries and enclosures

Walls
New brick walls, well-constructed on sound footings, should need little attention over the years. From time to time, however, a coping stone may become dislodged or frost may cause damage. Old boundaries of this material, on the other hand, have a habit of keeling over and some form of buttressing may be necessary. You may also find that older walls play host to seedlings. Buddleias, for instance, are great seeders in walls. As charming as the effect undoubtedly is, the woody roots will begin to destroy the wall as they mature and so they should be eradicated.

Extremely old walls may have a problem with ivy, which can bore its way into older, softer lime mortar. It is also true, of course, that ivy can support a wall, so have a care when pulling it out.

Fences
Wooden fences will need rather more maintenance over the years. All panel fencing must be given a coat of preservative from time to time, when all climbers to which it is playing host should be removed. It will then be some time before they grow back again, since most preservatives are toxic. When removing climbers, check that they have not broken any

Fence weaknesses
The diagrams below point out the inherent weaknesses of post and rail or panel fences, and those details that require regular replacement.

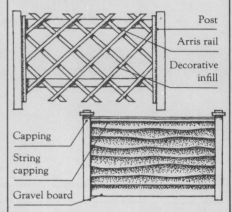

Post
Arris rail
Decorative infill

Capping
String capping
Gravel board

portion of the panel infill wood. Then check that the verticals to which your panels are attached have not rotted at ground level or been lifted by frost. Also check that the capping is sound and, most important of all, renew the gravel board running horizontal with the ground under the infill panel.

Fences with horizontal rails should be checked regularly, at the points where the rails join the posts. At the same time, check any gates through the fences and rehang any that have dropped.

All this type of maintenance work can be done during winter if there is no snow or immediately after it has cleared in spring if there is.

Buttressing
If you have a brick wall that is leaning or bowing you can stop further deterioration by adding buttresses, as in the diagrams below. The buttresses must be built on additional concrete foundations in materials that complement the existing walling. If the signs of weakness in a wall are advanced, you will have to demolish the offending section and rebuild it, including buttresses for increased structural strength.

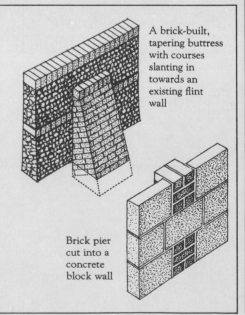

A brick-built, tapering buttress with courses slanting in towards an existing flint wall

Brick pier cut into a concrete block wall

Replacing a partly rotten post

Wooden fence posts sunk directly into earth or concrete will eventually rot at ground level. You can remedy this one post at a time without dismantling the fence, as shown below.

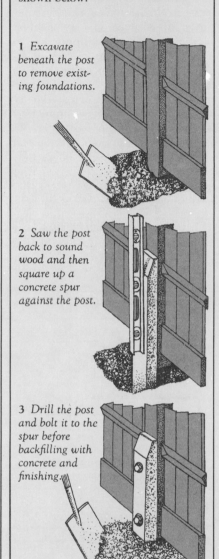

1 *Excavate beneath the post to remove existing foundations.*

2 *Saw the post back to sound wood and then square up a concrete spur against the post.*

3 *Drill the post and bolt it to the spur before backfilling with concrete and finishing.*

Replacing gravel boards

Gravel boards fit along the bottom of a fence, fixed to battens at the base of the posts. Simply unscrew the rotting boards, replace worn battens and screw on new boards.

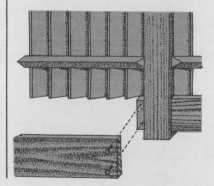

Changing levels

Retaining walls

Retaining walls in the garden should be inspected after heavy rain or snow for this is when they are supporting the maximum weight of wet earth. When there is any likelihood of collapse, excavate at the rear of the wall to reduce the pressure before rebuilding the offending section and backfilling with a good proportion of ash or hardcore behind the new construction to improve drainage. Also check that there are weep-holes at the base of the wall to allow any accumulation of water to escape. Depending on the structure of the wall, you should check its components and capping.

Steps

Stepped changes of level should be checked at the end of summer to ensure that treads have no movement in them and that there is a water run-off, either forward or to the side of the steps. Without this, water and then ice will form, which is extremely dangerous.

The precise nature of any wear in a flight of steps depends on the original construction material. Wooden steps need constant checking for signs of loosening, cracking or moss growth. Remove moss with a wire brush as this can make a very slippery surface. Poured concrete treads can chip away at the leading edges and you should consider constructing new edges in a harder wearing material. Treads made from units, such as pre-cast paving slabs, can become unstable if the jointing around the units loosens. In this case, the offending units should be removed and relaid.

You might find that the original detailing of your steps has proven inadequate. If you are unhappy about an encroaching bank, for example, try one of the solutions proposed below.

Edging chipped treads

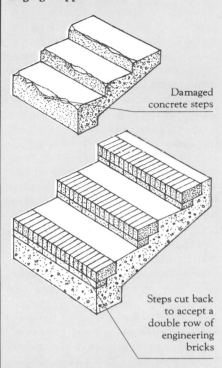

Damaged concrete steps

Steps cut back to accept a double row of engineering bricks

Rethinking step margins

After use, your step margins may have become difficult to maintain, either presenting a difficult mowing edge or over-spilling soil, as in the diagram, right. Two solutions are shown in the diagram, below right. A retaining wall now holds back the bank on one side of the flight, while "L"-shaped extensions to the risers contain the soil for successful planting on the other. A recessed brick edging makes mowing much easier.

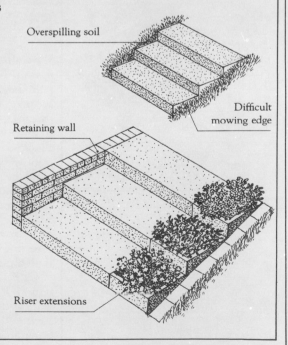

Overspilling soil

Difficult mowing edge

Retaining wall

Riser extensions

Banks

Changes of level divided by newly planted earth banks should be regularly checked. Ensure that the bank has not washed down after heavy rain or snow. To retain a new bank, especially one established at a steep angle, peg wire or plastic netting over the surface at regular intervals and plant ground cover through it to hold the bank with its roots.

Grassed banks which have been mown throughout the season should be examined in autumn for patches that the mower might have shaved too closely. Cut out any dead turf and replace with new, taken from another part of the lawn where a bare patch will not be so noticeable. Tamp the replacement turf down and keep it well-watered until the repair turf is established. Fill the gap left in the secluded part of the lawn with a mixture of soil and sand, incorporate a little grass seed in the surface and level off the patched area, similarly tamping it to match the surrounding turf.

Retaining an unstable slope

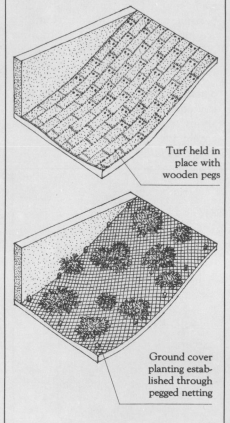

Turf held in place with wooden pegs

Ground cover planting established through pegged netting

Drainage

After wet weather you should also ensure that there is no standing water at the base of any contouring. If there is, a drain run should be dug which will direct surplus water to a convenient soakaway (dry well).

All drains should be checked in spring to ensure that they are doing their work properly. Temporary forms of drainage, mole or open trench drains, have only a short span anyway, but your type of soil, whether sticky or dry, will also make a difference. An open drain in clay soil will obviously last longer than one in sandy soil, which will quickly silt up or collapse.

When you have standing water or excessive moss in your lawn, you may need to drain it. Before going to this expense, however, ensure that there is not an impervious consolidated layer below the surface which might have formed during garden construction, especially if heavy machinery was used. If this is the case, you can cure the condition by forking straight down and working the fork about at regular intervals across the lawn, then brushing grit into the holes to facilitate drainage. You can pierce the lawn with your garden fork or use a purpose-built hollow-tined lawn perforator. There are many such tools available, of contrasting designs. They all cut out narrow cores of turf in a regular pattern across the lawn.

It is essential that any drainage you make is laid to a fall, and connected to a drainage outlet.

Surfaces

Hard surfacing

From time to time it is necessary to rethink your areas of hard paving. In autumn, consider whether the terrace area was large enough for your summer activities and whether you should increase it. If the terrace was planned with a specific purpose in mind, be critical as to how it fulfilled that function. A seating area, for example, should have provided a comfortable space for the garden furniture upon it. If it has not, you will have to go back to your original garden plan with its guiding grid (see p. 40) before revising the size of the terrace. Check, too, whether its surface is sound, whether any area has sunk and whether there is standing water after rain. Autumn is the time

for all this work, before the earth becomes wet and is therefore more difficult to work.

An existing terrace that falls short on any of these points might need to be taken up and relaid on a sound new foundation with new pointing between the paving elements. Sometimes, of course, only small areas need lifting and reinstating.

Check the pointing of any surfacing from time to time, and also check that the retaining brick or curb which holds a surface material together has not crept outwards, loosening other elements. It is into any weak joints in the surfacing that rain, then frost, infiltrates, causing

Re-planning a terrace

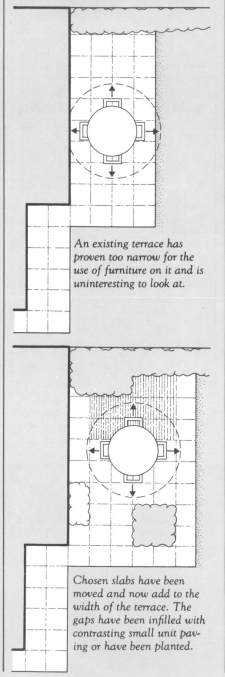

An existing terrace has proven too narrow for the use of furniture on it and is uninteresting to look at.

Chosen slabs have been moved and now add to the width of the terrace. The gaps have been infilled with contrasting small unit paving or have been planted.

the materials of which the surface is made to decompose rapidly.

You might also check whether pathways are wide enough to do their job and that they are routed correctly. Check that your stepping stones through grass or water are correctly distanced from each other.

Before winter, you may need to clean down brick or stone paving to prevent its becoming slippery. Use salt if there are no plants growing in the vicinity or a mild detergent. This operation may need to be done again in spring, when the surface should be hosed down.

Soft surfacing

Loose gravel surfaces will need weeding from time to time, either by hand or by the application of a weed killer. If using the latter method, the application must not be allowed to damage any plants growing in the medium. Weed killer may be applied as liquid from a watering-can or under pressure by spray. It can also be applied in granular form.

Decking

Wooden paving, or decking, when used in a moist climate that does not allow the material to dry out in summer, should be scrubbed with salt or a proprietary cleaner and hosed down, in autumn and spring, to prevent its becoming slippery. A wire brushing to roughen wooden paving surfaces is helpful. Wood will, however, wear relatively quickly in areas that take a high level of pedestrian traffic, such as steps. You should replace badly worn or split boards that might cause someone to trip. If you have room, it is a good idea to store some replacement decking timber outside so that it weathers at the same rate as the original deck and will make any necessary repairs a good match. Occasionally check the condition of the substructure of your deck to make sure that its boards are sound.

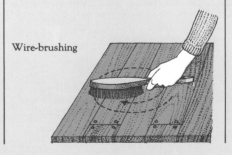

Wire-brushing

Features

Rockeries

You should have divided alpines after their spring flowering. Then, in autumn, give a more general clearance to the rockery outcrop. Study the configuration of rocks in your rockery and compare it with your experience of natural outcrops of rock. Make sure that there are no rocks sticking out of the ground vertically, nor groups of unnaturally small pieces of rock, nor areas where rocks are arranged in a random, unconnected way.

Lift rocks to dig out invasive weeds, cut back shrubby conifers and remove superfluous leaves and rubbish which invariably build up within a rockery. Ensure that paths and stepping stones are soundly bedded. A rockery is one of the first features in a garden to come to life in spring, with miniature bulbs and early alpine flowers, so have your clearance work completed in readiness for this.

Pools

A garden pool with clear water resulting from a well-balanced community of plants, fish, insects and amphibians should not need to be emptied during its first few years, but one which has not been cleared out for a long period, even if it has an oxygenating plant, fish and snail population, should be. This is because leaves will inevitably fall into a pool in autumn and will cause decay and pollution which the natural balancing elements of pond life cannot eradicate.

Netting a pool

Netting, or caging, over a pool always looks unsightly. If your pool is a regular shape, however, you can submerge netting just below the surface on a non-corrosive frame.

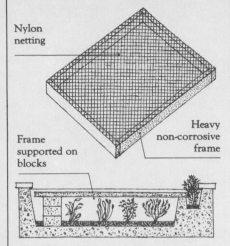

Nylon netting

Frame supported on blocks

Heavy non-corrosive frame

If there is no built-in outlet to the pool, you can syphon out the water to a lower part of the garden through a hose. If you have not first removed your fish, tie some gauze over the pipe outlet so they will not be sucked up. Lower the pool to a water level of 100 mm (4 in), then stop the syphon and take out the livestock before clearing completely, prior to cleaning and replacement.

When it is not possible to site a new pond away from the overhang of trees, you will need to net the pond in autumn to prevent leaves falling into it and so avoid the above procedure. In certain areas, nets over a pool, or just below the water's surface, are necessary to prevent herons and other predators from eating the fish and other pond life.

Draining a pool

If your pool does not have a purpose-built outlet pipe, the easiest way to drain it is to set up a syphon using a hose pipe. It is best to make a filter, shown right, using a funnel and gauze. Several meters (10 ft) of hose are required below the level of the pool.

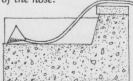

Gauze

Funnel

Hose

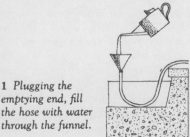

1 *Plugging the emptying end, fill the hose with water through the funnel.*

2 *Fit the gauze, place the filter beneath the surface and unplug the emptying end of the hose.*

Relining a pool

A poorly-constructed concrete pool may crack and present you with the alternatives of expensive re-building or lining the existing cracked pool with a heavy duty plastic (PVC) sheet. Technique for folding and disguising the liner is shown right and below.

1 *Stretch the liner so that the pool is centered beneath it.*

2 *Let the sheet fall into the pool and fold the excess at each corner (as below).*

3 *In each corner, pinch the sheet together to leave the excess outside the water enclosure.*

4 *Cut away the excess from the corner of the sheet and slit the remainder to ground level.*

5 *Fold the sheet down on either side of the corner to make a straight seam.*

6 *Cover the sheet overlap with slabs so that they overhang the water to disguise its level.*

Ponds and pools constructed of concrete that has cracked are difficult to repair satisfactorily. It is sometimes better to empty the whole container and line it with heavy plastic (PVC) sheeting, which can be ordered to fit particular shapes. You may need to modify the coping surround to the pond to hide the edge of the plastic sheet. Any existing outlet and inlet pipes serving a cracked concrete pool that you decide to line in this way, will become defunct. You will have to remove protruding pipes and make sure that there are no rough edges that would puncture the plastic sheet. An existing onshore pump will also become inoperable once the pool is lined and will have to be removed or disguised.

Swimming-pools

Autumn is a good time to empty a Gunite swimming pool in order to clean it. However, this major project is only required every few years or so. Vinyl-lined in-ground pools are not emptied as without the water pressure the pool will collapse. All pools should be covered over winter. Furniture, umbrellas and loose cushions must be stored unless they are designed in waterproof materials to be left out over winter.

Recreational areas

In spring you should check the surfacing of your children's play area, add more peat bark where necessary and ensure that the area is dry and free of standing water.

Examine all the swings, slides and climbing frames, making sure that they are sound. Check that tree boughs with ropes attached are strong enough, and be sure that tree houses are secure. Wooden equipment should be sandpapered down to remove splinters and checked for splits that expand or contract under strain, since they can easily trap small fingers. This is especially true of sections of wooden climbing frame.

As your children grow, reassess the usefulness of purpose-built play equipment and play areas as a whole. Requirements change quickly and garden space is usually too precious to waste on unused areas and features. If you utilized a sawn tree trunk as a play frame (see p. 146) you can always retain it as a sculptural feature or saw it up for other constructional purposes or, as a last resort, for firewood.

In autumn, sandpits should be covered over. Then, in spring, ensure that drainage is satisfactory and fill the pit with fresh sharp sand.

Barbecue areas

The remains of a summer barbecue can look depressing in winter. Moveable barbecues should be cleaned, dried and stored, together with their equipment. Built-in barbecues should also be thoroughly cleaned. Barbecues are used for burning leaves and garden trash in Europe and England, but this practice is discouraged and in fact is illegal in most regions of the USA because of concern for the additional air pollution it will cause.

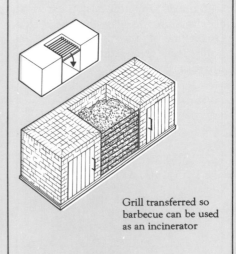

Grill transferred so barbecue can be used as an incinerator

Structures

Conservatories, greenhouses and cold frames

All wooden structures require regular maintenance. If they are painted, they will need recoating every two years or so and redwood houses should similarly be given an application of preservative. Metal structures need less attention, which is one of their attractions.

Glass should be kept clean so that it transmits as much light as possible. It should be thoroughly washed down in spring to remove grime that has built up through the winter. Do not attempt to crawl over a conservatory or greenhouse roof, however well it is supported, unless you can construct a safe ladder rest, as shown below. It is best to use a long-handled brush and a hose from the eaves. Always keep spare panes of glass in reserve: broken glass must be replaced immediately, since wind penetrating even a small aperture will reduce the temperature in the conservatory or greenhouse.

Before winter, check that glass fixtures are in order and that there are no leakages to dissipate your expensive heating. In spring, ensure that hinges to opening ventilation windows are sound.

Locating greenhouse leaks

Light a proprietary smoke pellet in your greenhouse (when it is free of plants), close the door and watch for escaping smoke.

Leak

Smoke pellet

Climbing on to a greenhouse

It is not safe to rest a ladder directly on to a greenhouse roof. You must first tie planks across the entire width of the frame to distribute the weight of you and the ladder as widely as possible. Adjust the ladder so that it matches the slope of the pitch of the greenhouse roof and make sure that it cannot slip.

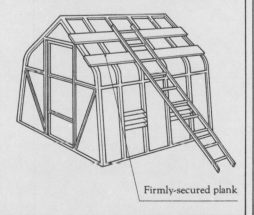

Firmly-secured plank

Replacing panes of glass

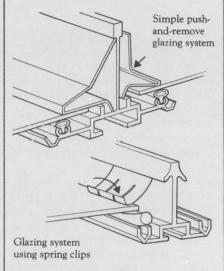

Simple push-and-remove glazing system

Glazing system using spring clips

Keep your structures clean and sound inside and out and check brickwork for any signs of dampness that might indicate a faulty damp proof course or leaking from above.

Snow can be a significant problem where structures comprise large expanses of glass. Clear falls of snow from roofs before the weight of snow builds up. Ensure there can be no sudden heavy falls of melting snow from overhanging foliage or masonry on to a glass roof.

In late autumn, clean out gutters, removing silt and leaves, and ensure that all gulleys are running freely. Blockages will result in leaks during the winter. Make sure that any drains that serve conservatories are free from debris and that greenhouse drainage systems are working well.

Pergolas

Let climbing plants down from pergolas in autumn so that you can check for any rotting sections in the structure. If you do find rot, replace boards as necessary. Treat the woodwork with preservative or paint. This is the time to prune climbing plants

(see p. 358) before tying them back to their support. Freshly applied preservative will burn foliage.

Roof gardens

Roof gardens can take an enormous battering from snow, wind and rain throughout winter and it is essential to give them a thorough reappraisal before this. Furniture and fittings should go into storage; then thoroughly check the structure of the garden, including the planting areas, surrounds, any overhead structures, and electric wiring on walls. The most important task is to ensure that drainage is efficient, with good cross falls to outlet channels and then to clear downpipes.

After clearing your annuals planted for color and cutting back shrubs (for they should be low-growing and sturdy), either replace tired earth and compost in permanent beds or thoroughly feed them with an organic manure. Sacks of finely shredded horse manure, compost, peat moss or other organic feed are obtainable and their contents are both easy and clean to apply. This should then be lightly forked in.

Balconies

Much of the forementioned maintenance of roof gardens also applies to balconies. More attention will be necessary, however, to the plant containers for they are inevitably smaller than those on a roof garden and their nutrient will be exhausted. Replace growing mixes, incorporating plenty of fine organic matter to act both as a soil conditioner and as food. This will also help to retain moisture. All this should be undertaken in autumn if you are planting the containers for a winter effect, but if you seek a summer display do the work in the spring.

Spring is also the time to check decorative finishes for signs of frost damage. The glaze of ceramic tiles can be damaged by unexpectedly cold weather and lightweight flooring tiles can lift. Also check to see how paintwork and varnish finishes have weathered. However, if possible, it is best to leave painting and varnishing until late summer or autumn so that new coats will harden completely before facing the heat of the mid-summer sun.

Cultivation

Gardeners seldom agree on the best methods of plant cultivation. Some, indeed, consider that none is necessary, since plants flourish naturally. It is true that once plants are established in a decorative garden, cultivation can be reduced to a minimum, often little more than the removal of unwanted weeds. However, most gardeners will agree that cultivation of some sort must be periodically undertaken to maintain plantings.

Autumn is the best time for a major clearance of the garden, for the application of organic compost and for a thorough dig-over before the ground becomes too heavy with moisture. Frost will break down the large clods of earth (organic feed will also help to do this) to provide a spring tilth for planting. Lighter soils will need a more gentle forking over in autumn, when organic compost or uncomposted soft organic waste can be incorporated to give the soil a more cohesive quality.

Most gardeners now dig only one spit deep (to the depth of the blade of the spade) and turn that over. In earlier generations, when labor was cheap and plentiful, gardens were dug two spits deep, which produced deeper cultivation. The system of digging you choose to employ must depend on your type of soil and the use to which you will put the land you are cultivating. Heavy soils (see p. 16) require more cultivation than light ones as they have to be encouraged to crumble and they hold perennial weed roots tightly. Soil that is to be used again and again for vegetable production requires more cultivation to replace soil nutrients than soil used for a perennial display. Digging also depends on the state of cultivation you inherit.

Hand-operated rotary cultivators working with rotary blades, it is claimed, can now penetrate the ground to one spit deep, but surfaces must be level since they are heavy and difficult to move.

Borders and beds should be lightly forked over in autumn and again in spring, turning in leaves and organic matter. If you dig these areas too deeply you will disturb the plants' small feeder roots.

Much cultivation is simply to tidy your garden when you have open beds and exposed earth, since newly turned earth looks fresh and attractive. By planting ground cover in bare areas, this chore is avoided.

Tools for the task

There is an abundance of garden equipment on the market but your needs are, in fact, very simple. Avoid too much gadgetry and choose only essential tools. However, it is advisable to buy the best, for good quality garden tools can last a lifetime even if given extremely hard use. Your basic equipment should include a spade, fork, rake, hoe, a trowel and hand-fork, a watering-can, pruners, a wheelbarrow and a hose.

It is important that you clean your garden equipment after use, particularly if you cannot afford stainless steel. Brush off all earth, clean blades with an oily rag and then store spades, forks and all other equipment in a dry place.

Spades

Spades vary in size. The largest may have a blade 290×190 mm ($11\frac{1}{2} \times 7\frac{1}{2}$ in) wide, while the smallest a mere 260×160 mm ($10\frac{1}{4} \times 6\frac{1}{4}$ in). If you are not strong, or have heavy soil, go for the smaller size. The best blades are made of stainless steel. These slice through the earth, are easy to keep clean and will not rust. Stainless steel is expensive, however. The shaft of the spade may be of a synthetic material for lightness but wooden shafts should be close grained and smooth. Handles will either be D- or T-shaped, so test them to see which suits you better.

A spade is the most important of all garden tools, for it is used not only for digging and trenching but for planting trees and large shrubs. It is therefore advisable to get the best, if you can. It is sometimes advisable to have more than one spade, not only of different blade sizes but also

---

The cultivation cycle

When land is used for vegetable and fruit growing, or for other plants grown on a seasonal basis, the soil needs tending so that it is ready for the planting of seeds or seedlings. This tending involves incorporating compost, digging to remove weeds and raking to a tilth. So as to make the best use of the good effects of frost on the soil, digging and composting is done in the autumn so that raking can follow in the spring immediately prior to planting. When you establish permanent planting this process is only necessary once. The soil between plants can thereafter be hoed and dressed with compost, if this is necessary.

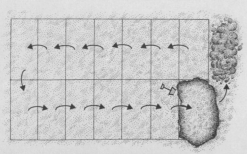

Single digging Bisect large areas and work down one side and up the other, moving earth from the first trench across ready to fill the final trench.

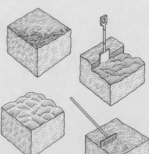

1 Spread well-rotted manure or organic materials.

2 Dig to remove weeds and incorporate manure.

3 Leave the soil in clods over winter.

4 Break the clods and rake to a fine tilth in spring.

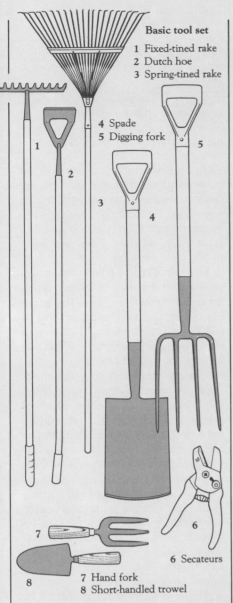

Basic tool set
1 Fixed-tined rake
2 Dutch hoe
3 Spring-tined rake

4 Spade
5 Digging fork

1
2
3
4
5

6 Secateurs
7 Hand fork
8 Short-handled trowel
6
7
8

of different construction. Most wooden-handled examples have a strapped socket with three rivets, but for heavier work, such as uprooting a tree, a stronger spade with longer straps and five rivets is better.

Forks
A digging fork usually has square tines, each narrowing to a point. Forks with flattened tines are specifically for digging potatoes. Like spades, the best forks are made of stainless steel with either a wooden or synthetic shaft and handle. The length of fork tines varies from 300 mm (12 in) to 260 mm (10 in), so select what you can manage. For forking through you will not need a large fork.

Rakes
A garden rake is invaluable for general clearance, though for raking leaves in autumn you will need a finer, more springy type than the

normal one with short rigid tines. Many gardeners also invest in a large, wooden hay rake, which can not only be used for clearing dead leaves but also for levelling ground.

In the vegetable garden, a rake will help you create a fine tilth for seed sowing. You can also use your rake to keep gravel areas looking fresh. Sizes vary from 400 mm (16 in), as do shaft lengths; try them and buy what suits you.

Hoes
We tend to overlook the old Dutch hoe, but it is extremely useful for keeping weeds down between rows of vegetables and elsewhere. You can also use this hoe to make seed drills, dragging it along a line of string stretched between pegs.

Other types of hoe include the draw hoe, the more modern scuffle hoe and, especially useful for awkward corners, the triangular hoe. It is important that you always keep your hoe blade not only clean but sharp.

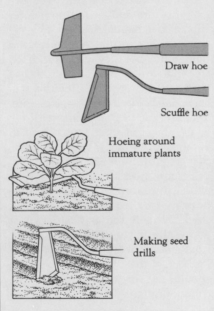

Draw hoe

Scuffle hoe

Hoeing around immature plants

Making seed drills

Trowels and handforks
These invaluable small tools for planting and hand weeding are best made of stainless steel. Quite apart from its greater efficiency, you invariably lose track of such small items in the garden and stainless steel will not rust when left outside for any length of time.

Pruners
There is an enormous range of pruners available. Always get the best, for cheap pruners do not cut cleanly and can cause damage to a branch, which in time may induce rot or disease.

Tool systems
Tool systems are available where a single handle locks on to a variety of attachments. The durability of the connection between handle and attachments is important.

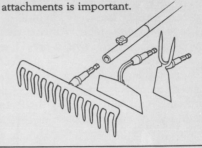

Other tools
When buying a wheelbarrow, get one that holds a reasonable amount and is strong but light enough for you to manage when loaded. The wheel should have a rubber covering.

Hoses should be of rubber or rubberized material for, despite manufacturers' assurances, plastic tends to buckle and block the flow of water.

Lightweight galvanized metal wheelbarrow

You may find that where you are growing crops of fruit or vegetables you need a pressure spray. Hand and knapsack versions are available.

There are also tools for specialist tasks. For example, if you have a number of fruit trees it is worth buying long-handled pruners and, where a lawn leads directly on to flower beds, edging clippers will eliminate stooping. Finally, a stiff garden broom is vital, particularly if you have a terrace, since hard areas will need to be cleared of moss and debris periodically.

Spray gun

Wind-up hose

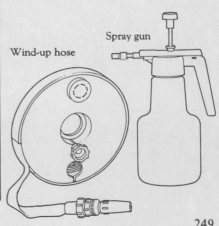

Plant care

Many gardeners make work by choosing plants and cultivation methods that need considerable attention; others prefer planting that requires a minimum of work. The choice is entirely yours. If you elect to grow plants that require regular replacement, such as vegetables or annuals, you will need to dedicate hours of work to gardening on a regular basis; on the other hand, a more casual treatment, with borders of shrubs and random planting through gravel, will only require periodic maintenance.

Trees, in most cases, fall between these two extremes. As a general rule, they require attention at the planting stage and many need care until they are established, which may be a year or two. After that, however, they should thrive with little or no interference until they are old, when special treatment may be necessary. Exceptions to this rule are the fruit trees, for they are usually trained for decorative purposes, for crop quality and ease of harvesting.

Tree maintenance

Newly planted trees
Careful maintenance during the period following planting is crucial if a healthy, vigorous specimen is to become established. The larger the tree, the more important the care. Semi-mature trees, newly planted, need regular watering, but the soil around their roots must not become waterlogged. Mulching the soil throughout summer to the extent of the trees' root runs will help to retain

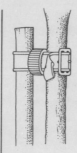

Support ties *Check support ties after windy and wet weather. Make sure the ties are neither too tight nor broken.*

moisture, and will help to keep down weeds which otherwise rob the soil of valuable nutrients. It is also vital that the guy ropes supporting a top-heavy specimen are regularly checked to ensure that there is no root movement. Such care is necessary for all newly established trees for at least two years. Certain conifers, such as pines, need longer attention.

Smaller trees, though staked rather than guyed, need to have their supports checked in spring to ensure that they are still firm after winter winds. Ties should be carefully examined to ensure that they are not too tight; if they are they will cut into the tree and weaken it. Nor should they chaff the bark in wind, for this will cause damage and encourage disease.

From time to time, look critically at the shape of your tree. Then, in autumn, prune by taking out limbs that are growing the wrong way.

Certain trees, particularly fruits and many weeping forms of tree, have been grafted on to another root stock. Usually the graft shows just above the ground. Suckers sometimes grow out from the root stock just below the original graft. These should be cut back flush to the trunk of the tree.

Older trees
Trees are living and as they get older need more specific attention, possibly tree surgery. Most gardeners do not understand the skill of tree surgery. Specialist firms practice this craft, however, employing skilled men with the correct equipment. Before employing such a firm, it is wise to ensure that they are covered by third party and public liability insurances if your trees adjoin a public right of way.

The work that a tree surgeon can perform (and you, to a lesser degree, on smaller trees) includes the pruning and removal of limbs, bracing of old limbs, treatment of hollows to avoid moisture settling and causing further rotting, and feeding trees.

Pruning and removing limbs are the most common operations necessary when a tree gets older. In either case, the limb or branch should be cut right back to the main trunk of its leader. When properly treated the remaining short stub will die and rot back into the tree, where the wound will heal naturally. The time for this in most regions is autumn and winter.

Extremely heavy branches are removed in two pieces to avoid the full weight of the branch, when partially cut, tearing the bark away on the lower parts of the tree.

All newly sawn surfaces should be cleaned at the edges with a sharp knife, and then painted with a commercial preparation which includes a bitumen emulsion with an added fungicide. This forms a seal until the raw area has grown over with callus.

Pruning free-growing trees, or any plant material for that matter,

Pruning for shape
The purpose of general autumn pruning is to create an attractive, open head to the tree. Drastic, clumsy cutting will produce a mass of unsightly new growth. Remove crossing branches, any dead wood and weak growth, then prune lightly to leave a predetermined framework.

Before pruning

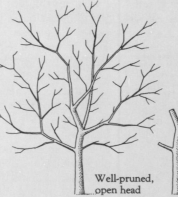

Well-pruned, open head

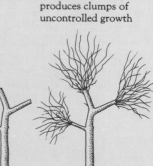

Insensitive hacking produces clumps of uncontrolled growth

seldom necessitates the severe clipping treatment so loved by the ill-informed gardener. When you clip a branch you substitute for one main growth half a dozen other lesser ones, which by the end of the following season will have compounded your problem.

Older trees, particularly when exposed to wind, may have grown in an unattractive way, probably due to having lost their leader growth in their youth. In high winds, different parts of the tree may sway in different directions, thereby causing stress and eventual cracking of the tree where the trunk forks. To prevent this, limbs may be braced together with wire bands, but this is work for a specialist. Failing this, the sensitive removal of one limb of the tree will reduce wind stress.

Removing limbs

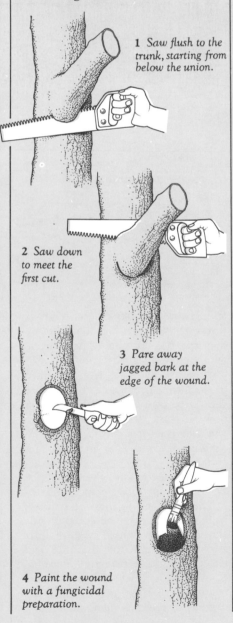

1 *Saw flush to the trunk, starting from below the union.*

2 *Saw down to meet the first cut.*

3 *Pare away jagged bark at the edge of the wound.*

4 *Paint the wound with a fungicidal preparation.*

Pleaching

The classic pleached screen of trees is started against supporting posts and wires. A row of young trees is encouraged to grow in one plane only, so that their branches can be intertwined. Each autumn, vertical growth is stopped above pairs of chosen buds that are left to grow horizontally along each wire, until the desired height is reached. Subsequent growth on this framework will merge to form a mass of foliage in the summer that is then clipped to shape.

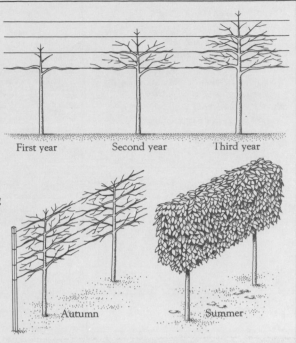

First year   Second year   Third year

Autumn   Summer

Where hollows develop in old trees they should be cleared out and any rotting wood removed. Clean with an antiseptic and then allow to dry. When possible, build up the hole with layers of the material used to seal tree wounds, mixed with sawdust or hardwood chippings. When weathered off, the tree callus will grow over the hole and its bung.

Old trees that have been neglected may benefit from root feeding. Into holes drilled about 230 mm (9 in) into the soil 600 mm (24 in) apart under the tree's overhang, apply a feed consisting of five parts by weight of sulphate of ammonia, five parts of superphosphate and one and a half parts of sulphate of potash. Pour this into each hole and cover with soil.

Special pruning

Pleaching deciduous trees to create a hedge requires considerable seasonal maintenance. This involves pruning, supporting and intertwining in autumn and clipping the overall foliage shape through the summer.

"Top-worked" fruit trees will not only make attractive forms (see p. 183) but will produce a quality crop and one that is easier to harvest. Training the trees is, however, time consuming. One method is fan training (see p. 252), in which the young tree is cut back to 600 mm (24 in). Then train the main branches on wires to the shape of a fan. Growth forwards and backwards from the plane of the fan is cut out. In time, subsidiary branches are trained to the same fan shape and unsuitable growth eliminated.

Another method, allowing many varieties of fruit tree to grow in a small area, consists of restricting a tree to one stem grafted on to dwarfing stock and trained obliquely. Every year, the tree (cordon) must be cut back as it grows longer, so that the entire crop is always within reach.

The espalier form (see p. 183) is perhaps the most effective for fruit trees but it, too, involves considerable yearly maintenance. An advantage of the espalier form is that it can be used for free-standing trees with the support wires strung between posts. In this way a row of espalier-trained fruit trees can be used to divide the garden. As with a pleached avenue of trees, growth away from the line of the supporting wires is removed annually.

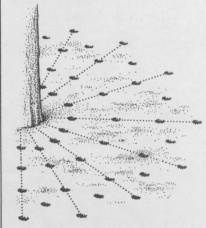

Root feeding *230 mm (9 in) bore holes, made at 600 mm (24 in) intervals.*

251

Fan training fruit trees

Fan training is a useful form of top-working fruit trees, especially cherries, plums and peaches. The fan shape of growth is usually tied against wires and temporary canes attached to a wall. The main stem of a maiden tree is removed above two buds that will grow to form the chief pair of fan ribs.

Year one *Prune the main stem to about 600 mm (24 in), above two healthy opposing buds.*

Year two *Tie the ribs to canes and, in the winter, prune both to 450 mm (18 in), above a bud. Leave 4 buds on each rib.*

Year three *Tie subsidiary ribs to canes as they grow and, in winter, prune the 8 ribs to 750 mm (30 in), above a bud.*

Allow three shoots from each of these ribs to make the 32 ribs of a complete fan in the fourth year.

Hedges

Maintenance of a formal hedge varies according to type. Certain varieties, particularly the fast growing ones, such as privet (*Ligustrum* sp.), thorn (*Crataegus* sp.) and *Lonicera nitida*, need trimming from time to time throughout the year in order to keep them tidy. Other species should be trimmed during July or August and then again in October to remove the secondary growth made after the initial trim. This group includes box (*Buxus* sp.), hornbeam (*Carpinus* sp.), Lawsons cypress (*Chamaecyparis lawsoniana*), *Cotoneaster simonsii*, *Cupressus* sp., *Escallonia* sp., beech (*Fagus* sp.), holly (*Ilex aquifolium*), *Pyracantha* sp., rosemary (*Rosmarinus* sp.), yew (*Taxus baccata*) and *Viburnum tinus*.

Some hedges need to be trimmed only once a year. These include *Aucuba japonica*, *Berberis stenophylla*, *Elaeagnus pungens*, bay (*Laurus nobilis*), laurel (*Prunus laurocerasus*) and Portuguese laurel (*Prunus lusitanica*). The larger-leaved of these should be trimmed with pruners

Once established, it is important that you feed and water your hedge from time to time. Where evergreens are packed extremely tightly to form a screen, they also provide a canopy that shields their roots from rain; in these cases leave a hose dribbling at their roots in high summer.

The shape that you hope your hedges will ultimately achieve is important, for they should be correctly trained from the start. Formal hedges should be trimmed to provide foliage right to the ground and be shaped so that the top is slightly narrower than the base, to prevent damage from wind and snow. A top-heavy hedge, with snow on it, will be pried open at the center and will ultimately collapse. Harder trimming will provide a denser hedge.

Informal and flowering hedges, which should have a much looser shape, are pruned to remove old and dead wood but should not be trimmed, as you will inevitably cut off flower buds. Therefore pick your time carefully. As with shrubs in a border, some hedging shrub flowers appear on young wood formed the same year. These should be pruned in winter or spring and include *Buddleia davidii*, *Cistus* sp., *Fuschia*

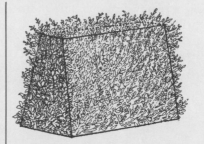

Formal hedge before trimming

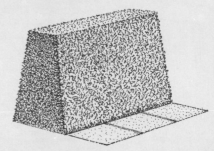

Ideal formal shape with path for easy maintenance

sp., *Hydrangea paniculata* 'Grandiflora', *Hypericum patulum*, *Lavandula* sp., *Rosa rubrifolia*, *Rosa rugosa* and *Santolina chamaecyparissus*.

Others flower on wood formed during the previous year. These should be pruned immediately after flowering and include *Berberis darwinii*, *Berberis stenophylla*, *Ceanothus dentatus*, *Chaenomeles japonica*, *Forsythia* sp., *Hippophae rhamnoides*, *Mahonia aquifolium*, *Prunus × blireiana*, *Ribes* and *Weigela* sp.

The third and final group consists of those that flower on spurs or side shoots. These, which require little attention except for thinning and shaping, include *Berberis thunbergii*, *Cotoneaster franchetii*, *Cotoneaster microphylla*, *Hebe traversii*, *Rhododendron* sp., and *Skimmia japonica*.

Laying a hedge *Old deciduous hedges can be rejuvenated by cutting half through main woody stems and intertwining and staking their bent-over tops.*

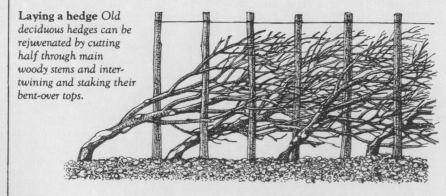

Shrubs

Transplanting

It is possible to transplant most shrubs, even when they are old, provided their roots are prepared and the plant itself cut back. Conifers, however, are notoriously difficult to move when large.

A plant's roots are composed of those which anchor it in the soil so that it is not blown over by wind, and by finer feeder roots located at the tip of the anchorage system. Some shrubs have one or two enormous tap roots, which grow to a considerable depth; most have a system not unlike their branches. As a general guide, you can assume that the shrub's underground feeder root system extends outwards at least as far as its overhead branch system.

By digging close to a shrub, prior to moving it, you will break both its feeding and its anchorage rooting systems. The larger and older the subject, the greater the problem. Up to two or three years of age, shrubs have a small root system and light anchorage since they have no bulk to hold. They can be moved easily, though the more earth you take with the root system the less root disturbance there will be.

Older, larger shrubs should be prepared a year before you propose moving them by slicing down hard around the shrub with a spade at a 500 mm (20 in) radius from the stem to encourage a tighter root ball of young feeder roots, which can be more easily moved the following spring. Older shrubs should also have their heads cut back to reduce loss of moisture through transpiration, since you are limiting their intake of water at the roots.

Temporary heeling in

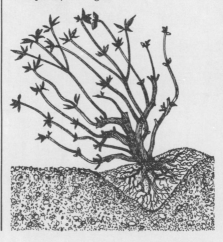

Before lifting a shrub of whatever size, dig the hole in which you are going to replant it. Make the hole wide and deep. It is most important that the moving operation is as swift as possible, so that the exposed root system does not dry out. Ideally, plant in overcast, windless weather, for both sun and wind are injurious.

Prepared for transplanting

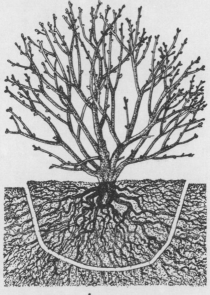

Transplanted and cut back

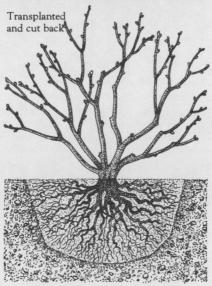

Heel the lifted shrub into a temporary trench if there is any delay in planting.

To lift a shrub, dig around the roots as gently as possible with a fork to ease them. You will then have to chop off extensive roots cleanly with a spade. Work your way around the plant, gradually loosening the soil underneath it and levering upwards.

When the shrub is free of its surround and you can examine its root system, adjust the size of the hole into which it is to be planted. Before replanting, fork into the base of the new position some organic manure or compost with a handful of bone meal. Transfer the shrub with as much earth attached to it as possible. Spread out its root system, cut broken roots cleanly with pruners and fork back the previously excavated soil. Shake the shrub up and down occasionally to allow soil to settle around the roots.

Before finally topping off, hammer in a stake but be careful not to damage the roots. Then complete the backfilling process, heeling down the earth as you go. The final earth height should be at the same position on the stem as it was in its original planting position. If the earth is dry, water the shrub heavily to ensure that earth has enveloped the root system. Finally, fix your shrub to its stake with a plastic tie.

Subsequent maintenance

Newly-planted shrubs need careful treatment. They must be regularly watered to ensure that roots do not dry out, evergreens being particularly susceptible to drought.

After frost or snow, newly planted shrubs should be firmed into the soil by treading around them. New beds should be kept clean and friable by hoeing or light forking through the growing season. This will also assist rain penetration. During early spring, more rotted manure or mulch can be spread on the soil.

The time of year at which you transplant shrubs, and their subsequent maintenance, will vary according to your location. In milder areas the work can be undertaken through autumn, winter and spring, provided the earth is not frozen. Transplanting is safer in spring in regions with short autumns and long severe winters and this is especially true for conifers. However, in most northern regions, gardeners can gain by moving plants in autumn. The weather is cooler and rainfall often more plentiful and plants are approaching their dormant period.

Weather may change in spring quite quickly, however; if the soil dries out, it is essential to keep shrubs well watered with a hose or a can without a fine nozzle. Wind will also dry your soil. Depending on species, you should be quite brutal in cutting back the head of the shrub to make it gain new growth quickly.

When you have moved shrubs in autumn, be sure to check the stability of the subject regularly and reheel in if necessary.

Pruning shrubs

Shrubs will generally flower quite well if left alone. Pruning should only be undertaken to regulate the height of the shrub, its shape and the thickness of its growth, and to establish the level at which you want its flowers. Therefore, decide upon your aims before you start.

Left to themselves, shrubs grow upwards and outwards with flowers early in the season formed on previous years' wood, or flowers towards the end of the season on the current year's wood. You should prune the shrubs to prevent the blossom getting higher and higher each year. Take care when you do this: it is no use pruning a spring flowering specimen in autumn for you will only cut off the next spring's flowers. Prune such shrubs after they have flowered in the spring so that they grow throughout summer to produce the wood on which the following year's flowers will grow. In autumn you should only prune shrubs which flower on the following year's growth.

You can shape your shrubs in the autumn but keep the outline relaxed and only clip dense shrubs, such as box (*Buxus* sp.) and holly (*Ilex* sp.). Use pruners to thin and prune shrubs, making clean cuts just above a node or joint, or cut back flush to the main stem.

Shrub roses need no pruning and floribunda roses only shaping and the removal of dead wood, but hybrid tea roses must be severely pruned back to the second or third bud on each major lateral stem. You must also prune to establish an open, well-shaped bush. New growth will extend from the buds you retain, so prune with ultimate shape in mind. In hard climates, this should be done in spring.

Pruning is a straightforward process but if you are in any doubt, do nothing. Then analyze your plant next season and ascertain what should be done to achieve a shape that will blend harmoniously with adjoining species. Remember that you will seldom kill a shrub by cutting it; you are much more likely to invigorate it. However, you can kill half-hardy roses by pruning too early in the season. You can take out or prune back the center of many shrubs, particularly those with a strong leader shoot, to achieve a more flattened shape.

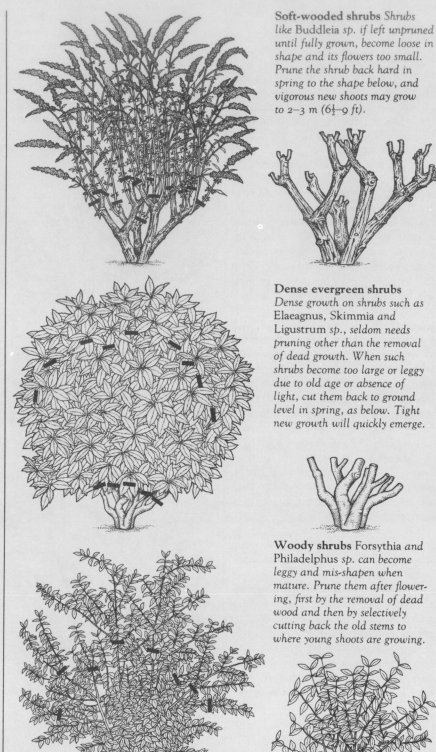

Soft-wooded shrubs *Shrubs like Buddleia sp. if left unpruned until fully grown, become loose in shape and its flowers too small. Prune the shrub back hard in spring to the shape below, and vigorous new shoots may grow to 2–3 m (6½–9 ft).*

Dense evergreen shrubs
Dense growth on shrubs such as Elaeagnus, Skimmia and Ligustrum sp., seldom needs pruning other than the removal of dead growth. When such shrubs become too large or leggy due to old age or absence of light, cut them back to ground level in spring, as below. Tight new growth will quickly emerge.

Woody shrubs Forsythia *and* Philadelphus *sp. can become leggy and mis-shapen when mature. Prune them after flowering, first by the removal of dead wood and then by selectively cutting back the old stems to where young shoots are growing.*

Pruning cuts

When pruning a stem it is important to make a clean cut close above a healthy bud, with the sloping face made away from the bud itself.

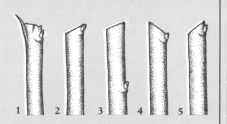

1 Too ragged   2 Too near bud
3 Too far from bud   4 Wrong slope
5 Correct cut

Perennials

Most herbaceous plants will grow in all but extreme soil conditions. They are cheap to buy but need rather more attention than shrubs. They grow quickly, however, and if you are just starting your garden they have the advantage of achieving their ultimate dimensions in one season. It is a mistake, however, to suppose that perennials live for ever; all vegetation ultimately dies of old age, but life span varies from one species to another. Lupines, for example, seldom enjoy more than two years of healthy life, while peonies can survive for 10 years or more. You can be fairly rough when dividing your herbaceous plants in autumn as there is little chance of your killing them. If you do not divide the plants until spring, you may not recognize them since they will have no foliage. You may also destroy their crown or growing point at that time of year.

Many herbaceous plants will self-seed and one of the pleasures of the mixed border is the casual appearance of something you had not intended. The results are invariably far more interesting than the designed areas. Unlike woody shrubs, herbaceous perennials have soft stems which tend to die down to the ground at the end of their growing season. These are the plants that form the mainstay of a flower border and they are the summer glory of the traditional cottage garden. Many herbaceous plants will flower quite happily alongside shrubs, and indeed their inclusion in a shrub border is easier than their cultivation in a strictly herbaceous border.

The herbaceous perennial border needs to be wider than twice the height of its tallest occupants, which are usually two meters (6½ ft) high. This arrangement will look correct in its proportions. These dimensions are often a surprise and to achieve them you may have to enlarge an existing bed in autumn. Perennials tend to flop over and when this happens on to grass it makes lawn maintenance difficult. You may want to edge the area with paving stone or brick to avoid having to support the heads each time you mow.

The ground should be prepared several weeks in advance of planting perennials so that it can settle and consolidate. Cultivate the ground as deeply as possible, incorporating organic feed and some bone meal in the top spit of earth. Ideally, prepare your planting area in autumn to plant the following spring. On particularly light soil, with an equable climate, you can plant in autumn.

The planting hole for each specimen must be large enough to accommodate the root spread and the crown or growth point set to the correct depth. Planting distances within groups of plants should be 230–300 mm (9–12 in) between small species, like primulas, 300–380 mm (12–15 in) for medium species like *Erigeron* sp., while stronger-growing species, such as delphiniums, should be 460–600 mm (18–24 in) apart.

Subsequent maintenance of perennials involves staking the plants at the height of their growth, where wind is likely to blow them over. After flowering, dead heads must be cut off. Plants that flower early, such as lupines, may then produce a second crop of flower heads.

Divide your plants in autumn when they become too large, for herbaceous plants tend to grow outwards and a hole develops quite quickly in their center. Extract any invasive weeds and then, with two forks pushed back to back in the mass, force it apart by levering. Those with fleshy tubers, such as peonies should be lifted, then cut apart with a knife, allowing three to five buds per new division.

Dividing fibrous-rooted perennials

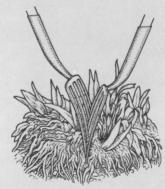

Dividing tuberous perennials

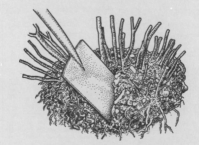

Annuals

Annuals are in general spectacular and, because their life span is short, require little attention once established. Many annuals are now sold as seedlings in spring. However, with a sterile growing medium and fluorescent lights, you can bring on annuals yourself from seed to be hardened off before planting out. Other, larger seeds, such as nasturtiums, can be sown where you want them to flower.

Prepare the ground by light cultivation, no deeper than 100 mm (4 in), and remove all surface weeds and weed roots. Where your seeds are small, as with *Eschscholzia* sp. for example, broadcast over the prepared ground by gently shaking the seed packet. For easier distribution, many seeds are now pelleted within a sterile medium. This not only makes them less subject to rotting but, since they are larger, more manageable. After sowing, gently rake over the ground and water, using a fine mist of water. Seedlings should appear after about 14 days or so, depending on your soil type and its temperature, and will probably need to be thinned.

If you have sown your annuals early in the year, cut them back with shears after they have flowered and you may well get a second flowering later in the growing season.

Broadcasting annual seeds

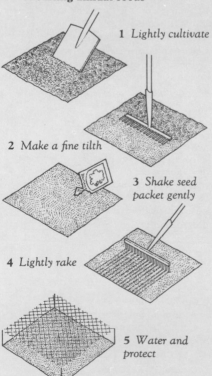

1 *Lightly cultivate*

2 *Make a fine tilth*

3 *Shake seed packet gently*

4 *Lightly rake*

5 *Water and protect*

Lawns

Grass makes a most attractive natural surface but has some disadvantages. In the first place, lawns need a great deal of attention during the growing season. Moreover, grass will not thrive in areas of heavy shade or in any situation where it is subjected to constant human traffic. During periods of drought, some grass species will dry out completely and go dormant. Excessive heat also wrecks many summer lawns. Lastly, grass can play host to organisms that are detrimental to its own growth; if the grass succumbs to disease it results in a poor sward.

If you are prepared to undertake the necessary maintenance tasks, however, there is no better garden surface. Essential maintenance, such as mowing, watering, feeding and weeding, will not only keep a garden looking trim and attractive but will increase the health and vigor of your grass, which in turn will inhibit invaders such as moss and weeds.

Mowing is an essential weekly task throughout the growing season. The blades of your mowing machine must be sharp, properly set and at the correct height, as shown in the diagram showing height of cut.

Watering will be necessary after about seven days of drought in summer and 10 days in spring, or your lawn will look brown and dull and lose its springiness underfoot. As with all watering, give the lawn a good soaking (see Irrigation, p. 105); too light an application will only encourage surface rooting, which compounds your problem.

Feeding your grass will be necessary, since constant cropping of the foliage drains the nutrient reserves in the soil. Do this in spring, when the grass starts to grow, using a lawn fertilizer, applied by a cyclone or drop-type spreader.

Raking with a spring-tined rake will remove surplus and dead surface foliage and open up the thatch of matted stems, which otherwise encourages moss and weed invasion and forms an impassable canopy for air and moisture. (Use a bamboo rake to remove light debris such as fallen leaves.)

Moss and weed eradication is a continuous process. Excessive moss is usually a sign that your lawn needs drainage; small areas of moss are not unexpected, however, after a period of heavy rain. Apply a weed and moss killer as soon as there is an obvious invasion.

Worm casts are a nuisance if your lawn takes much wear, for when crushed underfoot the bare earth makes a seed bed for weeds. When casts appear, scatter them with a bamboo rake before mowing.

Whether you edge your grass or not is an aesthetic consideration. A paved edging eliminates the need for

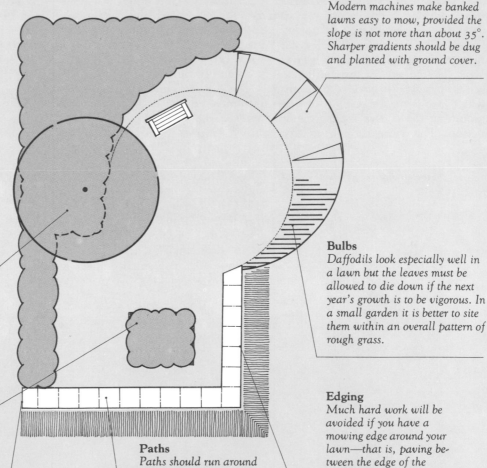

Maintaining features associated with lawns

Areas beneath trees
An area of lawn beneath a tree with dense leaves will inevitably suffer, for it will be deprived of food, water and sunlight. Removing the tree's lower branches will help but even so yearly reseeding of grass may be necessary. One solution is to turn the area into a bed and plant it with shrubs and perennials that welcome shade. Alternatively, surround the base of the tree with a pattern of brickwork.

Isolated beds
An isolated bed must be in proportion to the lawn. Wherever you site it, however, it will inevitably make the lawn appear smaller unless its shape is related to the surrounding pattern in which it sits. Reshape the bed if it is necessary.

Access areas
Ensure that the entry to your lawn is of generous proportions; if not, the area will quickly become worn and unsightly with constant use.

Banks
Modern machines make banked lawns easy to mow, provided the slope is not more than about 35°. Sharper gradients should be dug and planted with ground cover.

Bulbs
Daffodils look especially well in a lawn but the leaves must be allowed to die down if the next year's growth is to be vigorous. In a small garden it is better to site them within an overall pattern of rough grass.

Edging
Much hard work will be avoided if you have a mowing edge around your lawn—that is, paving between the edge of the grass area and surrounding walls and buildings. Paths should be slightly below the lawn level for the same reason.

Paths
Paths should run around a lawn rather than into it, for the junction of path and grass will otherwise rapidly become worn.

regular clipping but defines the lawn and whatever it abutts with an unnecessarily hard edge. Much clipping can be reduced if you ensure that your mower can get into all the corners and over the edge of the grass.

There are several other necessary but less frequent tasks. You can aerate the lawn with a spike or fork to break up the surface layer, which with use and mowing may become compacted. The spiking will also help aerate your grass and improve its drainage (see p. 244). This should be done at least once a year if moss becomes a nuisance.

Top-dress your lawn in autumn to improve the ground on which it feeds, particularly if your topsoil is poor. The dressing should be a mixture of peat, loam and sand. Minor hollows must be filled to give you an even surface for mowing. You should also feed your lawn in autumn with a balanced fertilizer, formulated for the season, to build

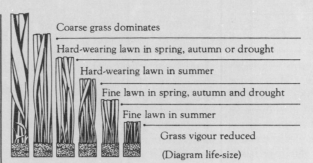

Coarse grass dominates
Hard-wearing lawn in spring, autumn or drought
Hard-wearing lawn in summer
Fine lawn in spring, autumn and drought
Fine lawn in summer
Grass vigour reduced
(Diagram life-size)

Height of cut
Maintain your lawn at the requisite height of cut according to the time of year, weather conditions and the type of grass established.

up the root system and increase resistance to disease. Autumn, in most sections of the country, is a good time to apply limestone, if soil tests show its need.

One task that is seldom necessary is rolling, which will compact your lawn if done at the wrong time of year. The only time to roll is in spring, when the surface of the lawn is dry although the soil beneath still damp, and you need to firm turf that has been lifted by frost.

Ground cover

As with all aspects of gardening, the secret of easy maintenance with ground cover is thorough preparation of the area to be planted. Once established, ground cover will largely eliminate weeding because no plant, however hardy, can survive if totally deprived of sunlight, but do not be deceived into thinking that ground cover will rapidly smother weeds for you. Much time and labor will be saved over the years if you first destroy all weeds by digging out or chemicals. If you can afford the time leave the area unplanted for two or three summer months to ensure that the eliminating process has been thorough.

Nevertheless, weeds will inevitably appear and from time to time plants will need to be lifted and the root systems cleared of pernicious weeds. Some plants will not only need to be lifted occasionally but also divided and replanted, for creeping plants, particularly perennials, such as *Thymus* sp., *Armeria* sp. (thrift) and *Stachys lanata*, grow away from their original center, which then becomes bare. Lift the whole plant, pull off the young growths (which will probably have developed their own root systems) and replant them. Other plants become invasive and their runners should be removed. An example is *Lamium maculatum*. If not held in check, this plant grows into,

and ultimately smothers, adjacent shrubs. Various species of *Rubus* also become invasive in this way, as do certain large-leaved forms of *Hedera*.

If you are not seduced into planting ground cover material that is too rampant for the area you wish to establish, maintenance tasks are not demanding. There are always slower-growing alternatives; the shrubbier junipers, for instance. So study your plants and their growth pattern before using them. You must also consider the site and its exposure. For instance, junipers will not grow in shade and shade is usually the reason why we seek plants other than grass. Both *Vinca minor* and pachysandra thrive with little care in shade.

Certain plants, such as *Hypericum calycinum* and bamboo (*Arundinaria* sp.), will need to be restrained, particularly if you are trying to establish a precise pattern. To do this, sink 300-mm (12-in) strips of slate into the ground to foil underground runners, though even this will sometimes fail to restrain coarse bamboo. In this case, sheet metal (preferably aluminium, which will not rust) provides a flexible, resilient and less penetrable guard, but it is expensive. If your ground cover is keeping within its bounds it will still need attention, either with shears or pruners, to keep the growth low and horizontal.

There are certain plants, such as ground cover roses and ivy, that need their runners directed to infill bare earth. Either pin the runner down with a stone or, more efficiently, make hoops of wire and use these to pin the stems firmly into the earth where you want them.

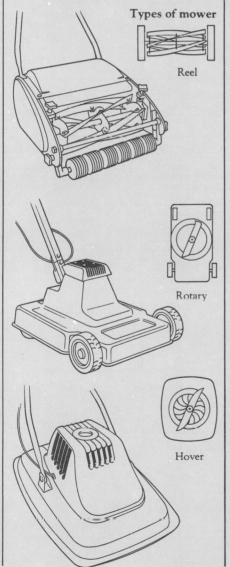

Types of mower

Reel

Rotary

Hover

Climbing plants

The manner in which climbers grow is the key to how they should be treated at the end of the season. The treatment you give will also depend on how high you want them to grow and flower, for you may want them to cover structures ranging from a low fence to the wall of a house. You can control the height at which flowers appear in that they generally appear on new growth. In general, the harder you prune a flowering climber, the lower new growth will appear and so the lower flowers will be. Flowering also depends on pruning at the right time of year. Prune spring-flowering climbers when they have finished flowering, for if you cut them in autumn, when the other climbers are pruned, you will cut off next spring's flowering buds.

Many tropical climbers, such as *Solanum jasminoides*, can be cut back each autumn, for they make enormous growth in the course of one year. In the same way, cut winter jasmine (*Jasminum nudiflorum*) in the spring. Outside decorative vines (*Vitis* sp.) should also be shortened to their main leader in autumn. Rambler roses must have all the year's growth removed in autumn. Tie new growth in a fan shape to make next year's pruning easier.

Woody climbers, such as *Solanum crispum*, are usually pruned in autumn, when they should also be shaped. Take out old and dead wood to encourage new growth. Be bold for you will get the best results by cutting back fairly hard. If you give a

weak snip here and there, you will get a lot of fuzzy end growth that will neither flower nor be in the true character of the plant. To maintain the height of a climbing rose, for example, tie in all the vigorous old growth, take out dead portions and shorten the growths of intermediate length to encourage flowering lower down the plant. In autumn, remove any suckers and rogue growths from the root stock, taking them off with secateurs to the main stem.

Clematis, including the species and many hybrids, require mainly corrective pruning to cut back winter-killed wood or to restrict over-vigorous growth that is making the vines a tangle. For northerners, clematis varieties that bloom on new wood are safer. *Wisteria* sp. must have their rampant twining leaders shortened after flowering in July or August, and must then be trained, tied in and shaped during autumn. For detailed instructions on pruning and shaping a particular species, refer to specialist books on climbers and their maintenance.

Autumn is the ideal time to replace hardware, wires and trellises when pruning your climbers. You may need to let your plants down to give them thorough treatment, and it is sensible to do any replacement necessary then. At this stage, when a plant has a considerable amount of growth, you will see that, unless you have a particularly well-made trellis, it is uncertain whether the climber is holding your trellis up or the trellis the climber. It is for this reason that wires are a more efficient form of horizontal support.

Pruning deciduous climbing and clinging plants

Deciduous climbers must sometimes be cut back to prevent a mat of growth. Prune low to the ground above healthy buds. Clinging plants, such as climbing hydrangeas, should be detached from their supports before removing lateral growth back from the main stems and re-attaching to the support.

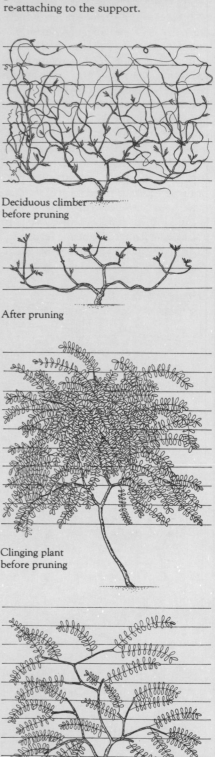

Deciduous climber before pruning

After pruning

Clinging plant before pruning

After pruning

Pruning roses

Cut out recent year's growth from rambler roses to leave a fan shape of vigorous, established wood. With climbing roses, take out dead wood and shorten new growth to leave a clear framework.

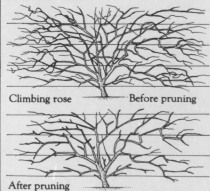

Climbing rose — Before pruning

After pruning

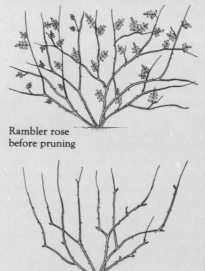

Rambler rose before pruning

After pruning

Water plants

It is neither necessary nor desirable to empty and clean a pool frequently, for every time you do it will need to re-establish a natural balance between water and pond life, including plants. A simple method of removing leaves from small ponds is to thread some wire netting into the tines of a digging fork and then use it like a ladle. You must remove leaves to prevent the choking of water plants. In full sun, algae growing in the water become a nuisance and must be cleared with a fine net, although proprietary chemicals are available that help.

When you do eventually need to empty and clean your pool, take the opportunity to divide your plants before replanting them, the best time being in late spring. Wash the plants thoroughly and cut out any weak or spindly growth. Strong stock should be divided and the tubers of water lilies cut into pieces, leaving one good crown to each plant. You need leave only a few inches of tuber to each crown and some of the old, fleshy roots must be cut away.

Plants and fish will be quite safe below ice during winter, provided your pool is deep enough (500–600 mm (20–24 in)). You should nevertheless maintain a hole in the ice 500 mm (24 in) across, admitting air to the water and enabling the fish to be fed. Tropical water lilies will not survive freezing and must be treated as annuals in the North. Hardy water lilies should survive if their roots are below the ice layer.

Very small ponds can quickly freeze solid in severe weather, injuring or even killing fish and lilies. Life within the pool can be protected by wooden boards, to which old mats

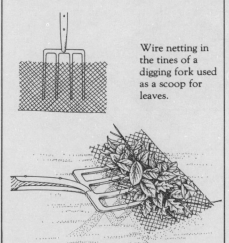

Wire netting in the tines of a digging fork used as a scoop for leaves.

Dividing water plants
When you come to divide water plants, use the method to suit the type of plant. Marginal plants with lower stems like celery are divided by pulling the elements of the root stock apart. Marginals with creeping rhizomatous roots should be cut to separate rooted sections and tuberous-rooted plants, such as water lilies, should be pulled apart.

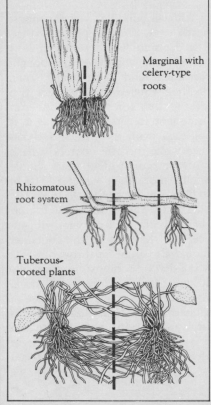

Marginal with celery-type roots

Rhizomatous root system

Tuberous-rooted plants

or a layer of straw is attached. These are then left to float on the surface but as soon as the weather improves in spring they must be removed or plants will be forced into premature growth. Alternatively, cover the pool with boards and place sacks or straw on top of them. Easier and almost a necessity in most northern regions is an electric immersion heater controlled by a thermostat.

Plants growing in damp soil at the edge of ponds and pools should be cut down during winter, much as you do with perennials and mixed border material. The crowns of the enormous *Gunnera manicata* can be protected by folding back one of its leaves over the crown and then covering this with evergreen boughs or with straw.

Herbs

Maintenance of herbs includes cutting back annual growth and dead heads and generally shaping bushes. In mild climates, do this in autumn but in the North spring is preferable. Sage, for example, becomes very straggly after two or three years and will need to be cut back to the main stem or dug up and replaced with new stock. Some climbing herbs, such as sorrel, will need to be lifted and divided or they will swamp the area. If you plant mints in open ground they must be dramatically restrained or their rampant growth will swamp the herb garden.

Many herbs, especially those with umbelliferous flowers, like lovage, seed extensively and the plants must be removed each year. Fennel and angelica, for instance, should always be treated in this way. If the ripe seeds are left to fall into the soil and germinate, they grow through other species and can then be very difficult to remove.

If you wish to collect herb seeds, remove the entire plant with its seed heads before they have dried out, then tie them in bundles and hang them upside-down from a stake over a prepared bed into which the seeds will drop. This method is especially successful with chervil, angelica, fennel and dill.

You must also remove annual herbs, such as dill and sweet basil, at the end of the season for they will not reappear the following year and you will need to utilize the space for new planting. Chives have an unfortunate habit of hosting grass roots, so lift the clumps when necessary, divide them and then replant after removing any entwined, foreign roots. The leaves of some herbs, such as basil and marjoram, may be harvested for immediate use. Remove the center tip, as this will produce bushy side growth. With herbs such as parsley and lovage you must take the outside leaves and their stalks, leaving the crown.

Other herbs need to be dried and stored after harvesting. Take only as much as you can manage to dry at one time, as delay after cutting reduces the strength of their essential oils. Annuals and perennial herbs will give two or even three crops in a season, but make your last cut in autumn to allow new growth to harden before the cold weather.

The organic cycle

In most conditions in the northern hemisphere plants will flourish without artificial additives, for nature has made adequate provision with her various cycles. The "water cycle", for example, is simply the process by which water evaporates from seas, lakes and rivers, is carried about the atmosphere by winds and is ultimately deposited as rain or snow to percolate through the earth and fill rivers and lakes again. In the same way, the "nitrogen cycle" (dead animal and vegetable tissue decomposing into the soil eventually releases nitrogen for the use of plants, which in turn provide food for animals) gives adequate soil nutrition. If you step in clumsily, adding synthetic, inorganic fertilizers and pesticides for instant results in your garden, you can easily ruin the long term fertility of your soil and disrupt the natural chains of life that will otherwise keep a rough balance. Establish your own compost heaps to re-use vegetable waste and introduce animal manures to increase the nitrogen content.

Leaf clearance
On still autumn days a regular task is to clear leaves from lawns, paths and plants. Do this regularly before they accumulate, as they can smother grass. Use the leaves for rotting down into leaf mold or include them in your compost heap. Beech and oak leaves, which take some time to rot, may be used directly, with other organic matter, as a mulch to protect tender perennials. Place the leaves around the base of the plants, leaving the tops uncovered if they are still green for only the crown of the plants and the roots need protection. Then place twigs over the mulch to hold it in place.

Compost heaps

A compost heap can be open or enclosed. In a well-composed heap, spring waste will be compost by summer and summer waste by autumn. An autumn heap will take longer to break down but will still be ready by spring.

You can build your own compost heap or buy a pre-shaped container. The decision will depend on how much waste you have, for bought containers tend to be small. When building your own, construct two areas so that you will have one area to contain vegetable waste as it is collected from the garden and kitchen while the other compost heap is decomposing. The heap should not be more than a meter (3 ft) or so high. The base of the heap should be slightly raised to allow for air circulation (a layer of twigs will suffice) and the sides of the container should also allow air through.

Build your compost heap in 150–200 mm (6–8 in) layers of waste. Poisonous leaves, including those of rhubarb, must be excluded. Spread farmyard manure, organic activator or sulphate of ammonia at rate of 15 g (.53 oz) to every square meter

(10 ft²) over alternate layers and a sprinkling of lime over intervening ones. Water each layer as you build the heap. Finally, add a 200 mm (8 in) layer of soil.

Some gardeners pre⋅ leave the rotting process undisturbed, but there is some evidence to suggest that the rotting process is improved by turning the heap every month or so and watering any dry areas. Compost is ready for use when its components can no longer be distinguished, but can be used sooner.

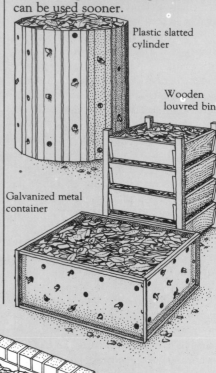

Plastic slatted cylinder

Wooden louvred bin

Galvanized metal container

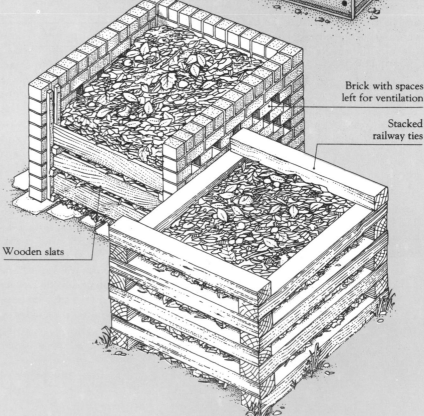

Brick with spaces left for ventilation

Stacked railway ties

Wooden slats

APPENDIX

Plant lists and selection guides
Mortar mixes and concrete mixes
Paving coverages
Grass seed blends

Broad-leaved trees

The trees below are deciduous unless indicated evergreen. More than one entry under "size" in the selection guide indicates a wide size range.

Acer griseum (Paperbark Maple). Outstanding small tree for small properties. Shredding orange-red bark, compound foliage that colors to bright red and orange in late autumn.
Acer negundo (Box Elder). Spreading, open, fast-growing tree. Pinnate, irregularly-toothed leaves, which do not color in autumn. Drought- and cold-tolerant.
Acer platanoides (Norway Maple). Magnificent, round-headed, fast-growing tree. Sharply-lobed leaves turn yellow or red in autumn. Yellow flowers open April, before leaves.
Acer pseudoplatanus (Common Sycamore). Wide-spreading, densely-leaved tree. Deep green leaves.

Aesculus (Horse Chestnut). Handsome, wide-spreading, densely-leaved trees. Big, palmate leaves turn yellow in autumn. "Candles" of flowers in May. "Conkers" in autumn.

Ailanthus altissima (Tree of Heaven). Elegant, oval-headed tree with long, ash-like leaves. A "weed" tree but very useful in cities and at seashore.

Alnus (Alder). Fast-growing conical trees with leaves lasting long into autumn. Catkins in March before leaves, their buds conspicuous in winter.

Amelanchier canadensis (Shadblow). Lovely, round-headed tree, also grown as shrub. Leaves unfold pink and turn scarlet in autumn. Clusters of starry, white flowers in spring. Purple edible fruits ripen in July. Gray bark.

Betula (Birch). Graceful, open trees with white or brown bark in maturity. Yellow autumn leaves. Catkins in early spring.

Carpinus (Hornbeam). Beech-like forest trees. Beautiful gray, fluted bark. Strongly ribbed and toothed leaves, yellow in autumn, often persisting winter.

Catalpa bignonioides (Indian Bean Tree). Wide, low tree with big, heart-shaped leaves. White yellow and purple foxglove-like flowers, summer. Fruits like beans in autumn.

Cornus florida (Flowering Dogwood). Ever popular small tree with white or pink flowers in spring and autumn colors. Attractive winter form.

Crataegus (Hawthorn). Densely-leaved, very hardy trees. White flowers late spring. Profuse red berries lasting into winter.

Cytisus battandieri (Moroccan Broom). Open, many-branched tree with silky gray leaves, pineapple-scented flowers, July. For mild climates only.

Eucalyptus gunnii (Cider Gum). Fast, open, vertical tree with handsome bark. Silver-blue young foliage. Evergreen. For mild climates.

Fagus (Beech). Majestic, large-domed trees with silvery-gray bark. Leaves gold/copper in autumn as nuts produced.

Fraxinus (Ash). Open, fast trees with ascending branches. Pinnate leaves, green until they fall. Fruit ripens to brown in October and into winter.

Gleditsia Elegant foliage trees with barbed trunks and branches. Delicate, bipinnate leaves appear late and yellow in autumn. Most popular forms 'Moraine' and 'Sunburst'.

Koelreuteria paniculata (Goldenrain Tree). Rounded tree with long pinnate leaves, red in spring, turning slowly yellow, green and finally gold in autumn. Yellow midsummer flowers. Bladder-like fruit.

Laburnum (Golden Chain). Graceful trees with arching branches famed for their long racemes of bright yellow flowers, spring. Brown pods with poisonous black seeds.

Liquidambar styraciflua (Sweet Gum). Broad-domed handsome tree with maple-like leaves, which color richly in the autumn.

Liriodendron tulipifera (Tulip Tree). Fast, beautiful tree with distinctive squared-off leaves, gold in autumn. Mature trees have yellowish-green, tulip-shaped flowers.

Magnolia kobus Young trees cone-shaped, broader when mature. Shiny leaves. After 15 years, white, fragrant flowers appear profusely.

Malus (Flowering Crabs). Densely-crowned, wide trees with attractive pink/red/white flowers in spring. Some varieties color richly in autumn when most bear fruit which can be made into jelly.

Oxydendrum arboreum (Sourwood). Eastern USA native that is slow growing. Long lasting drooping "lily-of-the-valley" flowers in the summer.

Parrotia persica (Persian Ironwood). Wide trees with gray, peeling bark similar to the London plane's. Beech-like leaves, crimson/gold in autumn. Red, tufted flowers January/March before leaves.

Platanus (Plane). Particularly handsome, fast trees with high-domed crown. Distinctive flaking bark. Maple-like leaves sometimes color in autumn.

Populus (Poplar). Tall, slender trees ideal for screens. Young leaves red or bronze and often scented. Many have attractive catkins. Not to be placed near buildings due to thirsty roots.

Prunus cerasifera (Cherry Plum). Open tree with profuse small white flowers in February/March. Mature trees bear edible fruits.
Prunus dulcis (Almond). Open tree with ascending branches and pointed leaves. Large, pink flowers, March, before leaves. Nuts in autumn.
Prunus padus (Bird Cherry). Elegant tree, rounded in maturity with slender racemes of scented white flowers that appear in late May.
Prunus persica (Peach). Shrubby tree with pale pink flowers, April. Edible fruits. Must be sprayed against peach leaf curl and other pests.
Prunus serrulata (Japanese Cherry). Stiffly-branched tree with profusion of white or

Acer platanoides

Ailanthus altissima

Catalpa bignonioides

Eucalyptus gunnii

Gleditsia triacanthus

pink flowers in spring. Young leaves often bronze. Some forms color in autumn.

Pyrus (Pears). Very hardy, round-domed trees with plentiful white flowers, April. Apart from fruiting forms, there are ornamental varieties with good autumn color.

Quercus (Oak). Tall, wide, stately trees needing a lot of space. Some varieties color richly in autumn. Most produce acorns.

Robinia Very hardy, fast trees with light, open crown, noted for beautiful foliage (pinnate). Fragrant, white flowers in June.

Salix (Willow). Diverse, vigorous genus. Early slender leaves, often silvery. Many have colorful bark and stems in winter. Catkins.

Sorbus aria (Whitebeam). Compact tree with ascending branches. Attractive gray-green foliage turns red/gold autumn. White spring flowers. Conspicuous red berries.

Sorbus aucuparia (Rowan or Mountain Ash). Irregularly-shaped, oval-headed tree with delicate pinnate leaves and

Liquidambar styraciflua

Liriodendron tulipifera

Pyrus communis

Robinia pseudoacacia

Sorbus aria

SELECTION GUIDE
Broad-leaved trees

	SOIL TOLERANCE				LOCATION		SIZE			
	Acid	Alkaline	Well-drained	Damp	Full sun	Semi-shade	Over 60 ft	35–60 ft	15–35 ft	Provides dense shade
Acer griseum	●		●		●	●			●	
Acer negundo	●	●	●		●	●		●		
Acer platanoides		●	●		●	●	●			●
Acer pseudoplatanus	●	●	●	●	●	●	●			
Aesculus	●	●	●		●	●	●			●
Ailanthus altissima		●	●		●	●		●		
Alnus	●	●		●	●	●	●			
Alemanchier lamarckii	●			●	●	●			●	
Betula	●	●	●		●	●		●		
Carpinus	●	●		●	●	●	●	●		
Catalpa bignonioides		●		●	●	●		●	●	●
Cornus florida	●		●	●	●	●		●		
Crataegus	●	●		●	●	●			●	
Cytisus battandieri	●	●	●		●				●	
Eucalyptus gunnii	●	●			●			●		
Fagus		●	●		●	●	●			●
Fraxinus	●	●			●	●	●			
Gleditsia	●	●	●		●	●		●	●	
Koelreuteria paniculata		●	●		●	●			●	
Laburnum		●	●		●				●	
Liquidambar styraciflua	●			●	●	●	●	●		●
Liriodendron tulipifera	●		●		●	●	●			
Magnolia kobus	●	●	●	●	●	●			●	
Malus	●	●	●	●	●	●			●	
Oxydendram arboreum	●		●	●	●	●		●		
Parrotia persica		●	●	●	●	●			●	
Platanus	●	●	●	●	●	●	●			●
Populus	●	●	●	●	●		●			
Prunus cerasifera	●	●	●		●	●		●	●	
Prunus dulcis	●	●	●		●	●			●	
Prunus padus	●	●	●	●	●	●		●	●	
Prunus persica	●	●	●		●	●			●	
Prunus serrulata	●	●	●		●	●			●	
Pyrus	●	●			●	●		●	●	
Quercus	●	●		●	●	●	●			●
Robinia		●	●		●	●		●		
Salix	●	●		●	●	●		●		
Sorbus aria	●	●	●		●	●			●	
Sorbus aucuparia	●	●	●		●	●			●	
Tilia	●	●			●	●	●	●	●	●
Ulmus	●	●			●	●	●	●		●

263

white, scented flowers in May. Bright autumn berries.

Tilia (Lime or Linden). Narrow-crowned trees with ascending branches and glossy, green, heart-shaped leaves. Scented yellow flowers hang in cymes, June.

Ulmus (Elm). Tall, elegant trees, now greatly reduced due to Dutch elm disease.

Conifers

My selection of conifers, below, is largely restricted to the larger growing genera. Forms of conifer are included in many other classifications.

Abies (Silver Fir). Handsome, conical trees whose name refers to their imposing, lofty stature. Erect cones, in some species blue when young. Dislikes pollution.

Cedrus (Cedar). Conical at first, spreads later. Huge trees with barrel-shaped cones. Leaves in rosettes, in some species blue or silvery-blue. There are dwarf forms.

Chamaecyparis (False Cypress). These differ in their flat branches and small cones from the true Cypress, which has rounded branches and large cones. A varied genus,

often with attractive foliage. Recommended: the range of cvs of *C lawsoniana*.

× **Cupressocyparis** varieties. Columnar, extremely vigorous trees, ideal as hedge or screen. Some have unusual and attractive leaf color.

Cupressus (Cypress). Handsome, conical trees with wide variety of colors.

Ginkgo biloba (Maidenhair Tree). The only survivor of a group of trees flourishing 200 million years ago. Beautiful, slow tree with lovely fan-shaped leaves, yellow in autumn. Long lived.

Juniperus (Juniper). Large genus. Most forms have gray-green berries and aromatic leaves, poisonous to cattle.

Larix (Larch). Fast, deciduous trees with bright green leaves in spring, yellow in autumn. Dense linear leaves.

Metasequoia (Dawn Redwood). Beautiful, conical, deciduous trees becoming rounder in maturity. Fern-like foliage, coloring pink and gold in autumn.

Picea (Spruce). Dense, conical trees with sharp, pointed leaves. Pendulous cones. Genus includes Christmas Tree.

Pinus (Pine). A large and varied genus with long, sharp leaves. Many forms have handsome, colored bark.

Taxodium distichum (Deciduous Cypress or Swamp Cypress). Conical trees with reddish bark. Feathery green foliage, bronze before falling.

Taxus baccata (Yew). Long-lived, dark green-leaved tree, particularly useful for hedges.

Tsuga canadensis (Canada Hemlock). Native over wide area of Northeast. Large, handsome tree with soft needles, small cones. Many dwarf forms.

Hedges

I have selected both deciduous and evergreen hedge plants below. The flowering species will only produce blooms if trimmed at the right time of year (see p. 252).

Berberis (Barberry). Large and varied genus of prickly shrubs, both evergreen and deciduous. Yellow/orange spring flowers. Most have autumn fruits.

Buxus (Box). *The* evergreen hedge where winters are mild to moderate. *B. sempervirens* best but hardier forms exist.

Abies alba

Ginkgo biloba

Metasequoia glyptostroboides

Taxodium plicata

Thuja plicata

SELECTION GUIDE **Conifers**	SOIL TOLERANCE				LOCATION			SIZE		
	Acid	Alkaline	Well-drained	Damp	Full sun	Semi-shade	Total shade	Over 60 ft	35–60 ft	15–35 ft
Abies	●	●		●	●	●		●		
Cedrus	●	●	●	●	●	●		●		
Chamaecyparis	●	●	●	●	●	●		●	●	
× Cupressocyparis	●	●	●	●	●	●		●	●	
Cupressus	●	●	●		●	●		●	●	
Ginkgo biloba	●	●	●		●			●		
Juniperus	●	●	●		●	●			●	●
Larix	●	●	●	●	●	●		●	●	
Metasequoia	●	●	●	●	●	●		●	●	
Picea	●	●	●	●	●	●		●	●	
Pinus	●	●	●		●	●	●	●	●	
Taxodium distichum	●	●		●	●	●		●		
Taxus baccata	●	●	●		●	●	●		●	●
Tsuga Canadensis	●		●	●	●	●				

SELECTION GUIDE
Hedges

	SOIL TOLERANCE				LOCATION			SIZE		
	Acid	Alkaline	Well-drained	Damp	Full sun	Semi-shade	Total shade	Over 10ft	5–10ft	3–5ft
Berberis	●	●	●		●	●		●	●	●
Buxus	●	●	●	●	●	●		●		●
Carpinus	●	●		●	●	●		●		
Cotoneaster	●	●	●	●	●	●	●	●	●	●
Escallonia		●	●		●				●	●
Euonymus	●	●				●	●			●
Fagus		●	●		●	●		●		
Hebe		●	●		●	●				●
Hippophae	●	●	●	●	●			●	●	
Ilex	●	●	●			●	●	●	●	
Ligustrum	●	●	●	●	●	●	●	●	●	●
Lonicera	●	●	●		●	●			●	●
Potentilla	●	●	●		●	●			●	●
Pittosporum	●	●	●		●	●		●		
Prunus laurocerasus	●	●	●			●	●	●		
Prunus lusitanica	●	●	●			●	●	●		
Pyracantha	●	●	●			●		●		
Rhamnus	●	●	●		●	●		●	●	
Syringa	●	●	●		●			●		
Coniferous hedges										
Chamaecyparis	●	●	●		●	●		●	●	
× Cupressocyparis	●	●	●		●	●		●	●	
Cupressus	●	●			●	●		●	●	
Taxus baccata	●	●	●		●	●	●	●	●	
Thuja plicata	●	●	●		●	●		●		

Berberis × stenophylla

Cotoneaster lacteus

Escallonia illinita

Euonymus alatus

Pyracantha 'Watereri'

Rosmarinus officinalis

Taxus baccata

Thuja occidentalis

Carpinus (Hornbeam). Deciduous trees whose yellow-brown, oval leaves remain throughout winter when clipped as hedge.

Cotoneaster These are deciduous and evergreen shrubs noted for spring flowers, bright berries and, in some forms, autumn foliage.

Escallonia Generally evergreen shrubs (semi-evergreen in colder districts) with profuse summer flowers. Good coastal plant in California.

Euonymus (Spindle). Most varied genus of evergreen and deciduous shrubs, often with conspicuous fruits and, in deciduous forms, provides autumn color.

Fagus (Beech). Deciduous tree useful as all-year screen. Retains brown leaves all winter as clipped hedge.

Hebe (Veronica). Slightly tender evergreen shrub with plentiful flowers carried in small spikes through summer.

Hippophae Silver or sage-green-leaved shrubs with profuse berries throughout winter. Ideal on coast.

Ilex (Holly). Prickly, evergreen genus, many forms with bright berries. Most are tender.

Ligustrum (Privet). Either evergreen or semi-evergreen fast-growing shrubs. Grow in all conditions.

Lonicera (Honeysuckle). Dense, evergreen and deciduous shrubs of the same family as the better-known climbers. All have fragrant, usually cream, flowers.

Pittosporum Dense, evergreen shrubs; elegant, oval foliage. Small, fragrant flowers in May.

Pontentilla (Cinquefoil). Compact, long-flowering shrubs with pretty, white/red/orange/yellow flowers.

Prunus laurocerasus (Cherry Laurel). Vigorous evergreen shrubs with glossy leaves, white spring flowers and black fruits. Good for shade, tender.

Prunus lusitanica (Portuguese Laurel). Similar to Cherry Laurel, with purple fruits and, though hardier good in shade.

Pyracantha (Firethorn). Handsome, thorny evergreens with white spring flowers and profuse red/orange/yellow autumn berries.

Rhamnus frangula 'Columnaris' (Tallhedge). A superior deciduous hedge plant because of its hardiness, fast growth and neat form. Does not need as much pruning as privet.

Syringa (Lilac). Where space is ample the common lilac makes an informal screen and windbreak.

Coniferous hedges

Chamaecyparis (False Cypress). Hardy genus with fan-like foliage. *See Conifers*

× **Cupressocyparis** varieties. Adaptable, very vigorous. × *C. Leylandii* is fast growing in Washington, D. C. area.

Cupressus (Cypress). Fast-growing genus, including forms with blue-gray, green, gold and blue foliage.

Taxus baccata (Yew). Slow tree, excellent as clipped hedge, with dark green foliage (there are also gold and variegated forms). Poisonous seeds.

Thuja occidentalis (American Arborvitae). Adaptable tree which makes good, thick hedging. Foliage forming fan-like sprays.

Shrubs

My selection of shrubs provides a range of mild climate as well as hardy kinds. Note the column denoting "architectural form" in the selection guide.

Abelia × **grandiflora** Graceful shrub with glossy, green leaves and abundant, tubular, white/pink flowers, late summer.

Acacia dealbata (Mimosa). Beautiful shrub with fern-like foliage and yellow, fragrant flowers, winter. Tender and requires considerable protection from frost.

Acer japonicum Handsome shrubs with palmate leaves. Glorious purplish-red autumn color. Recommended: *A. j.* 'Aureum' a slow-growing form with soft yellow leaves growing to form a rounded bush.

Acer palmatum (Japanese Maple). Similar to *Acer japonicum* with elegant, 5/7-lobed leaves, splendid purplish-red autumn colors. Recommended: *Dissectum* group, all having deeply-cut leaves and dense, round habit. Green, purple or bronze-tinted leaves, all with autumn color.

Aesculus parviflora A shrubby relative of the Horse Chestnut, with similar leaves. White "candles" with red anthers, late summer.

Amelanchier canadensis *See Trees.*

Aralia elata (Japanese Angelica Tree). Spiny, many-stemmed shrub with huge, palm-like leaves. White flowers in plumes show through autumn. Often treelike.

Arbutus (Strawberry Tree). Evergreens with white, pitcher-shaped flowers and red, strawberry-like fruits. Recommended: *A. unedo* bears flowers and fruits simultaneously in autumn.

Aronia arbutifolia (Red Chokeberry). Hardy, dependable, tolerant of moist soil. Red berries, leaves in autumn.

Arundinaria (Bamboo). Fine evergreens for shade. Recommended: *A. nitida* has arching, purple canes, contrasting well with delicate, narrow leaves that rattle in the wind.

Aucuba japonica Handsome, rounded evergreens with red berries. Some forms have attractive gold-splashed foliage.

Berberis A variable genus with evergreen and deciduous members, noted for its profuse flowers (usually yellow) and autumn berries. Evergreens are spiny and have dense, glossy leaves. Deciduous forms have fine autumn foliage. Recommended: *B. thunbergii* 'Rose Glow'. Leaves start purple, turning silver-pink, then purple again. Deciduous.

Buddleia (Butterfly Bush). Graceful shrubs, whose long racemes of scented flowers (June/July) attract butterflies. Recommended: *B. davidii* offers red, white, violet or blue flowers; *B. fallowiana* 'Alba' has silver-gray leaves and highly-scented white flowers with an orange eye. Tender.

Camellia japonica Beautiful, evergreen, winter/spring-flowering shrubs. Glossy green leaves and sumptuous flowers. Hardy, to Washington, D.C. and like climates.

Caryopteris (Blue Spiraea). Aromatic, gray-green, low shrubs with blue flowers in late summer. Recommended: *C.* × *clandonensis*, hybrid with several cultivars.

Ceanothus (Californian Lilac). Large family of evergreen and deciduous shrubs, usually with bright blue flowers from July onwards. Recommended: *C. thyrsiflorus repens* is mound-forming ground cover with light blue flowers. Tender.

Ceratostigma (Hardy Plumbago). Autumn-flowering, low shrub with blue flowers and often rich autumn foliage color. Recommended: *C. willmottianum.*

Cercis siliquastrum (Judas Tree). Slow-growing, half-hardy large shrub with pink pea-flowers, spring. Red seed pods from July. According to legend, the tree from which Judas hanged himself.

Chaenomeles (Japonica or Flowering Quince). Very hardy, spiny shrubs invaluable for their lovely, very early flowers. Recommended: *C.* 'Cameo', which has apricot flowers.

Chimonanthus (Winter Sweet). Sweetly-scented, winter-flowering shrubs. For mild climates. Recommended: *C. praecox* has yellow flowers with purple or red centers.

Choisya ternata (Mexican Orange Blossom). Glossy, aromatic, tender evergreen shrub with fragrant, white flowers, late spring.

Cistus (Sun Rose). Half-hardy, evergreen shrubs with masses of very pretty, short-lived, saucer-shaped flowers. Recommended: *C* × *corbariensis* is a hybrid form with crimson-ringed buds, opening white.

Clethra alnifolia (Summersweet). Very hardy native shrub with fragrant white flower panicles in summer.

Cordyline australis (Cabbage Tree). Palm-like evergreen with trunk and long, sword-like leaves. Small, scented, cream flowers, summer. Tender.

Cornus (Dogwood). Large, mainly deciduous family. Attractive foliage, often richly colored in autumn, and bright stems through winter. Recommended: *C. stolonifera* 'Flaviramea' has yellow stems, white flowers.

Arbutus unedo

Aucuba japonica

Choisya ternata

Cotoneaster horizontalis

Euonymus japonica

Cortaderia (Pampas Grass). Evergreen perennial with tall autumn plumes and arching, narrow leaves. Recommended: *C. argentea* has silvery-white plumes.

Cotinus (Smoke Tree). Handsome, foliage shrubs with rich autumn colors. Best in poor soil. Recommended: *C. coggygria* has smooth, green leaves and fawn/pink, wispy inflorescences in summer.

Cotoneaster *See Trees and Hedges* Mainly evergreen genus. Recommended: *C. horizontalis* 'Variegatus' is a ground cover form with spreading, "herringbone" branches, small, cream, variegated leaves, bright fruit and autumn foliage.

Cytisus (Broom). Free-flowering shrubs with yellow, pea-shaped flowers, spring. Recommended: *C. scoparius* includes many unusual colors.

Daphne Very fragrant, deciduous and evergreen shrubs, spring flowering. Recommended: *D. odora aureomarginata* has early, purple-pink flowers and large, lanceolate leaves which are variegated yellow and green.

Deutzia Pretty, June-flowering shrubs with narrow leaves and profuse clusters of white flowers along stems. Recommended: *D. discolor* has scented, rose-tinted flowers.

Elaeagnus Vigorous, very hardy, deciduous and evergreen shrubs with small, fragrant flowers and fine foliage. Recommended: *E. ebbingei* has silvery flowers, autumn, orange, silver-speckled fruits, spring.

Escallonia *See Hedges* Recommended: *E.* 'Iveyi' has large, glossy leaves and white autumn flowers. Not hardy.

Eucalyptus gunnii *See Trees*

Enkianthus campanulatus (Red-vein Enkianthus). Hardy, elegant shrub. Background or specimen. Red autumn color.

Euonymus *See Hedges* Tender. Recommended: *E. alata* has corky, winged branches and good autumn color; *E.*

fortunei is evergreen ground cover with some lovely variegated forms.

Fatsia japonica Exotic-looking evergreen with large, palmate leaves and globular, cream flowers on stalks. Not hardy.

Forsythia Hardy shrubs with plentiful, golden-yellow flowers in early spring on bare branches. Recommended: *F. suspensa* is a vigorous, handsome wall shrub.

Fothergilla. Southeastern natives hardy to Boston. Fuzzy white flowers in spring. Fragrant. Good autumn leaf color. Use in woodland garden.

Fuchsia Hardy summer/autumn flowering shrubs with handsome, pendulous blooms. Recommended: *F.* garden hyb. 'Riccartonii' has scarlet and purple flowers.

Garrya elliptica Graceful evergreen with handsome, midwinter catkins on male plants. Vigorous. Not hardy.

Gaultheria Evergreen ground cover with white, urn-shaped flowers, spring/summer. Recommended: *G. procumbens* has bright red autumn berries.

Genista Broom-like shrubs with yellow, summer flowers. Recommended: *G. aetnensis* is a vigorous, free-flowering form to 6 m high.

Griselinia littoralis Leathery-leaved evergreen, not hardy. Small, green flowers and apple-green leaves. Some variegated forms.

Hamamelis (Witch-hazel). Lovely shrubs with fragrant, spidery winter flowers. Usually fine autumn foliage. Recommended: *H. mollis* 'Pallida' has dense clusters of sulphur-yellow flowers.

Hibiscus Syriacus (Rose of Sharon) Splendid, hardy summer/autumn-flowering shrubs with hollyhock-like flowers of blue, red or white. The last color is particularly recommended.

Hippophae *See Hedges* Recommended: *H. rhamnoides*

has masses of orange-red berries and silver leaves.

Hydrangea Varied genus with domed or flat flowering heads. Pink, red, blue or white flowers, summer/autumn. Recommended: *H. villosa* (Lacecap) has large lilac-blue flowers. Also *H. serrata*.

Hypericum (St. John's Wort). Evergreen, deciduous shrubs with bright yellow flowers, summer/autumn. Recommended: *H. androsaenum* has black berries and often good autumn color.

Ilex (Holly) *See Hedges* Recommended: *I. aquifolium* includes variegated forms and interesting berry colors.

Kalmia latifolia (Mountain-laurel). Outstanding native evergreen noted for late spring flowers. Prefers part shade and needs acid soil.

Kerria japonica Attractive shrubs with bright yellow, buttercup-like flowers on arching stems. Recommended: *K. j.* 'Variegata' has creamy-white variegated leaves.

Kolkwitzia amabilis (Beauty Bush). Hardy, dependable. A fountain of beauty in early summer with its pink flowers. Pretty, soft green foliage.

Laurus nobilis (Sweet Bay). Aromatic, oval-leaved evergreens with small, yellow flowers, April. Not hardy.

Ligustrum (Privet) *See Hedges.* Recommended: *L. ovalifolium aureum* has rich yellow leaves with green blotch, semi-evergreen.

Lonicera (Honeysuckle) *See Hedges* Recommended: *L. nitida* 'Baggensen's Gold' has gold-yellow leaves, turning greenish in autumn.

Magnolia Varied genus with evergreen and deciduous forms and magnificent flowers. Recommended: *M. grandiflora* has long, glossy leaves and big, scented, cream flowers, summer/autumn.

Mahonia Prickly, compound-leaved evergreens with racemes of fragrant yellow, winter flowers. Blue/black berries.

Garrya elliptica

Griselinia littoralis

Kerria japonica

Laurus nobilis

Ligustrum ovalifolium

Foliage burns in winter north of Washington, D.C.

Myrica pensylvanica (Bayberry). Leathery aromatic foliage that gives a billowy effect. Gray berries. Seaside subject.

Myrtus communis (Myrtle). Aromatic, tender leafy evergreens with profuse, white summer flowers and purple berries. M.c. lechleriana has white berries.

Nandina domestica (Sacred Bamboo). Erect shrub with white summer flowers and red autumn berries. Pinnate foliage crimson in spring and autumn. Half hardy.

Pachysandra terminalis Evergreen ground cover with diamond-shaped leaves and greenish-white winter flowers.

Paeonia (Tree Paeony). Handsome foliage shrubs with glorious flowers when established. Recommended: P. lutea ludlowii has saucer-shaped, golden flowers. May/June.

Parrotia persica See Trees

Pernettya mucronata Evergreen ground cover with profuse, white spring flowers and white berries. Some forms have pink/red berries.

Perovskia Aromatic shrubs with gray, deeply-cut foliage and panicles of blue flowers, autumn. Recommended: P. atriplicifolia 'Blue Spire'.

Philadelphus (Mock Orange). Invaluable, fragrant, white-flowered shrubs. Recommended: P. coronarius has richly-scented summer flowers, and some variegated forms with cream-margined green leaves.

Phlomis fruticosa Semi-evergreen shrubs, like giant sage. Bright yellow flowers, late summer. Tender.

Phormium tenax Handsome evergreens with sword-like leaves and bronze-red flowers in panicles, late summer. There is a form with bronze-purple leaves. A New Zealand native for California and like climates.

SELECTION GUIDE — Shrubs

	SOIL TOLERANCE				LOCATION			SIZE			
	Acid	Alkaline	Well-drained	Damp	Full sun	Semi-shade	Total shade	Over 10ft	5-10ft	Under 5ft	Architectural form
Abelia × grandiflora	●	●	●		●				●	●	
Acacia dealbata	●		●		●			●			●
Acer japonicum	●		●		●	●		●		●	●
Acer palmatum	●		●		●	●		●		●	●
Aesculus parviflora	●	●	●		●	●		●			●
Amelanchier canadensis	●			●	●	●		●			
Aralia elata	●	●	●		●			●			●
Arbutus		●	●	●	●	●		●			●
Aronia arbutifolia	●			●	●	●			●	●	
Arundinaria	●	●	●	●	●	●	●	●		●	
Aucuba japonica		●	●		●	●	●	●	●	●	●
Berberis	●	●	●		●	●		●	●	●	
Buddleia	●	●	●	●	●	●		●	●		
Camellia japonica	●			●		●	●		●		●
Caryopteris		●	●		●	●			●		
Ceanothus		●	●		●			●	●		
Ceratostigma		●	●		●					●	
Cercis siliquastrum		●	●		●			●			●
Chaenomeles	●	●	●		●	●			●	●	
Chimonanthus		●	●		●					●	
Choisya ternata	●	●	●		●	●	●		●		●
Cistus		●	●		●				●	●	
Clethra alnifolia	●			●	●	●		●			
Cordyline australis	●	●	●		●	●		●			●
Cornus	●	●	●	●		●	●	●	●		
Cortaderia	●	●	●	●	●	●	●	●			
Cotinus		●	●		●	●		●			
Cotoneaster	●	●	●		●	●	●	●	●	●	
Cytisus	●	●	●		●			●	●	●	●
Daphne		●	●		●	●				●	
Deutzia	●	●	●		●	●			●	●	
Elaeagnus	●	●	●		●			●	●		
Escallonia		●	●		●			●	●	●	
Eucalyptus gunnii	●	●	●	●	●			●			●
Enkianthus campanulatus	●		●	●		●		●			●
Euonymus	●	●	●		●	●		●	●	●	●
Fatsia japonica	●	●	●			●			●		
Forsythia	●	●	●	●	●	●			●		
Fothergilla	●		●	●	●			●		●	
Fuchsia		●	●	●	●	●			●	●	
Garrya elliptica	●	●	●		●	●		●			●
Gaultheria	●	●	●		●	●				●	
Genista	●	●	●		●			●			
Griselinia littoralis	●	●	●		●	●		●			●
Hamamelis	●		●	●	●			●			●
Hibiscus		●	●		●			●	●		
Hippophae	●	●	●	●	●			●			●
Hydrangea	●	●		●		●	●	●	●	●	

	SOIL TOLERANCE				LOCATION			SIZE			
	Acid	Alkaline	Well-drained	Damp	Full sun	Semi-shade	Total shade	Over 10 ft	5–10 ft	Under 5 ft	Architectural form
Hypericum	●	●	●	●		●	●		●	●	
Ilex	●	●	●			●	●	●	●		●
Kalmia latifolia	●		●	●	●	●			●	●	
Kerria	●	●	●	●	●				●	●	
Kolkwitzia amabilis	●	●	●		●			●			●
Laurus nobilis	●	●	●		●				●	●	●
Ligustrum	●	●	●	●	●	●	●	●	●	●	
Lonicera	●	●	●	●	●	●			●	●	
Magnolia	●	●	●	●	●			●	●	●	●
Mahonia	●	●	●		●	●			●	●	●
Myrtus communis		●	●		●				●	●	●
Nandina domestica		●	●		●					●	●
Pachysandra terminalis	●	●		●			●			●	
Paeonia		●	●	●					●		
Parrotia persica	●		●	●	●	●		●			●
Pernettya mucronata	●		●	●			●			●	●
Perovskia		●	●		●					●	●
Philadelphus	●	●	●		●	●			●	●	●
Phlomis fruticosa		●	●		●					●	●
Phormium tenax		●	●		●				●		●
Pieris	●		●	●		●			●		
Pittosporum	●	●	●		●	●		●			●
Potentilla	●	●	●			●	●		●	●	
Prunus	●	●	●	●	●	●		●	●	●	
Pyracantha	●	●	●	●	●	●	●	●			
Rhamnus alaterna	●	●	●	●	●	●	●	●	●		●
Rhododendron (inc. Azalea)	●			●		●	●		●		
Rhus typhina	●	●	●		●	●			●		●
Romneya		●	●		●				●		●
Rosa	●	●	●		●	●			●	●	
Rosmarinus		●	●		●				●	●	
Rubus	●	●	●		●	●	●		●	●	
Ruta graveolens		●	●		●					●	●
Salix	●	●		●	●	●		●	●	●	
Sambucus	●	●	●	●	●	●	●		●	●	
Santolina		●	●		●				●		
Sarcococca humilis	●	●				●	●			●	
Skimmia japonica	●	●	●		●	●	●			●	●
Spartium junceum	●	●	●		●				●	●	
Spiraea	●	●	●		●				●	●	
Stephanandra incisa	●	●	●		●	●			●		●
Symphoricarpus	●	●	●	●	●	●	●		●	●	
Syringa	●	●	●		●				●	●	
Teucrum fruticans		●	●		●				●		
Ulex europaeus		●	●		●	●			●		
Viburnum	●	●	●	●		●	●		●		
Vinca	●	●	●			●				●	
Weigela	●	●	●		●	●			●	●	
Yucca		●	●		●				●	●	●

Pieris Lovely evergreens with white lily-of-the-valley-type flowers in spring. Bright red young foliage. Recommended: P. 'Forest Flame', leaves turn red, pink, cream, green. P. floribunda most hardy.

Pittosporum See Hedges Recommended: P. tenuifolium has dark purple, honey-scented spring flowers. Not hardy.

Potentilla See Hedges Recommended: P. fruticosa.

Prunus laurocerasus Prunus lusitanica See Hedges

Pyracantha See Hedges Recommended: P. angustifolia, orange-yellow berries all winter; P. crenato-serrata.

Rhamnus alaterna Narrow, densely glossy evergreens with yellowish-green flowers and red fruits. Hardy to Washington, D.C.

Rhododendron (including **Azalea**) Huge group of beautiful deciduous and evergreen shrubs with glorious flowers. Some have fine foliage and some deciduous forms have autumn color. Recommended: Azalea pontica (Rhododendron luteum) has funnel-shaped, fragrant, yellow flowers, May, and fine autumn color; A. 'Palestrina' is an evergreen, flowers white with faint green stripes.

Rhus typhina (Stag's Horn Sumach). Easily-grown shrub with fine pinnate foliage and glorious autumn color. Dark red spikes of fruit persist all winter.

Romneya (Californian Tree Poppy). Fine foliage shrubs with large, white, late summer flowers with gold stamens. Slow to establish and needs protection. Recommended: R × hybrida, more vigorous.

Rosa (Shrub Rose). Easily cultivated, very varied shrubs which can offer abundant flowers over a long season, decorative foliage and colorful hips. Broadly divided into modern garden, old garden and wild types.

Rosmarinus See Hedges Recommended: R. officinalis

has a dense habit and gray-green leaves. Tender.

Rubus (Ornamental Bramble). Prickly, deciduous and ever-green shrubs, offering attractive foliage and flowers. Fruits edible but generally flavorless. Recommended: *R. × tridel* 'Benenden' is a vigorous, spineless, arching form to 3 m (10 ft) with large, white, scented flowers, May.

Ruta graveolens (Rue). Low, aromatic evergreen with fern-like leaves and small, yellow summer flowers.

Salix *S. purpurea* 'Nana' is a very low-growing form with blue leaves.

Sambucus (Elder). Handsome foliage/fruit shrubs with ornamental pinnate leaves. Recommended: *S. nigra* 'Aurea' has cream flowers, June, black berries, autumn.

Santolina (Cotton Lavender). Delicate, silvery evergreens with button, yellow flowers, July. Half hardy. Recommended: *S. virens* has vivid green, filigree leaves.

Sarcococca humilis Dense, evergreen ground cover with glossy foliage and small, white, fragrant flowers in winter.

Skimmia japonica Easily-grown, ornamental evergreens with white fragrant spring flowers and bright red fruits on female plants.

Spartium junceum (Spanish Broom). Almost leafless, rushlike stems bears fragrant, yellow pea-flowers all summer.

Spiraea (Spirea). Large genus with white, pink or rose flowers, mostly in summer. *S. × arguta* is very hardy, bears white garlands of shortlived flowers in spring.

Stephanandra incisa (Cutleaf Stephanandra). 'Crispa' is low-growing, mounding, with indifferent flowers but fernlike foliage. Fine on banks.

Symphoricarpus Range of ornamental shrubs with white/pink berries, autumn/winter. Recommended: *S. × doorenbosii* 'White Hedge' is vigorous.

Syringa (Lilac). Lovely, spring-flowering shrubs, often frag-rant. Recommended: *S. vulgaris* 'Miss Ellen Willmott' has large panicles of scented, pure white flowers.

Teucrium fruticans (Shrubby Germander). Tender evergreen with terminal racemes of pale blue flowers in summer.

Ulex europaeus (Gorse). Spiky, dense shrub, ablaze with golden flowers in spring and intermittently thereafter.

Viburnum Evergreens have ornamental leaves, deciduous have rich autumn color. Fragrant, white and/or pink flowers. Recommended: *V. × carlcephalum*, white fragrant flowers in spring; *V. × burkwoodii* (evergreen), dark shiny leaves and flowers January–May; *V. davidii* (evergreen), bright turquoise berries when grown in groups; *V. plicatum*, double rows of florets May/June; *V. rhytido-phyllum* is a vigorous form with red fruits, turning black; *V. tinus* has metallic blue berries.

Vinca (Periwinkle). Evergreen ground cover with blue flowers. Recommended: *V. minor* has bright blue flowers, spring then intermittently.

Weigela Shrubs with fresh green leaves and funnel-shaped flowers June/July. Recom-mended: *W. florida* 'Eva Supreme' has a compact habit with attractive leaves and deep red flowers.

Yucca Arresting, half-hardy shrub with sword-like leaves and spectacular panicles of cream-white flowers, late summer. Recommended: *V. gloriosa* has a trunk-like stem and sharp leaves.

Perennials

By the term "perennials" most gardeners refer to the hardy herbaceous perennials used in borders and mixed planting schemes. My selection em-phasizes "architectural form" and color.

Acanthus (Bear's Breeches). Stately plants with dark green, deeply-cut leaves

and mauve, white-lipped summer flowers. Recom-mended: *A. mollis.*

Achillea (Yarrow). Yellow, flat flowering heads and feathery, pungent leaves (60–80 cm/24–30 in). *A. millefolium* 'Moonshine' has clear yellow flowers, May–August, and silver foliage.

Agapanthus (African Lily). Clumps of long, slender leaves with 80 cm (30 in) flower stems towering above them. Blue/white, lily-like flowers, July/August. Not hardy. In North store in cool, frost-free room over winter.

Alchemilla (Lady's Mantle). Mounds of lovely, gray-green leaves and feathery sprays of yellow-green, starry flowers (30 cm/12 in). Recommended: *A. mollis.*

Anemone japonica (× hy-brida) (Japanese Anemone). Clumps of dark green, vine-like foliage and lovely autumn flowers in white or pink (60–90 cm/2–3 ft). Recom-mended: *A.j.* 'September Charm'.

Anthemis Parsley-like leaves, daisy-like white/yellow flowers, summer (75 cm/30 in). Recom-mended: 'Moonlight' has yellow flowers.

Artemisia (Wormwood). Silver, fern-like foliage and insignificant flowers, late summer (60 cm–1.5 m/2–5 ft). Recommended: *A. ludoviciana* 'Silver King'.

Aster Late summer-flowering, bushy plants (30 cm–1.2 m/1–4 ft). Blue/pink, daisy flowers, including Michaelmas Daisies. Recommended: *A. amellus* 'Triumph' has light blue flowers and low, woody stems.

Bergenia (Elephant's Ears). Round, evergreen leaves. Spikes of pink/white flowers, (30–45 cm/12–18 in). Recom-mended: *B.* 'Silberlicht' is slightly smaller and has white flowers. Autumn foliage is tinged pink.

Brunnera macrophylla Blue, flowers like forget-me-nots, through spring/summer. Large, soft heart-shaped leaves. Good ground cover (45 cm/18 in).

Pyracantha atalantoides

Skimmia japonica

Viburnum opulus

Campanula (Bellflower). Large genus of lovely plants with purple/blue/white funnel or bell-shaped flowers, summer (15 cm–1.5 m/½–5 ft). Recommended: *C. latifolia* has long blue funnels of flowers, July, and is one of the tallest varieties; *C. l. alba*, white flowers.

Chrysanthemum Very varied, summer-flowering (60–90 cm/24–36 in). Single or double daisy flowers, toothed leaves. Recommended: *C. uliginosum.*

Crambe Big (1.8 m/6 ft), eye-catching plant with huge, dark, limp leaves and clouds of white, scented, starry flowers, summer. Recommended: *C. cordifolia.*

Cynara Tall (1.8 m/6 ft), handsome, purple flowers, late summer, and gray, decorative foliage. Tender. Recommended: *C. cardunculus.*

Dianthus (Pink). Pretty, carnation-like flowers with bluish foliage (15–45 cm/6–18 in). Recommended: *D. deltoides* has scarlet/pink/white flowers.

Dierama Half-hardy plant with sprays of pink, summer flowers and long, rush-like leaves (75–90 cm/2½–3 ft).

Digitalis (Foxglove). Tall spikes (60 cm–1.5 m/2–5 ft) of trumpet-like, pink/purple flowers. Recommended: *D. ambigua* has soft, yellow flowers. Short lived. Self sows.

Echinops (Globe Thistle). Prickly plants with statuesque, round, blue flowers, summer (1–1.4 m/3–4½ ft). *E. ritro* has steel-blue flowers.

Euphorbia (Spurge). Bushy plants (15 cm–1 m/½–3 ft) with greenish/yellowish flowering heads, spring. Recommended: *E. wulfenii* has handsome, glaucous foliage.

Gaillardia Hardy with yellow/orange/brownish-red, daisy flowers, profuse all summer (90 cm/35½ in).

Geranium (Cranesbill). Indented foliage and plentiful, blue/pink, spring/summer flowers (45–90 cm/18–35 in).

SELECTION GUIDE **Perennials**	SOIL TOLERANCE				LOCATION		
	Acid	Alkaline	Well-drained	Damp	Full sun	Accepts shade	Architectural form
Acanthus	●	●	●		●	●	●
Achillea	●	●	●		●		●
Agapanthus	●	●	●		●		●
Alchemilla	●	●		●		●	●
Anemone japonica	●	●	●		●	●	●
Anthemis	●	●	●		●		
Artemisia	●	●	●		●		●
Aster	●	●	●		●		
Bergenia	●	●				●	●
Brunnera	●	●	●			●	
Campanula	●	●		●	●	●	
Chrysanthemum	●	●			●		
Crambe	●	●	●	●	●		●
Cynara	●	●	●		●		●
Dianthus	●	●	●		●		
Dierama	●	●		●			●
Digitalis	●	●	●	●	●	●	
Echinops	●	●	●	●	●		
Euphorbia	●	●	●	●	●		
Gaillardia	●	●	●		●		
Geranium	●	●	●		●	●	
Helenium	●	●	●	●	●		
Helleborus	●	●		●		●	●
Hemerocallis	●	●	●	●	●		
Hosta	●	●		●		●	●
Iris	●	●	●	●	●	●	●
Kniphofia	●	●	●		●		
Libertia	●	●	●		●	●	
Ligularia	●	●		●	●	●	
Macleaya	●	●	●		●		●
Oenothera	●	●	●		●		
Paeonia	●	●		●	●	●	●
Papaver	●	●	●		●		
Phlox	●	●		●		●	
Rheum	●	●		●	●	●	●
Rudbeckia	●	●	●		●		
Salvia	●	●	●		●		●
Sedum	●	●	●		●		●
Sisyrinchium	●	●	●		●		
Stachys	●	●	●		●		
Veronica	●	●	●	●	●		
Zantedeschia	●	●		●	●		●
Grasses							
Arundo	●	●	●		●	●	●
Carex	●	●	●	●	●	●	●
Festuca	●	●	●		●		●
Helictotrichon	●	●	●		●		●
Lasiagrostis	●	●	●		●		●
Miscanthus	●	●	●	●	●	●	●
Pennisetum	●	●	●		●		●
Stipa	●	●	●		●	●	●

Acanthus mollis

Agapanthus umbellatus

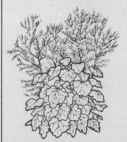

Crambe cordifolia

Dierama pendulum

Macleaya cordata

Helenium (Sneezewort). Useful daisy-like, summer and early autumn flowers with pronounced centers, yellow/orange/copper/mahogany. The last is particularly recommended (60–90 cm/24–36 in).

Helleborus Fascinating family of winter/early spring-flowering plants with attractive foliage (30–60 cm/12–24 in). Recommended: *H. corsicus* has pale green flowers, February; *H. orientalis* (Lenten Rose) has white/pink/purple flowers, November/March.

Hemerocallis (Day Lily). Mound of strap-like, bright green leaves and, above, plentiful though short-lived, lily-like flowers, red/orange/yellow (60–90 cm/24–36 in).

Hosta (Plaintain Lily). Beautiful foliage plants (60–120 cm/2–4 ft) with lily-like flowers, summer. Recommended: *H. plantaginea* has fragrant, white flowers; *H. sieboldiana* has bluish-gray leaves and lilac-white flowers.

Iris A vast range of glorious flowers generally blue/purple/white but also pink, red and copper in bearded varieties. There are many worthy species but most practical for today's gardens are Siberian, Japanese and bearded types.

Kniphofia (Red-hot Poker). Striking, red/orange flowers, summer/autumn, above grass-like mounds of evergreen leaves (60 cm–1.8 m/2–6 ft). Slightly tender. Recommended: *K.* 'Springtime' has yellow flowers with red tips.

Lavandula (Lavender). Evergreens with fragrant, blue or purple flowers in spikes, summer. Recommended: *L. angustifolia* 'Munstead' has dark blue flowers.

Ligularia (Ragwort). Vigorous, sturdy plants with bright yellow/orange flowers, summer (60 cm–1.5 m/2–5 ft). Recommended: *L. dentata* has huge leaves and daisy-like flowers.

Macleaya Tall (1.8 m/6 ft) plants with gray, lobed leaves and plumes of buff flowers. Recommended: *M. cordata*.

Oenothera (Evening Primrose). Bright spring shoots and saucer-shaped, yellow summer flowers (20–45 cm/8–18 in). Recommended: *O. cinaeus* has bronze-pink shoots.

Paeonia (Peony). Glorious spring flowers, attractive foliage (60–90 cm/2–4 ft). *P. mlokosewitschii* has yellow flowers, April.

Papaver (Poppy). Deeply-cut, usually hairy foliage and big, fiery flowers (60–90 cm/2–3 ft). Recommended: *P.* 'May Sadler'.

Phlox Broad panicles of bright flowers all summer (60–90 cm/2–3 ft). Recommended: *P. divaricata* has pointed leaves and fragrant, lilac flowers, in spring.

Rheum Tall (1.5 m/5 ft), red flower spikes, early summer. Deeply-cut foliage. Recommended: *R. palmatum* 'Rubrum' has young leaves, pink/purple, green later.

Rudbeckia (Coneflower). Drooping-petalled, yellow/orange, late summer flowers (60 cm/2 ft). Recommended: *R.* 'Goldsturm'.

Salvia officinalis (Sage). Aromatic, semi-evergreen herb with blue flowers in whorls, summer. Variegated forms include *S. o.* 'Tricolor'.

Sedum (Iceplant). Glaucous, fleshy foliage plants (30–60 cm/1–2 ft), with broad flowering heads, pink/yellow. Recommended: *S. maximum atropurpureum* has maroon leaves and dark pink flowers, autumn.

Stachys Evergreen ground cover with woolly leaves and pink/purple/white flowers, summer (30–60 cm/1–2 ft). *S. lanata* (Lamb's Ears) has silvery leaves and small, pink flowers.

Veronica (Speedwell). Blue spikes flower for long summer season above leaf mats/mounds (30–60 cm/1–3 ft). Recommended: *V. spicata*.

Zantedeschia (Arum Lily). Beautiful, white/yellow/red, spring flowers, tender. Can be grown in water. Recommended: *Z. aethiopica* has dark, arrow-shaped leaves.

Grasses

Arundo Magnificent form, with bamboo-like stems and large, arching leaves. Recommended: *A. donax* is one of the longest of the grasses (1 m/3 ft). Native to S. Europe. Clump forming, non-invasive.

Carex Striped, gold-green evergreen leaves. Flowers in spikes (30–90 cm/1–3 ft).

Festuca Blue, dainty grass, erect growth. Recommended: *F. amethystina* is a densely-tufted perennial, grayish blue/green (up to 45 cm/18 in).

Helictotrichon sempervirens Blue clumps with flower spikes above, June (75 cm/30 in).

Lasiagrostis Handsome, buff-colored plumes with clumpy growth (90 cm/3 ft). Recommended: *L. splendens* is one of the largest species (2 m/6½ ft); drought resistant, evergreen perennial. Purplish flowers May–July.

Miscanthus Upright, slow-spreading grasses (1 m/3–5 ft). *M. sinensis* has narrow, graceful leaves with a white central stripe.

Pennisetum Soft, gray-white leaves below flower spikes (30–90 cm/1–3 ft). *P. orientale* has purple-green flowers, late summer.

Stipa Handsome plumes above dark evergreen foliage (90 cm/3 ft). *S. gigantea* has purple plumes, turning golden. Gray foliage.

Paeonia mlokosewitschii

Sisyrinchium striatum

Arundo donax

Pennisetum orientale

Annuals

Annuals are those plants that are planted afresh in the spring. Examples from my selection, below, will infill mixed borders and decorate boxes and hanging baskets.

Ageratum Superb bedding plants, generally blue (some pink), fluffy flower heads and soft, hairy leaves (23 cm/9 in).

Alyssum (Lebularia). Edging plants with profuse white/purple summer flowers. Recommended: 'Carpet of Snow', (4 in).

Antirrhinum (Snapdragon). Bright, often bi-colored, half-hardy bedding plants with dark, narrow leaves (30–90 cm/1–3 ft). *A. majus*, most cvs, rust resistant

Calendula (Pot Marigold). Hardy bedding/edging plants with pale green leaves and, generally, bright yellow/orange flowers over a long season. Recommended: C. 'Pacific Beauty' is most drought resistant.

Callistephus (China Aster). Bedding and cut flower source. Rich colors on low to tall plants. Midsummer.

Cheiranthus (Wallflower). Hardy, spring-flowering biennials, white/yellow/red/rust (30 cm/12 in). Recommended: *C. cheiri* acts as a perennial in mild areas.

Cosmos. Single or semi-double daises and fine-cut foliage. Pink, white or yellow to orange range.

Dianthus (Pink). *See Perennials* Recommended: *D. chinensis* has fringed petals and dark centers. Many varieties.

Dimorphotheca (Cape Marigold). Hardy, daisy flowers, yellow/orange/pink/white, summer (30 cm/12 in). Sow seed early.

Eschscholzia (Poppy). Brilliant, flame-flowered, hardy bedding plants (30 cm/12 in). *E. californica* has fern-like leaves and yellow flowers. Scatter seeds in early spring.

Gazania Handsome foliage – evergreen when grown in mild areas as perennials – with yellow/orange/red daisy-flowers (30 cm/12 in). Recommended: G. 'Sunshine' has big, sun-loving flowers and is heat resistant. Likes dry soil.

Helianthus (Sunflower). Giant, golden, daisy-like flowers up to 3 m (10 ft) high, late summer. Recommended: *H. annuus* has flowers 30 cm (12 in) wide.

Heliotropium (Heliotrope). Bedding plants with flat heads of scented, violet flowers, summer/autumn. Can be grown as perennials in frost-free districts (90 cm/3 ft).

Iberis (Candytuft). Hardy, edging, bedding or cutting annuals. White/pink/red, bushy flowers, summer (30–40 cm/12–16 in).

Impatiens (Busy Lizzie). Fast-growing, generally pink/red-flowered plants which can overwinter indoors for following year.

Limnanthes Small annuals, native to West Coast. *L. douglasii* has saucer-shaped, yellow/white flowers, spring and summer.

Lobelia Lovely edging/rockery plants with bright blue flowers over a long season (15 cm/6 in). 'Sapphire', trailing; 'White Lady'; 'Crystal Palace', dark blue with dark leaves.

Lunaria (Honesty). Mauve-flowered biennials with large, coarse leaves and very attractive, silver-transparent seed heads (60 cm/2 ft). Plants will self-sow.

Matthiola (Stock). Spikes of scented, colorful flowers, spring. Hardy bedding plants (40 cm/16 in). Recommended: *M. bicornis* has heady-scented flowers, opening at night.

Mesembryanthemum Daisy-like half-hardy edging/rockery plants for sunny position (8 cm/3 in). Very popular on the West Coast.

Molucella (Shell Flower). Shell-shaped sepals surround tiny, white flowers on these unusual bedding plants (50 cm/20 in). Popular as cut flowers.

Calendula officinalis

Gazania × splendens

Mollucella laevis

Nicotiana affinis

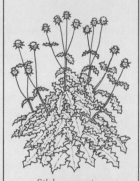
Papaver alpinum

Silybum marianum

Zinnia elegans

SELECTION GUIDE
Annuals

	SOIL TOLERANCE				LOCATION	
	Acid	Alkaline	Well-drained	Damp	Full sun	Semi-shade
Ageratum	•	•		•	•	
Alyssum	•	•	•		•	
Antirrhinum	•	•			•	
Calendula	•	•			•	
Callistephus	•	•			•	
Cheiranthus		•	•		•	
Cosmos	•	•			•	
Dianthus	•	•			•	
Dimorphotheca	•	•			•	
Eschscholzia	•	•	•		•	
Gazania	•	•	•		•	
Helianthus	•	•	•		•	
Heliotropium	•	•			•	•
Iberis	•	•			•	•
Impatiens	•	•			•	•
Limnanthes	•	•			•	
Lobelia	•	•		•		•
Lunaria	•	•	•			•
Matthiola	•	•	•		•	•
Mesembryanthemum	•	•			•	
Molucella	•	•		•	•	
Nicotiana	•	•			•	
Nigella	•	•		•	•	
Papaver alpinum	•	•			•	
Pelargonium	•	•		•		•
Petunia	•	•			•	
Reseda		•			•	
Tagetes	•	•			•	
Tropaeolum	•	•			•	
Zinnia	•	•			•	

Nicotiana (Tobacco Plant). Strongly-scented, long-flowering bedding plants in many colors, including lime-green. Half-hardy (90 cm/ 3 ft). Recommended: *N. affinis*, white flowers.

Nigella (Love-in-a-mist). Hardy bedding plants with pale blue flowers, spring, and lovely ferny foliage (30 cm/12 in).

Papaver alpinum (Poppy). Colorful, summer-flowering annuals with lovely saucer-flowers and delicate foliage (30 cm/12 in). Scatter seeds early.

Pelargonium (Geranium). Free-flowering bedding plants which will winter indoors for following year. Big heads of varied color (60 cm/2 ft).

Petunia Showy bedding plants for hot, dry position. Innumerable colors of funnel-shaped, scented flowers In mid-summer, pinch back plants to force new bushy growth and flowers until frost.

Reseda (Mignonette). Yellow stars of scented, summer flowers on annuals which can be perennial in mildest areas (60 cm/2 ft). Recommended: *R. alba* has white flowers.

Tagetes (Marigold). Mainstay of annual garden and long-lasting cutflower. Yellow, orange, rusty red and near white ('Snowbird').

Tropaeolum (Nasturtium). Trailing, sometimes climbing, hardy annuals with pretty, round leaves (edible in salads) and bright orange tubular flowers. Prefers poor soil (Spread 1.2 m/4 ft). Recommended: *T. majus* offers a variety of shades of yellow and red.

Zinnia Dahlia-like, summer flowers in bright colors. Versatile annual in wide range of forms and heights.

Ground cover

In this category, I include some shrubs that, despite their height, grow down to ground level in addition to the usual ground-smothering plants.

Ajuga (Bugle). Carpet of bright blue flower spikes from leaf mat. Recommended: *A. reptans* 'Atropurpurea'.

Alchemilla *See Perennials* Recommended: *A. mollis* (Lady's Mantle) forms mounds of light green leaves with sulphur-yellow flowers in loose sprays, summer.

Anthemis *See Perennials* Recommended: *A. marshalliana*, gray foliage, daisy flowers.

Artemisia *See Perennials*

Recommended: A. 'Silver Mound' has attractive gray foliage forming a low mound.

Aubrieta Spring flowers with long season. Blue/pink/red/ purple. Recommended: *A. deltoidea*.

Asperula odorata (Sweet Woodruff). Whorled foliage.

Berberis *See Shrubs* Recommended: any low-growing forms. *B. candidula* (evergreen) makes glossy mounds with purple berries; *B. thunbergii* (deciduous) has red berries and good autumn foliage color.

Bergenia *See Perennials* Recommended: all forms.

Choisya *See Shrubs* Recommended: *C. ternata* (Mexican Orange Blossom) has scented white flowers. Tender.

Alchemilla mollis

Bergenia cordifolia

Hypericum calycinum

SELECTION GUIDE **Ground cover**	SOIL TOLERANCE				LOCATION			SIZE		
	Acid	Alkaline	Well-drained	Damp	Full sun	Semi-shade	Total shade	Over 5 ft	2–5 ft	Under 2 ft
Ajuga	●	●	●	●	●	●				●
Alchemilla	●	●		●		●	●			●
Anthemis	●	●	●		●				●	
Artemisia	●	●	●		●	●			●	●
Aubrieta	●	●	●		●					●
Asperula	●	●	●	●	●	●	●	●	●	●
Berberis	●	●	●		●	●		●	●	
Bergenia	●	●				●	●			●
Choisya	●	●	●		●	●	●	●		
Cornus	●	●	●	●	●	●		●	●	
Cotoneaster	●	●	●	●	●	●		●	●	●
Dianthus	●	●	●		●					●
Elaeagnus	●	●	●		●			●	●	
Epimedium	●	●	●	●	●	●	●			●
Erica	●		●		●				●	●
Escallonia		●	●		●	●		●	●	
Euonymus	●	●	●		●	●		●	●	●
Euphorbia	●	●	●	●	●	●				●
Festuca	●	●	●		●					●
Gaultheria	●			●	●	●			●	
Genista	●	●	●		●				●	
Geranium	●	●	●		●	●				●
Hebe	●	●	●		●				●	
Hedera	●	●	●		●	●	●			●
Helianthemum		●	●		●					●
Helleborus	●	●		●		●	●			●
Heuchera	●	●	●	●	●	●			●	●
Hosta	●	●		●		●	●			●

Santolina chamaecyparissus

Stachys lanata

Tiarella cordifolia

Cornus *See Shrubs* Recommended: *C. alba* (Red Barked Dogwood) has many interesting forms with rich autumn color. Stems red in winter months.

Cotoneaster *See Shrubs* Recommended: all prostrate to medium-sized varieties, especially *C. dammeri*.

Dianthus *See Perennials.*

Elaeagnus *See Shrubs* Recommended: all evergreen forms. *E. pungens* 'Maculata', gold/green variegated leaves.

Epimedium (Barrenwort). Heart-shaped, evergreen leaves with small, yellow/pink/white, May/June flowers.

Erica (Heath). Large evergreen family with variable leaf and flower colors and flowering seasons.

Escallonia *See Shrubs* Recommended: *E. iveyi* has dark, glossy leaves and white autumn flowers.

Euonymus *See Shrubs* Recommended *E. fortunei* has some brilliantly colored variegated forms.

Euphorbia *See Perennials* Recommended: *E. myrsinites* has silvery foliage in rosettes and light green flowers; *E. wulfenii* has larger, yellowish flowers (1.3 m/4 ft).

Festuca (Fescue) *See Grasses* Tufted, glaucous grass. There is a blue-green variety.

Gaultheria *See Shrubs* Recommended: *G. procumbens* has scarlet berries and dark green leaves.

Genista *See Shrubs* Recommended: *G. hispanica* (Spanish Gorse) is a prickly shrub with bright yellow, early summer flowers.

Geranium *See Perennials* Recommended: all forms.

Hebe Recommended: all forms where hardy.

Hedera *See Climbers* Recommended: all forms.

Helianthemum (Rock Rose). Lovely, small, profuse flowers in summer. Protect in North.

Helleborus *See Perennials*

Heuchera (Coral Flower). Low, heart-shaped leaves, often mottled with tall spikes of pink/red bell flowers above them, summer.

Hosta *See Perennials*

Hydrangea *See Shrubs* Recommended: *H. petiolaris* has flat heads of greenish-white flowers, June.

Hypericum *See Shrubs* Recommended: *H. calycinum* (St. John's-wort) has big golden flowers.

Juniperus *See Conifers* Recommended: *J. horizontalis* are wide-spreading, low shrubs with many vareties offering blue-green/gold/yellow/bright green, ferny, evergreen foliage.

Lamium (Deadnettle). Nettle-like perennial for shade with interesting leaf variegations. Purple, yellow, white flowers.

Liriope Blue spikes of flowers, late summer.

Lonicera *See Shrubs* Recommended: *L. pileata* has cream flowers and violet berries.

Pachysandra *See Shrubs* Recommended: *P. terminalis* is evergreen, likes shade.

Polygonatum (Solomon's Seal). Arching stems with broad leaves and, hanging beneath them, tiny white bells.

Potentilla *See Shrubs* Recommended: all forms.

Prunus laurocerasus *See Shrubs* Recommended: *P. l.* 'Zabelliana' has profuse white flowers with narrow leaves.

	SOIL TOLERANCE				LOCATION			SIZE		
	Acid	Alkaline	Well-drained	Damp	Full sun	Semi-shade	Total shade	Over 5 ft	2–5 ft	Under 2 ft
Hydrangea	●	●		●	●	●		●	●	
Hypericum	●	●	●	●	●	●			●	●
Juniperus		●	●	●	●	●		●	●	
Lamium	●	●	●	●	●	●	●			●
Liriope	●		●		●	●				●
Lonicera	●	●	●		●	●		●	●	
Pachysandra	●		●	●			●			●
Polygonatum	●	●		●		●	●		●	●
Potentilla	●	●	●		●	●			●	●
Prunus laurocerasus	●	●	●	●		●			●	
Rhododendron	●			●		●		●	●	●
Ribes	●	●	●		●	●			●	●
Rosmarinus		●	●		●				●	●
Ruta		●	●		●					●
Salix	●	●		●	●	●		●	●	●
Sambucus	●	●	●	●	●	●		●	●	●
Santolina		●	●		●					●
Sarcococca	●	●	●			●				●
Saxifraga	●	●	●			●	●			●
Sedum	●	●	●		●	●				●
Senecio	●	●	●		●				●	●
Stachys	●	●	●		●	●				●
Symphoricarpus	●	●	●		●	●	●	●		●
Teucrium		●	●		●					●
Thymus	●	●	●		●					●
Tiarella	●	●	●	●		●	●			●
Viburnum davidii	●	●	●	●	●	●		●	●	●
Vinca	●	●	●			●	●			●

Rhododendron *See Shrubs* Recommended: all forms especially low, small-level.

Ribes (Flowering Currant). Evergreen and deciduous shrubs with yellow or pink spring flowers.

Rosmarinus *See Hedges* Recommended: *R. officinalis* has blue summer flowers.

Ruta *See Shrubs* Recommended: *R. graveolens* has mustard-yellow flowers, pungent leaves.

Salix *See Shrubs* Recommended: *S. repens argentea* is very good for coastal areas; *S. hastata* 'Wehrhahnii' has silvery male catkins in spring, slowly turning yellow.

Santolina *See Shrubs* Recommended: all forms.

Sarcococca *See Shrubs* Recommended: *S. humilis* has dark shiny leaves, white/pink flowers and black berries.

Saxifraga (Saxifrage). Rosettes of leaves with pink, starry, summer flowers.

Sedum *See Perennials* Recommended: all forms.

Stachys *See Perennials*

Symphoricarpos *See Shrubs* Recommended: *S. albus* has oval leaves, pink flowers and white berries.

Teucrium *See Shrubs* Recommended: *T. fruticans* has downy leaves and blue summer flowers. Requires winter protection.

Thymus (Thyme). Aromatic, gray foliage with pink/white/mauve summer flowers. Used in cooking.

Tiarella Round, pale green evergreen leaves, bronze in winter. White/pink, starry spring/summer flowers carried on stems high above leaves.

Viburnum davidii *See Shrubs*

Vinca *See Shrubs* Recommended: *V. minor* spreads easily and has attractive blue spring flowers.

Bulbs

You will see below that my selection of bulbous plants provides flower color and form for spring, summer and autumn. The selection guide indicates "architectural form".

Allium This family includes onions, shallots and garlic, generally having strap-leaves with clusters of summer flowers (blue/white/purple) on long stems (15–60 cm/6–24 in). Choice: *A. giganteum* for its spectacular, violet flower heads, July.

Anemone Delightful spring flowers (white/blue/purple/red), with attractive foliage (15–30 cm/6–12 in). Recommended: *A. blanda* flowers in early spring. Good for naturalizing.

Arum Extraordinary, spiky flowers held in a leaf-like shield or spathe (15 cm/6 in). Recommended: *A. italicum* has bright red, autumn berries.

Chionodoxa (Glory of the Snow). Starry, bright blue, very early flowers. Strap-like leaves. At their best when naturalized in rough grass (15 cm/6 in).

Colchicum (Meadow Saffron). Pink/lilac autumn flowers, similar to crocus (often known as Autumn Crocus). Leaves appear in spring, die back in summer (25 cm/10 in). Recommended: *C. speciosum*, lilac-rose to red-purple range and also white.

Crinum Handsome, lily-like flowers (white/red/pink), generally hardy in south-facing bed. Strappy leaves (90 cm/3 ft). Recommended: *C. × powellii* 'Album'.

Crocus Large and varied genus of spring and autumn flowering bulbs. Main colors purple/gold/white, (10 cm/4 in). Recommended: *C. tomasinianus* has rich purple flowers.

Eranthis hyemalis (Winter Aconite). Bright yellow, early spring flowers. Pale green, finely-cut leaves. Ideal for naturalizing (5–10 cm/2–4 in).

Eremurus (Foxtail Lily). Tall spikes (1.2–2.4 m/4–8 ft) of star-shaped summer flowers. Strappy leaves.

Allium giganteum

Crinum x powellii

Fritillaria imperialis

Galtonia candicans

Leucojum aestivum

SELECTION GUIDE
Bulbs

	Soil Tolerance				Location		
	Acid	Alkaline	Well-drained	Damp	Full sun	Semi-shade	Architectural form
Allium	●	●	●	●	●		
Anemone	●	●	●	●	●	●	
Arum	●	●	●	●	●		
Chionodoxa	●	●	●	●	●	●	
Colchicum	●	●	●		●		
Crinum	●		●			●	●
Crocus	●	●			●		
Eranthis hyemalis	●	●	●		●		
Eremurus	●	●	●		●		
Fritillaria	●	●	●		●	●	
Galanthus		●	●	●	●	●	●
Galtonia candicans	●	●	●		●		●
Hyacinthus	●	●	●		●	●	
Leucojum	●	●	●		●		
Lilium candidum	●	●	●		●	●	
Muscari	●	●	●		●	●	
Narcissus	●	●	●		●		
Nerine	●	●	●			●	●
Scilla		●	●		●	●	
Tulipa	●	●	●		●		●

Fritillaria Pendulous spring flowers on leafy stems. Recommended: *F. imperialis* has imposing red/orange/yellow flowers, hanging beneath a whorl of leaves (1.2 m/4 ft).

Galanthus (Snowdrop). Charming, very early white flowers (10–20 cm/4–8 in). Force in pots. Recommended: *G. nivalis* is particularly good for naturalizing in grass.

Galtonia candicans (Summer Hyacinth). Long, narrow leaves and white, hyacinth-like flowers, summer (1.2 m/4 ft).

Hyacinthus (Hyacinth). Ideal for garden or indoor forcing, bright blue/purple/white/pink/yellow spring flowers with heady scent.

Leucojum (Snowflake). White snowdrop-like flowers spring, some species in autumn. Recommended: *L. aestivum* flowers in late spring.

Lilium candidum (Madonna Lily). Large, white, delightful flowers, fragrant, summer (60 cm–1.8 m/2–6 ft).

Muscari (Grape Hyacinth). Clusters of tiny blue flowers, late spring (15 cm/6 in). Recommended: *M. armeniacum* has tight clusters of blue flowers, April–May.

Narcissus (Daffodil). Bright yellow/white, trumpet flowers, spring. Hardy and easy to grow, there are thousands of cultivars of this genus.

Nerine Handsome, pink/red, late summer flowers, hardy only in mildest areas but otherwise need greenhouse protection (30–60 cm/1–2 ft).

Scilla (Bluebell). Lovely blue spring flowers (also white/pink), naturalizing well in half-shade (15–30 cm/6–12 in). Many varieties. Recommended: *S. (Endymion) campanulata* (Wood Hyacinth) flowers early in mixed colors.

Tulipa Innumerable varieties of brightly-colored, spring flowers, often bi-colored. Recommended: Lily-flowered has tall (60 cm/24 in) flowers with petals bent inwards or outwards.

Climbers

Some climbers cling without help, some ramble and need to be tried, others will grow against a support if trained. The selection guide, below, separates them under the heading "nature".

Abutilon Unusual, handsome wall shrubs with bell-shaped, hanging flowers. Recommended: *A. megapotamicum* has red and yellow summer flowers. Tender.

Actinidia Vigorous climbers. Recommended: *A. chinensis* (Chinese Gooseberry) has cream, late summer flowers and produces fruit in full sun. This is the "kiwi" from New Zealand and it is tender in the North.

Akebia Purple/red-flowered climber with handsome foliage. *A. quinata* occasionally produces dark purple fruits. Fragrant flowers.

Aristolochia Pipe-shaped, yellow, summer flowers and heart-shaped leaves. Recommended: *A. macrophylla* (Dutchman's Pipe) is vigorous.

Campsis Eye-catching, red/orange trumpet flowers, late summer. Recommended: *C. radicans* (Trumpet Vine) has strikingly bright flowers.

Ceanothus *See Shrubs* Recommended: *C. thyrsiflorus* has light blue flowers, early summer. Mild climates only.

Chaenomeles *See Shrubs* Recommended: *C. speciosa* has a wide choice of colors.

Clematis Huge range of species and hybrids with handsome flowers and often attractive seed heads. Recommended: *C. montana* 'Alba' has pure white, early summer flowers and, being vigorous, is ideal for growing into the branches of established trees.

Eccremocarpus Tender climbers. Recommended: *E. scaber* is hardy in mild districts and very vigorous. Red/orange/yellow tubular summer flowers. The leaves are small and fern-like.

Clematis montana

Hydrangea petiolaris

Jasminum nudiflorum

Wisteria sinensis

SELECTION GUIDE
Climbing plants

	SOIL TOLERANCE				LOCATION			NATURE		
	Acid	Alkaline	Well-drained	Damp	Full sun	Semi-shade	Shade	Clinger/twiner	Wall shrub	Rambler
Abutilon		●	●		●				●	
Actinidia	●	●			●			●		
Akebia	●	●	●		●	●		●		
Aristolochia	●	●	●	●	●			●		
Campsis	●	●			●			●		
Ceanothus		●	●		●				●	
Chaenomeles	●	●	●	●	●				●	
Clematis	●	●			●					●
Eccremocarpus	●	●			●					●
Euonymus fortunei	●	●				●				●
Garrya elliptica	●	●				●	●		●	
Hedera	●	●	●			●	●	●		
Humulus lupulus	●	●			●	●		●		
Hydrangea petiolaris	●	●			●	●		●		
Jasminum	●	●	●		●	●		●		
Parthenocissus	●	●	●		●	●		●		
Passiflora	●	●			●			●		
Polygonum	●	●	●		●	●	●	●		
Rosa	●	●			●	●				●
Solanum		●	●	●	●				●	
Wisteria	●	●	●		●				●	

Euonymus fortunei *See Shrubs*

Garrya elliptica *See Shrubs*

Hedera (Ivy). Easy, hardy evergreens with great variety of leaf color and shape. Recommended: *H. colchica* 'Dentata Variegata' has very large, cream-edged leaves.

Humulus lupulus (Hop). Small flowers followed by hops in late summer. Recommended: *H. l.* 'Aureus' has handsome, yellow leaves.

Hydrangea petiolaris Large, flat heads of white flowers, June. Vigorous.

Jasminum (Jasmine). Small, white/yellow, fragrant flowers. Recommended: *J. nudiflorum* (Winter Jasmine) has scentless, yellow flowers on bare branches, November–March.

Parthenocissus (Virginia Creeper). Handsome-foliaged climber with glorious autumn color. Recommended: *P. quinquefolia* has large leaves and spectacular autumn color.

Passiflora (Passion Flower). Large, exotic flowers. Vigorous, but tender. Recommended: *P. caerulea* has blue, purple and white, fragrant flowers. Semi-evergreen.

Polygonum Hardy, very vigorous climber, any situation. Recommended: *P. baldschuanicum* (Russian Vine) has cream, pink-tinged flowers, summer/ autumn.

Rosa Innumerable varieties, broadly divided into climbing and rambler roses, from the three types: modern garden, old garden and wild.

Solanum Handsome, late-summer flowers, usually blue/purple. Tender. Recommended: *S. crispum* 'Glasnevin' has purple, yellow-centred flowers; *S. jasminoides* (Jasmine Nightshade) has gray-blue flowers.

Wisteria Lovely blue/pink/white flowers in long racemes, spring. Recommended: *W. sinensis* bears fragrant, lilac racemes on bare branches, late spring.

Water plants

I have subdivided this list into submerged aquatics (oxygenators), floating aquatics and bog and waterside plants, that need various degrees of moisture.

Bog and waterside

Acorus calamnus (Sweet flag). Greenish-white flowers, sword-leaves. There is a handsome variegated form.

Alisma Hardy perennials, sprays of white/pink flowers.

Aponogeton distachyus (Water Hawthorn). Fragrant white flowers, floating leaves.

Butomus umbellatus (Flowering Rush). Umbels of pink flowers, June, Narrow, twisted leaves tinted purple when young.

Calla palustris (Bog Arum). Flowers very similar to Arum *See bulbs*, including red, autumn beries. Dark green, heart-shaped leaves.

Caltha palustris (Marsh Marigold). Golden, spring flowers, heart-shaped leaves.

Juncus (Rush). Stately plants with insignificant flowers.

Mentha aquatica (Water Mint). Blue, late summer flowers, lemon-scented leaves.

Menyanthes trifoliata (Bog Bean). Lovely, pink-budded white flowers, bean-like leaves.

Myosotis scorpiades (Water Forget-me-not). Sky-blue summer flowers.

Sagittaria (Arrowhead. *See Submerged Aquatics* Recommended: *S. lancifolia*.

Typha latifolia (Great Reed Mace). Also called Bulrush. Very tall (2.4 m/8 ft).

Floating aquatics

Azolla (Fairy Moss.) Floating perennial forming carpet of red-tinted moss-like growth. Tender.

Eichornia (Water Hyacinth). Glossy, heart shaped leaves, lilac flowers with gold. Winter indoors.

Nymphae (Water Lily). Glorious, exotic summer flowers, generally divided into:
a) Extra strong growing (75 cm–1 m/2½–3 ft). Recommended: *N. alba*.
b) Strong (50–75 cm/19–30 in). Recommended: *N. gloriosa*.
c) Medium (30–50 cm/12–19 in). Recommended: *N. odorata alba*, white flowers.
d) Small (10–30 cm/4–11 in). Recommended: *N. pygmaed*.

Submerged aquatics

Callitriche (Water Starwort). Some varieties grow completely submerged, some prefer shallow (15 cm/6 in) water, producing rosettes of foliage on the surface.

Elodea (Canadian Pondweed). Excellent oxygenators.

Hottonia (Water Violet). Lovely, ferny foliage. Whorls of pale lilac flowers, May.

Myriophyllum (Water Milfoil). Finely-cut foliage, some varieties with red stems.

Potamogeton Wavy-edged, reddish-green, translucent leaves, like seaweed.

Sagittaria (Arrowhead). Arrow-shaped leaves 60 cm (24 in) above surface.

Butomus umbellatus

Calla palustris

Caltha palustris

Sagittaria lancifolia

SELECTION GUIDE **Bog and waterside**	SOIL TOLERANCE				SIZE	
	Acid	Alkaline	Full sun	Semi-shade	Over 1 ft	Less than 1 ft
Acorus calamnus	•	•	•	•	•	
Alisma	•	•	•	•		
Aponogeton distachyus	•		•	•		•
Butomus umbellatus	•	•	•		•	
Calla palustris	•	•	•	•		•
Caltha palustris	•	•	•	•	•	
Juncus	•	•	•	•	•	
Mentha aquatica	•	•	•	•	•	
Menyanthes trifoliata	•	•	•	•	•	
Myosotis scorpiades	•	•	•	•	•	
Sagittaria	•	•	•	•	•	
Typha latifolia	•	•	•	•	•	

Mixes and coverages

Gardeners interested in do-it-yourself will need to know what quantities of materials to order when constructing the garden. If you have drawn up your garden layout to scale, however (see pp. 40–41), you can easily calculate the quantities required by taking measurements from your scale drawing, but the charts below and overleaf give a useful guide to coverages. They will also help you to decide on the exact mix of constituents for mortar, concrete and lawn depending on location, climate and expected wear and tear.

It is always cheaper to buy constituents separately and to mix them yourself. Weigh this saving against the savings in time and labor offered by ready-mixed products.

Paving coverages

The chart on the right will help you to work out the number of paving elements you require to cover a particular area. If you intend to mix more than one material, there is really no substitute for counting the numbers required from a scale drawing. If the area has odd corners (something to avoid), you will need more elements to allow for cutting. Thinner elements tend to break during unloading so you should allow for this. It is anyway a good idea to have a few spare elements that can weather at the same rate as those laid, to replace breakages due to frost damage.

A   Paving slabs (700 mm²/28 in²)
B   Paving slabs (460 mm²/18 in²)
C   Paving slabs (305 mm²/12 in²)
D   Granite blocks (240 × 110 mm/ 9½ × 4.4 in)
E   Paving bricks (220 × 110 mm/ 8.8 × 4.4 in)
F   Tiles (150 mm²/6 in²)

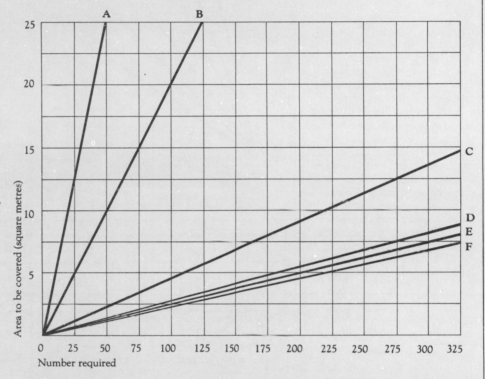

Mortar mixes

Mortar consists of sand and a binding agent. The binding agent is cement or lime, or a mixture of the two. Using all cement makes a strong mix that dries quickly but is liable to crack, while using all lime makes a weak mix that dries slowly but is less likely to crack. Mortar should not be stronger or weaker than the material it joins. Aerated mortar is made with cement and a proprietary plasticizing agent that forms air bubbles in the mortar, making the mix more workable and resistant to frost. Add plasticizer as indicated by the manufacturer.

Use	Cement mortar	Cement-lime mortar	Aerated mortar
Retaining walls, engineering bricks	1 part cement 3 parts sand		
Cappings, step treads and risers	1 part cement 3 parts sand	1 part cement ½ part lime 4½ parts sand	1 part cement 6 parts sand Plasticizer as indicated
Exterior walls, work below damp proofing	1 part cement 3 parts sand	1 part cement 1 part lime 6 parts sand	1 part cement 6 parts sand Plasticizer as indicated
Exposed walls above damp proofing		1 part cement 1 part lime 6 parts sand	1 part cement 6 parts sand Plasticizer as indicated
Internal walls		1 part cement 2 parts lime 9 parts sand	1 part cement 8 parts sand Plasticizer as indicated

Concrete mixes and coverage

The thickness and mix of concrete you use depends on its function – mainly the weight of the traffic upon it. You have the choice of buying aggregate and sand separately or paying a little more for mixed aggregate and sand. Aggregate is available in different grades from fine to coarse. In general, the thicker the concrete required, the courser the aggregate you should use. Finer aggregate is required, however, for smooth surface finishes.

Sharp sand is required for mixing concrete as opposed to the soft builder's sand used in mortar mixes. If a large quantity of concrete is required, for say a driveway, consider contacting a firm that supplies ready-mixed concrete to you direct. Ready-mixed concrete has the advantage of being aerated (see p. 279) and so is more resistant to frost than hand-mixed concrete. It is essential, however, that you are well-prepared for the delivery with curbs or temporary forms in position, since ready-mixed concrete starts to harden within an hour and a cubic meter (35.31 ft³) equals 40 wheelbarrow loads. You will need assistance.

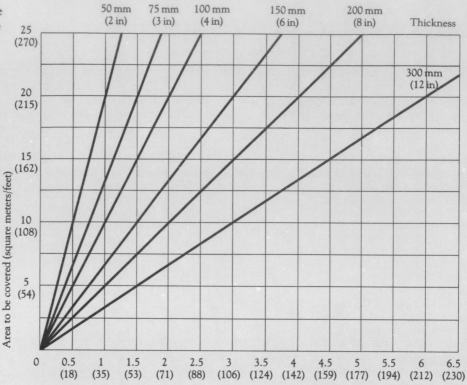

Use	Cement	Aggregate	Sand
Foundations, driveways, garage floors, surfaces for heavy wear	1 part cement	4½ parts all-in aggregate (max. size 20 mm/0.8 in)	
(Separate aggregate alternative)	1 part cement	4 parts coarse aggregate (max. size 20 mm/0.8 in)	2½ parts sand
Paths, surfaces for pedestrian traffic	1 part cement	3½ parts all-in aggregate (max. size 10 mm/0.4 in)	2½ parts sand
Bedding for slabs	1 part cement		3 parts sand
Pond linings	1 part cement	4 parts aggregate (max. size 10 mm/0.4 in)	

Grass seed mixtures

You can buy grass seed mixes to suit most locations. Broadly there are six grasses that have various qualities of wear and appearance. Most grass seed is sold in mixes formulated for various uses and climates and often contains perennial rye grass. Ryegrass is a coarse, fast growing tufted plant that will take heavy wear and is useful for lawns on which children will play. In the USA, state and federal regulations control the formulations of grass seed and label information. St. Augustine and Zoysia are available as sod or plugs rather than seed.

Grass type	Disease Resistance	Winter Hardiness	Drought Resistance	Shade Tolerance
Bent	poor	good	poor	fair
Fescue	good	good	very good	good
Perennial Ryegrass	good	good	good	poor
Kentucky Bluegrass	good	very good	fair	poor
St. Augustine	poor	poor	very good	fair
Zoysia	very good	fair to good	very good	fair

Index

Acknowledgments

Author's acknowledgments
I must thank those that have helped me in this compilation: Hilary Bryan-Brown, who has typed up my appalling script so patiently, David Lamb, who has edited it so knowledgably and Steven Wooster, who has presented it so handsomely. I would also like to thank Ivan Ruperti for the use of his photographs.

Dorling Kindersley would like to thank the following for their help in producing this book:

Michael Runge (landscape designer) and James Seymour of Seymours Garden and Leisure Centre, Ewell, who provided most of the materials photographed in *Constructing your garden* and *Finishing touches*.

Peter Morter, for the color illustrations in the *Garden-by-garden guide*.

Alison Chappel; Geoff Dann for special photography; Polly Dawes; Debbie Lee; George Perkins (Cement and Concrete Association) and Anna Selby.

Ben Knott, Ron Phillimore and Geoff Owens of Adroit Photo Litho.

Photographs were provided by:
Molly Adams: 136
Architectural Association: 22T
A–Z Botanical Collection Ltd: 124T
Michael Boys: 2, 6, 39TR, 50, 62, 100, 131, 149B, 150T, 212L, 217, 235TL (Susan Griggs Agency): 9T, 24, 27, 90, 130B, 151, 155L, 156, 164B, 182BL, 213B, 228B, 231B, 237T, 237BL
John Brookes: 18B, 118, 149T, 158T, 173B, 188T, 189T, 229B, 232BL, 232BC, 238L
Karl-Dietrich Bühler: 4, 11T, 13B, 19T, 43, 44, 47, 48, 54, 74, 88, 120, 121, 140, 141T, 143T, 145T, 145B, 154, 157R, 169, 192, 201, 206T, 211T, 214, 216B, 230B
Camera Press: 14, 15, 19B, 26T, 33, 39B, 45, 46, 56, 66, 70, 72, 76, 80, 86, 94, 110, 119, 128, 130T, 137, 142, 148, 159B, 170, 172, 175, 179, 202T, 212R, 228T, 236B, 240T
Michael Crockett (EWA): 82
Cam Culbert (Susan Griggs Agency): 23
Geoff Dann: 30, 109, 114, 115, 132, 133, 230T, 231CL, 232C, 232BR, 233B, 234B, 235C, 235B, 236TL, 236TR, 237BR, 229TL, 229TR
Richard Davies (EWA): 26B
Michael Dunne: 127C, 144
EWA: 134T

Roberta Frateschi Bosetti: 147, 161TR
Iris Hardwick Library of Photographs: 117C, 139, 157L
Pamela J. Harper: 12BR, 22B, 58, 60, 96, 107B, 111B, 112B, 116, 117B, 123, 126, 134BL, 153T, 155R, 163T, 195, 206BL
Peter Hayden: 21
Clive Helm (EWA): 98
Ann Kelly (EWA): 166
Landscape Institute: 112T
Georges Leveque: 12BL, 37, 186B, 203, 207
Neil Lorimer (EWA): 9B
Michael McKinley: 10, 28T, 34, 111T, 122, 125T, 127T, 127BR, 129T
Tania Midgley (Vision International): 17CL, 17CR, 36B, 52, 125B, 138T, 143BR, 152, 158B, 181BR, 185, 198, 199B, 200, 205R, 234T
Michael Nicholson (EWA): 160, 162, 239T
Ian O'Leary: 150B
George Perkins: 130C, 134BR, 240BL
Spike Powell (EWA): 145C
Ivan Ruperti: 49
Scala: 20
John Sims: 235TR
Harry Smith Agency: 8, 36T, 143BL, 164T, 168, 189B, 215T, 223T, 232T
Anthea Sieveking (Vision International): 146
Tim Street-Porter (EWA): 25, 28B, 124B, 135R, 159T
George Taloumis: 13T

Friedhelm Thomas (EWA): 84
Pamla Toler: 17T, 17BL, 17BR, 18T, 35, 64, 68, 117T, 127BL, 141B, 163B, 165, 171, 174, 178, 180, 182BR, 183, 184, 186T, 193, 194, 197, 205L, 206BR, 208, 210, 211C, 215B, 223BR, 233T, 233C
Jerry Tubby (EWA): 11B, 108, 135L, 153B, 161B, 202BL, 231T
Steven Wooster: 39TL, 106, 107T, 129B, 138B, 161TL, 181TL, 181TR, 181BL, 188B, 202BR, 213T, 213C, 216T, 231CR, 238R, 239B, 240BR
George Wright: 78, 92, 173T, 199T, 220, 223BL, 223BC

T = top, B = bottom, L = left, R = right, C = centre

Illustrations by:
David Ashby
Will Giles
Jim Robins
Saxon Artists
Les Smith
Eric Thomas
Venner Artists
John Woodcock

Typesetting
MS Filmsetting

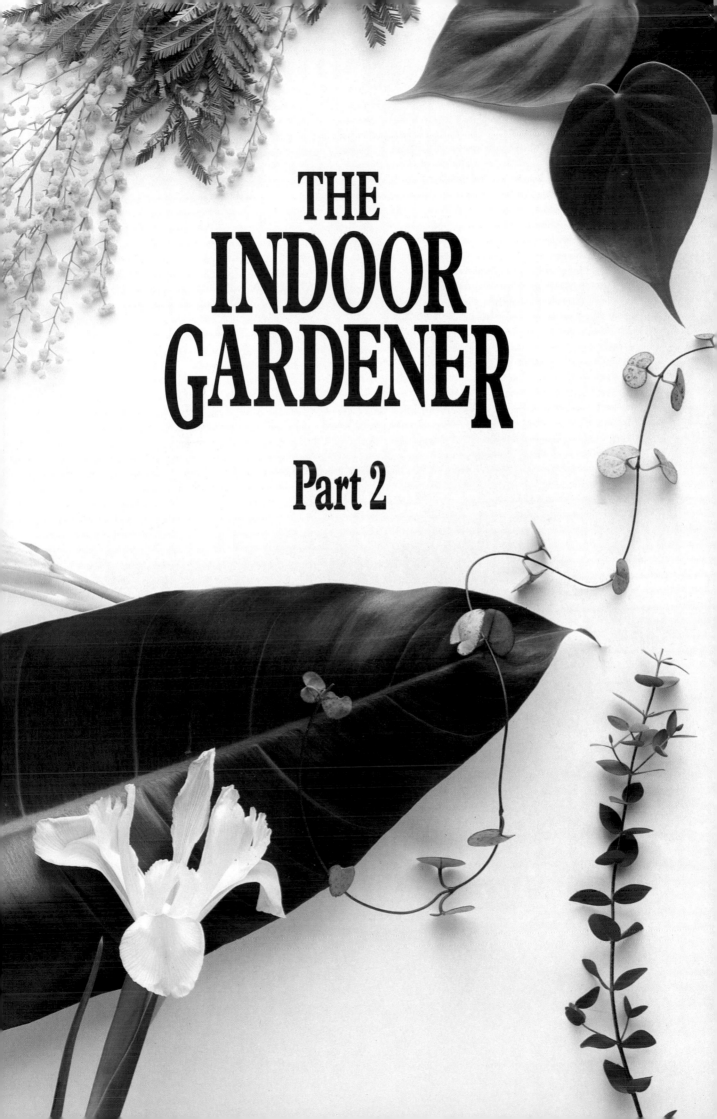

THE
INDOOR
GARDENER

Part 2

Part 2: Contents

Introduction **6**

Introduction

For those of us living in the colder parts of the northern hemisphere, the long months of winter sometimes stretch from October to April—nearly half the year. While green thoughts and nursery catalogues may sustain some plantsmen through this long period, others may seek a more practical outlet for their horticultural interests, or just the sight of greenery and flower color in their home. And for those residing in towns, this yearning for a contact with nature lasts throughout the year. It is to all these that *The Indoor Garden Book* is directed.

Indoor plants provide contact with nature for they are living growing things, and interesting because of it; at the same time they will enhance almost any interior by adding natural forms, colors and fragrances. However, used at random they look messy and may be at odds with the decoration of a room. Professional designers are well aware of the decorative qualities of plants and how they can be used to complement a decorating scheme. But this skill in matching plants to interior decoration, and in placing them effectively in a room, can be easily learned through practice and through an appreciation of the different decorative qualities of plants and flowers. This book sets out to show you how to get to know your plants and flowers and appreciate their shapes, colors, sizes, textures and seasons within an interior setting.

How to use your indoor plants

Begin your decorating by thinking about the sort of space you want to fill with plants. Do you want one large dramatic plant to act as a single focal point or a smaller group of

A Victorian flavour
The classic late nineteenth-century interior is dark and cluttered with heavy draperies and over-stuffed furniture. Several large Kentia palms (*Howea belmoreana*) might be placed in the room, with gloxinias (*Sinningia* sp.) clustered on side tables. Here, a series of hanging baskets helps to break up the large expanse of window and lightens the gloom of the dark wooden panelling.

Period romanticism
A more romantic approach to the interior appeared around the turn of the century, combined with a re-appraisal of simple garden flowers. This torso is surrounded by a group of poinsettias (*Euphorbia pulcherrima*) whose lush flowers echo the color of the sculpture; the effect is rich and voluptuous.

Traditional country-house style
Though modern, this room is a scaled-down version of a traditional, grand, country-house interior with bright colors, a fireplace, deep upholstery and an arrangement of garden flowers. Strongly colored exotic house plants would appear alien in this setting, and although some orchids (*Cymbidium* sp.) have crept in here, their color is sufficiently delicate to blend in with the decoration.

plants to contrast shapes, colors or textures? Perhaps you only have space to use plants in a hanging basket, or trained round a piece of furniture, or round part of the structure of the room. Step-by-step projects in the chapter on *Plant Display* show you how to put these ideas and many more into practice. A simple arrangement of fresh flowers will immediately lighten the mood of a room and, in the *Cut-Flower Arranging* chapter, a selection of cut flowers and foliage, including commercially available material and garden varieties, have been used to create a series of seasonal displays. In winter, cut flowers are expensive, so it is worth considering the use of dried material in the home to sustain the colors and mood of summer and autumn. The chapter on *Dried-Flower Arranging* shows you how to make trees, wreaths and decorations as well as flower arrangements. In *The Plant Finder's Guide*, decorating tips are given on how to use each of the featured plants to best effect, while *The Room-by-Room Guide* shows how plants and flowers can be used in a variety of novel and exciting ways in different parts of the house.

Styling with plants

Never has there been such a range of styles for living as there is today. Yet all—even the most modern—are subtly influenced by the past. Recognizing the component parts of a style of décor helps to define the qualities you need in a plant to enhance that style. To illustrate this, and show how to approach your decorative schemes, I have chosen a selection of contemporary styles of decoration and analyzed them, to show how plants contribute to the overall styling.

American colonial style
Another trend in interior decoration is one which is strongly influenced by the houses and artefacts of colonial North America. The early homesteaders were gardeners, and this is reflected in the way that herbs and vegetables, along with country flowers, are used for decoration in this style. The daisy bushes (*Chrysanthemum frutescens*) in rough wicker baskets used in this bedroom are typical.

Simple rustic style
In Britain, nostalgia for a rural past took another turn when stripped-pine furniture and small-print fabrics appeared in the 1960s. The style is comfortable and unpretentious, with much allusion to country pursuits. Country flowers, such as these daffodils (*Narcissus* sp.), and dried flowers find a place here.

The influence of the exotic
The hippy movement of the 1960s brought the east closer to the west, and fabrics, carpets and ornaments from the east have now found their way into many homes. The rich patterns and colors of many ethnic textiles suit the strong forms and bold colors of tropical and semi-tropical plants.

The history of indoor plants

Plants have been used indoors for many centuries. The Dutch interest in painting interiors and flower-pieces went hand-in-hand with an increasing interest, throughout the western world, in the cultivated plant. Again, the Dutch tulip craze of the 1630s must have influenced other countries, but travellers, since the returning Crusaders, would also have brought plants home and fostered them indoors prior to the advent of glass. We know, too, that herbs were used extensively indoors: for strewing, medicinal and culinary purposes. In the seventeenth century, orangeries, structures made of brick or stone with large south-facing windows, were built to shelter orange trees in winter. But it was not until the introduction of glass structures, which could be heated, that plants could be grown inside to any degree.

Tropical fruit was initially cultivated in primitively heated houses; pineapples, guavas and limes were grown—and also the first camellias. Later, there followed the date palm and banana. Succulents, such as the aloe and agave, were also raised for medicinal purposes and to decorate terraces in summer. During the nineteenth century, the conservatory became a standard addition to larger houses; house plant cultivation moved into the realms of fashion, with fern houses, palm houses, and houses for exotic plants being all the rage. Simple potted plants too began to escape from the conservatory to become the necessary accompaniment to the heavy, draped look of the late nineteenth-century interior—although the smoke from open fires did the plants little good. Floristry became a fashionable lady's accomplishment.

One reaction to this style was to seek inspiration from what

The influence of the 1930s
This contemporary bathroom looks back to the 1930s in its monochromatic color scheme and the geometric form of the metal-framed mirror. The simplicity calls for plants with a strong form, and these dragon trees (*Dracaena marginata*) add softness and interest to a setting which might otherwise look clinical.

The oriental look
This modern interior is heavily influenced by the austerity of a traditional Japanese home. Colors are largely neutral and are offset by carefully positioned areas of bright color— the pink leaf margins of the ti plant (*Cordyline terminalis*) in the foreground pick up the color of the cushions. The bare branches are chosen for their linear forms.

Linear austerity
The evolution of the Modern movement in architecture and interior design was complex, with influences from Japan, Scandinavia, Italy and America. But it was typified by more severe linear forms, a lack of pattern, and "designer" furniture in laminated wood or metal and leather. This type of hard-edged interior is softened and enriched by the use of large plants, such as these Kentia palms (*Howea belmoreana*)— which here also help to link indoors with outdoors.

must have been a continuing, unsophisticated, cottage tradition of keeping temperate plants indoors to root or over-winter, and of hanging herbs from the rafters to dry. An alternative Modernist movement at the beginning of this century used specific plants in its interiors—the lily being a great favorite. But the real origins of the use of house plants lie in Scandinavia where, traditionally, plants were brought indoors to relieve the bleakness of a long winter; and it was not until after the Second World War that they really became part of the modish interior. It was then that house plants as we know them started to make their appearance, with species from Asia, Africa and tropical America becoming available. Since then, new varieties have been bred that need less maintenance and, with the right environment and management, they can be kept very successfully indoors.

Choosing plants

The plants, which are or are not suitable for you, will depend on the particular type of decoration you have, for currently there are a number of interior styles. Your selection will depend on personal taste and on what it is practical to maintain—given the specific limitations of day- and night-time temperatures, light availability, the presence of drafts, children and pets, and, of course, available space.

The industrial style
During the 1970s, a new style of design appeared, which made use of industrial artefacts. The hard lines and strong colors of this style called for the use of large plants with distinctive shapes, and flowers with strong forms and colors.

A softer approach
In the 1980s, a softening of the high-tech style has occurred with the introduction of subtle pastel colors. In this interior, the rooms blend into each other to create a feeling of space and light, and large plants, such as these weeping figs (*Ficus benjamina*), can be used in an architectural way to link the spaces.

Classical eclecticism
Another current mood is a classic look characterized by discreet colors and patterning, and bold pieces of furniture which may be modern or traditional. Plant groupings are strong and simple; they are part of the overall conception of the room, but punctuate rather than dominate the setting.

·1·

THE DECORATIVE QUALITIES OF PLANTS

The photographs in this opening chapter demonstrate the astounding diversity of plant form—from striking architectural plants with bold foliage to relatively inconspicuous ground creepers. There is a tremendous range of growing habit, as well as leaf and flower size, shape, color and texture. Cut flowers, too, provide a kaleidoscopic array of colors—rich and vibrant or subtle and subdued. The flower heads may be large or small, flat, spiky, spherical or more complex, and these shapes themselves may suggest an appropriate way to display the material.

Bear these decorative qualities in mind when choosing plants and flowers, so that their characteristics will enhance the mood of your home. Think about the form and size of a plant if you want it to be part of the landscape of your room, or link parts of the room that have different functions. When planning smaller groups of plants, or arrangements of flowers, consider their colors and textures in conjunction with wall colors and fabric textures, so that the display and its setting show a sense of overall harmony.

Infinite variety
One of the principal joys of using plants in the home is the diversity of decorative qualities they provide. Here, a random selection of freshly cut flowers, leaves and berries gives some indication of the range of color, texture, size and shape available.

Plant form

Of all plant characteristics it is shape that probably creates the strongest initial impression. Shape is primarily to do with the general outline of the plant, but it also embraces other characteristics that contribute to the plant's overall form: the density of the growth, the size and number of individual stems and branches, the way the leaves or leaflets are arranged and the "weight" of the foliage. Of course, shape is always changing as a plant grows, but certain generalizations can be made and throughout this book I have used a system of classification that divides plants into eight different shape categories: upright, arching, weeping, rosette-shaped, bushy, climbing, trailing and creeping. These are the categories used in *The Plant Finder's Guide* and here you will find a plant to illustrate each one of them.

Coconut palm
Cocos nucifera (see p.169)
This plant has an *arching* shape, as do most of the palms and ferns; its sword-shaped fronds have a hard outline.

Japanese fatsia
Fatsia japonica (see p.181)
The overall shape of this plant is *bushy* but the large fingered leaves have a strong individual outline.

Creeping fig *Ficus pumila* (see p.193) With its spreading shape, this *creeping* plant resembles a green carpet when allowed to ramble; it can also trail or climb.

Heartleaf philodendron
Philodendron scandens (see p.188)
Plants usually combine different elements of
shape; this *trailing* philodendron has beautifully
shaped leaves as well as stems that trail
in an attractive way.

Algerian ivy
Hedera canariensis (see p.184)
The shape of its support will
dictate the overall shape of a
climbing plant, but individual
foliage will give an outline that
may be delicate or bold.

Stick yucca
Yucca elephantipes (see p.167)
Plants with *upright* growth and
spiky leaves have a simple
bold shape.

Ponytail
Beaucarnea recurvata (see p.171)
The soft shape of this *weeping* plant is created by
the mass of drooping, grasslike leaves.

Bird's nest bromeliad *Nidularium innocentii*
(see p.175) Most *rosette-shaped* plants
have a strong outline that demands attention.

Leaf size

In many fields successful design often relies on the simple repetition of elements of similar sizes. This principle holds good for the arrangement of plants but impressive effects can also be achieved by emphasizing differences in scale.
For example, the delicate tracery of small climbing plants can be highlighted by juxtaposing them with broad expanses of leaf of an uncomplicated shape.

Dwarf coconut palm
Microcoelum weddellianum
(see p.170) Juxtapose these small slender fronds with other larger palms.

Kentia palm
Howea belmoreana (see p.170)
Display large plants on their own, or in groups with spiky-leaved plants.

Rosary vine
Ceropegia woodii (see p.201)
A plant which looks best on its own; allow the stems
to trail from a hanging basket or shelf.

Elephant's ear philodendron
Philodendron hastatum
(see p.187)
A large-leaved climber best
used as a feature plant or as a
foil for low-growing plants.

Heartleaf philodendron
Philodendron scandens
(see p. 188)
Use in a hanging basket or
arrange around a large-leaved
philodendron.

Leaf shape

Leaf shape is a very strong visual characteristic of a plant and a striking display can be achieved by concentrating solely on either contrasting or harmonizing leaf shapes. There is a great variety of leaf shapes to choose from—lance-shaped leaves, oval leaves, heart-shaped leaves, wavy-edged leaves and even leaves shaped like a violin. The shape of its leaves can be the most important feature of a plant or it can be a secondary charm.

Pothos vine
Scindapsus pictus "Argyraeus" (see p.188) Heart-shaped leaves with acutely pointed tips.

Swiss cheese plant
Monstera deliciosa (see p.187) The large oval leaves become perforated as the plant gets older.

Passion flower
Passiflora caerulea (see p.185) Fan-shaped leaves with many deeply cut lobes.

Grape ivy
Cissus rhombifolia (see p.186) The leaves have pointed tips and scalloped edges.

Fiddle-leaf philodendron
Philodendron bipennifolium (see p. 169) The young irregularly shaped leaves become violin-shaped when mature.

Asparagus fern
Asparagus setaceus (see p.183) Wiry stems carry triangular sprays made up of feathery branchlets.

Dumb cane
Dieffenbachia exotica
(see p.163)
The long oval leaves have wavy
margins and a distinct point at
their tip.

Weeping fig (see p.171)
Hcus benjamina (see p.171)
Small, slender, oval leaves with
curved edges and pointed tips.

Stick yucca
Yucca elephantipes
(see p. 167)
Long, narrow, spiky leaves with
finely toothed edges.

Silk oak
Grevillea robusta (see p.166)
The leaves are highly divided
giving a delicate fernlike
appearance.

Boston fern
Nephrolepis exaltata
"Bostoniensis".
(see p. 170)
The fronds are divided into
narrow leaflets giving a graceful
feathery appearance.

False aralia
Dizygotheca elegantissima
(see p.165)
Narrow leaflets with saw-
toothed edges radiate like
spokes from the top of
each stem.

Leaf color

The range of color found in leaves is startling: from the variety of different greens to leaves with all-over colors from silver-white to deep purple, as well as those which are patterned or mottled with contrasting colors. Dramatic displays can be made with foliage plants by concentrating on the interplay between two, or at most three; colors.

Wandering Jew
Zebrina pendula (see p. 189)
The leaves are finely marked with two translucent green stripes.

Nerve plant
Fittonia verschaffeltii
(see p. 193)
Carmine-red veins traversing olive-green leaves create a dramatic color contrast.

Angel wings
Caladium hortulanum hybrids (see p.182)
Paper-thin leaves with very delicate markings in combinations of red, pink, white and green.

Painted nettle
Coleus blumei
(see p.177)
Leaf color and pattern varies, with rich mixtures of yellow, red, orange, green and brown.

Croton
Codiaeum variegatum pictum
(see p.164) Leaves in a range of warm exotic colors mottled with spots, blotches and veins.

Blushing bromeliad
Neoregelia carolinae "Tricolor" (see p. 174)
Green- and cream-striped leaves which become suffused with red at flowering time.

Peacock plant
Calathea makoyana (see p. 165)
Leaves which look as if they
have been hand-painted with a
spectacular pattern of dark
blotches.

English ivy
Hedera helix hybrids
(see p.190)
The mid-green leaves have
darker green blotches and
cream margins.

Ti plant
Cordyline terminalis (see p.163)
The striped leaves are outlined
in a vivid pink.

Angel wings
Caladium hortulanum hybrids
This young leaf, from the same
plant as the leaf to its left, shows
the color variation that can
occur on the same plant.

Silvered spear
Aglaonema crispum
"Silver Queen" (see p.164)
Beautiful dark-green leaves
heavily marked with silvery-
green blotches.

Eyelash begonia
Begonia "Tiger Paws"
(see p. 193)
The bright-red markings on the
undersides of the emerald-green
leaves show through as brown
on the upper surface.

Strawberry geranium
Saxifraga stolonifera "Tricolor"
(see p.190)
Olive-green leaves with a pink
margin and fine pink hairs.

Polka-dot plant
Hypoestes phyllostachya
(see p.179)
Dark olive-green leaves which
are heavily spotted with pink.

Leaf texture

There are as many variations in leaf texture as in shape, size or color. Very few leaves have no textural quality and textures can vary from glossy to matt, from hairy to wrinkled, from ribbed to quilted, each variation giving added interest to the plant. Subtle displays can be made by juxtaposing plants with contrasting leaf textures.

Norfolk Island pine
Araucaria heterophylla (see p.166)
Tiers of needle-covered branches give an overall filigree lightness.

Cast-iron plant
Aspidistra elatior (see p. 165)
Distinctive ribbing marks run along the length of these leathery leaves.

Bird's nest fern
Asplenium nidus
(see p.173)
The lance-shaped leaves are extremely smooth and shiny with a central rib.

Emerald ripple peperomia
Peperomia caperata
(see p.180)
The heart-shaped, dark-green leaves have a corrugated surface with a waxy feel to them.

Painted-leaf begonia
Begonia rex-cultorum (see p.183)
The highly decorative foliage is covered in pimples giving it a curious rough texture.

Delta maidenhair fern
Adiantum raddianum
(see p.183)
Leaves have a soft filmy texture
and are arranged on gracefully
drooping fronds.

Purple velvet plant
Gynura aurantiaca (see p.191)
The toothed leaves are covered
in soft purple hair, giving them a
furry texture.

Staghorn fern
Platycerium bifurcatum (see p.191)
The antler-shaped fronds are
covered with fine, white,
feltlike scurf.

Prayer plant
*Maranta leuconeura
erythroneura* (see p.178)
Bright-red veins stand out from
the surface of the satiny leaves.

Columnea
Columnea "Banksii" (see p.189)
The dark-green paired leaves are
fleshy with a waxy texture.

Flower size

The beauty of flowers does not depend solely on their color, although it is an important factor. Size contributes to the unique appeal of a particular bloom and is a major consideration when planning an arrangement. Use flowers which are in scale with one another and, when choosing a container, make sure that its size is suitable for your flowers.

Mimosa
Acacia longifolia (see p.212)
This evergreen shrub produces
short-stemmed clusters of
fragrant, golden-yellow flowers
the size of peas.

Delphinium
Delphinium elatum (see p.217)
The tall spikes of these cut
flowers are suitable for any kind
of large arrangement.

Chrysanthemum
Chrysanthemum hybrids (see p.222)
These flowers, the largest
of the numerous cut varieties of
chrysanthemum, are the size of
grapefruits.

Poinsettia
Euphorbia pulcherrima (see p.178)
These striking house plants have large,
bright-red bracts which form a circle
around the insignificant flowers.

Cornflower
Centaurea cyanus (see p.217)
The single, small, round heads of
these cut flowers are the size
of golfballs.

Anemone
Anemone coronaria (see p.222)
These brightly colored, poppy-
like flowers have heads as large
as tennis balls

Flower shape

Flowers come in an immense variety of shapes from the simple petalled blooms of the primrose to the exotic, petalless, globular flowers of the nodding pincushion. Successful flower arrangements depend upon an appreciation of shape, and the natural outline of the flower can be used as a key to the overall design. Use long, thin flower spikes for outline and rounded shapes for focal point in large displays.

Bells-of-Ireland
Moluccella laevis (see p.217)
These are long spikes of small white flowers surrounded by green cuplike bracts.

Kalanchoe
Kalanchoe blossfeldiana (see p.196)
The small flowers of this house plant grow in dense clusters and may be cut and used in a vase.

Painter's palette
Anthurium andraeanum (see p.182)
These strange-looking blooms consist of a waxy, shield-shaped bract and a protruding cylindrical flower spike.

Baby's breath
Gypsophila paniculata (see p.213)
The loose clusters of tiny single or double flowers create a hazy effect which is emphasized by displaying them alone in a glass container.

Transvaal daisy
Gerbera jamesonii (see p.217)
These large single or double flowers come in vivid colors and provide focal interest in mixed arrangements.

Pansy
Viola wittrockiana (see p.213)
These attractive heart-shaped flowers have layers of soft, lobed petals.

Bird-of-paradise
Strelitzia reginae (see p.164)
These unusual flowers consist of a green bract supporting orange-and-blue flowers which stand erect like the crest of a tropical bird.

Zonal geranium
Pelargonium hortorum
hybrids (see p.178)
These rounded clusters of small flowers are available in a wide range of colors.

Orchid
Dendrobium sp. (see p.223)
These long-lasting flowers grow
in arching sprays that bloom
right down the stems.

Peruvian lily
Alstroemeria pelegrina (see p.213)
The trumpet-shaped flowers are
borne at the ends of the
long stems.

African violet
Saintpaulia hybrids (see p.175)
The single or double flowers of
these house plants grow in
clusters on a
short stem.

Gentian
Gentiana sp. (see p.217)
These small flowers are
shaped like a funnel.

Sword lily
Gladiolus sp. (see p.215)
These elegant cut flowers
have tall, one-sided spikes
of single florets.

German violet
Exacum affine (see p.178)
The flowers of this house plant
are small and saucer-shaped
with a single layer of petals.

Tuberous begonia
Begonia tuberhybrida
(see p.176) These house plants
carry both single and double flowers
which are large and roselike.

Nodding pincushion
Leucospermum nutans (see p.221)
These unusual globular blooms
are covered with protruding spikes.

Carnation
Dianthus caryophyllus
(see p.215) These double flowers,
which grow on clustered stems, have a
"ruffled" appearance.

Poison primrose
Primula obconica (see p.181)
This house plant has clusters of
brightly colored blooms on a
single stalk.

·2·
PLANT DISPLAY

The arranging, grouping and positioning of plants and flowers is an art, not a science. It is a matter of taste, and therefore not an area in which there are hard-and-fast rules. However, there are guidelines, and it is possible to give advice on what is likely to look good and what is not.

Perhaps the most important thing to remember is that every plant arrangement must be designed in context. This means taking into account not only the appearance of the plant itself, but also the container you intend to put it in, the background against which it will be seen, and the room features or items of furniture by which it will be surrounded. Arrangements may consist of a single plant in a simple pot, a formal grouping of associated plants, a jungle-like garden room or conservatory overflowing with greenery, a single vase of bright, colorful, cut flowers, or a mixed display that incorporates any or all of these elements. In each case, the first thing to do is to look at the plants and flowers themselves and see them in terms of the qualities described in the previous chapter. Only then turn to the choice of container and make your selection not just on the basis of choosing the right size for your plant's health, but also in terms of how the container can add to your display, and how it can enhance the mood you want to create.

Co-ordinating plants and containers
The color of flowering house plants can be picked up, and reinforced, by the color of their containers. Here, the color of the containers holds the group together and, at the same time, because they are a less assertive pink than the flowers, attention is focused on the plants.

Matching plants to containers 1

The criteria to be borne in mind when selecting a container for your plant are many and complex, and for every rule formulated it is possible to show an example that breaks it successfully. In every case the decision will be tempered by personal taste and preference but it is worth setting down some basic guidelines.

The most important consideration is the proportion of the container to the plant. In general, the smaller the plant the more it should equal the height of its container. To find out what combinations will work together it is best to try various permutations of container with your plant, standing back to appreciate the result in each case. Having selected a container whose proportions suit the plant, make sure that both together will suit the particular place

in which you want to put them. This is fundamental to the success of the arrangement for not only the container, but also the plant inside it, must be suitable for the setting both practically and aesthetically.

It is essential to choose a style of container and a type of plant that will reflect and enhance the ambience of the room for which they are intended. The style of the container depends on the material of which it is made and on its shape, color and texture. The style of a plant can be analyzed in a similar way: for instance, the spiky-leaved yucca has a hard-edged modern look to it, while a begonia with lush flowers and a soft outline will suit a more traditional setting. So do not be tempted to buy a yucca in an aluminium pot if you have a period house decorated with chintzes.

Containers for different-shaped plants

Scarlet star
Guzmania lingulata

Pothos vine
Scindapsus pictus
"Argyraeus"

English ivy
Hedera helix hybrids

Conical glass bowl
The crisp linear form of this bowl complements the red flowers and strong outline of these rosette-shaped plants.

Spherical ceramic pot
The trailing pothos vine hangs attractively over the edge of this rounded pot. The simplicity of the pot, both in shape and color, shows off the silver variegation in the leaves.

Tall terracotta pot
An English ivy displayed in this way needs a tall pot to show off its trailing stems. A tall upright plant would look out of proportion in such a container.

Boston fern
Nephrolepis exaltata
"Bostoniensis"

Button fern
Pellaea rotundifolia

Ponytail
Beaucarnea recurvata

Classical lead urn
The height of this imitation lead urn sets off the Boston fern's arching fronds. The combination has a formal look reinforced by the urn's classical design.

Round ceramic pot
The simple shape of this container sets off the delicate outline of the button fern's arching fronds. The dark matt-green leaf color goes well with the blue of the pot.

Low terracotta dish
The bizarre shape of the weeping ponytail plant calls for a plain container such as this terracotta dish. As the roots like to be pot bound, the container is very small for a plant of this size.

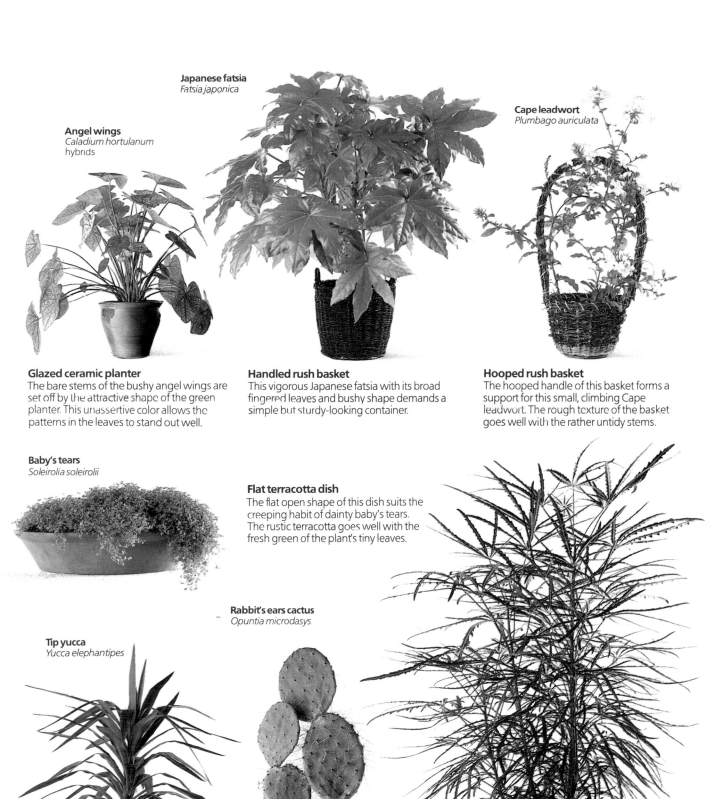

Japanese fatsia
Fatsia japonica

Angel wings
Caladium hortulanum
hybrids

Cape leadwort
Plumbago auriculata

Baby's tears
Soleirolia soleirolii

Rabbit's ears cactus
Opuntia microdasys

Tip yucca
Yucca elephantipes

False aralia
Dizygotheca elegantissima

Glazed ceramic planter
The bare stems of the bushy angel wings are set off by the attractive shape of the green planter. This unassertive color allows the patterns in the leaves to stand out well.

Handled rush basket
This vigorous Japanese fatsia with its broad fingered leaves and bushy shape demands a simple but sturdy-looking container.

Hooped rush basket
The hooped handle of this basket forms a support for this small, climbing Cape leadwort. The rough texture of the basket goes well with the rather untidy stems.

Flat terracotta dish
The flat open shape of this dish suits the creeping habit of dainty baby's tears. The rustic terracotta goes well with the fresh green of the plant's tiny leaves.

Square fiberglass planter
The austere form of the upright spiky-leaved yucca is shown off by the extreme simplicity of its white fiberglass container.

Rustic wooden barrel
The arresting shape of this upright cactus requires a container with a simple form. The rough wooden barrel goes well with its vigorous spiny texture.

Large terracotta planter
The success of this combination relies on the contrast between the solidity of the terracotta pot and the filigree effect of this upright plant's bronze-colored foliage.

Matching plants to containers 2

Groups of containers

One of the ways of adding interest to the layout of a room is by grouping pots and other containers with plants, as incidental points of interest. You can use containers of the same color to hold a group of plants together and to stabilize the mood of an area within a room. Few groupings of this sort are important enough to become the focal point in a very large room, but can work well in a smaller area.

When choosing your containers, think carefully about how they will match your plants, and about how plants and containers will work together as a group, both in terms of themselves and in terms of their setting.

Counterpoint with color *right*
These containers were chosen to set up a pleasing interplay of color between themselves and the plants. The black and red containers pick up and complement the leaf colors of both plants.

Painted-leaf begonia
Begonia rex-cultorum

Croton
Codiaeum variegatum pictum

Black aluminium planter

Red plastic container

Baby's tears
Soleirolia soleirolii

Terracotta pots

Terracotta pots *above*
A simple classical grouping of containers that share the same style and color helps control the random, profligate growth of the plants, and contributes to the effect of a balanced arrangement.

Playing with scale *above*
This group works through the repetition of container shape and texture set off by a dramatic contrast in scale of the containers. The use of the same plant in each pot contributes to the satisfying unity of the group.

Tall and small *right*
Here, the contrast in shape and scale between the two containers is enhanced by the use of the same plant in each. The monochromatic color scheme of the pots helps to hold the group together and picks up the silvery-gray leaf variegation in the pothos vine.

Grey ceramic container

Repetition *below*
A small plant in a small pot may need reinforcement: this can be achieved by using a larger specimen of the same plant in a larger pot. These pots pick up the very dark-green color of the polka-dot plants' leaves and contrast well with their pink variegation.

Polka-dot plant
Hypoestes phyllostachya

Pothos vine
Scindapsus pictus
"Argyraeus"

White ceramic pot

Black ceramic containers

Unusual containers

Many containers are expensive to buy, particularly if you are thinking of using several of them. It is worth having a look at everyday household objects—wastepaper baskets, preserving pans, galvanized buckets, coal scuttles, kettles, watering cans, china and enamel bowls—which can take on a new look and a new lease of life if used imaginatively. There are no rules for improvisation, it is just a question of what looks right for the plants and for the style of setting they are to inhabit. Experiment with putting potted bulbs in wicker shopping baskets, ivies and other trailing plants in shiny ice coolers, small cacti in colorful pencil holders and any other combinations that suggest themselves. Even an old chimney pot can make an attractive container for a rustic setting (either stand the plant on top of it, in its own planter, or rest the planter on a pile of bricks inside the chimney pot). If you use a container without drainage holes, line it with a layer of gravel, vermiculite or clay pot fragments before planting.

A bird-cage *right*
The delicate bars of the cage provide an elegant framework for the creeping fig (*Ficus pumila*) to ramble over. This plant will climb and trail, as well as creep, and all three habits of growth can be seen here.

An animal container *below*
An out-of-the-ordinary container can attract attention, add an element of humor, and greatly increase the impact of a single plant display—as this rhinoceros pot clearly demonstrates.

A china bust *right*
You can use an object as a container to set up an association and convey a particular mood. Here the combination of fronds of ivy trailing over a classical head recalls overgrown antique statuary.

The principles of arrangement 1
Balancing groups

Making an arrangement of growing plants means both grouping plants together with their containers, as you might on a shelf or table-top for example, as well as placing plants in a room. Special advice for arranging plants in room settings appears in *The Room-By-Room Guide*; but it is easiest to start looking at good groupings of plants together with their planters.

The key to a good arrangement is that it should have visual balance. As a simple rule of thumb, a larger plant has more visual weight than a smaller one. However, certain plants have striking leaf color, shape or texture which attracts the eye instantly; so a small example of such a plant will have as much visual weight as a large example of a less dramatic plant.

Symmetrical arrangements

Symmetry
Two identical creeping figs (*Ficus pumila*) either side of a Norfolk Island pine (*Araucaria heterophylla*) create a perfectly symmetrical arrangement. If a vertical line ran through the middle of the group each side of the line would exactly mirror the other.

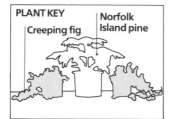

PLANT KEY | Norfolk Island pine
Creeping fig

Asymmetrical arrangements

Asymmetry
The pine has more visual weight than a single creeping fig and needs to be balanced by two of the latter. Space can be used to adjust balance: here, merging the two trailing plants together a little gives them more visual weight than when they are separated.

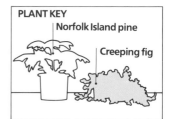

PLANT KEY | Norfolk Island pine
Creeping fig

Balancing plants and objects *left*
Two striking bromeliads stand on a console table, either side of a centrally placed urn. To hold this group together, and to highlight the sense of symmetry, ashtrays have been positioned either side of the urn. The success of the arrangement is reinforced by the way the red of the flowers and the green of the urn echo colors in the painting behind them.

Formal balance through symmetry *above*
In general, perfectly symmetrical arrangements suit plants with a very regular shape and rather formal look, such as the common myrtles (*Myrtus communis*) placed either side of this mirror. Bay trees or orange trees would also be appropriate in this context. The simple table arrangement is made of a single flamingo flower (*Anthurium* sp.) and palm frond (*Howea* sp.).

The principles of arrangement 2
Using contrast

If a successful arrangement is one that balances visually, what makes it not merely successful but outstanding? The answer: contrast—the setting off of opposites against one another. You can use bold contrasts of shapes and scale or more subtle contrasts of textures and colors. Compose your groups by experimenting with several different plants—choosing ones which like similar conditions—relying upon your eye to tell you what works and what does not. When planning a group, the best way to use contrast is to restrict it to just one, or at most two, elements. The effect of contrast will always be stronger if it is part of an arrangement that displays some sense of overall order and harmony.

Shape

The upright, spiky-leaved yucca (*Yucca elephantipes*) contrasts with the low, rounded forms of the cacti. The strong form of the yucca gives it a visual weight that needs to be balanced by a number of small cacti. The introduction of the spiky-leaved but low-growing queen agave (*Agave victoriae-reginae*) on the left creates a pleasing link between the two dominant elements in the composition.

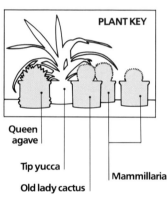

PLANT KEY

Queen agave

Tip yucca

Old lady cactus

Mammillaria

Texture *left*

The filigree lightness of the large delta maidenhair fern (*Adiantum raddianum*) has a similar visual weight to the dense mass of the emerald ripple peperomia leaves (*Peperomia caperata*) because of the different sizes of the plants. The plants balance visually simply by being placed side-by-side.

Maidenhair fern

Emerald ripple peperomia

PLANT KEY

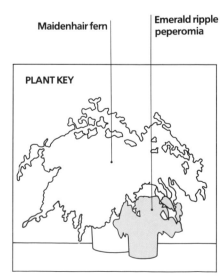

Scale

The three plants in this group share the same sort of shape and the same sort of texture— they are all spiky-leaved. Yet they vary enormously in scale. The small queen agave (*Agave victoriae-reginae*) is only a few inches high, whereas the large stick yucca (*Yucca elephantipes*) rises to a height of about 5 ft. Their similarity in shape and texture, and the fact that they are displayed in all-white containers, serve to emphasize the contrasts in scale. Another way of using contrasts of scale effectively is to group plants in a row—along a mantelpiece or shelf for example—using plants of the same kind but of different heights.

PLANT KEY

Stick yucca

Tip yucca

Queen agave

Color *right*

Three pink elatior begonias (*Begonia* "Elatior" hybrids) are offset by a single white-flowered variety. By slightly overlapping the three pink plants and setting the white one a small distance away, neither color predominates but each is strengthened by the element of contrast. Another way of using color is to juxtapose a plant with variegated leaves with a flowering plant that picks up one of the colors in the leaves.

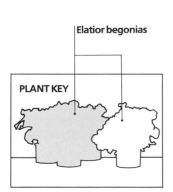

Elatior begonias

PLANT KEY

Lighting plants

The chances are that your plants are seen as often in the evening, when they are lit by artificial light, as they are during the day. In addition to background lighting, you can use directional lighting to highlight plants and flowers. This type of lighting, where the beam of light is narrow enough to pick out a single object, throws plants into relief, accentuating shape, defining color and emphasizing texture. Dramatic effects can be achieved through the interplay of light and shade created by directional lights, and the most ordinary of plants can be made into something outstanding.

Another consideration is the quality of light that you want. Incandescent tungsten bulbs, which are the most popular, give out a warm light which emphasizes yellows and reds; while tungsten halogen bulbs give out a more concentrated beam of colder light. To increase the warmth of a light, buy color-coated bulbs or translucent shades in warm colors. Plants should not be placed right next to the light source, as the heat transmitted by the bulb will damage the leaves. A safe distance is about 2 ft away from a 100 watt incandescent bulb.

Natural light

Light acts on the green pigment chlorophyll, which is present in all plants, to start the process called photosynthesis. The violet/blue and red wavelengths are most important for plant growth: the blue stimulates foliage and the red flowering. Incandescent bulbs are low in blue wavelengths and have only a limited effect on plant growth; but there are special lights which can be used as a substitute for daylight (see pp.258-9).

The amount and quality of daylight that a plant needs depends upon its original habitat in the wild. Some plants need full sunlight, some prefer filtered light, which can be given by diffusing daylight with Venetian blinds, lace or muslin, and others good indirect light. The quality of the natural light in your room will dictate the areas in which you can display your plants. At the same time, think about how they will be lit at night, so that their position allows enough natural light for healthy growth and for a directional light to show them off in the evening.

Using a window as a frame *left*
The filtered light received from this tiny window suits the Japanese fatsia (*Fatsia japonica*) and silhouettes its brilliant-green foliage. The scale of the plant and the window are perfectly matched.

Sun on a windowsill
below
A symmetrical group of a white Cape primrose (*Streptocarpus* sp.) set between two carved birds is arranged on a wide windowsill. The light emphasizes the brilliant white of the flowers, and gives a translucent quality to the leaves which fall directly in its path.

Lighting effects 1

Downlighting
Use a downlight or pendant light over a table to direct light on to a central decoration, such as a flower arrangement, or to hold together a group of small plants.

Using a pendant light *left*
A pendant light suspended a little way above a terracotta bowl of baby's tears (*Soleirolia soleirolii*) picks up the detail of the foliage.

Using a downlight *right*
A downlight recessed into the ceiling casts an intense beam of light over the plants and objects arranged on this table. It illuminates a bowl of pinks (*Dianthus* sp.), a large bromeliad (*Portea petropolitana extensa*) and a maple tree (*Acer* sp.), which has been brought inside for a temporary display.

LIGHTING SET-UP   Down light

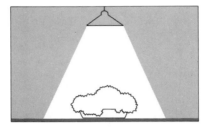

Uplighting
Lighting a single plant or a group of plants from below, with an uplighter or floor-mounted spotlight, throws strong shadows on to the wall and ceiling above. The quality of the shadows can be controlled by the position of the lights.

LIGHTING SET-UP   Side view

Back light   Front light

Uplighting from behind
An uplight placed behind the plant creates an abstract pattern of dramatic but distorted shadows, and reduces the plant itself to an attractive silhouette.

Uplighting from in front
Placing the lamp in front of the plant reveals detail and color in the plant itself, and creates a shadow which echoes the plant's natural shape and form.

Lighting effects 2

Frontlighting and backlighting

By using a spotlight on a table or shelf, you can create a dramatic lighting effect in a small area. Frontlighting will give strong shadows which will enhance the natural shape of plants or flowers, while backlighting produces a softer effect.

LIGHTING SET-UP   Side view

Back
light

Front
light

Backlighting *above*
This light creates an overall warm, translucent quality.

Frontlighting *below*
The shadows enhance the tulips' (*Tulipa* hybrids) distinctive shapes.

Sidelighting

Use a wall- or ceiling-mounted spotlight to beam light on to a plant or flower arrangement. With this flexible type of lighting, the angle of beam can easily be adjusted.

Sidelighting from above *below*

This angled light illuminates the soft texture and filigree pattern of the delta maidenhair fern's (*Adiantum raddianum*) foliage.

LIGHTING
SET-UP

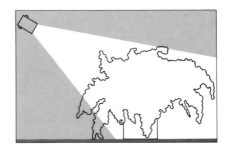

Side
light

Sidelighting dried flowers

Kitchens are rooms where different types of lighting are needed: bright lights to illuminate working areas and softer, moodier lights for eating areas. Here, two angled spotlights focus beams of light on to dried flowers, revealing their colors and textures. The candles on the table add another warm light.

Styling with plants 1

Few of us have the opportunity of designing a room from scratch—in one go selecting all the materials, furniture, decorative objects and plants needed to create a recognizable style of interior decoration. In spite of practical limitations on the scope of your ideas, it is well worth looking at how plants can be used to evoke and enhance particular decorative styles. Plants and flowers are an integral part of many styles, often being the inspiration for decorative motifs of all kinds. On the following pages you will find an analysis of some of the most popular contemporary styles of interior decoration, combined with advice on what types of plants and flowers to display with them.

Country style

Country style seeks to bring the garden into the house. Flower patterns are everywhere—on wallpaper, curtains, cushions and china—and can be given added freshness by the presence of fresh flowers. Country style can be formal or relaxed, suitable for the town as well as the country. Objects do not have a particular place but rely on number to create a comfortable, lived-in atmosphere. Nostalgia for rural values is an important ingredient of this style which prizes well-crafted wooden furniture, homely designs, natural fabrics and warm colors.

Plants for a country kitchen *right*
Simple glazed pots are filled with an informal array of variegated English ivy (*Hedera helix* hybrids), thyme (*Thymus vulgaris*) and a sickle-thorn asparagus fern (*Asparagus falcatus*).

Elements of formal country style *left*
Color is more important than shape in country style. Here, foliage and flowering plants with a soft shape complement the patterns found on wallpaper, china and fabric, as do the fresh flowers which are those commonly found in an old-fashioned garden. This type of country style is more formal in feel than that featured opposite. The textures—of bone china and chintz—have more luster than those of terracotta and unvarnished wood.

PLANT KEY

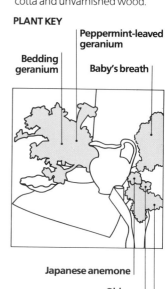

Peppermint-leaved geranium

Bedding geranium

Baby's breath

Japanese anemone

Old rose

Stocks

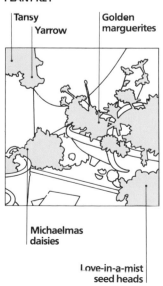

Floating flower-head table display *above*
Many types of geranium heads (*Pelargonium* sp.) have been floated in water on two plates to make a colorful display suitable for a center-piece on a country dining table.

Echoing floral patterns *left*
Flowers are everywhere—on fabric, on china and massed together in dried bunches to create a crowded effect reminis-cent of a well-stocked country garden.

Elements of informal country style *right*
Again, the shape of plants or flowers is less important than their color. Flowers such as these Michaelmas daisies (*Aster novi-belgii*) are fresh and warm in color, without being vibrant. Dried seed heads have rough textures and monochromatic colors that mix well with the colors and textures of wood, terracotta and basketry. Dried flowers have an immediate asso-ciation with the countryside, and their soft yellows and blues pick up the colors on the hand-painted ceramics.

PLANT KEY

Tansy
Yarrow
Golden marguerites

Michaelmas daisies

Love-in-a-mist seed heads

Styling with plants 2
Ethnic style

The many manifestations of what can be termed "ethnic" style reflect the traditional cultures of various groups throughout the world. It is based on artefacts made by traditional methods and characterized by the use of lively patterns, which can be abstract or figurative.

Using ethnic textiles *above*
A beautiful kilim is the inspiration for this arrangement; its colors are echoed in the ceramic dish and the ochre-colored centers of the marguerites (*Chrysanthemum frutescens*).

South-American style *left*
The brilliant flowers and strong form of this Easter cactus (*Rhipsalidopsis gaertneri*) show up well against the rough texture of the stone shelf and stone carving.

Elements of ethnic style *left*
Plants with a strong outline and solid shape are needed to stand up against the abundance of patterns. Cacti are an obvious choice, particularly with objects of South-American origin as shown here. Colors should be warm to harmonize with the colors of natural dyes. Dried flowers, pebbles and bleached driftwood would all fit in to this decorative scheme.

PLANT KEY

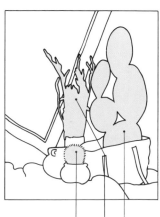

Mammillaria

Chilli peppers

Rabbit's ears cactus

Oriental style

The Far East has been a source of inspiration for decoration over several hundred years. As a decorative style it can be interpreted in a number of different ways, since each area—China, Malaya and Japan—has its own recognizable national style influenced in part by the indigenous flora.

Contrasting textures in the Japanese style *left*
The spiky leaves of the bonsai are echoed by the floating chrysanthemum heads and the harsh texture of the rock is offset against the smooth ceramic plate.

Oriental simplicity *above*
Another simple group which relies on strong forms and contrasting textures for its effect. The spiky-leaved iris (*Iris pallida*) and simple fans have an abstract quality very much in an oriental style.

Elements of oriental style *right*
A key element in oriental style is the concentration on a few simple shapes and large areas of neutral color, offset by focal points of bright color. Here, the contrast in texture between the coarse-weave bamboo mat and the glistening lacquer table is typically oriental. The feathery umbrella plant (*Cyperus* sp.) suggests bamboo while the vivid basket plant (*Aeschynanthus lobbianus*) adds a more tropical Malaysian feel to the group.

PLANT KEY

Miniature gladioli

Basket plant

Spider chrysanthemums

Umbrella plant

Styling with plants 3
High tech

This is a style based on the utilitarian shapes and materials of industrial products. Decoration is minimal and the overall effect is hard and clinical looking; it is the antithesis of anything organic. Plants need to have a vigorous outline, and flowers must be strong in color so that they are not swamped by gleaming metallic surfaces and vibrant primary colors.

Using vivid colors *above*
Use flowers with clearly defined shapes and strong colors such as this flamingo flower (*Anthurium andreanum* hybrids). The flowers look almost "unreal" as the texture of the deep-red bracts resembles shiny plastic.

Using strong forms *left*
The aggressive form of a Peruvian apple cactus (*Cereus peruvianus*) emerges in the foreground of this picture. Bright lighting and the reflective white tiling call for large, dominant plants such as the umbrella plant (*Cyperus* sp.) in the background.

Elements of high tech *right*
Suitable plants are those with a great deal of visual weight, such as large agaves, yuccas and cacti. Here, the plants have a well defined shape and foliage whose plain-green color goes well with the red plastic container and red rubber flooring.

PLANT KEY

Staghorn fern | Cast-iron plant

Art deco

The art deco style of the 1920s and 1930s is still a source of inspiration for interior decoration. It is characterized by the use of strong geometric forms, monochromatic colors and reflective surfaces, such as chrome and lacquered wood.

Informal art deco *above*
Tulips (*Tulipa* hybrids) have a strong shape which suits this style—particularly when they are massed together in a vase of the period.

Formal art deco *right*
This picture shows the geometric shapes, shiny textures and monochromatic colors which are all hallmarks of the style. The regal lilies (*Lilium regale*) in the circular vase, and the ponytail, with its bold shape, hold their own against the strong outlines of the chairs.

Elements of art deco *left*
Plants with a strong outline are needed to complement the hard lines and solid forms of this style. Here, the hard-edged shape of the sculpture is repeated in the form of the lily flowers. The white of the flowers is in keeping with the monochromatic color scheme. The linear form of the silvery-mauve rosary vine (*Ceropegia woodii*) in the ceramic light fitting is silhouetted against the wall.

PLANT KEY

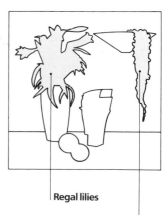

Regal lilies

Rosary vine

Grouping plants in a single container 1

For a large arrangement, quite dramatic effects can be achieved by grouping several plants together in a single container. Plants grow better when they are grouped together; a micro-climate is established with the moisture given off by one plant becoming available to its neighbor. The individual plants tend to grow into each other and show each other off.

The plants may either be all of the same kind, or they may form a mixed group of several different types with similar growing needs. They can either be knocked out of their pots and planted in a common potting mixture, as shown here, or, if they are for a temporary display, they can be left in their individual pots and stood in moist peat. If you are potting the plants, select a fairly deep container, so that the potting mixture does not dry out too quickly, and always include a layer of porous material at the base of the container if it is without drainage holes. This method has the advantage that it usually gives the plants a bigger root run, but it does make it more difficult to remove an ailing plant, or to group plants with different watering needs. Sometimes a combination of the two methods is best, allowing you to give a single plant special treatment.

An alternative planting with begonias

A striking and colorful foliage group can be made by planting together a number of painted-leaf begonias (*Begonia rex-cultorum*). These plants have extremely decorative leaves with striking patterns in red, silver, green and black. Choose specimens with different sorts of leaf patterns and textures to create a subtle interplay of colors. Plant them in peat-based potting mixture and put them in a warm part of the house in indirect light.

Equipment and materials

China planter

Trowel

Peat-based potting mixture

Urn plant
Aechmea fasciata
(see p.173)

Charcoal

Clay pellets or vermiculite

Planting a large container

In general, the strongest arrangements of this type are the simplest ones. Often, mixed plantings do not work because they show too much variation in shape and texture; the overall effect is untidy and difficult to place in a room. Here, I have chosen to group together several exotic-looking urn plants. Their vigorous shape called for a simple container and I chose a white china planter whose color picked up the white sheen on the leaves of the plants.

The finished arrangement
To keep the urn plants in good condition, put them in a warm, sunny place and keep their natural "vase"— formed by the rosette of leaves—filled with water. Small pale-blue flowers will emerge from the pink bracts; these do not last for long but the bracts will remain attractive for up to six months.

Building up the arrangement

1 Line the bottom of the planter with ¾in of porous clay pellets or vermiculite and scatter pieces of charcoal over them. Fill the planter half-full with potting mixture and place one of the plants on the mixture to check that the top of its pot is level with the top of the planter.

2 To remove the urn plant from its pot, first water it well and then, holding the plant between your first and second finger, hit the pot hard against the edge of a table, or strike the base hard with your fist.

3 Build up the potting mixture at the back of the planter, and as you position each plant in the potting mixture tilt it out slightly so that the rosette of leaves and flower heads can be appreciated.

**PLANTS
Mini-climate 1**
Warm, sunny

An alternative planting with saffron spikes
Grouping saffron spikes (*Aphelandra squarrosa* "Louisae") in the same china planter makes another simple and effective group. Their strong shape and exciting leaf and flower color are intensified when the plants are massed together.

Grouping plants in a single container 2
Arranging plants in a basket

The choice of a basket as a container will dictate the types of plants which are suitable to be displayed in it. A rush basket calls for unsophisticated plants such as cinerarias (*Senecio cruentus*) and German violets (*Exacum affine*), as well as the examples illustrated here. Potted bulbs can be used in spring and should be massed together in the basket just before they begin to flower.

The plants which you select are for a temporary arrangement as you display them for their flowering period, or when their foliage is at its best. Given that their moment of glory is short there is no need to unpot the plants into a potting medium; and, since they are in separate pots, you can choose to group together plants with different watering needs so long as they like similar amounts of light and heat.

An alternative display with kale

These ornamental kale (*Brassica oleracea acephala*) look like giant flowers when grouped together. Their leaves of rich purple or ivory, both edged with green, can be frilled or plain and are shown off to great effect when several plants are packed together as shown here. Ornamental kale are available in late summer and autumn and, provided that they are given plenty of light and kept in a cool place, they will remain fresh for several weeks.

PLANTS
Mini-climate 5
Cool, filtered sun

Equipment and materials

Rush basket

Plastic lining

Clay pellets or vermiculite

Peat

English ivy
Hedera helix hybrids
(see p.190)

Scissors

Building up an arrangement with primroses and ivy

1 Place a piece of plastic (a trash can liner is suitable) in the basket to form a watertight skin. Cut it to shape allowing a small overhang which will eventually be tucked in. Cover the bottom of the basket with a layer of porous clay pellets or vermiculite about 1 in deep.

2 Fill the basket with 2in of damp peat. Stand the pots inside and start to build up the composition. Put the three taller, salmon-pink poison primroses at the back, packing peat around the pots as you go, then let the variegated ivy trail down one side to soften the overall shape.

3 Finally, put the remaining primroses at the front of the basket. Make sure that all the pots are standing upright because you will still need to water them—the primroses in particular like plenty of water. To keep the display looking fresh, take off individual flowers as they fade and remove any yellowing leaves. These primroses should last from 6-8 weeks provided they are kept in a cool place.

Poison primrose
Primula obconica
(see p.181)

An alternative display with begonias
Another filling, suitable for a warmer place in the house, would be a collection of small-leaved eyelash begonias (*Begonia* "Tiger Paws"). Their striking green-and-bronze foliage creates a strong enough pattern for them to stand on their own.

Training climbing plants 1

Making a moss-pole

Climbing plants need to be provided with some kind of support in order for them to grow upright. Plants that use aerial roots to climb, such as the philodendrons, Swiss cheese plants (*Monstera deliciosa*) and pothos vines (*Scindapsus pictus* "Argyraeus"), like to grow over a constantly moist medium. A pole made out of wire netting stuffed with sphagnum moss is an excellent, sturdy support, and particularly suitable for climbing plants with thick stems and large leaves. Plants which climb by means of curly leaf tendrils, such as passion flowers (*Passiflora caerulea*) and ivies (*Hedera* sp.), can be trained on canes, wire hoops and trellis work.

Equipment and materials

Moss-poles can be bought ready-made, but if you make your own with wire netting you can provide far moister moss for the roots of climbing plants. You will need about three or four small plants to grow up a moss pole about 3ft high. Once it is made, remember to keep the moss constantly moist, otherwise the aerial roots will not grow into it.

Sphagnum moss

Bamboo sticks

Terracotta half-pot

Tamping stick

Wire cutters

Roll of corrugated paper

Chicken wire

Drainage dish

Peat-based potting mixture

Trowel

Heartleaf philodendron
Philodendron scandens
(see p.188)

PLANTS
Mini-climate 3
Warm, shady

Wires

Building up the arrangement

1 To form the shape of the moss-pole, take a roll of corrugated paper and wrap chicken wire round it. Cut the wire so that it is 2in wider than the paper. Join the two cut edges together to form a column shape.

2 Cut two lengths of bamboo, thread them through the netting about 1½in from the bottom. Lash them together where they cross each other, and to the wire column, then wedge them into the pot.

Training plants in the house

Climbing plants can be trained up a blank wall, to make it an attractive feature, and trained round mirrors, doors and windows, to frame them with fresh greenery. To provide support for the plant, string runs of wire or strong nylon cord between nails or screw eyes, and then attach the plant to the support with plant ties, to help maintain the shape that you want.

Training a plant up a wall *right*
The emerald fern (*Asparagus densiflorus* "Sprengeri") is often displayed as a trailing plant, but here its soft, feathery stems have been trained round a picture.

Training a plant round a mirror *above*
A grape ivy (*Cissus rhombifolia*) makes an unusual frame for this large mirror. This attractive vine clings to any support with its wiry tendrils and grows very rapidly—about 2-3ft a year. It is an extremely tolerant plant which thrives in a wide range of conditions.

3 Fill the pot two-thirds full with potting mixture. Start to fill the empty column of chicken wire with sphagnum moss, using a wooden stick to pack it together tightly, and continue until it is full.

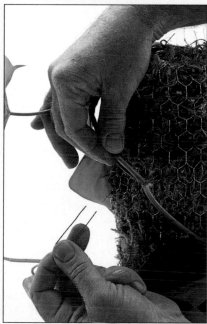

4 Pot the heartleaf philodendrons and attach their stems to the pole with wire, bent to form a hairpin shape.

5 Water the sphagnum moss and the potting mixture well before putting the moss-pole in a warm, shady position. Spray the pole every day to keep the moss thoroughly moist.

Training climbing plants 2
Making a wire support

Many plants suitable for indoor use are rampant climbers in the wild. They are often bought trained round a wire support which is soon outgrown. It is then a good idea to open the plant out and train it round a larger support which will show off foliage and flowers more effectively. Try to match the scale of the plant to the scale of the support: here I trained passion flowers round hoops of wire which suited the delicate tracery of the plants' foliage.

Equipment and materials

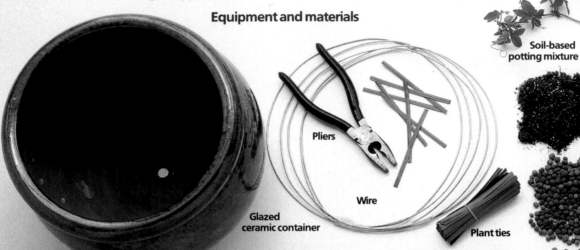

Glazed ceramic container

Pliers

Wire

Plant ties

Soil-based potting mixture

Clay pellets or vermiculite

Passion flower
Passiflora caerulea
(see p.185)

PLANTS
Mini-climate 1
Warm, sunny

The finished arrangement
Covering one hoop less thickly than the others made the arrangement a more interesting shape. It also gave it a lightness of effect which will make the transitory opening of the curious flowers more visible. You will need to tie in the shoots very regularly in order to maintain the overall shape of the display. If you cut the plants back, as far as the main stems, at the beginning of winter and put them in a cool, frost-free place they should grow back again in the spring.

Building up the arrangement

1 Cut two lengths of wire of the same size to form two hoops. Place them in the container to check that they are in scale with it. Put the hoops to one side; they will be held in place by the potting mixture once you have started planting.

2 If your container has a drainage hole, place a piece of broken shard over it; then line the pot with 1in of vermiculite or clay pellets and fill three-quarters full with potting mixture. Unwind a passion flower from its previous support and repot it, firming potting mixture around its roots. Place one hoop in the pot and wind the plant's stems around it.

3 Place the other wire hoop in the container at a 90 degree angle to the other and fix the pair together with plant ties. Remove any dead leaves or unwanted shoots as you go. Plant the last passion flower, training one stem up the remaining bare hoop, and arranging the other stems on the opposite side.

Other ornamental supports

Using bamboo, rattan or wire you can make many different shapes of support. Bamboo stakes can be made into trellis or, for a more unusual effect, into obelisks. Rattan is flexible and can be used to make any sort of rounded form.

Trellis work *below*
Woodland strawberries (*Fragaria vesca* "Alpine") bear small fruit and make an attractive display.

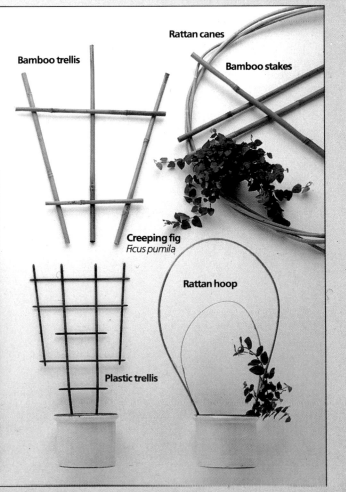

Rattan canes

Bamboo trellis

Bamboo stakes

Creeping fig
Ficus pumila

Rattan hoop

Plastic trellis

Planting hanging baskets 1

Most of us are familiar with hanging baskets displayed on terraces, balconies or porches, but seldom see them used indoors to advantage. When selecting a basket for an indoor display think carefully about its setting: a wire basket is only suitable for a room with a water-resistant floor, such as a conservatory. A practical, but less attractive, alternative is a solid plastic basket with a raised platform inside, a filling tube and water-level indicator, or another type which incorporates a drip-tray. But there is nothing to stop you using a terracotta container or rush basket, if you make your own rope hangings, or using a wall basket in an appropriate material.

It is important to secure the basket properly because it will be very heavy when wet. The chain or rope support should hang from a hook firmly anchored in a ceiling joist, not set into the plaster.

When deciding upon a planting scheme for a basket, remember that you are trying to blend the arrangement with your décor. Limit yourself to one type of plant unless your setting is very plain. For an outdoor planting you can afford to be less restrained with your color, but it is sensible to choose species which are used to heat and the drying effect of wind.

Planting a wire basket

The attraction of a wire basket is that, once the plants are established, it becomes a spherical mass of flowers or foliage. Here, I set out to create the effect of a large ball of flowers by planting white and blue Italian bellflowers. These should flower continuously from August to November provided they are watered well in warm weather—a good reason for putting this display in a conservatory.

Cross-section of the planted basket

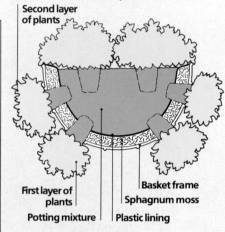

Second layer of plants

First layer of plants

Potting mixture

Basket frame

Sphagnum moss

Plastic lining

Bucket

Plastic lining

Wire basket

A garden room filled with hanging baskets

This light garden room provides an excellent setting for an array of hanging baskets. A dramatic staghorn fern (*Platycerium bifurcatum*) is the focal point of the display. This is flanked on the left by a grape ivy (*Cissus rhombifolia*) in a wicker basket and an impatiens (*Impatiens* sp.), and on the right by several spider plants (*Chlorophytum comosum* "Vittatum"). Notice the wicker wall baskets—one containing dried flowers, the other another grape ivy.

Building up the arrangement

1 Rest the basket on the rim of a flat-bottomed bowl or bucket. Line it with a 2in layer of damp sphagnum moss. Then, cut a circle of plastic sheeting to fit inside, leaving an overlap of 4in. Make a circle of holes in the plastic 2in up from the bottom.

2 You will need to divide some of the larger plants into two to fit them through the holes. First, water the plants before taking them out of their pots; then, holding the plant in both hands, plunge your thumbs into the middle of the potting mixture and pull apart. Insert the divided plants from the outside, pushing the roots through the sphagnum moss and the holes in the plastic.

4 Fill the gaps in the top with blue-flowered plants and, when the basket is filled, tuck in the overhanging plastic. Water the basket well before replacing the chains and hanging it in a sunny place.

3 Push one row of plants around the bottom of the basket, cover with a layer of potting mixture, firming it down around them, and then place more plants higher up the sides of the basket to fill the gaps. Plant several large white specimens in the top.

PLANTS
Mini-climate 4
Cool, sunny

Italian bellflower
Campanula isophylla
(see p.191)

Equipment and materials

Scissors

Peat-based potting mixture

Trowel

Sphagnum moss

Planting hanging baskets 2

Planting a wicker basket

Hanging baskets can add freshness and color to a room, particularly where space at floor level is limited. Think about the place where your basket is to hang and select your plants with an eye to the decorative effect you want, bearing in mind that the plants should like the place you have chosen and be broadly compatible in their requirements. The container you use should not detract from the natural colors of the plants. I felt a wicker basket suited this display where I have chosen to group ferns together, accentuating contrasts of plant form and leaf shape.

Equipment and materials

Wicker basket

Floral foam matting

Foil

PLANTS
Mini-climate 2 Warm, filtered sun
Mini-climate 3 Warm, shady

Clay pellets or vermiculite

Trowel

Peat-based potting mixture

Charcoal

Asparagus fern
Asparagus setaceus
(see p.183)

Emerald fern
"Asparagus densiflorus "Sprengeri"
(see p.191)

Scarlet star
Guzmania lingulata
(see p.174)

Bird's nest fern
Asplenium nidus
(see p.173)

Boston fern
Nephrolepis exaltata
"Bostoniensis"
(see p.170)

Cretan brake
Pteris cretica
(see p.183)

Delta maidenhair fern
Adiantum raddianum (see p.183)

Sphagnum moss

The finished arrangement
The final addition of the scarlet stars creates a splash of color and links the display to its setting by echoing the red of the poppies in the painting. After completing the planting I placed the rope hangings round the basket and hung it from the ceiling by a north-facing window. It is a good idea to use a hook with a universal joint so that the basket can be rotated to ensure plants get an even supply of light.

Building up the arrangement

1 Line the basket with foil to prevent rotting, then place foam matting on top and trim to fit. Put some pieces of gravel at the back of the basket to form a higher area for planting. Line the basket with porous clay pellets or vermiculite.

2 Fill the basket with peat-based potting mixture, adding about a handful of charcoal to prevent the mixture turning sour. Allow enough room at the top for watering. Position the first plant where the compost has been built up over the gravel. Use a bushy asparagus fern with delicate feathery fronds to give height to the arrangement.

3 At this stage, it is a good idea to plan the rest of the arrangement by positioning your plants, still in their pots, until you are satisfied with the design. Here I put two trailing emerald ferns either side of the asparagus fern.

continued over

4 To give more substance to the back of the design put two more Boston ferns either side of the asparagus fern. When planting, tilt the ferns out to the side so that their fronds overhang the sides of the basket.

5 To fill the foreground add a delta maidenhair fern and a Cretan brake. The delicate fronds of the delta maidenhair fern and the unusual branching of the Cretan brake provide further variation in leaf shape and color.

6 Placing a bird's nest fern on the left sets up a pleasing contrast between its broad straplike leaves and the surrounding feathery fronds. Finally, add the two scarlet stars, cover any visible potting mixture with damp moss and water well before hanging.

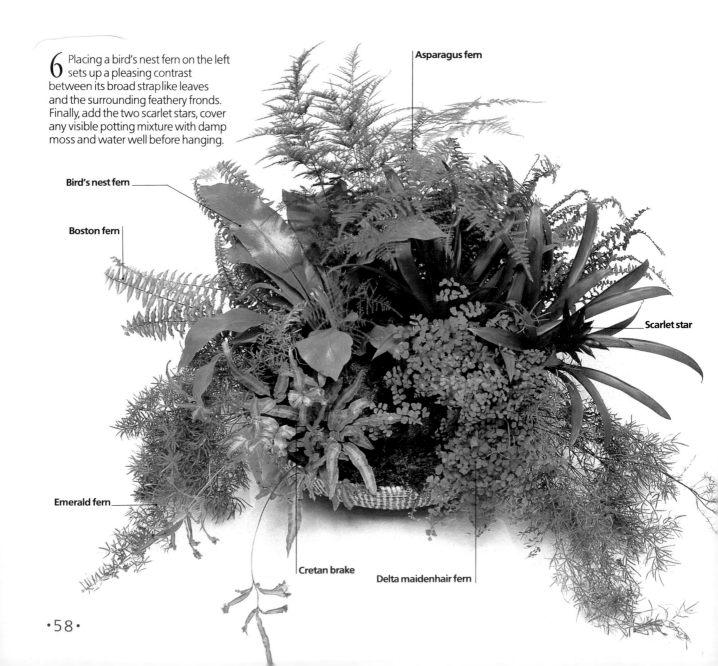

Asparagus fern

Bird's nest fern

Boston fern

Scarlet star

Emerald fern

Cretan brake

Delta maidenhair fern

Growing bulbs indoors 1

A mass of temporary flowering bulbs can make a beautiful grouping, particularly when there is little other color around. Most bulbs can be grown in containers without drainage holes, as well as conventional pots. Plant them in soup tureens, vegetable dishes, china pots or glass vases using potting mixture, or grow them hydroponically in pebbles and water.

When garden bulbs are grown in the house they have to experience an artificial "winter" before they will bloom. They will not flower properly unless they are kept cool (30-45°F) and dark for eight to ten weeks. You can buy "prepared" bulbs which do not need to be kept in the dark (although they must be kept cool) but these are more expensive. Buy bulbs as soon as you see them on sale—usually in early autumn—and plant them right away. It is a good idea to buy several types so that you can keep replacing fading specimens with fresh ones. Plant bowls of early-flowering crocuses which can be white, yellow, bronze, mauve or purple. Plant hyacinths for their scent as well as their large flowers. Choose daffodils for their fresh and cheerful colors, and lily-flowered and kaufmannia tulips for their strong shapes and colors.

A windowsill of bulbs *above*
Amaryllis (*Hippeastrum* hybrids), daffodils (*Narcissus* hybrids) and hyacinths (*Hyacinthus orientalis* hybrids) line a windowsill. This is a good place to display your bulbs since the cooler the plants are kept, the longer they will last.

Crocuses in a basket *below*
A mass of bulbs and foliage spilling over the edges of a basket can look stunning. Here, brilliant white crocuses (*Crocus* hybrids) have been mingled with the graceful grasslike foliage of the bulrush plant (*Scirpus cernuus*).

Growing bulbs indoors 2

Although bulbs can be bought from retailers, there is such an enormous range of hybrids available that it is worth looking through a specialist catalogue to select bulbs whose colors and shapes particularly appeal to you. For fresh color and delicate fragrance, daffodils are a good choice. Certain species of daffodils, including *Narcissus* "Cragford" which I have used here, can be grown in gravel or stones instead of potting mixture or bulb fiber. Plant

them in glass containers which allow the texture of the gravel to be seen. If you plant the daffodil bulbs in October, and "winter" them as shown below, they should be in flower by Christmas.

Indoor bulbs which flower later in the spring or in the summer include the amaryllis (*Hippeastrum* hybrids), which has huge, trumpet-shaped flowers, and several lilies including the fragrant, white Easter lily (*Lilium longiflorum*).

Equipment and materials

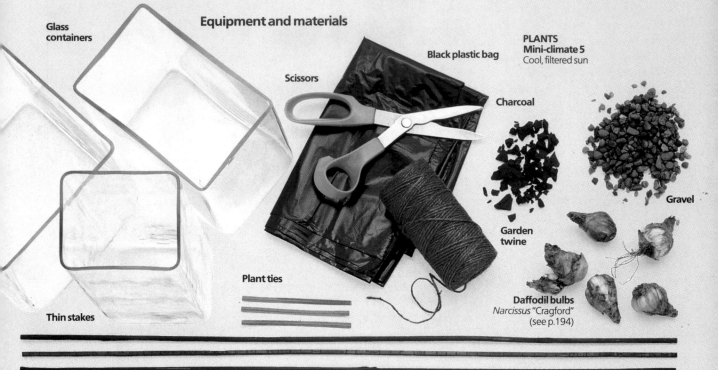

Glass containers

Scissors

Black plastic bag

**PLANTS
Mini-climate 5**
Cool, filtered sun

Charcoal

Gravel

Garden twine

Plant ties

Daffodil bulbs
Narcissus "Cragford"
(see p.194)

Thin stakes

Building up the arrangement

1 Mix some gravel with about 20 small pieces of charcoal, having first washed the gravel to remove any dirt which would cloud the water. Fill the container so that it is about three-quarters full of gravel and start planting the first bulbs, making a depression with your finger for each bulb to sit in.

2 Place the bulbs in position with their "noses" coming out of the medium. You should be able to fit about nine bulbs in a container of this size, but make sure that the bulbs do not touch each other. Fill the spaces between the bulbs with more gravel and add water until it is close to, but not touching, the bottom of the bulbs.

3 If you use prepared bulbs or those of the paper white narcissus, they can grow in the light, but other bulbs must be kept in the dark. Cut a black plastic bag in half, secure it round the container with garden twine or string and stand in a cool, dark place. Look at the bulbs after about four weeks to see if they need more water.

4 After eight to ten weeks, about ½in of growth should be visible and the bulbs can be brought out into the light. Once the daffodils have reached their maximum height, some of their stems and leaves will need support. Attach any untidy leaves or bending stems to thin green stakes with plant ties. Alternatively, use the stakes at an early stage—when about 4in of top growth has appeared—to support the stems and leaves as they grow.

5 Most spring bulbs do not like very warm rooms. If temperatures are high, their stems become elongated and the leaves soft and sappy. When the flowers have died, remove the dead heads and plant the daffodil bulbs outdoors.

Other indoor bulb displays

It is best to plant one color of a flower per pot because different colors may flower at different times. Hyacinth (*Hyacinthus orientalis* hybrids) bulbs vary so much that it is safest to plant single bulbs in 3in pots. Once the flower buds are well developed, group bulbs together at the same stages of development.

Hyacinths in full bloom *left*
Hyacinths have large flower heads and, when planted en masse, make an eye-catching and fragrant display.

Pots of daffodils *above*
A cheerful display of daffodils (*Narcissus* sp.) in clay pots. Grass seeds have been sown on the surface of the potting mixture for decoration.

Planting window-boxes 1

Window-boxes are usually thought of as outdoor containers but there is no reason why they cannot be used indoors, provided you have a window which opens outwards or upwards with a suitable sill. There are many types of boxes: plastic is a light, cheap material suitable for use indoors or out and, if planted with trailers, will hardly be visible through the greenery; fiberglass comes in authentic-looking imitations of lead and stone, and is extremely light but correspondingly expensive; stone is always attractive but is too heavy for most sills and better used on the ground; terracotta suits period houses and formal interior settings; wood is a very useful material for an outdoor box as it can be made to measure and, if fitted with a waterproof zinc liner which can be lifted out, is easy to replant with the new season's flowers.

Your window-box should have holes at the bottom to prevent the lower layers collecting sour water and causing roots to rot. Wooden, stone and terracotta boxes have holes drilled and plastic ones have indentations which you can tap out with a screwdriver. Always fit a drip-tray underneath the box to prevent any surplus water overflowing. Whether your box is to go indoors or out, select one that is as deep as is practical; this will prevent the potting mixture from drying out too quickly, although you will find that any box will need very frequent watering in warm weather. If your box is placed high-up where it could fall and cause damage below, secure it in place with a brace on either side attached to the window surround, or within an angled bracket fixed to the wall or window. Never use window-boxes on weak or rotten sills.

Types of window-box

The material of your window-box should be in keeping with the style of your house—if it is to go outside—and the style of your room—if it is to go inside. In either case, it is best to choose a box which is as low-key as possible to show off the plants. If you use a purpose-made wooden box it can be painted to match the color of your walls. Your choice of plants will depend on the season in which you are planting, and on the orientation of your window.

A cedarwood box *left*
This deep, wooden window-box sits snugly on its sill. Its simple planting of scarlet geraniums (*Pelargonium hortorum* hybrids) will flower for almost all the year and makes an eye-catching display set against the deep-yellow wall.

A painted wooden box *below*
This box of painted wood is almost completely obscured by the purple lobelia (*Lobelia erinus pendula*) trailing over it. Deep-pink primroses (*Primula obconica*) and marguerite daisies (*Chrysanthemum frutescens*) complete a colorful summer planting attractively framed by the wrought-iron sill-surround.

A brass box *above*
The glistening brass of this indoor window-box is set off by the austere, white-leaded window. It is planted with blue German violets (*Exacum affine*) whose golden stamens pick up the color of the brass. Other alternatives suitable for a brass box would be a bronze-leaved wax begonia (*Begonia semperflorens-cultorum*) or impatiens (*Impatiens wallerana* hybrids), rust-colored florist's chrysanthemums (*Chrysanthemum morifolium* hybrids) or a collection of richly colored painted nettles (*Coleus blumei*).

Planting an indoor window-box

Begin by thinking about what types of plants will like the quality of light offered by your window and make sure that those you choose have similar growing needs. For this summer group I used a plain white plastic window-box and chose pink and purple Cupid's bowers and a tradescantia with pink stripes to pick up the color of the flowers. Alternative plantings for a spring box would be bulbs or herbs and for a winter box you could use daffodils.

Building up the arrangement

1 Line the box with a layer of shards making sure that the pieces face downwards so that water will drain off them (if you do not have any broken terracotta pots, most garden centers will supply shards free of charge). Add a 2in layer of potting mixture, putting more at the back to give height to the back of the arrangement.

2 Set the plants out in the box and experiment with the design until you are satisfied that it looks balanced. Begin by planting six purple Cupid's bowers along the length of the box, leaving room between them for the pink-flowered kinds and the trailing foliage of the tradescantia.

3 Place a tradescantia in the center of the box, letting some stems trail down in front and threading the others through the Cupid's bowers. Finally, fill the remaining spaces with pink Cupid's bowers and another tradescantia.

The finished arrangement
Both plants like a sunny position and will be happy on a south-facing windowsill. The Cupid's bowers will flower from June until October and, as they grow, will trail attractively over the edge of the box.

Equipment and materials

PLANTS
Mini-climate 1
Warm, sunny

Shards

Tradescantia
Tradescantia fluminensis
"Variegata"
(see p.189)

Soil-based potting mixture

Cupid's bower
Achimenes grandiflora
(see p.181)

Window-box and drip-tray

Trowel

Pruners

Planting window-boxes 2

Planting an outdoor window-box

Winter is the season when you long to see greenery and colorful flowers. One way of improving the view from your windows, particularly if you live in the city, is to plant a window-box using plants with colorful berries and evergreens with attractive foliage. The window-box I have planted below will need protection from the frost, since the Christmas cherries and florist's chrysanthemums are not hardy; put it at a window where it can easily be brought inside in cold weather or, alternatively, use it as an indoor window-box for a cool place.

Building up the arrangement

1 Line the window-box with 1in of clay pellets (you can also use shards or gravel) to provide drainage. Place a layer of potting mixture over the pellets to a depth of about 2in.

2 With the plants still in their pots, experiment with the design, putting the Christmas cherries in the middle and the chrysanthemums at the edge. Place the ivies in the box to see where their trailing stems will look best.

3 Take the plants out of their pots and shake off excess potting mixture. Put two Christmas cherries in the center of the box and plant the florist's chrysanthemums on either side. Let the four small ivies trail down at the sides and in the front of the box. Firm potting mixture around the plants and water well before putting in position.

Florist's chrysanthemum
Chrysanthemum morifolium
hybrids (see p.181)

Equipment and materials

**Clay pellets
or vermiculite**

Trowel

**Peat-based
potting mixture**

English ivy
Hedera helix hybrids
(see p.190)

**Terracotta
window-box**

PLANTS
Mini-climate 4
Cool, sunny
Mini-climate 5
Cool, filtered sun

Christmas cherry
Solanum capsicastrum
(see p.180)

Other ideas for window gardens

There are other ways to decorate windows besides using window-boxes. You can set potted plants on tiers of glass or plastic shelves across a window, or use wooden shelves lined with metal to protect them from water. Your choice of plants will depend upon the orientation of your window. Place sun-loving desert cacti and succulents and tropical species at a south-facing window, flowering plants at west- and east-facing windows, and plants which like indirect light at north-facing windows. Alternatively, it is possible to build a special window for plants, similar to a miniature conservatory.

Tiers of plants *right*
Rows of plants ranged on glass shelves obscure the view but make an attractive display in themselves. Placing all the plants in the same type of container introduces a sense of order into a crowded arrangement. Most of the plants shown here are desert cacti and succulents which are used to bright sunlight in the wild. Plants with variegated leaves, such as the polka-dot plant (*Hypoestes phyllostachya*) on the bottom shelf, will also thrive in good light, which will intensify the color of their foliage.

A miniature conservatory *below*
Plants benefit from being grouped together and, if they are also given good light, they will grow fast. In a glass box, such as the one shown here, it is necessary to provide some form of shade from the summer sun, to ensure good ventilation, and to increase the humidity, particularly when it is hot. To do this, stand plants on trays filled with moist pebbles.

Planting bottle gardens

Bottle gardens provide optimum growing conditions for plants which like a humid atmosphere, so it makes sense to plant particularly slow-growing specimens if you want your garden to look attractive for a year or more. Tempting as it may be to plant African violets (*Saintpaulia* hybrids), it is not a good idea since, once the flowers fade, they can look very dull. It is best to create a colorful effect by using plants with variegated leaves and to build an interesting group with contrasts of shape and texture. Any sort of bottle is suitable, provided plants can be passed through the neck. If the bottle is made of colored glass it will block out some light and, to compensate for this, you should move the garden into brighter light than would be normal for the plants inside.

Circle of paper

Funnel

Glass bottle

Maidenhair fern
Adiantum raddianum microphyllum
(see p.183)

Sphagnum moss

Clay pellets or vermiculite

Peat-based potting mixture

Charcoal

Equipment and materials

Miniature trowel

Little nerve plant
Fittonia verschaffeltii argyroneura "Nana"
(see p.193)

Sponge

Spool

Fork

Spoon

Nerve plant
Fittonia verschaffeltii
(see p.193)

Building up the arrangement

Australian maidenhair fern
Adiantum hispidulum
(see p.183)

**PLANTS
Mini-climate 3**
Warm, shady

1 Cut a circle of paper the same size as the planting area of the bottle and experiment with the design—placing the taller plants at the back and the low-growing ones in the foreground.

2 Pour a 1in layer of clay pellets or vermiculite into the bottle through a funnel made of stiff paper. Add a handful of charcoal, and fill the bottle with 2-3in of damp peat-based potting mixture.

3 Build up the potting mixture at the back of the bottle to give more height to the group. Use the spoon to smooth out the surface of the mixture and make a hole at the back for the roots of the first plant.

4 Remove a maidenhair fern from its pot and shake off excess potting mixture. Stick the fork into the root ball and lower the plant into the hole made for it. Release the plant, cover the roots and gently firm down the potting mixture around it.

5 Put another maidenhair fern at the back of the group and then add an Australian maidenhair to vary the outline. Make sure that the plants are not too close together—leave about 2in between them to allow room for growth.

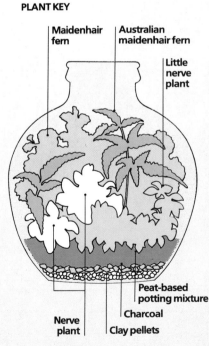

PLANT KEY

Maidenhair fern

Australian maidenhair fern

Little nerve plant

Peat-based potting mixture

Charcoal

Nerve plant

Clay pellets

6 Place the little nerve plants in the foreground. Their solid silver-veined leaves provide a pleasing contrast to the mass of delicate fronds above them. Then, to give the arrangement a focal point and to add color, plant a nerve plant with red leaf veins in the centre. Finally, decorate any bare area of potting mixture with sphagnum moss, and pour a cup of water into the bottle by directing it against the glass. You can put a cork in the top to make the atmosphere more humid, but it will make the glass mist up more quickly.

Planting terraria

Terraria are glass cases that offer the same humid environment as bottle gardens, since the moisture given off by the leaves of the plants inside condenses and runs back into the soil. As it is easier to prune and remove plants from a terrarium than from a bottle garden, you can use suitable fast-growing kinds such as the mosses and polka-dot plants planted in the terrarium opposite. For the same reason, small flowering plants such as miniature gloxinias (*Sinningia pusilla*) can be planted, and replaced when they have faded. Here, I used a leaded-glass terrarium resembling a tiny conservatory which suggested the choice of palms to form the background of the group.

Equipment and materials

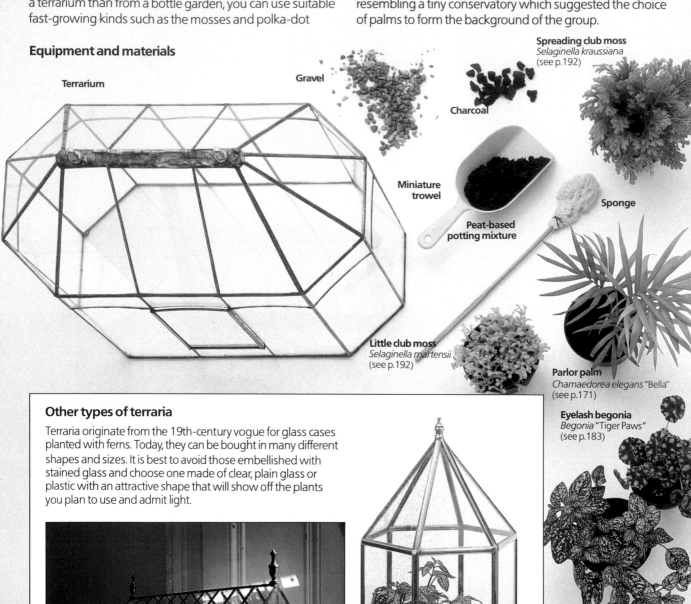

Terrarium

Gravel

Charcoal

Spreading club moss
Selaginella kraussiana
(see p.192)

Miniature trowel

Peat-based potting mixture

Sponge

Little club moss
Selaginella martensii
(see p.192)

Parlor palm
Chamaedorea elegans "Bella"
(see p.171)

Eyelash begonia
Begonia "Tiger Paws"
(see p.183)

Polka-dot plant
Hypoestes phyllostachya
(see p.179)

**PLANTS
Mini-climate 2**
Warm, filtered sun

Other types of terraria

Terraria originate from the 19th-century vogue for glass cases planted with ferns. Today, they can be bought in many different shapes and sizes. It is best to avoid those embellished with stained glass and choose one made of clear, plain glass or plastic with an attractive shape that will show off the plants you plan to use and admit light.

A pagoda *above*
One species of plant massed together looks very effective in a small terrarium.

A miniature greenhouse *left*
Moss-covered rocks make an interesting addition to this group.

Building up the arrangement

1 Line the terrarium with ½in of gravel, spread lumps of charcoal over it and then fill with 2in of damp potting mixture. Place some of the plants you have chosen inside the terrarium and plan your group.

2 Make a depression and plant the tallest parlor palm, spreading the roots out horizontally and gently packing potting mixture around them. This will not harm the plant and will slow down its growth.

3 Plant another parlor palm at the back of the terrarium on the left. Then, beneath it place an eyelash begonia next to a little club moss which matches the brilliant green in the begonia's leaves.

PLANT KEY

Parlor palm

Spreading club moss

Polka-dot plant

Little club moss

Eyelash begonia

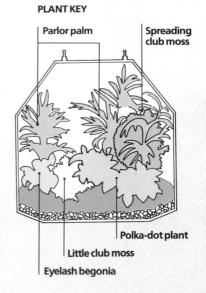

4 Put another little club moss in the front of the terrarium and a spreading club moss behind the larger parlor palm to give it more bulk. Then, fill the remaining spaces around the palm with polka-dot plants, and decorate any bare potting mixture with gravel. Mist-spray plants and potting mixture and close any aperture.

Cleaning the terrarium
Use a small sponge attached to a bamboo stake to remove condensation or algae from the inside surface of the glass.

Cacti and succulent gardens

Cacti and succulents with similar growing needs can be planted together to make a miniature desert landscape. As they do not have deep root systems, they can be planted in shallow containers. If your container does not have drainage holes, line it with porous material to prevent the roots from rotting, and water the plants more sparingly than is recommended in *The Plant Finder's Guide*.

Queen agave
Agave victoriae-reginae
(see p.200)

Bishop's cap
Astrophytum myriostigma
(see p.198)

Equipment and materials

Coarse sand

Trowel

Gravel

Soil-based potting mixture

PLANTS Mini-climate 4
Cool, sunny

Powder-puff cactus
Mammillaria bocasana
(see p.199)

Terracotta dish

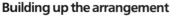

Building up the arrangement

1 Line the container with 1in of gravel. Mix coarse sand and soil-based potting mixture together in measures of one part of sand to two of soil. Spread a 1in layer of this mixture over the gravel.

2 With the plants still in their pots, experiment with the design. Consider any decorative pebbles which can be used on the surface of the potting mixture.

Mammillaria
Mammillaria sp.
(see p.199)

3 Fold up a piece of brown paper, wrap it round the spines of the cactus and lift the plant out with one hand, pulling the pot away with the other.

4 Lift the queen agave out of its pot and place it at the back of the dish. Plant the two bishop's caps and mammillarias, trickling the potting mixture gently around their roots.

Brown paper

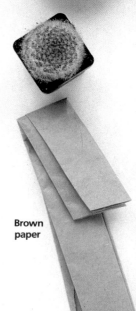

Decorative finishes

Most nurseries and garden centers stock a wide variety of stone chippings, pebbles and gravel that can be used to decorate the surface of the potting mixture. Marble chips can be obtained from stone masons, and aquarium dealers often have a good selection of colored pebbles. Coverings of pebbles and gravel tend to look best with cacti and succulents, since they are in keeping with the plants' arid or semi-arid natural habitat, but try out other finishes as well.

Pebbles

Shells

Coarse-grade blue glass

Limestone chips

Fine-grade green glass

Decorating a cactus garden

A large area of potting mixture between plants looks dull. Cover it with stone chippings and interestingly shaped pebbles, which resemble rocks, and you have a suitably rugged and arid-looking miniature landscape for these desert plants.

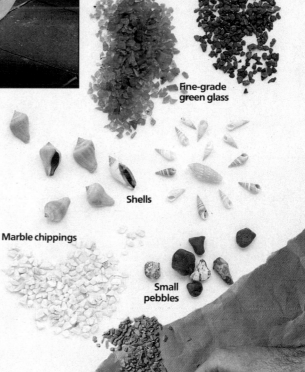

Shells

Marble chippings

Small pebbles

Patterns and textures *above*

Building up a series of decorative concentric rings made out of contrasting colors or materials is simple and effective. The sharp conical shells are arranged to mimic the spines of the cactus.

Adding a decorative finish *right*

Using a small scoop or spoon, add a thin layer of decorative material to the top of the potting mixture.

Making water gardens

Hydroculture is a relatively new name for an old practice of growing plants in containers filled with water and aggregate to which soluble plant foods are added. In place of soil, plants are held in position by the aggregate. Special containers are available (see pp.260-1) but you can make a simple and attractive planting in a glass vase.

It is best to use plants that have already made roots in water before putting them into the new medium, since the roots made in water are quite different from those made in soil. "Prepared" plants can be bought, or you can use cuttings of soft-stemmed plants that have been rooted in water. If you do transfer a plant from soil to water you must wait for the old roots to be replaced by new succulent ones. This process takes between 8-12 weeks and, during this time, the plant will need to be encased in a plastic bag to keep it in a warm and humid atmosphere.

Equipment and materials

Glass containers

Pothos vine
Scindapsus pictus
"Argyraeus"
(see p.188)

PLANTS
Mini-climate 1
Warm, sunny

Tradescantia
Tradescantia albiflora
"Albovittata"
(see p.187)

Pebbles

Charcoal

Aggregate

Miniature trowel

Building up the arrangement

1 Line the container with ¾-1 in of aggregate which has previously been soaked to wash away impurities. Place a layer of pebbles over it and add some charcoal to keep the water sweet.

2 Fill the container two-thirds full with aggregate. Pour in enough water to fill the container one-third full and let the aggregate absorb the water.

3 Place the plant inside the container and trickle aggregate around its roots. If you are moving a plant grown in potting mixture carefully wash all traces of it away before planting.

The finished arrangement
A pothos vine and a trades-cantia have been planted in aggregate decorated with pebbles to create layers of different textures in the transparent containers. Plants are fed by adding food in the form of a powder or a sachet which releases nutrients into the water when they are needed (see p.260).

Alternative arrangements

Almost any plant can be successfully grown by hydroculture. It is a technique that has several advantages over conventional methods: it is convenient for apartment dwellers since potting mixture does not have to be stored; it is less messy; watering and feeding are simpler; growth is more vigorous; and plants are not subject to soil-borne pests and diseases.

A vegetable garden *above*
The sweet potato (*Ipomoea batatas*) is usually grown for its tuberous edible roots; here the root is growing in water and decorative heart-shaped leaves rise from it.

An oriental garden *left*
This umbrella plant (*Cyperus* sp.) likes boggy conditions in the wild and is therefore a natural candidate for hydrocul-ture. Here, I built up a layer of white pebbles at the front of the container and filled the rest of it with the aggregate.

Caring for bonsai

The word bonsai means literally "plant in a tray". It is a technique by which any tree or shrub can be turned into a dwarf specimen by restricting its growth, and by pruning its roots and branches. As developed by the Japanese and Chinese, the technique was applied mainly to hardy trees of all kinds, such as maple, silver birch, beech, larch and pine. Today, these are referred to as "outdoor" bonsai since they need to spend most of the year outdoors. They should not be brought into a heated room for more than a few days in winter, but in summer, when the temperatures inside are similar to those outside, they can be brought in more frequently. A new development is the "indoor" bonsai: these are tropical or semi-tropical species which are happy to be kept indoors all the year round.

All bonsai need a great deal of light and, as their roots are restricted in a very small container, they must be watered frequently, particularly in warm weather.

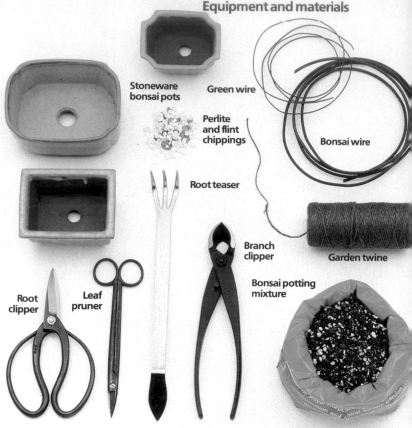

Equipment and materials

Stoneware bonsai pots

Green wire

Perlite and flint chippings

Bonsai wire

Root teaser

Branch clipper

Garden twine

Bonsai potting mixture

Root clipper

Leaf pruner

Indoor and outdoor trees

Bonsai can be grown from seed or cuttings, or bought as young and mature plants. If properly cared for, these trees can live for many years; their price depends on age and the complexity of the shape of the tree.

Bonsai should be grown in shallow frost-proof pots with large drainage holes. Imported from Japan, these pots come in a variety of shapes and in plain, subtle colors which do not detract attention from the trees.

An outdoor bonsai
This Japanese maple (*Acer palmatum* "Dissectum") has a double twisted trunk and graceful upright shape. The leaves turn this beautiful, coppery-pink color in autumn.

An indoor bonsai
This fig (*Ficus retusa*) is 15 years old and its trunk has splayed roots with an interesting shape. Display at an east- or west-facing window, but provide shade for it from the late afternoon sun.

Training and pruning

The Japanese have many different styles of bonsai, named according to their shape and the angle of the trunk in the pot. You can train your tree to grow in unusual shapes with wires, and by pruning the branches and leaves. To wire branches, it is best to use specially imported bonsai wire, which is very stiff, to hold branches rigid in the position you want to train them to follow. Training and pruning should be done in the very early spring, just before the new growth appears. Leaf pruning can be done all through the growing season and will encourage the growth of smaller leaves, which are in scale with the tree.

Complementary shapes *left*
Before you start to train and prune your tree, decide what shape you want it to have. If you want to display it with another tree, put the two together. Here, the smaller tree is to be trained to a fan shape with a flat top to complement the taller specimen behind it.

1 Loop the bonsai wire round the trunk of the tree and push it into the shape you want the branch to follow. Secure the branch to it with thinner garden wire.

2 Prune the stem back almost to the point at which it is wired. Cut just above the leaf axil as this is where new growth will develop.

3 Continue to prune the tree, cutting out all unwanted branches and shortening any long branches by half. Shorten all stems, and where there are multiple shoots crowded together leave just one.

Root pruning and repotting

Established bonsai need repotting every two or three years in spring in order to replenish the potting mixture, and to restrict their roots. They should not be moved into a larger pot because this will encourage them to grow bigger. Use a special soil-based potting mixture which is well-aerated and rich enough to sustain active growth. If you plan to prune your tree as well as repot it, leave three weeks between each operation so that the plant can recover its strength.

1 Take the plant out of its pot. Remove excess potting mixture by gently teasing it from the roots with a special tool or kitchen fork.

2 Prune the roots with a pair of root clippers, cutting away about half the growth and any damaged roots.

3 Line the pot with perlite and flint chippings. Tie the roots up with garden twine and thread the ends through the drainage holes to hold the plant rigid until new roots appear.

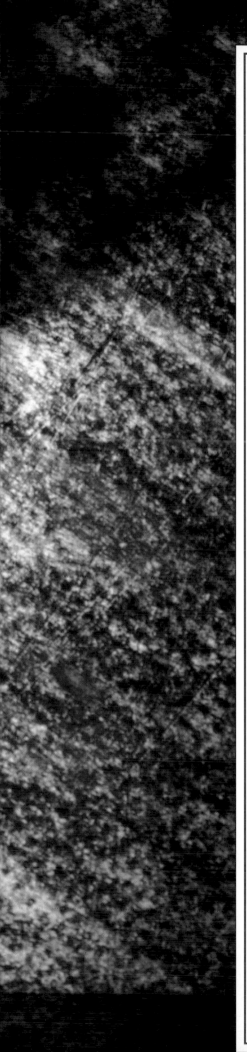

·3·
CUT-FLOWER ARRANGING

There is a special joy in using cut flowers in the house; they have an immediate freshness which house plants seldom achieve. Many books have been written about the techniques of flower arranging but, apart from the Japanese *ikebana* arrangements, where different combinations of flowers have symbolic meanings, it cannot be learned by following a set of rules.

The beauty of an arrangement is in the flowers themselves, and the way they are arranged should enhance their inherent qualities rather than impose a formal structure at odds with their natural habit of growth. My personal preference is for simple, informal arrangements which allow the natural shapes, colors and textures of the flowers to be appreciated.

While flower arranging cannot be learned systematically, you will find that, through practice and experiment, you will discover the qualities of different flowers and foliage and acquire an instinctive feeling for how to arrange them. The design of a flower arrangement depends on an appreciation of shape, color and texture and an ability to orchestrate these qualities to produce a harmonious group.

Always think about the setting for your arrangement before you choose the flowers and, at the same time, decide whether it is to be a dramatic display for a special occasion or an informal day-to-day display. These considerations will dictate the size, shape and overall color scheme and help you to create a display which complements its surroundings.

A simple arrangement of orchids
The vibrant color of these orchids
(*Phalaenopsis* hybrids) is set off by the black
vase. The simple lines of the container
allow the intricate shape of the
flowers to stand out.

Using the color wheel

Successful flower arranging depends upon an appreciation of color. The ability to mix colors together comes with experience, and, by experimenting with colors yourself, you will soon develop an instinctive feeling for how to use them. It is also useful to know a little about color theory. Here, a selection of cut flowers and foliage has been arranged in a circle with the colors following the same order as the spectrum—this is known as the color wheel.

Triadic color schemes
Orange, violet and green are secondary colors produced from an equal mixture of the two primary colors either side of them on the wheel. Used together they form a triadic color scheme, as they are equidistant from each other on the color wheel. You can put red, blue and yellow together for a strong triadic combination or, for a more subtle effect, use shades of orange, violet and green.

BLUE
Primary

GREEN
Secondary

YELLOW
Primary

The color wheel
The wheel is composed of primary and secondary colors and each segment of color represents a whole family of tints (the color plus white), shades (the color plus black) and tones (the color plus gray).

Complementary color schemes
Each secondary color is the complementary color of the one primary not used in its make up. For instance, violet, which is formed from red and blue, is the complementary of yellow. Use two complementary colors, in a variety of shades and tones, as the theme of an arrangement.

Analagous color schemes
Analagous, or related, colors are harmonizing colors from adjacent sections of the wheel. Strong reds, oranges and yellows may look harsh together, so use shades of each color for a more subtle scheme. Monochromatic color schemes use various shades of the same color, and very beautiful and sophisticated displays can be made by using a variety of plant material in just green or gray.

VIOLET
Secondary

RED
Primary

ORANGE
Secondary

PLANT KEY

Carnation · Rose · Transvaal daisy · Lily · Chrysanthemum · Chrysanthemum · Rose · Daffodil · Cypress · Fern · Iris · Brodiaea · Hyacinth · Statice · Anemone

Cutting and preparing flowers

It is important to realize when you cut a flower that it is still alive and growing. The best time to cut flowers is in the morning, when they contain most fluid. Failing this, cut your flowers in the evening, when the plant will have been producing food all day, giving it a reservoir of nutrients to help it survive in the container. Once picked, slit the stems and put them straight into deep water, then leave them in a cool place for several hours.

When choosing flowers at the florist, make sure that petals are firm and colors are strong, and that foliage is green and not beginning to wilt. A good way of telling how fresh flowers are is to look at their stamens. If they are hard, this indicates that the flower has only recently opened. Never buy flowers that have been left outside in hot sun.

Cutting soft stems

When a freshly cut flower is left out of water, the water-transporting tubes start to close up. To help a soft stem take up water, cut the stem as cleanly as possible by using a sharp knife or florist's scissors. If you have only a few flowers to arrange, cut the stems in water so that water, not air, is drawn up immediately.

1 Cut the stem at a 45 degree angle to increase the surface area for water intake. It will also stop the stem resting flush against the bottom of the vase, thus cutting off its water supply.

2 Make a vertical slit about 2in long to further increase the area capable of taking up water. Put the cut stems in deep water for a long drink before arranging. This ensures that they become full of water (turgid), and will therefore last longer.

Cutting woody stems

Cut woody stemmed flowers and foliage at a 45 degree angle using pruners. If the stem is very hard, remove the bark from the base of the stem as well. Do not hammer the stems, since this reduces their capacity to take up water. Strip off all the leaves that will be underwater in your vase, as they will rot and foul the water.

1 With stems which are particularly woody, such as roses (*Rosa* sp.), lilac (*Syringa* sp.) and foliage sprays, scrape off 2in of bark with a sharp knife.

2 Make a 2in slit with pruners or a sharp knife to increase the surface area for water intake.

Sealing bleeding stems

Daffodils, euphorbias, poppies (*Papaver* sp.) and many other plants bleed when cut, exuding either a sticky or milky juice. (The milky juice of euphorbias can cause skin irritation.) This sap flow results in a loss of nutrients to the flower head and, if lost into the flower water, will block up the water-conducting tubes of the stem and encourage bacteria; so spend a little extra time conditioning flowers which bleed, before using them in an arrangement.

1 Seal bleeding stems by first cutting them at an angle and then either dipping them in boiling water or placing them in a flame for 30 seconds. This will not prevent them from taking up water.

2 Place the treated stems, by themselves, in warm water until they have finished bleeding. They can then be arranged with other flowers.

Useful tips

● To prolong the life of flowers with hollow stems, such as delphiniums (*Delphinium* sp.) and Cape lilies (*Crinum* sp.), fill each stem with water and plug the end with cotton wool.

● Harden weak stems by putting them in water containing a special florist's conditioning solution. Leave in a dark place where water loss by transpiration will be reduced.

● Condition young foliage by immersing it completely in water for two hours before arranging.

● To remove thorns from roses, rub the stems very hard with the back of a pair of scissors. Roses are much easier to arrange once the thorns have been removed.

● Add one or two drops of household bleach to your arrangement water, as this will help prevent the growth of bacteria. Dissolve a teaspoonful of sugar in warm water to provide flowers with valuable glucose.

● Add water to your arrangement daily. You will find that certain flowers, such as dahlias (*Dahlia* hybrids), asters (*Aster novi-belgii*) and stocks (*Matthiola incana*), foul their water very quickly, so it is worth changing their water completely once a day.

● Remove any dying heads immediately, as they emit an ethylene gas which will cause wilting in other flowers.

● Position your arrangements away from bright sunlight, heat and drafts. These will all shorten the life of your flowers, since they increase transpiration.

● Mist-spray your flowers daily with a fine spray of luke-warm water. This will make them last longer.

Removing an airlock

If your flowers have been out of water for some time, it is possible that air may be trapped in the stems. Air-bubbles prevent water from being taken up into the stem and lack of water will cause the flowers to wilt prematurely.

Preparing tulips

Forced tulips (*Tulipa* hybrids) have weak stems which droop in an awkward way, making them difficult to arrange. They can be straightened by wrapping them in paper and putting them in warm water containing a conditioning solution.

Pricking a tulip to remove an airlock
To release trapped air, sterilize a needle in a flame, then prick the stem just below the flower head.

1 Having cut and slit the stems, and removed some of the leaves, wrap the flowers in brown paper, newspaper or waxed florist's tissue which will retain its rigidity in water.

2 Stand the tulips in warm water for several hours. To assist the process and strengthen the stems, add special florist's conditioning solution to the water; this contains sugar for food and a bactericide.

Supports for flower arrangements

Using wire netting

Crumpled chicken wire is an effective stem holder, particularly for woody stems or heavy flowers. It can be used on its own— and is the best anchor for flowers which will only last if arranged in deep water—or it can be used with floral foam for extra support. You can buy chicken wire by the foot in various gauges: use the fine gauge for slender stems and the wider gauges for more robust flowers and foliage. If you need to support one, or several, very heavy stems, secure them on a pinholder attached to the bottom of the container with adhesive clay, using wire netting as well if necessary.

1 Cut a piece of wire netting with wire cutters to make a square several times larger than the aperture of the container. You can use ordinary household objects, such as this mixing bowl, as a water-tight container inside a more decorative outer container, such as a wicker basket.

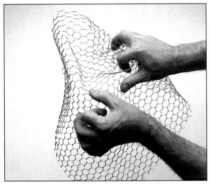

2 Crumple the wire in your hands molding it so that it will fit into the bowl and have an uneven surface. Be careful to avoid scratching yourself against the raw edges of the metal.

3 Place the crumpled wire in your container. For larger arrangements it may be necessary to secure the netting in place by passing wires, or pieces of color-less adhesive tape, over it, and securing them beneath the container.

4 Place the mixing bowl filled with crumpled wire inside the basket, and insert the first stems through the layers of netting which will secure them.

Using floral foam

Water absorbent floral foam is another useful stem holder which will support flowers in place at any angle. It is available in several shapes and sizes: in large bricks for large arrangements and in cylinders and squares for smaller displays. The foam can be used whole, or cut to fit any shape of container. Floral foam should be soaked in water for half an hour before use, since it will otherwise suck water out of the flowers as they are being arranged. If you are arranging long- or heavy-stemmed flowers, you may need to secure the foam in position with clear adhesive tape. A block of floral foam can be re-used several times.

1 Place the floral foam in the container. For a low arrangement (shown made up on p.85), trim down the floral foam so that it is flush with the side of the container. If you want to insert stems at an angle, so that they will point downwards, allow several inches of floral foam to extend above the rim of the container.

2 Having soaked the floral foam in water, insert the stems by pushing them carefully into the foam. Top up the container with water once all the flowers are in position.

The principles of arrangement 1

Where do you begin with a flower arrangement if you are starting from scratch? First of all, think about where the arrangement is to go, and plan it with the setting in mind. Consider how it will be lit and the angle from which it will be seen. Then think about a suitable container for the place you have chosen. Containers range from kitchen bowls, jugs and baskets to purpose-made vases in all sorts of shapes and materials. Before you start to arrange your flowers, look at their shapes, textures and colors and work out a design based on a simple shape. Prepare and condition the flowers as described on pp.80-1, and select the first stems to establish the basic outline for the arrangement. Then fill out the shape, placing the largest foliage and flowers at the bottom and the most slender at the top. Position the most striking material in the center of the arrangement.

Making a large informal arrangement *right*
For a large arrangement, avoid following a shape too rigidly; allow the natural outlines of the flowers to show. Here, I have established the outline with foliage, white lilac (*Syringa* sp.) and baby's breath (*Gypsophila paniculata*), and added red flowers for focal interest.

A triangular arrangement

Fill the vase with floral foam or wire netting. First, establish the apex of the triangle and the outline of the two sides with chrysanthemum (*Chrysanthemum* hybrids) sprays. Then strengthen the shape with holly (*Ilex aquifolium*), choosing branches with a suitable outline and good berries. Add the corn-shaped heads of chincherinchee (*Ornithogalum thyrsoides*) for outline, and use some large chrysanthemum heads for focal point.

FLOWER KEY

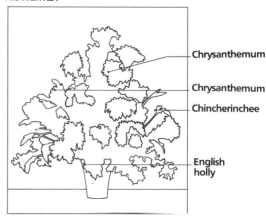

Chrysanthemum

Chrysanthemum

Chincherinchee

English holly

The principles of arrangement 2

A circular arrangement

This shape of arrangement suits all types of cottage flowers. Put floral foam inside the vase so that it is flush with the top. Establish the shape with baby's breath (*Gypsophila paniculata*) and then strengthen it with white lilac (*Syringa* sp.). Then add sprays of white daisy-shaped chrysanthemums (*Chrysanthemum* hybrids), orange lilies and pink-and-green Peruvian lilies (*Alstroemeria* sp.).

FLOWER KEY

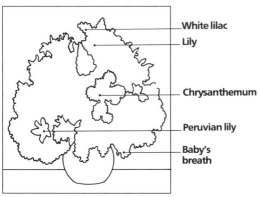

White lilac
Lily
Chrysanthemum
Peruvian lily
Baby's breath

A semi-circular arrangement

This thin, lozenge-shaped container and the bare twigs suggested a stark, modern arrangement. Insert wire netting into the top of the container and let it extend a little way over the edge, so that stems can be inserted at an angle. Establish a semi-circular shape with the twigs, letting one trail down in front. Insert the orchid stems so that they follow the lines of the twigs.

FLOWER KEY

Dogwood | Orchid

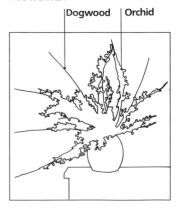

A vertical arrangement

FLOWER KEY

White iris
Iris leaves

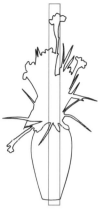

The stiff, linear form of the iris (*Iris* sp.) and vertical container suggested this oriental-style arrangement; sword lilies (*Gladiolus* hybrids) would also be suitable. Fill the vase with floral foam so that it extends about 1 in above the edge. Insert one stem to establish the height and arrange the others at different heights.

A low triangular arrangement

I have used irises again to make this low horizontal arrangement. Establish the outline on both sides with blue flowers, then add iris leaves for outline. Cut the stems of the white irises short and insert them in the middle at varying heights for focal interest.

FLOWER KEY

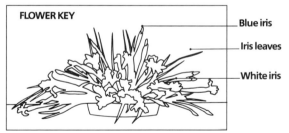

Blue iris
Iris leaves
White iris

A spring flower arrangement

Daffodils (*Narcissus* hybrids) are simple flowers that look best arranged informally; they do not mix well with other flowers in a more formal display. I like to arrange them so that their stems curve outwards, mimicking the way they grow in clumps in the wild. Mass the flowers together in a simple wicker basket and include some of their own foliage to increase the natural look of the display. Put the arrangement on a side table, or use it as a centerpiece for a country kitchen table. If you place the arrangement in a cool spot, the flowers will last much longer.

Building up the arrangement

1 Place a glass mixing bowl inside a circular reed basket and cut a block of floral foam to fit inside so that it is flush with the top. Cut a large piece of wire netting, mold it into peaks, and secure it around the edge of the basket.

Equipment and materials

Wire netting

Reed basket

Mixing bowl

Large-cupped daffodil
Narcissus "Fermoy"

Daffodil
Narcissus "Barrii"

Small-cupped daffodil
Narcissus "Soleil d'Or"

Large-cupped daffodil
Narcissus "Armada"

Floral foam

Florist's scissors

Wire cutters

Daffodil
Narcissus "Golden Harvest"

Daffodil
Narcissus medioluteus hybrids

Large-cupped daffodil
Narcissus "Ice Follies"

2 Daffodils have stems which exude a sticky juice, so seal them before arranging (see p.80). Begin by outlining a semi-circular shape, arranging the flowers with their leaves.

3 Continue to fill in the basic shape, using the larger daffodils and leaves, cutting the stems to the height you want. Rotate the arrangement as you work, for, if used as a centerpiece, the display will be seen from all angles.

4 Use small daffodils, also known as jonquils, to fill in any obvious spaces. Add more large flowers and leaves to emphasize the outline and give body to the arrangement; bend down some of the lower stems below the line of the basket to give a slightly more rounded shape. Other flowers can be cut down and positioned to give body to the middle of the arrangement. Cut a few of the smaller ones very short and insert them around the edges of the basket so that they disguise the wire netting.

A summer flower arrangement

There is such a profusion of flowers in the summer that you should think carefully about the setting for your arrangement, and the effect you wish to create, before picking or buying the flowers. Here I wanted to create a display with a light and airy feel suitable for a side table or an alcove.

I chose to contrast strong shades of blue and golden yellow against a subtle background of gray and white flowers and green foliage. Taking an asymmetrical triangle as my basic shape, I selected a white oval casserole dish as a container since it will be obscured by the flowers.

Building up the arrangement

1 Cut a block of foam to extend above the rim of the container and secure in position with adhesive clay. Form the outline with the strongest shapes—the cylindrical globe thistles and the dried sea holly.

2 Fill the shape out laterally with eucalyptus and, at the front of the arrangement, push sprigs of foliage into the foam so that they hang down over the edge of the container. Add the deep yellow flowers of St John's wort to create focal points of color.

Equipment and materials

Florist's scissors

Pruners

Golden marguerite
Anthemis tinctoria "E.C. Buxton"

Stub wires

Eucalyptus
Eucalyptus gunnii

Tutsan St John's wort
Hypericum androsaemum

Marguerite daisy
Anthemis cupaniana

Casserole dish

Sea holly
Eryngium giganteum

African lily
Agapanthus "Headbourne Hybrids"

Yellow yarrow
Achillea filipendulina "Coronation Gold"

White yarrow
Achillea sp.

Floral foam

Globe thistle
Echinops ritro

Butterfly bush
Buddleia davidii "White Cloud"

3 Now strengthen the yellow areas by adding several golden yarrow heads to create yellow focal points in the middle of the design. As you position each flower, you will need to cut the stem to an appropriate length to maintain the overall shape. Place the most dominant yarrow head right into the center of the group, cutting its stem short so that your eye is led into the design. Add a couple of sprigs of white yarrow to fill out the base of the arrangement.

4 The largest flowers should be positioned at the base of the arrangement. Use the long and heavy heads of the sweetly scented butterfly bush at the front, and at the sides, to give them more bulk. As the arrangement fills out in all directions, the foam and the casserole dish become obscured by the delicate mass of flowers and foliage.

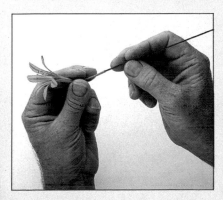

5 Since a full African lily head would be out of scale with the other flowers, pull off the individual florets and wire them by pushing a fine-gauge stub wire up the length of each stem.

6 Lighten the design with touches of golden and white marguerite daisies. Finally add the wired African lily florets, concentrating them on the right-hand side of the design to balance the daisies on the left.

An autumn flower arrangement

The colors of autumn are much darker than those of spring and summer. Here I chose to contrast russet- and gold-colored flowers and berries with deep-purple foliage, highlighted with scarlet dahlias and rose hips. I decided to make a horizontal arrangement designed to be seen from above—either on a low table or as a table centerpiece—

where the addition of fruit would enhance the autumnal feel of the display. Since the arrangement may be put on a table where people eat, it should be low enough to allow conversation across it. I chose a wooden basket, whose natural color harmonized with the flowers, and fitted a glass pie dish inside the basket to act as a watertight container.

Equipment and materials

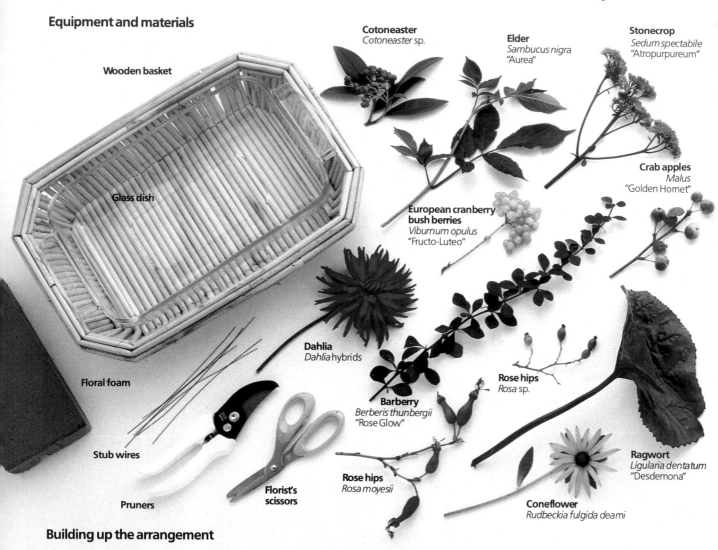

Wooden basket

Glass dish

Floral foam

Stub wires

Pruners

Florist's scissors

Cotoneaster
Cotoneaster sp.

Elder
Sambucus nigra "Aurea"

Stonecrop
Sedum spectabile "Atropurpureum"

Crab apples
Malus "Golden Hornet"

European cranberry bush berries
Viburnum opulus "Fructo-Luteo"

Dahlia
Dahlia hybrids

Barberry
Berberis thunbergii "Rose Glow"

Rose hips
Rosa sp.

Rose hips
Rosa moyesii

Ragwort
Ligularia dentatum "Desdemona"

Coneflower
Rudbeckia fulgida deami

Building up the arrangement

1 Cut a piece of foam to fit the glass container, allowing it to extend above the rim so that stems can be pushed in horizontally. Lay two purple elder branches and two circular ragwort leaves over the foam to establish the overall shape which will relate, of course, to where you plan to put the arrangement.

2 Once you are satisfied with the outline, decide whether you are going to look down on your arrangement or whether it will be seen from the side, and plan the design accordingly. Slide the foliage into the foam, then, to give bulk to the arrangement, add the purple stonecrop flowers.

3 Add the golden coneflowers for focal interest and open out the arrangement by adding a couple of stems of barberry, following the lines established by the elder. Put a sprig of cotoneaster berries at the front to fill an empty space. The flowers and branchlets which you are using should have been cut at an angle, and the stems split, to provide a greater area for water intake. Be careful not to push the cut stems flush with the side or bottom of the container as this will reduce the amount of water available to them.

4 Wire several stems of crab apples together and add the bunch to the arrangement. Add dahlias to create bold points of color and echo their scarlet tones with stems of rose hips placed at one end of the display. At this stage, fill the bowl with cool water and move it to its setting. You will need to top up the water after a day or so as the floral foam absorbs a considerable amount.

5 European cranberry bush berries are sparsely distributed on their stems, so wire two sprigs together. Hold the stems tightly and wrap a fine-gauge stub wire around them. The wired bunch can easily be pushed into the foam.

6 Add several bunches of the wired berries to fill the hole at the front of the display and reinforce the red area on the right by adding another stem of rose hips. Place a bunch of grapes and a few crab apples beside the arrangement.

A winter flower arrangement

Flowers are at a premium in winter, but in the garden you will find a surprising amount of material suitable for arrangements. Some of the autumn berries remain, much of the variegated foliage is in good condition, small buds are beginning to open on shrubs and trees, and the early flowering hellebores appear after Christmas. Here, I have made a predominantly green arrangement, exploiting the different shapes of the foliage and adding white and yellow flowers and orange berries for color. An old pottery jug makes a suitable container for this unsophisticated display.

Building up the arrangement

1 Shave the sides off a block of floral foam so that it will fit inside the jug, and push it in so that it is flush with the top. Begin the arrangement by inserting branches of witch hazel and cypress.

Equipment and materials

Floral foam

Pruners

Pottery jug

Hellebore
Helleborus corsicus lividus

Winter-flowering cherry
Prunus subhirtella
"Autumnalis"

Laurustinus
Viburnum tinus

Stinking iris
Iris foetidissima

Persian ivy
Hedera colchica
"Paddy's Pride"

Mahonia
Mahonia sp.

Black calla
Arum italicum
"Pictum"

Silk tassel bush
Garrya elliptica

True cypress
Cupressus glabra

Witch hazel
Hamamelis mollis

2 Position a large branch of mahonia in the center of the arrangement and a tall spray of the silk-tassel bush, covered with some early catkins, behind; this establishes the height and basic triangular shape of the display.

3 Insert a large flower head of hellebore in the center as a focal point, after trimming off all the lower leaves and some of the upper ones. Place a spray of laurustinus to fill out the space at the back of the arrangement.

4 Now position the yellow-and-green ivy leaves and place the bright-orange iris berries at the top of the arrangement. Add the narrow, spiky iris leaves to contrast with the heavier forms of the other foliage, and place a branch of winter-flowering cherry behind the cypress on the left. Finally, include the highly patterned black calla leaves to provide interest at the base of the container. This arrangement should remain attractive for about a fortnight, providing you put it in a cool place and top up the water level every day.

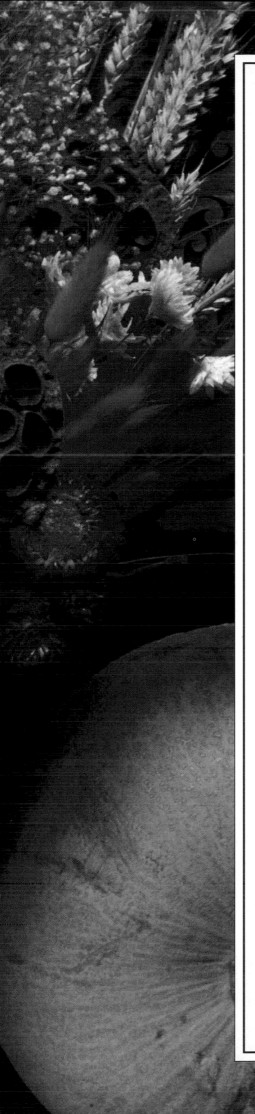

$\cdot4\cdot$
DRIED-FLOWER ARRANGING

Living plants require regular care and a particular environment in order to thrive, and the beauty and freshness of cut flowers lasts for a few weeks at most. But dried flowers need neither water nor light and, once arranged, they do not flop or drop their petals. Dried arrangements can be put anywhere and, through the winter, when fresh material is hard to come by, will evoke the abundance of the summer season. As with fresh flowers, the principles of proportion and use of color, texture and shape apply to each display. Containers are important: baskets—plain or painted— terracotta pots and glass vases all help show dried flowers to their best advantage. Do not restrict yourself to flower arrangements—garlands and wreaths are simple to build up with dried material. Make a dried-flower tree, or mix up a fragrant pot-pourri whose heady scent may be reminiscent of a late spring meadow or warm summer night. Drying herbs and bunches of flowers in your kitchen will also bring back the smells of summer.
If dried displays catch your imagination, enjoy discovering all the different forms they can take. As well as flowers, you can include leaves, grasses, berries, cereals, fruits and seed heads, to give countless variations of color and texture. You will soon develop a "collector's eye"—scanning every garden, bank and hedgerow for suitable materials to be dried and incorporated in your arrangements.

An informal arrangement of dried flowers
A collection of dried flowers, grasses and seed heads have been massed together in a simple terracotta container. The arrangement is held together by its autumnal color scheme and complemented by the orange pumpkin placed beside it.

How to dry flowers 1

Drying flowers requires neither time-consuming techniques nor expensive equipment. Many plants need only to be collected at the right time, tied in bunches and hung up to dry. Others, depending on their shape, can be dried upright or laid flat. The more delicate garden flowers, or those likely to lose their color if air-dried, may be put in an airtight box and covered with a suitable desiccant.

Although the techniques by which plants are dried are not difficult to follow, you will find that, however careful you are, your results will vary from year to year as the process is affected by the weather conditions. Pick flowers only when the weather is dry, and begin the drying process as soon as possible after you have picked them. Avoid putting them in direct sunlight, as this causes colors to fade.

Air-drying

This technique is suitable for most flowers, grasses and seed heads. Arrange them in small bunches, hanging large flowers, such as hydrangeas (*Hydrangea* sp.), separately so that they do not touch each other. Check after a day or two and if those with fleshy stems, such as delphiniums (*Delphinium* hybrids), are not drying, apply moderate heat.

Drying in bunches

1 Strip the leaves off the stem as far as the flower head, unless they form a natural rosette around the flower, as those of straw flowers (*Helichrysum bracteatum*) do, in which case leave them so the stems do not look so naked.

2 Tie up the flowers with an elastic band so that the bunch stays together as the stems contract. Do not make your bunches too large, otherwise the flowers in the middle will fail to dry and will become moldy.

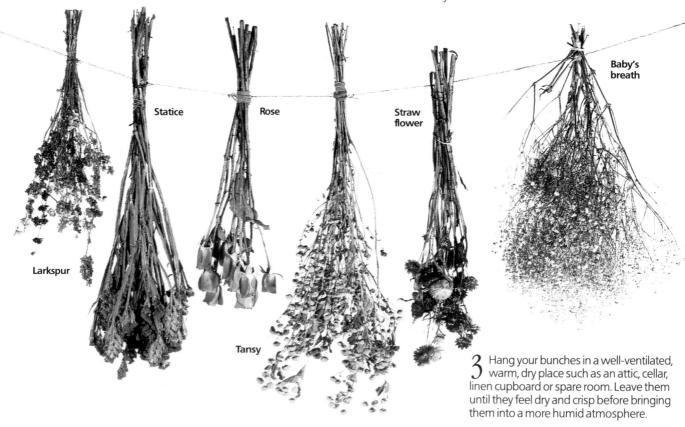

Larkspur

Statice

Rose

Tansy

Straw flower

Baby's breath

3 Hang your bunches in a well-ventilated, warm, dry place such as an attic, cellar, linen cupboard or spare room. Leave them until they feel dry and crisp before bringing them into a more humid atmosphere.

Drying upright

Most flowers which can be air-dried can also be dried upright. Use this method for flowers or grasses with particularly delicate heads, as it will preserve them better. Leave the flowers standing in a little water until they have absorbed it all and become crisp to the touch.

Drying flat

Most seed heads, grasses and seed pods can be dried in open boxes or laid flat on newspaper or brown paper.

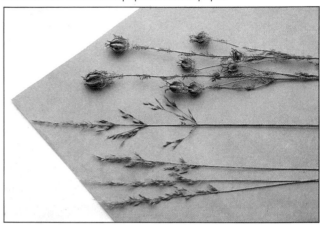

Preserving in desiccants

This is a slightly more complicated process, but it is worth using on more delicate flowers and on roses, which lose some of their color when air-dried. You need an airtight container, such as a biscuit tin or plastic food box. It need only be large enough to dry the flower heads; as wire stems are attached once they are dry.

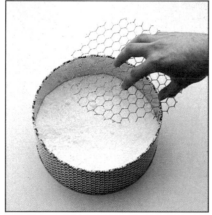

1 Line your container with 1 in layer of equal parts of borax and alum. Alternatively, use silver sand and silica gel crystals, and heat the mixture to eradicate moisture.

2 Cut a piece of wire netting to fit the container and lay it on top of the desiccant mixture. This will keep the flower heads upright.

3 Take a flower, such as a Transvaal daisy (*Gerbera* sp.) and cut about 1 in below the head, leaving enough stem to insert the wire into, when the flower has dried.

4 Place the flower heads in the netting, making sure that they do not touch. Dry flowers of one type together so that they will be ready at the same time.

5 Add more of the desiccant powder, sieving it over the flower heads to avoid damaging them. Continue until they are covered by about 1 in of powder.

6 Seal the container and leave undisturbed in a warm, dry place for four to fourteen days, depending on the density of the flowers.

How to dry flowers 2

Preserving in glycerine

This is a preserving, rather than a drying, method which can be used for whole branches of foliage, berries and large leaves. It is also suitable for preserving long flower spikes, such as foxgloves (*Digitalis* sp.). The stems are placed in a mixture of glycerine and near-boiling water and left until they have absorbed enough of the solution. This takes about a week for light foliage, and from six to eight weeks for heavy foliage. The leaves gradually become deeper and richer in color, and when

drops of glycerine appear on them they will have absorbed enough of the solution. Remove them, as excessive absorption will cause wilting, and wipe them clean. Immerse single leaves and very tall branches, when the top stems might not take up the mixture, in a bath of glycerine and water solution.

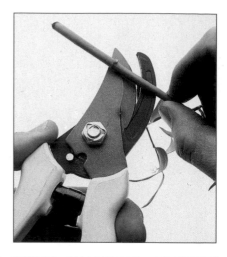

1 Remove the lower leaves from the stems with pruners. Cut them at a 45 degree angle, pare away any bark from woody stems, and make a 2in slit to increase the area for glycerine intake.

2 Mix one part of glycerine with two parts of near-boiling water in a narrow container and stir the solution vigorously.

3 Pour the glycerine and water solution into a heatproof container. Fill to a depth of 4in, so that it will cover the prepared part of the stems.

4 Stand the stems in the solution and place the container with the foliage in a cool, dark room until the leaves have absorbed sufficient glycerine.

Pressing

Most leaves—including ferns, gray-tinted shrubs and maples (*Acer* sp.)—can be dried by pressing. Only a little pressure is needed for large leaves and ferns, otherwise they become too brittle to arrange. Once covered in blotting paper or newspaper, they can be put under a carpet or mattress and left to dry for about a week. Smaller leaves, bracts and the delicate heads of wild flowers can be put in a bought press and left for a fortnight.

Two methods of pressing leaves
Place large leaves between pages of blotting paper, and small leaves and flowers between the absorbent sheets of a bought flower press.

Making pot-pourri

Pot-pourri means "rotten pot"—the original method was to mix dried petals with salt so that they fermented, giving off a strong scent. Although its smell is more fugitive, the dry pot-pourri is much easier to make.

Rose petals

Larkspur
Delphinium consolida

Rose petals for decoration

Hop-clover
Trifolium agrarium

Juniper berries

Pot-pourri essence

Bay leaves
Laurus nobilis

Dried lemon peel

Sea holly
Eryngium maritimum

Orris root powder

Lemon-scented geranium leaves
Pelargonium crispum

Larkspur
Delphinium consolida

Lavender
Lavandula sp.

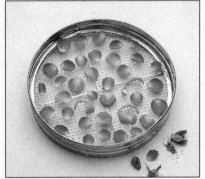

1 Dry petals, leaves and the lemon peel on a surface that allows plenty of air to circulate round them. It will take up to ten days for them to become crisp.

2 Mix all the petals and leaves together. Crush the lemon peel into small pieces and add it to the mixture with the spices and a few drops of essence.

3 Add dried flower heads and rose petals dried in borax for decoration. Seal the container and leave it for six weeks to mature, shaking it occasionally.

Ingredients for pot-pourri

Sachets have been filled with dried flowers and leaves from the terracotta bowls. These bowls contain some of the most popular ingredients for making pot-pourri. Lavender has a strong scent and is an ingredient of many pot-pourris. Sweet-scented roses are often used as the base of a pot-pourri and the whole heads, as seen here, can be added for decoration. The small grape hyacinth florets (*Muscari* sp.) are intensely blue and help to give color to a pot-pourri.

Arranging flowers in a basket

The place where you decide to put an arrangement will help to suggest an appropriate size and shape. I selected a windowsill where the flowers would be attractively framed by the window. For a display such as this, which will not be seen in the round, I chose a flat-backed asymmetrical triangle as my basic shape.

I decided to use blues, whites, creams and yellows, adding cereals and seed heads to give substance and texture to the design. Let an arrangement reflect the natural growth of the flowers themselves. Here, the graceful curve of the barley lent itself to trailing over the sill, contrasting with the stiffer wheat used to outline the shape.

Equipment and materials

Basket

Floral foam

Knife

Florist's scissors

Stub wires

Dried moss

Wheat
Triticum vulgare

Larkspur
Delphinium consolida

White statice
Limonium sinuatum

Barley
Hordeum vulgare

Everlasting
Helipterum roseum

Sea lavender
Limonium latifolium

Blue statice
Limonium sinuatum

Baby's breath
Gypsophila paniculata

Poppy seed heads
Papaver sp.

Lady's mantle
Alchemilla vulgaris

Oregon grape
Mahonia aquifolium

Sea holly
Eryngium maritimum

Oats
Avena sp.

Heath
Erica sp.

Rose
Rosa sp.

Love-in-a-mist seed heads
Nigella damascena

Dyed baby's breath
Gypsophila paniculata

Straw flower
Helichrysum bracteatum

The finished arrangement
This light and delicate arrangement suits the small window with its pretty lace pelmet and neutral-colored curtains. Think carefully about the décor of your room before selecting flowers and a container so that the colors and style of your display will be in keeping with its surroundings.

Building up the arrangement

1 Cut one block of foam—using the stiffer variety made for dried flowers—for the center of the basket and two smaller ones to fit either side. Press the foam down firmly and shear off all edges with a knife. Cut some wires into thirds and bend to form a hairpin shape. Cover the foam with dried moss secured with the wire pins. Position the wheat to establish the shape of the design.

2 Having established the height using the basket as a guide—it should be a third of the overall height—start to establish the shape of the arrangement with the sea lavender. When you cut the foam, make sure that it extends above the rim of the basket so that flowers can be inserted downwards.

continued over

3 Introduce color and tone with larkspur and blue statice to the left and white statice to the right. Take a few blue flowers over to the right to help link the two sides of the design.

4 Elongate the design with barley and everlastings wired into small bunches (see p.110). Add lady's mantle and baby's breath and position the poppy seed heads and the sea holly in the center for focal interest.

5 Cross the design with love-in-a-mist seed heads and infill with oats to give bulk to the paler side of the group. Fill the spaces with the darkest elements in the design—Oregon grape, dyed gypsophila and heath. Add the roses and the straw flowers which should be wired to give them extra length. Then, having put the display in its setting, stand back and adjust the outline as necessary.

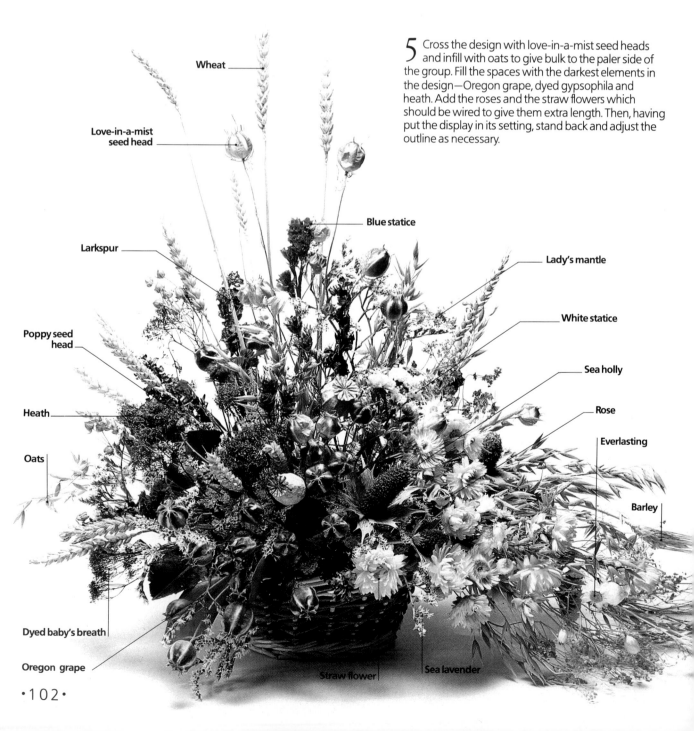

Wheat

Love-in-a-mist seed head

Blue statice

Larkspur

Lady's mantle

Poppy seed head

White statice

Sea holly

Heath

Rose

Oats

Everlasting

Barley

Dyed baby's breath

Oregon grape

Straw flower

Sea lavender

Further ideas for arrangements

There are an enormous number of ways in which dried flowers can be arranged. For informal displays use baskets of any kind, or earthenware pots, as containers. Try filling a large basket with grasses, seed heads and cereals in creams, beiges and very pale greens, inserting stems at an angle so that the flowers appear to radiate from the center. Alternatively, fill an earthenware pot with bunches of flowers.

Neutral tones *below*
A tall container can set off a rounded mass of flowers, and frosted glass will disguise stems and wires. Here the neutral colors of the vases do not overshadow the delicate flowers of sea lavender (*Limonium latifolium*) on the right and flowering onion (*Allium* sp.) on the left.

Still life *above*
Arrange dried hydrangeas (*Hydrangea macrophylla*) in a simple vase and the subtlety of their color and texture is enough to make an attractive display. The figs, grapes and pomegranates complete a still life group which looks good enough to paint.

Informal groups *left*
Bunches of flowers placed in baskets can look very effective in the right kind of setting. Here, the neutral tones and rough textures of the love-in-a-mist (*Nigella damascena*) and poppy (*Papaver* sp.) seed heads suit the coarse-weaved basket. A sheaf of ribbed seed pods in the foreground picks up the textures of the baskets.

Making dried-flower trees

Dried-flower trees are much easier to make than you might imagine and, once you have mastered the basic techniques, you can experiment with different types of flowers and different shapes of tree. Here, I have used pink, blue and white flowers and parchment-colored seed heads to make a light and delicate tree.

Equipment and materials

Blue larkspur
Delphinium consolida

Bells-of-Ireland
Moluccella laevis

Blue statice
Limonium sinuatum

Sea lavender
Limonium latifolium

Winged everlasting
Ammobium alatum

Poppy seed heads
Papaver sp.

Everlasting
Helipterum roseum

Straw flower
Helichrysum bracteatum

Pink larkspur
Delphinium consolida

Wire cutters

Ribbon

Baby's breath
Gypsophila paniculata

Plastic pot

Pink statice
Limonium sinuatum

Stub wires

Ball of floral foam

Sea holly
Eryngium maritimum

Stones

Fresh moss

Interior wall filler

Bamboo stick

Building up the arrangement

1 Take a plastic plant pot 4½-5in in diameter, line it with foil and fill with stones in order to secure a bamboo stick about 14in high. Spoon a mix of wall filler into the pot until it reaches the surface.

2 Push the ball of floral foam on to the bamboo stick. Make sure that the stick only goes half-way through the foam. Pack moss around the outside of the ball.

3 Attach the moss to the foam with pins, made by cutting stub wires into thirds and bending the pieces over. As you work, be careful not to push down too hard on the foam ball.

4 Start to outline the shape with the blue larkspur and blue statice. You will find that you need to break small branches of flowers off the main stems to achieve the right scale for this size of tree.

5 Break off some small segments of sea lavender, and place them where they will be seen. Wire together some winged everlastings to form small bunches, and add to cover the surface of the tree. Infill with pink statice and pink larkspur.

6 Add the round heads of straw flowers and pink everlastings to fill some of the gaps. Place poppy seed heads, sea holly and small pieces of bells-of-Ireland to give texture, and finally add small sprigs of baby's breath to soften the outline.

7 Place the completed tree in a white pot and put some moss and a few flower heads over the stone base. You can leave the bamboo stick plain, or decorate it with ribbon to create a maypole effect. Take two strips of ribbon, glue them to the top of the stick and twine them round it, securing at the bottom with sticky tape.

Other types of dried-flower tree

For a strong and simple country-style tree, use the flat heads of golden yarrow (*Achillea filipendulina*) to form the tree itself and use a plain terracotta pot for the base. To create a different type of tree, take a branch with an interesting outline and decorate it with rough-textured flowers, cereals and seed heads in creams, browns and greens.

A tree for Christmas
The basic form of this tree is the same as the one featured above. Instead of flowers, I have covered the foam base with wired pine cones, and added a few artificial fruits to add color and give it a more festive look.

Decorating a basket of pot-pourri

The art of making pot-pourri is experiencing something of a revival. Consequently, there are many bought varieties to choose from or it is possible to make your own by following the recipe on p.99. Pot-pourri is valued not only for its subtle smell but also for the attractive colors and textures of the dried petals from which it is made. Put it in a pretty basket decorated with dried flowers and you will have a delicate and sweet-smelling display with many decorative uses. If you wish to add a spicy quality to the fragrance of the pot-pourri, place a pomander in the middle of the basket. Alternatively, these can be decorated with ribbon and hung around the house or put in drawers.

Equipment and materials

Wicker basket

Dried flower heads

Pot-pourri

Pomander

Larkspur
Delphinium consolida

Chicken wire

Binding wire

Cotton wool

Wire cutters

Pot-pourri essence

Rose
Rosa sp.

Adding a decorative finish

If you want to give the basket a Victorian aura put a pomander in the center and encircle it with deep-crimson rose heads. Spread a layer of freshly dried daisy and forget-me-not heads over the pot-pourri to set a cool pattern of blue and white against the warm tones of the other flowers.

Building up the arrangement

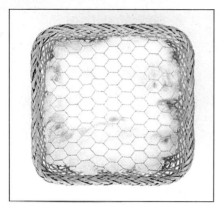

1 Line the basket with a thin layer of cotton wool. Cut a piece of fine chicken wire to fit inside the basket resting on the cotton wool. This will keep the pot-pourri dry and stop it becoming "fusty" by allowing air to circulate underneath it.

2 Sprinkle a few drops of bought pot-pourri essence (or use your own essential oils distilled from fresh flowers) to enhance the existing natural fragrances. Fill the basket two-thirds full with pot-pourri made from rose petals, lavender, scented-leaved geraniums, dried lemon peel and orris root (see p.99).

3 To make the garland, take three stems of larkspur and bind them together using fine binding wire. Arrange the stems so that the flowers are equally distributed along the garland and wrap the wire around the stems being careful not to damage the flowers.

4 Continue to make the garland until it is long enough to fit right round the basket. As an alternative to the pink larkspur you could use blue larkspur mixed with deep red straw flowers or immortelles.

5 As the garland is flexible, adjust it to the shape of your basket and secure it in position with wire. The illustration opposite shows how to add a decorative finish using blue and white dried flower heads and a pomander centerpiece.

Making a pomander

Take an orange—preferably a Seville orange—and, if you are planning to hang up your pomander, place masking tape on the orange where the ribbons will go. Stick the cloves into the orange and then roll it in the orris root and cinnamon. Put it in a dark, well-ventilated place for several weeks.

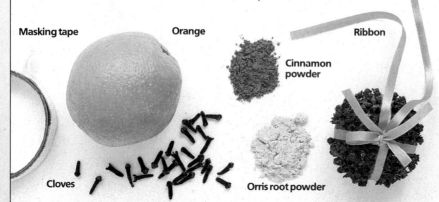

Masking tape   **Orange**   **Ribbon**

Cinnamon powder

Cloves   **Orris root powder**

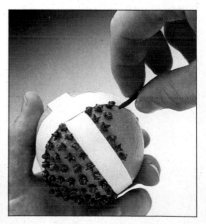

Inserting the cloves *above*
Stick the cloves into the orange leaving the width of one head between them.

Making wreaths

Wreaths made out of dried materials can be used in a number of ways. They can be hung on a door, on a wall, or from the ceiling, or used flat to make a table decoration. Here, I have made a rough-textured wreath with brown nuts and neutral-colored grasses, highlighted with the warm tones of yellow, orange and red flowers.

Equipment and materials

Immortelle
Xeranthemum annuum

Stub wires

Wire cutters

Old-man's-beard stems
Chionanthus virginicus

Sea holly
Eryngium maritimum

Artificial fruits

Yarrow
Achillea filipendulina

Poppy seed heads
Papaver sp.

Oats
Avena sp.

Wheat
Triticum vulgare

Beech nuts
Fagus sp.

Straw flower
Helichrysum bracteatum

Larch cones
Larix sp.

Everlastings
Helipterum roseum

Chestnuts
Aesculus hippocastanum

Pine cones
Pinus sp.

African daisy
Lonas inordora

Other types of wreath

Floral foam also makes a useful base for a wreath. You will need to buy a large brick so that you can form the shape out of it. Once you have cut out the shape, cover the foam with moss and then insert your flowers. As an alternative to flowers, dried grasses and cereals will make a wreath of subtle color and texture, arrange them so that their heads radiate out in natural curves.

Country-style wreath

The rich textures and colors of this wreath suit a background of natural wood. Radiating lines of pink everlastings (*Helipterum roseum*) are interspersed with the deep-red tones of love-lies-bleeding (*Amaranthus caudatus*) and sea lavender (*Limonium latifolium*) dyed pink. The striped seed heads of love-in-a-mist (*Nigella damascena*) add further texture to this tightly packed wreath.

Building up the arrangement

1 Make the circular base of the wreath with old-man's-beard stems. Wrap the thickest stems around each other about four times, forming a circle, then wrap the thinner parts of the stems over this. Vine prunings can also be used as the base.

2 Beech nuts, chestnuts, pine cones, and straw flowers need to be wired. To wire a pine cone, insert a wire between the scales of the cone and twine the shorter side of the wire around the longer.

3 Encircle the wreath with wired pine cones. Wire the chestnuts by pushing a stout needle through the center to make a hole (see step 2). Wire the beech nuts in the same way as the pine cones.

4 Add groups of wired chestnuts to the wreath. Insert larch cones on their short stems, wired beech nuts, poppy seed heads, sea holly, wheat and oats to create the main body of the wreath.

5 Add everlastings, yellow, orange and red straw flowers, immortelles, yarrow and African daisies wherever there are holes which need filling.

6 You can leave the wreath as it is or, if you want to decorate it for Christmas, add some red artificial fruits and a large red ribbon to attach it to a door knocker.

Larch cone

Pine cone

Chestnut

Wheat

Immortelle

Beech nut

Poppy seed head

Straw flower

African daisy

Yarrow

Sea holly

Oats

Everlasting

Making decorations

Dried flowers can be used to make decorations for festive occasions. Floral balls, corn stars and "snowy" pine cones make unusual tree decorations and a brightly colored chain of straw flowers can be hung on a tree or chimneypiece.

Floral balls

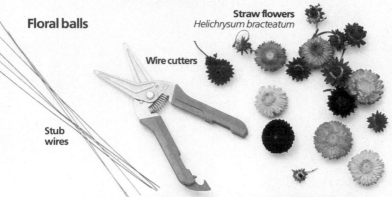

Straw flowers
Helichrysum bracteatum

Wire cutters

Stub wires

1 Push a wire through the center of each flower, bending it over at the top and pulling it back through the flower head.

2 Wire five flowers, then arrange them so that they form a ball. Twist one of the wires around the others to secure them.

Corn stars

Wire cutters

Everlasting
Helipterum roseum

Wheat
Triticum vulgare

Ribbon

1 Cut the corn stalk between the nodes to make 4in lengths, and strip off the outer sheath. Make a slit in one stalk and slip another through it at 90 degrees.

2 Continue until you have a star with as many points as you require. Take the ribbon and twist it under and over each prong of the corn to make a central disc.

Snow-covered pine cones

Pine cones
Pinus sp.

Washing powder

Stub wires

Wallpaper paste

1 Wire the pine cones as shown on p.109; dip each one into a solution of wallpaper paste until half of the cone is covered in paste. Take it out and shake well to remove the excess paste.

2 When the paste feels tacky, dip the cones in the washing powder, making sure that they receive an even covering of white. Shake off any excess and leave them to dry before hanging on the tree.

A chain of dried flowers

Crochet thread

Darning needle

Straw flowers
Helichrysum bracteatum

Cut a piece of thread to the length that you require. Thread the darning needle and push it through the center of each straw flower. As you thread each flower, make sure that its front faces the back of the one it is next to on the chain; this will ensure a more even effect.

·5·
THE ROOM-BY-ROOM GUIDE

Pot plants and flowers have been used to decorate rooms since as early as the seventeenth century, but it was the start of the nineteenth century that saw a vast influx of exciting new plants into Europe. This was when the first painted-leaved begonias, paper flowers and a large array of tropical foliage plants arrived, and those who could afford them began to display them in their homes and conservatories. However, it is only recently that an enormous range of plants have become available to everyone.

The following pages display the different rooms in the house and show how plants can be actively incorporated into the decorative scheme of a room, rather than being merely random extras. Each room in the home has a different function and its practical use will determine the sort of environment, or *mini-climate*, it can offer to plants. Each room also has a specific mood and plants can be used to enhance this particular atmosphere.

The period of your house and the style of your room will determine the way in which you display your plants. A traditional interior calls for plants to complement an existing setting and, for instance, co-ordinate with fabrics or a collection of objects. A modern interior may call for plants to be used in an architectural way, as an integral part of the landscaping of the room.

Using plants and flowers in a room
These two milkbush plants (*Euphorbia tirucalli*) are used as a counterbalance to the large bookcase, and are of a scale to match it. They like the warm conditions of a living room and are easy to keep provided they are not overwatered. The vase of flowers on the table is part of an incidental coffee table grouping.

Mini-climates in the home

Throughout this book I have used a system of mini-climates to identify the different environments offered by the average home. Each plant featured in *The Plant Finder's Guide* has a mini-climate reference indicating its optimum levels of heat and light. This need not be interpreted too rigidly; a great attribute of many of our most popular house plants is their tolerance of a wide range of growing conditions. In much of the USA and Canada where summer temperatures run very warm indoors and outdoors it is impossible to provide consistent summer indoor temperatures of 50°-60°F. One solution is to summer the plants outdoors in light shade. Also, plants grown in city apartments may not receive the suggested amount of light. A solution is to provide artificial light, usually from fluorescent tubes (see p.244 and p.258).

Winter sunshine will not harm any plant grown in northern latitudes, and one that ideally needs filtered sun when the sun is high may need direct sunlight in winter, when the sun is weaker and days shorter.

Very few plants will suffer if placed in a higher temperature than that recommended—as long as higher levels of humidity, and probably a little more water, are provided for them. Water plants less if you grow them cooler than the given mini-climate, and remember that it is much better to underwater than to overwater.

Very high summer temperatures often cannot be brought down without the aid of air conditioning units, which dry the air. A high level of humidity, adequate watering and frequent mist-spraying will all help to counteract this but, in any case, do not keep plants near an air conditioning unit.

When choosing plants to group together indoors, it is not enough merely to consider their decorative qualities; if the display is to remain attractive, you must also ensure that the mini-climate requirements of the plants are compatible. A plant which likes direct sunlight can be put quite happily with a plant that likes filtered light, but it is not sensible to group a tropical shade-lover with a temperate flowering plant.

Mini-climate 1
Warm, sunny

A *warm* room is one kept at a temperature of 60°-70°F—a range preferred by many house plants. Ideally, for the comfort of people, the day temperatures are 65°-70°F and the night range between 60°-65°F or even lower, which the plants can tolerate.

A *sunny* position is one that gets direct, unobstructed sunlight for part of the day. A plant standing in or very near to a south-facing window is in a sunny position; those in east- or west-facing windows receive less sun each day.

White walls contribute to brightness of the room by reflecting light.

Hanging basket receiving direct light, but away from heat rising from stove.

Two large windows provide plenty of direct sunlight for plants and flowers.

Steam rising from kettle increases humidity in the kitchen.

Timber ceiling absorbs heat, preventing sudden temperature changes.

Hot air rises, creating warm conditions for these tropical plants.

Bare brick wall catches light and has heat-retaining qualities.

Full-length windows provide the amount of light needed for this large, plant-filled room.

Mini-climate 2
Warm, filtered sun

A *warm* room is one kept at a temperature of 60°-70°F—a range preferred by many house plants. Ideally, for the comfort of people, the day temperatures are 65°-70°F and the night range between 60°-65°F or even lower, which the plants can tolerate.

A room receiving *filtered sun* may face south, east or west (or south-east or south-west) but direct sunlight is baffled by translucent blinds or curtains, a tall building or leafy tree outside a window.

Sub-tropical plants thrive in these conditions.

Fine net curtain serves as filter for sunlight.

White fittings and large mirror over bath reflect light, greatly increasing room brightness.

Steam rising from bath provides high levels of relative humidity.

Leafy tree outside window serves to baffle sunlight.

Venetian blind needed to filter direct light by the coast or in lower latitudes.

Wall-mounted mirror reflects sunlight and increases brightness of the room.

Umbrella plant benefits from filtered sun and humidity of the bathroom.

Mini-climate 3
Warm, shady

A *warm* room is one kept at a temperature of 60°-70°F—a range preferred by many house plants. Ideally, for the comfort of people, the day temperatures are 65°-70°F and the night range between 60°-65°F or even lower, which the plants can tolerate.

A *shady* position, in our definition, receives no direct or filtered sunlight, but does not have "poor" light (which is too low for healthy plant growth). Plants that like some shade can be grown away from the window in a room that is well-lit, or in the window of a room that is not well-lit.

Conditions are ideal for this thriving Swiss cheese plant.

Light filtered by trees outside and curtains.

There is not enough light in this corner of the room for healthy plant growth.

Dark floor absorbs light, reducing brightness in the room.

Curtain serves to reduce light entering large window.

Staghorn fern thrives when suspended out of direct light.

Dark furnishings absorb light reflected by pale floor and walls.

Large pot catches the drips from watering.

Mini-climate 4
Cool, sunny

A *cool* room is one kept at a temperature of 50°-60°F. This is the range preferred by many temperate zone plants, although plants from warmer climates may also be able to thrive—and temporary flowering house plants often live longer—at these temperature levels.

A *sunny* position is one that gets direct, unobstructed sunlight for part of the day. A plant standing in or very near to a south-facing window is in a sunny position; those in east- or west-facing windows receive less sun each day.

The large leaves of this banana plant require strong direct sunlight, but this plant can tolerate temperatures as low as 50°F.

Cool, airy landing with high ceiling is ideal environment for large-scale feature plants.

Spacious, open-plan staircase forms part of very large, unenclosed area of cool air.

Very large, unshaded window provides plenty of light for this assortment of plants.

Mini-climate 5
Cool, filtered sun

A *cool* room is one kept at a temperature of 50°-60°F. This is the range preferred by many temperate zone plants, although plants from warmer climates may also be able to thrive—and temporary flowering house plants often live longer—at these temperature levels.

A room receiving *filtered sun* may face south, east or west (or south-east or south-west) but direct sunlight is baffled by translucent blinds or curtains, or a tall building or leafy tree outside a window.

Creeper outside window prevents strong light being reflected from white wall.

Heavy draped curtains may be partially drawn to keep room temperature down.

This thriving ivy is shielded from the window by the mass of the arrangement.

Suitable plants for these conditions include Japanese fatsia.

This plant can be given the amount of shade it requires by the Venetian blind.

White walls and bed linen contribute to the cool environment by reflecting heat.

Full-length blinds filter the sunlight entering the room.

Living rooms 1

For most people, the living room is the show-piece of the home and the room in which most entertaining takes place. A considerable amount of money may be spent on furnishings, fabrics and general decoration. Broadly speaking, living rooms may be traditional or modern, with elements of one style being adapted and combined with those of others. Plants provide a restful background and fresh colors, and should enhance the layout of the room without dominating it. Living rooms usually contain large items of furniture, and plants should be of an appropriate size to counterbalance them: one or two large ones usually look much better than a clutter of smaller ones. Arrangements of cut or dried flowers and small-scale plants can be used for incidental groupings on coffee tables, side tables and shelves.

Position your plants away from radiators or open fires, in a place which provides adequate light for their specific needs, and where you can water them easily. It is very important that plants should not be in the way of people moving about, both for the convenience of the human inhabitants and the protection of the plants themselves. So, once you have decided on the type of plant and the scale you need, work its positioning into your basic plan making sure that plant and container are an integral part of your design concept.

Linear forms *below*
A classic modern interior of oriental simplicity, composed of linear forms —the table, sofas and pictures—and muted colors without patterns. The focal point of the room is the arrangement of dried twigs on the table, which is counter-balanced by the ornament and bonsai. The large rainbow plants (*Dracaena marginata*) soften what might otherwise be too spartan a room.

Black and white

The placement of the furniture in this severe, modern interior is governed by the position of the chimney breast and the view of the terrace. The plants used inside are very low-key, but nonetheless link the two spaces effectively. It is interesting that the designer felt that this uncompromisingly robust interior should be softened by a trailing tradescantia (*Tradescantia* sp.). The all-white flower arrangement is in keeping with the overall color scheme, and picks up the white of the floor and walls in an area where black predominates.

Pattern and color

A softer decorative look permeates this room with much use of fabric in the full drop of the curtains and the table covering. Bright colors and patterns call for large plant forms that will accompany, but not dominate, decoration. Behind the sofa stands a European fan palm (*Chamaerops humilis*) and part of a fishtail palm (*Caryota mitis*) can be seen in the foreground. The central feature is the low coffee table with its clutter of books and the large bowl, whose shape is cleverly echoed by the smaller bowls on the corner table, and contrasted with the curving leaves of an orchid in flower.

Living rooms 2

Rustic style
In this cottage living room the overall effect is cluttered and without a single dominant feature. Spectacular tropical species would be out of character, but small-leaved temperate plants are used to good effect, as are the bowl of pot-pourri and bird's nest in the foreground. Rustic wooden furniture, botanical prints and floral patterns are all in keeping with the gentle mood of this type of decoration.

Bold color contrast *left*
Compared to the room above, the overall impression here is one of severity, although all the furniture is, in fact, highly decorative. The strong color contrast of black, red and white is brought together in the patterned carpet, and given a final flamboyant touch with the addition of the vase of huge cut amaryllis (*Hippeastrum* sp.) which echo the red of the canvas.

Low-key *right*
The blinds in this room give it a soft lighting effect which creates a tranquil mood not disturbed by heavy patterns or assertive colors. The gentle green foliage of the bamboo (*Arundinaria* sp.) is in keeping with the relaxed atmosphere. The cut flowers and small house plant are additional features which serve as minor points of interest.

Size, shape and color co-ordination *right*
The large leaves of the African hemp (*Sparmannia africana*) are in accord with the geometric wall patterning behind the plant. The foliage of the foreground Kentia palm (*Howea belmoreana*) is similar to the leaf shape in the painting, and the soft colors of the room are repeated in the table arrangement of cut flowers.

Horizontal lines *below*
Downlighters pick out the colors of the simple furniture and patterned fabric, echoed by the flowers, plants and objects. The bold horizontal patterning of blinds and floor unify the diverse points of interest.

Living rooms 3

Part of creating a comfortable, inviting living space is building up one or more attractive seating areas which draw the visitor into the room. Whether these are in the corners of the room, at one end, or in alcoves, window bays and recesses, house plants can play a large part in making the most of them. Plants can highlight a fabric, either by forming a total contrast or by echoing colors and patterns in the curtains or soft furnishings. Alternatively, the shape and form of plants can enhance and soften these settings—gracefully overhanging a sofa or armchair perhaps, complementing a picture, or providing a solid background for a group of cane or wicker chairs in a corner.

Making a feature of the ceiling *right*
Distinctive roof supports are something of a feature in this room, and the shiny spotlights are certainly there to be noticed. So two trailing plants set up high enhance the effect and save space in the room.

Sofa in a window bay
above
A tall golden-feather palm (*Chrysalidocarpus lutescens*), arching its delicate fronds over the sofa, makes the whole area more inviting. Light filtered from the window gives the plant a strong silhouette. The two other house plants are a small parlor palm (*Chamaedorea elegans* "Bella") and white calla lily (*Zantedeschia aethiopica*).

Modern sofa setting
right
This cushion seating is backed by a window in a modern living room. The effect is clean and sharp but, at the same time, softened by the arrangement of creamy-white hydrangeas (*Hydrangea* sp.) on the left.

Making a plant grouping for a corner of a room

Here, I have set out to compose a little period piece to accompany the easy chair and draped curtain. The site is a corner of a living room decorated in neutral shades, next to an east-facing window. Since the room is not in constant use, and therefore not always heated, I needed plants suited to a cool room. When you are aiming to create a particular atmosphere like this, you may find that certain of your possessions suggest themselves as "props".

The setting and overall styling
below and right
This is an attractive corner, but the décor shades are muted and monotone, and something bright and colorful is needed to guide the eye towards the large window. An arrangement of plants or flowers will look well on the graceful occasional table. As the room is not used very often, an arrangement of potted plants will enhance the corner for longer than an arrangement of cut flowers. The arrangement needs to be large, without dominating the corner. To continue the period feel, I added a pair of Victorian dolls and a small footstool. The red of the foot-stool and the velvet cushion picks up the exact red of the cyclamen.

Making up the arrangement
I used a plastic tray in which to stand the various pots, so that the plants can be watered according to their individual needs. I planned the arrangement around the two cyclamen (*Cyclamen persicum* hybrids), making sure they were offset by the solid greenery of the Japanese fatsia (*Fatsia japonica*). Then I added a spiky green spider plant (*Chlorophytum comosum*) to provide outline interest, and lightened the whole effect with trailing stems of variegated ivy (*Hedera helix* hybrids) to mask the edge of the table. Finally, just for fun, I included a bunch of grapes, and these actually have the effect of "lifting" the green/red/beige scheme.

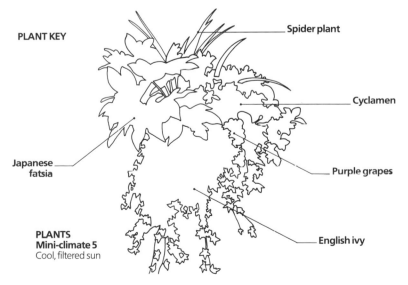

PLANT KEY

Spider plant

Cyclamen

Japanese fatsia

Purple grapes

English ivy

PLANTS
Mini-climate 5
Cool, filtered sun

Living rooms 4
Focal point

Sometimes, plants are allowed to become the dominant feature of a room. Whereas strong patterning and bold colors tend to obscure vegetation by competing with it visually, simple fabrics, plain colored walls and the long, low lines of modern furniture all serve to draw attention to house plants or flower arrangements.

Bold leaves *below*
A plant with small leaves would look weak in this airy setting, but the massive fiddle leaf fig (*Ficus lyrata*) looks superb and automatically becomes the focal point of the room. Such a sizeable plant easily draws attention from the large studio windows.

Small-scale setting *right*
This ponytail (*Beaucarnea recurvata*) is a fairly dominant plant which has been used here with a table and a lamp to make an interesting group. The pebbles on the table and floor help to link the treelike plant to its setting.

On a grand scale *right*
The imposing banquette is surmounted by an arching Kentia palm (*Howea belmoreana*), providing a magnificent central feature. The palm's graceful lines are echoed by the pair of white sails (*Spathiphyllum* "Clevelandii") on the console table, and combine with the panelled door and ornate coving to make this room evocative of past grandeur.

Splash of color *left*
Almost minimalist in style, this dark-colored furniture makes a restrained setting for an arrangement of larkspur (*Delphinium consolida*) in a glass vase. Thus the simple colorful display immediately becomes a focal point.

Contrasting textures *right*
Here, the arrangement is one of scale, line and textural contrast. The hard geometry of the dark-colored beams is emphasized by the soft hanging English ivy (*Hedera helix* hybrids) and the graceful clumps of the umbrella plant (*Cyperus alternifolius*).

Living rooms 5
Table-top ideas

In any style of living room there will usually be side tables and coffee tables that can be made into smaller focal points of interest. Plants and flowers should relate to other objects, such as ornaments, books or lamps, which may in themselves suggest the choice of a plant or group of flowers.

A question of scale *right*
A small plant would be swamped by this bold interior, but the magnificent painted nettle (*Coleus blumei*) is large enough to demand attention. The red markings of the foliage pick up the color of the sofa.

Mellow tones *above*
A basket of dried flowers and grasses blends in with the warm colors of leather-bound books and polished wood, bringing a touch of summer to a library setting.

Graceful lines *above*
The graceful curved neck of this decoy swan is echoed in the lines of the tulip stems and the shape of the central pot. The soft colors match those of the sofa.

Contrasting forms *above*
The basket of dried lavender and the cluster of spherical wooden objects combine with the dominant, oriental lamp base to form a pleasing group.

A dominant feature *above*
Mosslike baby's tears plants (*Soleirolia soleirolii*) arranged in a basket make a dominant central display that needs to be surrounded by low-key furnishings that do not vie for attention.

Imposing order *left*
In this eclectic mixture of furnishings, an eye-catching arrangement of Swiss cheese plant leaves (*Monstera deliciosa*) and foxtail lilies (*Eremurus* sp.) serves to unify the diverse features.

Living rooms 6

Although designed expressly for putting things on, shelves and mantelpieces do not usually promote the long-term well-being of plants. Lack of space and light means that arrangements of cut or dried flowers are usually the best choice, or, perhaps, flowering annual plants or bulbs.

Shelves of cacti *left*
Because of their simple, compact shapes, cacti look good ranged on shelves. Moreover, a set-up like this alcove—with an overhead light source, backing mirror and glass shelves—will help to maximize the impact of the group. The overhead lighting has the effect of highlighting any fluffy down or dramatic spikes on the cacti. Notice how glass shelves look green in cross section (due to refraction), which enhances the plant display—try for a similar effect with a collection of tumbling greenhouse plants, or a collection of ferns, making sure there is sufficient light.

Using dried flowers
above
Five bunches of dried flowers provide a lower-edge "frame" for this large over-mantel mirror. They form part of the "ordered clutter" of objects and ornaments around and on the marble mantelpiece. When displaying dried flowers for any length of time, blow the dust off them occasionally.

Using wild flowers *right*
Wild flowers are easy on the eye and, in general, have softer-hued flower heads than garden varieties. Too strong an arrangement of plants in this gothic setting would have been out of character, but two light, feathery bunches of wild flowers do not detract from the delicate tracery of the wall decoration. Beneath this shelf is a radiator, which should be turned off when any fresh flowers are displayed on the shelf. Wild flowers, especially, wilt very quickly if not kept in cool conditions. (Grow your own rather than picking from the wild.)

Making wreath decorations for mantelpieces

An open fireplace easily becomes the focal point of a room. But when there is no fire lit, a mantel decoration can counteract the empty void below.

The setting *right*
This dried wreath succeeds in echoing the style and natural colors of the fireplace and the remainder of the décor—the books, wooden decoy ducks and an old straw hat. The wreath is positioned off-center and is balanced by the objects on the left.

PLANT KEY

Old-man's beard stems

Bracken

Straw flower

Oats

Bells-of-Ireland

Lady's mantle

Wheat

Baby's breath

Yellow statice

Decoration for a special occasion *right*
This idea for a festive occasion includes fresh flowers, so do not light the fire, unless the blooms only need to last a few hours for a party. The two swags are made of white-painted magnolia (*Magnolia* sp.) leaves, pampas grass (*Cortaderia* sp.) and lemons, wired to a base of crumpled netting, which is filled with damp moss into which yellow chrysanthemums (*Chrysanthemum* sp.) have been pushed.

Living rooms 7
Plants and pictures

Various styles of painting will suggest different types of display; by using plants or flowers in conjunction with a picture, you can recreate a still life with fresh material or pick up the patterns, textures or colors in a painting. Each composition may be a little set piece on its own or, if you are working with a large painting, it may dominate the whole room.

Old and new *above*
Lilies (*Lilium auratum*) and Transvaal daisies (*Gerbera jamesonii*) in a modern vase make a humorous contrast with a traditional still life.

Linking textures *above*
There is a textural harmony between the painting, the table inlay and the mottled leaves of the leopard plant (*Ligularia* sp.).

Picking up a color *above*
It is color that unifies this triangular mantelpiece display—the yellow of the painted sun is echoed by that of the lilies (*Lilium* hybrids).

Using a dominant color *right*
Color again provides the association here, between the flowers in the painting and those in the vase. The vibrant yellow stands out in a monochromatic setting.

Dining rooms 1

It is not easy to be specific about current styles of interior decoration for any room, as there are so many styles about and the dividing lines between them are often not exact.

Styles for dining rooms show the same range as living rooms. One of the most popular current styles is based on fabrics inspired by eighteenth- and nineteenth-century prototypes and casual country furniture. Temperate plants, fresh garden flowers and dried flowers will all enhance this type of room. Offshoots of this style are the informal American colonial look and an eclectic ethnic style based on imports from the Far East and India. Another style of interior decoration has its origins in industrial high-tech, which first appeared in the late 1970s. It still has a utilitarian look, but one which has been adapted by popular chain stores to furnish a sophisticated urban market. Large, architectural plants used with this décor continue the austere effect. Another style currently in vogue is a softer look, full of pastel colors and the use of draperies, which recalls the 1920s.

Country style *above*
This dining room epitomizes country style in its furniture, floor covering and small-print curtain fabric. Large baskets of dried flowers are in keeping with the rustic mood and their subdued colors harmonize with the rich, dark colors of the antique furniture.

Softening sharp angles *right*
The wiry, angular shapes of the lamp and chairs in this eating area are reminiscent of popular furniture in the 1950s. Their harshness is softened by the large leaves of the avocado pear plant (*Persea americana*).

Hard-edged sophistication *above*
This glass table increases the impact of a flower arrangement, and the shape of the dining chairs is repeated in the curved glass bowls. Red tulips (*Tulipa* hybrids) contrast spectacularly with the furniture.

Using a mantelpiece *above*
A softer, period look with a froth of baby's breath (*Gypsophila paniculata*) as a central feature on the polished table. Delicate baby's tears plants (*Soleirolia soleiroleii*) line the mantelpiece.

Dining rooms 2

Opulence on a small scale
right
This attic dining room, although small, has a baronial feel. The tapestry-covered dining chairs and gleaming silver table accessories are complemented by two large, bushy crotons (*Codiaeum variegatum pictum*). The predominant colors of the decoration —red and green—are repeated in the leaves of the plants.

Large-scale dining space
below
This interesting, airy setting is overhung by a footbridge on the upper level. At one end of the dining table, a luxuriant mass of the cut-leaved finger plant (*Philodendron bipinnatifidum*) and ferns is a fittingly dramatic backdrop. The plants look equally attractive viewed from above.

Successful decoration with two plants *left*
The spectacular palm dominating one corner of this dining room catches your eye immediately. But the smaller bushy foliage plant, cleverly placed on a lower level, has the effect of drawing the eye down and towards the table which, after all, is the focal point of the room.

Thematic table setting *below*
For a special occasion, display cut flowers or flowering house plants which match your china. Here, yellow and white flowers echo the colors of the table mats and plates, while a huge African hemp (*Sparmannia africana*) brings fresh greenery into the room.

Dining rooms 3

The focal point of a dining room must be its table. Floral centerpieces should be in the mood of the table setting but should not impede conversation across the table. Just a few flower heads floating in water will make an attractive display, particularly if they complement the colors of the food. Other arrangements in the room should not distract attention from the centerpiece.

An elegant still life *left*
A charmingly simple still life composition on a dining room side table which is not too demanding on the eye. The arrangement is enlivened by the addition of a regal lily (*Lilium regale*) in a narrow vase.

Echoing floral motifs
right
Even without its centerpiece, this dining room setting conjures up a mood of summer with its vibrant colors and abundance of greenery. An ivy patterned wallpaper, a floral tablecloth and two weeping figs (*Ficus benjamina*) on either side of a fireplace set the scene for a stunning central arrangement of red trumpet honeysuckle (*Lonicera brownii*) mixed with English ivy (*Hedera helix* hybrids) in a basket.

Co-ordinating colors
right
In certain situations artificial flowers are perfectly acceptable, and perhaps the dining table is one of them. The chance to recreate a summer arrangement in midwinter is always welcome. Here, the bright colors provide a strong contrast to the predominantly white table setting and furniture. The mixture of orange, white and purple flowers and green foliage picks up the colors in the floral pattern of the china perfectly.

Kitchens 1

Kitchens can be of two types: working galley kitchens and kitchens to live in. By definition, the worktop surfaces are practical and do not lend themselves to too much decoration—add to this the hazards of steam and constantly changing temperatures and you may not have ideal growing conditions. However, some plants will prefer the added humidity and warmth of the kitchen environment. Arrangements of dried flowers, and bowls of gourds, fruit and vegetables, can be most attractive as long as they do not impede the cook. Window-ledges can be utilized, but plants must be protected from the fall in temperatures at night if there is no double glazing. Plants can be displayed in hanging baskets, but only in places where it is easy to water them frequently.

Period feel *below*
Something of a period mood has been created here with copper pans, wooden spoons and basketware—all visually strong in themselves. However, the white tulips (*Tulipa* hybrids) are the focal point.

Strong primaries *left*
Cut chrysanthemums (*Chrysanthemum* hybrids) make a bright addition to the edible strawberries, lemons, peppers and tomatoes which complement the strong primary color scheme of this streamlined kitchen unit. The location of the display makes imaginative use of the concealed, split-level lighting.

Practical and decorative *left*
The typical type of clutter one might expect to find on the wide sill of a country kitchen. Drying herbs hang in a swathe above the window, their presence serving both a practical and a decorative use. The bowl of fruit and the cyclamen (*Cyclamen persicum* hybrids) on the sill itself contribute to the overall impression of a warm, welcoming room and a place of work.

Casual and homely *left*
This breakfast area is enlivened by an informal arrangement of garden flowers, foliage and grasses in a jug, and a heartleaf philodendron (*Philodendron scandens*) trails attractively over the shelves which house a collection of American blue-and-white spatterware. These plants like a warm and humid atmosphere, as their natural habitat is the tropical rain forest.

Square patterns *right*
A high-tech kitchen which has ingeniously utilized squared wire mesh for hanging utensils above the sink, and repeated the motif as a support for a mosaic of climbers against the window. These are positioned in such a way as to benefit from the light of the window whilst not interfering with the work of the cook. The square pattern is repeated in the wall and floor coverings, but the angular style of the kitchen is softened by the presence of the plants.

Utilizing a high ceiling
right
The ceiling of a large kitchen which does not get too steamy makes an ideal place to hang and dry summer flowers and herbs. When the ceiling is high, bunches of flowers can make the room seem less bare and are in no danger of getting in the way of the cook. In this country kitchen, baskets, rattan blinds and a bird cage complement the simple pine furniture and complete the styling.

Kitchens 2

In a compact kitchen, the chances are that you will not want any plants cluttering up your valuable worktops. Yet it seems a pity to do without greenery, and there are several ways of solving the problem practically and safely, while keeping plants off surfaces and away from kitchen appliances.

Making a feature of a plain wall *right*
People hang pans and utensils in the kitchen, and there is no reason why you cannot hang up plants. A plastic-coated grid attached to the wall makes an attractive base to which you can fix a selection of small potted herbs so that they are to hand when you are cooking.

Decorating an eating area *above*
This kitchen eating area is enlivened by an Algerian ivy (*Hedera canariensis* hybrids). The simple white décor focuses attention on the green foliage.

A kitchen corner *below*
Several house plants enliven this kitchen, but none of them occupies a working surface. The luxuriant Boston fern (*Nephrolepis exaltata* "Bostoniensis") is suspended by a chain from the ceiling.

Decorating a kitchen dresser

A collection of blue-and-white china looks very appealing ranged on the dresser of a traditional country kitchen. But perhaps the scene is a little stark. Dresser shelves are quite narrow and normally used for display, rather than as functional shelves for much-used kitchen items. So a dresser is an ideal "showcase" for plants, provided you observe the rules of lighting and watering, and change the plants when necessary.

The setting *below*
The areas of white wall behind the dresser look rather austere and would benefit from some "filling in". But introducing a random collection of plants would interrupt the subtle styling of the kitchen.

PLANT KEY

PLANTS **Christmas cherry**
Mini-climate 4
Cool, sunny

Making up the arrangement
As a solution, I selected five plants of the same variety—the Christmas cherry (*Solanum capsicastrum*). Its orange berries provide a color contrast, without being too distracting to the eye, and complement the china collection.

The overall styling *above*
Within the country-style setting of this kitchen interior, the Christmas cherries, with their bright berries and small, pretty leaves, warm and soften what could easily be too severe a room-scheme.

Looking after the plants *left*
This useful little winter berrying plant, which has insignificant flowers earlier in the year, lasts up to two months. Given a coolish interior, it appreciates a degree of humidity and should be misted every day or so. Since the dresser does not offer the direct light these plants prefer, move them to a sunny position for several hours a day.

Bedrooms 1

Your bedroom is a highly personal part of your house and one where you can indulge your most imaginative ideas about decoration. An arrangement of fresh or dried flowers in a guest room is a thoughtful touch, too. Yet displays must still be practically planned. If space is a problem, consider fixing up a hanging arrangement in the form of a wreath or garland, or using a pedestal to support a plant or flower arrangement in one corner.

Balancing vibrant colors *below*
This unusual bedroom is decorated in bright colors and excitingly lit. A stylish combination of artificial white tulips in two large, yellow vases and a tall euphorbia (*Euphorbia pseudocactus*) help reinforce the whole effect.

Art-deco style bedroom *right*
A large house plant sits on a beautiful ceramic jardiniere, totally in keeping with the collection of art-deco paraphernalia and the floral design of the window blind. Place pedestals like this where they will not be knocked over.

Creating a romantic mood *left*
A nostalgic bedroom is reflected in this floor-length mirror decorated with garlands of dried flowers. The bed's brass corner poles are adorned with ribbons and bunches of artificial rosebuds.

Maintaining a spacious feel *below*
A magnificent weeping fig (*Ficus benjamina*) stands in a sunny corner of this airy bedroom. Although large, the plant is positioned well out of the way and adds to, rather than detracts from, the feeling of lightness and space.

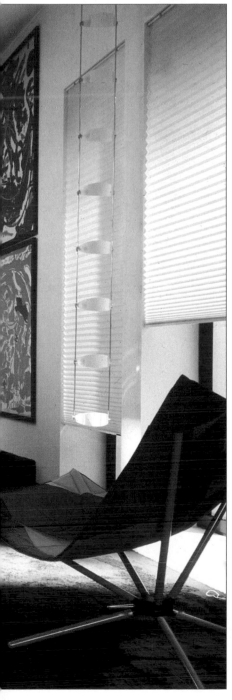

Bedrooms 2

Complementing a picture *above*
The chest of drawers provides a solid support for a single cineraria (*Senecio cruentus* hybrids) which subtly reinforces the subject of the picture hanging directly above it.

A conservatory corner *above*
Sunlight flooding through a bedroom window illuminates this collection of plants. A large fuchsia (*Fuchsia* sp.) contributes to the "conservatory" feel.

A place for artificial flowers *left*
Occasionally, people may be physically averse to plants or fresh flowers in the room where they sleep. Instead, try an artificial, but informal, decoration such as this enchanting basket filled with artificial forget-me-nots. Country-style bedrooms can be enhanced by using painted or stencilled baskets as containers for flower arrangements.

A romantic bedroom
right
A vase of lilac (*Syringa* hybrids) seen through a mirror fills a softly pretty bedroom with fragrance. The lilac complements the lace-covered pillows and delicate pink-and-white wallpaper. Always place bedroom vases somewhere safe, where they will not be knocked over while you dress or make the bed. Use other fragrant flowers and plants as they come into season.

Co-ordinating color scheme *right*
In a carefully put-together period room, a tall vase of dried Chinese lanterns (*Physalis alkekengi* "Gigantea") stands on the mantelpiece, helping to make a focal point of the fireplace area and the cosy coal fire. The green and orange lanterns coordinate perfectly with the color scheme of the bold designs on the wardrobe, fabric and wallcovering.

Bathrooms 1

The relaxing surroundings of a bathroom can form a stylish setting for some of your more striking plants, and matching containers to the bathroom fittings ensures a successful display.

Provided that they have good light, bathrooms come nearest to providing the ideal growing conditions for a number of the most popular house plants. They are generally warm places and, two or three times a day, the air becomes saturated with moisture. Quite a high level of humidity can continue for some time after someone has taken a bath, while damp towels dry out and moisture on surfaces and fabrics gradually evaporates. Even if obscured glass is fitted to windows, there is little light loss; direct sunlight becomes bright, filtered light.

A "jungle-look" corner *above*
In this Victorian-style bathroom, an empty corner provides a good home for a large Swiss cheese plant (*Monstera deliciosa*), which offsets the white, antique bath. This plant loves warmth and humidity, so it is an ideal bathroom plant.

Oriental-style bathroom *left*
There is a Japanese feel about this bathroom, with its clean black and white surfaces. The fine, filigree foliage of an umbrella plant (*Cyperus alternifolius*), which needs to be grown in a constantly wet medium, is shown to perfect advantage on the windowsill.

A fragrant bathroom *right*
An elegant bathroom with potted gardenias (*Gardenia* sp.) standing on the bath surround. Their perfume will dominate the bathroom and they thrive in a moist atmosphere.

A temporary display *below*
Although you will need to change a plant such as this African lily (*Agapanthus campanulatus*) every three weeks or so (there being no natural light), it makes a beautiful addition to the bathroom.

Cut flowers in the bathroom *left*
The fresh pink, green and white color scheme of this bathroom is picked up by the cut flowers at the window and on the edge of the bath.

The small bathroom *right*
Mirrors are a superb device for increasing the apparent size of a small bathroom. Green plants used as decoration will have double the effect. Here, a pair of stick yuccas (*Yucca elephantipes*) add the final touch to a smart, masculine bathroom.

Bathrooms 2

Although space may be at a premium in the bathroom, different styles of plant decoration are possible. There is a "cluttered" look, with various small plants appearing among the soap and toothpaste; or, for a more dramatic effect, just one or two large plants can be used.

Using shelves *right*
Ferns like the warm and humid conditions of a bathroom, and small shelves above a basin surround make a suitable home for various potted specimens including a bird's nest fern (*Asplenium nidus*).

Country-style simplicity *above*
In this traditional, stencilled bathroom, a wall shelf-unit is balanced by a plant arrangement either side of the head of the bath. The rather bare, bleached feel of the room lends itself to plant decoration.

Real and painted *left*
Two exquisite viridiflora tulips (*Tulipa* hybrids) stand in an elegant vase against a mural which continues the floral theme of this bathroom.

A flower-filled bathroom *above*
The design of the blind fabric has been continued on the walls with hand-painted primroses and rose sprigs. Fresh flowers and potted plants add to the effect.

Displaying airplants in a bathroom window recess

Airplants make a fascinating display in a bathroom. Most bromeliads are native to the tropical regions of the Americas, where they cling to rocks or trees. Their roots are used merely for support—the plants survive on moisture in the air, so spray them regularly with water.

Making up the arrangement *right*
Single airplants are difficult to display well; the best approach is to mass them together. A collection of shells and coral provides decorative support for the plants and gives them an underwater look suitable for the bathroom.

The setting *below*
Airplants like the moist air in a bathroom and, despite their delicate appearance, are very tolerant. This well-lit window recess with glass shelves makes an ideal setting.

PLANT KEY

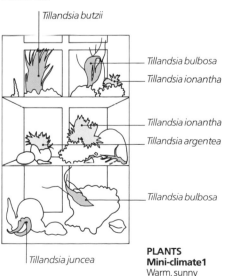

Tillandsia butzii

Tillandsia bulbosa
Tillandsia ionantha

Tillandsia ionantha
Tillandsia argentea

Tillandsia bulbosa

Tillandsia juncea

PLANTS
Mini-climate1
Warm, sunny

Details of the airplant arrangement *above left and right*
Mounted on coral, shells, pieces of wood, cork or minerals, airplants have a magical feel. Here, the delicate gray-green leaves contrast with the strong shapes of the shells and coral. The glass shelves allow light to filter between the plants and reflect the pearly sheen of the shells. Tuck or gently tie the plants into the shells, or use a special airplant fixative; in time they will probably attach their roots to the support.

Halls and entrances 1

Front doors and entrance halls are the first areas you see on entering the house. Decorated attractively, they can be warm and welcoming, drawing the visitor into the heart of the house. So first impressions are important, yet halls and lobbies often have poor light and fluctuating temperatures. You will need to plan displays for the hall using the most tolerant house plants. Cast-iron plants (*Aspidistra elatior*) and mother-in-law's-tongues (*Sansevieria trifasciata*) are good choices. Dried flowers and foliage are particularly useful for displaying in any hall or entrance with a lighting problem. People pass through the hall at standing height, so scale up plants accordingly and avoid using trailing plants in awkward places. Any plant which is constantly brushed against will inevitably become damaged.

Decorations for a large entrance hall *above*
The plain brick walls of this hall are softened by a mass of dried beech leaves (*Fagus sylvatica*) whose warm tones harmonize with the mellow brick. Two stick yuccas (*Yucca elephantipes*) stand either side of the door, and a bowl of gourds relieves the expanse of bare table-top.

Framing a doorway *left*
Two sturdy yuccas frame the doorway leading into the conservatory beyond. Tumbling light-green foliage makes an inviting transition between the two rooms.

An impressive focal point *right*
A magnificent staghorn fern (*Platycerium bifurcatum*) dominates the center of an entrance hall. A large pot standing underneath catches drips from watering and prevents people from walking too close to the plant and damaging it.

Halls and entrances 2

If you have a hall large enough to furnish, you will have the opportunity to go for maximum effect in your plant and floral arrangements. However, even in a hall which is little more than a passageway, there are several devices you can use to make sure your decorations do not go unnoticed by people passing through.

If space is a real problem, make up a swag using wire netting with dried flower heads entwined in it. Wreaths are also pretty and festive, especially at Christmas.

Using a mirror *above*
A huge mirror placed behind the side table doubles the effect of the two plants—a dragon tree (*Dracaena marginata*) and a glossy grape ivy (*Cissus rhombifolia*). Also, the mirror enlarges the apparent size of the hall and reflects light on to the plants.

Using a shelf *right*
A pretty marble shelf bracketed to the wall provides the perfect surface for an arrangement of dried roses and grasses. Two small vases containing more roses stand on either side of the central glass vase, and a tall mirror makes the most of the arrangement.

Scaling up to fill a space
left
Because it is likely to be cooler than a living room, the hall is often a good place to site an arrangement of fresh-cut flowers to help them last longer. Here, a large, informal arrangement of day lilies (*Hemerocallis* sp.) and fennel (*Foeniculum* sp.) helps to fill an area of bare whitewashed wall in a country cottage hall. The flowers, which stand on a beautiful black inlaid chest, pick up the warm colors in the furnishing fabric, helping to make the hall cosy and welcoming.

Making a winter arrangement for a hall

In a rather dull corner of this hall, in front of some pine doors opening to a seldom-used cupboard, I sited a winter arrangement of red and yellow cut flowers, including berries, early flowering shrubs and evergreen foliage to soften the effect. I used a mixing bowl and a large block of floral foam 6in higher than the container.

The setting *above*
This corner of the hall is well lit from the side and gives easy access for replacement of water. The honey-colored stripped pine makes a pleasing background for the arrangement whose triangular outline helps to soften the vertical lines of the area. As the pedestal is turned slightly to one side, emphasis is drawn towards the light source.

Making up the arrangement

A triangular arrangement
To outline the shape, I used bold Oregon grape sprays, and then I added the large chrysanthemums—yellow at the outer edge, deepening to bronze-red at the core. More sprays of jasmine, freesias and evergreen foliage added dimension.

FLOWER KEY

Crab apple

Chrysanthemum

Winter jasmine

Oregon grape

Freesia

Spider chrysanthemum

Cotoneaster

Daffodil

Japanese fatsia leaves

Persian ivy

Stairs and stairwells

The staircase may not be the first place you think of for displaying plants but, if you follow the principles outlined for halls and entrances, the results can be effective. Stairs and stairwells can be cold and drafty so select the hardier house plants.

The stairs themselves should normally be kept free of obstructions, but there may be space on a wide turn of the stairs for a large specimen plant or a collection of smaller ones. If the staircase turns round a central well, and receives some daylight, try placing a tall, upright plant or a climber in the otherwise redundant space.

Landing windowsills and skylights at the top of the stairs are two possible light sources which can help plants thrive. Large hanging baskets filled with easy-care plants such as tradescantias (*Tradescantia* sp.), spider plants (*Chlorophytum* sp.) and Swedish ivies (*Plectranthus australis*), can be secured to the framework of a skylight. The plants will soon cascade impressively, several feet down the stairwell.

Making a feature of a landing *left*
This landing halfway up a flight of stairs is well lit and deep enough for a large display of plants. Furniture, pictures and ornaments are all of the period and the twin vases of tall pampas grasses (*Cortaderia* sp.) enhance the Victorian flavor, as does trailing greenery framing the lower portion of the window.

A landing on the grand scale *right*
This imposing period staircase leading on to a wide, sunny landing is a fine enough setting for the massive foliage of a banana plant (*Musa* sp.). The huge bay window means a selection of large plants can be housed on the landing, and the back-lighting from the sun shining through the different leaf shapes creates a dramatic effect.

Making use of a skylight
Suspended plants dominate this small Edwardian landing, which is toplit from the large skylight. The arrangement of green plants, which include spider plants (*Chlorophytum* sp.) and ferns (*Nephrolepis* sp.), is reflected in a wall mirror, increasing the "cluttered" effect which is in keeping with the style of the period.

A cascade of greenery
This cool, wide stone staircase is filled with hanging plants, but has an open, spacious feel. A magnificent ladder fern (*Nephrolepis cordifolia*) dominates the foot of the stairs, while great swathes of grape ivy (*Cissus rhombifolia*) hang from the upper balcony and are silhouetted by the toplighting.

Flowers on a landing
A peaceful corner of the stairs is brought into focus by an informal arrangement of garden flowers, illuminated by sidelighting from the landing window. The flowers balance the picture above, while still maintaining the neutral tones of the rest of the interior.

Sunrooms and conservatories 1

Traditionally, the conservatory was a place in which to display plants that had been raised in the greenhouse, where they were returned when the display started to deteriorate. The modern sunroom is more a place in which people relax and enjoy the warmth, but it is also one that suits plants. Real fanatics may transform the room into something resembling a jungle, where greenery takes over, but fewer plants, well displayed, can be just as effective.

Rooms like these provide light and airy conditions, a moist atmosphere and space for plants to spread. With careful watering in winter, many plants can be grown in a room with a night temperature of 50°F, but somewhat higher during the day. However, most sunrooms are warmer than this.

Furnishing a dining area with plants *right*
This conservatory-like house extension has a tall, airy feel. This has been maintained by using a relatively small number of plants to furnish it, and soften the architectural lines. The majority of these sit on waist-level shelves fitted all round the outer edge of the room. A large rubber plant (*Ficus elastica*) stands in one corner. The conservatory is one place where large-leaved plants like this can be given their head and allowed to fill as much space as they want.

A warm sunroom *below*
This spectacular room needs to maintain a considerable temperature in winter to sustain the tropical plants growing here. Windows must be double-glazed to prevent heat loss through the large areas of glass. Huge plants are placed in pots, baskets and specially constructed brick troughs. The hanging platform which provides extra space for a suspended "island of greenery" is a most unusual, and practical, feature, since it can be lowered for watering and maintenance.

An elegant conservatory *below*
This pretty room with its distinctive glazing bars contains a selection of flowering plants, as well as a citrus tree. Color accents are provided by a poinsettia (*Euphorbia pulcherrima*) and a cactus (*Schlumbergera* sp.).

Plant-filled sunroom *above*
Here, the living space extends through sliding glass on to a sunroom floored with white decking. The large plants include a dumb cane (*Dieffenbachia* sp.) and a thriving chestnut vine (*Tetrastigma voinieranum*).

Sunrooms and conservatories 2

The sunroom windowsill *left*
This windowsill is flooded with light all day, and four attractively shaped fans are used to shade the cyclamen (*Cyclamen persicum* hybrids) and Kafir lily (*Clivia miniata*) from bright light. The small cacti (*Mammillaria* sp.) are happy in full sun.

Variety for a rustic-style sunroom *below*
At least ten different varieties of green plants decorate this sunroom. The green of their leaves contrasts vividly with the warm apricot wash on the walls. A bunch of dried flowers hangs upside-down above the riot of foliage.

Conservatory shelves *above*
An idea for making the most of a group of impatiens plants (*Impatiens* sp.) is to combine the plants with a collection of glass or china such as these colored glass vases.

Decorating a corner *right*
An array of plants and cut flowers establishes the conservatory theme in this well-lit corner. On the table stand lilies (*Lilium* hybrids), white sails (*Spathiphyllum* "Clevelandii") and English ivy (*Hedera helix* hybrids). A huge stone vase of flowering onion (*Allium giganteum*) and a basket of white chrysanthemums (*Chrysanthemum morifolium* hybrids) complete the arrangement.

A place for herbs indoors *left*
A well-lit, cool conservatory can be a home for potted herbs. There is attractive color variation in this studied arrangement of fennel (*Foeniculum vulgare*), chives (*Allium schoenoprasum*), feverfew (*Chrysanthemum parthenium*), parsley (*Petroselinum crispum*) and lady's mantle (*Alchemilla vulgaris*).

A green oasis *right*
Consider what your conservatory looks like from inside the house. This one, glimpsed through an arch, has a hanging curtain of greenery which makes a charming transition from the interior.

·6·
THE PLANT FINDER'S GUIDE

The first function of *The Plant Finder's Guide* is to provide a catalogue of the various forms of plant material that can be used in the house. There are sections dealing with cut flowers and foliage and all kinds of dried matter, as well as nearly 150 of the most popular house plants. Color photographs provide a visual guide, and advice is given on how to display your material. Additionally, the guide gives special care advice, by way of readily recognizable symbols.

In the case of house plants, the symbols indicate the preferred light, temperature, watering and humidity levels of each plant, plus the relative ease of its cultivation. The entries are classified according to the basic shape of each plant—a prime factor in determining its decorative use in the home—and information is given regarding the probable dimensions of mature specimens. Similarly shaped plants of the same genus are listed, where appropriate, and briefly described. The amount of light and heat needed by each plant is described in terms of its *mini-climate:* a system that enables you to see, at a glance, which plants are compatible. Using this, you can determine which upright plants, for example, would be suitable for a warm and sunny position, or for a warm and shady one—thus allowing you to choose easily between different plants that are suitable for a given position.

Choosing plants and flowers
Plants come in such an overwhelming variety of shapes, sizes and colors and, depending on their origins, need a variety of different conditions: in order to choose the right ones for your home, you need to be aware of both their decorative qualities and growing needs.

How to use The Plant Finder's Guide

For easy reference, *The Plant Finder's Guide* is divided into three separate guides: one for house plants, one for cut flowers and one for dried flowers.

The guide to house plants contains almost 150 color photographs of the most widely used indoor plants, each with a detailed entry. Most of the entries are arranged in eight different shape categories: upright, arching, weeping, rosette-shaped, bushy, climbing, trailing and creeping. Of course, plants change shape as they grow and these categories are generalizations only. Each category is then sub-divided according to the shape and size of the leaves: large-leaved plants are those with leaves over 6in in length; small-leaved plants have leaves less than 6in in length; and com-pound-leaved plants have leaves divided into two or more leaf segments. There are separate sections in the guide for flowering bulbs, and for cacti and succulents, which are arranged according to their own shape categories. At the end of the house plant section there is a photographic color guide to a selection of flowering house plants, running through the spectrum from white to violet, and there is also a seasonal guide, in the form of a chart, to indicate their flowering or fruiting periods.

Within *The guide to cut flowers*, the flower entries are arranged according to season and the foliage entries are organized according to color. Each entry describes how to use and prepare the material and, of the 100 entries, 85 have a color photograph.

The guide to dried flowers is separated into flowers themselves, arranged according to color, and into other dried material, arranged according to type. A total of 65 species have been photographed and each has an entry giving advice on how to use it and on the best method of drying.

Symbols give additional information in all three guides.

SAMPLE PAGES

The guide to house plants

The plants are classified by their pattern of growth and foliage characteristics. An introduction to each group describes the main characteristics of the plants contained within it. Every plant has a color photograph. A key to the symbols used in the guide is given.

Common name in bold type. Scientific name (genus and species) in italics, fol-lowed by hybrid/cultivar name where applicable

A general description of each plant, mentioning its main decorative qualities and how to use it

Size entry gives the maximum dimensions of the plant and tells you in what form it is offered for sale

Feeding entry gives advice on the most suitable fertilizer and how often to use it

Potting entry gives compre-hensive advice on when and how to pot the plant, and the type of potting mixture to use

ELATIOR BEGONIA
Begonia "Elatior" hybrids

These begonias flower for most of the year. The large, rose-like flowers range in colour from deep red through pink to yellow and white. They are best treated as annuals and discarded when flowering has finished. The foliage is usually pale green but plants with deep-red foliage are sometimes available. As their flowers are quite large, these begonias can be displayed as specimen plants or grouped together in a shallow pan. Elatior begonias do best in light, well-ventilated rooms.

Mini-climate 2 Warm, filtered sun.
Size "Elatior" begonias are usually erect with a maximum height and spread of 35-40cm. Small bushy plants are offered for sale from mid-spring to early autumn.
Feeding Feed with standard liquid fertilizer every two weeks in spring and summer.
Potting Repot two or three times during summer and autumn using a mixture of half soil-based potting mixture and half leaf mould or coarse peat moss. If you don't want to move an older plant into a larger pot topdress instead.
Special points Protect from powdery mildew by supplying adequate ventilation.

Similar-shaped species
Begonia tuberhybrida has large, double flowers of red, pink, white or yellow.

Plant care symbols give a pictorial summary of each plant's needs: temperature, light, humidity, watering and ease of care

Mini-climate categorization enables you to see at a glance which plants are compatible and can be displayed together

Special points (where applic-able) for keeping a plant in a healthy state

Similar-shaped species entry (where applicable) lists similar plants of the same genus and describes how they differ from the featured plant

How to use the symbols

The guide to house plants

Temperature

Cool with winter rest Keep plants cool from spring to autumn, 50°-60°F being ideal, and 45°-50°F in winter if possible.

Cool The plants, which thrive in a cool climate, prefer a year-long temperature around 50°-60°F, if possible.

Warm These plants, which prefer warmth, thrive between 60° and 70°F all year, but endure higher or lower ranges for reasonable periods.

Light

Sunny A sunny position is one near a south-, east- or west-facing window which receives unobstructed direct sunlight.

Filtered sun This is indirect sunlight, which shines through a translucent curtain or blind, or is baffled by a leafy tree outside a window.

Shady A shady position is one close to a north-facing window, or to the side of an east- or west-facing one which receives no direct or indirect sun.

Humidity

Low humidity The air surrounding the plant should be approximately 30-40 per cent saturated with water. Few plants tolerate low humidity.

Moderate humidity The air surrounding the plant should be approximately 60 per cent satu-rated with water.

High humidity The air surrounding the plant should be approximately 80 per cent saturated with water.

Watering

Water sparingly This involves barely moist-ening the whole mixture, and allowing it to dry out almost completely each time.

Water moderately This refers to moistening the entire mixture, but allowing the top inch or so to dry out before watering again.

The guide to cut flowers

Cut flowers and berries are classified according to their seasonal availability, and foliage is classified according to its color. An introduction to each section describes the variety of material available. A key to the symbols used in the guide is given.

The guide to dried flowers

Dried material is classified according to color or type. An introduction to each section describes the variety of material available and gives general suggestions on how to use it. Color photographs show examples. A key to the symbols used in the guide is given.

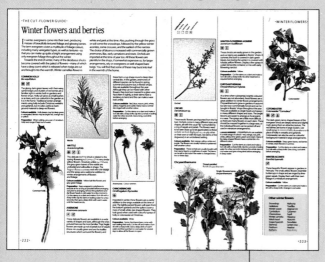

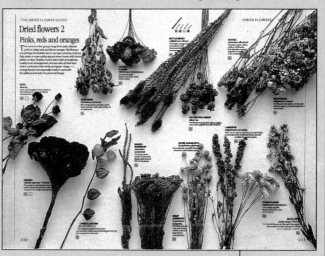

Common name in bold type. Scientific name (genus and species) in italics followed by hybrid/cultivar name of flower or foliage where applicable

Symbols show whether the flowers are fragrant, long-lasting, have useful foliage or are suitable for drying

Description of how to use the flowers/ foliage and what to mix them with

Colors available (flowers only)

Advice on how to prepare and condition the flowers/foliage

ANEMONE
Anemone coronaria

These delicate flowers are available in a wide variety of shapes and sizes, although the ones pictured here are the most familiar. Their fragile flowers are made up not of petals but of sepals (these are usually green and are the leaf like structures which surround the flower), and these form a cup shape round a deep-blue central disc. In the garden, anemones of different species can be found in spring, summer and autumn but, in florists' shops, they are available throughout the year. Although they can be mixed with other flowers, they look best massed in a glass vase. Pack them in tightly, as their stems have a tendency to bend and this can make a vase look untidy.

Colours available Red, blue, mauve, pink, white, yellow, magenta and scarlet. Many have a central disc ringed with another colour.

Preparation Cut the stems on a slant and make a 5cm slit with a sharp knife. Dip the cut ends in boiling water for a few seconds. Give a long, cool drink before arranging.

Common name in bold type. Scientific name (genus and species) in italics followed by hybrid/cultivar name where applicable

Advice on decorative uses, and details of any other colors which are available

Symbols give the most suitable method of drying the material

CELOSIA
Celosia argentea "Cristata"
The purple or pink blooms have a mossy texture and provide dramatic focal point for a large arrangement.

Water plentifully This means keeping all of the potting mixture moist at all times, not letting even the surface dry out.

Care

Easy Plants which are termed "easy" to care for are those which can be grown successfully with only the minimum of attention.

Fairly easy Plants in this category require the basic care plus some attention to their individual growing needs.

Challenging These plants must be provided with their very specific growing needs or they will not thrive.

The guide to cut flowers

Long lasting Flowers or leaves which remain attractive for a particularly long time when cut.

Useful foliage Flowers whose own leaves are suitable for using in any arrangement, with or without that particular flower.

Fragrant Flowers which have a pleasant scent.

Suitable for drying Flowers, or their seed heads, or foliage which can be successfully preserved and used in dried displays.

The guide to dried flowers

Air-dried This refers to plant material dried naturally, without the use of chemicals, and usually involves hanging material upside-down in bunches.

Glycerine method This method involves standing foliage stems, or immersing leaves, in a solution of glycerine which, when absorbed by plant cells, preserves them.

Silica/borax This process uses desiccants which absorb moisture from the plant material, retaining its lifelike appearance when dried.

Pressing This is a mechanical method which preserves leaves or flowers by means of compression but does not retain the original shape.

Upright plants 1

These are plants with a distinctly vertical habit of growth. They vary in size from the treelike crotons and large-leaved rubber plants to relatively low-growing species such as the pileas and calatheas. Some of the treelike plants in this category, such as the yucca, have a central unbranched stem with leaves at the top only. Others, such as the Norfolk Island pine and the false aralia, have a central, upright stem with branches at intervals along it. Not all upright plants have both stems and leaves. The mother-in-law's tongue is stemless, with the leaves rising directly out of the potting mixture. Many upright plants, which otherwise grow too tall for a domestic setting, can be made into shorter, rounder shrubs by pinching out the main growing shoot or tip and allowing side-stem growth to develop; the rubber plant is a good example of this. Leaf shape differs widely within the group and leaf size varies from under 6in to over 2ft. Leaf color is also well represented; from the green-and-cream leaves of the spotted dumb cane to the red leaf markings of the croton. There are some beautiful flowering upright plants including the spectacular bird-of-paradise flower and the delicate flowering maple. With this range of form and size you can find plants for very different situations: imposing specimen plants, such as the Norfolk Island pine, which look best displayed on their own; plants of more modest size which contrast well with low-growing, creeping or trailing plants, and spiky-leaved plants which mix well with the rounded shapes of some cacti.

SMALL-LEAVED UPRIGHT PLANTS

CALAMONDIN ORANGE
Citrofortunella mitis

These ornamental orange trees bear fragrant flowers, unripe green fruits and ripe orange fruits all at the same time. The oranges produced are small and bitter but are excellent for making marmalade. The plants will fruit when still quite young and are best as specimen plants or arranged in formal groups.

Mini-climate 4 Cool, sunny.
Size Orange trees take several years to reach a maximum height of 3-6ft with a similar spread. Small specimens bearing fruit are offered for sale.
Feeding Feed every two weeks with a tomato-type fertilizer all year except in winter.
Potting Repot in spring using soil-based potting mixture but only if the roots have completely filled the existing pot. If you don't want to move an older plant into a larger pot topdress instead.
Special points Susceptible to scale insects. Prune to keep plants shapely and compact.

Similar-shaped species
Citrus limon will produce lemons of up to 3in in diameter.
Citrus sinensis is the only species which produces sweet fruit. Its stems have sharp spines.

ALUMINIUM PLANT
Pilea cadierei

The raised, silver leaf markings give the foliage of these attractive plants a quilted look. This effect is caused by pockets of air under the upper surface of the leaf. Group them with other attractively marked plants, or mass dwarf varieties together in a shallow bowl or in a bottle garden or terrarium.

Mini-climate 2 Warm, filtered sun.
Size Aluminium plants will reach a height of about 1ft in one year. A dwarf variety is available, which reaches a maximum height of about 6in.
Feeding Feed with standard liquid fertilizer every two weeks in spring and summer.
Potting Repot every spring using a mixture of two-thirds peat moss and one-third coarse sand or perlite. Once plants are in 3in pots topdress instead.

Similar-shaped species
Pilea spruceana has triangular, quilted, bronze-green leaves with a silver stripe down the middle.

FLOWERING MAPLE
Abutilon hybridum "Canary Bird"

Flowering maples are pretty, woody plants which can be trained when young. They have maplelike leaves from whose leaf-joints come the bell-shaped flowers. The flowers of the hybrids are red, pink, yellow or white. Flowering maples are long-lasting, making them suitable for use as feature plants, especially in front of a window.

Mini-climate 1 Warm, sunny.
Size Flowering maples may reach a height and spread of 3ft in three years. Pinch out growing tips to maintain bushy growth.
Feeding Feed with standard liquid fertilizer every two weeks in summer.
Potting Repot every spring using soil-based potting mixture. Once plants are in 10in pots topdress instead.
Special points Water more sparingly in winter and cut back any untidy stems in spring.

Similar-shaped species
Abutilon pictum "Thompsonii" has green and yellow variegated leaves and flowers which may be composed of one color, two colors or two shades of the same color.

LARGE-LEAVED UPRIGHT PLANTS

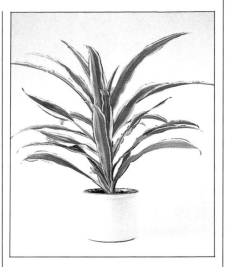

TI PLANT
Cordyline terminalis

These plants have large leaves patterned in red or green. The patterns of leaf coloring vary from plant to plant and ti plants look impressive when massed together to form a tapestry of color in a warm room containing richly colored fabrics.

Mini-climate 2 Warm, filtered sun.
Size Ti plants can grow to a height of 4ft with a spread of 1½ft. Small plants are offered for sale.
Feeding Feed with standard liquid fertilizer every two weeks from April to September.
Potting Repot every two years in spring using soil-based potting mixture. If you don't want to move an older plant into a larger pot topdress instead.
Special points Water more sparingly in winter. Clean leaves with a damp sponge.

RUBBER PLANT
Ficus elastica

The shiny, dark-green leaves are oval in shape with a pronounced point at their tip. The growth point is covered in a pink sheath for protection. Rubber plants have a strong shape and look best displayed as specimen plants in a modern setting.

Mini-climate 3 Warm, shady.
Size Rubber plants can grow up to 6ft in height. Plants of all sizes are offered for sale.
Feeding Feed with standard liquid fertilizer every two weeks in spring and summer.
Potting Repot in spring using soil-based potting mixture but only if the roots have completely filled the existing pot. If you don't want to move an older plant into a larger pot topdress instead.
Special points Clean older leaves regularly with a damp sponge. Do not clean young leaves.

Similar-shaped species
Ficus lyrata has huge puckered leaves which are shaped like a violin.

BELGIAN EVERGREEN
Dracaena sanderana

Also known as "ribbon plants", these are the most dainty of the dracaenas. They are slender, upright plants with narrow, cream-striped leaves. Because they rarely branch, three or four specimens should be planted together in a pot to create an interesting spiky mass of leaves.

Mini-climate 2 Warm, filtered sun.
Size Belgian evergreens are slow-growing but will reach a maximum height of 3ft. Small plants, usually three to a pot, are offered for sale.
Feeding Feed with standard liquid fertilizer every two weeks from mid-spring to early autumn.
Potting Repot every two or three years in spring using soil-based potting mixture. Once plants are in 4½-5in pots topdress instead.
Special points Water more sparingly in winter.

SPOTTED DUMB CANE
Dieffenbachia maculata

Spotted dumb canes are bold feature plants with handsome, variegated leaves. Older plants tend to lose their lower leaves giving a solitary plant a bizarre look; but several plants grouped together make a dramatic display in a modern setting.

Mini-climate 3 Warm, shady.
Size Spotted dumb canes will grow to a height of 5ft and a spread of 2ft. Plants of all sizes are offered for sale.
Feeding Feed with standard liquid fertilizer every two weeks from early spring to mid-autumn.
Potting Repot every spring using soil-based potting mixture in clay pots. Once plants are in 8in pots topdress instead.
Special points The sap is poisonous and can cause severe inflammation of the mouth.

Similar-shaped species
Dieffenbachia amoena has 1½ft long, pointed leaves which are dark green with herringbone markings in cream.
Dieffenbachia "Exotica" has 10in long dark-green leaves marked with white and pale green.

Upright plants 2

LARGE-LEAVED UPRIGHT PLANTS continued

CROTON
Codiaeum variegatum pictum

Crotons are striking, highly colored, tropical shrubs with many variations in leaf shape, size and color. Young leaves have a green color; reds, oranges and purples develop with age. Crotons naturally drop their lower leaves with age but will retain them longer in a humid atmosphere. Mass plants with different colored leaves for a vivid display.

Mini-climate 1 Warm, sunny.
Size Crotons rarely grow larger than 3ft tall, with a similar spread. Small and medium-sized plants are offered for sale.
Feeding Feed with standard liquid fertilizer every two weeks from spring to autumn.
Potting Repot every spring using soil-based potting mixture. When plants are in 8-10in pots topdress instead.
Special points Stand plants on trays filled with moist pebbles to increase humidity.

AFRICAN HEMP
Sparmannia africana

Also known as "indoor limes", these plants have large, apple-green leaves, covered in fine, white hairs. A plant blooming in a cool room can produce clusters of small, white flowers nearly all year round. African hemp plants look best displayed on their own as feature plants in both modern and traditional settings.

Mini-climate 4 Cool, sunny.
Size African hemps grow to about 5ft in height with a spread of 3ft wide in two years. Small plants are offered for sale.
Feeding Feed with standard liquid fertilizer every two weeks.
Potting Repot in spring using soil-based potting mixture but only if the roots have completely filled the existing pot. Once plants are in 12in pots topdress instead.
Special points Water more sparingly in winter.

SILVERED SPEAR
Aglaonema crispum "Silver Queen"

The beautiful foliage of these plants is green only at the margins and main veins; the rest of the leaf is silvery-white and cream. As plants age they lose some of their lower leaves and develop a short, trunklike stem. They are excellent as part of a bold, leafy arrangement, particularly if contrasted with dark-green foliage plants.

Mini-climate 2 Warm, filtered sun.
Size Silvered spears reach a maximum height of 3ft with a spread of about 2ft.
Feeding Feed with standard liquid fertilizer once a month from spring to autumn.
Potting Repot every spring using soil-based potting mixture. Once plants are in 6in pots topdress instead.

BIRD-OF-PARADISE
Strelitzia reginae

These plants have spectacular orange-and-blue crested flowers which emerge in succession over a period of several weeks from a beak-shaped bud. Birds-of-paradise are unusual specimen plants for a modern interior; a large-scale setting is best as leaves and flowers become very big.

Mini-climate 1 Warm, sunny.
Size Birds-of-paradise will grow to 3ft in height with a spread of 2ft. Young plants are offered for sale but will not flower until they are five years old.
Feeding Feed with standard liquid fertilizer every two weeks in spring and summer and once a month in autumn and winter.
Potting Repot every spring using soil-based potting mixture. Once plants are in 12in pots topdress instead.
Special points Clean leaves with a damp sponge.

Temperature 50°–60°F spring to autumn, 45°–50°F in winter 50°–60°F 60°–70°F

Light sunny filtered sun shady

Humidity low moderate high

Watering sparingly moderately plentifully

Care easy fairly easy challenging

CAST-IRON PLANT
Aspidistra elatior

As their name suggests, cast-iron plants will tolerate a certain amount of neglect. They were much used by the Victorians as specimen plants, but despite these associations, cast-iron plants can be used to great effect, either massed together or grouped with other, smaller plants. They are ideal plants for filling difficult, darker spaces.

Mini-climate 5 Cool, filtered sun.
Size Cast-iron plants have a maximum height and spread of 3ft. Small plants are offered for sale.
Feeding Feed with standard liquid fertilizer every two weeks in spring and summer.
Potting Repot every three years using soil-based potting mixture but only if the roots have completely filled the existing pot. If you don't want to move an older plant into a larger pot topdress instead.

TREE IVY
Fatshedera lizei

Also known as "aralia ivies", these plants have palmate, glossy-green leaves and can be displayed as upright feature plants, either alone or to give height to a group of smaller plants. They will also climb and can be trained, if tied to supports, to cover staircases and balcor and to frame windows.

Mini-climate 5 Cool, filtered sun.
Size Tree ivies can grow upright to a height of 3ft with a similar spread. If allowed to wander over a support their growth will be unlimited.
Feeding Feed with standard liquid fertilizer every two weeks.
Potting Repot every spring using two-thirds soil-based potting mixture and one-third peat-moss. If you don't want to move an older plant into a larger pot topdress instead.

PEACOCK PLANT
Calathea makoyana

The leaves of peacock plants look as if they have been hand painted with dark-green patterns. They look best in a mixed group of foliage plants. Smaller plants can be used in bottle gardens and larger terraria.

Mini-climate 3 Warm, shady.
Size Peacock plants can grow to a height of 3ft with a spread of about 2ft. Plants of all sizes are offered for sale.
Feeding Feed with standard liquid fertilizer every two weeks during spring and summer and once a month during autumn and winter.
Potting Repot every spring using a mixture of two-thirds soil-based potting mixture and one-third leaf mold or peat. Once plants are in 6in pots topdress instead.
Special points Stand plants on trays filled with moist pebbles to increase humidity.

COMPOUND-LEAVED UPRIGHT PLANTS

FALSE ARALIA
Dizygotheca elegantissima

Also known as "finger aralias", these plants are elegant, open shrubs made up of many narrow leaflets. Leaf color changes with age from bronze to a very deep green and the leaf texture becomes coarser. The dark tracery of the palmate leaves makes a delicate background to set off bolder foliage, or several plants can be grouped together to create a lacy mass of leaves.

Mini-climate 2 Warm, filtered sun.
Size False aralias reach 7ft in height with a spread of 2ft. Pinch out growing tips to encourage bushy growth. Plants of all sizes are offered for sale.
Feeding Feed with standard liquid fertilizer every two weeks in spring and summer.
Potting Repot every two years in spring using soil-based potting mixture. If you don't want to move an older plant into a larger pot topdress instead.
Special points Stand plants on trays filled with moist pebbles to increase humidity.

Upright plants 3

COMPOUND-LEAVED UPRIGHT PLANTS continued

NORFOLK ISLAND PINE
Araucaria heterophylla

Also known as "Christmas tree plants", these pines are at their best when four years old. Because of their starkness, they seldom look well mixed with other plants, but a most striking effect can be created by grouping several of these conifers together to give a Japanese look.

Mini-climate 5 Cool, filtered sun.
Size Norfolk Island pines are slow-growing: a ten-year old plant rarely exceeds 6ft in height and 4ft width.
Feeding Feed with standard liquid fertilizer every two weeks in spring and summer.
Potting Repot every two or three years in spring using soil-based potting mixture. Once plants are in 9-10in pots topdress instead.
Special points Water more sparingly during the winter rest period.

SILK OAK
Grevillea robusta

Silk oaks are treelike evergreen shrubs with finely divided, fernlike leaves. The leaves are bronze when they first appear, turning green later. They look good grouped with other plants and, when they are large enough, displayed as specimen plants.

Mini-climate 4 Cool, sunny.
Size Silk oaks are fast growing and will reach 5ft high in two or three years. Encourage bushy growth by pinching the main shoot when young. Young plants are offered for sale.
Feeding Feed with standard liquid fertilizer every two weeks during spring and summer.
Potting Repot every spring using lime-free soil-based potting mixture. If you don't want to move an older plant into a larger pot topdress instead.
Special points Water more sparingly in winter.

UMBRELLA PLANT
Cyperus alternifolius "Gracilis"

The radiating grasslike bracts of these plants resemble the spokes of an open umbrella. The tall stems are very brittle and should be handled with care. Umbrella plants have a Japanese look and suit stark modern interiors.

Mini-climate 2 Warm, filtered sun.
Size Umbrella plants will reach a height of 4ft given suitably wet conditions.
Feeding Feed with standard liquid fertilizer once every month.
Potting Repot in spring using soil-based potting mixture with added charcoal, but only if the roots have completely filled the existing pot. Ensure plants are repotted at the same soil level. If you don't want to move an older plant into a larger pot topdress instead.
Special points Stand permanently in a water-filled saucer to keep the roots saturated.

SPIKY-LEAVED UPRIGHT PLANTS

BOAT LILY
Rhoeo spathacea "Variegata"

These plants are also known as "Moses-in-the-cradle", referring to the boat-shaped cups which encase the small, white, three-petalled flowers. The long, rather stiff leaves are beautifully colored, having yellow and cream stripes on their upper surface and purple on their lower surface. Boat lilies are best displayed on their own so that the unusual flower-cups can be seen.

Mini-climate 2 Warm, filtered sun.
Size Boat lilies reach a maximum height of 1ft with a spread of 1½ft. Plants of this size are offered for sale. Maintain as an upright plant by pinching off basal shoots.
Feeding Feed with standard liquid fertilizer every two weeks in spring and summer.
Potting Repot every second year in spring using soil-based potting mixture. If you don't want to move an older plant into a larger pot topdress instead.

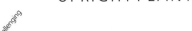

EUROPEAN FAN PALM
Chamaerops humilis

Also known as "dwarf fan palms", these handsome, low-growing palms have wide, fan-shaped fronds. These are made up of rigid, sword-shaped segments with split ends. There is no recognizable stem, except in very mature plants, the fronds being held upright on long leaf stalks. These are ornamental plants with an oriental look to them to be used as specimens or in groups depending on their size.

Mini-climate 2 Warm, filtered sun.
Size European fan palms are slow-growing, but will reach 5ft in height with a similar spread when mature. Plants of all sizes are offered for sale.
Feeding Feed with standard liquid fertilizer once a month in spring, summer and autumn.
Potting Repot every two years in spring using soil-based potting mixture. Once plants are in 12in pots topdress instead.
Special points Stand plants outside in a sheltered place in summer. Water more sparingly in winter.

MOTHER-IN-LAW'S TONGUE
Sansevieria trifasciata "Laurentii"

The upright leaves of this plant emerge in a cluster from an underground stem. The thick, leathery leaves are marbled with dark green and have golden bands along their margin. Display large plants as specimens or group them with other spiky-leaved plants in a modern setting.

Mini-climate 2 Warm, filtered sun.
Size The leaves of mother-in-law's tongues can grow to a height of about 3ft. Plants of all sizes are offered for sale.
Feeding Feed with half-strength standard liquid fertilizer once a month.
Potting Repot in spring or early summer, using a mixture of one-third coarse sand or perlite and two-thirds soil-based potting mixture, but only when a mass of roots appears on the surface. If you don't want to move an older plant into a larger pot topdress instead.
Special points Water more sparingly in winter.

RAINBOW PLANT
Dracaena marginata "Tricolor"

The name "rainbow plant" is derived from the leaf markings, which form stripes of green, cream and pink. In mature plants, the topknot of leaves emerges from the bare, woody stem, giving plants a palmlike look. Three or four specimens planted in the same pot make a good display in a modern setting.

Mini-climate 2 Warm, filtered sun.
Size Rainbow plants will grow to 5ft with a spread of 1½ft. Lower-growing plants are offered for sale, but there is more demand for older plants with bare stems.
Feeding Feed with standard liquid fertilizer every two weeks in spring and summer, and once a month in autumn and winter.
Potting Repot every spring using soil-based potting mixture. If you don't want to move an older plant into a larger pot topdress instead.
Special points Water more sparingly in winter.

STICK YUCCA
Yucca elephantipes

These plants have a very distinctive appearance. Many are specially grown from logs which, when planted, produce roots and leaves. The leaves are long and narrow, and can appear in clumps at any point of the upright stem. Yuccas have a strong shape and should be displayed on their own, or with other spiky-leaved plants in a modern setting.

Mini-climate 1 Warm, sunny.
Size Yuccas up to 6½ft in height with a spread of 1½ft are offered for sale. The spread increases as more leaves are produced. Plants can also be bought which are virtually stemless; these are known as "tip yuccas".
Feeding Feed with standard liquid fertilizer once every month.
Potting Repot every spring using soil-based potting mixture. If you don't want to move an older plant into a larger pot topdress instead.
Special points Water more sparingly in winter.

Arching plants 1

The overall shape of the plants in this category is determined by the way the stems, leafstalks or fronds branch out in an arch from the base of the plant. Because of this, most of the arching plants take up a great deal of space when fully grown and are best displayed on their own. Indeed, the largest arching plants, with their strong architectural shapes, make striking additions to the modern interior. Also in this category are three plants, the ponytail, West Indian holly and weeping fig, whose leaves hang downwards to give a "weeping" effect.

There is a great variety of leaf shape and texture in this category, ranging from the smooth, lance-shaped leaves of the white sails to the deeply cut leaves of some philodendrons and the delicate leaflets of the ferns and palms.

The diversity of leaf shape among arching plants compensates for the lack of colorful foliage in the group, and some species, such as the wax plant and white sails, produce very attractive flowers.

The graceful lines of the Boston and hare's foot ferns are produced by the arching fronds and are best appreciated when viewed at eye-level, as is the flat-topped button fern: display them in an urn, a tall terracotta pot or hanging basket. Plants such as the bamboo palm, the Kentia palm and the coconut palm can grow to quite a size and older plants are dominant enough to become the focal point of a room. Arching plants are among the most elegant of plants and should ideally be displayed in a position where they can be seen from all angles.

SMALL-LEAVED ARCHING PLANTS

FUCHSIA BEGONIA
Begonia foliosa miniata

These delicate-looking begonias have small, oval leaves with a glossy texture. The leaves are borne on long, thin stems which begin to arch over as they get longer. Small, waxy, succulent-looking, shell-pink flowers appear in clusters between autumn and spring. The plants need some kind of support if they are to be seen to best effect. Display with green foliage groups in an informal setting.

They are attractive if allowed to trail from a hanging basket.

Mini-climate 1 Warm, sunny.
Size Fuchsia begonias can grow to about 3ft in height, with a spread of about 20in. Pinch out growing tips to maintain bushy growth. Small plants are offered for sale.
Feeding Feed with standard liquid fertilizer once every two weeks during the flowering period.
Potting Repot every spring using an equal-parts mixture of soil-based and peat-based potting mixture. If you don't want to move an older plant into a larger pot topdress instead.
Special points Water more sparingly in winter.

BUTTON FERN
Pellaea rotundifolia

These unusual-looking ferns have low, spreading fronds making them one of the few ferns with an almost horizontal outline. The pinnae of the fronds are also most unfernlike, consisting of leathery, button-shaped leaflets arranged in a row, one on either side of a stiff midrib. These leaflets weigh the fronds down to give an arching appearance. Button ferns make excellent infill plants to hide foreground pots in groups of plants. Display with plants of varying leaf texture in a modern setting for best effect. They can also be used in bottle gardens and terraria.

Mini-climate 3 Warm, shady.
Size The individual fronds of button ferns grow to a maximum of 1ft long, giving the plant a wide but very flat shape.
Feeding Feed with standard liquid fertilizer every two weeks.
Potting Repot in spring using fern potting mixture in a shallow pot, but only if the roots have completely filled the existing pot. If you don't want to move an older plant into a larger pot, prune the roots to curb growth.
Special points Button ferns can be placed outside in a sheltered shady spot in summer. Stand plants on trays filled with moist pebbles to increase humidity.

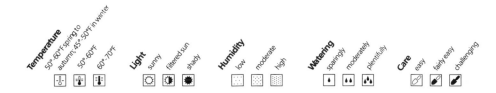

LARGE-LEAVED ARCHING PLANTS

FINGER PLANT
Philodendron bipinnatifidum

The leaves of these plants are heart-shaped in outline with deeply cut edges. The leaves are borne on stout stalks radiating from a central stem and unlike most of the other philodendron species these plants do not climb. They make dramatic feature plants for a large room.

Mini-climate 3 Warm, shady.
Size Finger plants can reach a height and spread of about 3-6ft. Plants of all sizes are offered for sale.
Feeding Feed with standard liquid fertilizer every two weeks in spring and summer.
Potting Repot in spring using half soil-based potting mixture and half leaf mold, but only if the roots have completely filled the existing pot. Once plants are in 12in pots topdress instead.
Special points Destroy any scale insects you find.

WHITE SAILS
Spathiphyllum "Clevelandii"

The striking arumlike flower heads of the white sails are produced from May to August. Each flower lasts for six weeks or more, turning from white to an attractive pale green. Their elegant shape makes them ideal specimen plants for the modern interior.

Mini-climate 3 Warm, shady.
Size Mature white sails can reach a height and spread of 3ft. Plants in flower are offered for sale.
Feeding Feed with standard liquid fertilizer every two weeks from early spring to late summer.
Potting Repot every two years in spring using peat-based potting mixture. Once plants are in a 6-8in pot root prune instead.
Special points Stand plants on trays filled with moist pebbles to increase humidity.

COCONUT PALM
Cocos nucifera

These most striking looking plants grow directly from the nut which sits on top of the potting mixture. From the nut sprout the upright stalks which bear the once-divided, arching fronds. These fronds are heavily ribbed. The coconut palm makes a striking specimen plant for a stark modern interior.

Mini-climate 2 Warm, filtered sun.
Size Coconut palms can reach more than 5ft in height. Large plants are offered for sale.
Feeding Feed with half-strength liquid fertilizer every two weeks in spring and summer.
Potting Repotting is unnecessary.
Special points Coconut palms only last about two years in the home as they resent root disturbance.

COMPOUND-LEAVED ARCHING PLANTS

HARE'S FOOT FERN
Polypodium aureum "Mandaianum"

These plants derive their common name from the furry rhizome from which the fronds arise. The fronds are carried on long, arching stems and each bears up to ten silvery blue-green leaflets. Each leaflet has a ruffled edge. Since their color is so attractive, hare's foot ferns should be displayed as feature plants when they are large enough. Smaller plants mix well with other ferns.

Mini-climate 3 Warm, shady.
Size The fronds of the hare's foot fern can grow to about 2ft in length giving the plant a large spread. Plants of all sizes are offered for sale.
Feeding Feed with half-strength standard liquid fertilizer once a week from spring to autumn.
Potting Repot in spring using half soil-based potting mixture and half leaf mold in a shallow container, but only if the rhizomes have completely filled the existing pot. Once plants are in 8in pots root prune instead.
Special points Stand plants on trays filled with moist pebbles to increase humidity.

Arching plants 2

COMPOUND-LEAVED ARCHING PLANTS continued

KENTIA PALM
Howea belmoreana

These slender palms were great favorites in the 19th century, adding soft grace to large rooms. The arching fronds are borne on upright stems giving the plant an elegant look. Always specimen plants, Kentia palms can be difficult to place due to their large size but seem to thrive in a range of conditions found in the home.

Mini-climate 2 Warm, filtered sun.
Size Kentia palms can grow to 10ft with a spread of 8ft. Medium and large plants are offered for sale.
Feeding Feed with standard liquid fertilizer once a month from spring to autumn.
Potting Repot every second year in spring using soil-based potting mixture. Once plants are in 12in pots topdress instead.
Special points Clean leaves with a damp sponge.

Similar-shaped species
Howea forsterana is very similar and can only be told apart by the greater, flat-topped spread and wider gaps between the frond leaflets of this species.

DWARF COCONUT PALM
Microcoelum weddellianum

These compact palms have shiny fronds which are deeply divided into many threadlike leaflets arranged in a herringbone fashion. Although the fronds look feathery they are quite tough to the touch. Dwarf coconut palms have no true trunk; the fronds arise from a short, thickened base. They are not as arching as the larger types and are therefore suitable for use on table tops or shelves.

Mini-climate 2 Warm, filtered sun.
Size Dwarf coconut palms reach a maximum height and spread of 3ft. Small plants are offered for sale all year.
Feeding Feed with standard liquid fertilizer once a month in summer.
Potting Repot every two years in spring using soil-based potting mixture. If you don't want to move an older plant into a larger pot topdress instead.

BAMBOO PALM
Rhapis excelsa

Also known as "little lady palms", these plants have stems which cluster together giving the plant a crowded look. The leaves are composed of five to nine, often blunt-tipped segments giving an overall fan-shaped look. Each segment is deeply cut. Display the bamboo palm with other dark-green foliage plants. Older plants lose their lower leaves making them suitable for displaying on their own.

Mini-climate 2 Warm, filtered sun.
Size Bamboo palms are slow-growing taking several years to reach a height of 5-10ft tall with a similar spread. Medium and large plants are offered for sale.
Feeding Feed with standard liquid fertilizer once a month during the active growing period.
Potting Repot every second year in spring using soil-based potting mixture. Once plants are in 12in pots topdress instead.

BOSTON FERN
Nephrolepis exaltata "Bostoniensis"

These lush but graceful ferns have swordlike fronds which are available in several forms: some with crested fronds, others with very finely divided leaf sections. Boston ferns make elegant specimen plants, used either on a pedestal or in a hanging basket, and suit almost any type of setting.

Mini-climate 3 Warm, shady.
Size Boston ferns have fronds that are often 3ft long and can grow to 6ft. Plants of all sizes are offered for sale.
Feeding Feed with standard liquid fertilizer every two weeks when actively growing, otherwise feed once a month.
Potting Repot in spring using fern potting mixture but only if the roots have completely filled the existing pot. If you don't want to move an older plant into a larger pot topdress instead. Or divide it.
Special points Stand plants on trays filled with moist pebbles to increase humidity.

Similar-shaped species
Nephrolepis cordifolia is smaller; its fronds will grow up to 2ft long.

Temperature
50°-60°F spring to
autumn, 45°-50°F in winter
50°-60°F
60°-70°F

Light
sunny
filtered sun
shady

Humidity
low
moderate
high

Watering
sparingly
moderately
plentifully

Care
easy
fairly easy
challenging

PARLOR PALM
Chamaedorea elegans "Bella"

These palms have dainty, deeply divided fronds arching from the central stem. The fronds are fresh green when young and darken with age. Mature plants produce small sprays of tiny, yellow, beadlike flowers. Parlor palms thrive in the conditions of a bathroom, and small plants add interest to bottle gardens and terraria.

Mini-climate 2 Warm, filtered sun.
Size Parlor palms are dwarf palms reaching a height of about 3ft after several years, with a spread of 1½ft. Young plants are offered for sale.
Feeding Feed with standard liquid fertilizer once a month from spring to autumn.
Potting Repot in spring using soil-based potting mixture but only if the roots have completely filled the existing pot. Once plants are in 6-8in pots topdress instead.
Special points Water more sparingly in winter.

Similar-shaped species
Chamaedorea erumpens forms a clump of slender stems, knotted at intervals like bamboo and with sections of bare stem. They can grow to about 6-8ft in height.

WEEPING ARCHING PLANTS

WEST INDIAN HOLLY
Leea coccinea

These plants have deep-green, holly-shaped leaves which are often tinged with a coppery-red. The plant has a very open appearance as the leaves are twice divided. West Indian hollies can be used as specimen plants or as a foil for low-growing foliage plants.

Mini-climate 2 Warm, filtered sun.
Size West Indian hollies reach a maximum height of about 5ft with a similar spread. Plants of about 1ft tall with a similar spread are offered for sale.
Feeding Feed with standard liquid fertilizer every two weeks from spring to autumn.
Potting Repot every spring using soil-based potting mixture. If you don't want to move an older plant into a larger pot topdress instead.
Special points Water more sparingly in winter.

WEEPING FIG
Ficus benjamina

These plants are the most elegant of the ornamental figs with their graceful, gray-barked arching stems bearing the dangling, pointed leaves. The arrangement of the leaves gives the plant an open appearance; good for both modern and period interiors.

Mini-climate 3 Warm, shady.
Size Weeping figs have a maximum height of 5ft with a spread of about 4ft if given enough room. Medium-sized and large plants are offered for sale.
Feeding Feed with standard liquid fertilizer every two weeks in spring and summer.
Potting Repot in spring using a soil-based potting mixture but only if the roots have completely filled the existing pot. If you don't want to move an older plant into a larger pot topdress instead.
Special points Water more sparingly in winter.

PONYTAIL
Beaucarnea recurvata

These are most bizarre-looking plants, having a ponytail-like tuft of narrow, green leaves sprouting from the top of a fat or long, woody stem. The swollen base adds to the unusual appearance of the plant. Ponytails are ideal plants for displaying in a modern interior and will thrive in any centrally heated room.

Mini-climate 2 Warm, filtered sun.
Size Ponytails reach a maximum height of 5ft with a spread of 2ft. Small and medium-sized plants are offered for sale.
Feeding Feed with standard liquid fertilizer every month during summer.
Potting Repot every three or four years in spring using soil-based potting mixture. Ponytails thrive in small pots.
Special points Can easily be killed by overwatering.

Rosette-shaped plants 1

This category is made up of plants whose leaves radiate from a central growing point and overlap each other, forming a circular cluster of leaf bases, usually at potting mixture level. Plants can be small and low-growing, or tall with large leaves: the shape of the cluster varies from the flat-leaved rosette of low-growing plants, such as African violets and earth stars, to the tall, arching rosette of the bird's nest fern and the blue-flowered torch. Another variation is the spiky-leaved rosette formed by the variegated pineapple plant and the scarlet star. These plants look good displayed on their own as they have such strong shapes. Flat-leaved rosette-shaped plants should be massed and placed where they can be seen from above.

Many of the plants in this category are from the bromeliad family and originate from tropical America. They are striking, exotic-looking plants which often have bold and unusual flower spikes, or leaves which become suffused with strong color prior to, and during, the flowering period. The leaves of many bromeliads, such as the urn plant and the bird's nest bromeliad, form a cup-shaped central reservoir which should be kept topped with fresh water if the plant is to remain in good condition.

Many bromeliads are epiphytic; in their native tropical environment they grow on trees—using them only as a means of support, not as a source of nutrients. An effective way to display them, therefore, is on a natural-looking support such as a dried branch covered in moist sphagnum moss, or attach them to a large piece of cork or bark.

ARCHING ROSETTE-SHAPED PLANTS

URN PLANT
Aechmea fasciata

When three or four years old, these plants produce a drumstick-shaped inflorescence which rises from the center of the rosette. This flower head comprises many spiny, pink bracts through which peep short-lived, pale-blue flowers. The head remains attractive for about six months. The leathery leaves are marked with white cross-banding on a gray-green background. Display large plants as specimens, or grow small plants on a dried branch covered with sphagnum moss.

Mini-climate 1 Warm, sunny.
Size The leaves of urn plants reach 2ft long and the flower spikes grow 6in above the leaves. Small plants grown from offsets and mature plants are offered for sale.
Feeding Feed with half-strength standard liquid fertilizer once a month in spring and summer. Apply feed to the center of the rosette as well as the roots.
Potting Repot in spring using bromeliad potting mixture but only if the roots have completely filled the existing pot. Once plants are in 6in pots topdress instead.
Special points Keep the center of the rosette filled with fresh water. Change the water once a month.

FLAMING SWORD
Vriesea splendens

These bromeliads have exotically marked leaves; they are shiny green banded with deep purple. The leaves form an upright vase, from the center of which a bright-red spike of bracts emerges when the plants are several years old. Small, yellow flowers poke through the red bracts. Several plants massed make a spectacular display; alternatively, include the flaming sword with strong foliage plants or use small specimens on a dried branch covered with sphagnum moss.

Mini-climate 2 Warm, filtered sun.
Size Flaming swords can reach a height and spread of about 1½ft. The flower spike can reach 2ft in height. Plants of all sizes are offered for sale.
Feeding Feed with half-strength standard liquid fertilizer once a month. Ensure the feed gets on the leaves, roots and the central cup.
Potting Repot in spring using bromeliad potting mixture but only if the roots have completely filled the existing pot. Once plants are in 6in pots topdress instead.
Special points Keep the center of the rosette filled with fresh water except when the flower bud first appears. Change the water once a month.

Similar-shaped species
Vriesea fenestralis is a little larger with paler green leaves covered in brown markings.
Vriesea psittacina has shorter leaves which are plain green with mauve shading towards the center of the rosette.
Vriesea saundersii has a squat rosette of gray-green leaves with a dull rose-pink underside and a yellow flower spike.

QUEEN'S TEARS
Billbergia nutans

These plants have tough leaves with toothed edges. There may be many plants in the same pot, as production of offsets is prolific. During the short flowering season in May and June, the foliage is interspersed with trailing, bright-pink bracts which are very attractive. These bracts open to display the small yellow, green and purple flowers. Queen's tears are best displayed at eye-level as feature plants.

Mini-climate 1 Warm, sunny.
Size The leaves of queen's tears reach about 2ft in length. Spread depends on the number of offsets produced. Small plants are offered for sale.
Feeding Feed with standard liquid fertilizer once every two weeks during spring and summer.
Potting Repot every spring using bromeliad potting mixture. Once plants are in 6in pots topdress instead.
Special points The rosette of leaves should be cut away at the base after flowering to allow the offsets around it to develop.

BLUE-FLOWERED TORCH
Tillandsia cyanea

These are medium-sized bromeliads with stiff, arching, grassy leaves arranged in a loose rosette. When mature, the plants produce a fleshy spear-shaped flower head, made up of pinky-green overlapping bracts. This unusual flower head is flat and wide and will remain decorative for some months. Three-petalled, bright violet-blue flowers appear in succession from between the bracts. Display blue-flowered torches as feature plants.

Mini-climate 1 Warm, sunny.
Size The leaves of blue-flowered torches reach about 1ft in length. Offsets give the plant a large spread. Small plants are offered for sale.
Feeding Feed with half-strength standard liquid fertilizer once a month. This can be applied to the leaves as a foliar feed.
Potting Repot every spring using bromeliad potting mixture. Once plants are in 4in pots topdress instead.
Special points Place in a sheltered part of the garden in summer to encourage flowering.

BIRD'S NEST FERN
Asplenium nidus

These plants have shiny, apple-green fronds arranged in an upward-spreading rosette at whose base is a circle of young leaf fronds. These slowly unroll from the fibrous core of the plant. Large bird's nest ferns are too bold in shape to display with other ferns and look best either arranged on their own, or included in a mixed group of large-leaved foliage plants.

Mini-climate 3 Warm, shady.
Size The fronds of bird's nest ferns can reach 1½ft long. Young plants are offered for sale.
Feeding Feed with standard liquid fertilizer once a month.
Potting Repot in spring using fern potting mixture but only when a mass of roots appears on the surface of the potting mixture. If you don't want to move an older plant into a larger pot root prune instead.
Special points Stand plants on trays filled with moist pebbles to increase humidity.

SPIKY-LEAVED ROSETTE-SHAPED PLANTS

VEITCH SCREW PINE
Pandanus veitchii

These plants get their name from the way the leaf bases spiral round the stem but, despite their name, they are unrelated to the pine family. The long, arching leaves are a rich dark green edged in cream and have a fine-toothed edge which can rasp the skin. Use these handsome specimens in a modern setting for a dramatic effect.

Mini-climate 1 Warm, sunny.
Size Screw pines can reach a height and spread of about 3ft. Plants of all sizes are offered for sale.
Feeding Feed with standard liquid fertilizer every two weeks during spring and summer and once a month during autumn and winter.
Potting Repot every spring using soil-based potting mixture. If you don't want to move an older plant into a larger pot topdress instead.
Special points Thick, stiltlike aerial roots form after two years and lift the plant base away from the potting mixture. These roots should be encouraged to grow into the potting mixture for improved anchorage.

Rosette-shaped plants 2

SPIKY-LEAVED ROSETTE-SHAPED PLANTS continued

VARIEGATED PINEAPPLE
Ananas comosus "Variegatus"

These plants are prized for their stiff, spiny leaves, which curve gracefully outward, giving them a symmetrical shape. When five or six years old they produce striking pink flower heads, followed by a pink fruit, which is unlikely to ripen and be edible. Large plants displayed in an urn suit formal interiors.

Mini-climate 1 Warm, sunny.
Size Variegated pineapple plants grow to a maximum height of about 3ft with a spread of up to 6ft. Fruiting plants are offered for sale.
Feeding Feed with standard liquid fertilizer every two weeks during spring and summer.
Potting Repot in spring every two years using bromeliad potting mixture. Once plants are in 6-8in pots topdress instead.
Special points In direct sunlight, a rich-pink hue enhances the variegation of the leaves.

Similar-shaped species
Ananas bracteatus striatus is the variegated form of the wild pineapple and has boldly striped leaves which become pink if grown in bright light.
Ananas nanus is much smaller with plain, dark-green leaves and produces small, inedible fruits. It can be bought in fruit in a 4in pot.

FLAT-LEAVED ROSETTE-SHAPED PLANTS

SCARLET STAR
Guzmania lingulata

These winter-flowering bromeliads have centers made up of bright-orange or scarlet bracts filled with small, yellow flowers. The arching leaves are soft, glossy and bright-green in color. These are strongly colored plants which suit bold, modern interiors. Mass several plants in a shallow glass bowl or display in pairs for a symmetrical arrangement.

Mini-climate 2 Warm, filtered sun.
Size The scarlet star reaches about 10in in height and has a spread of up to 1ft.
Feeding Feed with half-strength standard liquid fertilizer once a month. Ensure the feed gets onto the leaves and roots and into the central cup.
Potting Repot in spring using bromeliad potting mixture but only if the roots have filled the existing pot.
Special points Empty the central cup and fill with fresh water every month.

EARTH STAR PLANT
Cryptanthus bivittatus

These small plants have some of the most beautifully colored foliage found in the bromeliads. The sharply pointed leaves have two distinctive cream stripes running along their length, which turn pink or even a strong red if placed in the direct sun. Clusters of small white flowers are hidden by the leaves. These stemless plants can be massed in shallow bowls or terraria.

Mini-climate 1 Warm, sunny.
Size Earth stars are slow-growing and will reach 6-8in across by the time they flower.
Feeding Feed occasionally by splashing with half-strength standard liquid fertilizer.
Potting Repotting is hardly ever necessary.
Special points Some time after flowering has finished cut away the parent plant to allow the offsets around its base to develop.

BLUSHING BROMELIAD
Neoregelia carolinae "Tricolor"

These flat-topped bromeliads have striking foliage; young leaves are a soft green striped with ivory white. As the plants mature the leaves become suffused with pink, and just before flowering the center becomes bright red. Display within a group of bold foliage plants for best effect.

Mini-climate 2 Warm, filtered sun.
Size Mature blushing bromeliads grow to about 8in in height with a spread of about 1½ft.
Feeding Feed with half-strength standard liquid fertilizer once a month. Apply on to the leaves, into the cup and on to the potting mixture.
Potting Repot in spring using bromeliad potting mixture but only if the roots have completely filled the existing pot. Once plants are in 5in pots topdress instead.

AFRICAN VIOLET
Saintpaulia sp. and hybrids

These plants have an impressive range of flower colors from white and pink to purple, magenta and violet. The flowers are held in clusters above the rosette of furry leaves. With this range of color African violets can be used in both modern and period interiors. One of the most effective ways to display them is massed in a shallow bowl. Miniature varieties can be displayed in a terrarium.

Mini-climate 2 Warm, filtered sun.
Size African violets will form a flat rosette of about 8in diameter. Flowering plants are available all year. Named varieties run into thousands.
Feeding Feed with specially prepared African violet liquid fertilizer, used at one-quarter strength, at each watering throughout the year.
Potting Repot only when the roots have completely filled the existing pot. Use a mixture of equal parts peat moss, perlite and vermiculite in half pots or shallow pans.
Special points Avoid wetting the hairy leaves when watering and feeding as they will become stained.

BIRD'S NEST BROMELIAD
Nidularium innocentii

These plants form low, spreading rosettes of straplike, dark-green leaves. The center of the rosette becomes very dark red, sometimes almost black, at flowering time. The small, white flowers form a clump in the center of the water-filled vase and last only a short time, although the colored center remains attractive for some months. Bird's nest bromeliads can be grouped with other bold-leaved plants.

Mini-climate 2 Warm, filtered sun.
Size Bird's nest bromeliads grow to a height of about 8in with a spread of 16in. Three or four year old plants about to flower are offered for sale.
Feeding Feed with half-strength standard liquid fertilizer once a month. Apply on to the leaves, into the cup and on to the potting mixture.
Potting Repot in spring using bromeliad potting mixture but only if the roots have completely filled the existing pot. Once plants are in 4in pots topdress instead.
Special points Some time after flowering has finished cut away the parent plant to allow the offsets around its base to develop.

Similar-shaped species
Nidularium fulgens is of similar size with dark-spotted, spiky-edged leaves.

CAPE PRIMROSE
Streptocarpus "John Innes" hybrids

These small plants have primrose-like leaves and large, tubular flowers on long stalks. Flowers may be white, pink, red, mauve or blue. Attractive twisted seed pods appear but these are best cut off to encourage more flowers. These plants can be treated as annuals and discarded when flowering has finished. Like primroses and African violets, Cape primroses should be massed together in a shallow bowl placed on a low table.

Mini-climate 5 Cool, filtered sun.
Size Cape primroses grow to about 1ft in height with a spread of 1 ½ft. Small plants in bud are offered for sale.
Feeding Feed with half-strength, high-phosphate liquid fertilizer every two weeks from early spring to late autumn.
Potting Repot every spring using an equal-parts mixture of sphagnum peat moss, coarse grade perlite and vermiculite. Add half a tablespoon of limestone chips to every cup of mixture. Once plants are in 6in pots root prune instead.

GLOXINIA
Sinningia speciosa hybrids

The large, downy leaves have a bold pattern of veins on them but are eclipsed by the large, showy flowers. They are borne in a cluster on top of the rosette of leaves. Trumpet-shaped with frilled edges they can be white, pink, red or purple, and are often margined in white. Although gloxinias can be treated as annuals they have a tuber which can be dried off in autumn and repotted in spring. Gloxinias are best in period rooms, displayed either singly or in a group.

Mini-climate 2 Warm, filtered sun.
Size Gloxinias can attain a height and spread of about 1ft. Plants in bud are offered for sale.
Feeding Feed with high-phosphate liquid fertilizer once a month during the flowering period.
Potting Repot the tubers in spring using equal parts of peat-based potting mixture, vermiculite and perlite. Repotting once the plant is flowering is unnecessary.

Similar-shaped species
Sinningia pusilla is very small, no higher than 1in or so, but has relatively large, pale-lavender flowers. Many attractive named varieties exist.

Bushy plants 1

Bushy plants are difficult to describe precisely as this category covers a vast range of flowering and foliage plants. Their common feature is a tendency to grow outwards as much as they grow upwards. This gives them a spread nearly equal to their height, and is why they are often displayed on their own, or in twos, rather than in groups with different plants—although some of the more upright bushy plants can make good foils for trailing plants. Many of the flowering bushy plants look good when several of the same species are massed in a shallow bowl. A large number of the flowering bushy plants are annuals, bought for their display of flowers and then discarded

when flowering has finished. Many kinds branch naturally, regularly producing side shoots, others branch freely only if their growing tips are regularly pinched out. Form and size range from the small, low-growing peperomias and hypoestes to the tall and shrubby spotted laurel. Leaf texture, shape, size and color are also well represented; from the smooth, fleshy leaves of the florist's cyclamen to the large and pimpled leaves of the painted-leaf begonia. Colorful leaves are found on plants such as the painted nettle, polka-dot plant, and angel wings. Bushy plants are well suited to period décor or places where an informal atmosphere prevails.

SMALL-LEAVED BUSHY PLANTS

AMETHYST VIOLET
Browallia speciosa

Also known as "bush violets", these are showy plants with violet-blue or white flowers that appear in early summer to autumn, depending on climate and when the seeds were started. They are usually treated as annuals and discarded when flowering has finished. Several strains are available, including the "Troll" and "Bells" series. The stems tend to droop so display plants at eye level in hanging baskets or massed on a low table.

Mini-climate 1 Warm, filtered sun.
Size Amethyst violets grow to 10-12in tall with a similar spread. Pinch out growing tips to encourage bushy growth. Seedlings can be bought in spring, or grow your own from seeds sown early indoors under fluorescent tubes.
Feeding Feed with standard liquid fertilizer every two weeks.
Potting Repotting is unnecessary.
Special points Destroy any greenfly you may find.

Similar-shaped species
Browallia viscosa is only half the size of *B.speciosa*, with smaller leaves and flowers. The leaves are slightly sticky.

ELATIOR BEGONIA
Begonia "Elatior" hybrids

These begonias flower for most of the year. The large, roselike flowers range in color from deep red, through pink, to yellow and white. They are best treated as annuals and discarded when flowering has finished. The foliage is usually pale green but plants with deep-red foliage are sometimes available. As their flowers are quite large these begonias can be displayed as specimen plants or grouped in a shallow pan. Elatior begonias do best in light, well-ventilated rooms.

Mini-climate 2 Warm, filtered sun.
Size "Elatior" begonias are usually erect with a maximum height and spread of 14-16in. Small bushy plants are offered for sale from mid-spring to early autumn.
Feeding Feed with standard liquid fertilizer every two weeks in spring and summer.
Potting Repot two or three times during summer and autumn using a mixture of half soil-based potting mixture and half leaf mold or coarse peat moss. If you don't want to move an older plant into a larger pot topdress instead.
Special points Protect from powdery mildew by supplying adequate ventilation.

Similar-shaped species
Begonia tuberhybrida has large, double flowers of red, pink, white or yellow.

WAX BEGONIA
Begonia semperflorens-cultorum

These are small plants grown for their profusion of flowers. Single- and double-flowered varieties are available. The white, pink or red flowers begin blooming in spring and continue well into the winter. They are best treated as annuals and discarded when flowering has finished. They make excellent display plants when grouped in shallow containers or mixed with colorful foliage plants. These begonias do best in light, well-ventilated rooms.

Mini-climate 1 Warm, sunny.
Size Wax begonias never reach more than 1ft in height when fully grown. They are offered for sale in spring as seedlings and for the rest of the year as mature plants.
Feeding Feed with standard liquid fertilizer every two weeks in spring and summer.
Potting Repot as needed, perhaps two or three times during summer and autumn, using a mixture of half soil-based potting mixture and half leaf mold or coarse peat moss. If you don't want to move an older plant into a larger pot topdress instead.
Special points Protect from powdery mildew by supplying adequate ventilation.

LEMON GERANIUM
Pelargonium crispum "Variegatum"

These geraniums are grown for their aromatic leaves rather than the flowers they produce. The foliage is pale green with a cream-colored wavy edge, and plants can be trained to many shapes by appropriate pinching out of the growing tips. Place in a position where the leaves will be brushed against for maximum aromatic effect. Geraniums have a pretty, "cottage" look and suit period rooms which are not too formal.

Mini-climate 4 Cool, sunny.
Size Lemon geraniums can grow to 2-3ft tall or be kept small and bushy. Small rooted plants are offered for sale.
Feeding Feed with half-strength standard liquid fertilizer twice in summer.
Potting Repot in spring using soil-based potting mixture on top of a small layer of rough drainage material, but only if the roots have completely filled the existing pot.
Special points Do not overwater in winter as plants become susceptible to black stem rot.

PAINTED NETTLE
Coleus blumei

These plants have soft textured leaves in a range of vivid colors, from red and bronze to cream and purple, some incorporating three or more colors. Although the serrated leaves closely resemble those of the stinging nettle, the two plants are not related. Painted nettles are best treated as annuals and discarded after one year. Their brightly patterned foliage is suited to period rooms containing richly colored fabrics.

Mini-climate 1 Warm, sunny.
Size Painted nettles will grow to a height of 18in in one year with a similar spread. Pinch out growing tips to encourage bushy growth.
Feeding Feed with standard liquid fertilizer every two weeks in spring and summer, and once a month during autumn and winter.
Potting Repot every two months using soil-based potting mixture. If you don't want to move an older plant into a larger pot topdress instead.
Special points Leaf color is stronger if plants are placed in a sunny position.

EGYPTIAN STAR CLUSTER
Pentas lanceolata

These attractive plants are winter-flowering shrubs, although they may flower at any time of year. They have lance-shaped, hairy leaves and clusters of tiny, star-shaped flowers which can be mauve, white or pink in color. The almost flat-topped flower heads can be nearly 4in across. Egyptian star clusters look best when several plants are massed in an informal room.

Mini-climate 1 Warm, sunny.
Size Egyptian star clusters reach between 1ft and 1½ft in height. Pinch out growing tips to encourage bushy growth. Small plants are offered for sale.
Feeding Feed with standard liquid fertilizer every two weeks during the flowering period.
Potting Repot every spring using soil-based potting mixture. If you don't want to move an older plant into a larger pot topdress instead.
Special points Water more sparingly in winter.

IMPATIENS
Impatiens wallerana hybrids

The flower color of these ubiquitous plants ranges from white, through pink, to red; some flowers are striped with another color. The foliage and thick, succulent stems also vary in color from pale green to bronze. Impatiens will begin flowering when only six weeks old and continue throughout the summer. They are best treated as annuals and discarded when flowering has finished. These plants look particularly attractive if grouped in a hanging basket or window-box.

Mini-climate 1 Warm, sunny.
Size Impatiens are fast-growing, some hybrids reaching a maximum height of 14in. Pinch out growing tips to encourage bushy growth. Seedlings and small and medium-sized plants are offered for sale, or start seeds indoors.
Feeding Feed with standard liquid fertilizer every two weeks in spring and summer.
Potting Repot every spring using soil-based potting mixture but only if the roots have completely filled the existing pot. Once the plants are in 5in pots topdress instead.

Bushy plants 2

SMALL-LEAVED BUSHY PLANTS continued

CHINESE HIBISCUS
Hibiscus rosa-sinensis

Large, funnel-shaped flowers and glossy, dark-green leaves make Chinese hibiscuses spectacular plants. Flowers can be red, pink, white, yellow or orange and appear singly, usually in spring and summer. Use in a bright, sunny setting for an oriental look, either individually or by grouping several plants of different colors together.

Mini-climate 1 Warm, sunny.
Size Chinese hibiscuses are fast-growing, quickly reaching 5ft in height. Plants with opening buds are usually offered for sale in spring.
Feeding Feed with high-potash liquid fertilizer every two weeks in spring and summer, and once a month in autumn and winter. If flowers are not produced freely, increase the frequency of feeding (not the strength of the fertilizer).
Potting Repot every spring using soil-based potting mixture. If you don't want to move an older plant into a larger pot topdress instead.
Special points Water more sparingly in winter.

GERMAN VIOLET
Exacum affine

Also known as "Persian violets", these are small, bushy plants with fragrant blue flowers with yellow eyes and shiny, olive-green leaves. They bloom in summer and the flowers can last for up to two months. They are best treated as annuals and discarded when flowering has finished. To display German violets, mass them in a large bowl, as they make an eye-catching show in any setting—traditional or modern.

Mini-climate 2 Warm, filtered sun.
Size German violets will quickly grow stems up to 1ft long. Young plants are rarely available so grow your own from seeds sown early indoors.
Feeding Feed with standard liquid fertilizer every two weeks while the plant is in flower.
Potting Repot using soil-based potting mixture but only if the plant was bought in a very small pot. Further repotting is unnecessary.
Special points Stand plants on trays filled with moist pebbles to maintain high humidity.

REGAL GERANIUM
Pelargonium domesticum hybrids

These geraniums have large flower heads that range in color from white to red, many are bicolored or tricolored. The flowering season is short, lasting only from spring to midsummer, but the showiness of the flowers compensates for this. Very much at home in indoor window-boxes, they look equally good as specimen plants.

Mini-climate 4 Cool, sunny.
Size Regal geraniums can be grown as single-stemmed plants of up to 2ft tall, or as small bushy shrubs. Plants of all sizes are offered for sale.
Feeding Feed occasionally with standard liquid fertilizer during spring and summer.
Potting Repot every spring using a soil-based potting mixture. Once plants are in 6in pots topdress instead.
Special points Cut off faded flower heads to encourage new growth.

Similar-shaped species
Pelargonium hortorum has ball-like clusters of flowers almost all year round.

PRAYER PLANT
Maranta leuconeura erythroneura

Prayer plants, also known as "red herringbone plants", are so-called because of the way pairs of leaves close together at night. They are remarkable for their beautiful leaves marked with deep-red, raised veins. The red midrib is surrounded by a pale-green stripe on the olive-green leaf. Prayer plants are amongst the showiest of plants and should be displayed in a prominent position. They can also be trained to grow up short, moss-covered poles.

Mini-climate 3 Warm, shady.
Size Prayer plants will grow to a maximum of 6-12in tall with a 16in spread. Small plants are offered for sale.
Feeding Feed with standard liquid fertilizer every two weeks during spring, summer and autumn.
Potting Repot every spring using soil-based potting mixture in half-pots or other shallow containers. If you don't want to move an older plant into a larger pot topdress instead.

CINERARIA
Senecio hybridus

Cinerarias have large, daisy-shaped flowers clustered in the center of the fleshy leaves. The flowers can be of orange, red, magenta, pink, blue or purple, often with a circle of white surrounding the central disc. The leaves are furry to touch and are often tinged with blue on their undersides. Cinerarias are best treated as annuals and discarded when flowering has finished. A bold display can be made with several cinerarias of the same color massed in a china dish or basket. They suit both traditional and modern rooms.

Mini-climate 4 Cool, sunny.
Size Budding cineraria plants up to 1ft tall and of similar spread are offered for sale throughout winter and spring.
Feeding Feeding is not required for these temporary pot plants.
Potting Repotting is unnecessary.
Special points To keep plants in a decorative state for as long as possible, ensure that the potting mixture does not dry out too much. Water is easily lost through the large leaves and the plant will collapse if the roots dry out. Destroy any aphids or whitefly you may find.

POINSETTIA
Euphorbia pulcherrima

With their flamboyant red, pink or creamy-white bracts, poinsettias are welcome at Christmastime. The bracts remain decorative for two months. After this they should be cut hard back and kept for their foliage alone, as it is not easy to get these plants to bloom for a second year. The poinsettia is essentially a specimen plant; the common red form is particularly striking, but can look good when mixed with dark-green foliage plants.

Mini-climate 1 Warm, sunny.
Size Poinsettias are available in many sizes, ranging from 1 to 5ft. They are offered for sale in winter.
Feeding Feed with standard liquid fertilizer once every month.
Potting Repotting of first year plants is unnecessary. If keeping the plant for a second year, repot in the same pot with fresh soil-based potting mixture.
Special points Poinsettias have a sap which can cause irritation of the skin in some people.

POLKA-DOT PLANT
Hypoestes phyllostachya

These are pretty plants with unusual foliage. The leaves, which range from olive-green to very dark green, are spotted with pale-pink dots. They are best treated as annuals and discarded after one year. New forms, as they are quite small, look more dramatic if several plants are grouped together, either in separate pots or planted in a shallow pan.

Mini-climate 2 Warm, filtered sun.
Size Polka-dot plants can grow quite tall but will become straggly, so it is advisable to limit growth to 1ft tall by pinching out the growing tips. Small, bushy plants of 3-5in tall are offered for sale.
Feeding Feed with standard liquid fertilizer every two weeks from early summer to mid-autumn.
Potting Repot in spring but only if the roots have completely filled the existing pot. Once plants are in 5in pots topdress instead.
Special points Spray leaves occasionally with tepid water to discourage red spider mites.

AZALEA
Rhododendron simsii

Azaleas produce clusters of brightly colored flowers atop a mass of shiny, green leaves. Flower color ranges from white to magenta, including almost every shade of red and pink. Some flowers are bicolored. They are best treated as annuals and discarded when flowering has finished. Mass azaleas in a shallow bowl and place in a prominent position in a hallway or other cool place.

Mini-climate 5 Cool, filtered sun.
Size Azaleas vary in size according to age and variety. Budding plants are offered for sale in winter and spring. After flowering, trim back new growth to maintain bushiness.
Feeding Feed with standard liquid fertilizer once every two weeks from spring to autumn.
Potting Repot as necessary using one part soil-based potting mixture, two parts peat moss, and one part coarse sand.
Special points To keep plants in a decorative state for as long as possible, keep the potting mixture permanently moist and display in a cool place.

Bushy plants 3

SMALL-LEAVED BUSHY PLANTS continued

FLORIST'S CYCLAMEN
Cyclamen persicum hybrids

Florist's cyclamens flower in late autumn, winter and early spring. Many varieties are available, with the color of the swept-back flowers ranging from white, through red, to purple. Some varieties have frilled or perfumed flowers. Although usually treated as an annual, if the tubers are dried off in the late spring and rested during the summer months, cyclamens can last for many years. Cyclamens do not mix well with other plants. They are ideal for colorful displays in entrance halls or period rooms where conditions are not excessively hot.

Mini-climate 5 Cool, filtered sun.
Size Cyclamens rarely grow larger than 8-10in tall. Budded plants are offered for sale from September until Christmastime.
Feeding Feed with standard liquid fertilizer every two weeks when in flower.
Potting Repotting of first year plants is unnecessary. Repot a rested tuber in soil-based potting mixture in September. Use the same pot each year.
Special points Never pour water directly onto the tuber; instead stand the pot in water for ten minutes.

CHRISTMAS CHERRY
Solanum capsicastrum

Marble-sized, orange-red berries make these small, shrubby plants an autumn favorite. The berries will last for several months if kept in a sunny but cool place; hot, dry air considerably shortens their lives. Placed on a low table or in a window-box, the Christmas cherry adds color and interest to a group of foliage plants.

Mini-climate 4 Cool, sunny.
Size Christmas cherries reach a height of 1½ft. Plants bearing berries are offered for sale.
Feeding Feed with standard liquid fertilizer every two weeks.
Potting Repot in spring using soil-based potting mixture. To keep for a second fruiting season cut away half the growth and move them outside in 5in pots for the summer.
Special points Mist-spray daily to increase humidity and aid pollination when in flower. The berries are not edible, so keep the plants away from small children.

EMERALD RIPPLE PEPEROMIA
Peperomia caperata

These small plants have very distinctive, deeply ridged, heart-shaped leaves. The low-growing form of the leaves is offset by the vertical, white flower spikes which emerge from the rosette of leaves. Peperomias look good when included in foliage groups with plants of contrasting sizes and textures.

Mini-climate 2 Warm, filtered sun.
Size Emerald ripple peperomias are compact plants, rarely growing taller than 6in with a similar spread. Young plants and a miniature form for use in bottle gardens are offered for sale.
Feeding Feed with half-strength standard liquid fertilizer once a month from mid-spring to autumn.
Potting Repot in spring using a peat-based potting mixture but only if the roots have completely filled the existing pot.
Special points Do not overwater peperomias as they are liable to rot.

CHRISTMAS PEPPER
Capsicum annuum

An increasingly popular plant bearing brightly colored fleshy berries which appear in autumn and remain decorative until after Christmas. The most familiar berries are orange-red in color but white, yellow, green and purple-berried varieties are also available. They are best treated as annuals and discarded when the fruiting has finished. They make colorful Christmas displays and are striking massed as a table decoration.

Mini-climate 1 Warm, sunny.
Size Christmas peppers are available at 12-14in height and spread.
Feeding Feed with standard liquid fertilizer every two weeks in the fruiting season.
Potting Repotting is unnecessary.
Special points To keep plants in a decorative state for as long as possible, stand plants on trays filled with moist pebbles to increase humidity. The fruits are edible but very hot.

FLORIST'S CHRYSANTHEMUM
Chrysanthemum morifolium hybrids

Also known as "pot chrysanthemums", these plants are offered for sale with flowers of every color but blue. The flowers and foliage have a distinctive scent. They will remain in flower for about six weeks, and are best treated as annuals and discarded when flowering has finished. Several plants grouped together in a shallow basket or pan on a low table look particularly attractive.

Mini-climate 5 Cool, filtered sun.
Size Florist's chrysanthemums have been specially cultivated to reach no more than 1ft in height. They are offered for sale in flower throughout the year.
Feeding Feeding is not required for these temporary plants.
Potting Repotting is unnecessary.
Special points When buying chrysanthemums make sure the flower buds show color as tightly closed green buds often fail to open.

POISON PRIMROSE
Primula obconica

This is one of the prettiest flowering plants, blooming between Christmas and summer. The long-stalked clusters of flowers are white, pink, salmon or mauve with a distinctive green eye. Poison primroses are best treated as annuals and discarded when flowering has finished. Use singly or massed in a shallow pan or basket in any cool area.

Mini-climate 5 Cool, filtered sun.
Size Poison primroses rarely grow taller than 1ft with a spread of 10in. Plants in flower are offered for sale.
Feeding Use liquid fertilizer every two weeks.
Potting Repotting is unnecessary.
Special points Leaves can cause painful skin rash.

Similar-shaped species
Primula malacoides is a very delicate plant with small white, rose pink or lilac flowers.

CUPID'S BOWER
Achimenes grandiflora

Also known as "magic flowers", these plants have hairy, upright, green or red stems and dull-green leaves which are also hairy. Flowers can be pink, purple or yellow in color, with white throats. The flowering period lasts from summer to autumn. These are very useful infill plants for an indoor window-box.

Mini-climate 1 Warm, sunny.
Size Cupid's bowers grow to 1½ft in height. Tubers or small plants are offered for sale in spring.
Feeding Feed with phosphate-rich liquid fertilizer at one-eighth strength when watering during the flowering period.
Potting Repot every spring using an equal-parts mixture of peat moss, coarse sand or perlite, and vermiculite. Divide older plants every spring.
Special points Dry off and rest in winter.

LARGE-LEAVED BUSHY PLANTS

JAPANESE FATSIA
Fatsia japonica

An evergreen shrub which has been used for over a century as an indoor and outdoor plant. It has attractive, shiny, fingered leaves whose color and texture contrast with the stem which becomes gnarled and woody with age. The plant can be moved outside in summer, where the leaves become a deeper shade of green. Japanese fatsias can look extremely decorative in an architectural setting.

Mini-climate 5 Cool, filtered sun.
Size Japanese fatsias are fast-growing shrubs, reaching 1.5m in height and spread in two years. Small plants are offered for sale.
Feeding Feed with standard liquid fertilizer every two weeks during spring and summer.
Potting Repot every spring using soil-based potting mixture. Clay pots are best because fatsias tend to be top-heavy. If you don't want to move an older plant into a larger pot topdress instead.

Bushy plants 4

LARGE-LEAVED BUSHY PLANTS continued

SPOTTED LAUREL
Aucuba japonica "Variegata"

Also known as "Japanese laurels", these plants were much used by the Victorians in their shrubberies and greenhouses. The modern hybrids are more cheerful, having leaves strongly variegated with yellow. Spotted laurels can be used in window-boxes and in foliage arrangements for cool rooms as they tolerate a certain amount of neglect, poor light and drafts.

Mini-climate 5   Cool, filtered sun.
Size   Spotted laurels can reach 3-4ft in height. Plants of about 8in high are offered for sale.
Feeding   Feed with standard liquid fertilizer once a month in summer.
Potting   Repot every spring using soil-based potting mixture. Once plants are in 8in pots topdress instead.
Special points   Clean leaves regularly with a damp sponge. Plants can be put outside in summer.

ANGEL WINGS
Caladium hortulanum hybrids

Angel wings send up long, fleshy stalks bearing the paper-thin, heart-shaped leaves. The variety of leaf colors and patterns is immense—besides green leaves with red veining, white and cream leaves veined with pink or green are also available. Angel wings are highly ornamental, especially if several different leaf colors are grouped together.

Mini-climate 3   Warm, shady.
Size   The mainly green-leaved angel wings grow to a maximum height of 8-10in. Varieties with colored leaves may reach 1½-2ft high. Plants in full leaf are offered for sale.
Feeding   Feed with half-strength liquid fertilizer every two weeks in spring and summer.
Potting   Repot a rested tuber in spring using peat-based potting mixture. Make provision for good drainage. Use 5in pots and cover the tuber with about 1in of potting mixture.

SAFFRON SPIKE
Aphelandra squarrosa "Louisae"

These are dual-purpose flowering and foliage plants. For about six weeks the plant has unusual flower heads of overlapping yellow bracts. When flowering has finished, pinch off the dead blooms and use the saffron spike as a foliage plant. The leaves are large and glossy and marked with large, white veins. Mix with plain-leaved plants for a contrasting display in a modern living-room.

Mini-climate 2   Warm, filtered sun.
Size   Saffron spikes grow to about 1ft in height with a similar spread. Plants already in flower are offered for sale.
Feeding   Feed with standard liquid fertilizer every week from spring to early autumn.
Potting   Repot every spring using soil-based potting mixture. Once plants are in 6in pots topdress instead.

FLAMINGO FLOWER
Anthurium scherzeranum hybrids

The exotic flower heads consist of a bright scarlet bract encircling a tail-like flower spike. They last for several weeks and can appear at any time between February and July. When in flower, groups of several plants make an attractive display; when not in flower, the leaves harmonize with those of other tropical plants suitable for shady spots.

Mini-climate 3   Warm, shady.
Size   Flamingo flowers grow to about 2ft in height. Small plants are often offered for sale.
Feeding   Feed every two weeks with standard liquid fertilizer.
Potting   Repot every spring using a mixture of one-third soil-based potting mixture, one-third coarse peat moss, and one-third coarse sand. Once plants are in 7in pots topdress instead. Cover any exposed roots in peat moss.
Special points   Water more sparingly in winter. Stand plants on trays filled with moist pebbles to increase humidity.

Temperature 50°-60°F spring to autumn, 45°-50°F in winter   50°-60°F   60°-70°F   **Light** sunny   filtered sun   shady   **Humidity** low   moderate   high   **Watering** sparingly   moderately   plentifully   **Care** easy   fairly easy   challenging

PAINTED-LEAF BEGONIA
Begonia rex-cultorum

Also known as "rex begonias", these are among the most handsome begonias, grown for the beautifully colored leaves rather than their flowers, which tend to be insignificant. The heart-shaped leaves, which can be up to 1ft in length, bear striking patterns made up of variations of red, black, silver and green. Leaf texture also varies: some hybrids have smooth leaves; this one has a rippled or pimpled surface.

Mini-climate 3 Warm, shady.
Size Painted leaf begonias can grow up to 1ft in height with a 3ft spread. Young plants 2-3in high are offered for sale.
Feeding Feed with standard liquid fertilizer every two weeks in spring and summer.
Potting Divide overcrowded rhizomes and repot in spring every three years using peat-based potting mixture in a shallow container.
Special points Water very sparingly in winter. Destroy any powdery mildew you may find.

Similar-shaped species
Begonia masoniana has a deep-red, cross-shaped pattern in the middle of its pale-green leaves.

COMPOUND-LEAVED BUSHY PLANTS

DELTA MAIDENHAIR FERN
Adiantum raddianum

Delta maidenhair ferns have delicate, pale-green fronds borne on black, wiry stalks. They mix well with both foliage and flowering house plants and are useful for softening the outline of many arrangements. They also look very attractive on their own. Small plants can be planted in terraria.

Mini-climate 3 Warm, shady.
Size These ferns grow to 1ft in height with a similar spread. Plants of all sizes are offered for sale.
Feeding Feed with standard liquid fertilizer once a month during spring and summer.
Potting Repot in spring using fern potting mixture but only when a mass of roots appears on the surface of the potting mixture.
Special points Stand plants on trays filled with moist pebbles to increase humidity.

Similar-shaped species
Adiantum raddianum microphyllum has minute, dark-green, wedge-shaped leaflets.
Adiantum hispidulum is very small and has fingerlike fronds.

ASPARAGUS FERN
Asparagus setaceus

Asparagus ferns have light, feathery foliage made up of tiny branchlets on wiry stems. Taller growing kinds may be trained up thin canes to form a delicate column shape. Trained around east- or west-facing windows they can give a charming "cottage" effect. They can also be included in fern groups in a hanging basket.

Mini-climate 2 Warm, filtered sun.
Size Asparagus ferns can produce stems up to 4ft long. Small plants are offered for sale.
Feeding Feed with standard liquid fertilizer every two weeks in spring and summer, and once a month in autumn and winter.
Potting Repot every spring using soil-based potting mixture. If you don't want to move an older plant into a larger pot topdress instead.

Similar-shaped species
Asparagus asparagoides is a vigorous climbing vine with leaflet-like branchlets up to 2in long.
Asparagus falcatus is similar but has sickle-shaped spines on its stems.

CRETAN BRAKE FERN
Pteris cretica

Also known as "table ferns", these plants form clumps of striped fronds which grow from short, underground rhizomes. Each frond is hand-shaped, the individual pinnae looking like fingers. Cretan brake ferns mix well with other plants, especially if used as pot hiders at the front of plant groupings. They are ideal for a north-facing conservatory or plant window collection.

Mini-climate 3 Warm, shady.
Size Cretan brake ferns grow to 14in in height with a similar spread. Small plants of about 5in in height are offered for sale.
Feeding Feed with half-strength standard liquid fertilizer once a month.
Potting Repot in spring using fern potting mixture but only if the roots have completely filled the existing pot. If you don't want to move an older plant to a larger pot topdress instead.

Similar-shaped species
Pteris tremula looks like bracken. It is fast-growing, with fronds up to 2ft long and 1ft wide.

Climbing plants 1

Climbing plants usually have stems that are too weak to grow unaided in an upright position, but will grow in any direction provided they have a support to cling to. Many climbing plants can be displayed equally effectively as trailers, and vice-versa. The species, which bear aerial roots, such as the philodendrons and the Swiss cheese plant, usually produce quite thick stems and their fleshy leaves can be large and weighty, so they are best grown on a stout moss-covered pole. Some climbing plants naturally scramble through other plants, gaining some support by sending out tendrils or by just "leaning" on their neighbors. Others which produce curly leaf tendrils can be trained on canes, wire hoops and trellis work. Although the tendrils may look thin and frail they are usually very strong. Climbing plants can also be trained to frame windows, mirrors or archways or used to create a foliage screen dividing areas in a room. Many have attractive foliage, such as the scalloped leaves of the kangaroo vine and the yellow-and-green variegated leaves of the Cape ivy and Algerian ivy. A number of climbers have flowers, including the Cape leadwort whose blooms are a striking sky-blue and the jasmine, with its small but heavily scented white flowers. Most spectacular of all are the large, showy flowers of the passion flower.

SMALL-LEAVED CLIMBING PLANTS

ALGERIAN IVY
Hedera canariensis

Also known as "Canary Island ivies", these plants have slightly lobed dark-green leaves with patches of gray-green variegation. They are vigorous climbers and can easily be trained up any kind of support. They make good specimen plants when very large and are most suitable for use in cool places such as halls and stairways.

Mini-climate 5 Cool, filtered sun.
Size Algerian ivies are fast-growing with an unpredictable maximum height and spread; certainly 6ft. Leaves can be as much as 6in long and 6in wide. Plants of all sizes are offered for sale.
Feeding Feed with standard liquid fertilizer every two weeks when actively growing.
Potting Repot in spring using soil-based potting mixture but only if the roots have completely filled the existing pot. Once plants are in 4½-6in pots topdress instead.
Special points Water more sparingly in winter.

CAPE IVY
Senecio macroglossus

These plants are very similar to the English ivies, but their leaves are smoother, softer and more fleshy. The leaves are borne on purple stems and are green marked with pale-cream streaks and patches. In some cases, where variegation is very strong, all the leaves on a shoot may be predominantly cream-colored. Cape ivies should be trained around hoops of bamboo cane or wire, or planted in small hanging baskets.

Mini-climate 1 Warm, sunny.
Size Cape ivies grow up to 3ft in height and spread. Pinch out growing tips to maintain bushy growth. Small plants are offered for sale.
Feeding Feed with standard liquid fertilizer every two weeks during spring and summer.
Potting Repot every spring using a mixture of one part coarse sand to three parts soil-based mixture. Once plants are in 6in pots topdress instead.
Special points Water more sparingly in winter. Destroy any aphids you may find.

GRAPE IVY
Cissus rhombifolia

These plants have deeply toothed leaves. New leaf growth appears to be silver due to a fine covering of hairs on both surfaces. Older leaves have undersides covered in fine, brown hairs. Trained up a simple framework of bamboo canes, grape ivies can become quite large feature plants relatively quickly. They also make an excellent display in large hanging baskets.

Mini-climate 2 Warm, filtered sun.
Size Grape ivies grow to 6ft in height in around two years and can reach 10ft in ideal conditions. Pinch out growing tips regularly to encourage bushy growth. Plants of all sizes are offered for sale.
Feeding Feed with standard liquid fertilizer every two weeks in spring and summer.
Potting Repot every spring using soil-based potting mixture. Once plants are in 6-7in pots topdress instead.

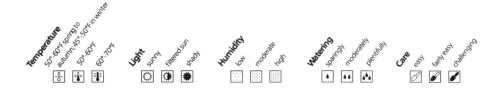

PASSION FLOWER
Passiflora caerulea

These exotic-looking plants have beautiful flowers. Each consists of five pinkish-white petals and five pinkish-white sepals encircling a ring of purple-blue filaments. These filaments encircle the golden anthers. The flowers may appear at any time during the summer and autumn. The foliage is dark-green and stems should be trained over a wire support to make an attractive shape. Passion flowers make striking specimen plants for conservatories or large, bright windowsills.

Mini-climate 1 Warm, sunny.
Size Passion flowers have a maximum height and spread of about 30ft. Plants of all sizes are offered for sale.
Feeding Feed with standard liquid fertilizer every two weeks during spring, summer and autumn.
Potting Repot every spring using soil-based potting mixture. Once plants are in 8in pots topdress instead.
Special points To keep plants in a decorative state for as long as possible, prune heavily in spring.

WAX FLOWER
Stephanotis floribunda

These plants have dark-green, glossy leaves carried on woody stems, which twine readily round any support, and delightfully scented, waxy, white flowers. The flowers grow in clusters of ten or more and each is tube-shaped, flaring out into five pointed lobes. They appear from spring until autumn. Wax flowers may be trained to climb a trellis or, if space is more limited, round a hoop of wire or cane inserted into the pot.

Mini-climate 1 Warm, sunny.
Size Wax flowers are vigorous growers. Height and spread is variable, but is usually about 10ft. Pinch out growing tips to encourage bushy growth. Plants of all sizes are offered for sale.
Feeding Feed with standard liquid fertilizer every two weeks during spring and summer.
Potting Repot every second year in spring using soil-based potting mixture. Once plants are in 8in pots topdress instead.
Special points Stand plants on trays filled with moist pebbles to increase humidity. Water more sparingly in winter.

PLUSH VINE
Mikania ternata

These small plants have soft, slaty-green foliage covered in fine, purple hairs. The underside of the leaves and the stems are purple. Plush vines can be used in much the same way as ivies—either as trailers or climbers—although they do not grow as tall. Their unusual coloring provides a contrast to light-green plants in a mixed foliage arrangement.

Mini-climate 2 Warm, filtered sun.
Size Plush vines have a maximum height and spread of about 10ft. Small plants are offered for sale.
Feeding Feed with standard liquid fertilizer every two weeks from spring to autumn.
Potting Repot in spring using soil-based potting mixture. Discard the plant after the second repotting.
Special points Do not wet the hairy foliage.

BLACK-EYED SUSAN VINE
Thunbergia alata

Black-eyed Susan vines have attractive bright-orange flowers with a characteristic deep chocolate-brown "eye". The large, round blooms are produced from spring to late autumn. Black-eyed Susan vines look particularly good when trained to climb up strings in front of a window.

Mini-climate 4 Cool, sunny.
Size Black-eyed Susan vines may reach over 6ft in height. Buy young plants or grow your own from seed.
Feeding Feed with standard liquid fertilizer every two weeks.
Potting Repot in spring using soil-based potting mixture but only if the roots have completely filled the existing pot. Once plants are in 6in pots top-dress instead.
Special points To keep plants in a decorative state for as long as possible, pinch out any faded flowers.

Climbing plants 2

SMALL-LEAVED CLIMBING PLANTS continued

KANGAROO VINE
Cissus antarctica

Relatives of the grapevine, these are scrambling foliage plants whose glossy, dark-green leaves have marked veining and a scalloped edge. They can be used in many different ways: either trained up poles, used as specimen plants or displayed in hanging baskets.

Mini-climate 2 Warm, filtered sun.
Size Kangaroo vines grow to 6ft tall with a spread of 2ft in about two years. Plants of all sizes are offered for sale.
Feeding Feed with standard liquid fertilizer every two weeks in spring and summer.
Potting Repot every spring using soil-based potting mixture. Once plants are in 6-8in pots topdress instead.
Special points Stand plants on trays filled with moist pebbles to increase humidity. Mist-spray plants in hanging baskets.

CAPE LEADWORT
Plumbago auriculata

These plants produce clusters of up to 20 pale-blue flowers from spring to autumn. A narrow, darker blue stripe runs down each of the five petals which flare from a 1½in long tube. Training these plants round a trellis produces an attractive display, or they can be trained to cover a wall.

Mini-climate 1 Warm, sunny.
Size The stems of the Cape leadwort can reach over 3ft in length, but should be pruned every spring as the plants can become very straggly. Plants of all sizes are offered for sale.
Feeding Feed with tomato-type liquid fertilizer once every two weeks from spring until autumn.
Potting Repot every spring using soil-based potting mixture. Once plants are in 8in pots topdress instead.
Special points Water more sparingly in winter.

WHITE-SCENTED JASMINE
Jasminum polyanthum

Clusters of white, scented flowers are produced by these attractive plants in winter and spring. Jasmine are most delicate-looking, but are very vigorous climbers, easily trained round wire hoops or any other fine support. If planted in a conservatory border, they can be trained to cover a wall.

Mini-climate 4 Cool, sunny.
Size White-scented jasmine can reach 20ft if grown in a border, 3ft if grown in a pot. Spread depends upon the support used. Plants in flower are offered for sale in winter.
Feeding Feed with standard liquid fertilizer once a month in summer and autumn.
Potting Repot every spring using soil-based potting mixture. Once plants are in 8in pots topdress instead.
Special points Place plants outdoors in summer.

GOLDEN TRUMPET
Allamanda cathartica

These climbing plants produce bright, buttercup-yellow flowers over a period of many weeks during the summer. The oval leaves which are carried on long stems are a glossy dark-green color. If grown in a conservatory border, or in a tub, golden trumpets can be trained to cover a wall. For the smaller room, they can be grown in pots and trained over a wire framework of any shape.

Mini-climate 2 Warm, filtered sun.
Size Golden trumpets are fast-growing and can attain a maximum height and spread of 7ft. Plants should be cut back by as much as two-thirds in winter. Small plants are offered for sale in summer.
Feeding Feed with standard liquid fertilizer every two weeks in summer.
Potting Repot every spring using soil-based potting mixture. If you don't want to move an older plant into a larger pot topdress instead.
Special points Water more sparingly in winter.

Temperature	Light	Humidity	Watering	Care
50°-60°F spring to autumn, 45°-50°F in winter / 50°-60°F / 60°-70°F	sunny / filtered sun / shady	low / moderate / high	sparingly / moderately / plentifully	easy / fairly easy / challenging

PAPER FLOWER
Bougainvillea buttiana

Armed with sharp spines, these plants are woody-stemmed. The small, creamy-white flowers are insignificant in themselves but are surrounded by large, decorative, papery bracts which can be white, yellow, orange, pink, red or purple. These are produced in clusters of between 10 and 20, mainly during spring and summer. Although they are naturally climbing plants, paper flowers can be trained to remain bushy indoors. They are best grown in very sunny rooms or conservatories, since they require a large amount of light to encourage them to flower.

Mini-climate 1 Warm, sunny.
Size Paper flowers can reach a maximum height and spread of about 6ft. Pinch out growing tips to encourage bushy growth. Small plants are offered for sale.
Feeding Feed with standard liquid fertilizer every two weeks in summer.
Potting Repot every spring using soil-based potting mixture with extra peat moss mixed in. Once plants are in 8in pots topdress instead.
Special points Water more sparingly in winter. Destroy any mealy bugs you may find.

LARGE-LEAVED CLIMBING PLANTS

BURGUNDY PHILODENDRON
Philodendron "Burgundy"

These large-leaved philodendrons have bright-red leaf stalks and undersides to their leaves. They will flourish if trained around a moss-covered pole. Large specimens look best displayed on their own.

Mini-climate 3 Warm, shady.
Size Burgundy philodendrons are slow-growing; they eventually reach a height of 6ft.
Feeding Feed with standard liquid fertilizer every two weeks in spring and summer.
Potting Repot in spring using half soil-based potting mixture and half peat moss, but only if the roots have filled the existing pot. Once plants are in 6-10in pots topdress instead.

Similar-shaped species
Philodendron hastatum has deep-green leaves.

ARROWHEAD PLANT
Syngonium podophyllum "Imperial White"

These climbing plants are unusual in that the shape of the leaves changes as the plant matures. Young leaves have three deeply-cut lobes but, in older specimens, the leaves have five lobes. Arrowhead plants can be trained to climb up thin stakes, or up a moss-covered pole, or they can trail from a hanging basket.

Mini-climate 2 Warm, filtered sun.
Size The stems can grow up to 6ft. The spread depends on the support system used.
Feeding Feed with standard liquid fertilizer every two weeks from spring to autumn.
Potting Repot in spring using an equal-parts mixture of soil-based potting mixture and leaf mold, but only if the roots have completely filled the existing pot. If you don't want to move an older plant into a larger pot topdress instead.

SWISS CHEESE PLANT
Monstera deliciosa

These plants have undivided, heart-shaped leaves when young; the characteristic split edges and holes appear with age. Train Swiss cheese plants up a moss-covered pole so that the pencil-thick aerial roots can be guided into the moss; never cut these roots off as they take in nutrients. The scale of a mature plant makes it a good foil for large pieces of furniture.

Mini-climate 3 Warm, shady.
Size Swiss cheese plants can reach heights in excess of 8ft. Plants of all sizes are offered for sale.
Feeding Feed with standard liquid fertilizer every two weeks in spring and summer.
Potting Repot every spring using two-thirds soil-based potting mixture and one-third leaf mold. Once plants are in 8in pots topdress instead.
Special points Clean older leaves regularly.

Trailing plants 1

Most of these plants look best displayed with their stems hanging downwards, although some, such as ivies and philodendrons, can be trained to climb as well. Trailing plants are best displayed in hanging baskets, on pedestals, or on shelves, so that the tumbling foliage can be appreciated. They can also be used to soften the outline of any arrangement or to disguise the edges of a hanging basket, shelf or table. Within the group there is a wonderful range of leaf textures, from the light, feathery fronds of the emerald fern to the bold, fleshy fronds of the staghorn fern, and the delicate, dripping foliage of the strawberry geranium. A dramatic hanging display can be made using the large foliage of the staghorn fern contrasted with the heart-shaped leaves of the heartleaf philodendron. For color there are the red flowers of the columneas and the light-blue or white flowers of the Italian bellflower. The leaves of trailing plants can also provide color and different textures: for example, the furry, purple foliage of the purple velvet plant and the beautiful, silver-marked foliage of the pothos vine.

SMALL-LEAVED TRAILING PLANTS

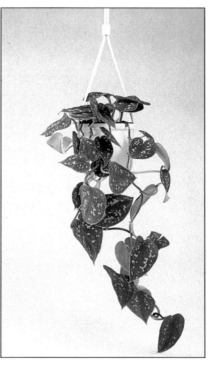

HEARTLEAF PHILODENDRON
Philodendron scandens

These small-leaved philodendrons are the easiest members of this genus to grow. The acutely pointed leaves are fleshy and attractively bronzed when they first appear, but become dark green and leathery with age. These plants can be trained up a support, such as a moss-covered pole, as well as being left to trail. They make good fillers for the front of groups, and are ideal for warm rooms which don't get too much sun.

Mini-climate 3 Warm, shady.
Size These philodendrons are fast-growing; maximum size is unpredictable but a 6ft length and a 20in spread can be reached. Pinch out growing tips to encourage bushy growth. Small plants are offered for sale.
Feeding Feed with standard liquid fertilizer every two weeks in spring and summer, and once every month in autumn and winter.
Potting Repot every spring using half soil-based potting mixture and half leaf mold or peat moss. Once plants are in 10-12in pots topdress instead.
Special points Stand plants on trays filled with moist pebbles to increase humidity.

POTHOS VINE
Scindapsus pictus "Argyraeus"

The most striking feature of these plants is their matt olive-green colored leaves covered with silver spots. The heart-shaped leaves are carried on thick stems which occasionally produce aerial roots. Mass several small plants together or put a large specimen in a hanging basket near a sunny window. Pothos vines also make attractive feature plants when trained up moist, moss-covered poles.

Mini-climate 1 Warm, sunny.
Size Pothos vines are slow-growing, but mature plants can reach 5ft in height with a similar spread. Pinch out growing tips in spring to encourage bushy growth. Plants of 4-6in in height are offered for sale.
Feeding Feed with standard liquid fertilizer every two weeks from spring to autumn.
Potting Repot in spring using soil-based potting mixture but only if the roots have completely filled the existing pot. Once plants are in 6in pots topdress instead.
Special points Water more sparingly in winter.

DEVIL'S IVY
Epipremnum aureum

These plants, also known as "Solomon Island's ivies", have yellowish-green, angular stems with aerial roots and large, bright-green leaves boldly and irregularly marked with yellow. Devil's ivy is impressive in hanging baskets, on high shelves, or when trained up moss-covered poles. Large specimens have large leaves and are best displayed on their own in a warm room.

Mini-climate 2 Warm, filtered sun.
Size The stems of devil's ivy grow to a maximum of 6½ft long with a 3ft spread. Pinch out growing tips to encourage bushy growth. Young, small-leaved plants are offered for sale.
Feeding Feed with standard liquid fertilizer every two weeks in spring and summer.
Potting Repot every spring using soil-based potting mixture. If you don't want to move an older plant into a larger pot topdress instead.
Special points Water more sparingly in winter.

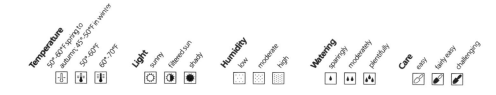

WANDERING JEW
Zebrina pendula

Also known as "inch plants", wandering Jews are highly decorative with attractive leaf coloring. The oval leaves have a striped, iridescent upper surface and a deep-purple underside. In spring and autumn, clusters of small, purple-pink flowers are produced. Wandering Jews make a fine display when massed in hanging baskets, but also look attractive trailing over the edge of a bowl in a mixed planting.

Mini-climate 1 Warm, sunny.
Size The stems of wandering Jews grow to 16in long with a spread of 1ft. Pinch out growing tips to encourage bushy growth. Small plants are offered for sale.
Feeding Feed with standard liquid fertilizer once every two weeks.
Potting Repot in spring using soil-based potting mixture but only if the roots have completely filled the existing pot. Discard the plant after the second or third repotting. Start new plants from cuttings.
Special points Remove stems with poorly colored leaves should they appear.

MINIATURE WAX PLANT
Hoya bella

These are spreading plants with drooping stems and dull green, fleshy leaves. The pure white, strongly scented flowers are grouped in star-shaped clusters of eight to ten, each flower having a curious purple center. Flowers appear through the summer. Miniature wax plants are best displayed in hanging baskets as the centers of the drooping flowers can only be seen from below. They look good in a sunny conservatory or modern interior.

Mini-climate 1 Warm, sunny.
Size Miniature wax plants grow to 1ft in height, the branches then begin to trail and produce a maximum spread of 1½ft.
Feeding Feed with high-potash liquid fertilizer every two weeks from spring to early autumn.
Potting Repot every spring using soil-based potting mixture making provision for good drainage. Once plants are in 5-6in pots topdress instead.
Special points Destroy any mealy bugs you may find.

COLUMNEA
Columnea banksii

These plants have striking scarlet flowers borne amongst the small, waxy leaves on long trailing stems. The flowers may be produced at any time of year and a large plant may have up to 100 flowers at any one time. Use large plants as specimens in plain containers or hanging baskets in a warm room.

Mini-climate 2 Warm, filtered sun.
Size The trailing stems of columneas reach a maximum length of 4ft. Young plants are offered for sale in spring.
Feeding Feed with one-quarter strength high-phosphate liquid fertilizer at every watering.
Potting Repot every spring using a mixture of equal parts peat moss, perlite and vermiculite. If you don't want to move an older plant into a larger pot prune the roots instead.
Special points Maintain high humidity throughout the year.

TRADESCANTIA
Tradescantia albiflora "Albovittata"

Tradescantias are very similar to zebrinas. The silver-and green-striped leaves are almost transparent. Mass plants in a hanging basket or allow a large specimen to trail from a shelf. They are useful for inclusion at the front of mixed arrangements in a suitably sunny room. Tradescantias will also climb.

Mini-climate 1 Warm, sunny.
Size Tradescantias are fast-growing, the stems reaching 1ft long. Pinch out growing tips to encourage bushy growth.
Feeding Feed with standard liquid fertilizer every two weeks from spring to autumn.
Potting Repot in spring using soil-based potting mixture but only if the roots have completely filled the existing pot. Discard the plant after the second repotting. Start new plants from cuttings.
Special points Remove any dried or poorly colored leaves.

Similar-shaped species
Tradescantia fluminensis "Variegata" has leaves which are a deep olive-green striped with cream and pink and covered with soft, velvety hairs.
Tradescantia sillamontana has peppermint-green leaves with long, white, woolly hair.

Trailing plants 2

SMALL-LEAVED TRAILING PLANTS continued

PICKABACK PLANT
Tolmiea menziesii

These plants, which are also known as "mother-of-thousands", derive their common names from the way that a number of mature leaves produce small plantlets on their upper surfaces. These weigh down the long leafstalks to give a trailing appearance. The fresh-green leaves and slender leafstalks are covered with soft hair. These are excellent plants to display in hanging baskets. They are easily kept in any cool place.

Mini-climate 5 Cool, filtered sun.
Size Pickaback plants are fast-growing and reach a height of about 1ft with a similar spread. Small plants are offered for sale.
Feeding Feed with standard liquid fertilizer every two weeks during spring and summer.
Potting Repot in spring using soil-based potting mixture but only if the roots have completely filled the existing pot. Discard the plant after the second or third repotting.
Special points Water more sparingly in winter.

SPIDER PLANT
Chlorophytum comosum "Vittatum"

These cultivars have a distinctive white or cream stripe down the center of each leaf. The narrow leaves arch over but the true trailing effect is produced by long stems bearing numerous plantlets. Well-grown spider plants make striking feature plants when displayed from a height, either on pedestals or in hanging baskets.

Mini-climate 5 Cool, filtered sun.
Size The leaves of spider plants can grow up to 2ft long. The spread depends on the number of plants growing in the same pot. Plants of all sizes are offered for sale.
Feeding Feed with standard liquid fertilizer every two weeks.
Potting Repot in spring using soil-based potting mixture but only if the roots have completely filled the existing pot. If you don't want to move an older plant into a larger pot topdress instead.
Special points Allow a 1in space at the top of the pot for the development of the fat roots.

STRAWBERRY GERANIUM
Saxifraga stolonifera

These plants produce many plantlets on threadlike stems. The mother plants are small and low-growing and the plantlets hang down from the center of the plant giving a trailing effect. Strawberry geraniums are best displayed in hanging baskets so that the red undersides to their leaves may be seen. Display in cool places, such as hallways, and ensure the delicate trailing stems are not brushed against.

Mini-climate 5 Cool, filtered sun.
Size Strawberry geraniums are fast growing, but reach no more than 8in high. The trailing stems grow to 2ft long.
Feeding Feed with standard liquid fertilizer once a month.
Potting Repot every spring using soil-based potting mixture. Discard the plant after the second repotting.
Special points Water more sparingly during the winter rest period.

ENGLISH IVY
Hedera helix hybrids

There are many hybrids of the English ivies, all forming low-growing bushy trailers, but with many variations in leaf shape and color.
Ivies may be used in a variety of ways: to infill the fronts of groups, as trailers in hanging baskets, or displayed along shelves. They can also be trained to climb.

Mini-climate 5 Cool, filtered sun.
Size Ivies can grow very large and straggly so pinch out growing tips to encourage bushy growth. Plants of all sizes are offered for sale.
Feeding Feed with standard liquid fertilizer every two weeks in spring and summer and once a month in autumn and winter.
Potting Repot in spring using soil-based potting mixture but only if the roots have completely filled the existing pot. If you don't want to move an older plant into a larger pot topdress instead.
Special points Water more sparingly during the winter rest period.

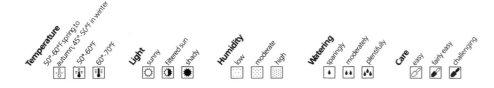

EMERALD FERN
Asparagus densiflorus "Sprengeri"

These plants have arching stems which begin to trail with age. Each frond is covered in tiny branchlets, giving the plants a delicate, fernlike appearance; in fact they are not true ferns but related to the lilies. Use them to soften the outline of arrangements, or group with true ferns in a hanging basket. Emerald ferns thrive in most conditions and have a fresh, informal look which makes them suitable for most types of setting.

Mini-climate 2 Warm, filtered sun.
Size The fronds of emerald ferns can grow up to 3ft in length. Small plants are offered for sale.
Feeding Feed with standard liquid fertilizer every two weeks in spring and summer, and once a month in autumn and winter.
Potting Repot in spring using soil-based potting mixture but only if the roots have completely filled the existing pot. If you don't want to move an older plant into a larger pot topdress instead.
Special points To keep plants in a decorative state for as long as possible, faded stems should be cut out as they appear.

PURPLE VELVET PLANT
Gynura aurantiaca

The tooth-edged leaves of these plants are covered in fine, purple hair and are at their most colorful when the leaves first open. The stems are upright at first but sprawl as they get longer. The downy leaves are seen to full advantage when the plants are massed in hanging baskets and viewed against a sunny window. A large plant looks good displayed in a room containing richly colored fabrics.

Mini-climate 1 Warm, sunny.
Size The trailing stems of purple velvet plants can reach over 3ft in length. Small, compact plants are offered for sale.
Feeding Feed with standard liquid fertilizer once every month.
Potting Repot in spring using soil-based potting mixture. Discard the plant after the second repotting.
Special points Water more sparingly in winter. Unpleasantly scented orange flowers are produced and should be removed before they open.

ITALIAN BELLFLOWER
Campanula isophylla

Italian bellflowers produce clusters of delicate-looking white or pale-blue flowers in early August and continue flowering until November. The flowers are normally so numerous that they completely hide the pale-green foliage. They are best treated as annuals and discarded when flowering has finished. Italian bellflowers are useful plants for massing in hanging baskets or window-boxes. They look good in conservatories or informal rooms.

Mini-climate 4 Cool, sunny.
Size The slender stems of Italian bellflowers reach a maximum length of 1ft. Pinch out growing tips to encourage bushy growth. Small plants are offered for sale in summer from some house plant specialists.
Feeding Feed with standard liquid fertilizer every two weeks during the flowering season.
Potting Repot every spring using soil-based potting mixture. When plants are in 5in pots topdress instead.
Special points Mist-spray plants in hanging baskets every day throughout summer and autumn.

LARGE-LEAVED TRAILING PLANTS

STAGHORN FERN
Platycerium bifurcatum

These are most unusual ferns. All plants have two types of frond: small fronds which clasp the plant's support and large, drooping fronds which give the fern its distinctive appearance. The fronds are dark green and covered with a fine, white, felty scurf. Staghorn ferns make striking specimen plants, particularly when displayed from a height.

Mini-climate 3 Warm, shady.
Size The fronds of the staghorn fern reach up to 3ft. Small plants are offered for sale.
Feeding Feed with standard liquid fertilizer once a month during active growth. Add feed to a bucket of water used to soak the pot or bark.
Potting Only small plants should be in pots—use fern potting mixture. Older plants should be grown on a piece of bark. Wrap the root ball in sphagnum moss and tie to the bark.
Special points Mist-spray regularly to maintain high humidity.

Creeping plants

These are plants with stems that grow just over the surface of the potting mixture. This ground-hugging habit creates a carpeting effect when they are allowed to spread. Creeping plants can be used successfully as ground cover around upright plants and to break up the hard lines of large containers. Some creeping plants, such as the little club moss, send roots down into the potting mixture whenever they touch it, virtually creating new plants; while others, such as the Swedish ivy, do no more than rest on the surface of the mixture.

Plants in this group tend to be small-leaved and most are small in overall size. Some will spread to become quite large with age, but will only do this if they are given adequate space. Certain species, like the versatile creeping fig, have a naturally creeping habit but can also be trained to climb up a support or trail from a hanging basket, as can the larger Swedish ivy.

Some of the plants in this category have unusual leaf-markings: the eyelash begonia has reddish-brown markings on lime-green leaves; the nerve plant has exotic, carmine-red leaf veins on a dark-green background; and the little nerve plant has silver leaf veins. The bead plant has pea-sized orange berries which remain decorative for several months. The colorful leaves and berries of the creeping plants compensate for the lack of flowers; any flowers which do appear are small and insignificant. Many of the creeping plants are particularly well suited to the humid atmosphere of bottle gardens and terraria.

SMALL-LEAVED CREEPING PLANTS

BABY'S TEARS
Soleirolia soleirolii

These pretty plants produce masses of tiny, bright-green leaves on thin stems, and will quickly carpet all available space in the pot. A number of these mossy mounds make an attractive display if they are arranged in a wicker basket They also look good filling in the front of foliage displays. Do not use them in bottle gardens or terraria as they quickly fill all the available space.

Mini-climate 4 Cool, sunny.
Size Baby's tears plants will not exceed 2in in height, but their spread is only limited by the size of the container in which they are grown. Trim the plant with a pair of scissors to maintain a neat shape. Small and medium-sized plants are offered for sale all year.
Feeding Feed with half-strength standard liquid fertilizer every two weeks in summer.
Potting Repot in spring using soil-based potting mixture. Discard the plant after the second repotting.
Special points Keep potting mixture damp at all times to prevent the leaves from turning brown.

BEAD PLANT
Nertera granadensis

The attractive bead plants have tiny, green leaves, but are prized for the profusion of pea-sized, bright-orange berries that develop from the insignificant, greenish-yellow flowers. The berries appear in late summer and last several months. They are best treated as annuals and discarded when the berries begin to die off. Bead plants make colorful table displays and are also suitable for growing in dish gardens, bottle gardens and terraria as long as they are kept small.

Mini-climate 4 Cool, sunny.
Size Bead plants form a low mound up to 3in high, with a maximum spread of around 6in. Small plants are offered for sale.
Feeding Feed with standard liquid fertilizer every two months while the berries are growing.
Potting Repot every spring using a mixture of two-thirds soil-based potting mixture and one-third peat moss. If you don't want to move an older plant into a larger pot topdress instead.
Special points Water more sparingly in winter. Bead plants can be placed outside, in a sheltered spot, in summer.

LITTLE CLUB MOSS
Selaginella martensii

These unusual plants have decorative, medium-green leaves which are packed round the branches like the scales of a fish. The creeping stems of little club mosses form a dense mat of foliage with a pleasant, soft texture. Roots are put down into the potting mixture at intervals. A terrarium or bottle garden is the best environment in which to display these small plants as they will thrive in the humid atmosphere.

Mini-climate 2 Warm, filtered sun.
Size The creeping stems of little club mosses may grow to 6in in length. Small plants are offered for sale.
Feeding Feed with one-quarter strength standard liquid fertilizer every two weeks.
Potting Repot every spring using a mixture of two-thirds peat-based potting mix and one-third coarse sand. Once plants are in 6-8in pots simply remove plants from their pots, clean and refill them with fresh mixture and replace the plants.
Special points Touch the plants as little as possible as this can damage the foliage.

Similar-shaped species
Selaginella apoda has shorter stems which branch more profusely, bearing fleshy, pale-green leaves.
Selaginella pallescens has white-edged leaves which grow on erect stems of up to 1ft long.

Temperature 50°-60°F spring to autumn; 45°-50°F in winter · 50°-60°F · 60°-70°F Light sunny · filtered sun · shady Humidity low · moderate · high Watering sparingly · moderately · plentifully Care easy · fairly easy · challenging

EYELASH BEGONIA
Begonia "Tiger Paws"

Eyelash begonias derive their name from the short, coarse hairs which grow around the edge of each lopsided, heart-shaped leaf. The attractive foliage is bright lime-green in color, marked with a bronze-red pattern which gives the leaves a patched or blotchy appearance. The stalks are also speckled with red and arise from a rhizome which creeps across the surface of the potting mixture. Arrange these begonias together in a basket or mix them with other foliage plants.

Mini-climate 2 Warm, filtered sun.
Size Eyelash begonias grow to about 6in in height with a 1ft spread. Small plants are offered for sale all year.
Feeding Feed with standard liquid fertilizer every two weeks during spring and summer.
Potting Repot every spring using an equal combination of soil-based potting mixture and leaf mold. If you don't want to move an older plant into a larger pot topdress instead. Discard the plant after several repottings.
Special points Stand plants on trays filled with moist pebbles to increase humidity. Protect from powdery mildew by supplying adequate ventilation.

NERVE PLANT
Fittonia verschaffeltii

These plants have oval, olive-green leaves which are covered by a network of fine, carmine-colored veins creating a mosaic effect. Yellow flower spikes may occasionally be produced. These plants are suitable for displaying together on a low table; they also look good in the forefront of a foliage group and are ideal for bottle gardens or terraria.

Mini-climate 3 Warm, shady.
Size Nerve plants reach a height of 6in with a spread of about 1ft. Pinch out growing tips to encourage bushy growth. Small plants are offered for sale all year.
Feeding Feed with half-strength standard liquid fertilizer every two weeks in spring and summer.
Potting Repot every spring using peat-based potting mixture in half-pots or other shallow containers. Once plants are in 4½in pots simply remove plants from their pots, clean and refill them with fresh mixture and replace the plants.
Special points Stand plants on trays filled with moist pebbles to increase humidity.

Similar-shaped species
Fittonia verschaffeltii argyroneura "Nana" has smaller leaves with silver veins and reaches a maximum spread of only 6in.

SWEDISH IVY
Plectranthus australis

Swedish ivies have fleshy, dark-green foliage borne on succulent, pink stems which lie flat on the potting mixture before they grow over the edge of the pot. The occasional pale-lavender flowers are insignificant and can be removed as they develop. Especially attractive in hanging baskets, the Swedish ivy also provides excellent ground cover for indoor window-boxes and other large groupings.

Mini-climate 1 Warm, sunny.
Size Swedish ivies are fast-growing; their stems quickly reach 3ft in length, with a height of 8in. Pinch out the growing tips to encourage bushy growth. Small plants are offered for sale.
Feeding Feed with standard liquid fertilizer every two weeks from spring to autumn.
Potting Repot in spring using soil-based potting mixture but only if the roots have completely filled the existing pot. If you don't want to move an older plant into a larger pot topdress instead.
Special points Water more sparingly in winter.

Similar-shaped species
Plectranthus oertendahlii has bronze-green leaves covered in soft hairs. The leaves have prominent white veins and are rosy-purple underneath.

CREEPING FIG
Ficus pumila

These plants have small, heart-shaped, slightly wrinkled leaves borne on long, wiry stems which spread out across the surface of the potting mixture. Creeping figs look good in shallow hanging baskets. Alternatively, they can be used as ground cover in indoor window-boxes. Small plants make good fillers in bottle gardens.

Mini-climate 5 Cool, filtered sun.
Size The stems of the creeping fig can reach 2ft in length. Spread depends on the mode of growth. Small plants are offered for sale.
Feeding Feed with standard liquid fertilizer every two weeks.
Potting Repot in spring using peat-based potting mixture but only if the roots have completely filled the existing pot.
Special points Stand plants on trays filled with moist pebbles to increase humidity. Never allow the potting mixture to dry out as the leaves will shrivel and never recover.

Bulbs

B ulbs and corms are the food storage organs of plants which have a distinct dormant period when all top growth dies down and no further growth takes place. Bulbs are made up of tightly packed modified leaves surrounding an embryo shoot and usually a complete embryo flower. Corms consist of modified stem bases covered in thin, papery scales and do not contain the young plant, but a bud from which the shoots and roots appear. Many bulbs and corms are "hardy", in that they need a period of wintering. Hardy bulbs are bought in their dormant state during autumn and early winter and, when potted up and provided with the right growing conditions, they start to come into flower in a matter of a few weeks. These special cold, dark conditions are known as "wintering" and it is during this period that roots are produced. To produce good flowers, the wintering recommendations for each bulb should be adhered to, as it is essential that adequate roots are established before flowering is induced. It should be noted that the care symbols for each entry refer to conditions applicable when the plant is in full flower. Some corms, such as crocuses, need to be kept cool right up to the stage when the flower buds start to show color, and their early development cannot be enjoyed in the home. Some spring bulbs, such as tulips, daffodils and hyacinths, especially those treated by the grower, can be potted up and most of their growth and development watched and enjoyed. The size of the plants produced ranges from the tiny crocus to the tall and elegant amaryllis.

Hardy bulbs and corms provide temporary house plants, but tender bulbs, such as the amaryllis, can be brought into flower season after season providing they are given a rest period in autumn.

DAFFODIL AND NARCISSUS
Narcissus sp. and hybrids

These bulbs have bright, graceful flowers, many of which are scented, with colors ranging through all shades of orange, yellow, cream and white. Many different shapes are available: trumpets, clusters, double-flowered and many other forms. The common name daffodil is used for most members of the genus, although some kinds are often called narcissi, especially those whose flowers have short trumpets. The flowers bloom naturally in late winter and early spring, but can be forced to flower earlier indoors. Many of the bulbs—including *N.* "Cragford" and *N.* "Paper-white"—can be forced in bowls filled with moist pebbles.

Mini-climate 4 Cool, sunny
Size Daffodils grow from 6-18in high, according to variety. Bulbs are sold in the autumn, the best quality being double-nosed bulbs, each bulb produces two or three flowers.
Feeding Feeding is unnecessary.
Potting Plant in early autumn in a peat-based potting mixture. Use about three bulbs of tall varieties in a 6in pot or several bulbs of miniature varieties to a smaller, squat pot. Allow the tips of the bulbs to show.
Special points Soak the pots of bulbs well before starting their "wintering" of eight to ten weeks. Forced daffodils—except for paper-whites—can be planted later in the garden.

AMARYLLIS
Hippeastrum hybrids

These plants have spectacular trumpet-shaped blooms up to four on a bare stem. Straplike leaves may be present or appear after the flowers. The flowers, which are produced in spring, can be white, red, orange or yellow, and are often striped or patterned. For a dramatic display, mass several plants together in a large bowl.

Mini-climate 1 Warm, sunny.
Size The flower stems of the amaryllis grow to 20in long, with flowers as much as 6in in diameter. Ordinary bulbs are offered for sale in autumn. Specially prepared bulbs, which will flower at Christmastime, are also offered for sale.
Feeding Feed with standard liquid fertilizer every two weeks from the time the flowers fade until mid-summer. Switch to high-potash fertilizer to ripen the bulb and to ensure flowering the following year. Stop feeding from early autumn.
Potting Plant new bulbs by themselves in 4½-6in pots using soil-based potting mixture. Bury only half of the bulb in the mixture. Repotting should only be necessary every three or four years or more.
Special points These tender bulbs should not be "wintered". During the autumn rest period, leave the bulbs in their pots and water very sparingly. Stand them outside in a sunny spot during summer and early autumn to help induce flowering the following year.

MINIATURE IRIS
Iris reticulata

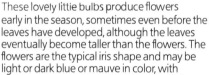

These lovely little bulbs produce flowers early in the season, sometimes even before the leaves have developed, although the leaves eventually become taller than the flowers. The flowers are the typical iris shape and may be light or dark blue or mauve in color, with bright-yellow markings. Each bloom rarely lasts more than two days, even if they are displayed in a cool place. However, their delicate fragrance makes it worth displaying them so that they can be appreciated close-up.

Mini-climate 4 Cool, sunny.
Size The flower stalks of miniature irises grow to about 6in in height, with leaves which are slightly longer. The tiny bulbs are sold dry in autumn or sometimes planted up and in leaf in winter.
Feeding Feeding is unnecessary.
Potting Plant the bulbs in the autumn in a shallow container using bulb fiber. Good drainage is essential as these tiny bulbs rot very easily. Plant them 2in deep and close together—about 12 in a 12in pot.
Special points Bulbs should be "wintered" for six weeks. Miniature irises can be planted out in the garden when flowering has finished.

Temperature			Light			Humidity			Watering			Care		
50°-60°F spring to autumn, 45°-50°F in winter	50°-60°F	60°-70°F	sunny	filtered sun	shady	low	moderate	high	sparingly	moderately	plentifully	easy	fairly easy	challenging

CROCUS
Crocus hybrids

The most commonly seen indoor crocuses are large-flowered Dutch hybrids which have green-and-white striped leaves and white, yellow, bronze, purple or striped blooms. These are cup-shaped and appear during winter and early spring. It is best to mass one variety of crocus in a shallow bowl.

Mini-climate 4   Cool, sunny.
Size   Crocuses grow to about 5in in height. Dry corms are offered for sale in late summer. Pre-planted pots are offered for sale at Christmastime.
Feeding   Feeding is unnecessary.
Potting   Plant several corms together in early autumn, using soil-based potting mixture or bulb fiber. Plant the corms just below the surface of the potting mixture.
Special points   Corms must be "wintered" for ten weeks and only brought into a warm room when the flower buds are seen.

TULIP
Tulipa hybrids

Tulips have an extraordinary variety of shapes, colors and patterns; even the leaves can be plain or variegated. The flowers are produced during late winter and early spring. It is best to plant just one variety of tulip in a pot rather than mixing the colors in the same container.

Mini-climate 4   Cool, sunny.
Size   Tulips grow to about 30in tall. Dwarf varieties grow to 8-12in tall. Most tulip bulbs are "rounds", producing only one flower. Specially prepared bulbs which will flower earlier are also offered for sale.
Feeding   Feeding is only necessary if the bulbs are to be planted outside the following season. Feed every ten days from the time the buds appear.
Potting   Plant in early autumn using either peat-based potting mixture or bulb fiber. Five or six bulbs should be planted close together, with just the tips exposed above the potting mixture.
Special points   Prepared bulbs should be "wintered" for eight weeks, ordinary bulbs for ten weeks.

GRAPE HYACINTH
Muscari sp.

The tiny bulbs of the grape hyacinth produce long narrow stalks topped with an elongated cluster of tiny blue or white flowers. Each individual flower is bell-shaped, and rimmed with a frilled white edge. The clusters of flowers open from the bottom upwards. The narrow leaves are strap-shaped and in the case of one species at least, are produced in autumn. Plant several bulbs in small pots and display them along a windowsill.

Mini-climate 4   Cool, sunny.
Size   Grape hyacinths reach a height of about 6in with leaves of nearly the same length. Bulbs already in leaf are offered for sale.
Feeding   Feeding is unnecessary.
Potting   Plant about twelve bulbs in a 6in pot in soil-based potting mixture or bulb fiber. Leave the tips of the bulbs above the potting mixture.
Special points   These bulbs should be "wintered" for ten weeks.

HYACINTH
Hyacinthus orientalis hybrids

Hyacinth flowers appear in spring and may be single or double, red, pink, yellow, blue or white. Their color and distinctive scent make them really welcome in the home. A group known as Roman hyacinths may produce two or even three flower stalks, but these are less tightly packed with the bell-shaped flowers. Bulbs of the same color should be massed in a shallow bowl for the best effect. They can also be cut and used in flower arrangements, combined with carnations, freesias and catkins, for example.

Mini-climate 5   Cool, filtered sun.
Size   The single flower stalks are 8-12in tall. Bulbs are sold according to size, in the autumn, and the size of the flower spike depends on the size of the bulb. Specially prepared bulbs which flower slightly earlier are offered for sale.
Feeding   Feeding is unnecessary.
Potting   Plant the bulbs "shoulder to shoulder" in soil-based potting mixture or bulb fiber. Leave the tips of the bulbs above the potting mixture. Hyacinths can also be grown in gravel, or water alone.
Special points   Prepared bulbs should be "wintered" for six weeks, ordinary bulbs for ten weeks.

Cacti and succulents 1

Cacti and succulents add a different range of shapes and textures to a collection of house plants. Most of the cacti have abandoned leaves and developed their unusual body shapes to prevent excessive loss of water. Some are ribbed or segmented and they may be covered with decorative spines, bristles or hairs. One species, the old man cactus, is so closely covered with white hair that it resembles a ball of wool. Desert cacti (usually covered in spines), such as mammillarias and rebutias, have the added attraction of striking flowers. The jungle cacti (often without spines), such as the orchid and Christmas cacti, have stems which are notched at intervals and respectively produce brightly colored flowers in early spring and mid-winter. Many cacti are relatively small reaching only a few inches in height; but others, such as the old man cactus, can grow to 10ft tall.

Succulents are those plants which have fleshy stems or leaves that store water. They come in a range of shapes and sizes as diverse as those of the cacti. Succulents may be upright and treelike in shape, or have thin trailing stems, or be spherical or columnar in outline. Some are just a few inches high; others can grow to 6ft tall and make large, striking plants. Leaf shape varies from the thick, succulent leaves of the Chinese jade and the silver crown to the thin, narrow leaves of the crown-of-thorns. Leaf color also varies from the green of the lace aloe and kalanchoe to the silvery-mauve of the rosary vine or the green and white of the queen agave.

UPRIGHT PLANTS

SILVER CROWN
Cotyledon undulata

These most unusual plants have fleshy, fan-shaped leaves with undulating edges and a dense covering of fine, silver-white scurf. Although orange-yellow flowers may appear on older plants in summer, it is for their leaves that they are grown. Mass several plants in a bowl on a low table.

Mini-climate 4 Cool, sunny.
Size Silver crowns are slow-growing reaching a height of about 20in in three years. Plants of all sizes are offered for sale.
Feeding Feed with standard liquid fertilizer once a month from spring to early autumn.
Potting Repot every spring using two-thirds soil-based potting mixture and one-third coarse sand, making provision for good drainage. Once plants are in 6in pots topdress instead.
Special points Avoid handling the plants as the meal will rub off. Water more sparingly in winter.

Similar-shaped species
Cotyledon orbiculata grows taller and has gray-green leaves edged with red, with just a little meal. Orange flowers appear in summer.

CROWN-OF-THORNS
Euphorbia milii

These succulent shrubs have horizontal branches bearing many sharp spines and relatively few leaves. The clusters of yellow or red "flowers" are in fact bracts which last for months, appearing in greatest profusion from February to September. Their interesting form and colorful bracts make them excellent specimen plants for the modern interior.

Mini-climate 1 Warm, sunny.
Size Crown-of-thorns can grow to about 3ft in height with a similar spread. Plants of all sizes are offered for sale.
Feeding Feed with standard liquid fertilizer once a month from spring to autumn.
Potting Repot young plants every second year in spring using half soil-based potting mixture and half coarse sand, making provision for good drainage. If you don't want to move an older plant into a larger pot topdress instead.
Special points These plants "bleed" a white latex if damaged: this latex should not be allowed to touch the eyes or the mouth.

KALANCHOE
Kalanchoe blossfeldiana hybrids

These attractive succulents flower in late winter and early spring, and remain in flower for about three months. The small flowers are grouped in closely packed flower heads borne on long stems. Each head has between 20 and 50 flowers. Color ranges from pink, through red, to orange and yellow. The fleshy leaves are dark green and often edged in red. Kalanchoes are best treated as annuals and discarded when flowering has finished. Use them massed on a low table for a splash of winter color.

Mini-climate 1 Warm, sunny.
Size Kalanchoes reach a maximum height of about 14in tall. A dwarf form is available and reaches 8in in height. Plants in flower are offered for sale all year but are particularly common around Christmastime.
Feeding Feed with standard liquid fertilizer once a month whilst in flower.
Potting Repotting is unnecessary.
Special points To keep plants in a decorative state for as long as possible remove flowers as they fade.

OLD MAN CACTUS
Cephalocereus senilis

The common name of these cacti is derived from the long, fine, white hair that shrouds the fleshy columnar body and hides the sharp spines. Flowers are only produced on older plants. Old man cacti look best massed with other cacti in a cactus garden.

Mini-climate 4 Cool, sunny.
Size Old man cacti are slow-growing and unlikely to grow taller than 10-12in. Plants of all sizes are offered for sale.
Feeding Feed with tomato-type fertilizer once a month from spring to mid-autumn.
Potting Repot in spring using three parts soil-based potting mixture and one part coarse sand, but only if the plant has completely filled the existing pot. If you don't want to move an older plant into a larger pot topdress instead.
Special points Do not water during the winter rest period. The long hairs may be washed in a weak solution of detergent to keep them clean.

PERUVIAN APPLE CACTUS
Cereus peruvianus "Monstrosus"

These cacti have bright-green columnar bodies which are twisted and contorted into most unusual shapes. They are in fact mutations of the true species. The yellow spines are short and inconspicuous. Large but short-lived white, scented flowers are produced in summer on older specimens. Their sculptural quality can be quite spectacular when several plants are grouped in a modern interior.

Mini-climate 4 Cool, sunny.
Size The Peruvian apple cactus is slow-growing and each mutation varies in maximum height and spread. Small plants are offered for sale.
Feeding Feed with tomato-type fertilizer once a month from spring to early autumn.
Potting Repot every spring using two-thirds soil-based potting mixture and one-third coarse sand. If you don't want to move an older plant into a larger pot topdress instead.

RABBIT'S EARS CACTUS
Opuntia microdasys

These arresting cacti are made up of flattened, oval segments which fit on top of one another. These segments are densely covered in tufts of tiny, yellowish spines. Yellow flowers are produced very occasionally. Rabbit's ears cacti have a spectacular outline and larger ones can be used as specimen plants. Group smaller plants in a cactus garden.

Mini-climate 4 Cool, sunny.
Size Rabbit's ears cacti can reach a maximum height of about 3ft and spread of about 2ft. Plants of all sizes are offered for sale.
Feeding Feed with tomato-type fertilizer once a month from spring to autumn.
Potting Repot in spring using two-thirds soil-based potting mixture and one-third coarse sand, but only if the plants have completely filled the existing pot.
Special points The tiny spines can be very painful if they touch the skin. Water more sparingly during the winter rest period.

CHINESE JADE
Crassula arborescens

These succulents have fleshy, almost round leaves which are gray in color and rimmed with red. They are borne on thick, branching, woody stems which are symmetrical in shape when the plant is mature. Small Chinese jades can be used as "trees" in dish gardens or miniature oriental gardens.

Mini-climate 4 Cool, sunny.
Size Very young Chinese jades are offered for sale; they will eventually reach 3ft or more in height, when the stems will resemble gnarled tree trunks.
Feeding Feed with standard liquid fertilizer once a month from spring to early autumn.
Potting Repot every spring using three parts soil-based potting mixture and one part coarse sand. Once plants are in 8in pots topdress instead.
Special points Water more sparingly in winter.

Similar-shaped species
Crassula ovata has shiny, jade-green succulent leaves and symmetrical branches.

Cacti and succulents 2

SPHERICAL PLANTS

FISH-HOOK CACTUS
Ferocactus latispinus

These cacti are noted for their fierce-looking spines which are grouped in clusters. Spines within individual clusters vary in size, shape and color, with one being broader and more prominently hooked than the others. Really mature plants can produce violet-colored flowers in summer. Large plants make good specimens—otherwise mix them with cacti of contrasting shapes in a cactus garden.

Mini-climate 4 Cool, sunny.
Size Fish-hook cacti can reach a maximum of 1ft in height and 8in across. Plants of all sizes are offered for sale.
Feeding Feed with tomato-type fertilizer once a month from spring to autumn.
Potting Repot in spring using a combination of two-thirds soil-based potting mixture and one-third coarse sand, but only if the plant has completely filled the existing pot.
Special points Do not water during the winter rest period or plants will rot.

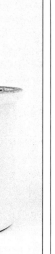

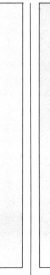

BISHOP'S CAP
Astrophytum myriostigma

These spherical cacti are divided into wide segments, each covered with a silvery meal instead of thorns. They look rather like de-spined sea urchins. The bright-yellow flowers resemble daisies and appear from the top of the plant in summer. Bishop's caps look good in cactus gardens or massed in a shallow bowl with a gravelly surround.

Mini-climate 4 Cool, sunny.
Size Bishop's caps are slow-growing, reaching about 10in in height with a spread of 5in. Plants of all sizes are offered for sale.
Feeding Feed with tomato-type fertilizer once a month from spring to autumn.
Potting Repot in spring using two-thirds soil-based potting mixture and one-third coarse sand, but only if the plant has completely filled the existing pot.
Special points Water more sparingly during the winter rest period.

GOLDEN PINCUSHION
Mammillaria rhodantha

These spherical cacti have bright-green bodies covered in small knobs which bear long, yellow-orange spines. They are arranged in circular groups over the whole body. Pink, daisylike flowers appear in a ring around the top of the body in summer. Display the golden pincushion in a cactus garden or group with other cacti.

Mini-climate 4 Cool, sunny.
Size Golden pincushions grow to about 4in in height and 3in in spread. Small plants are offered for sale.
Feeding Feed with tomato-type liquid fertilizer once a month from spring to autumn.
Potting Repot in spring using two-thirds soil-based potting mixture and one-third coarse sand, but only if the plant has completely filled the existing pot.
Special points Water more sparingly during the winter rest period.

RED CROWN
Rebutia minuscula

These small, white-spined cacti are almost completely round and quickly become surrounded by many offsets. They flower when very young and are crowned with red, funnel-shaped flowers from spring through the summer. The flowers open in the morning and close in the afternoon. Group flowering red crowns together for a spectacular display in a modern setting.

Mini-climate 4 Cool, sunny.
Size Red crowns are fast-growing and can make clumps 6in across in a year or two.
Feeding Feed with tomato-type fertilizer once a month from spring to mid-autumn.
Potting Repot in spring using three parts soil-based potting mixture and one part coarse sand, but only if the roots have completely filled the existing pot.
Special points Do not water during the winter rest period or plants will rot.

Temperature 50°-60°F spring to autumn, 45°-50°F in winter | 50°-60°F | 60°-70°F
Light sunny | filtered sun | shady
Humidity low | moderate | high
Watering sparingly | moderately | plentifully
Care easy | fairly easy | challenging

ROSE PINCUSHION
Mammillaria zeilmanniana

The spherical body of the rose pincushion is densely covered in regularly arranged yellow and brown spines. The numerous flowers are produced in summer and form a ring at the top of the body. They are reddish-purple in color. Allow the rose pincushion to form large clumps.

Mini-climate 4 Cool, sunny.
Size Individual rose pincushions grow to 2in in height but will form clumps of 10in across in around five years. Small plants are offered for sale.
Feeding Feed with tomato-type fertilizer once a month from spring to autumn.
Potting Repot in spring using two-thirds soil-based potting mixture and one-third coarse sand, but only if the plant has completely filled the existing pot.
Special points Water more sparingly during the winter rest period.

GOLDEN BARREL CACTUS
Echinocactus grusonii

These cacti are armed with stout, golden-yellow spines arranged in rows on the ribbed stems. Older plants develop the typical pattern of raised vertical ribs. Golden barrel cacti can be displayed with other cacti or foliage plants.

Mini-climate 4 Cool, sunny.
Size Golden barrel cacti grow quickly to 3-4in across, then it takes many years for the plant to double its size, though they can eventually reach a diameter of 8in. Small plants are offered for sale.
Feeding Feed with tomato-type fertilizer once a month from spring to autumn.
Potting Repot in spring using two-thirds soil-based potting mixture and one-third coarse sand, but only if the plant has completely filled the existing pot. When repotting is not necessary topdress instead.
Special points Do not water during the winter rest period or plants will rot.

OLD LADY CACTUS
Mammillaria hahniana

These globular cacti get their name from the white, silky hairs which cover and hide the grayish-green body and the sharp spines. When the cacti are about four years old, crimson flowers appear in early May. Group several old lady cacti together for a dramatic display or use in a cactus garden.

Mini-climate 4 Cool, sunny.
Size Old lady cacti grow to 4in tall with a spread of 3in. Small plants are offered for sale.
Feeding Feed with tomato-type fertilizer once a month from spring to autumn.
Potting Repot in spring using two-thirds soil-based potting mixture and one-third coarse sand, but only if the plant has completely filled the existing pot.
Special points Water more sparingly during the winter rest period.

SPIKY-LEAVED PLANTS

LACE ALOE
Aloe aristata

These stemless succulents are made up of many fleshy leaves arranged in tight rosettes. The triangular leaves are dark green and covered with raised white spots. The small orange-red flowers are borne on a long stalk which appears from the center of the rosette in summer and last only a few days. Offsets are readily produced from the base of mature plants. Group plants together and place them so that they are seen from above for maximum effect.

Mini-climate 1 Warm, sunny.
Size Lace aloes reach a maximum height of 6in. Spread is only limited by the size of the pot.
Feeding Feed with standard liquid fertilizer once a month from spring to autumn.
Potting Repot every spring using soil-based potting mixture. If you don't want to move an older plant into a larger pot topdress instead.
Special points Water more sparingly in winter. Avoid trapping water in the rosette of leaves.

Cacti and succulents 3

FLAT-LEAVED ROSETTE-SHAPED PLANTS

PAINTED LADY
Echeveria derenbergii

These pretty succulents have tightly packed bluish-gray leaves with a coating of silvery scurf and red margins. Yellow and orange bell-shaped flowers borne on spikes are produced in winter and early spring. They make good, small specimen plants for the kitchen windowsill all year round.

Mini-climate 4 Cool, sunny.
Size Painted ladies form cushions 4-6in across. Young single plants are offered for sale.
Feeding Feed with half-strength standard liquid fertilizer once a month from spring to autumn.
Potting Repot every second spring using four parts soil-based potting mixture and one part coarse sand. If you don't want to move an older plant into a larger pot topdress instead.
Special points Water more sparingly in winter.

MOLDED WAX PLANT
Echeveria agavoides

These succulents have triangular fleshy leaves which are light green with brown tips. Yellow flowers tipped with red are produced in spring. Molded wax plants should be viewed from above for best effect—place them on a low table, or use in a succulent garden.

Mini-climate 4 Cool, sunny.
Size Molded wax plants grow to about 3½in tall with a spread of about 6in. Plants of all sizes are offered for sale.
Feeding Feed with half-strength standard liquid fertilizer once a month from spring to autumn.
Potting Repot plants every second spring using four parts soil-based potting mixture and one part coarse sand. If you don't want to move an older plant into a larger pot topdress instead.
Special points Water more sparingly in winter.

QUEEN AGAVE
Agave victoriae-reginae

These succulents have three-dimensional scalelike leaves. Each fleshy leaf is dark green with a white margin and bears a sharp black spine at its tip. Queen agaves are the most attractive of agaves and should be displayed so that they can be seen from above.

Mini-climate 4 Cool, sunny.
Size Queen agaves are slow-growing, reaching a maximum height of 8in, but they can attain a spread of about 1½ft. Small plants are offered for sale.
Feeding Feed with standard liquid fertilizer once a month during spring and summer.
Potting Repot every second year in spring using two-thirds soil-based potting mixture and one-third coarse sand. If you don't want to move an older plant into a larger pot topdress instead.
Special points Water more sparingly in winter.

TRAILING PLANTS

CLAW CACTUS
Schlumbergera truncata

These jungle cacti have flattened, segmented stems which are notched at intervals. Bright-magenta, pink or white flowers are produced in late autumn. The stems are erect at first but begin to trail as more segments are produced. They make good specimen plants for hanging baskets or shelves.

Mini-climate 2 Warm, filtered sun.
Size The stems of claw cacti can grow to about 2ft in height and spread. Plants of all sizes are offered for sale.
Feeding Feed with tomato-type fertilizer once a month from early November to the end of flowering.
Potting Repot every second year in spring using two-thirds peat-based potting mixture and one-third coarse sand. Once plants are in 8-10in pots repot every year.
Special points Water more sparingly during the rest period following flowering.

Similar-shaped species
Schlumbergera "Bridgesii" is very similar but blooms later and has less sharply defined notches.

Temperature			Light				Humidity			Watering			Care		
50°-60°F spring to autumn, 45°-50°F in winter	50°-60°F	60°-70°F		sunny	filtered sun	shady	low	moderate	high	sparingly	moderately	plentifully	easy	fairly easy	challenging

ROSARY VINE
Ceropegia woodii

These small, tuber-forming succulents have trailing threadlike stems bearing heart-shaped leaves. These fleshy leaves, which appear in pairs at intervals along the stems, are marbled with silvery-gray and have purple undersides. Small, tube-shaped flowers appear amongst the leaves in summer. Several rosary vines displayed together in a small hanging basket in a warm room make an unusual display. Position them where they will not be brushed against. Alternatively, the stems may be coiled in the pot so the flowers stand upright.

Mini-climate 1 Warm, sunny.
Size Rosary vine stems do not usually grow longer than 3ft. Cut back any bare stems to encourage leafy growth. Small plants are offered for sale.
Feeding Feed mature plants with standard liquid fertilizer once a month in spring and summer.
Potting Repot young plants every spring using an equal-parts combination of soil-based potting mixture and coarse sand. Older plants thrive in 3-4in half pots. Hanging baskets should have a 1in layer of drainage material at the bottom.
Special points Water more sparingly in winter.

RAT'S TAIL CACTUS
Aporocactus flagelliformis

These cacti have long streamers of narrow, fleshy stems covered with many rows of fine, prickly spines. Striking crimson-pink flowers appear in spring; each bloom lasts several days and the flowering season extends for up to two months. Display them in hanging baskets or on shelves, and position them where they will not be brushed against, as the spines are very difficult to remove from the skin. They can also be displayed in a cactus garden, with their long stems trailing through an arrangement of rocks.

Mini-climate 4 Cool, sunny.
Size Rat's tail cacti are fast-growing and their stems can reach 3ft long (occasionally much more) in three or four years. Plants of all sizes are offered for sale.
Feeding Feed with tomato-type fertilizer once a month from late December to the end of flowering.
Potting Repot every spring after flowering using soil-based potting mixture. Once plants are in a 6-10in pot topdress instead.
Special points Water more sparingly during the rest period following flowering.

Similar-shaped species
Aporocactus mallisonii has stouter stems and flowers ranging from soft pink to deep crimson.

DONKEY'S TAIL
Sedum morganianum

These most unusual-looking plants have trailing stems which are densely packed with small, fat, succulent leaves. Each stem takes on the appearance of a rope as it is so thick. The individual leaves are a pale green, covered with a fine white bloom. Pink flowers may appear at the end of each "rope" in spring, but these plants do not flower readily in the house. Ideal plants for hanging baskets, donkey's tails should be displayed in a place where they will not be brushed against, as the leaves drop off very easily.

Mini-climate 1 Warm, sunny.
Size The stems of donkey's tails can grow to a maximum of 3ft in length. Plants of all sizes are offered for sale.
Feeding Feeding is unnecessary.
Potting Repot every spring using a combination of one-third coarse sand and two-thirds soil-based potting mixture. Donkey's tails grow best in half-pots or hanging baskets where they have room to spread. Once the plants have grown too big for an 8in pot, discard the plant and grow a new one from a cutting.
Special points Water more sparingly in winter.

The color guide to flowering house plants
Whites, creams and yellows

We all respond to the colors found in nature; bring them inside and they cannot fail to enhance almost any type of setting. Concentrate on related or contrasting schemes: combine plants in various shades of the same color for a subtle effect, or use exciting complementaries for a bold effect. Before you buy any flowering plants to decorate your home, always think about the location you have chosen for them and make sure that, however beautiful their color, they will enhance and harmonize with your existing color scheme.

The most colorful part of a plant is not always the flower itself: in some plants, such as the poinsettia and flamingo flower, it is the bract, or petal-like leaf, which surrounds the flowers; in others, such as the bead plant and Christmas pepper, it is the berries and fruits which appear after the flowers have faded.

WHITE SAILS
Spathiphyllum "Clevelandii" (see p.169)
White arumlike flower heads which turn pale green with age. The color of this plant suits any kind of interior decoration.

PRIMROSE
Primula obconica (see p.181)
Pure white flowers with green centers, also available with pink, red and mauve flowers. Use either singly, or massed in a bowl using different shades from white through to mauve.

ITALIAN BELLFLOWER
Campanula isophylla (see p.191)
Star-shaped white flowers, also available in several shades of blue. Use plants of one color, or mix blue and white together, and place on a high shelf or in a hanging basket.

WAX BEGONIA
Begonia semperflorens-cultorum (see p.176)
Small white flowers, also available with pink and red flowers. Arrange plants of the same color together or mix them with exotic-colored leaves.

MADAGASCAR PERIWINKLE
Catharanthus roseus
White flowers with carmine-red centers, also available with pink or all-white flowers. Use in groups with other plants or mass in a bowl or basket.

YELLOW ELATIOR BEGONIA
Begonia "Elatior" hybrids (see p.176)
Primrose-yellow double flowers, also available in many other colors. Mass plants of one color for a bold effect.

CHRISTMAS PEPPER
Capsicum annuum (see p.180)
The bright fruits may be orange, red or yellow and
will change color as they ripen. Use massed to
make a colorful winter table decoration.

WHITE ELATIOR BEGONIA
Begonia "Elatior" hybrids (see p.176)
Cream-colored double flowers, also
available in many other colors.

YELLOW TUBEROUS BEGONIA
Begonia tuberhybrida (see p.176)
Deep-yellow flowers, also available
with white, pink, red or orange flowers.

BLACK-EYED SUSAN VINE
Thunbergia alata (see p.185)
Bright orange-yellow flowers with a black central eye.
Leave them to ramble through other plants or train
them up a support to create a cascade of color.

See below left
AFRICAN VIOLET
Saintpaulia hybrids (see p.175)
Pure white flowers and white flowers
edged with purple, also available in
many shades of pink, blue and purple.
Mass plants of one color, or in
various shades of the same color, in
a shallow bowl on a low table.

YELLOW CHRYSANTHEMUM
Chrysanthemum morifolium
hybrids (see p.181)
Pale yellow daisylike flowers, available
in many other colors.

WHITE TUBEROUS BEGONIA
Begonia tuberhybrida (see p.176)
Ivory-colored flowers, also available
with pink, red, yellow or orange flowers.
Display individually or in
groups of one, or
several, colors.

**GOLDEN
CHRYSANTHEMUM**
*Chrysanthemum
morifolium* hybrids
(see p.181)
Dense golden flowers,
available in many
other colors.

**WHITE
CHRYSANTHEMUM**
Chrysanthemum morifolium hybrids (see p.181)
Dense creamy-white flowers, available in many other colors.
Mass in a large basket and display so they can be seen from above.

YELLOW FLOWERING MAPLE
Abutilon hybridum (see p.162)
Bell-shaped, creamy-yellow flowers,
available in many other colors.
Group several different colors
together or display as feature plants
when full grown.

See following page

Oranges and reds

CHRISTMAS PEPPER
Capsicum annuum (see p.180)
The bright fruits may be orange, red or yellow and
will change color as they ripen. Use massed to make a
colorful winter table decoration.

WHITE ELATIOR BEGONIA
Begonia "Elatior" hybrids (see p.176)
Cream-colored double flowers, also
available in many other colors.

BEAD PLANT
Nertera granadensis (see p.192)
Beadlike, deep-orange berries cover the plant.
Make a formal display on a table, or low shelf.

YELLOW KALANCHOE
Kalanchoe blossfeldiana hybrids (see p.196)
Long-lasting deep-yellow flowers, also available with
orange, pink and red flowers. Mass plants together
on a sunny windowsill for winter color.

ORANGE KALANCHOE
Kalanchoe blossfeldiana
hybrids (see p.196)
Long-lasting orange flowers,
also available in yellow, pink
and red.

PINK KALANCHOE
Kalanchoe blossfeldiana
hybrids (see p.196)
Long-lasting pink flowers
also available in yellow,
red and orange.

**GOLDEN
CHRYSANTHEMUM**
*Chrysanthemum
morifolium* hybrids
(see p.181)
Dense golden flowers,
available in
many other colors.

RED KALANCHOE
Kalanchoe blossfeldiana hybrids (see p.196)
Long-lasting scarlet flowers, also
available with yellow, orange and
pink flowers.

CHINESE HIBISCUS
Hibiscus rosa-sinensis
hybrids (see p.178)
Large deep-red flowers with a protruding stamen, also
available with white, yellow, pink or orange flowers.
Use either singly or in a group with different-colored forms.

PINK IMPATIENS
Impatiens wallerana hybrids (see p.177)
Deep-pink single flowers, also available with white, red, orange or bicolored flowers. Mass plants of the same color together in a hanging basket or window-box.

SCARLET STAR
Guzmania lingulata (see p.174)
Scarlet bracts surround small white flowers. Put plants together in a container or use them in a symmetrical arrangement. They may also be cut and wired for use in large floral arrangements.

BEDDING GERANIUM
Pelargonium hortorum
hybrids (see p.179)
Tight clusters of scarlet flowers, also available with white, mauve or pink flowers. Display in a row along a windowsill or group with foliage geraniums.

GLOXINIA
Sinningia speciosa
hybrids (see p.175)
Red trumpet-shaped flowers, also available with white or violet flowers. Mass plants together and display on a low table.

**PINK ELATIOR
BEGONIA**
Begonia "Elatior" hybrids (see p.176)
Deep-pink double flowers, also available in many other colors.

RED FLOWERING MAPLE
Abutilon hybridum (see p.162)
Scarlet bell-shaped flowers, available in many other colors. Group several different colors together or display as a feature plant when full grown.

See following page

Pinks, mauves and purples

PINK IMPATIENS
Impatiens wallerana hybrids (see p.177)
Deep-pink single flowers, also available
with white, red, orange or bicolored
flowers. Put plants of the same
color together in a hanging basket
or window-box.

FLAMINGO FLOWER
Anthurium andraeanum hybrids (see p.182)
A salmon-colored, shield-shaped bract surrounds
the central flower spike, also available with white or red flower
heads. Group plants together for an exotic display.

**RED WAX
BEGONIA** *Begonia semperflorens-cultorum* (see p.176)
Scarlet flowers with yellow centers, also available with pink or white
flowers. Mass plants of the same color together or mix with exotic-colored leaves.

PINK NEW GUINEA IMPATIENS
Impatiens "New Guinea" hybrids (see p.177)
Pinky-orange flowers and strongly variegated leaves, also available
with white, pink, orange
and bicolored flowers.

SHRIMP PLANT
Justicia brandegeana
White flowers emerge from
pink, shrimp-shaped
bracts. Show plants
together in a shallow
basket for a subtle
color effect.

PINK ELATIOR BEGONIA
Begonia "Elatior"
hybrids (see p.176)
Deep-pink double flowers,
also available in many
other colors.

CAPE LEADWORT
Plumbago auriculata (see p.186)
Clusters of small, blue flowers, also
available with white flowers.
Use trained round a window or
up a support.

PINK WAX BEGONIA
Begonia semperflorens-cultorum (see p.176)
Strong-pink flowers with yellow eyes,
also available in red and white.

ITALIAN BELLFLOWER
Campanula isophylla (see p.191)
Star-shaped, bluish-mauve flowers,
also available in other shades of blue
and white. Use plants of one color, or
mix blue and white together, and place
on a high shelf or in a hanging basket.

PURPLE AFRICAN VIOLET
Saintpaulia hybrids (see p.175)
Intense violet-colored flowers with yellow centers, also
available with pink, blue or white flowers. Mass plants of
one color, or several shades of the
same color, in a shallow bowl
on a low table.

GLOXINIA
Sinningia speciosa
hybrids (see p.175)
Purple blooms banded with white,
also available with white or red
flowers. Put plants of the same
color together on a low table.

**PINK
AFRICAN VIOLET**
Saintpaulia hybrids
(see p.175)
Deep-pink flowers with yellow
centers, also available with
blue, purple or
white flowers.

PASSION FLOWER
Passiflora caerulea (see p.185)
Curious white-petalled flowers with
purple-fringed filaments, also
available with pink and purple
petals. Train round a sunny
window or up a support.

URN PLANT
Aechmea fasciata (see p.172)
Short-lived, pale-blue flowers emerge
from pink bracts. Use as feature
plants or in a bold arrangement.

GERMAN VIOLET
Exacum affine (see p.178)
Tiny lilac-colored flowers with gold centers, also available
with white flowers. Mass several plants in a large bowl or
group with golden flowers for counterpoint.

PINK IMPATIENS
Impatiens wallerana hybrids (see p.177)
Sugar-pink single flowers, available with white,
red, orange or bicolored flowers.

The seasonal guide to flowering house plants

Key

Winter Spring Summer Autumn

Plant	Jan	Feb	Mar	Apr	May	Jun	Jul	Aug	Sep	Oct	Nov	Dec	Comments
Egyptian star cluster (see p.177)	■							■	■	■	■		Can flower at other times
Christmas cherry (see p.180)	■							■	■	■	■		Fruit
Tulip (see p.194)	■	■										■	Can flower at other times
Claw cactus (see p.201)										■	■		Can flower at other times
Poinsettia (see p.178)	■	■	■							■	■	■	
Hyacinth (see p.194)	■	■	■									■	
Daffodil and narcissus (see p.195)	■	■	■									■	
Crocus (see p.194)	■	■	■										
Scarlet star (see p.174)	■	■	■										
Florist's cyclamen (see p.180)	■	■	■	■						■	■		
White-scented jasmine (see p.186)	■	■	■	■									
Kalanchoe (see p.196)	■	■	■									■	Can flower at other times
Miniature iris (see p.194)	■	■	■										
Amaryllis (see p.194)	■	■	■	■	■								
Primrose (see p.181)	■	■	■	■	■	■							Can flower at other times
African hemp (see p.164)		■	■	■									
African violet (see p.175)		■	■	■	■	■	■	■	■				Can flower continuously
Powder-puff cactus (see p.198)			■	■	■	■							
Rat's tail cactus (see p.201)			■	■	■								
Azalea (see p.179)			■	■	■								Can flower at other times
Grape hyacinth (see p.195)			■	■									
Saffron spike (see p.182)			■	■	■	■							
Rose pincushion (see p.198)			■	■	■	■							
Regal geranium (see p.179)			■	■	■	■	■						
Bird-of-paradise (see p.164)			■	■	■	■	■						Only mature plants will bloom
Wax begonia (see p.176)			■	■	■	■	■	■	■				Can flower continuously
Columnea (see p.189)			■	■	■	■	■	■	■	■			Can flower continuously
Crown-of-thorns (see p.196)			■	■	■	■	■	■	■	■			Can flower continuously
Cineraria (see p.178)				■	■	■							
Red crown (see p.198)				■	■	■							
White sails (see p.169)				■	■	■	■						Can flower at other times
Wax flower (see p.185)				■	■	■	■						
Bishop's cap (see p.198)				■	■	■	■	■					
Chinese hibiscus (see p.178)				■	■	■	■	■	■				Can flower at other times
Flaming sword (see p.173)				■	■	■	■	■					Only mature plants will bloom
Paper flower (see p.186)				■	■	■	■	■	■	■			
Impatiens (see p.177)				■	■	■	■	■	■	■			Can flower continuously
Cape leadwort (see p.186)				■	■	■	■	■	■	■			
Calamondin orange (see p.162)					■	■	■	■					Can flower at other times
Bird's nest bromeliad (see p.174)					■	■	■	■	■				Only mature plants will bloom
Cape primrose (see p.175)					■	■	■	■	■	■			
Black-eyed Susan vine (see p.185)					■	■	■	■	■				
Gloxinia (see p.175)						■	■	■	■				
Blue-flowered torch (see p.172)						■	■	■	■				Only mature plants will bloom
Flowering maple (see p.162)						■	■	■	■				
Urn plant (see p.172)						■	■	■	■				Can flower at other times
Cupid's bower (see p.181)						■	■	■	■				
Flamingo flower (see p.182)						■	■	■	■				Can flower at other times
Elatior begonia (see p.176)						■	■	■	■				
Queen's tears (see p.173)						■	■	■	■				Can flower at other times
German violet (see p.178)						■	■	■	■				
Miniature wax plant (see p.189)						■	■	■	■				
Passion flower (see p.185)						■	■	■	■	■			
Bead plant (see p.192)							■	■	■				Fruit
Golden trumpet (see p.186)							■	■	■	■			
Blushing bromeliad (see p.174)							■	■	■				Only mature plants will bloom
Christmas pepper (see p.180)							■	■	■	■	■	■	Fruit
Amethyst violet (see p.176)								■	■	■	■		
Italian bellflower (see p.191)								■	■	■			
Florist's chrysanthemum (see p.181)									■	■	■		Can flower continuously

THE CUT-FLOWER GUIDE

Displays of cut flowers can transform a room with their shapes, colors and scents, and bring the freshness of the garden indoors at any time of the year. Arrangements need not be lavish; a few flowers arranged in an appropriate container can look just as effective as a large, complicated display.

On the following pages you will find a seasonal guide to the flowers and berries that are most useful to the flower arranger. Foliage is another essential ingredient of flower arrangements and, since much of it is available from spring to autumn, it has been grouped according to its color. Many of the types of foliage and flowers shown mix well together for striking seasonal arrangements. The entry for each featured plant contains advice on how to prepare the cut stems, and suggests how it can be used in arrangements.

Spring flowers 1

A quick appraisal of late winter and early spring color is of a ubiquitous dull brown, but on closer inspection you will find many interesting colors and textures. Quite early in the year the garden becomes infused with spots of white, lemon and pale green. As the season moves properly into spring, the colors intensify—and, against the fresh green of the new foliage, you see the many yellows of daffodils, followed by the subsequent rainbow colors of other cultivated bulbs and flowering trees.

Many garden shrubs also flower early; the sprays of the bright yellow forsythia, the white spiraea blossoms and the green clusters of European cranberry bush flowers can be cut and used to extend the outline of a simple spring arrangement. Later in the season, fruit blossoms, such as apple and pear, come into their own too, along with the earliest of the perennial material from the garden. These early perennials include some types of iris, violets, spurges, lilacs and rhododendrons.

LILY-OF-THE-VALLEY
Convallaria majalis

These delicate, bell-shaped flowers are easily grown in a shady spot in the garden. As they grow from a creeping rhizome, they quickly spread. Processed roots for forcing are sold by a few bulb dealers in winter. They look best arranged in bunches, with their own dark-green foliage, in a small glass vase. The heady scent of the flowers adds to their attraction. The white flowers are also very beautiful when mixed with other white flowers in a bridal bouquet.

Colors available White and pale pink.

Preparation Cut the stems on a slant and make a 2in slit with a sharp knife. Strip any foliage from the floral stems and give a drink in warm water for about an hour before arranging in deep water.

Daffodils **1** "Golden Ducat" **2** "Pheasant's Eye" **3** "Mrs Backhouse" **4** "Inglescombe" **5** "Cheerfulness" **6** "Mary Copeland"

DAFFODIL
Narcissus sp. and hybrids

This group of hardy spring bulbs includes many different species and hybrids. Daffodil is the common name used for most members of the genus, although some kinds are referred to as narcissi, especially those whose flowers have short center trumpets. Dwarf species are available, while the tallest varieties are nearly 2ft in height. The bulbs must be planted in the autumn but then reappear each spring. Use the flowers in country-style spring arrangements. They also go well with forsythia or catkins and look good when massed in a simple container for a bold color effect.

Colors available Daffodils are available in a wide range of combinations of white, cream, yellow, orange and peach.

Preparation Cut the stems on a slant and make a 2in slit with a sharp knife. Pass the cut ends through a flame to seal them. Give a deep drink for about an hour before arranging in shallow water.

FRITILLARY
Fritillaria sp. and hybrids

Fritillarys are not easily grown in the garden, but ones raised in a cool greenhouse can be bought from florists' shops. The size and shape of the fritillary flower depend upon the species—some have clusters of large flowers at the top of a tall stalk, others have small bell-shaped flowers which are borne singly on drooping stems. The leaves resemble those of a tulip in shape, although some plants can have very long, narrow leaves. Fritillarys are amongst the first long-stemmed flowers to bloom in spring and the clustered flowers look good in large arrangements. The smaller species have drooping heads, so look better arranged in a simple vase on their own.

Colors available Red, orange, yellow, white, maroon and purple. The flowers of the smaller species are usually checkered or spotted with another color.

Preparation Cut the stems with a sharp knife to avoid bruising. Give a deep drink in cool water before arranging.

Lilacs **1** "Katherine Havemeyer" **2** "Maud Notcutt" **3** "Massena"

LILAC
Syringa sp. and hybrids

Lilacs are woody shrubs, easily grown in the garden, which flower profusely in late spring. Forced lilac is also readily available in florists' shops in winter and early spring. It should only be bought on long stems, as short-stemmed flowers do not last as well. The tiny, highly fragrant flowers are arranged in elongated clusters and the full blossom heads look good mixed with other pastel-colored flowers, such as pale-colored poppies and peonies, in a simple vase. The yellow and white varieties can be used in soft-yellow and cream spring arrangements.

Colors available Purple, pink, white, whitish-green and yellow.

Preparation Cut the stems on a slant and make a 2in slit with a sharp knife. Strip any foliage from the floral stems and dip into boiling water before giving a deep drink in cold water overnight. Arrange on long stems in deep water.

Lily-of-the-valley

Lilies

LILY
Lilium hybrids

Lilies are amongst the loveliest of flowers, having an extremely elegant shape. Despite their fragile appearance, most lilies can be grown in the garden, usually among perennials. They should be arranged simply, with nothing to detract from the flower itself. Ivory-colored lilies are useful for wedding bouquets or church decoration.

Colors available Lilies are available in all colors except blue. Many flowers have two or more colors and most have dots or stripes of another color.

Preparation Cut the stems on a slant and make a 2in slit with a sharp knife. Strip any foliage from the floral stems and give a deep drink overnight in cold water before arranging.

TULIP
Tulipa sp. and hybrids

The vast range of color and shape makes the tulip useful for many different types of arrangement. Apart from the traditional single, cuplike form, tulips may be double, feathered, vase-shaped or shaped like a lily. Tulip stems have a tendency to twist and bend once they are cut so they are not suitable for very formal arrangements. Tulips mix well with many types of flowers and have colors to suit most arrangements. Possibly the best way of displaying them is to mass flowers of the same color in a vase with their own foliage.

Colors available Tulips are available in most colors, ranging from the almost black to pure white. Many are streaked with another color.

Preparation Cut off any white ends to the stems and all foliage, and roll the bunch in newspaper. Place the bundle in deep warm water for a few hours. This will straighten any curved stems. Prick each stem just below the head with a pin and arrange in water containing a teaspoonful of sugar.

Rhododendrons

RHODODENDRON
Rhododendron sp. and hybrids

Rhododendrons are large, robust flowers. Use flowers on long stems to give a focal point to large, textured arrangements; shorter-stemmed flowers can be used in small vases of snowdrops or primroses. The heads can be floated in shallow dishes of water.

Colors available White, pink, red and purple.

Preparation Cut the stems on a slant and make a 2in slit with a sharp knife. Strip any foliage from the floral stems and leave overnight in hot water. Arrange in fresh water containing a little household bleach.

Tulips

"White Triumphator"
"Aster Neilson"
"Dyanito"
"Blue Parrot"
"West Point"
"Flying Dutchman"
"Black Parrot"
"Greenland"
"May Blossom"
"Captain Fryatt"
"China Pink"

Spring flowers 2

Freesias

FREESIA
Freesia hybrids

Freesias are very delicate in appearance and can become "lost" in very large, fussy arrangements. Their elongated shape is best seen when a small spray is displayed on its own in a vase, although the large white freesias can be used in bridal bouquets. The double variety lasts longer than the single variety.

Colors available White, yellow, mauve, pink, red and orange.

Preparation Cut the stems on a slant and make a 2in slit with a sharp knife. Give a deep drink before arranging in deep water.

SPURGE
Euphorbia sp.

These small shrubby plants should be included in every flower arranger's garden, as they last well when cut and add an unusual range of colors, shapes and textures to country-style flower arrangements. The large

inflorescences are made up of tiny flowers surrounded by papery bracts and look good contrasted with feathery grasses or foliage.

Colors available Orange, red, yellow and green.

Preparation Cut the stems on a slant and make a 2in slit with a sharp knife. Scald the ends in boiling water or pass them briefly over a flame to staunch the flow of latex from the cut stem. Give a deep drink in cold water before arranging.

IRIS
Iris sp. and hybrids

These are very useful flowers, particularly if you grow them in your garden, as the foliage is as decorative as the flowers. The flowers are amongst the first to appear in spring. There are many varieties available, giving an enormous range of shapes, colors and sizes. Some irises grow very tall and have large flower heads suitable for large-scale flower arrangements. The smaller, early irises can be arranged with some of their own foliage and a few tulips.

Colors available Mauve, purple, yellow, brown, orange, gray and white. The flowers are usually spotted or striped with another color.

Preparation Cut the stems on a slant and make a 2in slit with a sharp knife. Strip any foliage from the floral stems and give a deep drink in cool water.

MIMOSA
Acacia dealbata

These delicate, fluffy flower heads mix well with all kinds of spring flowers. They can be used in formal bouquets, but look equally lovely massed in a terracotta pot with a few golden daffodils and their own foliage. The

feathery, gray-green leaves make good background material in many arrangements and the strong, heady scent adds to the attractiveness of this plant.

Colors available Yellow.

Preparation Keep wrapped in plastic to exclude air for as long as possible before arranging. Just prior to arranging, remove the plastic and dip flower heads in cold water for a few moments. Cut the stems on a slant and make a 2in slit with a sharp knife. Dip the stems in boiling water for a few seconds, then give a deep drink in warm water until the heads are dry.

Stocks **1** "Parma Violet" **2** "Yellow of Nice" **3** "Princess Alice"

STOCK
Matthiola incana

Stocks are widely available in both gardens and florists' shops. Those grown under glass are available for many months of the year.

Spurges

Euphorbia wulfenii

Euphorbia robbiae

Euphorbia griffithii "Fireglow"

Euphorbia characias

Euphorbia polychroma

Additional features
Long-lasting · Useful foliage · Fragrant · Suitable for drying

Their short spikes are packed with small, round flowers which can act as the focal point, or as filler material, in informal country-style arrangements.

Colors available White, yellow, crimson, mauve, purple, pink and orange.

Preparation Cut the stems on a slant and make a 2in slit with a sharp knife. Strip any foliage from the floral stems. Dip in boiling water for a few minutes before giving a deep drink in cold water. Arrange in deep water.

POLYANTHUS
Primula vulgaris

These small, bushy plants have tubular flowers which flare out into a round face with a prominent, colored eye. The variety of colors is immense, as new hybrids are being produced all the time. They can be grown in the garden but, for instant color, it is often easier to buy them in florists' shops in early spring. Choose polyanthus with short stems, as the longer ones wilt very easily. Simple bunches bound with their own foliage look good in plain containers. Alternatively, they can be used with other similarly colored flowers, such as hellebores or heaths, in a miniature arrangement.

Colors available Polyanthus are available in all colors including blue. Many varieties have a yellow ring surrounding the eye.

Preparation Cut the stems short with a sharp knife. Dip the ends in boiling water for a few minutes and then give a deep drink. Prick each stem just below the head to allow any air bubbles to escape. This helps the water to rise freely up the stem.

BABY'S BREATH
Gypsophila paniculata

These delicate sprays of flowers were once looked upon as foils for other, more robust flowers. They do add a pretty, hazy effect to arrangements of roses and carnations, but a generous amount massed in a glass vase or urn can look very striking in a modern setting. Baby's breath is commonly used in bouquets.

Colors available White and pink.

Preparation Cut stems on a slant and make a 2in slit with a sharp knife. Strip any foliage from the floral stems and give a deep drink in hot water before arranging. Spray the arrangements with setting spray as the flowers fall easily. Change the water regularly to prevent fouling.

Baby's breath

Peruvian lily

PERUVIAN LILY
Alstroemeria pelegrina

These elegant, eye-catching flowers are hard to grow in the garden but are available in florists' shops for most of the year. They have stiff, upright stems at the top of which are the groups of flowers, making them ideal for massing in a vase, with just a few of their own leaves, for a striking display.

Colors available White, pink, red, orange and lilac. Some may be marked with red-purple dots.

Preparation Cut the stems on a slant and make a 2in slit with a sharp knife. Strip any foliage from the floral stems and give a deep drink in cool water before arranging.

CALLA LILY
Zantedeschia aethiopica

It is possible to grow these beautiful flowers outside in a sheltered spot, but the best specimens come from the greenhouse. They have thick, fleshy flowers borne on erect stalks. The heart-shaped leaves are a rich green and just a few blooms, displayed with their own foliage in a round glass bowl, make an elegant display. The strong shape of calla lilies makes them a good focal point in any green group; they are also useful for formal displays which need to be seen from a distance.

Colors available White, yellow, green and pink.

Preparation Cut the stems on a slant and make a 2in slit with a sharp knife. Give a deep drink in warm water before arranging. Soak the leaves in a starch solution for twenty-four hours to make them last longer.

Flowering fruit trees **1** *Prunus serrulata* **2** *Prunus serrulata* "Ukon" **3** *Pyrus calleryana* "Chanticleer" **4** *Malus eleyi* **5** *Prunus serrulata* "Shirotae" **6** *Prunus serrulata* "Kwanzan"

FLOWERING FRUIT TREES
Prunus sp. and *Malus* sp.

This is a large group of ornamental and fruiting trees which bear delicate clusters of flowers in early spring. Masses of flowers make excellent background material for displays of pink tulips or yellow daffodils. A Japanese effect can be created by displaying a few stems of a white-flowered variety in a red and black setting.

Colors available Red, pink and white.

Preparation Cut the stems on a slant and make a 2in slit with a sharp knife. Give a cool drink before arranging in deep water.

PANSY
Viola wittrockiana

Pansies are pretty flowers whose round heads are usually marked with appealing, facelike blotches. Their small, delicate size suits them to table-top or miniature arrangements in small containers. Many are subtly scented.

Colors available Pansies are available in all colors, including blue and black. There are many plain-colored varieties and many marked types.

Preparation The soft stems should be cut with a sharp knife to avoid bruising them. Dip the heads in water for a few minutes before arranging.

Other spring flowers

Crocus	Honesty
Hawthorn	Blazing star
Rosemary	Azalea
Bluebell	Wallflower
Forsythia	Magnolia
Clematis	Arctic poppy
Spirea	Buttercup
Kafir lily	Primrose
Alyssum	Love-in-mist
Jasmine	Broom
Hyacinth	Jew's mallow
Cowslip	Quince

Summer flowers 1

Summer brings flowers and foliage in abundance, of every shape, size, color and texture. The overall colors of summer move from the pale yellows, pastel pinks, peaches and white of the carnations and foxgloves, to the deeper tones and warmer colors of peonies and sweet Williams. Many summer flowers, such as the poppy, sweet pea and rose, are available in a wide range of colors, and can be used in many different arrangements. Moreover, flowers are often accompanied by an equally wide range of different shaped and colored foliage—of which the hostas, ivies and privets must be among the most useful.

While much available material is herbaceous or perennial, there is an equally large range of flowering shrub material: use these branches either on their own or with cut flowers for bigger, grander displays, choosing from weigela, viburnum or mock orange, amongst many others.

Summer arrangements should make use of this abundance of material, and flowers should be arranged *en masse*. Most summer flowers have a heady fragrance which makes them doubly welcome in the home.

LADY'S MANTLE
Alchemilla vulgaris

These plants are easily grown in the garden but are not commonly seen in florists' shops. Lady's mantle is very versatile: the blooms can be used in both formal and informal arrangements, and the lovely, yellow-green heads mix well with almost every color of flower and foliage. They also look good massed on their own or arranged with feathery grasses and foliage in a simple glass or dull metal container. The round, umbrella-like leaves are soft and downy and contrast beautifully with red or bronze leaves in an arrangement.

Colors available Yellow-green.

Preparation Cut the stems on a slant and make a 2in slit with a sharp knife. Strip any foliage from the floral stems and arrange in deep water immediately. This will prevent air bubbles forming in the stem.

Lady's mantle

Peonies **1** *Paeonia lactiflora* **2** *Paeonia officinalis* "Rubra-plena" **3** *Paeonia officinalis*

PEONY
Paeonia sp.

The most commonly seen peony is the large-flowered, deep-magenta variety. Although very beautiful, it needs to be used thoughtfully as it can be dominating in flower arrangements; it looks good arranged with red or yellow-green foliage. There are many other kinds of peony, all of which can be used as focal points in arrangements. Red peonies mix well with other red flowers, and the delicate pinks look ravishing with the salmon-pink spikes of foxgloves or gladioli. Larger peonies can be used in large arrangements that are meant to be seen from a distance.

Colors available Shades of pink, red, magenta, yellow and white.

Preparation After cutting, peonies can be left out of water for several days if placed in a cold room. If put in plastic bags in a cold room they will keep fresh for some weeks. Prior to arranging, cut the stems on a slant and make a 2in slit with a sharp knife. Give a long, warm drink before arranging.

FOXTAIL LILY
Eremurus sp.

These long spikes are covered in densely packed, small, star-shaped flowers. The flowers open from the bottom of the stem upwards and, as the stems can range in height from 2-6ft, they can look majestic arranged in a long, narrow vase with some stiff, lance-shaped leaves.

Colors available White, yellow, pink and orange.

Preparation Cut the stems on a slant and make a 2in slit with a sharp knife. Give a deep drink in cool water before arranging.

CARNATIONS AND CLOVE PINKS
Dianthus caryophyllus hybrids

Carnations and pinks present a great challenge to the grower, as they hybridize very easily and new hybrids are always appearing on the market. These new hybrids may be bigger, smaller, more fragrant, have brighter colors, or be formed with a new mixture of colors—the range to choose from is vast. Although pinks and carnations look very similar, they can be told apart by the fact that carnations have larger flowers, wider leaves and longer stems than the pinks. Carnations and pinks are very formal flowers, especially the shop-bought ones with very straight stems. They can be used in all kinds of summer arrangements, but do look good on their own in a simple, tall-necked vase. Use the delicate pink or white flowers with gray foliage such as eucalyptus or artemisia.

Colors available Available in almost every color except blue. Many are marked with another color.

Preparation Cut the stems on a slant between the nodes (bumps on the stems). Make a 2in slit with a sharp knife and strip any foliage from the floral stems. Give a long deep drink before arranging them in warm water.

"Purple Frosted"

"Crowley Sim"

Additional features
Long-lasting   Useful foliage   Fragrant   Suitable for drying

Sword lilies **1** "Albert Schweitzer" **2** "White Angel" **3** "Madam Butterfly"

SWORD LILY
Gladiolus hybrids

With their elegant shape, gladioli are extremely useful for all types of arrangement. They are also easy to grow in the garden. There are many varieties of gladiolus, varying in size, color and floret type, although all the florets face the same way on the flower spike. Arrange the smaller, soft-colored gladioli with pink roses or other small flowers. Three or four spikes of the tall, bright-red gladioli look good in a long, elegant vase in a prominent position.

Colors available A wide range of colors including red, orange, yellow, pink and white.

Preparation Cut the stems on a slant and make a 2in slit with a sharp knife. Cut stems under water and, to make the blooms last longer, cut off a small piece of the stem every four or five days. If you don't want to use these flowers immediately, keep them in a cold place for about a week.

POPPY
Papaver sp. and hybrids

The popular conception of the poppy is of a bright-red, large-petalled flower. There are, however, many hybrids and cultivars available in a wide range of colors and sizes. Poppies have very delicate petals so they are not really suitable for formal arrangements. They are very short-lived, usually lasting only one day Use the bright-red flowers with dark-green foliage. All the pastel shades mix well with other muted flowers—lilacs, roses and delphiniums.

Colors available Many shades of red, pink, orange, yellow, cream and white.

Preparation Cut the stems with a sharp knife. Dip the ends in boiling water or pass them over a flame to seal them and prevent the sap from clouding the water. Give a long, deep drink before arranging.

Sweet Williams

SWEET WILLIAM
Dianthus barbatus

Fragrant varieties of sweet William are available in florists' shops and are very easy to cultivate in the garden. Their round, flat heads consist of many small flowers tightly packed together. The bright colors mix very well with other summer flowers in informal arrangements, and they look particularly attractive when massed together in a wicker basket.

Colors available Flowers are usually a mixture of two or more of the following colors: red, pink, crimson and white, arranged in rings of color around the center of the flower.

Preparation Cut the stems on a slant and make a 2in slit with a sharp knife. Strip any foliage from the floral stems. Give a long, cool drink before arranging.

Carnations and clove pinks

"Zebra"

"Portrait"

"Joker"

"Allwood's Cream"

"Arthur Sim"

"Fragrant Ann"

"Comoco Sim"

"Inchmery"

Summer flowers 2

Chinese delphinium

DELPHINIUM
Delphinium sp. and hybrids

Delphiniums are popular as both florists' flowers and garden plants, and many new hybrids are coming on to the market, extending the range of colors and sizes available. The long spikes are laden with small, fragrant flowers and are good for arrangements in tall vases. Use the tall, white varieties for large-scale decorations. If you don't have room for large arrangements, there are shorter hybrids available in all the colors, and these can look

Foxgloves

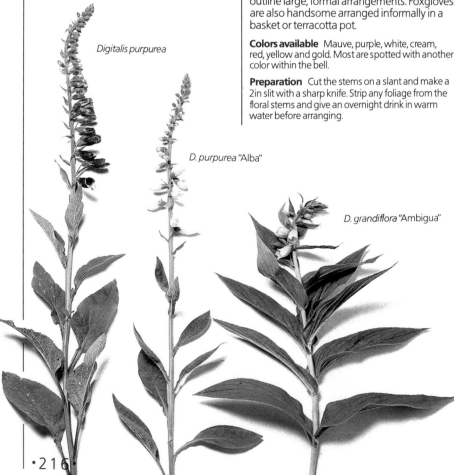

Digitalis purpurea

D. purpurea "Alba"

D. grandiflora "Ambigua"

very attractive massed together with some of their own feathery foliage.

Colors available Many shades of blue and mauve. Also pink, white and cream.

Preparation Cut the stems on a slant and make a 2in slit with a sharp knife. Give a long drink in cool water before arranging. To make the flowers last longer for a special occasion, it is worth filling the hollow stems with water and plugging the ends with cotton wool.

FLOWERING ONION
Allium sp.

These members of the onion family bear numerous tiny flowers in often large, ball-like clusters. Use as focal points in an arrangement of large-headed flowers.

Colors available Yellow, purple, pink and white.

Preparation Cut the stems on a slant and make a 2in slit with a sharp knife before arranging in deep water. Add a teaspoonful of bleach to the water to remove the onion smell.

FOXGLOVE
Digitalis sp. and hybrids

These beautiful, mostly biennial, flowers on tall, stately plants have always been popular in gardens or in semi-wild sites where they selfsow freely and tolerate all soil types. Grow your own from seed as they are rare in florists' shops. They are useful in arrangements as they retain their petals for some considerable time after cutting. Their delicate colors mix well with other pastel-colored flowers and their elongated form can outline large, formal arrangements. Foxgloves are also handsome arranged informally in a basket or terracotta pot.

Colors available Mauve, purple, white, cream, red, yellow and gold. Most are spotted with another color within the bell.

Preparation Cut the stems on a slant and make a 2in slit with a sharp knife. Strip any foliage from the floral stems and give an overnight drink in warm water before arranging.

Rose hybrids **1** "Message" **2** "Goldgleam"
3 "Pascali" **4** "Margaret Merrill"

HYBRID ROSES
Rosa hybrids

The variety of roses available is never-ending as new cultivars appear each year. The only drawback has been the loss of fragrance from some introductions. Hybrid tea, floribunda and miniature roses all have compact bushes with mainly high-centered double flowers. Some varieties have attractive hips. Roses of one color, massed in a basket, are lovely. So is one flower in a bud vase. Use the foliage as background material.

Colors available Roses are available in just about every shade of every color except blue.

Preparation Cut the stems on a slant and make a 2in slit with a sharp knife. Strip any foliage from the floral stems and dip stems in boiling water for a minute. Give a long drink in cold water before arranging.

Yarrow "Coronation Gold"

FERN LEAF YARROW
Achillea filipendulina

These informal-looking, flat-headed flowers are available in a range of sizes as well as colors. They are easily grown in the garden and commonly found along roadsides and in hedgerows. Use large, bright-gold heads as

Additional features

Long-lasting · Useful foliage · Fragrant · Suitable for drying

Sweet peas

focal points in large arrangements and smaller, pale-yellow or white heads in arrangements of white flowers, such as roses, or with variegated plantain lily leaves. As the petals do not fall and the flowers dry well, they can be included in dried-flower arrangements whilst still fresh.

Colors available Many shades of yellow and gold, and white.

Preparation Cut the stems on a slant and make a 2in slit with a sharp knife. Strip any foliage from the floral stems and give a deep drink before arranging.

TRANSVAAL DAISY
Gerbera jamesonii

These large, brightly colored, daisy-shaped flowers have soft, furry petals and soft, gray-green stems which are leafless. They can be greenhouse-grown and are becoming more readily available in florists' shops. The yellow and orange flowers look good arranged with white spider chrysanthemums and eucalyptus leaves, and can also be used to effect in autumnal dried-flower arrangements, as their color complements the warm tones of the dried material. Contrast the round heads with iris spikes, gladioli, or delphiniums of the same color.

Colors available Purple, crimson, red, pink, white, yellow and orange.

Preparation Cut the stems on a slant and make a 2in slit with a sharp knife. Dip the ends of the stems in boiling water, then give a long drink in cool water before arranging.

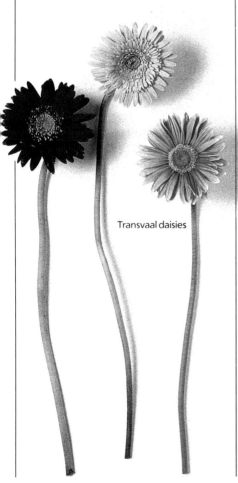

Transvaal daisies

African lily

AFRICAN LILY
Agapanthus africanus

These evergreen plants have smooth, lance-shaped leaves and tall, succulent stems. The individual flowers are small and borne in a ball-shaped cluster at the top of the stem, giving a large inflorescence. They can be grown in tubs outdoors in a sheltered spot and wintered indoors in cold regions. African lilies can be used in large arrangements and make a lovely, cool, summer arrangement if their round heads are mixed with tall, white, spiky flowers such as irises or gladioli.

Colors available Blue and white.

Preparation Cut the stems on a slant and make a 2in slit with a sharp knife. Arrange in deep water.

SWEET PEA
Lathyrus odoratus

These delicate flowers are well known for their sweet scent which can quickly fill a room. They are easily grown in the garden, where their climbing stems will need to be supported if they are to bloom profusely. They are often found in florists' shops during summer. There are usually four or five blooms to a stem and a large bunch of flowers of the same color can be very eye-catching. Sweet peas also look lovely arranged informally with roses of the same color. This gives a very fragrant display.

Colors available A wide range of shades of red, pink, purple, apricot and white.

Preparation Sweet peas should be handled as little as possible. Cut long stems with a sharp knife and give a deep drink in cool water for several hours before arranging.

Other summer flowers

Bells-of-Ireland	Snapdragon
Gentian	Lupine
Angelica	Candytuft
Cornflower	Marigold
Columbine	Clarkia
Brodiaea	Loosestrife
Zinnia	Lavender
Anthemis daisy	Hollyhock
Marguerite daisy	Petunia
Geranium	Clary
Bellflower	Perennial phlox
Mock orange	Day daisy

Autumn flowers and berries 1

The colors of autumn flowers are deeper than those of spring and summer. Purples, reds, browns and golds predominate among both flowers and foliage. Deep-yellow sunflowers and coneflowers, and fiery red-hot pokers provide rich and vibrant colors, while the many types of dahlia offer a splendid range of hues and shapes. When the flowers are over, the fruits, berries and vegetables of autumn can be used in arrangements. Vegetables, such as globe artichokes, can add interesting texture and color to a display. Berries and fruits, such as rose hips and crab apples, add rich color to arrangements and can look very attractive displayed informally by themselves or with some foliage. Autumn foliage is well worth using as the supply of home-grown flowers diminishes. Some foliage changes color, turning to shades of red, orange, coppery-brown and deep purple. Towards the end of the season it may be worth investing in some flamboyant imported material. One or two of the large South African nodding pincushion heads are enough to prolong the displays of autumnal flowers for a little longer, adding variety in shape and color.

CONEFLOWER
Rudbeckia sp. and hybrids

These pretty, daisy-shaped flowers have lovely, rich coloring. The round face is centered by a dark cone. Single and double flowers are available, and flowers of different colors massed in a terracotta pot bring the colors of autumn indoors. Coneflowers look equally good with red or yellow foliage.

Colors available Yellow, orange and brown, often ringed with red. The centers are dark brown.

Preparation Cut the stems on a slant and make a 2in slit with a sharp knife. Strip any foliage from the floral stems and dip the cut ends into boiling water for a few minutes. Give a deep drink before arranging.

CAPE LILY
Crinum powellii

These elegant plants have clusters of trumpet-shaped flowers borne at the top of a thick, succulent stem. The flowers are produced in succession and should be picked off as they fade. Use the Cape lily in large, formal arrangements where a certain elegance is required. The white variety is ideal for wedding displays. It also looks good arranged in a simple, white, porcelain vase with sprays of delicate flowers, such as twigs of lime from which all the foliage has been removed.

Colors available Pink and white.

Preparation Cut stems on a slant and make a 2in slit with a sharp knife. Give a long drink before arranging. The hollow stems can be filled with water and the ends plugged with cotton wool to make the flowers last longer.

Cape lily

Crab apple "John Downie"

CRAB APPLE
Malus sp.

The fruits of the crab apple tree are small and round and usually inedible when raw. More often found in the garden or hedgerow than in florists' shops, the attractive coloring of the fruits and the coppery tones of the autumn foliage make them useful for autumn groups. Mix them with flowers of autumnal shades, such as dahlias, red-hot pokers or coneflowers, or with woody shrubs such as the flowering maple or spindle tree. The undried fruits are suitable for dried arrangements, although they will begin to shrivel after a time.

Colors available The fruits and leaves take on the shades of autumn—reds, yellows and oranges. The spring blossoms are red, pink or white.

Preparation Scrape the stems and make a 2in slit with a sharp knife. Give a long drink in deep water before arranging.

ST JOHN'S WORT
Hypericum inordorum

A popular garden shrub which is very easy to grow. Although common in gardens, it is not often seen in florists' shops. St John's wort is a semi-evergreen shrub: the leaves are retained in the winter but, instead of remaining green, turn a greenish-red and are aromatic if crushed. The yellow flowers are very delicate but will last until October, when they are followed by the clusters of oval berries. The sprays are most useful as background material in all kinds of arrangements and the berries fit into arrangements of autumn fruits and flowers.

Colors available Summer flowers are yellow and foliage green; autumn berries are red and the foliage a greenish-red.

Preparation Cut the stems on a slant and make a 2in slit with a sharp knife. Strip any foliage from the floral stems. Give a deep drink before arranging in cool water.

FLOWERING MAPLE
Abutilon hybridum

These woody shrubs are common in mild climate gardens, but are usually grown as house plants in cold winter regions. The delicate papery flowers are a wide-funnel shape and hang down from the leaf axils. The woody branches and pale-green, often mottled leaves, interspersed with the colorful flowers look good arranged on their own in a plain vase or with other delicate material.

Colors available The flowers are combinations of red, yellow, mauve and pale blue.

Preparation Cut the stems on a slant and make a 2in slit with a sharp knife. Strip any foliage from the floral stems and give a deep drink before arranging.

Flowering maple

Additional features
Long-lasting · Useful foliage · Fragrant · Suitable for drying

Globe artichoke

Spindle tree

SPINDLE TREE
Euonymus sachalinensis

The berries of this shrub are most unusual—
they are round and fleshy, suddenly bursting
open into a flowerlike shape to reveal a mass
of bright-orange seeds. The foliage is
deep green, fading to a green speckled with
white and yellow. Branches are best used
at the back of an arrangement.

Colors available The berries may be red, pink or
white, with bright-orange seeds.

Preparation Scrape the ends of the stems and
make a 2in slit with a sharp knife before arranging.

MICHAELMAS DAISY
Aster novi-belgii

Michaelmas daisies have upright main stems
which bear shorter stems topped with the

flower. Due to their ragged appearance, they
do not mix well with other flowers. For best
effect, mass flowers of one color and
place in a large copper pan, then position the
arrangement so it reflects the autumn sun.

Colors available White, purple and pink.

Preparation Cut the stems on a slant and make a
2in slit with a sharp knife. Strip any foliage from the
floral stems and dip the ends into boiling water for a
few seconds, then give a deep drink for twelve hours.

Michaelmas daisy hybrids **1** "Ada Ballard"
2 "Blandie"

GLOBE ARTICHOKE
Cynara scolymus

Globe artichokes are most useful in all stages
of their development. Apart from being good
to eat, the flower buds are made up of fresh-
green, overlapping bracts which add textured
interest to the base of autumnal groups. The
tufts of purple flowers emerge later. The seed
heads and the beautiful, fernlike foliage are
also most useful.

Colors available The flower buds are pale green;
the flowers are purple.

Preparation The flower heads need no special
preparation. The leaves last much longer if the stems
are held in boiling water for thirty seconds and then
the whole leaf submerged in cold water for an hour.

STRAW FLOWER
Helichrysum bracteatum

These flowers, which are most often seen
dried, can also be used in fresh flower
arrangements. The daisylike flower heads are
surrounded by papery bracts giving the
illusion of being dried, when in fact they are
quite fresh. The colors of the flowers are
ideally suited to informal autumn arrangements and look good with almost all types of
flowers. Mass the flowers, in baskets, then
use them to fill alcoves or unused fireplaces.
As the petals do not fall, allow the flowers to
dry out, to provide a dried arrangement.

Colors available. Yellow, red, orange, magenta,
purple and combinations of these colors.

Preparation Cut the stems with a sharp knife, and
dip in boiling water. Allow a long drink in cool water
before arranging.

Straw flowers

Autumn flowers and berries 2

Sunflower

Bear's breeches

SUNFLOWER
Helianthus annuus

Sunflowers are favorites in the garden as they are so easy to grow, and most rewarding as they reach such a size. The large heads can easily unbalance an arrangement of small flowers, so use them as a focal point with large flowers, or mix them with foliage and berries.

Colors available Golden-yellow petals with dark-brown central discs.

Preparation Cut stems on a slant and make a 2in slit with a sharp knife. Dip the ends of the stems into boiling water and give a long drink before arranging.

BEAR'S BREECHES
Acanthus spinosissimus

These unusual, tall spikes are formed by small flowers enclosed in leafy bracts all the way up the succulent stem. The spikes give a good outline to large, formal and informal arrangements of autumn flowers and foliage. They can also be contrasted with large, round flowers such as sunflowers and dahlias. The spiky foliage is very attractive, especially arranged in a vase with pink flowers.

Colors available Purple-pink flowers hidden amongst purple-green, leafy bracts.

Preparation Cut the stems on a slant and make a 2in slit with a sharp knife. Dip the cut ends in boiling water and give a deep drink in cold water for several hours. Leaf stalks should also be dipped in boiling

water for a few moments. The whole leaf should then be submerged in a weak solution of starch for about twelve hours.

DAHLIA
Dahlia hybrids

Dahlias are popular, easily grown garden flowers which are becoming more readily available in florists' shops. They come in many sizes, shapes and colors. All the various shapes have a different name—"cactus", "pompom", "quilled" and "fancy", to name but a few, and the range is ever expanding as growers experiment with new crosses and hybrids. Dahlias mix well in all types of arrangements as they have an attractive, round shape and a predominant "face", so that you know which way to place them in an arrangement. Use the peach- and apricot-colored flowers with autumn foliage arrangements and the vibrant reds in a vase of red roses or red-hot pokers. Mix the whites with other white flowers and deep-green foliage for a striking effect, or mass dahlias of the same color but different shapes for a textured, informal arrangement.

Colors available Dahlias are available in many different colors, and many shades of the same color, as new hybrids produce increasingly subtle tones. The only color not yet produced is blue.

Preparation Cut the stems on a slant and make a 2in slit with a sharp knife. Strip any foliage from the floral stems and dip the ends in boiling water for a few minutes. Give a cool drink overnight before arranging in deep water. For special occasions or formal arrangements, when the flowers have to look good for as long as possible, arrange in deep water containing a commercial preservative.

Dahlias

"Rokesley Mini"

"Authority"

"Little Conn"

"Super"

"Glorie van Heernstede"

Additional features
Long-lasting · Useful foliage · Fragrant · Suitable for drying

Rose hips **1** *Rosa* sp. **2** *R. moyesii* **3** *R. rugosa*

European cranberry bush berries

ROSE HIPS
Rosa hybrids

Autumnal hedgerows were once full of the bright-red hips of wild roses, but the supply of these is decreasing. Hips will form on all garden roses, but are often not given the chance as the plants are pruned back. They are, however, very beautiful and come in many different shapes and sizes, according to the type of rose. Rose hips look good in all autumn arrangements, especially those incorporating dark-red flowers and foliage. Hips can also be used to add a splash of color to arrangements of dried foliage and seed heads.

Colors available Rose hips may be many different shades of red, depending on the time of cutting.

Preparation Cut the stems on a slant and make a 2in slit with a sharp knife. Strip any foliage and thorns from the stems. Dip the cut ends into boiling water for a minute before giving a long drink.

FLOWERING TOBACCO
Nicotiana alata

Other kinds are grown commercially for their leaves which are used in tobacco production. The garden varieties are cultivated for their colorful flowers which are heavily scented. The flowers are tubular, flaring out into a star-shaped face. Their myriad colors make them useful in all kinds of informal arrangements. Use the vibrant colors with red flowers or foliage, or make a truly autumnal arrangement using the orange- and yellow-colored varieties. The lime-green flowers can add interest to a vase of delicate green foliage.

Colors available White, red, orange, yellow, crimson, lime-green, cream and pink.

Preparation The stems are very soft and should be cut with a sharp knife. Place in warm water before arranging in deep water.

RED-HOT POKER
Kniphofia uvaria

These easily grown garden plants are not often seen in florists' shops. They make good cut flowers, although their large size makes them a little difficult to arrange. Their colors are ideally suited to autumnal arrangements and they add spiky interest to large, informal displays. The succulent stems of red-hot pokers tend to grow on, even when cut; this causes the stems to twist, so you will have to rearrange the flowers if you want to retain a particular shape.

Colors available The heads of red-hot pokers are green when they first appear, but then turn red. Hybrids are now available in cream-and-yellow and cream-and-pink.

Preparation Cut the stems on a slant and make a 2in slit with a sharp knife, then give a long drink in cool water before arranging.

Red-hot poker

EUROPEAN CRANBERRY BUSH BERRIES
Viburnum opulus "Xanthocarpum"

The translucent, golden berries which appear in autumn are as useful as the white flowers which appear in spring. The berries are held in small clusters on branches which retain their leaves even when quite dry. This makes them useful for background sprays in arrangements of fresh or dried materials.

Colors available Berries are yellow in this cultivar. Spring flowers are white, in flat clusters. Foliage is bright green.

Preparation Scrape the stems and cut on a slant. Make a 2in slit with a sharp knife and dip the cut ends into boiling water for a few moments. Give an overnight drink in cool water before arranging.

NODDING PINCUSHION
Leucospermum nutans

These spectacular flower heads are members of the protea family and are imported from South Africa. The heads have a rounded shape covered with yellow spikes with red bulbous tips. Nodding pincushions add a focal point to large arrangements of fresh or dried materials.

Colors available Yellow-red.

Preparation Cut the stems on a slant and make a 2in slit with a sharp knife. Give a deep drink before arranging in cool water.

Other autumn flowers

Japanese anemone	Red valerian
Clematis	Chinese lantern
Hydrangea	Fleabane
Marigold	Montbretia
Sedum	Ageratum
Statice	Forget-me-not
Monkshood	Rose mallow
Cotoneaster	Verbena
Lilyturf	Autumn crocus
Shasta daisy	Scabiosa

Winter flowers and berries

In winter, evergreens come into their own, producing masses of beautifully textured foliage and glowing berries. The term evergreen covers a multitude of foliage colors, including many variegated types, as well as textures—so that you can make up quite a bright arrangement using only evergreen foliage throughout the winter.

Towards the end of winter, many of the deciduous shrubs become covered with the palest of flowers—many of which have a deep scent which is released when twigs are cut and brought into the warmth. Winter camellias flower in white, red, and pink at this time in mild climate regions. Also come the snowdrops, followed by the yellow winter aconites, some crocuses, and the earliest of the daffodils. The choice of blooms is increased with commercially grown anemones, lilac, early carnations and roses. Orchids are imported at this time of year too. All these flowers are plentiful in the shops, if somewhat expensive so, for larger arrangements, rely on evergreens or well-shaped bare twigs. You will find that some of these may burst into leaf in the warmth of the house.

ENGLISH HOLLY
Ilex aquifolium

The glossy, dark-green leaves with their wavy, spined edges and clusters of red berries are a familiar sight in winter, both in gardens and florists' shops. This holly can grow as bushes or as trees, and is as colorful in the garden as it is in the home. Traditional winter arrangements using holly include Christmas wreaths and garlands, but it is also useful as background material to deep-red flowers.

Colors available Holly leaves may be deep green or variegated. Berries may be bright red, orange-red or yellow according to the variety.

Preparation When cutting, use a pair of pruners. Holly lasts a short time if kept out of water.

English holly

Wattle

WATTLE
Acacia longifolia

This delicate-looking shrub is related to the spring-flowering mimosa and has very similar yellow flowers. However, unlike the mimosa, the gray-green leaves of this wattle are undivided and willowlike in shape. The fragrant flowers contrast well with the foliage and the sprays are a welcome addition to winter arrangements of flowers and foliage.

Colors available Yellow ball-like flowers and gray-green foliage.

Preparation Keep wrapped in plastic to exclude air for as long as possible before arranging. Just prior to arranging, remove the plastic and dip flower heads in cold water for a few moments. Cut the stems on a slant and make a 2in slit with a sharp knife. Dip the stems in boiling water for a few seconds, then give a deep drink with warm water until the heads are dry.

ANEMONE
Anemone coronaria

These delicate flowers are available in a wide variety of shapes and sizes, although the ones pictured here are the most familiar. Their fragile flowers are made up not of petals but of sepals (these are usually green and are the leaflike structures which surround the flower), and these form a cup shape round a deep-blue central disc. In the garden, anemones of different species can be found in spring, summer and autumn but, in florists' shops, *Anemone coronaria* is the species available in winter. Although they can be mixed with other flowers, they look best massed in a glass vase. Pack them in tightly, as their stems have a tendency to bend and this can make a vase look untidy.

Colors available Red, blue, mauve, pink, white, yellow, magenta and scarlet. Many have a central disc ringed with another color.

Preparation Cut the stems on a slant and make a 2in slit with a sharp knife. Dip the cut ends in boiling water for a few seconds. Give a long, cool drink before arranging.

Anemones

CHINCHERINCHEE
Ornithogalum thyrsoides

Imported in winter, these flowers are a useful addition to the range available at this time of year. The tightly packed flowers will open from the bottom upwards and the spike is soon a mass of small, white, star-shaped flowers. They look good when used with colorful sprays of holly or cotoneaster at Christmas.

Colors available White.

Preparation Some chincherinchees come with wax sealing their ends. Cut this off and make a 2in slit with a sharp knife. Give a deep drink of warm water and then put them in cool water for several days to allow all the flowers to open.

Additional features
Long-lasting   Useful foliage   Fragrant   Suitable for drying

Orchid

ORCHID
Dendrobium sp. and hybrids

These exotic flowers are imported from the Far East. They come in many different sizes and shapes, all with the usual "lip" surrounded by a ring of sepals and petals. The flowers need to be seen close up to be appreciated, so these orchids are best displayed very simply, either on their own or with the bare, red stems of the dogwood, in an uncluttered setting.

Colors available Red, orange, yellow, white and purple. The flowers are usually marked or patterned with another color.

Preparation These orchids are usually bought in sprays or branches of flowers rather than as single flowers. They will last over a long period if the water is changed daily.

WINTER-FLOWERING JASMINE
Jasminum nudiflorum

These shrubs are easily grown in the garden, and cut stems are available in florists' shops. In summer, the bush is covered in dark-green leaves, but during the winter it is covered with tubular, yellow flowers. Display a few sprays in a plain terracotta container or mix with early flowering daffodils.

Colors available Yellow.

Preparation Cut the stems on a slant and make a 2in slit with a sharp knife. No other treatment is required before arranging.

CHRYSANTHEMUM
Chrysanthemum hybrids

At a time when substantial, brightly colored flowers are not abundant, these flowers are a great addition to winter flower arrangements. Chrysanthemums grow in gardens in autumn but are now commercially forced and can be bought in florists' shops throughout the year. They are available as single heads and sprays in many different shapes and sizes. The single blooms are easier to arrange as focal points in a vase. The sprays are a little more difficult, as there are many flowers on each stem. These should be massed together in a large vase, or the individual flowers can be picked off and used in miniature arrangements.

Colors available Chrysanthemums are available in a wide range of colors—red, orange, rust, pink white, yellow, lime-green, peach and cream. Many of the daisy-shaped flowers have a central disc of a different color.

Preparation Cut the stems at a slant and make a 2in slit with a sharp knife. Dip the cut ends in boiling water for a few seconds. Immerse the whole stem in cool water and give a long drink before arranging in deep water.

Cotoneaster

COTONEASTER
Cotoneaster "Cornubius"

The dark-green, lance-shaped leaves of this evergreen shrub are deeply veined and slightly matt, giving them an attractive texture. The red berries are borne in large clusters. Use small sprays in seasonal table decorations or in place of holly in wreaths and garlands. This cotoneaster can also be used as colorful background material in large arrangements.

Colors available Deep-green leaves, red berries in winter, cream flowers in summer.

Preparation Cut the stems on a slant and make a 2in slit with a sharp knife. Give a long cool drink before arranging.

WINTER ACONITE
Eranthis hyemalis

These little flowers appear in gardens in early spring. The yellow flowers resemble buttercups in shape and are ringed by lime-green sepals. Display them with their own foliage in a miniature arrangement.

Colors available Yellow.

Preparation Cut the stems on a slant and make a slit with a sharp knife. Arrange in cool water.

Chrysanthemums

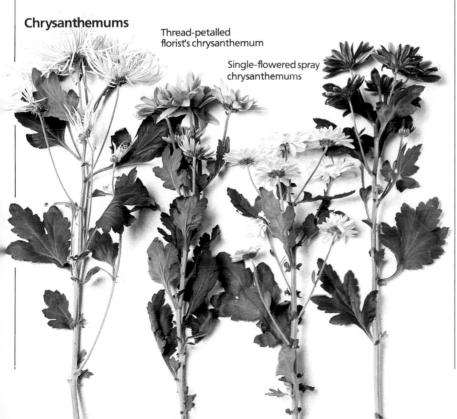

Thread-petalled florist's chrysanthemum

Single-flowered spray chrysanthemums

Other winter flowers	
Snowdrop	Mahonia
Hellebore	Toadflax
Winter sweet	Algerian iris
Cymbidium	Cyclamen
Chionodoxa	Squill
Winter camellia	Hepatica
Witch hazel	Hyacinth
Grape hyacinth	Snowflake
Skimmia	Lenten rose
Firethorn	Heath
Barberry	Snowberry

Foliage 1

Foliage plays as great a part in flower arranging as flowers themselves. Individual leaves or sprays can either be used as background or filler material in mixed arrangements, or the foliage can be used on its own to make an attractive display. While the choice of foliage available in florists' shops may be limited, gardens and woods can provide an enormous variety of leaves with a fascinating range of colors, shapes and textures with which to experiment. Plain-green leaves range from the forest-green of the pittosporum to the apple-green of the plantain lily; or leaves may be variegated with white, cream or yellow—they may be completely colored, like the golden-yellow leaves of the spindle tree, or marked only at the margins, like the variegated holly. Silver and gray foliage looks particularly attractive with yellow or pink flowers and can be used on its own—many different textures massed together in a monochromatic arrangement look very striking. Red and bronze leaves are usually associated with autumn, but many leaves have this color all year round. When planning arrangements, try to utilize the natural outline of the leaves or sprays as an integral part of a design. Use spikes of leaves as outline material, soft, arching ivies and ferns to add curves—either within the arrangement or trailing down from an arrangement placed on a pedestal—and bold leaves, such as those of the plantain lily and bergenia, to make a dramatic, modern display. Arrangements made up entirely of foliage can be just as attractive as arrangements of flowers.

To prepare cut foliage for display, condition it first by soaking it in water—overnight for older leaves and about two hours for younger leaves. Do not soak silver or gray foliage as it has a tendency to become soggy. Wash evergreen foliage in a solution of mild detergent to restore its shine. All foliage can be pressed; individual entries state which items can be air-dried or dried in glycerine.

GREEN FOLIAGE

VIBURNUM
Viburnum rhytidophyllum

These deep-green leaves have a distinctive wrinkled texture caused by the heavy veining on the upper surface. They mix very well with pansies and white or red dahlias, and can be used to vary texture in an all-green display. The evergreen leaves dry particularly well in air or glycerine.

SOFT SHIELD FERN
Polystichum setiferum

The leaves of this handsome fern have a soft texture and a good, bright-green color. They are finely divided and gently arching, providing an excellent foil for cut flowers. They mix well with teasel and driftwood in a modern arrangement. Soft shield fern is an evergreen that does not dry well.

MAGNOLIA
Magnolia grandiflora

These shiny, green leaves have a leathery texture and a rust-colored, feltlike underside. They can be used as a background for deep-red flowers. The evergreen leaves do not dry well.

PLANTAIN LILY
Hosta plantaginea

The leaves of this plant are large and broad and are a bright-green color. Their size and deeply grooved, glossy texture make them ideal for modern arrangements, and they combine well with large flowers such as lilies or poppies. Other kinds of hosta have especially attractive foliage.

COTONEASTER
Cotoneaster horizontalis

Tiny, delicate, dark-green leaves are arranged on stiff stems. The leaves have a glossy upper surface, and are gray and hairy beneath. The long, narrow spikes of leaves are suitable for establishing the outline of an arrangement; the tiny leaves complement larger and more dominant elements with their delicate appearance. This foliage is evergreen but turns red in autumn. These leaves can be air-dried or dried in glycerine.

JAPANESE ANGELICA
Aralia chinensis

The oval-shaped leaves are a rich-green color, and there is also a yellow-and-green variety. The number of leaflets on each spray makes them useful as filler material in all types of arrangement. They are deciduous leaves that can be air-dried.

BERGENIA
Bergenia sp.

The large, dark-green leaves of the bergenia have a smooth, shiny texture with bold ribbing. They are good for focal interest and are suitable for large-scale modern arrangements. These plants are perennial and are grown in colonies in part shade.

PITTOSPORUM
Pittosporum tobira

These attractive, tear-drop shaped leaves are a lustrous green and have a prominent central vein. Their thick, leathery texture contrasts well with rough or hairy leaves. As the leaves are small, pittosporum makes a good background material to cut flowers. This plant is an evergreen and can be used all year round.

Green foliage **1** Viburnum **2** Soft shield fern **3** Magnolia **4** Plantain lily **5** Cotoneaster **6** Japanese angelica **7** Bergenia **8** Pittosporum

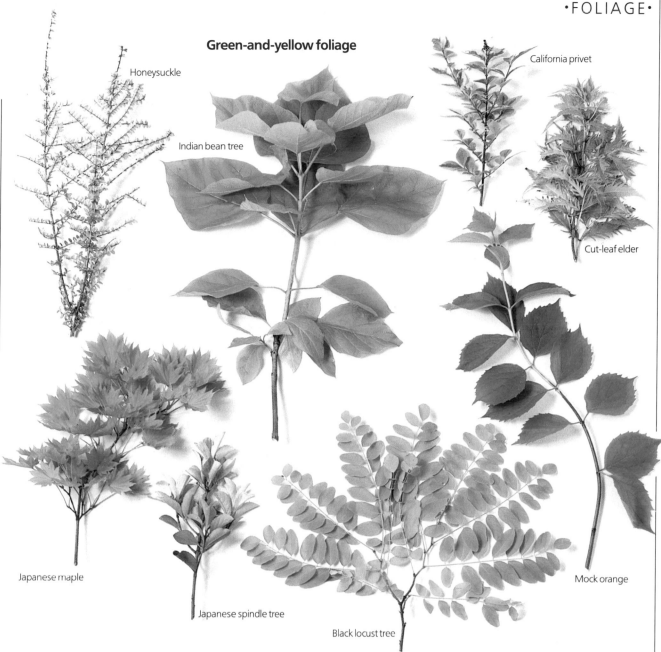

Green-and-yellow foliage

Honeysuckle

Indian bean tree

California privet

Cut-leaf elder

Japanese maple

Japanese spindle tree

Black locust tree

Mock orange

GREEN-AND-YELLOW FOLIAGE

HONEYSUCKLE
Lonicera nitida "Baggesen's Gold"

The rows of tiny, golden and pale-green leaves are borne in upright spikes. This shrubby form of honeysuckle can be used for outline, or as filler material in flower and foliage arrangements, and looks good with yellow roses. The evergreen leaves can be used fresh or air-dried at any time of year.

INDIAN BEAN TREE
Catalpa bignonioides

With its large, heart-shaped, pale yellow-green leaves, this foliage is useful for large-scale arrangements—though it does exude a pungent smell if crushed. Beanlike seed pods are produced in autumn. The leaves are at their best during summer. They do not dry well.

CALIFORNIA PRIVET
Ligustrum ovalifolium "Aureum"

This variety of privet is a pale-green color with wide borders of deep yellow. Other varieties of privet may be green or white and green. The leaves have a soft texture. The

evergreen leaves are borne in bushy spikes, and are useful in many types of arrangement, but do not dry well.

CUT-LEAF ELDER
Sambucus racemosa "Plumosa Aurea"

These unusual golden-yellow and green leaves have deeply serrated margins. The leaves are borne in sprays which are useful for giving a soft outline shape to a large arrangement. The cut-leaf elder produces berries in autumn, but the leaves are at their best in spring or summer. They do not dry well, but are very useful for fresh arrangements.

JAPANESE MAPLE
Acer japonicum "Aureum"

Deeply serrated margins give these large leaves a beautiful shape. The fresh, bright coloring and unusual "fan" shape make them a suitable focal point for a foliage display and are seen at their best in simple displays. The yellow leaves turn a rich crimson in autumn. They are especially attractive when pressed.

JAPANESE SPINDLE TREE
Euonymus japonica "Ovata-aurea"

The small, oval leaves are golden-yellow or yellow-green in color and have an attractive glossy texture. They grow in dense sprays and make good filler material in arrangements of small, yellow flowers. These are evergreen leaves that do not dry well.

BLACK LOCUST TREE
Robinia pseudoacacia

When they first appear, the leaves are golden-yellow, turning into a pale yellow-green in the summer. The "Frisia" variety has golden-yellow leaves throughout the season. The small leaflets are arranged in very regular pairs on thin branchlets. Display these leaves so that the natural fan shape and interesting texture can be used to best effect.

MOCK ORANGE
Philadelphus coronarius "Aureus"

When young, the foliage of this plant is bright golden-yellow, becoming dark green with age. The round leaves have a pointed tip and roughly toothed margins, and are at their best in spring. Use them to complement large flowers of any color.

Foliage 2

GREEN-AND-WHITE FOLIAGE

TARTARIAN DOGWOOD
Cornus alba "Elegantissima"

This mid-green foliage is irregularly edged with white and grows on red stems. The plain-green varieties often turn red or orange in autumn. All provide useful color for flower or foliage groups, mixing especially well with white flowers. The leaves are at their best in autumn. They do not dry well.

EUROPEAN ELDER
Sambucus nigra "Albo-variegata"

These slender, dark-green, pointed leaves are finely edged with pale yellow. They exude a disagreeable odor if bruised, but are an ideal background to a vase of yellow flowers. The leaves are at their best during spring and summer. They do not dry well.

COMMON PRIVET
Ligustrum vulgare "Aureo-variegatum"

These long, elegant leaves grow on densely packed branches which have an elongated overall shape. The smaller leaves are more prominently yellow, so a good color range is present on each stem. These evergreen leaves air-dry well.

ENGLISH HOLLY
Ilex aquifolium "Golden Queen"

The sharp, spiky, dark-green leaves have white or silver edging. Holly is an evergreen foliage traditionally used in Christmas garlands and wreaths. It can also be usefully combined with hellebores, red or white carnations, or ivy. Holly lasts longer if arranged without water and air-dries well.

GREATER PERIWINKLE
Vinca major "Variegata"

These leaves are oval in shape and are mid-green edged with white. They are arranged in pairs on slender, curving stems which can be allowed to trail or twine. Use these evergreen leaves as trailing material in a pedestal arrangement.

ENGLISH IVY
Hedera helix "Argento-variegata"

These small, heart-shaped leaves are mid-green with irregular, white edging. Ivies are evergreen trailers but can also be used to twine up through an arrangement. They contrast well with snowdrops and catkins in a winter arrangement, and can also be used effectively with freesias or foxgloves in shades of yellow for a fresh-looking display. The leaves are suitable for drying in glycerine.

Green-and-white foliage

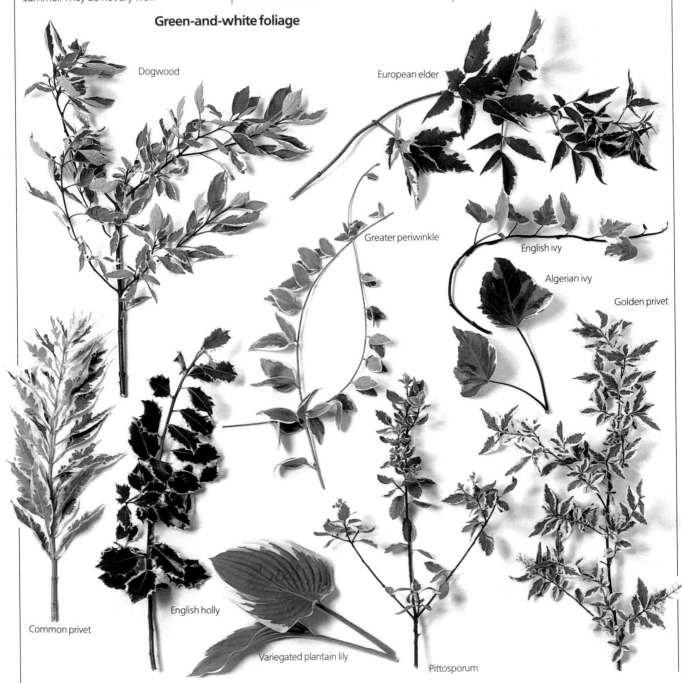

Dogwood

European elder

Greater periwinkle

English ivy

Algerian ivy

Golden privet

Common privet

English holly

Variegated plantain lily

Pittosporum

ALGERIAN IVY
Hedera canariensis "Variegata"

These large, leathery leaves are dark green edged with white. The heart-shaped leaves grow on red stems and look good in displays of large flowers, such as daffodils or yellow Transvaal daisies. Whole stems of these evergreen leaves can trail from arrangements. The leaves are suitable for drying in glycerine.

VARIEGATED PLANTAIN LILY
Hosta sp.

These large, broad leaves have a prominent pale-yellow margin. Their size and deeply grooved, glossy texture make them ideal for modern arrangements. They also combine well with large flowers, such as roses, or with ferns in a foliage display. They are at their best in spring.

PITTOSPORUM
Pittosporum tenuifolium "Garnettii"

These pale-green leaves have narrow, irregular yellow margins and are borne on black stems. They have an open appearance and make excellent filler material at any time of year. The leaves can be dried in glycerine.

GOLDEN PRIVET
Ligustrum ovalifolium "Albo-marginatum"

These glossy, mid-green leaves have wide, irregular, creamy-white borders. The spikes of leaves are good filler material, and a useful addition to a green foliage arrangement at any time of year.

GRAY FOLIAGE

EUCALYPTUS
Eucalyptus gunnii

The distinctive young foliage of this evergreen plant encircles the thin gray stems. (The leaves become elongated as they get older.) The color varies between blue-green and silvery-white. Eucalyptus leaves look good with pink or blue flowers in a modern setting, or with grasses and ferns in a dried arrangement. The fragrance is also attractive. These leaves can be used throughout the year but look best when still young. They can be dried in glycerine.

SEA KALE
Crambe maritima

The leaves of this spring vegetable are large, fleshy and brittle, and have a distinctive blue-green color. They have a crinkly outline that provides an interesting contrast with more formal shapes, or they can be used to good effect in more abstract arrangements of leaves of different textures. They are at their best in summer. They do not dry well.

COMMON WORMWOOD
Artemisia "Powis Castle"

A sprig of common wormwood resembles a tiny tree in shape. The delicate silver-gray leaves are deeply dissected into slender filaments which have a silky texture and provide an unusual outline for small groups. These are evergreen leaves which may prove difficult to dry.

GROUNDSEL
Senecio "Sunshine"

Two distinct colors and textures are displayed by these small, oval leaves. They have a dark-green, leathery upper surface and a pale-green and densely felted lower surface. They look good in both flower and foliage arrangements as both sides of the leaves can be displayed to effect. Although the leaves are evergreen, they are at their best in winter. They do not dry well.

WHITE WILLOW
Salix alba

These two-tone leaves are deep-green above and silky-white beneath. The leaves are long and narrow and borne in pairs on the woody stems. Used thoughtfully, the sprays of leaves can add interest to both flower and foliage groups. The leaves are at their best in summer. They do not dry well.

MULLEIN
Verbascum sp.

These large, pale-gray leaves have a soft texture and gentle shape that combines well with other soft-textured foliage. They look attractive when mixed with flowers, particularly with pale-pink, blue or green flowers for a pastel-colored arrangement. The evergreen leaves are at their best in summer. They do not dry well.

SENECIO
Senecio maritima

A fine, white down covers both surfaces of these deeply dissected leaves and gives them an attractive, silvery appearance. The leaves have a soft texture and they are ideal for adding an interesting shape to a small arrangement. They mix particularly well with pink roses and statice. The leaves are evergreen and are at their best in summer. They do not dry well.

ORNAMENTAL OATS
Helicotrichon sempervirens

These long, thin and slightly arching leaves are an intense blue-gray color. They provide dramatic definition and contrast and go well with bright-blue flowers, such as irises, delphiniums and larkspur in a stark, modern arrangement. Although evergreen, the leaves are at their best in summer.

BALLOTA
Ballota pseudodictamnus

The very unusual leaves of this plant grow densely on slim, upright stems. They are heart-shaped with slightly scalloped edges and are "woolly-gray" in color; they provide excellent textural variation for a fresh or dried all-foliage arrangement. The leaves are evergreen but are at their best in spring and summer. They do not dry well.

SAGEBRUSH
Artemisia "Douglasiana"

The linear leaves are borne on tall spikes and have a pale-gray underside with a slightly darker upper surface. The long, slender shape of the stems provides graceful lines and strong definition for mixed groups, whether used as focal point or as a background for pink or blue flowers such as roses, larkspur or cornflowers. These leaves are at their best in summer and are suitable for air-drying.

Gray foliage **1** Eucalyptus **2** Sea kale **3** Common wormwood **4** Groundsel **5** White willow **6** Mullein **7** Senecio **8** Ornamental oats **9** Ballota **10** Sagebrush.

Foliage 3

BRONZE FOLIAGE

ORNAMENTAL GRAPE VINE
Vitis vinifera "Purpurea"

These crimson-red leaves turn to a richer claret-red in the autumn. Pretty red-and-green variegated types are also available. The butterfly shape of the leaves is an attractive feature and as such should be arranged thoughtfully. The ornamental grape vine is useful in autumnal arrangements, mixing well with yellow and orange flowers and foliage of autumnal shades. The leaves do not dry well.

COPPER BEECH
Fagus sylvatica "Purpurea"

The delicate oval leaves have toothed edges and are a rich-copper color. They blend well with other foliage, provide an excellent backing for large displays, and look especially striking when arranged with white or red flowers. Use older foliage, as young foliage is green. The leaves are at their best in spring and dry well in glycerine.

JAPANESE BARBERRY
Berberis thunbergii "Atropurpurea"

Small, rich dark-bronze leaves grow in clusters on long tapering stems. They turn bright red in autumn, as does the variety which is mid-green for the rest of the year. This excellent and colorful outline foliage can be combined effectively with wood and pine cones in modern arrangements. The leaves are at their best in autumn and air-dry well.

NEW ZEALAND FLAX
Phormium tenax "Purpureum"

These straplike, stiff, leathery leaves may be red or green, and some varieties may be striped with yellow. They can grow to 10ft long, but at this length become rather unusable. The young, shorter leaves provide elegant lines for arrangements. The leaves have good color all year but do not dry well. They can, however, be used in short-term dried arrangements whilst still fresh.

NORWAY MAPLE
Acer platanoides "Goldsworth Purple"

Apart from the deep purple-crimson of this foliage, there are white-margined, pale-green and red varieties. The bold, pointed outline of maple leaves makes them suitable for large arrangements, and they make excellent filling material, combining well with large flowers such as yellow tulips or chrysanthemums. The leaves are at their best in autumn and can be dried in glycerine.

SMOKE TREE
Cotinus coggygria

These elliptical leaves grow in dense clusters. They are green with red veins, and assume a rich-red color in autumn. The delicate mass of flower stems emerging from these clusters creates an unusual "smoky" effect which can be used effectively in Japanese-style arrangements. They also mix well with orange flowers. The leaves are at their best in autumn. They do not dry well.

PURPLE-LEAVED FILBERT
Corylus maxima "Atropurpurea"

These large, round leaves grow on slim arching stems and are deep-purple in color. They make good foliage for large arrangements and combine well with round flowers of red, purple or mauve. They are at their best in autumn, but may prove difficult to dry.

STONECROP
Sedum maximum "Atropurpureum"

The green-and-red fleshy leaves are matched by clusters of tiny flowers of similar shades. Use them to instil texture and color in an arrangement of fresh or dried flowers of autumnal shades. They are at their best during late summer and can easily be air-dried.

Bronze foliage

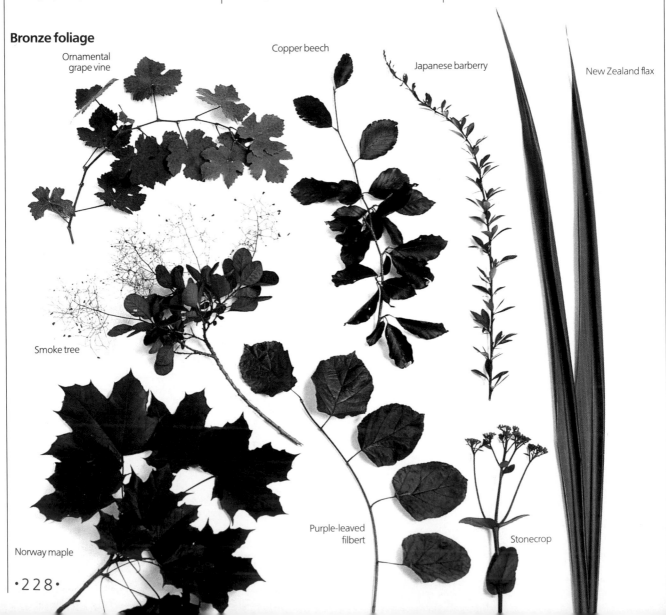

Ornamental grape vine

Copper beech

Japanese barberry

New Zealand flax

Smoke tree

Purple-leaved filbert

Stonecrop

Norway maple

THE
DRIED-FLOWER
GUIDE

Dried flowers have a charm that is independent of season, and create an appealing palette of pale and bright colors and of brittle and soft forms.

Flowers are not the only suitable materials; many other sorts of dried matter can be used, offering a great variety of shapes, textures and colors. The soft, neutral colors of grasses and cereals are a useful foil to flowers. The rich colors of autumnal foliage can be mixed with flowers and grasses, and both familiar and exotic seed heads offer unusual shapes and textures.

On the following pages you will find a selection of dried flowers (arranged according to their color), foliage, cereals, grasses, seed heads and fruits, all of which can be used to make attractive and long-lasting displays. Advice is offered on how to use each item of dried material and, for each entry, the most effective method of drying is given.

Dried flowers 1
Whites and yellows

This range of colors, from the muted tones of the greenish-whites to the brilliant snow-whites and vibrant yellows, adds freshness and light to any arrangement. They mix well with other colors, and can be used either to evoke the brilliance of summer sunshine, when used with other brightly colored dried flowers, or to reflect the mellow tones of autumn, when combined with flowers, foliage and grasses in shades of orange and brown. Their colors blend well with wicker baskets, terracotta and frosted glass.

Methods of drying
Air-drying Glycerine Silica/borax Pressing

LADY'S MANTLE
Alchemilla vulgaris
The delicate, yellow-green flowers blend well with grasses, cereals and seed heads.

TUMBLEWEED
Amaranthus albus
These green spikes look good in both flower and foliage arrangements.

WHITE BUTTON FLOWERS
Chrysanthemum hybrids
When the petals have been removed the central parts of the flowers can be dyed to any color.

STATICE
Limonium sinuatum
The yellow, white, purple, pink or red flowers look attractive massed in a terracotta container.

TANSY
Tanacetum vulgare
The bright-yellow, buttonlike flowers add a splash of color to an arrangement.

EVERLASTING
Helipterum roseum
White flowers with yellow centers add delicate color to small arrangements and wreaths.

STRAW FLOWER
Helichrysum bracteatum
The yellow, white, orange or red daisylike flowers should be wired before drying.

EVERLASTING
Helipterum humboldtianum
These attractive bright-yellow flowers add color to winter arrangements.

PEARL EVERLASTING
Anaphalis margaritacea
Clusters of ivory-white flower heads that may be sprayed or dyed for display.

GOLDEN MARGUERITE
Anthemis tinctoria
These versatile yellow flowers can be dyed or sprayed to any color.

YARROW
Achillea filipendulina
The flat-headed yellow or white flowers provide focal point in a group.

BABY'S BREATH
Gypsophila paniculata
The white or pink flowers are often used in bouquets and wreaths, but also look good on their own.

Dried flowers 2
Pinks, reds and oranges

The colors in this group range from pale, delicate pinks to deep reds and flame oranges. Red flowers are perhaps the boldest and most eye-catching of all, but they attain a more subtle appeal when toned with brown, yellow or blue. Shades of pink add a light and delicate quality to an arrangement, and are seen at their best when contrasted with white and green. Deep, rich-orange flowers are especially lovely if used with the yellows and reds of autumnal foliage.

ROSE
Rosa sp.
Mass roses in low baskets or tall containers to create an intense focal point of color.

STRAW FLOWER
Helichrysum bracteatum
The orange, daisylike flowers should be wired before drying.

FALSE SAFFLOWER
Carthamus tinctorius
Red-orange flowers and gray-green leaves provide a stiff outline shape for arrangements.

MARSH ROSEMARY
Limonium suworowii
The long, narrow clusters of rose-pink flowers add unusual lines to any group.

CELOSIA
Celosia argentea "Cristata"
The purple or pink blooms have a mossy texture and provide a dramatic focal point for a large arrangement.

CHINESE LANTERN
Physalis alkekengi
The orange and green flower pods can be used in mixed autumnal arrangements, but also can stand on their own.

Methods of drying

Air-drying Glycerine Silica/borax Pressing

BOTTLE BRUSH
Callistemon citrinus
The bright-orange heads shine forth in both flower and foliage arrangements.

STATICE
Limonium sinuatum
The pink, purple, yellow, white or red flowers look attractive when massed together in a terra-cotta container.

EVERLASTING
Helipterum roseum
Pink flowers with yellow centers add delicate color to small arrangements and wreaths.

FLOWERING ONION
Allium sp.
The flowers may be pink, blue or yellow. Mass them together in a tall container.

LARKSPUR
Delphinium consolida
Pink, mauve, blue or white flowers add height to arrangements of delicate flowers and are excellent for small wreaths.

GLOBE AMARANTH
Gomphrena globosa
These delicate, cloverlike flowers should be wired before drying.

JOE PYEWEED
Eupatorium purpureum
Use these delicate rose-pink flowers as filler material in larger flower arrangements.

STRAW FLOWER
Helichrysum bracteatum
The pink, daisylike flowers should be wired before drying.

ROCK CRESS
Arabis alpina "Rosea"
The tiny pink flowers can be used in bouquets and wreaths, but also look good on their own in a delicate container.

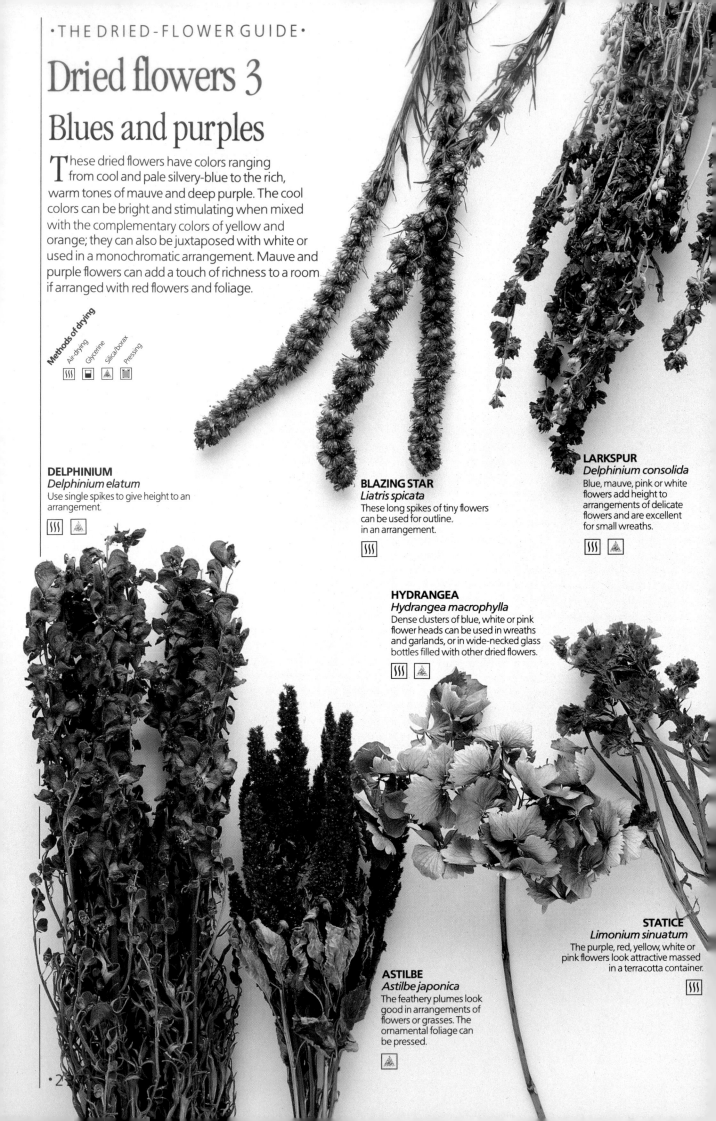

Dried flowers 3
Blues and purples

These dried flowers have colors ranging from cool and pale silvery-blue to the rich, warm tones of mauve and deep purple. The cool colors can be bright and stimulating when mixed with the complementary colors of yellow and orange; they can also be juxtaposed with white or used in a monochromatic arrangement. Mauve and purple flowers can add a touch of richness to a room if arranged with red flowers and foliage.

Methods of drying

Air-drying Glycerine Silica/borax Pressing

DELPHINIUM
Delphinium elatum
Use single spikes to give height to an arrangement.

BLAZING STAR
Liatris spicata
These long spikes of tiny flowers can be used for outline. in an arrangement.

LARKSPUR
Delphinium consolida
Blue, mauve, pink or white flowers add height to arrangements of delicate flowers and are excellent for small wreaths.

HYDRANGEA
Hydrangea macrophylla
Dense clusters of blue, white or pink flower heads can be used in wreaths and garlands, or in wide-necked glass bottles filled with other dried flowers.

STATICE
Limonium sinuatum
The purple, red, yellow, white or pink flowers look attractive massed in a terracotta container.

ASTILBE
Astilbe japonica
The feathery plumes look good in arrangements of flowers or grasses. The ornamental foliage can be pressed.

DOCK
Rumex acetosa
These rust-purple plants make excellent filling material, or can be used to make a rustic group if massed in a rush basket.

IMMORTELLE
Xeranthemum annuum
These purple, lilac, white or pink flowers should be wired together in bunches for use in arrangements.

LAVENDER
Lavandula angustifolia
The fragrant purple flowers may be used in small bouquets, wreaths, pot-pourris and herbal pillows.

GLOBE THISTLE
Echinops ritro
The rounded blue heads mix well with yellow flowers.

SEA HOLLY
Eryngium maritimum
The silver-blue stems and heads can be used to add texture to an arrangement.

THRIFT
Armeria maritima
The ball-like, silver-pink flowers provide focal point in a group.

GLOBE AMARANTH
Gomphrena globosa
These delicate, cloverlike flowers should be wired before drying.

Dried foliage, cereals and grasses

Foliage, cereals and grasses should be considered essential dried-flower arranging materials. Certainly, very few arrangements are produced without one or more of these ingredients to add some variation in shape, color or texture. But they are more than a mere foil to brightly colored flowers; with a little imagination they can provide an attractive display by themselves.

BRISTLE BENT
Agrostis curtisii
This gray-green grass has a dense flower head and is suitable for many arrangements, including wreaths.

HARESTAIL GRASS
Lagurus ovatus
This delicate grass can be used with flowers or with leaves, seed heads and other grasses.

QUAKING GRASS
Briza media
The delicate, nodding flower heads add lightness to small arrangements.

REED MACE
Typha latifolia
The hard-edged spikiness of this relation of the bullrush is useful in large groups.

PLATYLOBIUM
Platylobium angulare
The unusual foliage can be used as background material in arrangements of delicate flowers.

GREVILLEA
Grevillea triternata
These interesting fernlike leaves have an unusual spiky quality that adds variety to an arrangement.

EUCALYPTUS
Eucalyptus sp.
The red or brown leaves add strong shape and color to foliage arrangements.

PAMPAS GRASS
Cortaderia selloana
A useful background material for large groups, pampas grass looks attractive when displayed on its own in an urn.

Methods of drying

Air-drying Glycerine Silica/borax Pressing

BEECH
Fagus sylvatica
These attractive, copper-coloured
leaves provide an excellent background for large displays.

BROME GRASS
Bromus sp.
This wild grass adds an attractive feathery texture to any
dried arrangement.

BARLEY
Hordeum vulgare
This grass provides traditional
arrangements with an interesting
variation in shape and texture.

OATS
Avena sp.
This pale-green grass can
be mixed with other grasses
and foliage or used in flower
arrangements.

BENT GRASS
Agrostis sp.
This pale grass adds a delicate light-
ness to grass or foliage arrangements.

BRACKEN
Pteridium aquilinum
All ferns add a delicate outline to
dried-flower groups.

237

Dried seed heads and fruits

Dried material is not restricted solely to flowers, grasses and foliage; seed heads and fruits add to the already extensive range. Many plants have attractive seed heads which are only revealed when the flower itself has died. These are extremely useful, providing exciting variations of shape, color and texture. Fruits can be wired for use in an arrangement or can be placed to create interest around the base of a container.

ORNAMENTAL GOURD
Cucurbita pepo ovifera
Many colors, shapes and textures are available. Dried gourds can be waxed or varnished and can be massed in a bowl or mixed with real fruits. Gourds retain their shape by varnishing.

POPPY
Papaver sp.
A great assortment of differently shaped pods is available. The heads can be wired and used in wreaths.

PROTEA
Protea sp.
These heads are for large, dramatic arrangements. Several heads massed together in a rush basket look effective.

COTTON
Gossypium sp.
These fluffy, white tufts are an unusual and interesting addition to displays of grasses or foliage.

BANKSIA
Banksia menziesii
These deep-brown seed heads are excellent for inclusion in modern abstract arrangements.

Methods of drying

Air-drying Glycerine Silica/borax Pressing

BEECH NUTS
Fagus sylvatica
These rich-brown nuts can be contrasted with delicate grasses in an arrangement or wired for use in wreaths.

SCABIOUS
Scabiosa caucasica
These delicate heads can be used in autumn foliage arrangements, or mixed with dried flowers for a light effect.

CHILLI PEPPER
Capsicum annuum
These red, orange or yellow fruits add outline shape and vivid color to autumn foliage arrangements. Wire the heads for use in wreaths.

CARDOON BALLS
Cynara cardunculus
The handsome, fluffy heads provide height and texture for large arrangements.

MAIZE
Zea mays
The whole stems can be used in large seed pod and foliage arrangements or the heads can be wired for smaller arrangements.

LOVE-IN-A-MIST
Nigella damascena
The rosebud-shaped heads may have red or purple streaks. The frilly foliage around the heads adds a misty look to delicate arrangements.

TEASEL
Dipsacus fullonum
Distinctively shaped heads which may be cut in half to provide a starlike "flower". The heads can be wired for use in wreaths.

7.

PLANT CARE

Outdoors, plants are able to fend very much for themselves, needing only occasional assistance on our part. In the indoor garden, however, plants depend on us to meet all their needs: we decide what level of light and humidity they are given, the quantity and regularity of watering and feeding, how big a root-run they should be allowed, and what the minimum winter temperature should be. Successful gardeners and those whose house plants thrive are said to have green fingers or, at the very least, a green thumb. Certainly, some people seem to have a built-in feel for what plants need, and how they should be cared for, while others fail totally with their charges. There is, however, no mystery about growing plants successfully; good results can be achieved by anyone who is prepared to understand the needs of particular plants and establish a routine for looking after them. Always remember that you are dealing with living things; unhealthy specimens are a sorry sight and act as a reproach to us for failing to give them enough attention. Caring for plants is more likely to be a joy—as opposed to a chore—if you choose them carefully. Decorative qualities are, of course, important, but you should also be confident of your ability to look after the plant and be sure that it is capable of flourishing under the conditions you have to offer in your house or apartment.

Potting up your own plants
Plant care need be neither complicated nor time-consuming. Potting up young plants, such as these variegated bedding geraniums (*Pelargonium* hybrids), is quick and easy, and should result in healthy growth if you use the correct size of pot and the right kind of potting mixture.

Requirements for healthy plants

The plants we grow in our homes come from temperate, sub-tropical and tropical areas where widely differing growing conditions exist. For example, some are exposed to direct sunlight, others are protected from the fierce rays of the tropical sun by neighboring plants or are given some shade from overhanging trees, while still more grow on the forest floor in considerable shade. This diversity of natural habitat explains why different plants require different conditions when grown indoors.

Having said this, however, the ability to adapt to unfamiliar conditions is a major reason for the popularity of many common house plants. Most generally dislike widely fluctuating temperatures, although a drop of 5°-10°F at night is natural when the thermostat is lowered at bedtime and is preferred by most indoor plants; those that produce flowers require this change to form buds. Such a drop is similar to nature's pattern: temperatures fall as the sun goes down. A warmer house during daytime also follows nature's pattern—as the sun rises, the environment becomes warmer.

There is much pleasure and fulfillment to be derived from growing and looking after house plants. Maintaining healthy and attractive plants does not involve complicated or time-consuming procedures but just sensible and sensitive attention to the plants' basic needs. To thrive, plants need adequate light at the preferred intensity and for the right duration, a comfortable temperature, and the right level of atmospheric humidity. They have to be watered when they start to dry out a little, and some need a dormant period during the winter when the water supply needs to be curtailed—allowing the plant to rest and often encouraging flower-bud production. Food must be provided, the right kind of growing medium made available and, as the roots fill the pots, plants will need potting on. These and other needs are described in the sections that follow.

Basic tools and equipment for the indoor gardener

Fork

Trowel

Pruners

Anvil pruner

Scissors

Knife

Wooden stakes

Wooden plant supports

Bamboo stakes

Twine

Photosynthesis

This is the process undertaken by the parts of plants containing the green pigment chlorophyll, in which light energy is used to produce carbohydrates from water and carbon dioxide. During daylight hours, carbon dioxide is taken from the air through the pores (stomata) of the leaves—situated mainly on the leaf undersides. Photosynthesis occurs through the action of light on the chlorophyll in the leaves. The light energy is used to split water molecules into oxygen and hydrogen. The hydrogen is then combined with the carbon dioxide taken in through the stomata to form carbohydrates, such as glucose, which provide the plant with food. Certain minerals are required for these complex chemical reactions to occur, and these are taken up, with water, by the roots.

The essential processes
Photosynthesis occurs during the day, or whenever light is available to the green parts of a plant. This diagram shows the movements of carbon dioxide, oxygen, water and minerals during this process. Photosynthesis cannot take place in the dark and the flow of oxygen and carbon dioxide is reversed as the plant respires or "breathes".

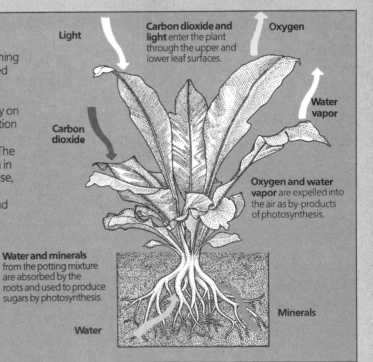

Light

Carbon dioxide and light enter the plant through the upper and lower leaf surfaces.

Oxygen

Carbon dioxide

Water vapor

Oxygen and water vapor are expelled into the air as by-products of photosynthesis.

Water and minerals from the potting mixture are absorbed by the roots and used to produce sugars by photosynthesis.

Minerals

Water

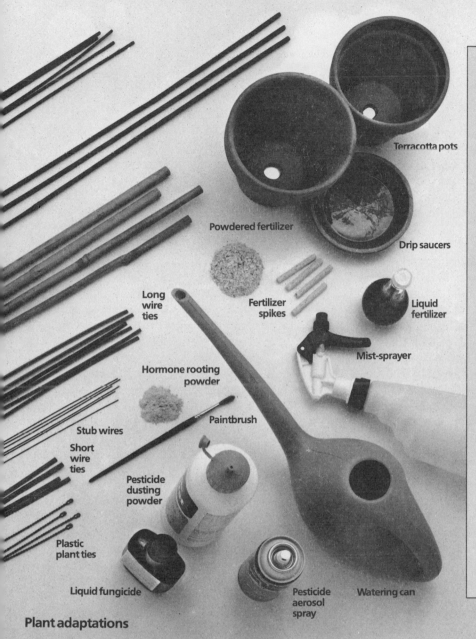

Terracotta pots

Powdered fertilizer

Drip saucers

Long wire ties

Fertilizer spikes

Liquid fertilizer

Hormone rooting powder

Mist-sprayer

Paintbrush

Stub wires

Short wire ties

Pesticide dusting powder

Plastic plant ties

Liquid fungicide

Pesticide aerosol spray

Watering can

Signs of ill-health

Slow or sluggish growth
If symptom occurs during summer months:—
Are you overwatering? (see p.251)
Are you underfeeding? (see p.252)
Does the plant need repotting? (see p.257)
If symptom occurs during winter months:—
Is this a natural rest period?

Wilting
Is the potting mixture very dry? (see p.251)
Are you overwatering? (see p.251)
Is there adequate drainage? (see p.255)
Is the location too sunny? (see p.245)
Is the temperature too high? (see p.246)

Drooping leaves and wet soil
Are you overwatering? (see p.251)
Is there adequate drainage? (see p.255)

Brown leaf tips/spots on leaves
Are you overwatering? (see p.251)
Is the plant too close to the sun or another
source of heat? (see p.246)
Is the humidity level too low? (see p.247)
Is the plant standing in a draft? (see p.246)
Are you overfeeding? (see p.252)
Have you splashed water on the leaves?
(see p.249)

Falling flowers, leaves and buds
Are you overwatering? (see p.251)
Are you underwatering? (see p.251)
Is the temperature inconsistent? (see p.246)
Is the light inconsistent? (see p.245)
Is the humidity level too low? (see p.247)

Variegated leaves turning green
Is the plant getting enough light? (see p.245)

Rotting at the leaf axils
Has water lodged in the axil? (see p.249)

Leaves turn yellow
If growth is straggly:—
Are you overwatering? (see p.251)
Is the plant getting enough light? (see p.245)
Is the temperature too high? (see p.246)
Are you underfeeding? (see p.252)
Does the plant need repotting? (see p.257)
If leaves fall off the plant:—
Are you overwatering? (see p.251)
Is the plant standing in a draft? (see p.246)
Is the humidity level too low? (see p.247)
Is the temperature too low? (see p.246)

Plant adaptations

Thin, delicate-looking leaves
These usually indicate that plants come from
tropical regions where they are protected
from the extremes of great heat or cold.

Leathery or waxy leaves
These usually indicate that plants come from
hot, dry areas, since such plants store water
more effectively, reducing the amount of
water lost through transpiration.

Spines or fuzzy hair
These usually indicate that plants come from
desert areas as they help to baffle hot desert
sunshine—the spines take the place of leaves
and the stem becomes thick and succulent.

Light

Light is essential to all plants. Without enough light, growth suffers, and leaves become small and pale. Healthy growth depends on the process of photosynthesis, triggered off by the action of light on the green pigment chlorophyll. This pigment is present in red, bronze, purple and gray leaves as well as green ones; the other color is just an overlay to the green beneath. Variegated-leaved plants, however, are at a disadvantage as the yellow, cream or white sections on their leaves contain no chlorophyll. For this reason, variegated-leaved plants generally need brighter light if their strong leaf color contrast is to be maintained.

Indoor light levels

Plants in their native habitats have adapted to a wide range of different light levels. Indoors, you should try to provide the light intensity preferred by each plant as far as possible. To do this, you need to assess the amount of light present in various parts of any particular room. This can be difficult because the human eye is not a good judge of light intensity; it compensates for different light levels to give the impression of even overall lighting. The only really accurate way of measuring light intensity is to use a small hand-held photographic light-meter, or a camera with a built-in meter, which both give a good indication of light levels. You will probably be surprised at how low the levels of light are indoors: on a south-facing windowsill your plants will only get about half as much light as they would if they were growing outside, due to reflection from the glass. And as little as 3ft into the room there is only about three-quarters as much light as at the window. Having said this, however, most popular house plants are extremely tolerant, their adaptability being the main reason for their popularity.

Day length

In addition to intensity, light duration or day length is an important factor in determining how much light a plant receives. Most plants need about 12 to 16 hours of daylight to sustain active growth. Foliage house plants fall into two main groups: those that stop growing in the late autumn and need resting during the winter, and those that will continue to grow throughout the winter and remain attractive. Foliage plants from the tropics which, in the wild, receive around 12 hours of sunlight each day throughout the year, will only continue to grow all the year round in more temperate regions if they are given as much light as possible in winter, by using supplementary artificial light, and when kept in a warm room. Plants from more temperate regions stop growing (or slow down their growth very considerably) with the onset of winter and a shorter day.

In general, flowering plants need more light than foliage plants in order to initiate flower bud production and to allow the buds to develop properly. In many plants, flower production is triggered off by day length. These plants fall into two groups: long-day plants and short-day plants. Long-day plants flower when they have received more than 12 hours of light a day over a certain period. (It does not matter whether the light is natural or artificial—African violets (*Saintpaulia* hybrids) can be induced to flower at any time of year under artificial light.) Short-day plants flower

·244·

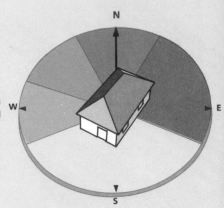

Light intensity and orientation
Levels of light intensity striking a house from all points of the compass. The lightest area corresponds to the strongest light, and the darkest area to the weakest, (assuming the sun is shining from the south). By finding out the orientation of your house, you will be able to place plants in appropriately lit positions.

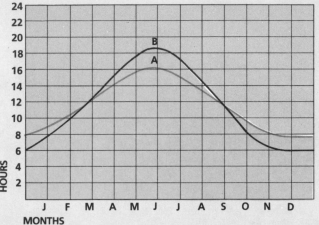

MONTHS
Daylight levels
In northern regions (B) plants receive more but less intense daylight in summer and less adequate light in winter than those further south (A).

when they receive less than 12 hours light a day over a certain period. Poinsettias (*Euphorbia pulcherrima*), chrysanthemums (*Chrysanthemum* hybrids), azaleas (*Rhododendron simsii*) and claw cacti (*Schlumbergera* sp.) are short-day plants which flower naturally in the autumn, but chrysanthemums can now be bought all through the year because growers can simulate the short day and initiate flower production by covering the plants in black plastic for the requisite number of hours each day. Many plants appear to have no strong preference with regard to day length, and flower through most or all of the year. These are known as day-neutral plants.

How plants seek light

All plants turn their leaves towards the source of light, apart from stiff-leaved species such as mother-in-law's tongue (*Sansevieria* sp.), many palms and dracaenas, and rosette-shaped bromeliads. Rooms with white or pale-colored walls will reflect light back on to plants, whereas those decorated in darker colors absorb light and will cause plants to turn towards the window. To counteract this natural tendency, and to promote balanced, upright growth, you should turn your plants frequently.

Suitable light levels for different plants

In *The Plant Finder's Guide*, the light preference of each featured plant is indicated by one of three symbols. These stand for sunny, filtered sun and shady, and are described in detail on the following page.

Sunny

A sunny position is one that gets direct sunlight for all, or part of, the day. South-facing windows will receive sunlight for most of the day, east-facing windows receive sunlight for several hours in the morning, and west-facing ones for several hours in the afternoon. The strength of the sunlight will depend on latitude and on the orientation of the room. South-facing rooms receive more intense light, but in summer it reaches less far into the room than in east- or west-facing rooms. In lower latitudes, or at the coast where light is brighter due to reflection from the sea, some form of shading may be necessary at a large south-facing window in summer to prevent possible leaf scorching and too-frequent drying out of the potting mixture. This type of bright light is for plants such as desert cacti, succulents from open bush or savanna, hard-leaved bromeliads from the tree-tops and certain sun-loving flowering plants.

Filtered sun

Filtered sun is direct sun that has been filtered through a translucent curtain or blind, or baffled by a tree or building outside. This level of light is also found between 3 and 5ft from a window which receives sun for all, or part of, the day. Although no direct sun falls here, the general level of brightness is high. Filtered sun is about a half to three-quarters as intense as direct sunlight. If you are in any doubt about the amount of light your plant needs, place it in filtered light, as few plants like direct, hot summer sunlight. In general, too little light is less harmful than too much light. Palms, tropical rain forest plants, and shrubs, including dracaenas, ti plants (*Cordyline terminalis*), and false aralias (*Dizygotheca elegantissima*), and soft-leaved bromeliads, such as scarlet stars (*Guzmania lingulata*) and flaming swords (*Vriesea splendens*), prefer this kind of light, as it is similar to the dappled light they receive in their native forest.

Shady

This position is one that receives no direct or indirect sunlight, yet does not have poor light. This level of light is found in, or just a little distance from, a well-lit north-facing window. It is also found in shaded areas within sunny rooms—for instance, along side walls—where the plant is well out of reach of direct sunlight, yet no more than 5-6ft from a sunny window. Shady positions receive about a quarter as much light as sunny ones. This amount of light suits plants from low-down in the jungle canopy where they are shielded from the rays of direct sun. However, day length in tropical jungles is considerably greater than that in northern hemispheres in winter, and you may need to move shade-loving plants nearer to the source of light during our winter. No flowering plants, or foliage plants with variegated leaves, will be happy in a shady position. Without sunlight, they will lose most of their leaves, and those that remain will lose their variegation.

Levels of light intensity in a room

Different levels of light in a typical room, in the northern hemisphere, on a summer day when direct sunlight is not obscured by clouds. In lower latitudes the light would be brighter, but would extend less far into the room. Obviously, the amount of light entering a room will be affected by local factors such as the number and size of the windows, and the presence of nearby buildings and trees.

Curtains absorb light, reducing the levels on either side of the windows.

Blind for shading plants on the windowsill from hot summer sun.

East- or west-facing windows get good light all day and direct light for a few hours.

South-facing windows receive direct sun for much of the day.

Bird's nest fern
Asplenium nidus

Belgian evergreen
Dracaena sanderana

Stick yucca
Yucca elephantipes

Poor light	Shady	Filtered sun	Sunny
An area more than 6ft away from the source of light. No plant will thrive here, even though the area seems bright to the human eye.	A moderately-lit area 5-6ft away from a sunny window, usually along a side wall, or near a well-lit north-facing window.	A well-lit position 3-5ft inside a south-, east- or west-facing window, or one receiving direct sunlight filtered by a tree or curtain.	A position which receives direct sunlight for most, or part of, the day. The strength of the sunlight will depend on latitude.

Temperature and humidity

Temperature

House plants have a preferred temperature range in which they thrive, and usually another that they will tolerate. Most popular house plants are from tropical and sub-tropical areas and do best in a temperature range of 60°-70°F. (Seeds usually germinate best when temperatures reach 64°F or more; and tip-cuttings and divided sections root well at 64°-75°F.) Other types of plants—mainly temperate evergreens and flowering species—prefer cooler conditions in the range of 50°-60°F. These are the two temperature ranges described by the mini-climates in *The Plant Finder's Guide* as "warm" and "cool". Although these are the conditions to which the plants are best suited, they will almost certainly be tolerant of slightly higher or lower temperatures for at least part of the time.

Plants that grow naturally in cool places will grow faster when given higher temperatures. Some may adapt and thrive, perhaps growing more quickly than is convenient indoors, although the blooming period of certain short-term flowering plants is greatly reduced if they are given higher temperatures than they need. It is rare that plants from a warm place do well in much cooler conditions.

In general, a fall in temperature of 5°-10°F at night is natural in the wild and advisable indoors. Some plants, such as cacti, can tolerate a much sharper fall, but fluctuations of more than 15°-18°F between daytime and night-time temperatures should be avoided in the house.

Winter- and spring-flowering bulbs must have their "wintering" at around 40°-50°F—a period when root growth is encouraged and active top growth discouraged. In addition, many house plants, especially evergreen species, require a winter rest period, away from the steady winter warmth of most domestic rooms. If possible, it is best to set aside a specific room which can be kept reasonably cool for several months.

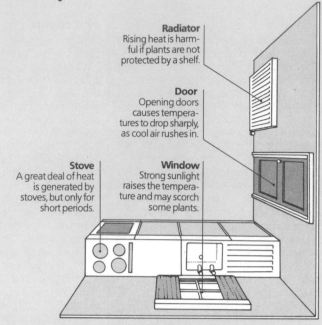

Radiator
Rising heat is harmful if plants are not protected by a shelf.

Door
Opening doors causes temperatures to drop sharply, as cool air rushes in.

Stove
A great deal of heat is generated by stoves, but only for short periods.

Window
Strong sunlight raises the temperature and may scorch some plants.

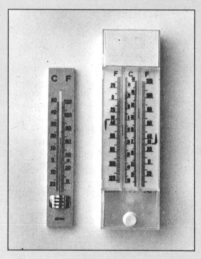

Variable temperatures *above*
This typical kitchen does not have a uniform temperature, and this factor should be borne in mind when positioning plants.

Monitoring temperatures *left*
It is always a good idea to monitor temperatures. The photograph shows a simple thermometer and a minimum/maximum thermometer which measures the daily fluctuation in temperature by recording the highest and lowest levels reached.

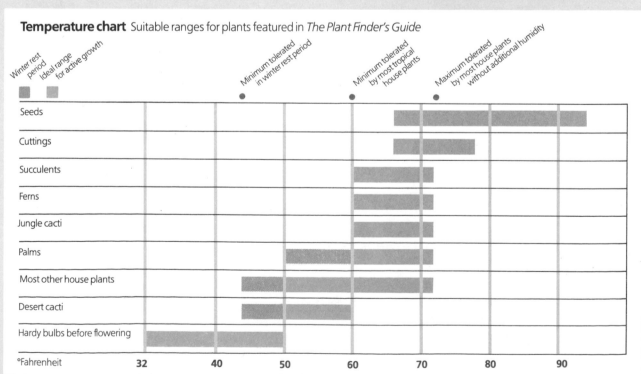

Temperature chart Suitable ranges for plants featured in *The Plant Finder's Guide*

	Winter rest period	Ideal range for active growth			Minimum tolerated in winter rest period		Minimum tolerated by most tropical house plants		Maximum tolerated by most house plants without additional humidity
Seeds									
Cuttings									
Succulents									
Ferns									
Jungle cacti									
Palms									
Most other house plants									
Desert cacti									
Hardy bulbs before flowering									

°Fahrenheit   32   40   50   60   70   80   90

Humidity

Humidity is the amount of water vapor contained in the air. It is affected by changes in temperature: warm air is capable of carrying more moisture than cold air, and it will cause water to evaporate from all available sources, including the leaves of plants. The amount of water in the air is measured on a scale of "relative" humidity—that is, the amount of water in the air compared to saturation point at a given temperature. 0 per cent equals absolutely dry air and 100 per cent equals absolutely saturated air. A relative humidity of at least 40 per cent is a requirement for most plants. To maintain this degree of humidity, a greater amount of water will need to be present in warm air than in colder air.

Cacti and succulents are used to a level of around 30-40 per cent, but the average tolerant house plant does best with a level of around 60 per cent. The thin-leaved jungle plants, such as delta maidenhair ferns (*Adiantum raddianum*) and painted nettles (*Coleus blumei*), however, enjoy a level nearer 80 per cent. These three figures correspond to the "low", "medium" and "high" humidity categories given in *The Plant Finder's Guide*. The relative humidity level of the average living room with the heating switched on, but with no humidifying device, is only around 15 per cent so the air in bathrooms and steamy kitchens makes them better homes for most plants than living rooms.

Signs of humidity deficiency

There are a number of signs which indicate that a plant is suffering from a lack of humidity: its leaves may begin to shrivel or show signs of scorching—watch out for the drying out of leaf tips on plants with long, narrow leaves, such as spider plants (*Chlorophytum comosum*) and palms; buds may fall off; or flowers may wither prematurely.

Plants lose moisture from the tiny pores (stomata) of the leaves. These open during the day to take in carbon dioxide from the air but, at the same time, water from the tissues of the leaves escapes; this process is known as transpiration. Low levels of humidity mean that plants lose more moisture through transpiration. House plants grown in warm rooms, therefore, suffer all the disadvantages: the warm air encourages them to grow, but "sucks" moisture from their leaves and causes water in the potting mixture to be taken up more quickly, making more frequent watering necessary. You can alleviate this condition by increasing the humidity.

How to increase humidity

Portable humidifiers powered by electricity can be bought to increase the level of humidity throughout the room. These are effective—keeping humidity levels between 30 and 60 per cent in heated homes—benefiting people and furniture as well as plants. Growing several plants in proximity helps to make the air around them more humid, as moisture transpired by one plant increases the humidity for its neighbor. Arrangements of plants in bowls and large containers therefore offer good growing conditions. Other methods of increasing humidity include mist-spraying and standing plants on trays filled with moist pebbles.

The ultimate solution for those plants which must have a very high level of humidity is to grow them in closed or almost-closed containers such as bottle gardens and terraria.

Ways of increasing humidity

Mist-spraying *left*
A hand-spray fitted with a fine mist nozzle, used once or twice a day, temporarily places a thin film of moisture over the leaf and stem surfaces. Spraying also washes off room dust and discourages certain insect pests.

Pebble-filled trays *right*
Stand pots on a tray lined with moist pebbles. The water evaporates into the surrounding air.

Burying pots in peat *below*
Bury pots up to their rims in a larger outer container filled with moist peat or vermiculite (see pp.48-9).

Lining baskets *right*
Line hanging baskets with sphagnum moss and wet it thoroughly by regular spraying (see pp.54-5). Periodically dunk the whole basket base in a bowl of water.

Temperature/humidity ratio
Water in grams

The higher the temperature the greater the amount of water the air can hold. If this water is not supplied artificially, moisture is "sucked" out of plants. Therefore, if the temperature is high, additional humidity must be supplied, unless the atmosphere is naturally very humid.

Watering 1

In the wild, water appears as rain, mist or fog and is taken up mainly by the root system. Plants in the home are reliant on us to meet all their watering needs. Water is essential to all plants; without it they will die. The length of time this takes may vary from one day for young seedlings to several months in the case of a succulent plant, but death will always occur eventually. Water acts as a transport medium, in the way blood does for animals, and it is also essential for the process of photosynthesis, which supplies the plant's food. Water from the potting mixture is passed by the roots to all parts of the plant, carrying with it the nutrients vital for the food-manufacturing process. It charges stems and leaves and makes them sturdy and plump (turgid); without it they cannot stay erect. Any shortage of water results in stems and leaves going limp and drooping, flowers fading quickly, and buds falling before they can open. A temporary drought often means that leaves shrivel and go brown at the edges and the tips, making the plants look unattractive.

When to water
Knowing when to water can be difficult but, as a general rule, you should water potted plants when they need it. This may seem to be an over-simplification, but it is accurate. The real problem is to judge when that is. Drooping leaves and limp stems are obvious signs that more water is needed, but you should not wait for such an advanced stage to be reached. There are more subtle signs: some plants' leaves take on a paler, translucent look when water is needed; on others, the flower buds dry and shrivel. Each plant has its own watering needs, dependent on its size, its natural environment and, most importantly, the time of year; actively growing plants need a lot of water, the same plants can manage with much less during the winter rest period. Never water routinely just because someone tells you to water every so many days. It is far better to test the potting mixture first, as this will indicate whether or not the plant needs watering. "Weighing" the pot in your hand regularly can also give an indication of the amount of water in the potting

mixture; a mixture that is saturated with water weighs more than one that is dry. This method is reliable, but it takes a little practice to gauge whether or not the plant needs water, and is not always practical with larger plants in bigger pots. Moisture gauges are available which record on a dial the exact moisture content of the potting mixture. Readings such as "wet", "moist" or "dry" can be seen at a glance and allow you to act accordingly. Quite simple small indicator "sticks" or probes can be bought which are pushed into the mixture and change color according to the moisture content. Generally, play safe and, if in doubt whether to water, wait a day or two before taking the decision.

How to water
Most plants prefer to be given a really thorough drink, and like the dose to be repeated only when a given amount of the potting mixture has dried out. To water frequently in dribbles is bad practice. To give too little often means that the water never reaches the lower layers of the mixture which become compacted around the roots; and to give too much often results in a waterlogged potting mixture. Waterlogging forces air out of the potting mixture and, as roots rot, produces the same wilting appearance as underwatering does.

Type of water to use
Tap water is safe to use on most plants, even though it can have a high lime content. It is always best to apply it when it is tepid, or at least at room temperature; stand a can filled with water overnight in the same room as the plant, to allow the water to reach room temperature and some of the chlorine to dissipate. Ideally, the water should be as lime-free as possible. Rain water is good if you live in the country but, if collected in towns, it is liable to be polluted by chemicals. Water can be boiled (and allowed to cool) for the real lime-haters such as azaleas (*Rhododendron simsii*); distilled water is also lime-free, but rather expensive for use on anything but the most precious of plants. Do not use water from an ordinary domestic water-softener, as this is full of chemicals and can cause serious damage.

Watering checklist
Plants needing plenty of water

● Plants which are actively growing.

● Plants with delicate-looking, thin leaves, e.g., angel wings (*Caladium hortulanum* hybrids).

● Plants in very warm rooms, especially those near windows in summer.

● Plants with many large leaves that clearly transpire a lot of water.

● Plants that have filled their pots with a mass of healthy roots.

● Plants that are grown in relatively small pots, e.g., African violets (*Saintpaulia* hybrids).

● Plants grown in dry air.

● Plants from bogs and marshy areas, e.g., umbrella plants (*Cyperus* sp.).

● Plants grown in free-draining potting mixes, including peat-based mixtures.

● Plants in clay pots.

● Plants with budding leaves and blossoms.

Plants needing less water

● Plants which are resting and those without buds or flowers.

● Plants with thick, leathery leaves, e.g., rubber plants (*Ficus elastica*).

● Plants grown in cooler rooms, especially in winter.

● Plants which are succulent and therefore naturally adapted to store water for future use, e.g., cacti; they transpire much less than leafy plants.

● Plants that have recently been repotted and whose roots have not yet penetrated all of the mixture.

● Plants that are given a high level of humidity, e.g., ferns, and those grown in a shady position or in bottle gardens and terraria.

● Plants grown in water-retentive potting mixtures, including soil-based mixtures.

● Plants grown in plastic and glazed clay pots.

● Plants that have thick, fleshy roots or water-storing sections on their roots, e.g., spider plants (*Chlorophytum comosum*), asparagus ferns (*Asparagus setaceus*) and the ponytail (*Beaucarnea recurvata*).

Methods of applying water

Topwatering *left*
Pour water on to the surface of the potting mixture; this gives more control over the amount of water the plant receives and flushes away any excess mineral salts that may have accumulated.

Watering from below *right*
Stand the pots in saucers filled with water. This method forces mineral salts to the upper layer of the potting mixture, but these can be flushed away with an occasional topwatering.

Bromeliad watering
Pour the water into the "cup" with a narrow-spouted watering can.

How much water to give

It is very important to choose the right amount of water, since damage to plants can occur by both underwatering and overwatering. Overwatering is probably more fatal to plants than underwatering (see also pp.250-1). In *The Plant Finder's Guide*, three symbols have been used to indicate the correct amount of water to give each plant shown; these recommend watering plentifully, moderately or sparingly. A detailed explanation of the three main instructions is given below. Although the illustrations show topwatering, details of how to water from below are also given.

Watering sparingly

Give enough water at each watering to barely moisten the potting mixture throughout. Do this in several stages, adding a little water each time. Never give so much water that it appears in any quantity through the drainage hole in the bottom of the pot. When watering from below, put no more than ¼in in the saucer at a time. Repeat if necessary.

1 Test the potting mixture with a stake. It is time to water when approximately two-thirds of the mixture has dried out.

2 Add just enough water to the surface of the potting mixture to allow percolation without water appearing in the saucer.

3 Test again with the stake. Add a little more water if you find any dry patches. Never leave water in the saucer.

Watering moderately

This involves moistening the mixture all the way through, but allowing the top ¼-1in to dry out between applications. When watering from below, stand pots in ¼in of water and repeat until the surface of the potting mixture becomes moist.

1 When the potting mixture feels dry to the touch, give the plant a moderate amount of water.

2 Pour on enough water to moisten, but not saturate, all of the potting mixture.

3 Stop adding water when drops start appearing from the drainage hole. Pour away any excess water from the saucer.

Watering plentifully

This involves keeping all of the potting mixture moist and not letting even the surface of the mixture dry out. Give enough water at each watering to let some flow through the drainage holes at the bottom of the container. If watering from below, keep re-filling the saucer until no more water is taken up. Half an hour is usually sufficient.

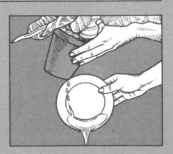

1 When the potting mixture feels dry to the touch, give the plant plenty of water.

2 Flood the surface of the potting mixture with water until it flows through the drainage hole.

3 Empty the saucer once the excess water has drained through the potting mixture.

Watering 2

Going away on vacation can present problems if you have a collection of healthy house plants and no-one to look after them. An absence of just a few days should not cause any harm to your plants; if they are given a thorough watering and moved into a cool room, they should quite happily survive. Increasing the humidity can also help at this time (see p.247). For longer periods, some form of self-watering system is required so that your plants do not suffer.

Certain of the methods shown below are better suited to plants in plastic pots; others are suited to plants in clay pots, as they need a larger, more constant supply of water. Automatic methods of watering are not suitable for plants in containers without drainage holes because of the risk of waterlogging the potting mixture. Happily, such containers are usually glazed and, therefore, water loss is much less than with porous clay pots. Plants in these kinds of containers should be well watered before departure on vacation, placed out of direct sun or strong light and stood on trays filled with moist pebbles or even a thick wad of wet newspaper—either of which will improve the humidity and allow a plant to survive a drought period.

Capillary mats
Place the capillary mat on a draining board or a shelf next to the bath and let at least half of it trail into the sink, or bath, which should be filled with water. As the mats are made of thick felt or felt rubber, the water will be carried up to the plants. The plants then take up what water they need by capillary action. Use capillary mats for plants in plastic pots; the thinness of a plastic pot and the many holes in its base allow the easy passage of water. Clay pots are too thick—the pot tends to absorb the water, rather than passing it to the plant.

Covering with transparent material *right*
Plants can be put into large plastic bags or into purpose-made domes. The processes of respiration and photosynthesis produce water vapor which condenses on to the sides of the bag or container. Do not use this method for long periods, as the plant may begin to rot.

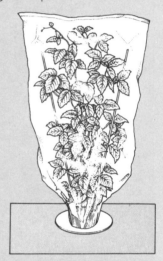

Temporary wicks *left*
Simple wicks for short-term use can be made using water-absorbent materials such as oil-lamp wicks, cotton shoe-laces or old tights. Place one end in a reservoir of water and the other firmly in the potting mixture. Capillary action should do the rest.

Making a "self-watering" wick

This type of wick, made in a similar way to a temporary wick, is actually embedded in the potting mixture and is suitable for permanent or long-term use. It enables the plants to take up their water needs automatically, by capillary action, and saves the grower time and effort. Some growers "wick" their plants throughout the year. However, regular checks should be made to ensure that the plant is not being overwatered or underwatered by the wick. If this happens, remove the wick immediately.

These wicks are suitable for plants in either clay or plastic pots. The reservoir can be any container which will safely support the plant pot and should be covered by a lid (pierce a hole for the wick) to prevent the water from evaporating.

1 Carefully remove the plant from its pot, taking care not to damage the root ball in any way as you do so.

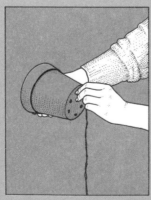

2 Make a wick using a strip of cotton or nylon material. Push it through one of the holes in the bottom of the pot.

3 Carefully push one end of the wick up into the root ball using a thin cane or a pencil.

4 Lower the plant back into the pot. Stand the pot over a reservoir, ensuring that the "tail" extends into the water.

Possible watering problems

If the watering instructions given in *The Plant Finder's Guide* are followed, your plants should receive the right amount of water for healthy growth. However, there are problems which arise if plants are underwatered, or overwatered—particularly during the winter rest period.

Watering in winter

At some time during the twelve month season, most plants need a period of rest. Many should be fed and watered more sparingly than during the rest of the year, others need no food or water at all. The rest period is brought on naturally by the reduced amount of light available to plants (so it coincides with winter), and to give too much water at this time stimulates growth which is not supported by adequate light. This results in poor, and often moldy growth, browning of leaves and early leaf fall.

Underwatering

Underwatering can still occur if you apply water "little and often", as the plant may need a large dose of water to thoroughly soak its roots. Should the potting mixture get over-dry (this happens particularly readily with peat-based potting mixtures), it can shrink appreciably, leaving a gap between root ball and pot sides. Any water applied to the plant just runs quickly away. The only solution is to soak the pot in a bowl or bucket of water until the mixture has swollen up again and the gap closed. The symptoms of underwatering are easily recognized and can often be arrested in time to save the plant. Plants particularly susceptible to problems if underwatered are those with succulent-looking stems, such as painted nettles (*Coleus blumei*), impatiens (*Impatiens* sp.), and all primroses and most ferns.

Overwatering

The symptoms of overwatering can take much longer to show themselves than those of underwatering. Again, watering "little and often" can lead to overwatering. Many plants need to start to dry out before they are re-watered and, if the potting mixture is kept permanently wet, the mixture soon becomes waterlogged. A warning sign that your mixture is waterlogged is the presence of green moss on the surface, since it will only grow in a constantly wet medium. Waterlogging leads eventually to plant death. The first indication that something is wrong with the plant is when a few leaves fall or become yellow, or when the plant makes poor growth. The lack of air and excess of water in the potting mixture cause the roots to become rotten, and cut off the supply of water and food to the plant. To save an overwatered plant, carefully remove it from the pot and check the roots; if they feel soft and come away easily, they are rotten and best removed. Replace the plant in the pot with some fresh potting mixture containing at least 25 per cent sand to aid drainage. Plants particularly susceptible to problems if overwatered include many of the cacti or succulents, whose bodies or leaves are adapted to store water.

Some plants, however, thrive on plenty of water. Their natural habitat is the swamp or bog and, consequently, their potting mixture should always be kept saturated.

Reviving a parched plant

If a plant does become parched and dried-out, it is often best to cut back the top growth and wait for next year's growth. If, however, you rescue it just in time, you could try the following emergency treatment.

Dried-out root ball

Root ball problems

Often, the root ball has shrunk away from the sides of the pot so that any water given runs away. Alternatively, the potting mixture often becomes compacted so that water cannot penetrate it.

Compacted root ball

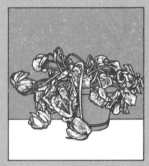

1 This plant has clearly wilted, as the drooping leaf and flower stalks can no longer support themselves.

2 Begin reviving the plant by using a fork to break up the dried-out potting mixture. Do not injure the roots.

3 Immerse the pot in a bucket filled with water until the air bubbles cease to rise from the potting mixture. Use a mist-sprayer on the leaves.

4 Allow any excess water to drain away, and put the plant in a cool place. Within a few hours the plant should begin to revive.

Danger signs

Too little water

- Leaves rapidly become wilted and limp.
- Leaf growth slows.
- Lower leaves become curled or yellow in color.
- Lower leaves fall prematurely.
- Leaf edges become brown and dried-out.
- Flowers fade and fall quickly.

Too much water

- Leaves develop soft, rotten patches on their surface.
- Leaf growth is poor.
- Leaf tips become brown.
- Leaves become curled or yellow in color.
- Plant remains wilted.
- Young and old leaves fall at the same time.
- Roots rot away.

Feeding

Plants are capable of manufacturing their own food but, in order to do so, they must have a supply of light, minerals and water. Minerals are present in garden soil and in most potting mixtures, and manufactured fertilizers are made up of a mixture of the minerals that plants need to carry out the essential processes in photosynthesis. The plant does all the work of converting the raw materials to form the food it needs for healthy growth (see p.242). When plants are bought ready potted, sufficient minerals should already be in the potting mixture to last the plant several weeks. Soil-based potting mixtures come from a variety of sources and some may be rich in nutrients. Their main advantage is that they release minerals over a period of several months, so plants grown in these mixtures will last longer without supplementary feeding than those grown in peat-based potting mixtures. However, the loam content of soil-based mixtures may vary considerably in its nutrient value.

Peat-based potting mixtures were introduced because of their convenience and efficiency for both nurserymen and gardeners. They contain a mixture of peat moss and sand to which is added perlite and vermiculite. The mixture has no food value, but some manufacturers add nutrients to the base and, by looking at the list of ingredients on the packet, you can check whether or not they are present. The nutrients that are added are of the slow-release kind and should feed plants for around eight weeks. However, some nutrients are soon leached away from the mixture by regular watering, or are used up quickly by the plants, so it is advisable to start giving supplementary feeds to plants grown in peat-based potting mixture about six weeks after purchase, or eight weeks after repotting.

Signs of a hungry plant

A hungry plant has an unhealthy "washed-out" look. Hunger signs are very slow—or a lack of—growth; weak stems; small, pale or yellowing leaves; lower leaves falling before they should, and few or no flowers. Ideally, plants should not be allowed to reach these extremes before you notice that they need feeding.

How often to feed

The Plant Finder's Guide recommends the feeding frequency for each featured plant. Fertilizer should only be applied during the active growth period, since feeding during the rest period will result in pale, spindly growth.

Feeding checklist

Too little fertilizer

● Slow growth, with little resistance to disease or attack by pests.

● Pale leaves, sometimes with yellow spotting.

● Flowers may be small, poorly colored or absent.

● Weak stems.

● Lower leaves dropped early.

Too much fertilizer

● Wilted or malformed leaves.

● White crust on clay pots and over the surface of the potting mixture.

● Winter growth is lanky while summer growth may be stunted.

● Leaves may have brown spots and scorched edges.

"Each-time feeding" is practiced by many specialist growers. It involves feeding at every watering with a considerably reduced strength of feed (half or quarter strength). This is a way of keeping a constant but weak supply of food always available—which is particularly important to plants that are grown in relatively small pots, and in peat-based potting mixture. It also prevents an unnecessary and harmful reserve of nutrients building up. New plants or recently repotted plants will not need feeding for some time: those in soil-based potting mixture should not need feeding for about three months; plants in soilless mixture (peat-based etc) will need feeding after about six weeks.

The feeding tips given in *The Plant Finder's Guide* assume that you are looking for the maximum of strong and vigorous growth. In some cases, you may feel that you would like to keep a plant at about its present size, but in a healthy state. Three feeds of standard liquid fertilizer spread over the active growth period (roughly, mid-March, mid-June and mid-September) would keep most plants healthy without encouraging rampant growth.

Feeding guidelines

● Fertilizer is not medicine for an ailing plant; feeding will often only make matters worse. If a plant looks unhealthy, examine it for possible causes, including pests and disease, before dosing it with fertilizer.

● Overfeeding can do as much damage as underfeeding. Feed only at the strength (or much less) given in the instructions on the label.

● Feed no more frequently than recommended on the label or in *The Plant Finder's Guide*.

Effects of fertilizers

Fertilizer	Supplied as	Effect	Use
N Nitrogen	Nitrates N	Manufacture of chlorophyll. Active leaf and shoot growth.	All foliage house plants, especially at start of growing season.
P Phosphorus	Phosphate P_2O_5	Healthy root production. Flower bud production.	All house plants, especially those grown for their flowers.
K Potassium	Potash K_2O	Healthy formation of leaves; flower and fruit production.	All flowering house plants, bulbs and plants grown for their berries.
Trace elements	Iron, zinc, copper, manganese, magnesium	Essential processes such as photosynthesis and respiration.	All house plants.

Types of fertilizer

Fertilizers can be bought in many different forms: as liquids, soluble powders and crystals, pills or tablets and "spikes" or "pins". Liquid fertilizers, bought in concentrated form, are very convenient, as the bottles are easy to store and the contents need only to be diluted with water. Water soluble powders and crystals are also easy to handle and only need a thorough stirring in the prescribed amount of water to be dissolved completely. "Spikes" and "pins" are cards impregnated with chemicals that release foods when watered. These are often called slow-release fertilizers, as they work over a period of three to six months, slowly giving up their stored nutrients. Their disadvantage is that they tend to produce "hot-spots"—concentrations of food around the pill or "spike"—which can burn nearby roots. In addition to fertilizers applied to the potting mixture, there are foliar feeds: fertilizers that are diluted with water and then sprayed on to the leaves of plants which do not readily absorb nutrients through their roots. Foliar feeds also have an immediate tonic effect on any plant that looks starved. Always follow the instructions given on the packet, as an excessive amount of fertilizer can damage roots and leaves.

What fertilizers contain

Balanced growth relies on three essential elements. Nitrogen (supplied as nitrates) is vital for producing energy-forming chlorophyll, and healthy leaf and stem growth. Phosphorus (supplied as phosphates) allows healthy roots to develop.

Potassium (supplied as potash) is essential for fruiting and flowering and the general sturdiness of the plant. The packaging of fertilizers always indicates the relative chemical contents (shown as percentages) of the three main foods and may mention other ingredients, such as iron, copper and manganese, often under the general heading of "trace elements". The three most important elements may be spelled out fully, as nitrogen, phosphorus and potassium, or be given the codes N, P and K. Sometimes, only the percentage numbers appear, but the coding is always arranged in the same order to avoid confusion.

What to feed

Fertilizers suitable for use with house plants are usually ones with an even balance of the essential nutrients. These are known as standard or balanced fertilizers and will promote generally good growth in most plants. There are, however, specialist fertilizers for more specific purposes. High-nitrate fertilizers encourage healthy leaf growth and are suitable for foliage plants. High-potash fertilizers are often called "tomato-type" fertilizers because they are used for tomatoes when they start to flower and fruit; these are useful for encouraging flowering and fruiting house plants that have reached a similar stage. High-phosphate fertilizers build up a strong, healthy root system and encourage the formation of flower buds, although foliage growth is slower. It is good practice to use a different fertilizer when the plant is flowering from the one used when it is not.

Methods of feeding

The method of feeding depends upon the type of plant you have and the form of fertilizer you have chosen to use. If you are using liquid fertilizer, or powders and crystals which have to be mixed with water, apply when watering the plant in the normal way. Before giving any type of food, ensure the potting mixture is already moist—to add food to dry soil is to risk root damage by "burning" with high concentrations of minerals. Foliar sprays are best applied with a mist-sprayer, used outside or in the bathtub to avoid inhalation and marking furnishings.

This type of food is rapidly absorbed, and will act very quickly on a plant with unhealthy foliage. Fertilizer pills are a very convenient form of feeding, as they can be inserted into the mixture and left to release their food gradually. Spikes, on the other hand, can be easily removed if you feel that a plant would benefit from a period without the stimulus of the fertilizer. Feeding mats are also now available; these are placed underneath the pot and the nutrients they contain are absorbed into the potting mixture.

Slow-release fertilizer spikes
As they tend to produce "hot-spots" of concentrated fertilizer, push the spike in at the edge of the potting mixture. Water well to help dissolve the food.

Foliar sprays
Always dilute to the correct concentration before spraying over both sides of the foliage with a mist-sprayer.

Liquid fertilizers
Add to the water you would give the plant at its normal watering time. These can be applied either from above or from below.

Slow-release fertilizer pills
These should be pushed deep into the potting mixture with the blunt end of a pencil. Try to avoid damaging the roots when pushing the pill in.

Pots and potting mixtures

Types of pot

Most house plants are sold in plastic pots, as this is the cheapest way of packaging them, but many other kinds are available including traditional, unglazed clay pots, and purpose-made ceramic and china pots. Almost any domestic container can be used to display plants effectively (see pp.28-31), but they may not all provide ideal conditions for healthy growth. All purpose-made containers will have one or more drainage holes to allow any excess water to drain away. It is possible to grow plants directly in bowls and other containers without drainage holes, but they need to be lined with drainage material and greater care is required when watering to prevent roots from rotting.

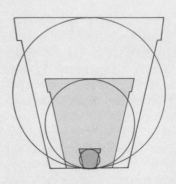

Pot shape *left*
In all pots, from the smallest available, with a diameter of 1½in to one of the largest, with a diameter of 12in, the depth is equal to the diameter of the rim.

Shards and gravel
These increase the drainage of a pot, and a layer is especially important in pots without drainage holes.

Gravel

Shards

Plastic pots
Plants grown in plastic pots need less frequent watering; plastic pots usually have several holes in their base.

Clay pots
Plants grown in clay pots dry out more quickly; the smaller sized clay pots have only one drainage hole in the base.

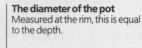

The depth of the pot
Measured from the top of the lip to the base, this is equal to the diameter.

The diameter of the pot
Measured at the rim, this is equal to the depth.

Standard pot dimensions

Always wider at its rim than at its base, and as deep as it is wide. Pots are usually round in shape, although square pots are also available and are useful for grouping several plants together.

2in

3in

4in

Half-pots *below*
Half-pots are less deep than broad, and come in a range of sizes up to 12in in diameter. Use them for seed sowing, rooting cuttings, and for plants with a shallow root system.

Drip saucers *right*
Made in a similar material, and a little larger than the base of the pot.

Pots with a built-in saucer base *below*
Made of a decorative plastic, these pots are supplied as hanging pots with a built-in drip tray.

Potting mixtures

Garden soil is usually not recommended for pots in the home. It is full of bugs, disease spores and weed seeds and its chemical content and physical make-up are uncertain. House plants should be grown in ready-prepared potting mixtures or a do-it-yourself mixture based on one of the standard prepared mixes. The contents of these have been very carefully tested as to their suitability to particular plants, and the ingredients have been sterilized to kill off unwanted visitors. The range of potting mixtures may seem large but a few basic potting mixtures will provide for the different needs of all the house plants featured in this book; details are given in *The Plant Finder's Guide*. There are two main mixtures, soil-based and peat-based. Soil-based mixtures have a heavy texture suitable for large plants; although sterilized, the soil contains some micro-organisms which break down organic matter into essential minerals, thus maintaining soil fertility. Peat-based mixtures are lighter and cleaner to handle but they often contain no built-in nutrients, so regular feeding is necessary.

Types of potting mixture

Potting mixtures are usually packaged in plastic bags of various sizes; the larger they are the more economical they become. The basic mixes are loam (soil) or peat. Specialized mixtures contain added ingredients. Additives for the mixes can be bought separately for home-made potting mixtures.

Bromeliad potting mixture *right*
Spongy and very porous, which suits the shallow root system of the bromeliads.

Bulb fiber *below*
Clean, light and drains well. Good drainage is essential to prevent the bulbs from rotting.

Soil-based potting mixture *left*
A heavy mixture. Suitable for large, top-heavy plants.

Charcoal *below*
Absorbs excess minerals and waste, keeping the mixture "sweet".

Peat-based potting mixture *right*
A lightweight, standardized mixture, containing very few nutrients.

Fern potting mixture *above*
Contains perlite or sand, and charcoal to keep it well drained.

Perlite *below*
Gives potting mixture an open texture for aeration and drainage.

Vermiculite *left*
Absorbs and retains nutrients and water.

Aggregate
Made of clay pellets, it has excellent water-retentive properties and is used for hydroculture and to provide drainage.

Sphagnum moss
Has excellent water-retaining properties.

Potting mixture recipes

Soil-based potting mixture
Best for large, established plants. A suitable home-made mixture consists of one-third sterilized fibrous loam, one-third medium-grade peat moss, leaf mold or tree bark and one-third coarse sand or fine perlite. A balanced fertilizer should also be added.

Peat-based potting mixture
A suitable mixture consists of one-third peat moss, one-third medium-grade vermiculite, and one-third coarse sand or medium-grade perlite. Add two tablespoonfuls of dolomite limestone powder to every two cups of the mixture to counteract the acidity of the peat.

Bromeliad potting mixture
A very open mixture, high in humus and almost lime free. A suitable mixture consists of half coarse sand or perlite and half peat moss. Specialist growers add other ingredients to the above mixture, including chunky pieces of partly composted tree bark (available in small bags) and pine needles (sometimes available locally)—all ensure that excess moisture drains away swiftly.

Fern potting mixture
A high-humus mixture which should have good drainage. A suitable mixture consists of three-fifths peat-based potting mixture and two-fifths coarse sand or medium-grade perlite. Add one cup of charcoal granules to every quart of the mixture (to help sweeten it) and add a balanced granular or powdered fertilizer (according to the instructions on the pack).

Bulb fiber
Use only for indoor bulbs; it does not contain enough nutrients for other pot plants. A suitable mixture consists of six parts peat moss, two parts crushed oyster shell and one part charcoal.

Useful additives

Humus (leaf mold)
Retains nutrients and gives an open texture.

Manure
Used as a dried powder, cow manure is nutrient rich.

Peat moss
Holds water and added fertilizer very well.

Tree bark
Holds water and added fertilizer very well.

Dolomite limestone powder
Acts to reduce the acidity of potting mixtures.

Eggshell/oystershell
Reduces the acidity and assists drainage of potting mixtures.

Limestone chips
Reduces the acidity and assists drainage of potting mixtures.

Coarse sand
Opens up potting mixtures for better aeration and drainage.

Rockwool
Holds moisture and allows air to penetrate.

Repotting and potting on

Plants in gardens have a free root run. Their roots spread as far as they need to in search of water and food. With a few exceptions (bromeliads and other epiphytic plants), most wild plants have roots that run under the surface of the soil, where some moisture and food is usually present and where the soil temperature (which is cool) stays fairly constant. By contrast, the roots of house plants are confined within a relatively small container. Young, healthy plants quickly fill their pots with roots, and then find that there is nowhere else for them to go but through the hole in the bottom of the pot, or over the surface of the potting mixture. When this happens, the mixture dries out quickly and needs very frequent watering and feeding. "Potting on", or planting in a larger pot, is then necessary.

Sometimes it is not obvious just by looking at plants that they need potting on, so you must take them out of their pots and examine the root ball and root system. Look to see whether the roots have penetrated all the available potting mixture; if they have, it is time to move the plant into a larger pot—usually the next size up; if not, return the plant to its original container. Some plants thrive in small pots, in which case the roots of the plants should be checked and the plant put back in the same pot with some fresh potting mixture. This is known as "repotting", but the same term is often used to describe moving a plant to a larger pot.

When the maximum pot size has been reached, or if the plant is very large, the potting mixture can be revitalized by removing the top few inches and replacing it with fresh mixture containing added fertilizer. This is called "topdressing".

As repotting and potting on can be a messy business, it is best to deal with several plants at the same time, protecting furniture and the floor with newspaper. Have ready all the materials you will need—potting mixtures, pots, fertilizers and drainage materials. Make sure all the pots are clean, and soak any new clay pots until the air bubbles stop rising; this will ensure the pot will not absorb water from the potting mixture.

Removing plants from their pots

This can be an awkward business if plants are large, an unusual shape, or have sharp spines. Cover the area where you are working with newspaper, and water the plant an hour before the operation; this will help it slide out of the pot more easily, avoiding root damage and spilling of dry potting mixture. Repot the plant as quickly as possible to avoid drying of the roots.

Removing a plant from a small pot

1 Place the palm of one hand on the surface of the mixture with the main stem between your fingers.

2 Turn the pot upside-down and gently tap the pot edge on the side of a table.

3 The plant and its root ball should then slide out easily into your hand.

Removing a plant from a large pot

 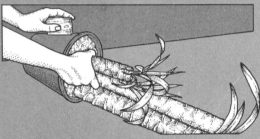

1 Gently run the blade of a blunt knife or spatula around the edge of the potting mixture.

2 Lay the pot on its side and tap it with a block of wood to loosen the potting mixture. Rotate the pot slowly, tapping it on all sides. Support the plant with one hand whilst doing this.

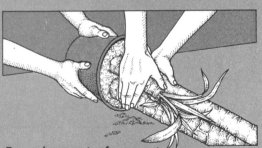

3 Make sure the plant is completely loose before attempting to remove it. If the plant is very large, two pairs of hands may be necessary—one to hold the plant steady, the other to pull the pot away.

Removing a cactus from a pot

1 With a prickly plant, such as a cactus, use a rolled up piece of paper to protect your hand.

2 Place the paper round the cactus, making sure the paper is long enough to make a "handle".

3 Holding the paper "handle" in one hand, gently pull the pot away with the other.

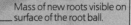

Potting on

The term "potting" refers specifically to the transfer of cuttings and seedlings to their first pot, while "potting on" is used to describe transferring a plant to a larger pot. It should be done at the beginning of the growing season. Do not pot on during, or just prior to, a rest period as no new root growth will be produced to penetrate the extra potting mixture; this will then become waterlogged and cause the existing roots to rot. Never pot on if the plant is unhealthy in any way (apart from being potbound), as this can cause unnecessary shock. Do not feed plants which have just been potted on for the first four to six weeks; instead let them send out new roots into the potting mixture in search of food.

A potbound plant

The earliest recognizable stage of a plant becoming potbound is when new roots start to cover the root ball. The roots will eventually become densely matted and form a thick spiral in the base of the pot. Potting on at this stage is essential.

Mass of new roots visible on surface of the root ball.

Roots begin to spiral at base.

Roots in a mass at the base of the pot, as they grow out of the drainage hole.

1 Remove any moss or other green surface growth from the top of the root ball.

2 Line the new pot with drainage material and ensure the plant will sit at the same level.

3 Prepare a mold by filling the space between the new pot and the old with potting mixture.

4 Insert the plant, fill in any gaps round the sides of the root ball and firm in gently to ensure it is supported.

Repotting

Plants do not always need potting on. If they are not potbound, or thrive better in a smaller pot, they may simply need repotting—taking them out of their pots and returning them to clean pots of the same size with some fresh potting mixture. Often, it is enough to gently tease away some of the old potting mixture and to supply the plant with a little fresh mixture which is high in nutrients. If the plant is growing too fast, or is already too big, the roots may need pruning to allow room for the new potting mixture.

1 Remove the plant from the pot gently. Watering about an hour before will help the plant to slide out.

2 To allow room for the new potting mixture, you may need to prune the roots by cutting slices off the root ball.

3 Place the plant in a clean pot of the same size. Fill in round the edges with new potting mixture and firm down.

Topdressing

Eventually, with well-established plants that have been potted on several times, it will not be practical to move them into larger pots. You must then find a way of providing them with extra nourishment. Topdressing each spring is the best way of doing this. The method also suits house plants, such as the amaryllis (*Hippeastrum* hybrids), which resent root disturbance and flower best when thoroughly potbound. Always use new potting mixture to which a slow-release fertilizer high in nutrients has been added.

1 Gently scrape away the top few inches of the potting mixture, with an old kitchen fork or similar implement, taking care not to damage the roots.

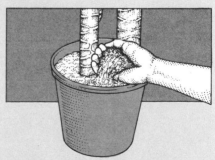

2 Refill the pot to its original level using fresh potting mixture of a suitable type. Firm this down to ensure the plant is properly anchored in the pot.

Growing plants in artificial light

The use of artificial light is becoming more widespread among indoor gardeners, either as a substitute or supplement for natural light, or to allow plants to be grown in places where the light level is otherwise too low for healthy plant growth or regular flower production.

Incandescent bulbs can scorch plants if placed too close to them, and do not produce enough light for a plant's growing needs if placed the right distance away to avoid scorch. Incandescent floodlights are more effective, as they concentrate a beam of light by means of built-in reflectors, but this is still only sufficient for display purposes.

Fluorescent tubes are the most satisfactory and economical way of providing artificial light for plants in the home. They are available in several different colors; the coating on the outside of the tube determines the color of the light. If you are using a fitting with two tubes, a combination of "natural white" and "daylight" gives the closest approximation to natural light. Plants require the violet/blue and red wavelengths: "daylight" bulbs are high in blue but low in red; "warm white" and "natural white" are high in red, but low in blue. The simplest units consist of a reflector which holds one or two tubes and is supported on legs, enabling plants to be positioned underneath the lights. Multi-layered units are also available which have lights under each shelf to illuminate the plants immediately below. Alternatively, you can provide lights for plants in a bookcase or shelf-unit, or in the space between a kitchen countertop and wall-hung cabinets. It is important that any home-constructed units be fitted by a competent electrician.

Plants vary in their light needs (see pp.244-5) in natural conditions, and equally so under artificial light tubes. If they are too close, the foliage will be scorched, if too distant they will become etiolated and flowering species will produce fewer blooms than they should. Plants grown for their flowers, such as African violets (*Saintpaulia* hybrids), need to be 7-8in from the tubes, but most foliage plants are better placed 1ft away. Pots can be lifted nearer to the tubes by standing them on blocks of wood or upturned empty pots, and those that prefer least light should be stood at the ends of the tubes. Cuttings can be raised very well under artificial lights, as long as they are positioned the right distance away from them.

To grow plants exclusively under lights, the tubes must be kept on for around 12-14 hours per day for foliage plants and 16-18 hours per day for flowering plants, unless they are short-day types—such as poinsettias (*Euphorbia pulcherrima*)—which require less light. Electric timer switches can be installed so that the lights will come on when it is most convenient. When using units to provide additional light in winter, plants should have as much normal daylight as possible, and then the tubes should be illuminated for around 5 or 6 hours in the evening.

Decorative and functional lighting *left*
This small light fixture is equipped with a special bulb which should provide the light needed to keep this Boston fern (*Nephrolepis exaltata* "Bostoniensis") healthy in a position which would otherwise be too dark for it. The light also serves a decorative purpose, casting an interesting shadow on to the wall behind.

Types of bulbs *below*
Fluorescent light tubes, in a range of lengths and wattages, are the most efficient means of artificially lighting your plants. Incandescent bulbs provide effective display lighting and have the advantage of maneuverability.

Simple but effective strip lighting *right*
A single, 6ft long fluorescent bulb suspended from the ceiling provides uncomplicated artificial lighting for the plants below. This type of bulb generates more light per watt than any other form of lighting and wastes less of its energy as heat. The attractive foliage of the plants is shown off to full advantage under the fluorescent light, which also fulfills their light needs.

Providing extra light *right*
A simple unit, like this one suspended from a wooden beam, is quick and easy to install. It can light a large number of plants in places which would otherwise be too dark for healthy plant growth.

Self-contained unit *below*
An illuminated unit filled with flowering plants can be a source of great pleasure through the dark months of winter. African violets (*Saintpaulia* hybrids), which naturally come into bloom in September, can be encouraged to flower all through the winter in this way.

Hydroculture

Hydroculture is the practice of growing plants in containers filled with water to which nutrients are added. Traditionally, the method was called hydroponics and can still be seen in its simplest form when hyacinth bulbs (*Hyacinthus orientalis* hybrids) are placed in bulb glasses filled with water; the bulbs sense the water is there and root down into it.

During the 1970s, growers started to market house plants growing in purpose-made, watertight containers filled with a special aggregate to support the roots of the plant, and chemically charged water to meet the plant's food needs. The special containers ranged in size from those suitable for housing a single plant to large, floor-standing models popular with establishments such as banks, libraries, hospitals and municipal offices, who liked the idea of bold, low-maintenance displays of plants. The beauty of hydroculture is that the plants need very little attention and virtually no expertise is required to cultivate them successfully (see also pp.72-3). Other advantages include vigorous and healthy growth, and freedom from soil-borne diseases and pests.

The basic materials for hydroculture are the aggregate, usually packed in plastic bags, and the container, which may be used on its own or have a liner. The aggregate must be clean and inert and can be grit, pea-gravel, perlite or, more commonly, a purpose-made granule composed of expanded clay. One name given to a particular aggregate is hydroleca—"hydro" meaning water, and "leca" standing for "lightweight expanded clay aggregate". This consists of lightweight pellets of varying sizes and fairly random shape that have been fired in a rotary kiln at extremely high temperatures. As a result, most of the clay has been forced to the outside wall of the pellet, leaving a honeycombed center. The great advantage of the pellets is that their outside cases conduct water from the reservoir sitting at the bottom of the container, thus moistening all the pellets. Another important feature is that there is plenty of air circulating between the upper pellets, where most of the plant's roots are.

Feeding methods

To feed plants grown in hydroculture, fertilizer is put into the water, but it can be put there in several different ways. The simplest way is to use a standard liquid fertilizer in the water used for filling the reservoir. The danger with this method is that nutrients which are not used immediately by the plants tend to crystallize out of the liquid on to the pellets and roots of the plant, and ought really to be washed out of the base periodically, which is rather a messy business. It is much simpler to use a specially designed hydroculture fertilizer bonded into a pad or disc, or packed in a sachet which is placed in the water. The advantage of these pads or discs is that they do not release multi-chemical fertilizer all the time, but only when the water lacks the particular element, and so no harmful build-up of chemicals is possible.

Containers for hydroculture

There are two main types of container that can be used—the single container and the double container. The single container may be made of any kind of watertight material (other than untreated metal that would affect the chemicals

Types of hydroculture

Hydroculture is easy to do and containers range from the simple bulb glass, to the more complex double container. Most plants can be grown in hydroculture and growth is usually vigorous.

Using a double container *below*
The plant is grown in the aggregate, but its roots may grow out of the inner container and come into direct contact with the reservoir of water.

Using a single container *above*
The plant is grown in the aggregate. Water is poured directly onto the aggregate.

Using a bulb glass *left*
This is a very old method of hydroculture. The bulb glass is specially designed to hold a column of water underneath the base of the bulb. Use a bulb that is large enough to support itself in the bowl of the glass; this prevents it toppling over when the top growth appears.

put into the water and would probably rust), ideally with a broad base to give stability. Glass is probably the best material to use. Apart from looking attractive, a glass container allows you to keep a check on the water level and the amount of roots in the container.

The double container has a similar watertight outer container into which fits a smaller container. The small container hangs on the rim of the larger container and holds the aggregate and plant. The inner container is usually made of plastic and has holes or large slits in its sides and base to allow air and water to circulate around the pellets and the roots of the plant.

In both cases, the water should only be in the lower regions, never in the upper ones. With the single container, the bottom quarter or third of the aggregate should be submerged; with the double container, it is normally enough that the inner container, filled with the aggregate, be in direct contact with the reservoir of water. A water gauge will indicate when more water is needed.

Potting up rooted cuttings in hydroculture

Cuttings that have made roots in water can be planted in hydroculture containers in much the same way as cuttings are planted in potting mixture. Hold the cuttings upright and gently trickle the aggregate around the roots, then tap the container gently to settle the aggregate. Never bury the cuttings deeper than you would if planting them in a potting mixture, and shade the planted cuttings for a few days until they have settled down in their new home. When they have made strong root growth, carefully transfer the pots to their permanent position.

Rooting cuttings in hydroculture *right* Cuttings of such plants as ivies (*Hedera* sp.), tradescantias (*Tradescantia* sp.), and wandering Jews (*Zebrina pendula*) can be rooted in "nursery beds"—small pots, filled with aggregate, which stand in deep saucers of water to which a little ordinary fertilizer at quarter strength has been added.

Potting on in hydroculture

A plant grown in hydroculture grows quickly but produces a much more compact root system than a plant grown in a potting mixture, so annual potting on is unnecessary. However, the plant will eventually need potting on as the roots grow to fill the container. Potting on in aggregate is a similar process to potting on in potting mixture, but much less messy and time-consuming. Always remember to pot on in a similar type of container—either single or double. If potting on in a double container, the size of the outer container needs to be increased as well as the size of the inner container to maintain the size ratio.

1 Cover the bottom of the new container with a layer of clean aggregate. Remove the plant from the old container. Do not pull the plant out as this will tear the roots.

2 Hold the plant over the new container of aggregate, making sure it is at the same level as before. Spread the roots out and trickle in the new aggregate.

3 Once the plant is properly anchored, fill with enough water to cover the bottom third of the new container, or until the water gauge indicates that it is "full".

Transferring a plant from potting mixture to hydroculture

It is not normally recommended that you transfer a well-developed or mature plant out of potting mixture into hydroculture because of the trauma it would suffer. However, it is possible. Because of the shock, it will be necessary to give the plant warmth and high humidity for 10-12 weeks to aid its recovery. A heated propagator provides the best conditions, but a warm greenhouse is also suitable, provided that the air around the plant is made very humid by the use of a plastic, tentlike cover and the temperature maintained at a constant level. During this time, all of the old, soil-adapted roots will die and new, succulent ones adapted to the semi-aquatic life will be made.

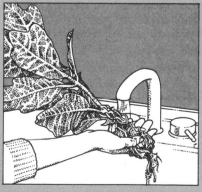

1 Using both hands, remove the mature plant from its pot, taking care not to damage the root ball. It is not advisable to use a rare or treasured specimen.

2 Supporting the plant with one hand, carefully tease apart the root ball, removing as much of the potting mixture as is possible without tearing the roots.

3 To remove the final traces of the potting mixture, wash the roots thoroughly under a gently running tap. Make sure the water is not too cold, as this will cause further trauma to the plant.

Pruning and training

House plants may need to be pruned periodically, or trained to the shape you wish them either to maintain or take on. They may become too big for the space available, or odd branches can start to grow in places where you do not want them, giving the plant an unbalanced look. Messy, tangled growth needs to be thinned out, and branches and stems induced to grow in a particular direction. Some plants need their growing points nipped out frequently to avoid unwanted leggy shoots and encourage a close, bushy shape. New growth on certain climbing plants will need to be supported as it is not capable of supporting itself.

The correct way to prune
Always cut just above the bud where you want the new shoot to form. Slope the cut downwards, away from the bud, and do not leave a long "snag", as this will be liable to rot.

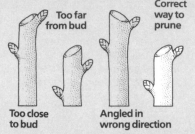

Too far from bud

Correct way to prune

Too close to bud

Angled in wrong direction

When to prune
Spring is the best time for pruning nearly all plants, as it is the season when new, active growth begins, but overlong stems can normally be cut back in the autumn if they get in the way or overcrowd the plant.

Some plants only make flower buds on the new season's growth and you can therefore cut away a lot of old growth in the spring, confident that you are not harming the prospect of flowers in the coming season. However, when cutting back woody-stemmed plants, it is usually safest to cut back into the previous year's growth and not beyond.

Whatever tool you use for pruning, it is important that it is sharp, to avoid bruising or otherwise damaging the remaining stem. A razor blade, scalpel or scalpel-like knife is excellent for soft-stemmed plants, and a finely pointed pair of scissors will allow you to get into the leaf axils of really bushy plants. For woody stems, pruners are essential.

Deadheading
Deadheading involves cutting away any dead or faded flowers on the plant. This encourages the plant to put more effort into producing new flowers rather than producing seeds, as would happen naturally.

Flowers on long stalks
Deadhead plants such as African violets (*Saintpaulia* hybrids), whose flower stalks arise from the base of the plant, by pulling and twisting out the whole stalk.

Flowers on short stalks
Deadhead flowers in clusters, or on short stalks arising from a main stem, by pinching them off between your thumb and index finger.

Cutting back

Cutting back is probably the most drastic form of pruning, but usually improves the attractiveness of a plant. It allows you to get rid of totally unwanted growth and lets you keep favorite plants that would otherwise become too big to be grown in the home. A drastic cutting back often improves growth by ridding the plant of old, weak sections and encouraging new, strong shoots with short gaps between the leaves. Citrus and azalea plants (*Rhododendron simsii*) benefit from this type of pruning.

Cutting back straggly growth
Fast-growing plants which climb, or are trained round hoops and canes, can lose their shape after one, two or three seasons' growth. Jasmine (*Jasminum* sp.) is a climber which needs particularly drastic cutting back. Do not be afraid to cut out all but the newest growth; if the plant is cut back in early spring, it will be covered with new growth by the summer.

1 If growth round the hoop becomes very straggly, cutting back will provide attractive, bushier new growth.

Cutting back to create close growth
Plants with long stems, such as ivies (*Hedera* sp.) or philodendrons, may develop large gaps between the leaves in winter. This may be due to insufficient light or overcrowding. To correct the condition, the stems affected must be cut back to allow new, close growth (the tips can be used as cuttings). The initial cause of the problem must then be identified and improved.

1 Stems with large gaps between leaves, particularly those of trailing plants, will look better if cut back.

Cutting back a tall plant
Cutting back usually encourages new growth, so merely snipping away the top 4-6in of a large plant will only prove a temporary solution. When a rubber plant (*Ficus elastica*) or rainbow plant (*Dracaena marginata*) almost reaches the ceiling, it needs shortening by about 3ft if you want to keep it indoors for a few more years. The plant may look odd for several weeks but once the new leaves appear the cutting back will have been worthwhile.

1 A favorite plant which has grown too tall can be cut back drastically and kept in the house for a few more years.

Pinching out

Growing tips should be pinched out frequently on plants that would naturally grow long unbranched stems, but which look better when growth is more compact. Pinching out also prevents climbers and trailers becoming too straggly.

How to pinch out *right*
Nip out the growing tip or point with your index finger and thumb.

2 Unwind the stems from the hoop and cut them off, using sharp scissors, until only two of the youngest stems remain.

3 Wind the remaining stems round the wire hoop and secure with wire plant ties.

2 Using sharp scissors, cut the stem back to the point (node) where tight growth exists, taking out the elongated, leggy growth.

3 If the plant is then given the correct growing conditions, the new growth will have short gaps between the leaves.

2 Use pruners to remove the head of a woody-stemmed plant. Cut down by as much as half its original height.

3 Staunch any flow of latex with a dusting of powdered charcoal. Give the plant the kind of growing conditions it needs to grow at its best and new leaves will be produced in four to six weeks.

Training plants

Many house plants can be trained to grow in a variety of shapes, by appropriate pruning or pinching out to obtain a bushy plant or a tall plant with a bare stem, known as a standard, or by training the plant to grow round a support. Most plants attain a rewarding shape within a few years.

Growing a standard

1 Remove all the side shoots that form on the main stem, but leave the foliage.

2 At the desired height, pinch out the growing tip. Remove foliage from the stem.

Growing a bushy plant

1 Pinch out the growing tips to encourage the development of side shoots.

2 Maintain the bushy shape by pinching out the growing points of new side shoots.

Training plants around a support

Support can be provided by fastening the stem of the plant to thin canes, bamboo, wire hoops or trellises pushed into the potting mixture. Ties made of twine, raffia, soft wire rings or wire-and-paper twists can be used. Fasten them so that they secure the stems, but not so tight that they will bite into the stems as they thicken.

Circular

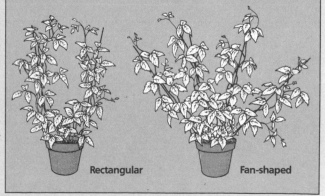

Rectangular   **Fan-shaped**

Propagation 1

All plants eventually reach the stage when they cease to be as attractive as they once were and need replacing with younger, more vigorous specimens. Propagating your own plants is a cheap and satisfying way of rejuvenating your house plant stock.

There are two main ways in which new plants can be produced—they may either be grown from seed (see p.269) or propagated vegetatively.

Vegetative propagation

This method of propagation involves taking a specific part of a plant and encouraging it to make roots of its own, so that it can establish itself and become a plant in its own right. Generally, but not always, plants propagated vegetatively look just like the original plant the section was taken from. Virtually any part of a plant can be used: plantlets that develop on leaf surfaces or on trailing stolons, offsets and stem or leaf cuttings. Alternatively, clumps may be divided (see p.267), or stems layered or air-layered (see p.268). You can propagate some plants by more than one of the methods mentioned, others can only be propagated in one particular way. Quick rooting and establishment is, in all cases, vital. The faster the section can make roots of its own and become established as a separate plant the safer it is; unrooted sections are at risk from wilting, rot and a number of other hazards. Special rooting mixtures are available for the propagation of cuttings—these hold plenty of air and water, but have few nutrients, which would scorch the new roots.

With practically all types of vegetative propagation, the best season to choose is the spring, just as new growth is starting.

Equipment for propagating plants

Jam jar propagator

Paintbrush

Plastic bag propagator

Plant labels

Hormone rooting powder

Labelling pencil

Peat tray

Peat pots

Peat pellets

Scissors

Widger or planting stick

Sharp knife

Electric heat propagator

Watering can

Seed tray

Cold propagator

Propagating from stem cuttings

Most house plants can be propagated from stem cuttings of one kind or another. Cuts should be made with a really sharp knife or razor blade, as bruised or split stems are liable to rot. If possible, water the plant about two hours before taking the cutting, as this ensures that the stems and leaves are fully charged with moisture. If you have to use a flowering stem, gently pinch off the flowers first. Coating the cut end of the stem with hormone rooting powder will hasten the rooting process.

Rooting a soft-stemmed cutting in water

1 Make a clean cut just above a leaf axil or node; the parent plant can then make new shoots from the top or upper leaf axils.

2 Make another cut immediately below the lowest node or leaf axil of the cutting and gently remove the lower leaves.

3 After approximately four weeks, 1-1½in of new root will have formed, and the cutting can then be transferred to its potting mixture.

Rooting a soft-stemmed cutting in potting mixture

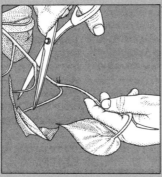

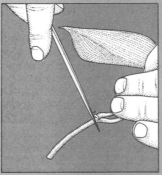

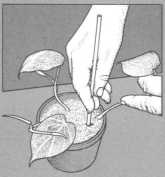

1 Select a healthy stem, with about three nodes spaced fairly close together, and make a clean cut, giving a 4-6in "tip" cutting.

2 Trim the cutting just below the lowest leaf node and remove the lower leaves to prevent them rotting in the rooting mixture.

3 Make some holes with a stick and plant several cuttings in the same pot, gently firming the mixture with your fingers.

Taking a woody-stemmed cutting

1 To propagate a woody-stemmed plant, remove any lower leaves that remain and cut the stem into short pieces, each of which should include at least one node. The rooting process may take several weeks longer than with a soft-stemmed plant.

2 Place the cuttings, horizontally or vertically, in rooting mixture. Roots will develop from buried nodes and new top growth from the nodes exposed to the air.

Propagation 2

Propagating from leaf cuttings

Some plants can be propagated from leaf cuttings. A complete leaf, with its leaf stalk attached, is pulled or cut from the parent plant and then grown in barely moist rooting mixture, or, in certain cases, water. The leaves should be inserted into the mixture at a 45 degree angle, and may be rested against the pot edge to give them maximum support; the cut end should not be buried too deeply. The new roots and shoots will develop from the cut end of the leaf stalk, or along the leaf edges (veins). Leaf cuttings may be planted singly in small pots, or a number may be planted together in larger pots or shallow trays. Enclosing the container in a plastic bag creates a humid atmosphere and usually eliminates the need for further watering. African violets (*Saintpaulia* hybrids) and rhizomatous begonias are examples of popular house plants which can be reproduced in this way. The leaves chosen should be neither too old nor too young, so—in the case of an African violet, for example—the extreme inner and outer leaves of the rosette should not be used. Large-leaved begonias should not have their leaves cut into sections, as they are then liable to rot, but the leaves can be used whole if their outer edges are trimmed off to reduce leaf area and loss of water by transpiration.

Rooting leaf cuttings in potting mixture

1 Remove one complete leaf with a sharp knife or razor blade, and trim the stalk to a length of 1½-2in.

2 Plant the leaf in barely moist rooting mixture and cover the pot with a plastic bag to increase humidity.

3 When new plantlets appear at the base of each leaf, cut away the parent leaf.

Rooting leaf cuttings in water

1 Remove a healthy leaf with a leaf stalk attached, and trim the stalk to a length of 1½-2in.

2 Cover a water-filled jar with plastic and insert leaves through holes punched in the plastic.

3 Roots and small plantlets will form underwater. These can then be separated and planted in potting mixture.

Rooting leaf sections in potting mixture

The leaves of certain plants, including the mother-in-law's tongue (*Sansevieria* sp.), Cape primrose (*Streptocarpus* hybrids) and emerald ripple peperomia (*Peperomia caperata*), can be cut into pieces, which are rooted separately to produce many new plants. A cluster of plantlets will push up through the mixture from a section of Cape primrose leaf and, most probably, just a single plantlet from the cut base of each piece of mother-in-law's tongue leaf. The segments of leaf must be inserted base downwards in the rooting mixture—otherwise no roots will develop.

Mother-in-law's tongue and Cape primrose leaves should be cut crosswise at 2-3in intervals and then planted almost vertically in a sandy rooting mixture, with between a quarter and a half of the section buried. Emerald ripple peperomia leaves should be cut into four sections (one cut down the leaf, one cut across it) and planted with a cut edge just in contact with a barely moist rooting mixture. If leaves from a variegated mother-in-law's tongue plant are used (as shown here), the new foliage which is produced will revert to plain green.

   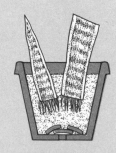

1 Remove the parent plant from its pot and select a healthy, mature leaf which is unblemished. Cut or break off the leaf at the base.

2 Cut the leaf crosswise, with a sharp knife, at 2-3in intervals. Each large leaf will provide several segments from which new plants can be propagated.

3 Plant the leaf cuttings together at a slight angle in the rooting mixture. They may be supported by plant labels or rested against the pot side, if required.

4 New roots will develop from the buried cut edge of each leaf section. When the plantlets are well-developed, pot them up and treat them as mature plants.

Propagating from plantlets

A number of house plants make "plantlets" —small replicas of themselves—on their leaves or at the ends of stolons or arching stems. Pickaback plants (*Tolmeia menziesii*) produce plantlets on their leaves, while strawberry geraniums (*Saxifraga stolonifera*) produce plantlets on stolons. If plantlets are left on the parent plant until they are well developed, they can usually be detached and potted up to develop roots of their own in a rooting mixture. Alternatively, strawberry geraniums and spider plants (*Chlorophytum comosum*) can be layered (see p.268), although plantlets may be less inclined to make roots of their own while they continue to be sustained by the parent through the linking stem.

1 Cut off a leaf or stolon (shown above) which bears a well-developed plantlet. Leave about 1in of the leaf stalk or stolon attached to the plantlet. Bury this stalk in a pot of rooting mixture with the plantlet resting on the surface.

2 Cover with a plastic bag to provide extra humidity. Roots should develop in three weeks.

Propagating from offsets

These are small plants which appear around the base of mature plants. Most grow directly from the stem but some may be produced on long stalks or stolons. Bromeliads and succulents often produce offsets at the base, and many of the spherical cacti make clusters of them. If offsets are to survive on their own, they should not be detached until they are well established and have developed the normal shape and characteristics of the parent. Well-developed offsets often have some roots of their own already formed, and this inevitably makes subsequent establishment easier and quicker.

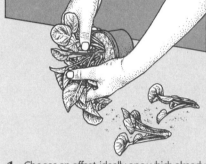

1 Choose an offset, ideally one which already has some roots attached, and gently break it off the main stem. This may be done at the same time as you repot the parent plant.

2 Plant the offsets in barely moist rooting mixture in separate pots. Place the pot in a plastic bag until active growth indicates that the offset is well rooted.

Propagating by division

Plants such as African violets (*Saintpaulia* hybrids), most ferns and some cacti can usually be divided by taking them out of their pots and firmly but gently pulling apart obviously separate sections, each comprising a single or small cluster of plants and a healthy root system. It may be necessary to tease or wash away some of the potting mixture so that you can see the separate sections. Sometimes these are joined together with tough thickened roots, and you may need a sharp knife to make the division. In addition, ferns often have densely packed fine roots that make pulling the sections apart difficult.

1 You may need to use a knife to start a division so that you can get your thumbs into the cut area and successfully lever the sections apart, dividing the root ball equally.

2 Pot up the divisions at the same level as previously, in a pot slightly larger than the root spread. Water sparingly until sections get established and new growth appears.

Propagation times

Soft-stemmed cutting in water: four to six weeks for adequate roots to form; then transfer to potting mixture.

Soft-stemmed cutting in potting mixture: three to four weeks for adequate roots to form.

Woody-stemmed cutting in potting mixture: eight to ten weeks for adequate roots to form.

Whole leaf in potting mixture: three to four weeks for adequate roots to form; then a further two to five weeks before new topgrowth appears.

Whole leaf in water: three to four weeks for adequate roots to form; then transfer to potting mixture.

Leaf section in potting mixture: four to six weeks for adequate roots to form; then a further four to eight weeks before new topgrowth appears.

Plantlet in potting mixture: three to four weeks for adequate roots to form; then a further two to five weeks before an attractive-looking new plant develops.

Offset in potting mixture: three to four weeks for adequate roots to form; then a further two to three weeks for a plant of a useful size to develop.

Division in potting mixture: two to three weeks for a plant of a useful size to develop.

Propagation 3

Layering

This is the process by which roots are encouraged to form on a trailing stem while it is still in contact with the rest of the plant. Layering is practiced in the garden when semi-woody stemmed shrubs have their stems bent down and held in contact with the soil to encourage them to make roots. It is not often practiced indoors except with heartleaf philodendrons (*Philodendron scandens*) and ivies (*Hedera* sp.)— both of which make aerial roots at the nodes or leaf joints. As with the propagation of plantlets (see p.267), the stems are brought into contact with a suitable rooting mixture in a nearby pot. Many creeping plants are constantly sending roots down into the potting mixture over which they grow. The new growths can be cut from the parent plants and potted up separately at virtually any time.

1 Bring the stem into contact with a pot containing suitable rooting mixture, securing it firmly in place with a hairpin or a piece of bent wire. Heap a little rooting mixture over the point of contact to further encourage rooting.

2 New roots form within three to four weeks at the node, and a young plant will begin to grow. When this happens, cut the new plant free, taking care not to spoil the shape of the parent. Several plants can be propagated in this way simultaneously.

Air layering

Air layering is a way of propagating a prized plant that has grown too big for convenience or one that has lost some of its lower leaves and is starting to look untidy. It is often used for woody-stemmed plants that do not root quickly from cuttings and are so stiff that their stems cannot be bent down for layering.

The woody stem is "injured" to encourage it to put forth roots at the point of injury; the top section is then cut off and potted up. One method involves making a single upward-slanting cut in the stem, but this puts it in danger of being broken off. A somewhat safer way of air layering is described here.

After

Before

1 Score out two rings, ½-¾in apart, just below the lowest healthy leaf on the stem. Peel off the bark between them, leaving the stem tissue undisturbed.

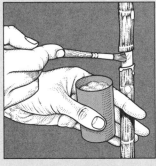

2 Brush the stripped area of stem with a thin layer of hormone rooting powder to encourage the rapid production of new roots.

3 Using insulating tape or strong thread, secure the end of an oblong piece of plastic around the stem, just below the point at which the stem is cut.

4 Pack the cuplike plastic sheath with moistened sphagnum moss. This is the most effective rooting medium for air-layering.

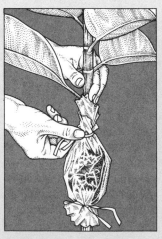

5 Lash the top of the plastic around the stem to ensure that the moisture cannot escape. The cut section of stem should now be completely covered.

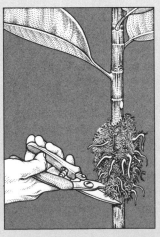

6 After several weeks, roots will appear through the moss. Remove the plastic cover and cut the stem cleanly, just below where the roots are growing.

7 Plant the new root ball in a pot large enough to allow a 2in space around it. Fill with a suitable potting mixture, and water sparingly until well established.

Growing from seeds

Very reliable strains of seeds are available for such popular house plants as wax begonias (*Begonia semperflorens-cultorum*), black-eyed Susan vines (*Thunbergia alata*), silk oaks (*Grevillea robusta*), German violets (*Exacum affine*) and impatiens (*Impatiens wallerana* hybrids), and the best hybrid forms can often be raised in this way.

Seeds are best sown in a suitable peat-based rooting mixture (see p.264). Use half-pots, pans or seed trays depending on the quantity of seed being sown. Very small seed, such as that of begonias (*Begonia* sp.) and African violets (*Saintpaulia* hybrids), resembles dust, and is best sprinkled over the surface of the rooting mixture. Slightly larger seeds can have a shallow layer of finely sieved mixture placed over them, and sizeable seeds should be buried at one and a half times their own depth. Once water has penetrated the outer coating of the seed, growth begins and, from that point onwards, a constant supply of moisture

is needed. Any drying out is fatal, but too much water will result in rotting, so a balance must be struck.

Temperatures above 60°F are needed for swift germination and some of the sub-tropical and tropical plants need much higher levels. Some seed germinates best in the dark, other types need light to grow—so always follow the instructions on the packet. It is very important to give small seedlings the quantity of bright light they need from the very earliest stages of growth. If a seedling starts to make elongated growth, due to insufficient light, it will never develop into a really satisfactory plant. Containers should be placed near to a source of bright light as soon as the first seedlings start to appear. However, it is important to avoid hot direct sunlight that could cause scorch and certainly dry up the surface of the mixture. It is a good idea to check trays, pots and pans every day to ensure the various needs of the seedlings are being met.

Sowing seeds

1 Spread a thin layer of gravel in the bottom of a tray—this provides good drainage and prevents waterlogging. Cover the gravel with a layer of suitable rooting mixture.

2 Mark out shallow furrows as a guide for sowing. Scattering seed indiscriminately over the whole surface will often result in overcrowding of seedlings.

3 Take small pinches of fine seed from a hand-held container and sprinkle them along the furrows. Larger seeds can be individually spaced at regular intervals in the furrows.

4 Cover the seeds, if appropriate, and thoroughly moisten the mixture with a fine mist-sprayer. Then place a sheet of glass or clear plastic on top and put the tray in a warm place.

Thinning out

1 At an early stage, carefully thin out seedlings growing very close together. This gives those that remain a better chance of thriving.

2 The spaces between remaining seedlings should be roughly equal to their height. Use your fingertips to carefully firm the mixture around each one.

3 When a seedling has developed at least two true leaves, gently remove it from the mixture using a plant marker, or something similar, to ease out the young roots.

4 Transfer each seedling to a pot containing mixture suitable for the adult plant. Ensure that the lower leaves are not buried and avoid handling the stem.

Problems, pests and diseases 1

Healthy, well-maintained house plants grow sturdily, look good and are less likely to develop problems or be attacked by pests or disease. Unhealthy plants are usually the result of poor environment, neglect or wrong treatment—actual pests or diseases are, in fact, rarely to blame.

The first step to ensuring that your plants remain in peak condition is to choose them carefully, bearing in mind the amount of time and effort you can devote to them and the conditions you have to offer. Buy a specimen which looks healthy and protect it on the journey home. A plant will also need a period of acclimatization to its new surroundings; try to ensure it is placed in a suitable position and not moved for a few days. It is unwise to introduce a new plant into an existing collection until it has been carefully examined; ideally, it should be isolated from your other house plants until it can be given a clean bill of health.

Preventive action
The successful way to care for any plant is to give it neither too much nor too little of the essential growth factors: water, food, light, warmth and humidity. Apart from meeting your plants' specific growing needs, though, it is well worth devoting a few minutes, every week or two, to cleaning them and generally looking them over. Turn over the leaves and examine the undersides carefully—this will help you

to spot any problems at an early stage. Should signs of ill health or pest infestation be apparent, immediate action must be taken if the plant is to be saved. Also pay close attention to the growing points; these, being soft and succulent, are more liable to attack by aphids than older, leathery leaves. In several flowering plants, such as the Cape primrose (*Streptocarpus* hybrids), the leaves are rarely attacked—it is the flower stalks and flower buds that are the susceptible parts. Some pests are a little choosy about their host plants, appearing only on certain species. Others are less discriminating and will attack any plant.

Routine maintenance
The action of cleaning a plant often dislodges the odd pest and may even prevent a real infestation. Household dust spoils the look of leaves and, to some extent, clogs the pores through which they breathe—it also reduces the amount of light which can be used for photosynthesis. See that plants are not crowded together so closely that air cannot circulate freely between them, or that some fail to get enough light because others are shading them. Remove any yellowing or damaged leaves and take off all flowers as they fade. Flower stalks should be taken off right to the base when all the individual blooms on the stalk are finished. Leaving sections of stalk behind can cause rotting in the plant's center.

Keeping plants clean
Plants which are kept indoors are bound to get dusty, so a regular cleaning program is essential. Clean leaves look more attractive and they allow a plant to function more efficiently. Various methods of cleaning are given below, depending on the size and texture of the plant's leaves. By far the most effective method of cleaning a plant of any shape or size is to stand it outside in a gentle shower, in a sheltered position, during the milder months. Rain water leaves no nasty white deposit behind and the leaves are thoroughly freshened by the experience.

Wiping with a damp cloth
Plants with large, smooth leaves can be cleaned with a damp sponge or soft cloth. Use a weak solution of soapy water and give a clear rinse afterwards. A shower will also benefit these plants, but ensure that the water pressure is not high enough to damage the leaves.

Removing faded leaves and flowers
Remove any faded flowers or yellowing leaves that are due to old age, taking them right off to the base. Snip off brown leaf tips with sharp scissors. As these are usually due to dry air, increase the level of humidity provided.

Routine checklist for ensuring healthy plants
In the majority of cases, ailments that affect house plants are not due to actual disease or infestation by pests. It may just be that one or more of the plant's growing needs are not being met. The following checklist will help you to determine the likely reason behind any

symptoms of ill health displayed by your plants. If more than one of the plant's growing needs are not being met, it will be necessary to correct them all, to ensure healthy plant growth. If any symptoms persist, examine for any likely pests or diseases.

- Are you overwatering?
- Are you underwatering?
- Is the plant getting the sort of light it prefers?
- Is the temperature too high or too low for proper growth?
- Is the level of humidity conducive to the plant's needs?
- Have you remembered to cater for any winter rest the plant may need?

- Does the plant stand in a draft?
- Is the pot size correct?
- Are the roots of the plant completely filling the pot?
- Is the plant growing in the right sort of potting mixture?
- Would the plant benefit from being grouped with others?
- Is the plant dusty and in need of a clean?

Cleaning a plant with hairy leaves
Hairy-leaved plants will be damaged if you attempt to clean them with a damp cloth, as the hairs trap the water, causing rotting. You can, however, "sweep" away any dust which may have accumulated by using a soft, dry ½in paintbrush.

Immersing a small plant
On warm days it is possible to wash leaves clean of dust by inverting a small plant and submerging it in a bowl of lukewarm water to which a little soap has been added. Swirl the plant around gently for a few seconds, remove it from the water and allow it to drain.

Examining for pests
It is a good idea to inspect your plants carefully at regular intervals. Pay particular attention to tender growing tips and the undersides of the leaves; scale insects and aphids are especially likely to congregate there. Watch out for the sticky honeydew that these pests exude, as this may encourage sooty mold.

Physiological problems

The most common problems met with in house plants are caused by overwatering, underwatering, fluctuating temperatures, drafts, strong sunlight causing leaves to scorch, cold water causing spotting on the foliage, and low levels of humidity.

Too much or too little water
Overwatering is a very common problem and can be a killer. The dangers of underwatering are less, but the signs of both faults are very similar: in each case the plant droops or wilts because it is not absorbing enough water. Consistent overwatering, when water is frequently given to an already moist potting mixture, means that air cannot reach the roots, so they stop growing and start to break down and die. With little or no roots, a plant cannot take up enough water to sustain it. To prevent overwatering, only water when the potting mixture starts to dry out, and wait until this happens again before giving more water. If a plant prefers a moist potting mixture, keep it moist all the time, but never sodden wet (see p.251).

If a plant is underwatered, it will be obvious that there is little or no water left in the mixture; there may also be a considerable gap between the root ball and the inside of the pot where the potting mixture has shrunk and, in the case of a soil-based potting mixture, the surface may become caked hard or even cracked.

Fluctuating temperatures
When temperatures fluctuate by more than 15°-18°F, leaf drop may occur. Aim at keeping the temperature fairly even, with only a slight fall at night. Avoid the opposite—cool days when the heating is turned off and warm evenings when the heating is turned on. It is better to keep all but the most warmth-loving plants at a lower temperature all the time, moving them to a room that is not directly heated at night.

When temperatures soar, African violets (*Saintpaulia* hybrids) and many other gesneriads will drop most or all of their flower buds; during a heatwave try to keep temperatures down and increase the level of humidity.

Drafts
Plants abhor drafts: the thin and more delicate fern fronds will be blackened by them, the leaves of angel wings (*Caladium hortulanum* hybrids) and painted-leaf begonias (*Begonia rex-cultorum*) will droop, and crotons (*Codiaeum variegatum pictum*) will drop their leaves. Avoid sites next to drafty or open windows and, at night, do not leave plants behind drawn curtains.

Sun scorch
The leaves of plants that prefer to grow in some shade can easily develop brown dehydrated patches if exposed to really strong sunlight. Those plants that can tolerate direct sun, but which are not used to it, can be scalded by sudden exposure. Always acclimatize plants gradually to brighter light.

Insufficient light
If a plant is not receiving enough light, its growth will be generally sluggish. Flowering plants will not bloom as they should, and flower buds may drop off. The new leaves of plants with variegated foliage will revert to a uniform green. To ensure that all parts of the plant receive sufficient light, turn plants regularly, or place them where a reflective surface can throw light on to the side facing away from the light source.

Cold water spots
African violets (*Saintpaulia* hybrids), gloxinias (*Sinningia speciosa*) and a number of other gesneriads can have their leaves marked with lighter colored patches if they are watered with cold water, or if water is allowed to collect on the leaves at the time of watering. Use tepid water and avoid wetting the foliage.

Incorrect humidity
Low levels of humidity can cause browning of leaf tips and leaf edges; this is particularly obvious on plants with thin leaves, such as peacock plants (*Calathea makoyana*), spider plants (*Chlorophytum comosum*) and many ferns. Increase humidity by regular mist-spraying and by standing plants on trays filled with moist pebbles.

Problems, pests and diseases 2

Pests

House plants are sometimes attacked by insects and other pests which eat their leaves, stems and roots or suck their sap. A minor infestation is hardly noticeable and often does little damage but, if left unchecked, numbers quickly build up and then serious harm can be done. The ways in which pests arrive on plants vary, but new plants should always be thoroughly checked and infested plants should be moved away from healthy ones. Some pests prefer to feed on particular plants and will leave others alone, while others are less discriminating. A few types, such as aphids and whiteflies, are very common—they thrive throughout the world, adapting to very different conditions, and are extremely difficult to get rid of—others need special conditions to do well and are therefore easily discouraged.

Aphids

Aphids, commonly called "greenflies" or "plant lice", which may be black, brown, gray or light yellow as well as green, suck sap and multiply at an alarming rate. They molt their skins, and the white cases are found on infested plants.

What they do Apart from sucking sap, which debilitates the plant and causes distortion, aphids carry incurable viral diseases and exude a sticky honeydew on which a black fungus called sooty mold can grow.

Susceptible plants All plants which have soft stems and soft leaves; these include cyclamens (*Cyclamen persicum* hybrids), impatiens (*Impatiens* sp.) and German violets (*Exacum affine*).

Treatment Individual pests can be removed by hand, but a suitable insecticide is needed in most cases.

Caterpillars and leaf rollers

Caterpillars, such as those found in the garden, rarely attack house plants but an infestation may occasionally be caused by moths or butterflies which fly in and lay their eggs on stems or leaves—usually the leaf undersides. Sometimes a problem on plants summered outdoors is the thin caterpillar of the tortrix moth.

What they do They roll themselves up in a young leaf, inside a protective web, and eat young stems and growing points, ruining the symmetry of a plant.

Susceptible plants All soft-leaved plants, such as Swedish ivies (*Plectranthus australis*), nerve plants (*Fittonia verschaffeltii*) and geraniums (*Pelargonium* sp.).

Treatment Individual caterpillars can be picked off by hand and destroyed, but a more serious attack will need treating with a suitable insecticide.

Fungus gnats or sciarid flies

Adult

Larvae

Also known as "mushroom flies", these are tiny, rather sluggish creatures that hover above the surface of the potting mixture and do no real harm.

What they do The flies lay their eggs in the mixture and the hatched larvae feed on dead matter, including decaying roots. The larvae are unlikely to damage live roots on mature plants, but will sometimes attack those on very young seedlings.

Susceptible plants Fungus gnats exist in practically all peat and peat-based products. This means that plants such as creeping figs (*Ficus pumila*), African violets (*Saintpaulia* hybrids) and most types of fern are especially likely to suffer from them.

Treatment The condition can be treated by drenching the mixture with an insecticide when it is relatively dry, but the flies are really more of a nuisance than a pest.

Mealy bugs and root mealy bugs

Mealy bugs

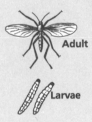

Root mealy bugs

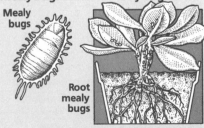

Mealy bugs resemble white woodlice; they are oval in shape and around ¼in long. They can wrap themselves in a sticky white "wool" which repels water (and insecticide).

What they do Mealy bugs are sap suckers and excrete honeydew. A severe attack can result in leaf fall. Root mealy bugs congregate on the roots and create little patches of white wool.

Susceptible plants Mealy bugs tend to attack citrus, cacti or succulents, but may appear on virtually any plant. Cacti, geraniums (*Pelargonium* sp.) and African violets (*Saintpaulia* hybrids) are particularly liable to attack from root mealy bugs.

Treatment Systemic insecticides can be effective against mealy bugs, if used repeatedly. For root mealy bugs, drench the potting mixture with an insecticide at least three times at two-weekly intervals.

Red spider mites

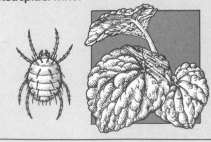

These minute reddish pests thrive in hot, dry air. The mites are barely visible to the naked eye, but their webs are the tell-tale indication of their presence.

What they do Red spider mites suck sap and spin very fine, silky webs on the undersides of leaves. Infestation results in leaves becoming mottled and rusty, new growth being stunted and, in severe cases, leaf fall occurring.

Susceptible plants English ivy (*Hedera helix* hybrids) and spider plants (*Chlorophytum comosum*) are two popular house plants which may be prone to attack.

Treatment As the mites dislike moisture, regular spraying with water will discourage a serious attack, but insecticides must be used in severe cases. Apply weekly, directing the spray on to both upper and lower leaf surfaces.

Scale insects

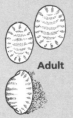

Adult

Most scale insects are brown or yellowish in color; they appear mainly on the undersides of leaves and are particularly partial to crevices. The young insects are very active and move about over the plant, but mature pests remain stationary, enclosed in their waxy cover, and appear as circular or oval raised discs.
What they do Both suck sap and excrete sticky honeydew—often the first sign that they are present is when this sticky residue is noticed on leaves or furniture. Honeydew may lead to infection by sooty mold.
Susceptible plants All plants are vulnerable to attack, but some types of scale insects prefer particular plants. The citrus family and ferns—especially bird's nest ferns (*Asplenium nidus*)—are most susceptible.
Treatment Spraying is not very effective, due to the hard protective coating of the adult insects, so systemic pesticides should be used.

Vine weevils

These pests are more common outdoors and in greenhouses. Adult weevils are large and almost black in color; their grubs are cream-colored.
What they do Adult pests bite pieces out of the foliage, leaving a permanent scar. The grubs eat roots, tubers and corms. Often, the first sign of their presence is when a plant droops and an inspection may reveal that it has no roots left at all!
Susceptible plants The most commonly affected plants include orchids, cyclamen (*Cyclamen persicum* hybrids), African violet (*Saintpaulia* hybrids) and all types of rosette-shaped succulents.
Treatment Adult pests can be removed by hand and destroyed, and the potting mixture should be drenched with a suitable insecticide. A plant without a root system cannot usually be saved.

Whiteflies

These tiny, white, mothlike creatures are sometimes found in the home, but are more common in greenhouses or conservatories. When whiteflies appear indoors, they have usually been brought in with temporary flowering pot plants.
What they do They settle mainly on the undersides of the leaves, sucking sap and depositing sticky honeydew. Their almost translucent larvae are often present in large numbers on the undersides of leaves.
Susceptible plants Whiteflies tend to attack certain flowering plants, such as fuchsias and geraniums (*Pelargonium* sp), grown during the summer in the garden.
Treatment These are persistent pests which may prove difficult to eradicate. Repeated applications of a spray insecticide for the larvae and a systemic kind for the adults will eliminate them in time.

Leaf miners

Leaf miners are the slim, sap-sucking maggots of a small fly. They can sometimes be seen if the leaves are examined closely.
What they do The grubs tunnel between the surfaces of the leaves of certain plants, causing a mosaic of irregular white lines. The progress of leaf miners is usually rapid and the appearance of a plant will quickly be spoiled if no action is taken.
Susceptible plants Chrysanthemums (*Chrysanthemum* sp.) and cinerarias (*Senecio cruentus* hybrids) are the most popular house plants likely to be attacked by these pests. Plants that are purchased are unlikely to be affected, but cinerarias grown by the amateur from seed can be at risk.
Treatment Damaged leaves should be picked off and a spray insecticide used on the leaves. Alternatively, a systemic insecticide can be applied to the potting mixture.

Earthworms

Although they are to be encouraged in the garden, where their feeding enriches the soil and their movements serve to aerate it, earthworms that get into the potting mixture of house plants can be a nuisance.
What they do Constant burrowing among the roots causes disturbance and loosens the potting mixture. Their presence is usually noticed when heaps of their casts appear on the surface of the mixture and plants seem loose in their pots.
Susceptible plants Worms may infest any plant which is left in the garden during the summer. They enter the mixture through the drainage holes in the pot.
Treatment Water affected plants with permanganate of potash solution and pick off any worms that surface. Tapping the pot will cause them to surface.

Slugs and snails

Slug

Snail

Slugs and snails will not survive in the home for long, as their presence is soon noticed and they can be easily picked off by hand and destroyed. They can, however, be troublesome in greenhouses and conservatories.
What they do Both are very fond of juicy stems, and can eat away large sections of them rapidly. They are most active at night and during prolonged wet spells outdoors.
Susceptible plants Plants that are left outside in summer and autumn can be seriously damaged by these pests. Christmas and Easter cacti (*Schlumbergera* and *Rhipsalidopsis* sp.) are especially at risk because of their succulent stems.
Treatment Protect all indoor plants while they are outdoors by sprinkling slug pellets around them. Renew pellets frequently as rain washes out the chemicals.

Problems, pests and diseases 3

Diseases

House plants are not prone to many air-borne diseases and, of those that are found, most gain a foothold because the plant has been overwatered, or because water has lodged in leaf axils causing conditions in which fungi and bacteria can thrive. Damaged leaves and bruised stems may spark off one of several bacterial diseases, and overcrowding, resulting in a lack of adequate air circulation, can also spell trouble. Many pests transmit diseases, and an infestation will, in any case, weaken a plant and make it more susceptible to disease. Always remove diseased sections as soon as you see them, and isolate an affected plant from the rest of your collection whilst treatment is being given.

Blackleg

This disease, also known as "black rot" and "black stem rot", strikes plants just where the stem meets the potting mixture, but spreads both upwards and downwards to the roots. An attack rarely occurs unless the potting mixture is kept too wet for too long, but stem cuttings are liable to be affected during propagation.
Susceptible plants This disease is most common on geraniums (*Pelargonium* sp.).

Treatment Always use free-draining potting mixtures and be particularly sparing with water during the period that geranium cuttings are rooting. Avoid damaging stems and always remove faded leaves. There is no cure for this disease but cuttings taken from the tops of stems that are unaffected can be rooted—dip the cut ends into hormone rooting powder containing fungicide.

Gray mold

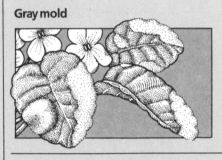

This fungus, which is also called "botrytis", usually starts growing on fallen leaves and flowers, but can also start when water lodges in the axils of the leaves. It strikes quickly when temperatures are low and the air is moist, and rarely in warmer weather and in dry air. Whole leaves or stems can be affected, assuming an unpleasant, fluffy-gray, moldy appearance.
Susceptible plants Gray mold affects plants with soft stems and leaves, such as African violets (*Saintpaulia* hybrids), cinerarias (*Senecio cruentus* hybrids), angel wings (*Caladium hortulanum* hybrids) and purple velvet plants (*Gynura aurantiaca*).
Treatment Fading leaves should be removed, and plants should be watered and mist-sprayed less frequently. A suitable fungicide may have to be used in severe cases, and to prevent further attacks.

Sooty mold

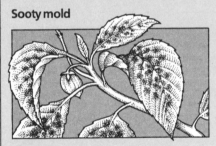

Sooty mold grows on the sticky honeydew secreted by pests such as aphids and scale insects. As such, it is a sure sign that a plant is infested with some sort of sap-sucker. The mold itself looks just like a thick layer of soot and feels sticky. Although sooty mold does not directly attack the leaves, its presence spoils the appearance of the plant, clogs the breathing pores of the leaves, and reduces photosynthesis by obscuring light.
Susceptible plants Citrus plants are particularly liable to be affected.
Treatment Regular washing of the leaves with soapy water avoids the possibility of an attack, and is the only way of washing off the objectionable mold once it appears. The best means of treatment is to attack the sap-sucking pests which deposit the sticky honeydew.

Mildew

Mildew appears as powdery white patches on leaves, stems and, occasionally, flowers. These patches can be distinguished from gray mold by the absence of fluffy growths. Stricken leaves become distorted and fall from the plant. Low temperatures combined with high humidity, poor air circulation and overwatering provide ideal conditions for mildew.
Susceptible plants Soft-leaved and succulent-stemmed plants, including some begonias, are particularly susceptible; other kinds of begonia, even when growing alongside affected plants, are not attacked.
Treatment To treat plants affected by mildew, pick off all affected leaves and spray the rest of the plant with a fungicide.

Stem and crown rot

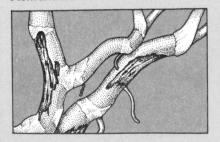

If the stem of a plant starts to go soft and slimy, the reason may be stem rot. Low temperatures and soggy potting mixture may cause plants to become infected. An attack of crown rot will cause the leaves to be eaten away from the center outwards.
Susceptible plants Plants with soft stems, such as impatiens (*Impatiens* sp.) and German violets (*Exacum affine*), are prone to stem rot. Other susceptible plants are cacti; when soft, dark-brown or black patches appear near to potting mixture level, it is likely to be stem rot. Rosette-shaped plants, such as echeverias (*Echeveria* sp.) and African violets (*Saintpaulia* hybrids), are liable to attack from crown rot.
Treatment An attack is usually fatal but unaffected sections may be dusted with sulphur and re-rooted if their shape justifies their being retained.

Diagnosis chart

The diagnosis chart below should enable you to determine what is wrong with your plant. Most problems occur because of incorrect growing conditions but, if the symptoms continue, check the plant for any likely pests and diseases, and treat accordingly.

Signs of pests

Symptoms	Cause
• Distorted stems and leaves • Damaged flowers • General air of lack-luster • Sticky "honeydew" substance on leaves and stems *Occurs throughout the year*	Aphids (plant lice or greenfly)
• Mottled or finely pitted leaves • Curled up leaf edges • Fine silky webbing on leaf undersides and leaf axils *Occurs throughout the year*	Red spider mites
• Sticky substance on leaves which may turn black • Waxy brown or yellow encrustations on leaf undersides *Occurs throughout the year*	Scale insects
• Yellowing leaves • General air of debility • Tufts of waxy, white wool in leaf axils and around areoles of cacti • "Honeydew" on leaves or on cactus stems *Occurs throughout the year*	Mealy bugs
• Poor growth and yellowing leaves • Clumps of white, waxy bugs on roots *Occurs throughout the year*	Root mealy bugs
• Crescent-shaped sections eaten out of leaf edges of plants with thick, succulent leaves *Occurs in spring and summer*	Vine weevils (adults)
• Wilting of the whole plant when potting mixture is still moist • Roots or tubers eaten away *Occurs in spring, summer and autumn*	Vine weevils (larvae)
• Sticky "honeydew" on leaves • Pure white insects resembling moths on leaf undersides *Occurs in summer and autumn*	Whitefly
• Minute, sluggish, brown flies circling above potting mixture • Piles of "soil" made by tiny larvae appear under the pot *Occurs throughout the year*	Fungus gnats
• Nibbled leaves and stems • Rolled up leaves with fine sticky webbing holding them together • Distorted growth caused by leaves or shoots being "stuck" to their neighbor *Occurs throughout the year*	Leaf rolling caterpillars

Signs of disease

Symptoms	Cause
• Fluffy gray mold on half-rotted leaves *Occurs from autumn to spring*	Gray mold (botrytis)
• Soft, slimy stems • Black or brown decayed areas *Occurs in autumn and winter*	Crown or stem rot
• Thin, black, sootlike deposit on leaves and stems growing on the "honeydew" secreted by sap-sucking insects *Occurs in summer and autumn*	Sooty mold
• Powdery white patches on leaves and stems • Twisted leaves • Leaf fall and possible total defoliation *Occurs in spring and autumn*	Powdery mildew
• Black shrivelled sections of stem just above the potting mixture *Occurs in late autumn and winter*	Blackleg

Other danger signs

Symptoms	Cause
• Pale elongated growth with large gaps between the leaves • Small new leaves, small or few flowers • Variegated leaves lose color contrast • New shoots that should be variegated appear plain green	Lack of sufficient light
• Large, irregularly shaped, light-brown patches on leaves • Drooping leaves and stems • Stunted flowers and unduly short or misshapen flower stalks	Too much sun or unaccustomed sun. Light too bright for those that prefer some shade
• Brown leaf tips and leaf edges • Some leaf curl	Air too dry and/or potting mixture allowed to dry out too much between each watering
• Blackening or shrivelling of small leaf sections • Serious leaf drop of large-leaved plants	Drafts or too cold a position
• Green slime on clay pots • Algae, moss and other plant growth on the surface of the potting mixture • Yellowing leaves and leaf drop • Wilting of plant	Overwatering

Problems, pests and diseases 4
Pesticides

All types of pesticide are labelled as to their contents and the pests or diseases they should be used against. Always follow strictly any specific instructions, such as the dilution ratio and the method of application.

Contact insecticides

Insecticides are most commonly applied in liquid form as a fine spray, so that they hit the pest directly and, with luck, kill it quickly before it has time to multiply. These "knock-out" sprays work on contact, affecting the insect's respiratory system or otherwise destroying it.

Most sprays have an unpleasant smell and should not be inhaled. Take plants to be treated out into the garden or on to a balcony, as good ventilation while spraying is essential.

Some insecticides are poisonous to animals, birds and fish, and need careful handling. Others may not be suitable for particular plants, or broad families of plants, since their chemical content could burn the leaves and possibly do more harm than the pests. The label should warn you of this.

Systemic insecticides

Systemic insecticides work in another way. They are taken up by the sap—either from the potting mixture or through the leaves—and the sap-sucking or leaf-chewing insect is poisoned. Some stay as a thin film on the surface of the leaves, killing the insects that eat them; these are often called "stomach insecticides". Systemics can be applied in a number of ways: they can be watered on to the mix, sprinkled over it in the form of granules or pushed into it as a "pin" or "spike". They can also be sprayed on to the foliage of plants; the active ingredients work their way into the sap and circulatory system of the plant and poison pests taking them in. All systemics are relatively long-lasting and they can kill "newcomers" (pests that arrive on the plants some time after the application of the chemicals), whereas contact sprays only affect insects that they make direct contact with.

Some insecticides combine both the knock-out effect and the long-term systemic coverage. New products are regularly appearing, which is just as well since some pests eventually develop a resistance to one chemical. Vary your insecticide from time to time to avoid the possibility of resistance build-up.

Fungicides and bactericides

The best way to prevent disease is to ensure that your plants are grown in the conditions they prefer. Because disease is less frequently met with than attack by pests, it can be controlled by a much smaller range of chemicals. These are known as fungicides, which combat fungal diseases, and bactericides, which combat bacterial diseases. Most of these act systemically and are therefore capable of combating disease which occurs in any part of a plant. They are also unlikely to harm healthy plants, as can unsuitable insecticides, and are not usually harmful to people.

Fungicides and bactericides are most effective when applied in advance of attack, and it does no harm to use them purely as a precautionary device.

Application methods

Insecticides, fungicides and bactericides are packaged in various forms and can be applied in a number of ways. In addition to the normal sprays, aerosols, dusts, granules and spikes, diluted chemicals can be used as a bath into which small plants can be dipped. When it is necessary to treat sub-soil pests by soaking the potting mixture, a watering can may be used to apply the insecticide. In all instances, great care should be taken to follow the manufacturer's instructions and to ensure adequate ventilation is provided when applying the chemicals.

Spraying
Coat all parts of the plant evenly, paying particular attention to the undersides of leaves. If possible, use sprays and aerosols outside so that the spray is not breathed in.

Soaking
Chemical solutions can be applied to the potting mixture using an ordinary watering can—but avoid splashing the leaves. Always use at the recommended strength.

Dusting
Dusting powders are especially useful on cut or bruised leaves. Give upper and lower surfaces a thorough coating. The potting mixture can also be dusted.

Sprinkling
Sprinkle granules evenly on to the potting mixture. The chemical is gradually released with each successive watering.

Inserting a spike
Push the spike into the potting mixture using a pencil or your finger. This method is quick and convenient.

How to apply pesticides

Key

◆ (filled drop)	Soaking
◇ (open drop)	Spraying
■	Dusting
▲	Granules
●	Pellets

Problem	Benomyl	Carbaryl	Diazinon	Dicofol	Dimethoate	Dinocap	Disulfoton	Malathion	Metaldehyde	Nicotine sulfate	Permanganate of potash	Pyrethrum with Resmethrin	Rotenone	Safer's Soap	Comments
Aphids			◆ ◇		◇		◇ ▲	◆ ◇		◇	◇	◆ ■	◇		
Blackleg															No known cure
Caterpillars		◇	◇		◆ ◇							◆ ◇			
Earthworms										◆					
Fungus gnats							◆ ◇			◆	◇		◇		
Gray mold (botrytis)	◇														
Leaf miners					◇		◇ ▲	◇							
Leaf rollers		◇	◇		◇										
Mealy bugs and root mealy bugs			◇		◆ ◇		◇ ▲	◆ ◇		◇	◆ ◇		◆ ◇		
Powdery mildew	◇					◇									
Red spider and other mites				◇	◆ ◇		◇ ▲	◆ ◇			◇			◇	
Scale insects					◆ ◇		◇ ▲	◆ ◇					◇		
Slugs and snails									●						
Sooty mold															Remove with a damp sponge
Stem and crown rot															No known cure
Vine weevils					◆ ◇										
White flies			◇		◆ ◇		◇ ▲	◆ ◇			◆ ◇	◆ ◇		◇	

Glossary 1

Adventitious roots Roots appearing in an unusual place, such as on stems or leaves, e.g., on the stems of cuttings placed in water or on the leaves of some succulent plants.

Aerial roots Roots that appear at nodes. They are mainly used for climbing but are also capable of absorbing moisture from the air. Many only develop properly if they can grasp a suitable rooting medium such as sphagnum moss, e.g., the philodendrons and their relatives the Swiss cheese plant, pothos vine, devil's ivy and arrowhead plant.

Annual A plant grown from seed that completes its life cycle in one season. Annuals must be thrown away once this cycle is complete. A number of perennial plants are treated as annuals (a recommendation is made in *The Plant Finder's Guide*), because of the difficulty of overwintering them or because they seldom look attractive in subsequent years, e.g., German violet. See also *biennial, perennial.*

Anther The male part of the flower which produces pollen.

Areole An organ unique to the cacti, consisting of a cushion or hump from which the spines and flowers arise.

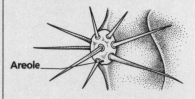

Areole

Axil The angle between the leaf or leaf stalk and stem from which new leaf or side-shoot growth and flower buds arise. Buds found here are known as axillary buds. Side-shoot growth is prevented if they are pinched out.

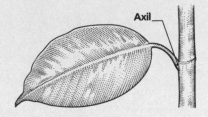

Axil

Berry A succulent fruit in which the usually small but hard seeds are embedded in the fleshy pulp. This pulp is usually brightly colored to attract animals and birds.

Biennial A plant grown from seed that takes two growing seasons to complete its life cycle. A rosette of leaves is produced in the first year, the flowers in the second. Biennials should be thrown away once this cycle is complete as it is difficult to make them flower again, e.g., foxglove. See also *annual, perennial.*

Bleeding When sap flows freely from a damaged stem. This is particularly obvious in such plants as the crown-of-thorns and rubber plant which bleed a milky-white latex. The flow can be staunched by applying powdered sulphur or charcoal. See also *latex.*

Bract A modified leaf, often colorful, which backs relatively insignificant flowers and acts as a method of attracting pollinating insects and birds, e.g., the petal-like red bracts of the poinsettia and the bell-shaped bracts of the paper flower.

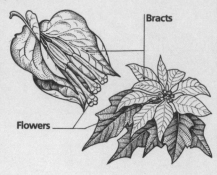

Bracts

Flowers

Bud An embryo shoot, leaf or an immature flower. A terminal growth bud is situated at the tip of a stem or side shoot, an axillary bud is one found in the axil of a leaf stalk. Growth buds are normally protected from damage and cold by closely overlapping scales or sheaths. See also *sheath, axil.*

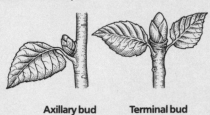

Axillary bud   Terminal bud

Bulb An underground storage organ containing a young plant. The organ stores food during the rest period and usually a complete embryo flower, e.g., tulip, daffodil. See also *corm, tuber.*

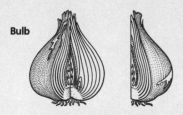

Bulb

Bulbil A small immature bulb attached to a parent bulb, it can also appear on the stems or leaves of the parent plant, e.g., some lilies.

Calyx The collective name for the ring of green sepals which surrounds the petals in most flowers. The calyx protects the developing flower buds. See also *sepal.*

Capillary action Also known as capillary attraction, this is the drawing up of water by a thread or hair. The term is also used to describe the way potting mixture draws up water when the pot and mixture are placed in direct contact with a dish or bowl of water.

Cereal Plants of the grass family cultivated for their seed as food, e.g., wheat, barley. See also *grass.*

Chlorophyll The green pigment found in the stems and leaves of plants.

Compound leaf A leaf divided into two or more segments, e.g., umbrella plant. See also *pinnate, palmate.*

Corm An underground storage organ made up of a thickened stem covered with a thin papery skin. At the top of the corm a bud produces both roots and shoots, e.g., crocus, sword lily. See also *bulb, tuber.*

Corm

Corolla The collective name for the ring of petals. The corolla may be made up of separate petals or the petals may be fused into one unit. See also *flower, petal.*

Crown The growing point of a plant, particularly of a rosette-shaped plant, e.g., African violet. The crown can also be the basal part of a herbaceous plant where the root and shoots meet. See also *root crown.*

Cultivar A type of plant or flower that has been developed in cultivation and named by the plant breeder. Cultivar names are enclosed by quotation marks to distinguish them from the scientific names. See also *variety.*

Cutting A term usually applied to a stem cutting. This is a section of stem, 3-4in long, (usually the growing tip), which is used in propagation to root and develop into a new plant.

Deciduous A plant that loses its leaves at the end of the growing season. These plants do not make good house plants as they are not decorative and usually need a cold resting period. New leaves appear in the spring. See also *evergreen.*

Dieback The death of a section of stem. This is often caused by faulty pruning.

Double flower Flowers having at least two layers of petals. Often the stamens and pistils at the center of the flower are replaced by more petals. Double-flowered forms are usually cultivars, e.g., modern roses. See also *single flower, semi-double flower.*

Double flower

Epiphyte A plant that grows on another plant but is not a parasite. Epiphytes use the host plant purely as an anchor and take no direct nourishment from it. Many bromeliads and ferns are epiphytes, producing strong, wiry roots which cling to tree trunks and branches, and other plants.

Etiolation The technical name for pale, sickly growth. The gaps between the leaves become greater and the flowers fewer. Insufficient light and overcrowding cause the condition.

Evergreen A plant which retains its leaves throughout the year. See also *deciduous*.

Exotic A plant introduced from abroad. The term is often applied to plants that have their origins in tropical and sub-tropical regions. Most house plants, therefore, are exotic.

Eye The center of a flower, which is often a different color to the rest of the bloom, e.g., black-eyed Susan vine, primrose.

Family A term used to describe a large association of plants in which certain characteristics are constant. Many genera make up one family, e.g., *Compositae* is the family name for all the plants with daisylike flowers. See also *genus, species.*

Filament The stalk supporting the anther. These two parts make up the stamen. Normally, many filaments are clustered together in the middle of the flower, e.g., passion flower. See also *stamen, anther.*

Floret A small flower among many others making up a flower head, e.g., most daisy flowers are made up of many florets.

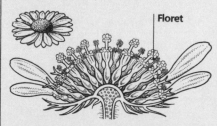

Floret

Flower Usually the most striking feature of a plant, this is an organ of very specialized parts concerned with sexual reproduction. Some plants produce flowers that carry only male parts (stamens), or female parts (pistils). These parts are usually surrounded by a ring of colored petals and green sepals, although there are many variations of this pattern. Some plants have both male and female flower heads on the same plant but, in most plants, both male and female parts are enclosed in the same flower head. Begonias are an example of a flower which is either male, when it is a collection of bright petals with pollen-filled stamens, or female, when it has a large winged seed sac backing the petals.

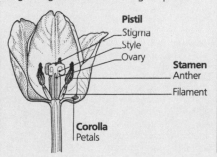

Pistil
Stigma
Style
Ovary

Stamen
Anther

Filament

Corolla
Petals

Forcing The technique of bringing a flower into growth ahead of its natural season. Usually a term applied to spring bulbs when they are encouraged to flower early. Azaleas and cyclamens are also "forced".

Frond Botanically, a term used to describe the deeply dissected "leaves" of ferns which bear spores and arise from a rhizome. It is also loosely applied to palm leaves.

Fruit A widely used term that describes any mature ovary bearing ripe seeds. The outer covering may be soft and fleshy, such as the berries of the Christmas cherry, or a dry pod with hard seeds inside, such as the seed pod of the Cape primrose. See also *nut, berry.*

Genus (pl. genera) A group of allied species. Usually a group of plants (though sometimes only one) which are similar in structure and which most probably evolved from a common ancestor. The genus name always begins with an upper case letter, e.g., English ivies belong to the genus *Hedera*. See also *species, family.*

Germination The first stage of a seed's development into a plant. The first visible stage is the sprouting of the new seedling. Germination can be swift (four to six days), or take many weeks or even months. It is a dangerous period as the seed is no longer protected by the hard outer casing, and strong roots and leaves have not yet developed.

Gourd The large, fleshy fruit of climbing and trailing annual plants native to tropical America. The dried fruits can be used in decoration.

Grass Annual or perennial plants of the family *Gramineae*. In the home, their decorative seed heads and threadlike stalks can be used in flower arrangements or dried for winter decoration. See also *cereal.*

Growing tip Also known as growing point, this is the tip of a shoot from which vigorous new growth emerges.

Hardy A plant capable of surviving outside throughout the year, especially in areas where there is the possibility of a sustained frost. English ivy and camellia are examples of hardy house plants.

Herbaceous A word usually associated with perennial plants whose growth dies down in the late autumn and is replaced with fresh growth the following spring. Plant material is stored as a bulb, corm, rhizome or tuber, e.g., begonia, daffodil. Herbaceous plants never have woody stems. See also *woody.*

Hip A fleshy type of fruit, especially common in the rose family.

Hybrid A plant derived from two genetically different parents. Cross fertilization is common between plants of different species within the same genus. Plants arising from such crossings are known as primary hybrids; they usually have some of the characteristics of both parents, but may favor one more than the other. Cross fertilization is possible, but rare, between plants of different genera, e.g., *Fatshedera* is a hybrid of *Fatsia* and *Hedera*. These crossings are known as bigeneric or intergeneric hybrids. Many naturally occurring hybrids are sterile.

Inflorescence A group of two or more flowers on one stem. An inflorescence may vary considerably in shape from the narrow and spikelike lavenders and sword lilies to the broad round heads of hydrangeas and Egyptian star clusters. See also *raceme, panicle, spike, umbel.*

Juvenile Usually applied to the leaves of a young plant that are different in shape from those of a more mature plant, e.g., eucalyptus foliage, which is round when taken from young plants and thin and pointed when taken from older trees. The leaves of young philodendrons may also be a different shape to those of older plants.

Latex A free-flowing, milky-white fluid which exudes from plants such as crown-of-thorns and rubber plants if stems are cut or damaged. See also *bleeding.*

Leaf The energy-producing organ of the plant. Light striking the green part of the leaf starts the process of photosynthesis. Sepals, petals, tendrils and bracts are thought to be modified leaves. In most cacti, the stems take over the function of leaves.

Leaflet A part of a compound, pinnate leaf, properly known as a pinna. See also *compound leaf, pinna, pinnate.*

Leaflet (pinna)

Leaf mold Partially decayed leaves used in potting mixtures to provide nutrients, bacterial activity and an open, free-draining consistency. More correctly known as humus, it may be difficult to buy but can be found under deciduous trees (leaf litter) or made by composting fallen leaves.

Margin The border of a leaf or flower petal. This may be lobed or toothed, or of a different color to the main body of the leaf.

Node A stem joint at which the leaves are borne. The node may be notched or swollen and is a point from which the new roots of such plants as ivies and philodendrons are commonly made.

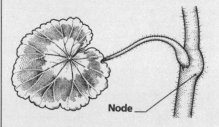

Node

Nut A type of fruit consisting of a hard or leathery shell enclosing a seed that is often edible. See also *fruit.*

Glossary 2

Offset Also known as an offshoot, this is a new plant produced by the parent at its base, or on short stolons, and is normally detachable from the parent. See also *stolon*.

Ovary The basal part of the flower in which the seeds are formed. The ovary wall becomes the fruit wall. See also *flower, fruit*.

Palmate A term applied to compound leaves with several leaflets arranged fanwise from a common point, shaped like a hand, e.g., false aralia. See also *compound leaf*.

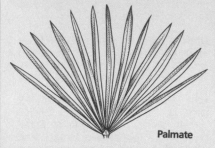

Palmate

Panicle A type of inflorescence consisting of a large branched cluster of flowers, each with a number of stalked flowers, e.g., lilac, most grasses. See also *inflorescence*.

Perennial A plant that lives for an indefinite period, e.g., African lily. Perennials can be herbaceous or woody. See also *annual, biennial*.

Petal Usually the showy part of the flower. Petals protect the center of the flower and, when colored, are intended to attract pollinating insects to the stamens and pistils. Sepals are often confused with petals. Petals may be few (three in many tradescantias) or many (as in a double-flowered rose). They are collectively known as the corolla. See also *sepal, stamen, pistil, flower, corolla*.

Photosynthesis The process by which carbon dioxide is converted into carbohydrates within the leaf. It is sparked off by light striking the green pigment in leaves and stems. See also *chlorophyll, leaf*.

Pinching out Also known as stopping. A form of pruning practiced by gently pulling off, with forefinger and thumb, the soft growing tips of shoots to induce bushiness.

Pinna An individual section of a much divided leaf or frond, commonly known as a leaflet. Used when describing fern fronds. See also *frond, leaflet*.

Pinnate A term used to describe a compound leaf that is divided into several or many pairs of oppositely arranged pinnae (leaflets), e.g., parlor palm. See also *compound leaf, leaflet, pinna*.

Pistil The female part of a flower, comprising stigma, style and ovary. See also *stigma, style, ovary, flower*.

Plantlet A young plant. The stage beyond that of a seedling, but also used to describe "offspring" that are produced on leaves or stolons, e.g., pickaback plant. See also *seedling*.

Raceme A type of inflorescence. An elongated, unbranched flower head, each flower having a short stalk. The flowers normally develop and open from the bottom of the raceme, higher ones opening as the lower ones fade, e.g., hyacinth. See also *inflorescence*.

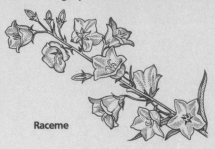

Raceme

Rest period A period within the 12-month season in which the plant should be allowed to become inactive, producing little or no leaf or root growth.

Rhizome A creeping stem, usually horizontal and often underground, from which leaves, side shoots and roots appear. It often acts as a storage organ to enable plants to survive through a short period of drought, e.g., painted-leaf begonia.

Rib A main or prominent vein of a leaf.

Root The lower part of a plant, normally in the potting mixture, which serves to hold it firm and pass nourishment and water to it from the potting mixture. There are two types of root: fine, fibrous roots and the larger, single tap roots. Most plants have one type of root or the other; few have both.

Root ball The mass of potting mixture interspersed with roots seen when a plant is taken from its pot. Examination of the root ball is a way of establishing whether a plant needs repotting or potting on.

Root crown The basal part of a plant, where the stem meets the roots.

Root hair The fine feeding hairs covering the surface of the roots. These are microscopic and cannot be seen with the naked eye.

Rosette An arrangement of leaves radiating from a distinct center, e.g., African violet.

Runner A creeping stem, running along the surface of the potting mixture, which takes root at its nodes and produces a new plant at that point. See also *stolon*.

Scurf Fine, scalelike particles on leaves or stems giving them a gray or silvered appearance, e.g., silver crown.

Seed The fertilized and ripened part of a flowering plant (ovule), capable of germinating and producing a new plant. Seeds range in size from very tiny to around 8in in diameter. Most seeds are pea-sized.

Seedling A young plant, raised from seed, which still possesses a single unbranched stem.

Semi-double flower A flower with more than one layer of petals but with fewer than a

fully double bloom, e.g., some African violets. See also *single flower, double flower*.

Semi-double flower

Sepal The outer part of a flower, often green, which protects the middle of the flower and the more delicate petals. Flowers such as the anemone are actually made up of sepals rather than petals. See also *calyx, petal*.

Sheath A protective wrapping for a growing point, e.g., rubber plant.

Shrub A woody-stemmed bushy plant, smaller than a tree and usually with many stems which branch near the ground. It is often difficult to define the difference between a large shrub and a small tree. Most house plants are shrubs rather than trees. See also *tree, woody*.

Single flower A flower with the normal number of petals, e.g., Marguerite daisy. See also *double flower, semi-double flower*.

Single flower

Spadix A small spike with minute flowers embedded in it, usually surrounded by a spathe, e.g., the center part of a flamingo flower. See also *spathe*.

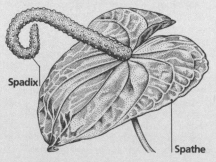

Spadix

Spathe

Spathe A prominent modified leaf or bract surrounding the spadix. Usually fleshy and white, sometimes colored, e.g., flamingo flower. See also *spadix*.

Species The members of a genus are called species. From its seed each persistently breeds true to type in its main characteristics. A plant's name is made up of at least two parts: the name of the genus and the name of the species, e.g., *Coleus* (genus) *blumei* (species). See also *genus, family*.

Spike A type of inflorescence, in the form of a long unbranched flower head. Very similar in appearance to a raceme except that the individual flowers of a spike have no stalks, e.g., sword lily.

Spike

Spore Minute reproductive bodies produced by ferns and mosses—the equivalent of seeds in a flowering plant. Spores are held in spore cases on the underside of some fronds (some fronds are sterile and do not bear spore cases) and may be arranged in a number of patterns—herringbone, marginal or scattered.

Stalk The organ supporting the flower (flower stalk), the leaf (leaf stalk) or the anther (filament). See also *filament*.

Stamen The pollen-bearing male organ of a flower, comprising a filament and two anther lobes containing pollen. See also *filament, anther, flower*.

Stigma The tip of the female reproductive organ (pistil) on which the pollen settles. See also *flower, pistil*.

Stolon A creeping stem that produces a new plantlet at its tip or wherever it touches the potting mixture. See also *runner*.

Stomata The pores through which gases enter and leave the plant. They are usually situated on the underside of the leaves.

Style The style supports the stigma, holding it in an effective place for pollination. See also *stigma, pistil, flower*.

Succulent A plant which has fleshy leaves or stems capable of storing water. Usually plants from arid areas, e.g., Chinese jade.

Sucker A shoot arising from below the surface of the potting mixture, usually from the roots of a plant.

Tendril A wiry projection from the stem that twines around a support and enables a plant to climb. The tendrils may be spiralled, e.g., passion flower, or forked.

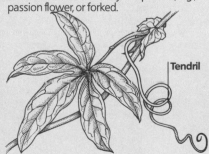

Tendril

Topdressing The process of replacing the top few inches of potting mixture with fresh mixture as an alternative to repotting. Topdressing is most useful for plants that have grown too large for moving into bigger pots. It involves carefully scraping away some of the old potting mixture in spring, doing as little damage as possible to the roots, and firming in fresh mixture.

Transpiration The continual, natural water loss from leaves. This may be heavy or hardly noticeable, depending on the time of day or time of year—factors which affect the relative humidity. Heavy transpiration in warm weather causes wilting, which is damaging to the plant.

Tree A woody-stemmed plant with an obvious trunk topped with branches. See also *woody, shrub*.

Tuber A thick, fleshy stem or root which acts as a storage organ. Some tuberous-rooted plants lose their leaves and stem in the autumn and the tuber stores food for renewed growth the following spring, e.g., begonia. Occasionally tubers are produced on stems, e.g., rosary vine. See also *corm, bulb*.

Tuber

Turgid A term applied to plants that are "crisp" and healthy as their cells are full of water. Also applied to cuttings that have obviously produced roots of their own and are taking up sufficient water for their needs.

Umbel A type of inflorescence. A flower head in which the individual flower stalks arise from a common point. Commonly known as a cluster, e.g., regal geranium, hydrangea. See also *inflorescence*.

Umbel

Undulate A leaf margin or petal that has a wavy edge. Undulate does not refer to toothed or serrated edges.

Variegated A term applied to leaves streaked or spotted with another color (usually cream or yellow). Variegation is usually the result of a mutation and is sometimes due to a virus infection; rarely is it natural or built-in. Variegated-leaved plants are popularly cultivated and need good light to maintain variegation. In some cases, cuttings from certain variegated-leaved plants produce plants with plain green leaves.

Variety A word used to refer to variations of the plant that have occured in the wild, but sometimes incorrectly used to describe a form developed in horticulture. Cultivar is a more accurate term for the latter. Varietal names are printed in italics. See also *cultivar*.

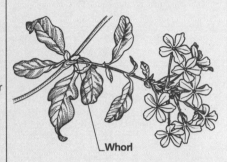

Whorl

Whorl A circle of three or more leaves or flowers produced at the nodes on a stem or stalk, e.g., Cape leadwort.

Wintering A term used to describe the simulation of winter conditions indoors to encourage winter- and spring-flowering bulbs to make good roots before top growth starts.

Woody Refers to plants which have hard stems which persist above ground all year, e.g., paper flower. See also *herbaceous*.

Index

·D·E·

·Q·R·

·S·

Acknowledgments

Author's acknowledgments

I should like to thank the following for their help:
Elizabeth Eyres who has edited the book and Jane Owen who has laid it out so delightfully.
Priscilla Ritchie who has given invaluable help in creating studio
shots in my absence, together with the photographer, Dave King.
Richard Gilbert who has performed monumental work on the horticultural
wants of plants—not my forté.
And lastly, Hilary Bryan-Brown, my secretary, who has coped amazingly
with both a new set of plant names and my handwriting!

Dorling Kindersley's acknowledgments

Richard Gilbert for all his tireless work and efficiency; Chris Thody for finding
plants; Helen Claire Young and Tina Vaughan for design assistance; Caroline
Ollard and Sophie Galleymore-Bird for editorial assistance;
Vickie Walters for picture research; Sue Brown and Sarah Hayes Fisher for styling;
Judy Sandeman for production; Richard Bird for the index;
Adrian Ensor for black and white prints; Sebastian von Mybourg at
The Flowersmith; Anmore Exotics; The Vernon Geranium Nursery; The Royal
Horticultural Society; Holly Gate Cactus Nursery; Syon Park Garden Centre; Clifton
Nurseries Ltd; Coolings Nursery; Bourne Bridge Nurseries; Inca (Peruvian Art and
Craft Ltd), 15 Elizabeth St, London SW1; The General Trading Company, 144
Sloane St, London SW1; Zeitgeist, 17 The Pavement, London SW4; Ceramic Tile
Design, 56 Dawes Rd, London SW6; Chris Frankham of Glass House Studios; Neal
Street East, London; and Habitat.

Illustrators

David Ashby Will Giles Tony Graham Nicholas Hall Coral Mula Sandra Pond James Robins Lorna Turpin

Photographic credits

EWA Elizabeth Whiting and Associates CP Camera Press SG Susan Griggs Agency DK Dorling Kindersley **T** = top, **B** = bottom, **L** = left, **R** = right, **C** = centre

1, 2, 3, 4, 5 Philip Dowell/DK; **6L** Ken Kirkwood/English Style (courtesy of Margot Johnson); **6C** Michael Boys; **6R, 7L & R;** Michael Dunne/EWA; **7C** Lucinda Lambton/Arcaid; **8L** Andreas Einsiedel/EWA; **8C** Richard Bryant/Arcaid; **8R** Michael Boys; **9L** Richard Bryant/Arcaid; **9C** John Hollingshead; **9R** Michael Dunne; **10, 11** Linda Burgess; **12, 13, 14, 15, 16, 17, 18, 19, 20, 21, 22, 23, 24, 25** Philip Dowell/DK; **26, 27** Linda Burgess; **28, 29** Dave King/DK; **30CL** Fuer Sie/CP; **30T, CR & B** Dave King/DK; **31T** Mon Jardin et Ma Maison/CP; **31BL** Schöner Wohnen/CP; **31BR** Michael Boys/SG; **32TL & TR** Dave King/DK; **32B** Michael Nicholson/EWA; **33** Jean Durand/The World of Interiors; **34T** Tom Dobbie/DK; **34B** Dave King/DK; **35T** Tom Dobbie/DK; **35B** Dave King/DK; **36T** Michael Boys/SG; **36B** John Vere Brown/The World of Interiors; **37L** Dave King/DK; **37TR** Michael Nicholson/EWA; **37BL & BR, 38T & B** Tom Dobbie/DK; **39T** Dave King/DK; **39B** IMS/CP; **40T** Fuer Sie/CP; **40B** Dave King/DK; **41TL & TR** Linda Burgess; **41B** Dave King/DK; **42TL** Michael Boys/SG; **42TR** Linda Burgess; **42B** Dave King/DK; **43L** Tom Dobbie/DK; **43R** Michael Boys/SG; **43B** Dave King/DK; **44TR** Linda Burgess; **44TL** Richard Bryant/Arcaid; **44B** Dave King/DK; **45TL** IMS/CP; **45TR** Schöner Wohnen/CP; **45B, 46, 47T & C** Dave King/DK; **47B** Geoff Dann/DK; **48, 49, 50** Dave King/DK; **51L** Michael Dunne/EWA; **51TR** Jessica Strang; **51B, 52, 53T & BR** Dave King/DK; **53BL** Hus Modern/CP; **54** Spike Powell/EWA; **55** Dave King/DK; **56, 57, 58** Trevor Melton/DK; **59T** Linda Burgess; **59B** Schöner Wohnen/CP; **60** Dave King/DK; **61BL** Pamla Toler/Impact Photos; **61BR** K-D Buhler/EWA; **62TL** John Moss/Colorific; **62TR & B** Pamla Toler/Impact Photos; **63, 64** Dave King/DK; **65T & B** Linda Burgess; **66, 67, 68T** Dave King/DK; **68BL** Michael Boys/DK; **68BR** Geoff Dann/DK; **69, 70, 71TL & R** Dave King/DK; **71BL & R** Tom Dobbie/DK; **72, 73T & BL** Dave King/DK; **73BR** Michael Boys; **74T & BR** Dave King/DK; **74BL** Schöner Wohnen/CP; **75** Dave King/DK; **76, 77**

Linda Burgess; **78, 79** Philip Dowell/DK; **80, 81, 82, 83, 84, 85, 86, 87, 88, 89, 90, 91, 92, 93** Dave King/DK; **94, 95** Linda Burgess; **96, 97, 98, 99T** Dave King/DK; **99B** Linda Burgess; **100, 101, 102** Trevor Melton/DK; **103TL** Jessica Strang; **103TR & B** Linda Burgess; **104, 105T & BL** Dave King/DK; **105 BR** Tom Dobbie/DK; **106, 107, 108T** Dave King/DK; **108B** Zuhause/CP; **109, 110, 111** Dave King/DK; **112, 113** Schöner Wohnen/CP; **114TL** Michael Dunne; **114TR** Bill McLaughlin; **114BL** Ron Sutherland; **114BR** Schöner Wohnen/CP; **115TL** Jessica Strang; **115BL** John Vaughan/The World of Interiors; **115C** Jacques Dirand/The World of Interiors; **115TR** Dave King/DK; **115BR** Femina/CP; **116** John Hollingshead; **117T** Schöner Wohnen/CP; **117B** Tim Street-Porter/The World of Interiors; **118T** Ken Kirkwood/English Style (courtesy of Tricia Foley); **118B** John Vaughan/The World of Interiors; **119TL** Michael Boys; **119TR** Schöner Wohnen/CP; **119B** Michael Boys; **120L** Schöner Wohnen/CP; **120R** Clive Helm/EWA; **120B** IMS/CP; **121** Dave King/DK; **122T** IMS/CP; **122C** Michael Boys; **122BL** Michael Dunne; **122BR** Ken Kirkwood/English Style (courtesy of Michael Baumgarten); **123** John Vaughan/The World of Interiors; **124TL** Ken Kirkwood/English Style (courtesy of Lesley Astaire); **124TR** Michael Boys; **124CL** Ken Kirkwood/English Style (courtesy of Lesley Astaire); **124CR & B** Michael Boys; **125** John Vaughan/The World of Interiors; **126TL** Ken Kirkwood/ English Style (courtesy of Stephen Long); **126TR** Schöner Wohnen/CP; **126B** Peter Woloszynski/The World of Interiors; **127** Dave King/DK; **128TL & TR** Michael Boys; **128TR** Michael Boys/SG; **128B** Jessica Strang; **129** Schöner Wohnen/CP; **130** Peter Woloszynski/The World of Interiors; **131TL** Michael Boys; **131TR** Ken Kirkwood/English Style; **131B** Schöner Wohnen/CP; **132T** M Deneux/Agence Top; **132B** Neil Lorimer/EWA; **133T** Hussenot/Agence Top; **133B** Schöner Wohnen/CP; **134T** Michael Boys; **134B** Kent Billequist/CP; **135** Tim Street-Porter/The World of Interiors; **136T** Richard Bryant/Arcaid; **136CL** Michael Dunne; **136CR** Jessica Strang; **136B** Ken Kirkwood/English Style (courtesy of Lesley Astaire); **137T** Schöner Wohnen/CP; **137B** Bill McLaughlin; **138TL** Suomen/CP **138R** Schöner Wohnen/CP; **138BL** Michael Dunne; **139** Dave King/DK; **140T** Spike Powell/EWA; **140B** Femina/CP

141T Lucinda Lambton/Arcaid (courtesy of Virginia Antiques, London W11); **141R** Schöner Wohnen/CP; **142TL** Lucinda Lambton/Arcaid; **142TR** Mon Jardin et Ma Maison/CP; **142C** Linda Burgess; **142B** Lucinda Lambton/Arcaid; **143** James Wedge/The World of Interiors; **144T** Jessica Strang; **144BL & BR** Schöner Wohnen/CP; **145TL** Lucinda Lambton/Arcaid (courtesy of Tessa Kennedy); **145TR** Bill McLaughlin; **145B** Clive Frost/The World of Interiors; **146TL** Lucinda Lambton/Arcaid (courtesy of Lyn le Grice Stencil Design, Bread St, Penzance, Cornwall); **146TR** Michael Boys/SG; **146BL & BR** Lucinda Lambton/Arcaid; **147** Dave King/DK; **148T & B** Michael Boys; **149** John Vaughan/The World of Interiors; **150TL** Bill McLaughlin; **150TR** Ken Kirkwood/English Style (courtesy of Philip Hooper); **150B** Jessica Strang; **151** Ken Kirkwood/English Style (courtesy of The Victorian Society); **152BL** Richard Bryant/Arcaid; **152BC** Michael Dunne; **152BR** Spike Powell/EWA; **153** Jacques Dirand/The World of Interiors; **154** Ron Sutherland; **155TL** Tim Soar/Arcaid; **155TR** Bill McLaughlin; **155B, 156TL** Linda Burgess; **156TR** Jessica Strang; **156B** Ken Kirkwood/English Style (courtesy of Matyelok Gibbs); **157TL** Linda Burgess; **157TR** Michael Boys; **157B** IMS/CP; **158, 159** Andreas Einsiedel/DK; **162, 163, 164, 165, 166, 167, 168, 169, 170, 171, 172, 173** Tom Dobbie/DK; **173TL** Dave King/DK; **174, 175, 176, 177** Tom Dobbie/DK; **177TL** Dave King/DK; **178, 179, 180, 181, 182, 183, 184, 185, 186, 187, 188, 198, 190, 191, 192, 193** Tom Dobbie/DK; **194, 195** Dave King/DK; **196, 197, 198, 199, 200, 201L** Tom Dobbie/DK; **201R** Dave King/DK; **202, 203, 204, 205, 206, 207** Ian O'Leary/DK; **209** Dave King/DK; **210, 211, 212, 213, 214, 215, 216, 217, 218, 219, 220, 221, 222, 223, 224, 225, 226, 227, 228** Trevor Melton/DK; **229** Dave King/DK; **230, 231, 232, 233, 234, 235, 236, 237, 238, 239** Philip Dowell/DK; **240, 241** The Design Group; **242, 246, 254, 255** Dave King/DK; **258L** IMS/CP; **258R, 259L** Dave King/DK; **259R & B** Femina/CP; **264** Dave King/DK.

Front cover photograph Dave King
Photograph of John Brookes Tom Dobbie